Compendium of Tourism Statistics

Data 2002-2006

2008 Edition

Compendium of Tourism Statistics – Data 2002–2006, 2008 Edition
ISBN 13: 978-92-844-1248-8

Published and printed by the World Tourism Organization, Madrid, Spain
First printing: 2008
All rights reserved

The designations employed and the presentation of material in this publication do not imply the expression of any opinions whatsoever on the part of the Secretariat of the World Tourism Organization concerning the legal status of any country, territory, city or area, or of its authorities or concerning the delimitation of its frontiers or boundaries.

World Tourism Organization
Calle Capitán Haya, 42
28020 Madrid, Spain
Tel.: (+34) 915 678 100
Fax: (+34) 915 713 733
Website: www.unwto.org
Email: omt@unwto.org

Permission to photocopy UNWTO material in Spain must be obtained through:
CEDRO, Centro Español de Derechos Reprográficos
Calle Monte Esquinza, 14
28010 Madrid, Spain
Tel.: (+34) 91 308 63 30; Fax: (+34) 91 308 63 27
cedro@cedro.org; www.cedro.org

For authorization of the reproduction of UNWTO works outside of Spain, please contact one of CEDRO's partner organizations, with which bilateral agreements are in place
(see: http://www.cedro.org/ingles_funcion_internacional.asp).

For all remaining countries as well as for other permissions, requests should be addressed directly to the World Tourism Organization. For applications see: http://www.unwto.org/pub/rights.htm

TABLE OF CONTENTS

Pages

Pages

TABLE OF CONTENTS

Pages

Pages

iv

TABLE OF CONTENTS

TABLE OF CONTENTS

Pages   Pages

TABLE OF CONTENTS

vii

INTRODUCTION

The Compendium of Tourism Statistics has been prepared by the UNWTO Department of Statistics and Economic Measurement of Tourism. It provides statistical information on tourism in 208 countries and territories around the world. This is the twenty-eighth in a series that began in 1975 as a biennial publication; it has been issued annually since 1986.

The present edition of the Compendium of Tourism Statistics is edited in English only, with countries classified according to English alphabetical order. For easy reference in Arabic, French, German, Russian and Spanish, the text of the basic indicators and the basic references has been printed in a separate pasteboard.

The statistical data published are those officially received from national tourism administrations, national statistical offices and international organizations (International Monetary Fund and World Bank).

All the data received are subject to different kind of controls and any discrepancies observed are consulted with the informing unit that confirms or rectifies, if necessary, the data previously sent.

Due to the rounding in the partial figures, the totals shown in the different tables of the Yearbook of Tourism Statistics may not coincide with the totals shown in the basic indicators of the Compendium of Tourism Statistics.

Statistical data on individual countries are grouped under:

* Inbound tourism
* Domestic tourism
* Outbound tourism
* Tourism industries
* Related indicators

Consequently, **the data included in this Compendium have an official character and have been entered in the UNWTO database as of 31 March 2008**. Therefore, any corrections or changes received after this date will be included in the next edition of the Compendium.

The Compendium is designed to provide a condensed and quick-reference guide on the major tourism statistical indicators in each country. Users who wish to obtain more detailed statistics than those presented here are invited to consult other statistical publications of UNWTO, or visit the UNWTO website: *http://www.unwto.org*.

The World Tourism Organization wishes to express its gratitude to the national tourism administrations, national statistical offices of the various countries and territories and the above-mentioned international organizations for their valuable co-operation.

Madrid, April 2008

INTRODUCTION

La Section Statistiques et mesure économique du tourisme de l'OMT est chargée d'élaborer le Compendium des statistiques du tourisme. Ce dernier fournit des informations statistiques sur le tourisme dans 208 pays et territoires du monde entier. Il s'agit de la vingt-huitième édition d'une publication bisannuelle lancée en 1975, qui est devenue annuelle à partir de 1986.

Cette édition du Compendium des statistiques du tourisme n'est publiée qu'en anglais, avec les pays classés dans l'ordre alphabétique anglais. Pour l'allemand, l'arabe, l'espagnol, le français et le russe, le texte des indicateurs de base et des références de base figure à part dans un fascicule.

Les données publiées sont celles officiellement reçues des administrations nationales du tourisme, des instituts nationaux de la statistique et d'autres organisations internationales (Fonds monétaire international et Banque mondiale).

Toutes les données reçues sont soumises à différents types de contrôle et les anomalies éventuellement relevées sont consultées avec l'unité chargée de l'information qui confirme ou, au besoin, rectifie les données envoyées.

Etant donné l'arrondissement des données partielles, les totaux qui apparaissent dans les différents tableaux de l'Annuaire des statistiques du tourisme peuvent ne pas correspondre aux totaux des Indicateurs de base du Compendium des statistiques du tourisme.

Les données statistiques des divers pays sont regroupées sous les rubriques suivantes :

- Tourisme récepteur
- Tourisme interne
- Tourisme émetteur
- Filières touristiques
- Indicateurs apparentés

En conséquence, **les données figurant dans le présent Compendium ont un caractère officiel et ont été introduites dans la base de données de l'OMT jusqu'à la date limite du 31 mars 2008.** Toute correction ou modification reçue après cette date sera incorporée à la prochaine édition du Compendium.

De par sa conception, le Compendium est un condensé rapidement consultable des principaux indicateurs statistiques du tourisme de chaque pays. Les utilisateurs souhaitant obtenir des statistiques plus détaillées que celles présentées ici sont invités à consulter les autres publications de l'OMT dans le domaine des statistiques ou à visiter le site Internet de l'OMT (*http://www.unwto.org*).

L'Organisation mondiale du tourisme tient à exprimer sa gratitude aux administrations nationales du tourisme, aux instituts nationaux de la statistique des divers pays et territoires et aux organisations internationales mentionnées plus haut pour leur précieuse coopération.

Madrid, avril 2008

INTRODUCCION

La Sección de Estadísticas y Evaluación Económica del Turismo de la OMT es la encargada de elaborar el Compendio de Estadísticas de Turismo. Esta publicación ofrece información estadística sobre el turismo en 208 países y territorios de todo el mundo. Este número es el vigésimo octavo de una serie que comenzó en 1975 como publicación bienal y siguió publicándose desde 1986 anualmente.

La presente edición del Compendio de Estadísticas de Turismo sólo se edita en inglés, con clasificación de los países en el orden alfabético correspondiente a este idioma. Para una fácil referencia en alemán, árabe, español, francés y ruso, el texto de los indicadores básicos y las referencias básicas han sido impresas sobre cartulina por separado.

Los datos publicados son los remitidos oficialmente por las administraciones nacionales de turismo, los institutos nacionales de estadística y las organizaciones internacionales (Fondo Monetario Internacional y Banco Mundial).

Todos los datos recibidos están sujetos a diversos controles y se consultan todas las discrepancias con la unidad informante, la cual confirma o rectifica, si es necesario, los datos remitidos.

Debido al redondeo de las cifras parciales, los totales que aparecen en los distintos cuadros del Anuario de Estadísticas del Turismo, pueden no coincidir con los totales que aparecen en los Indicadores Básicos del Compendio de Estadísticas del Turismo.

Los datos estadísticos correspondientes a cada país se agrupan de la siguiente forma:

- Turismo receptor
- Turismo interno
- Turismo emisor
- Actividades turísticas
- Indicadores relacionados

Así pues, **las cifras incluidas en este Compendio tienen carácter oficial y han sido introducidas en la base de datos de la OMT al 31 de marzo de 2008**. Por consiguiente, cualquier corrección o cambio recibido después de esta fecha aparecerá en la próxima edición del Compendio.

El Compendio está concebido como guía resumida y de referencia rápida sobre los principales indicadores estadísticos de turismo de cada país. Los usuarios que deseen obtener estadísticas más detalladas pueden consultar otras publicaciones estadísticas de la OMT o visitar el sitio de Internet: *http://www.unwto.org*.

La Organización Mundial del Turismo quiere expresar su gratitud a las administraciones nacionales de turismo, a los institutos nacionales de estadística de los diversos países y territorios y a las organizaciones internacionales mencionadas anteriormente por su valiosa colaboración.

Madrid, abril de 2008

Country tables
2002-2006

Basic Indicators	Units	2002	2003	2004	2005	2006
INBOUND TOURISM						
Arrivals						
1.1 Visitors	('000)	470	557	645	748	937
1.2 Tourists (overnight visitors)	('000)	36	41	32	48	60
1.3 Same-day visitors	('000)	..	..	..	..	..
1.4 Cruise passengers	('000)	..	..	..	..	..
Arrivals by region						
2.1 Africa	('000)	..	..	..	..	..
2.2 Americas	('000)	16	19	26	35	42
2.3 Europe	('000)	439	532	610	703	857
2.4 East Asia and the Pacific	('000)	3	4	4	5	8
2.5 South Asia	('000)	..	..	..	..	..
2.6 Middle East	('000)	1	1	1	1	1
Arrivals by means of transport used						
3.1 Air	('000)	80	87	103	128	151
3.2 Rail	('000)	..	..	..	..	..
3.3 Road	('000)	279	351	404	490	645
3.4 Sea	('000)	111	120	139	130	141
Arrivals by purpose of visit						
4.1 Leisure, recreation and holidays	('000)	262	310	415	430	696
4.2 Business and professional	('000)	100	88	63	68	48
4.3 Other	('000)	108	160	167	250	193
Accommodation						
5.1 Overnight stays in hotels and similar establishments	('000)	143	137	85	110	129
5.2 Guests in hotels and similar establishments	('000)	36	41	32	48	60
5.3 Overnight stays in all types of accommodation establishments	('000)	..	..	..	..	..
5.4 Average length of stay of non-resident tourists in all accommodation establishments	Nights	3.97	3.34	2.70	2.30	2.20
6.1 **Tourism expenditure in the country**	US$ Mn	492	537	756	880	1,057
6.2 "Travel" (*)	US$ Mn	487	522	735	854	1,012
6.3 "Passenger transport" (*)	US$ Mn	5	15	21	26	45
DOMESTIC TOURISM						
Accommodation						
7.1 Overnight stays in hotels and similar establishments	('000)	390	410	175	244	370
7.2 Guests in hotels and similar establishments	('000)	135	137	62	84	101
7.3 Overnight stays in all types of accommodation establishments	('000)	..	..	..	..	..
7.4 Average length of stay of resident tourists in all accommodation establishments	Nights	2.90	3.00	2.80	2.90	3.70
OUTBOUND TOURISM						
8.1 **Departures**	('000)	1,303	1,350	1,694	2,097	2,616
8.2 **Tourism expenditure in other countries**	US$ Mn	387	507	669	808	989
8.3 "Travel" (*)	US$ Mn	366	489	642	786	965
8.4 "Passenger transport" (*)	US$ Mn	21	18	27	22	24
TOURISM INDUSTRIES						
Hotels and similar establishments						
9.1 Number of rooms	Units	4,107	4,161	3,368	3,874	4,266
9.2 Number of bed-places	Units	7,996	8,420	6,600	7,642	8,362
9.3 Occupancy rate	Percent	41.00	42.00	39.00	46.00	60.00
9.4 Average length of stay	Nights	2.10	2.10	2.70	2.70	3.00
RELATED INDICATORS						
Share of tourism expenditure (6.1) in:						
10.1 Gross Domestic Product (GDP)	Percent	11.0	9.6	10.2	10.5	11.6
10.2 Exports of goods	Percent	149.1	120.1	125.4	134.1	133.3
10.3 Exports of services	Percent	84.1	74.6	75.4	75.5	70.3

(*) Balance of Payments items: 6.1 to 6.3 correspond to the "Credit" side (and are receipts for the country) while 8.2 to 8.4 correspond to the "Debit" side (and are expenditures in other countries).

ALGERIA

Basic Indicators		Units	2002	2003	2004	2005	2006
INBOUND TOURISM							
Arrivals							
1.1	Visitors	('000)	988	1,166	1,234	1,443	1,638
1.2	Tourists (overnight visitors)	('000)	..	..	..	..	..
1.3	Same-day visitors	('000)	..	..	..	..	..
1.4	Cruise passengers	('000)	..	..	..	..	..
Arrivals by region							
2.1	Africa	('000)	72	112	131	161	160
2.2	Americas	('000)	5	5	7	8	10
2.3	Europe	('000)	140	157	198	228	253
2.4	East Asia and the Pacific	('000)	9	8	9	15	19
2.5	South Asia	('000)	..	..	..	..	..
2.6	Middle East	('000)	24	23	23	29	37
Arrivals by means of transport used							
3.1	Air	('000)	456	..	..	..	..
3.2	Rail	('000)	..	..	..	..	..
3.3	Road	('000)	210	..	..	..	..
3.4	Sea	('000)	322	..	..	..	..
Arrivals by purpose of visit							
4.1	Leisure, recreation and holidays	('000)	..	240	267	323	321
4.2	Business and professional	('000)	..	65	101	118	146
4.3	Other	('000)	..	..	..	..	..
Accommodation							
5.1	Overnight stays in hotels and similar establishments	('000)	292	371	394	483	528
5.2	Guests in hotels and similar establishments	('000)	..	..	..	..	..
5.3	Overnight stays in all types of accommodation establishments	('000)	..	..	..	..	..
5.4	Average length of stay of non-resident tourists in all accommodation establishments	Nights	..	..	..	..	..
6.1	**Tourism expenditure in the country** (**)	US$ Mn	111	112	178	184	215
6.2	"Travel" (*)	US$ Mn	..	..	..	..	..
6.3	"Passenger transport" (*)	US$ Mn	..	..	..	..	..
DOMESTIC TOURISM							
Accommodation							
7.1	Overnight stays in hotels and similar establishments	('000)	2,959	3,948	4,149	4,222	4,376
7.2	Guests in hotels and similar establishments	('000)	..	..	..	..	..
7.3	Overnight stays in all types of accommodation establishments	('000)	..	..	..	..	..
7.4	Average length of stay of resident tourists in all accommodation establishments	Nights	..	..	..	..	..
OUTBOUND TOURISM							
8.1	**Departures**	('000)	1,257	1,254	1,417	1,513	1,349
8.2	**Tourism expenditure in other countries** (**)	US$ Mn	248	255	341	370	381
8.3	"Travel" (*)	US$ Mn	..	..	..	..	..
8.4	"Passenger transport" (*)	US$ Mn	..	..	..	..	..
TOURISM INDUSTRIES							
Hotels and similar establishments							
9.1	Number of rooms	Units	..	..	..	..	..
9.2	Number of bed-places	Units	72,567	77,473	82,034	83,895	84,869
9.3	Occupancy rate	Percent	..	..	..	..	..
9.4	Average length of stay	Nights	4.02	4.79	3.13	4.00	..
RELATED INDICATORS							
Share of tourism expenditure (6.1) in:							
10.1	Gross Domestic Product (GDP)	Percent	..	..	..	..	..
10.2	Exports of goods	Percent	..	..	..	..	..
10.3	Exports of services	Percent	..	..	..	..	..

(*) Balance of Payments items: 6.1 to 6.3 correspond to the "Credit" side (and are receipts for the country) while 8.2 to 8.4 correspond to the "Debit" side (and are expenditures in other countries).

(**) See Annex "Country notes".

Basic Indicators	Units	2002	2003	2004	2005	2006
INBOUND TOURISM						
Arrivals						
1.1 Visitors	('000)	..	..	..	..	..
1.2 Tourists (overnight visitors)	('000)	..	..	..	24.5	25.3
1.3 Same-day visitors	('000)	..	..	..	..	..
1.4 Cruise passengers	('000)	2.8	8.2	3.5	6.1	..
Arrivals by region						
2.1 Africa	('000)	..	..	..	..	..
2.2 Americas	('000)	..	..	..	6.9	7.2
2.3 Europe	('000)	..	..	..	0.4	0.4
2.4 East Asia and the Pacific	('000)	..	..	..	16.9	17.6
2.5 South Asia	('000)	..	..	..	..	..
2.6 Middle East	('000)	..	..	..	..	..
Arrivals by means of transport used						
3.1 Air	('000)	..	..	..	..	..
3.2 Rail	('000)	..	..	..	..	..
3.3 Road	('000)	..	..	..	..	..
3.4 Sea	('000)	..	..	..	..	..
Arrivals by purpose of visit						
4.1 Leisure, recreation and holidays	('000)	..	..	..	7.0	7.8
4.2 Business and professional	('000)	..	..	..	4.4	4.6
4.3 Other	('000)	..	..	..	13.1	12.9
Accommodation						
5.1 Overnight stays in hotels and similar establishments	('000)	..	..	..	..	..
5.2 Guests in hotels and similar establishments	('000)	..	..	..	..	..
5.3 Overnight stays in all types of accommodation establishments	('000)	..	..	..	..	..
5.4 Average length of stay of non-resident tourists in all accommodation establishments	Nights	..	..	..	..	..
6.1 **Tourism expenditure in the country**	US$ Mn	..	..	..	..	..
6.2 "Travel" (*)	US$ Mn	..	..	..	..	..
6.3 "Passenger transport" (*)	US$ Mn	..	..	..	..	..
DOMESTIC TOURISM						
Accommodation						
7.1 Overnight stays in hotels and similar establishments	('000)	..	..	..	..	..
7.2 Guests in hotels and similar establishments	('000)	..	..	..	..	..
7.3 Overnight stays in all types of accommodation establishments	('000)	..	..	..	..	..
7.4 Average length of stay of resident tourists in all accommodation establishments	Nights	..	..	..	..	..
OUTBOUND TOURISM						
8.1 **Departures**	('000)	..	..	..	35	41
8.2 **Tourism expenditure in other countries**	US$ Mn	..	..	..	..	..
8.3 "Travel" (*)	US$ Mn	..	..	..	..	..
8.4 "Passenger transport" (*)	US$ Mn	..	..	..	..	..
TOURISM INDUSTRIES						
Hotels and similar establishments						
9.1 Number of rooms	Units	143	243	243	257	..
9.2 Number of bed-places	Units	222	341	341	..	..
9.3 Occupancy rate	Percent	..	..	..	..	..
9.4 Average length of stay	Nights	..	..	..	..	..
RELATED INDICATORS						
Share of tourism expenditure (6.1) in:						
10.1 Gross Domestic Product (GDP)	Percent	..	..	..	..	..
10.2 Exports of goods	Percent	..	..	..	..	..
10.3 Exports of services	Percent	..	..	..	..	..

(*) Balance of Payments items: 6.1 to 6.3 correspond to the "Credit" side (and are receipts for the country) while 8.2 to 8.4 correspond to the "Debit" side (and are expenditures in other countries).

ANDORRA

Basic Indicators		Units	2002	2003	2004	2005	2006
	INBOUND TOURISM						
	Arrivals						
1.1	Visitors	('000)	11,507	11,601	11,668	11,049	10,737
1.2	Tourists (overnight visitors)	('000)	3,387	3,138	2,791	2,418	2,227
1.3	Same-day visitors	('000)	8,120	8,463	8,877	8,631	8,510
1.4	Cruise passengers	('000)	..	..	..	..	..
	Arrivals by region						
2.1	Africa	('000)	..	..	..	..	..
2.2	Americas	('000)	..	..	..	..	..
2.3	Europe	('000)	..	..	..	..	..
2.4	East Asia and the Pacific	('000)	..	..	..	..	..
2.5	South Asia	('000)	..	..	..	..	..
2.6	Middle East	('000)	..	..	..	..	..
	Arrivals by means of transport used						
3.1	Air	('000)	..	..	..	..	..
3.2	Rail	('000)	..	..	..	..	..
3.3	Road	('000)	11,507	11,601	11,668	11,049	10,737
3.4	Sea	('000)	..	..	..	..	..
	Arrivals by purpose of visit						
4.1	Leisure, recreation and holidays	('000)	10,439	10,253	10,156	9,522	9,681
4.2	Business and professional	('000)	601	626	691	645	493
4.3	Other	('000)	467	722	821	882	563
	Accommodation						
5.1	Overnight stays in hotels and similar establishments	('000)	6,765	5,581	5,525	5,199	4,911
5.2	Guests in hotels and similar establishments	('000)	..	..	..	..	..
5.3	Overnight stays in all types of accommodation establishments	('000)	9,336	7,745	7,322	6,762	6,284
5.4	Average length of stay of non-resident tourists in all accommodation establishments	Nights	2.87	2.68	2.62	2.80	2.82
6.1	**Tourism expenditure in the country**	US$ Mn	..	..	..	..	..
6.2	"Travel" (*)	US$ Mn	..	..	..	..	..
6.3	"Passenger transport" (*)	US$ Mn	..	..	..	..	..
	DOMESTIC TOURISM						
	Accommodation						
7.1	Overnight stays in hotels and similar establishments	('000)	..	..	..	..	..
7.2	Guests in hotels and similar establishments	('000)	..	..	..	..	..
7.3	Overnight stays in all types of accommodation establishments	('000)	..	..	..	..	..
7.4	Average length of stay of resident tourists in all accommodation establishments	Nights	..	..	..	..	..
	OUTBOUND TOURISM						
8.1	**Departures**	('000)	..	..	..	..	..
8.2	**Tourism expenditure in other countries**	US$ Mn	..	..	..	..	..
8.3	"Travel" (*)	US$ Mn	..	..	..	..	..
8.4	"Passenger transport" (*)	US$ Mn	..	..	..	..	..
	TOURISM INDUSTRIES						
	Hotels and similar establishments						
9.1	Number of rooms	Units	..	13,722	13,952	14,096	12,677
9.2	Number of bed-places	Units	..	34,522	38,310	38,957	31,515
9.3	Occupancy rate	Percent	..	..	..	..	..
9.4	Average length of stay	Nights	2.87	2.68	2.62	2.80	2.82
	RELATED INDICATORS						
	Share of tourism expenditure (6.1) in:						
10.1	Gross Domestic Product (GDP)	Percent	..	..	..	..	..
10.2	Exports of goods	Percent	..	..	..	..	..
10.3	Exports of services	Percent	..	..	..	..	..

(*) Balance of Payments items: 6.1 to 6.3 correspond to the "Credit" side (and are receipts for the country) while 8.2 to 8.4 correspond to the "Debit" side (and are expenditures in other countries).

Basic Indicators	Units	2002	2003	2004	2005	2006
INBOUND TOURISM						
Arrivals						
1.1 Visitors	('000)	..	..	..	..	..
1.2 Tourists (overnight visitors)	('000)	91	107	194	210	121
1.3 Same-day visitors	('000)	..	..	..	..	..
1.4 Cruise passengers	('000)	..	..	..	..	..
Arrivals by region						
2.1 Africa	('000)	17	31	42	43	19
2.2 Americas	('000)	15	15	34	36	21
2.3 Europe	('000)	52	55	101	110	63
2.4 East Asia and the Pacific	('000)	5	5	16	15	15
2.5 South Asia	('000)	1	..	..	2	2
2.6 Middle East	('000)	1	..	1	3	1
Arrivals by means of transport used						
3.1 Air	('000)	61	83	144	153	120
3.2 Rail	('000)	..	..	..	..	..
3.3 Road	('000)	27	21	46	52	1
3.4 Sea	('000)	3	3	4	5	..
Arrivals by purpose of visit						
4.1 Leisure, recreation and holidays	('000)	6	13	12	32	34
4.2 Business and professional	('000)	29	19	21	28	24
4.3 Other	('000)	56	75	161	150	64
Accommodation						
5.1 Overnight stays in hotels and similar establishments	('000)	183	212	143	176	199
5.2 Guests in hotels and similar establishments	('000)	..	..	92	120	64
5.3 Overnight stays in all types of accommodation establishments	('000)	207	217	149	182	231
5.4 Average length of stay of non-resident tourists in all accommodation establishments	Nights	..	..	..	..	..
6.1 **Tourism expenditure in the country**	US$ Mn	51	63	82	103	91
6.2 "Travel" (*)	US$ Mn	37	49	66	88	75
6.3 "Passenger transport" (*)	US$ Mn	14	14	16	15	16
DOMESTIC TOURISM						
Accommodation						
7.1 Overnight stays in hotels and similar establishments	('000)	34	78	61	72	54
7.2 Guests in hotels and similar establishments	('000)	..	..	48	47	36
7.3 Overnight stays in all types of accommodation establishments	('000)	133	124	87	124	79
7.4 Average length of stay of resident tourists in all accommodation establishments	Nights	..	..	..	..	..
OUTBOUND TOURISM						
8.1 **Departures**	('000)	..	..	..	..	..
8.2 **Tourism expenditure in other countries**	US$ Mn	52	49	86	135	393
8.3 "Travel" (*)	US$ Mn	19	12	39	74	148
8.4 "Passenger transport" (*)	US$ Mn	33	37	47	61	245
TOURISM INDUSTRIES						
Hotels and similar establishments						
9.1 Number of rooms	Units	8,262	9,244	9,358	9,593	9,593
9.2 Number of bed-places	Units	14,893	10,612	10,736	10,723	10,723
9.3 Occupancy rate	Percent	79.00	82.00	96.00	97.60	79.00
9.4 Average length of stay	Nights	4.00	4.00	..	..	..
RELATED INDICATORS						
Share of tourism expenditure (6.1) in:						
10.1 Gross Domestic Product (GDP)	Percent	0.4	0.5	0.4	0.3	0.2
10.2 Exports of goods	Percent	0.6	0.7	0.6	0.4	0.3
10.3 Exports of services	Percent	24.6	31.3	25.4	58.2	6.1

(*) Balance of Payments items: 6.1 to 6.3 correspond to the "Credit" side (and are receipts for the country) while 8.2 to 8.4 correspond to the "Debit" side (and are expenditures in other countries).

ANGUILLA

Basic Indicators	Units	2002	2003	2004	2005	2006
INBOUND TOURISM						
Arrivals						
1.1 Visitors	('000)	111	109	121	143	167
1.2 Tourists (overnight visitors)	('000)	44	47	54	62	73
1.3 Same-day visitors	('000)	67	62	67	81	94
1.4 Cruise passengers	('000)	..	..	..	..	..
Arrivals by region						
2.1 Africa	('000)	..	..	..	..	..
2.2 Americas	('000)	37	39	45	52	62
2.3 Europe	('000)	5	6	8	8	9
2.4 East Asia and the Pacific	('000)	..	..	..	..	..
2.5 South Asia	('000)	..	..	..	..	..
2.6 Middle East	('000)	..	..	..	..	..
Arrivals by means of transport used						
3.1 Air	('000)	30	28	24	32	33
3.2 Rail	('000)	..	..	..	..	..
3.3 Road	('000)	..	..	..	..	..
3.4 Sea	('000)	81	81	97	111	134
Arrivals by purpose of visit						
4.1 Leisure, recreation and holidays	('000)	40	43	50	57	66
4.2 Business and professional	('000)	4	4	4	5	7
4.3 Other	('000)	67	62	67	81	94
Accommodation						
5.1 Overnight stays in hotels and similar establishments	('000)	..	..	..	..	..
5.2 Guests in hotels and similar establishments	('000)	..	..	..	..	..
5.3 Overnight stays in all types of accommodation establishments	('000)	383	399	421	502	584
5.4 Average length of stay of non-resident tourists in all accommodation establishments	Nights	8.70	8.50	7.80	8.10	8.00
6.1 **Tourism expenditure in the country**	US$ Mn	..	..	..	..	..
6.2 "Travel" (*)	US$ Mn	57	60	69	86	107
6.3 "Passenger transport" (*)	US$ Mn	..	..	..	..	..
DOMESTIC TOURISM						
Accommodation						
7.1 Overnight stays in hotels and similar establishments	('000)	..	..	..	..	..
7.2 Guests in hotels and similar establishments	('000)	..	..	..	..	..
7.3 Overnight stays in all types of accommodation establishments	('000)	..	..	..	..	..
7.4 Average length of stay of resident tourists in all accommodation establishments	Nights	..	..	..	..	..
OUTBOUND TOURISM						
8.1 **Departures**	('000)	..	..	..	..	..
8.2 **Tourism expenditure in other countries**	US$ Mn	..	..	..	..	..
8.3 "Travel" (*)	US$ Mn	8	9	9	10	..
8.4 "Passenger transport" (*)	US$ Mn	..	..	..	..	..
TOURISM INDUSTRIES						
Hotels and similar establishments						
9.1 Number of rooms	Units	1,037	759	756	746	1,139
9.2 Number of bed-places	Units	..	..	..	..	..
9.3 Occupancy rate	Percent	43.95	45.50	52.00	..	..
9.4 Average length of stay	Nights	8.70	8.50	7.80	8.10	8.00
RELATED INDICATORS						
Share of tourism expenditure (6.1) in: (**)						
10.1 Gross Domestic Product (GDP)	Percent	..	..	..	..	..
10.2 Exports of goods	Percent	1425.0	1500.0	1150.0	573.3	..
10.3 Exports of services	Percent	86.4	87.0	88.5	90.5	..

(*) Balance of Payments items: 6.1 to 6.3 correspond to the "Credit" side (and are receipts for the country) while 8.2 to 8.4 correspond to the "Debit" side (and are expenditures in other countries).

(**) See Annex "Country notes".

Basic Indicators	Units	2002	2003	2004	2005	2006
INBOUND TOURISM						
Arrivals						
1.1 Visitors	('000)	528	623	791	734	745
1.2 Tourists (overnight visitors)	('000)	218	239	268	267	273
1.3 Same-day visitors	('000)	..	..	..	..	..
1.4 Cruise passengers	('000)	310	384	523	467	472
Arrivals by region						
2.1 Africa	('000)	..	..	..	..	..
2.2 Americas	('000)	108	122	129	126	139
2.3 Europe	('000)	82	99	113	106	107
2.4 East Asia and the Pacific	('000)	..	..	..	..	..
2.5 South Asia	('000)	..	..	..	..	..
2.6 Middle East	('000)	..	..	..	..	..
Arrivals by means of transport used						
3.1 Air	('000)	198	224	246	239	254
3.2 Rail	('000)	..	..	..	..	..
3.3 Road	('000)	..	..	..	..	..
3.4 Sea	('000)	310	384	523	467	472
Arrivals by purpose of visit						
4.1 Leisure, recreation and holidays	('000)	..	..	193	192	198
4.2 Business and professional	('000)	..	..	12	14	14
4.3 Other	('000)	..	..	41	33	42
Accommodation						
5.1 Overnight stays in hotels and similar establishments	('000)	..	..	..	..	..
5.2 Guests in hotels and similar establishments	('000)	..	..	..	..	..
5.3 Overnight stays in all types of accommodation establishments	('000)	..	..	..	..	..
5.4 Average length of stay of non-resident tourists in all accommodation establishments	Nights	..	10.00	9.37	9.26	9.54
6.1 **Tourism expenditure in the country**	US$ Mn	..	..	..	..	..
6.2 "Travel" (*)	US$ Mn	274	300	338	335	347
6.3 "Passenger transport" (*)	US$ Mn	..	..	..	..	..
DOMESTIC TOURISM						
Accommodation						
7.1 Overnight stays in hotels and similar establishments	('000)	..	..	..	..	..
7.2 Guests in hotels and similar establishments	('000)	..	..	..	..	..
7.3 Overnight stays in all types of accommodation establishments	('000)	..	..	..	..	..
7.4 Average length of stay of resident tourists in all accommodation establishments	Nights	..	..	..	..	..
OUTBOUND TOURISM						
8.1 **Departures**	('000)	..	..	..	..	..
8.2 **Tourism expenditure in other countries**	US$ Mn	..	..	..	..	..
8.3 "Travel" (*)	US$ Mn	33	35	38	40	46
8.4 "Passenger transport" (*)	US$ Mn	..	..	..	..	..
TOURISM INDUSTRIES						
Hotels and similar establishments						
9.1 Number of rooms	Units	..	..	3,373	..	..
9.2 Number of bed-places	Units	..	..	..	..	..
9.3 Occupancy rate	Percent	..	..	..	..	..
9.4 Average length of stay	Nights	..	..	..	..	..
RELATED INDICATORS						
Share of tourism expenditure (6.1) in: (**)						
10.1 Gross Domestic Product (GDP)	Percent	38.3	39.8	41.3	38.2	36.1
10.2 Exports of goods	Percent	805.9	666.7	593.0	408.5	..
10.3 Exports of services	Percent	69.5	71.8	70.9	68.6	..

(*) Balance of Payments items: 6.1 to 6.3 correspond to the "Credit" side (and are receipts for the country) while 8.2 to 8.4 correspond to the "Debit" side (and are expenditures in other countries).

(**) See Annex "Country notes".

ARGENTINA

Basic Indicators	Units	2002	2003	2004	2005	2006
INBOUND TOURISM						
Arrivals						
1.1 Visitors	('000)	..	..	..	..	..
1.2 Tourists (overnight visitors)	('000)	2,820	2,995	3,457	3,823	4,156
1.3 Same-day visitors	('000)	..	..	..	..	..
1.4 Cruise passengers	('000)	..	..	..	..	..
Arrivals by region						
2.1 Africa	('000)	..	..	..	..	..
2.2 Americas	('000)	2,420	2,425	2,722	2,984	3,271
2.3 Europe	('000)	324	456	546	631	658
2.4 East Asia and the Pacific	('000)	..	..	..	..	..
2.5 South Asia	('000)	..	..	..	..	..
2.6 Middle East	('000)	..	..	..	..	..
Arrivals by means of transport used						
3.1 Air	('000)	928	1,227	..	2,069	2,351
3.2 Rail	('000)	..	..	..	..	..
3.3 Road	('000)	1,617	1,430	..	1,436	1,417
3.4 Sea	('000)	275	339	..	318	388
Arrivals by purpose of visit						
4.1 Leisure, recreation and holidays	('000)	2,117	2,223	2,889	3,204	3,558
4.2 Business and professional	('000)	703	773	568	619	598
4.3 Other	('000)	..	..	..	..	..
Accommodation						
5.1 Overnight stays in hotels and similar establishments	('000)	..	..	..	9,482	9,782
5.2 Guests in hotels and similar establishments	('000)	..	..	..	..	..
5.3 Overnight stays in all types of accommodation establishments	('000)	27,636	31,148	36,576	40,097	45,547
5.4 Average length of stay of non-resident tourists in all accommodation establishments	Nights	9.80	10.40	10.58	10.49	10.96
6.1 **Tourism expenditure in the country**	US$ Mn	1,716	2,306	2,660	3,209	3,863
6.2 "Travel" (*)	US$ Mn	1,535	2,006	2,235	2,729	3,308
6.3 "Passenger transport" (*)	US$ Mn	181	300	425	480	555
DOMESTIC TOURISM						
Accommodation						
7.1 Overnight stays in hotels and similar establishments	('000)	..	..	..	28,569	32,965
7.2 Guests in hotels and similar establishments	('000)	..	..	..	..	..
7.3 Overnight stays in all types of accommodation establishments	('000)	..	..	..	..	..
7.4 Average length of stay of resident tourists in all accommodation establishments	Nights	..	..	..	..	..
OUTBOUND TOURISM						
8.1 **Departures**	('000)	3,008	3,088	3,904	3,894	4,009
8.2 **Tourism expenditure in other countries**	US$ Mn	2,744	2,997	3,208	3,564	4,078
8.3 "Travel" (*)	US$ Mn	2,328	2,511	2,604	2,790	3,131
8.4 "Passenger transport" (*)	US$ Mn	416	486	604	774	947
TOURISM INDUSTRIES						
Hotels and similar establishments						
9.1 Number of rooms	Units	170,746	176,685	182,444	191,840	195,267
9.2 Number of bed-places	Units	413,690	428,217	452,565	475,551	478,380
9.3 Occupancy rate	Percent	..	..	..	41.92	45.04
9.4 Average length of stay	Nights	..	..	..	..	..
RELATED INDICATORS						
Share of tourism expenditure (6.1) in:						
10.1 Gross Domestic Product (GDP)	Percent	1.7	1.8	1.7	1.8	1.8
10.2 Exports of goods	Percent	6.7	7.7	7.7	7.9	8.3
10.3 Exports of services	Percent	49.1	51.2	50.3	49.7	50.4

(*) Balance of Payments items: 6.1 to 6.3 correspond to the "Credit" side (and are receipts for the country) while 8.2 to 8.4 correspond to the "Debit" side (and are expenditures in other countries).

Basic Indicators	Units	2002	2003	2004	2005	2006
INBOUND TOURISM						
Arrivals						
1.1 Visitors	('000)	..	..	..	..	..
1.2 Tourists (overnight visitors)	('000)	162	206	263	319	381
1.3 Same-day visitors	('000)	..	..	..	..	..
1.4 Cruise passengers	('000)	..	..	..	..	..
Arrivals by region						
2.1 Africa	('000)	..	..	..	..	..
2.2 Americas	('000)	46	58	75	86	97
2.3 Europe	('000)	80	99	127	160	203
2.4 East Asia and the Pacific	('000)	3	6	9	14	16
2.5 South Asia	('000)	19	24	28	30	32
2.6 Middle East	('000)	14	19	23	28	33
Arrivals by means of transport used						
3.1 Air	('000)	135	173	196	225	270
3.2 Rail	('000)	2	3	14	19	19
3.3 Road	('000)	25	30	52	74	92
3.4 Sea	('000)	..	..	..	..	..
Arrivals by purpose of visit						
4.1 Leisure, recreation and holidays	('000)	126	160	204	235	246
4.2 Business and professional	('000)	31	39	46	67	114
4.3 Other	('000)	5	7	13	16	21
Accommodation						
5.1 Overnight stays in hotels and similar establishments	('000)	..	..	..	..	..
5.2 Guests in hotels and similar establishments	('000)	..	..	..	..	..
5.3 Overnight stays in all types of accommodation establishments	('000)	202	343	385	420	840
5.4 Average length of stay of non-resident tourists in all accommodation establishments	Nights	7.00	10.00	10.00	10.00	10.00
6.1 **Tourism expenditure in the country**	US$ Mn	81	90	188	240	307
6.2 "Travel" (*)	US$ Mn	63	73	171	220	271
6.3 "Passenger transport" (*)	US$ Mn	18	17	17	20	36
DOMESTIC TOURISM						
Accommodation						
7.1 Overnight stays in hotels and similar establishments	('000)	..	..	..	..	308
7.2 Guests in hotels and similar establishments	('000)	..	..	..	..	..
7.3 Overnight stays in all types of accommodation establishments	('000)	726	975	1,200	1,350	1,540
7.4 Average length of stay of resident tourists in all accommodation establishments	Nights	..	..	..	..	5.00
OUTBOUND TOURISM						
8.1 **Departures**	('000)	131	169	221	269	329
8.2 **Tourism expenditure in other countries**	US$ Mn	85	97	216	284	321
8.3 "Travel" (*)	US$ Mn	54	67	179	236	286
8.4 "Passenger transport" (*)	US$ Mn	31	30	37	48	35
TOURISM INDUSTRIES						
Hotels and similar establishments						
9.1 Number of rooms	Units	..	..	..	..	3,109
9.2 Number of bed-places	Units	12,578	13,774	14,964	17,387	19,590
9.3 Occupancy rate	Percent	25.00	50.00	58.00	59.00	61.00
9.4 Average length of stay	Nights	7.00	10.00	10.00	10.00	10.00
RELATED INDICATORS						
Share of tourism expenditure (6.1) in:						
10.1 Gross Domestic Product (GDP)	Percent	3.4	3.2	5.3	4.9	4.8
10.2 Exports of goods	Percent	15.8	12.9	25.5	23.9	30.0
10.3 Exports of services	Percent	44.0	43.5	56.5	58.4	63.3

(*) Balance of Payments items: 6.1 to 6.3 correspond to the "Credit" side (and are receipts for the country) while 8.2 to 8.4 correspond to the "Debit" side (and are expenditures in other countries).

ARUBA

Basic Indicators	Units	2002	2003	2004	2005	2006
INBOUND TOURISM						
Arrivals						
1.1 Visitors	('000)	1,225	1,184	1,304	1,286	1,285
1.2 Tourists (overnight visitors)	('000)	643	642	728	733	694
1.3 Same-day visitors	('000)	..	..	..	..	..
1.4 Cruise passengers	('000)	582	542	576	553	591
Arrivals by region						
2.1 Africa	('000)	..	..	..	..	..
2.2 Americas	('000)	595	585	665	666	630
2.3 Europe	('000)	44	55	60	63	62
2.4 East Asia and the Pacific	('000)	..	..	..	..	..
2.5 South Asia	('000)	..	..	..	..	..
2.6 Middle East	('000)	..	..	..	..	..
Arrivals by means of transport used						
3.1 Air	('000)	643	642	728	733	694
3.2 Rail	('000)	..	..	..	..	..
3.3 Road	('000)	..	..	..	..	..
3.4 Sea	('000)	..	..	..	..	..
Arrivals by purpose of visit						
4.1 Leisure, recreation and holidays	('000)	591	583	669	681	644
4.2 Business and professional	('000)	31	33	33	34	34
4.3 Other	('000)	21	26	26	18	16
Accommodation						
5.1 Overnight stays in hotels and similar establishments	('000)	3,945	4,059	4,615	4,735	4,515
5.2 Guests in hotels and similar establishments	('000)	567	568	647	653	619
5.3 Overnight stays in all types of accommodation establishments	('000)	4,863	5,098	5,640	5,695	5,471
5.4 Average length of stay of non-resident tourists in all accommodation establishments	Nights	7.57	7.90	7.80	7.77	7.90
6.1 **Tourism expenditure in the country**	US$ Mn	835.0	859.1	..	..	1,076.1
6.2 "Travel" (*)	US$ Mn	834	859	1,056	1,094	1,076
6.3 "Passenger transport" (*)	US$ Mn	1.0	0.1	..	..	0.1
DOMESTIC TOURISM						
Accommodation						
7.1 Overnight stays in hotels and similar establishments	('000)	..	..	..	..	..
7.2 Guests in hotels and similar establishments	('000)	..	..	..	..	..
7.3 Overnight stays in all types of accommodation establishments	('000)	..	..	..	..	..
7.4 Average length of stay of resident tourists in all accommodation establishments	Nights	..	..	..	..	..
OUTBOUND TOURISM						
8.1 **Departures**	('000)	..	..	..	..	..
8.2 **Tourism expenditure in other countries**	US$ Mn	172	214	248	241	256
8.3 "Travel" (*)	US$ Mn	159	189	218	217	233
8.4 "Passenger transport" (*)	US$ Mn	13	25	30	24	23
TOURISM INDUSTRIES						
Hotels and similar establishments						
9.1 Number of rooms	Units	7,040	7,731	7,206	7,966	9,062
9.2 Number of bed-places	Units	14,080	15,462	14,412	15,932	18,124
9.3 Occupancy rate	Percent	69.80	74.40	80.70	81.70	76.90
9.4 Average length of stay	Nights	..	..	..	..	..
RELATED INDICATORS						
Share of tourism expenditure (6.1) in:						
10.1 Gross Domestic Product (GDP)	Percent	43.7	..	..	..	..
10.2 Exports of goods	Percent	56.1	41.9	..	..	27.2
10.3 Exports of services	Percent	83.4	82.1	..	..	81.9

(*) Balance of Payments items: 6.1 to 6.3 correspond to the "Credit" side (and are receipts for the country) while 8.2 to 8.4 correspond to the "Debit" side (and are expenditures in other countries).

Basic Indicators	Units	2002	2003	2004	2005	2006
INBOUND TOURISM						
Arrivals						
1.1 Visitors	('000)	4,841	4,746	5,215	5,499	5,532
1.2 Tourists (overnight visitors)	('000)	4,420	4,354	4,774	5,020	5,064
1.3 Same-day visitors	('000)	43	30	23	26	35
1.4 Cruise passengers	('000)	..	..	..	..	..
Arrivals by region						
2.1 Africa	('000)	68	69	68	71	78
2.2 Americas	('000)	556	537	561	584	611
2.3 Europe	('000)	1,198	1,228	1,261	1,330	1,368
2.4 East Asia and the Pacific	('000)	2,924	2,812	3,205	3,375	3,315
2.5 South Asia	('000)	61	63	75	89	108
2.6 Middle East	('000)	31	34	43	49	52
Arrivals by means of transport used						
3.1 Air	('000)	4,819	4,730	5,201	5,486	5,514
3.2 Rail	('000)	..	..	..	..	..
3.3 Road	('000)	..	..	..	..	..
3.4 Sea	('000)	22	16	14	13	19
Arrivals by purpose of visit						
4.1 Leisure, recreation and holidays	('000)	2,401	2,441	2,685	2,952	2,887
4.2 Business and professional	('000)	873	900	999	1,104	1,218
4.3 Other	('000)	1,567	1,406	1,531	1,443	1,428
Accommodation						
5.1 Overnight stays in hotels and similar establishments	('000)	..	..	..	..	..
5.2 Guests in hotels and similar establishments	('000)	..	..	..	..	..
5.3 Overnight stays in all types of accommodation establishments	('000)	..	..	..	..	..
5.4 Average length of stay of non-resident tourists in all accommodation establishments	Nights	..	..	..	..	..
6.1 **Tourism expenditure in the country**	US$ Mn	13,624	16,647	20,453	22,566	23,729
6.2 "Travel" (*)	US$ Mn	9,971	12,438	15,214	16,868	17,854
6.3 "Passenger transport" (*)	US$ Mn	3,653	4,209	5,239	5,698	5,875
DOMESTIC TOURISM						
Accommodation						
7.1 Overnight stays in hotels and similar establishments	('000)	..	..	..	..	..
7.2 Guests in hotels and similar establishments	('000)	..	..	..	..	..
7.3 Overnight stays in all types of accommodation establishments	('000)	..	..	..	..	..
7.4 Average length of stay of resident tourists in all accommodation establishments	Nights	..	..	..	..	..
OUTBOUND TOURISM						
8.1 **Departures**	('000)	3,461	3,388	4,369	4,756	4,941
8.2 **Tourism expenditure in other countries**	US$ Mn	8,494	10,135	14,224	15,593	16,393
8.3 "Travel" (*)	US$ Mn	6,072	7,270	10,242	11,253	11,690
8.4 "Passenger transport" (*)	US$ Mn	2,422	2,865	3,982	4,340	4,703
TOURISM INDUSTRIES						
Hotels and similar establishments						
9.1 Number of rooms	Units	196,431	204,461	205,495	232,077	233,803
9.2 Number of bed-places	Units	563,779	580,252	586,217	659,731	673,792
9.3 Occupancy rate	Percent	58.70	63.50	63.70	64.50	66.90
9.4 Average length of stay	Nights	2.30	2.30	2.30	2.30	2.30
RELATED INDICATORS						
Share of tourism expenditure (6.1) in:						
10.1 Gross Domestic Product (GDP)	Percent	3.2	3.1	3.1	3.1	3.1
10.2 Exports of goods	Percent	21.0	23.6	23.5	21.1	19.0
10.3 Exports of services	Percent	69.5	70.1	71.8	72.7	71.7

(*) Balance of Payments items: 6.1 to 6.3 correspond to the "Credit" side (and are receipts for the country) while 8.2 to 8.4 correspond to the "Debit" side (and are expenditures in other countries).

AUSTRIA

Basic Indicators	Units	2002	2003	2004	2005	2006
INBOUND TOURISM						
Arrivals						
1.1 Visitors	('000)	..	..	..	..	..
1.2 Tourists (overnight visitors)	('000)	18,611	19,078	19,373	19,952	20,261
1.3 Same-day visitors	('000)	..	..	..	..	..
1.4 Cruise passengers	('000)	..	..	..	..	..
Arrivals by region						
2.1 Africa	('000)	26	27	32	42	43
2.2 Americas	('000)	647	599	674	692	780
2.3 Europe	('000)	16,984	17,387	17,446	18,031	18,257
2.4 East Asia and the Pacific	('000)	594	619	755	792	797
2.5 South Asia	('000)	39	30	40	39	50
2.6 Middle East	('000)	29	38	43	68	75
Arrivals by means of transport used						
3.1 Air	('000)	..	..	..	..	..
3.2 Rail	('000)	..	..	..	..	..
3.3 Road	('000)	..	..	..	..	..
3.4 Sea	('000)	..	..	..	..	..
Arrivals by purpose of visit						
4.1 Leisure, recreation and holidays	('000)	..	..	..	..	..
4.2 Business and professional	('000)	..	..	..	..	..
4.3 Other	('000)	..	..	..	..	..
Accommodation						
5.1 Overnight stays in hotels and similar establishments	('000)	60,249	60,622	60,746	62,396	62,789
5.2 Guests in hotels and similar establishments	('000)	14,165	14,489	14,853	15,363	15,765
5.3 Overnight stays in all types of accommodation establishments	('000)	67,346	68,217	68,270	69,733	70,017
5.4 Average length of stay of non-resident tourists in all accommodation establishments	Nights	4.60	4.53	4.40	4.40	4.30
6.1 **Tourism expenditure in the country**	US$ Mn	13,046	16,342	18,385	19,310	18,890
6.2 "Travel" (*)	US$ Mn	11,136	13,842	15,290	15,589	16,510
6.3 "Passenger transport" (*)	US$ Mn	1,910	2,500	3,095	3,721	2,380
DOMESTIC TOURISM						
Accommodation						
7.1 Overnight stays in hotels and similar establishments	('000)	19,302	19,634	19,800	20,329	21,184
7.2 Guests in hotels and similar establishments	('000)	6,444	6,603	6,766	7,072	7,569
7.3 Overnight stays in all types of accommodation establishments	('000)	26,424	27,023	26,980	27,298	28,112
7.4 Average length of stay of resident tourists in all accommodation establishments	Nights	3.50	3.50	3.40	3.40	3.30
OUTBOUND TOURISM						
8.1 **Departures**	('000)	3,907	8,384	8,371	8,206	10,042
8.2 **Tourism expenditure in other countries**	US$ Mn	10,300	12,894	13,411	12,755	11,035
8.3 "Travel" (*)	US$ Mn	9,460	11,757	11,834	10,994	9,348
8.4 "Passenger transport" (*)	US$ Mn	840	1,137	1,577	1,761	1,687
TOURISM INDUSTRIES						
Hotels and similar establishments						
9.1 Number of rooms	Units	282,735	282,614	290,491	289,879	282,002
9.2 Number of bed-places	Units	628,730	631,085	637,095	639,369	643,735
9.3 Occupancy rate	Percent	35.90	36.10	34.60	35.80	35.60
9.4 Average length of stay	Nights	3.86	3.81	3.72	3.69	3.60
RELATED INDICATORS						
Share of tourism expenditure (6.1) in:						
10.1 Gross Domestic Product (GDP)	Percent	6.3	6.4	6.2	6.3	5.9
10.2 Exports of goods	Percent	17.7	18.2	16.4	16.5	14.1
10.3 Exports of services	Percent	36.9	38.0	37.4	35.8	40.7

(*) Balance of Payments items: 6.1 to 6.3 correspond to the "Credit" side (and are receipts for the country) while 8.2 to 8.4 correspond to the "Debit" side (and are expenditures in other countries).

Basic Indicators	Units	2002	2003	2004	2005	2006
INBOUND TOURISM						
Arrivals						
1.1 Visitors	('000)	..	..	..	..	..
1.2 Tourists (overnight visitors)	('000)	834	1,014	1,349	1,177	1,194
1.3 Same-day visitors	('000)	..	..	..	..	..
1.4 Cruise passengers	('000)	..	..	..	..	..
Arrivals by region						
2.1 Africa	('000)	..	..	1	1	1
2.2 Americas	('000)	6	8	12	11	10
2.3 Europe	('000)	582	747	1,051	946	1,008
2.4 East Asia and the Pacific	('000)	3	4	6	7	7
2.5 South Asia	('000)	241	253	275	211	165
2.6 Middle East	('000)	2	2	2	2	2
Arrivals by means of transport used						
3.1 Air	('000)	798	950	1,260	1,100	1,116
3.2 Rail	('000)	5	8	12	11	10
3.3 Road	('000)	28	49	68	61	62
3.4 Sea	('000)	2	5	7	5	5
Arrivals by purpose of visit						
4.1 Leisure, recreation and holidays	('000)	8	16	23	21	22
4.2 Business and professional	('000)	775	915	1,230	1,065	1,076
4.3 Other	('000)	51	82	95	91	95
Accommodation						
5.1 Overnight stays in hotels and similar establishments	('000)	350	439	929	1,064	1,115
5.2 Guests in hotels and similar establishments	('000)	118	146	213	264	291
5.3 Overnight stays in all types of accommodation establishments	('000)	..	..	..	..	..
5.4 Average length of stay of non-resident tourists in all accommodation establishments	Nights	..	..	..	..	..
6.1 **Tourism expenditure in the country**	US$ Mn	63	70	79	100	201
6.2 "Travel" (*)	US$ Mn	51	58	65	78	117
6.3 "Passenger transport" (*)	US$ Mn	12	12	14	22	84
DOMESTIC TOURISM						
Accommodation						
7.1 Overnight stays in hotels and similar establishments	('000)	86	142	414	524	557
7.2 Guests in hotels and similar establishments	('000)	56	68	113	133	141
7.3 Overnight stays in all types of accommodation establishments	('000)	..	..	..	..	..
7.4 Average length of stay of resident tourists in all accommodation establishments	Nights	..	..	..	..	..
OUTBOUND TOURISM						
8.1 **Departures**	('000)	1,141	1,376	1,473	1,830	1,836
8.2 **Tourism expenditure in other countries**	US$ Mn	110	120	140	188	256
8.3 "Travel" (*)	US$ Mn	105	111	126	164	201
8.4 "Passenger transport" (*)	US$ Mn	5	9	14	24	55
TOURISM INDUSTRIES						
Hotels and similar establishments						
9.1 Number of rooms	Units	5,300	5,034	9,827	10,661	11,403
9.2 Number of bed-places	Units	9,591	9,569	21,144	22,492	24,706
9.3 Occupancy rate	Percent	..	..	..	..	..
9.4 Average length of stay	Nights	..	..	..	..	..
RELATED INDICATORS						
Share of tourism expenditure (6.1) in:						
10.1 Gross Domestic Product (GDP)	Percent	1.0	1.0	0.9	0.8	1.0
10.2 Exports of goods	Percent	2.7	2.7	2.1	1.3	1.5
10.3 Exports of services	Percent	17.4	16.2	16.1	14.6	21.4

(*) Balance of Payments items: 6.1 to 6.3 correspond to the "Credit" side (and are receipts for the country) while 8.2 to 8.4 correspond to the "Debit" side (and are expenditures in other countries).

BAHAMAS

Basic Indicators	Units	2002	2003	2004	2005	2006
INBOUND TOURISM						
Arrivals						
1.1 Visitors	('000)	4,406	4,594	5,004	4,779	4,731
1.2 Tourists (overnight visitors)	('000)	1,513	1,510	1,561	1,608	1,601
1.3 Same-day visitors	('000)	91	114	83	92	54
1.4 Cruise passengers	('000)	2,802	2,970	3,360	3,079	3,076
Arrivals by region						
2.1 Africa	('000)	1	1	1	1	1
2.2 Americas	('000)	1,406	1,393	1,455	1,485	1,484
2.3 Europe	('000)	80	94	84	86	83
2.4 East Asia and the Pacific	('000)	8	6	7	7	7
2.5 South Asia	('000)	..	..	..	..	..
2.6 Middle East	('000)	..	..	1	..	..
Arrivals by means of transport used						
3.1 Air	('000)	1,403	1,429	1,450	1,515	1,492
3.2 Rail	('000)	..	..	..	..	..
3.3 Road	('000)	..	..	..	..	..
3.4 Sea	('000)	3,003	3,165	3,554	3,265	3,239
Arrivals by purpose of visit						
4.1 Leisure, recreation and holidays	('000)	1,290	1,306	1,306	1,337	1,322
4.2 Business and professional	('000)	156	127	148	152	127
4.3 Other	('000)	67	77	107	119	151
Accommodation						
5.1 Overnight stays in hotels and similar establishments	('000)	..	..	..	..	..
5.2 Guests in hotels and similar establishments	('000)	1,086	1,098	1,152	1,188	1,157
5.3 Overnight stays in all types of accommodation establishments	('000)	8,704	8,957	9,898	10,297	10,269
5.4 Average length of stay of non-resident tourists in all accommodation establishments	Nights	5.75	5.90	6.30	6.40	6.40
6.1 **Tourism expenditure in the country**	US$ Mn	1,773	1,770	1,897	2,082	2,079
6.2 "Travel" (*)	US$ Mn	1,760	1,757	1,884	2,072	2,069
6.3 "Passenger transport" (*)	US$ Mn	13	13	13	10	10
DOMESTIC TOURISM						
Accommodation						
7.1 Overnight stays in hotels and similar establishments	('000)	..	..	..	..	..
7.2 Guests in hotels and similar establishments	('000)	..	..	..	..	..
7.3 Overnight stays in all types of accommodation establishments	('000)	..	..	..	..	..
7.4 Average length of stay of resident tourists in all accommodation establishments	Nights	..	..	..	..	..
OUTBOUND TOURISM						
8.1 **Departures**	('000)	..	..	..	..	..
8.2 **Tourism expenditure in other countries**	US$ Mn	338	404	469	528	541
8.3 "Travel" (*)	US$ Mn	244	305	316	344	385
8.4 "Passenger transport" (*)	US$ Mn	94	99	153	184	156
TOURISM INDUSTRIES						
Hotels and similar establishments						
9.1 Number of rooms	Units	15,145	15,393	15,508	14,800	14,929
9.2 Number of bed-places	Units	30,290	30,786	31,016	29,600	29,858
9.3 Occupancy rate	Percent	62.00	59.20	66.40	70.40	68.20
9.4 Average length of stay	Nights	4.43	4.47	4.88	..	..
RELATED INDICATORS						
Share of tourism expenditure (6.1) in:						
10.1 Gross Domestic Product (GDP)	Percent	32.8	32.2	..	..	..
10.2 Exports of goods	Percent	420.1	414.5	397.7	379.2	300.4
10.3 Exports of services	Percent	86.0	86.1	84.5	83.8	84.9

(*) Balance of Payments items: 6.1 to 6.3 correspond to the "Credit" side (and are receipts for the country) while 8.2 to 8.4 correspond to the "Debit" side (and are expenditures in other countries).

16

Basic Indicators	Units	2002	2003	2004	2005	2006
INBOUND TOURISM						
Arrivals						
1.1 Visitors	('000)	4,831	4,844	5,667	6,313	7,289
1.2 Tourists (overnight visitors)	('000)	3,167	2,955	3,514	3,914	4,519
1.3 Same-day visitors	('000)	1,664	1,889	2,153	2,399	2,770
1.4 Cruise passengers	('000)	..	..	..	..	..
Arrivals by region						
2.1 Africa	('000)	47	60	76	82	99
2.2 Americas	('000)	177	192	200	190	234
2.3 Europe	('000)	256	260	334	358	430
2.4 East Asia and the Pacific	('000)	187	212	268	287	374
2.5 South Asia	('000)	522	561	648	720	942
2.6 Middle East	('000)	3,642	3,559	4,141	4,676	5,210
Arrivals by means of transport used						
3.1 Air	('000)	920	974	1,176	1,301	1,544
3.2 Rail	('000)	..	..	..	..	..
3.3 Road	('000)	3,897	3,862	4,484	5,007	5,733
3.4 Sea	('000)	13	8	7	5	12
Arrivals by purpose of visit						
4.1 Leisure, recreation and holidays	('000)	3,642	3,769	4,005	4,187	5,087
4.2 Business and professional	('000)	419	542	647	627	868
4.3 Other	('000)	770	533	1,015	1,500	1,334
Accommodation						
5.1 Overnight stays in hotels and similar establishments	('000)	1,386	1,290	2,290	2,224	2,475
5.2 Guests in hotels and similar establishments	('000)	686	695	1,132	1,237	1,284
5.3 Overnight stays in all types of accommodation establishments	('000)	..	..	..	..	..
5.4 Average length of stay of non-resident tourists in all accommodation establishments	Nights	2.06	1.89	2.02	2.00	1.93
6.1 **Tourism expenditure in the country**	US$ Mn	985	1,206	1,504	1,603	1,786
6.2 "Travel" (*)	US$ Mn	740	720	864	920	1,048
6.3 "Passenger transport" (*)	US$ Mn	245	486	640	683	738
DOMESTIC TOURISM						
Accommodation						
7.1 Overnight stays in hotels and similar establishments	('000)	..	..	..	..	..
7.2 Guests in hotels and similar establishments	('000)	..	..	..	..	..
7.3 Overnight stays in all types of accommodation establishments	('000)	..	..	..	..	..
7.4 Average length of stay of resident tourists in all accommodation establishments	Nights	..	..	..	..	..
OUTBOUND TOURISM						
8.1 **Departures**	('000)	..	..	..	..	..
8.2 **Tourism expenditure in other countries**	US$ Mn	550	492	528	574	639
8.3 "Travel" (*)	US$ Mn	380	372	387	414	455
8.4 "Passenger transport" (*)	US$ Mn	170	120	141	160	184
TOURISM INDUSTRIES						
Hotels and similar establishments						
9.1 Number of rooms	Units	7,368	7,880	7,824	..	6,860
9.2 Number of bed-places	Units	10,314	10,759	..	..	..
9.3 Occupancy rate	Percent	53.72	44.68	54.78	56.30	57.40
9.4 Average length of stay	Nights	..	..	..	..	..
RELATED INDICATORS						
Share of tourism expenditure (6.1) in:						
10.1 Gross Domestic Product (GDP)	Percent	11.7	12.4	13.7	12.4	..
10.2 Exports of goods	Percent	16.7	17.9	20.0	16.0	15.4
10.3 Exports of services	Percent	92.2	95.7	96.5	96.5	96.6

(*) Balance of Payments items: 6.1 to 6.3 correspond to the "Credit" side (and are receipts for the country) while 8.2 to 8.4 correspond to the "Debit" side (and are expenditures in other countries).

BANGLADESH

Basic Indicators	Units	2002	2003	2004	2005	2006
INBOUND TOURISM						
Arrivals						
1.1 Visitors	('000)	..	..	..	..	..
1.2 Tourists (overnight visitors)	('000)	207	245	271	208	200
1.3 Same-day visitors	('000)	..	..	..	..	..
1.4 Cruise passengers	('000)	..	..	..	..	..
Arrivals by region						
2.1 Africa	('000)	1	2	2	2	2
2.2 Americas	('000)	18	31	37	19	25
2.3 Europe	('000)	47	64	77	49	57
2.4 East Asia and the Pacific	('000)	41	43	51	36	37
2.5 South Asia	('000)	97	102	100	99	75
2.6 Middle East	('000)	3	3	3	3	4
Arrivals by means of transport used						
3.1 Air	('000)	151	187	218	140	151
3.2 Rail	('000)	..	..	..	..	..
3.3 Road	('000)	56	58	53	68	49
3.4 Sea	('000)	..	..	..	..	..
Arrivals by purpose of visit						
4.1 Leisure, recreation and holidays	('000)	41	43	40	68	85
4.2 Business and professional	('000)	30	34	55	103	91
4.3 Other	('000)	136	168	176	37	24
Accommodation						
5.1 Overnight stays in hotels and similar establishments	('000)	..	..	..	..	..
5.2 Guests in hotels and similar establishments	('000)	..	..	..	..	..
5.3 Overnight stays in all types of accommodation establishments	('000)	..	..	..	..	..
5.4 Average length of stay of non-resident tourists in all accommodation establishments	Nights	5.50	4.50	4.50	4.50	4.50
6.1 **Tourism expenditure in the country**	US$ Mn	59	59	76	79	80.2
6.2 "Travel" (*)	US$ Mn	57	57	67	70	80
6.3 "Passenger transport" (*)	US$ Mn	2	2	9	9	0.2
DOMESTIC TOURISM						
Accommodation						
7.1 Overnight stays in hotels and similar establishments	('000)	..	..	..	..	..
7.2 Guests in hotels and similar establishments	('000)	..	..	..	..	..
7.3 Overnight stays in all types of accommodation establishments	('000)	..	..	..	..	..
7.4 Average length of stay of resident tourists in all accommodation establishments	Nights	..	..	..	..	..
OUTBOUND TOURISM						
8.1 **Departures**	('000)	1,158	1,414	1,565	1,767	1,819
8.2 **Tourism expenditure in other countries**	US$ Mn	309	389	442	375	444
8.3 "Travel" (*)	US$ Mn	113	165	161	136	140
8.4 "Passenger transport" (*)	US$ Mn	196	224	281	239	304
TOURISM INDUSTRIES						
Hotels and similar establishments						
9.1 Number of rooms	Units	4,550	4,565	4,575	4,590	4,590
9.2 Number of bed-places	Units	9,789	10,165	10,435	10,557	10,557
9.3 Occupancy rate	Percent	39.00	38.00	32.00	38.63	43.76
9.4 Average length of stay	Nights	..	..	..	..	..
RELATED INDICATORS						
Share of tourism expenditure (6.1) in:						
10.1 Gross Domestic Product (GDP)	Percent	0.1	0.1	0.1	0.1	0.1
10.2 Exports of goods	Percent	1.0	0.8	0.9	0.8	0.7
10.3 Exports of services	Percent	6.9	5.8	7.0	6.3	6.2

(*) Balance of Payments items: 6.1 to 6.3 correspond to the "Credit" side (and are receipts for the country) while 8.2 to 8.4 correspond to the "Debit" side (and are expenditures in other countries).

Basic Indicators	Units	2002	2003	2004	2005	2006
INBOUND TOURISM						
Arrivals						
1.1 Visitors	('000)	1,021	1,090	1,273	1,111	1,102
1.2 Tourists (overnight visitors)	('000)	498	531	552	548	563
1.3 Same-day visitors	('000)	..	..	..	..	..
1.4 Cruise passengers	('000)	523	559	721	563	539
Arrivals by region						
2.1 Africa	('000)	1	1	1	1	1
2.2 Americas	('000)	275	292	301	311	312
2.3 Europe	('000)	219	234	246	230	241
2.4 East Asia and the Pacific	('000)	2	4	3	3	3
2.5 South Asia	('000)	1	..	1	1	1
2.6 Middle East	('000)	..	..	..	..	..
Arrivals by means of transport used						
3.1 Air	('000)	492	526	546	544	557
3.2 Rail	('000)	..	..	..	..	..
3.3 Road	('000)	..	..	..	..	..
3.4 Sea	('000)	529	564	727	567	544
Arrivals by purpose of visit						
4.1 Leisure, recreation and holidays	('000)	417	436	445	432	470
4.2 Business and professional	('000)	58	65	70	72	60
4.3 Other	('000)	22	30	36	44	33
Accommodation						
5.1 Overnight stays in hotels and similar establishments	('000)	..	..	..	..	..
5.2 Guests in hotels and similar establishments	('000)	..	..	..	..	..
5.3 Overnight stays in all types of accommodation establishments	('000)	2,031	2,459	2,463	..	..
5.4 Average length of stay of non-resident tourists in all accommodation establishments	Nights	11.00	10.00	9.90	9.80	..
6.1 **Tourism expenditure in the country**	US$ Mn	666	767	785	905	..
6.2 "Travel" (*)	US$ Mn	658	758	776	897	978
6.3 "Passenger transport" (*)	US$ Mn	8	9	9	8	..
DOMESTIC TOURISM						
Accommodation						
7.1 Overnight stays in hotels and similar establishments	('000)	..	..	..	..	..
7.2 Guests in hotels and similar establishments	('000)	..	..	..	..	..
7.3 Overnight stays in all types of accommodation establishments	('000)	..	..	..	..	..
7.4 Average length of stay of resident tourists in all accommodation establishments	Nights	..	..	..	..	..
OUTBOUND TOURISM						
8.1 **Departures**	('000)	..	..	..	..	..
8.2 **Tourism expenditure in other countries**	US$ Mn	146	154	163	153	..
8.3 "Travel" (*)	US$ Mn	99	105	108	96	..
8.4 "Passenger transport" (*)	US$ Mn	47	49	55	57	..
TOURISM INDUSTRIES						
Hotels and similar establishments						
9.1 Number of rooms	Units	6,742	6,210	5,945	6,353	..
9.2 Number of bed-places	Units	13,050	10,770	11,237	12,417	..
9.3 Occupancy rate	Percent	42.50	49.90	49.70	53.80	..
9.4 Average length of stay	Nights	7.20	6.80	6.80	7.40	..
RELATED INDICATORS						
Share of tourism expenditure (6.1) in:						
10.1 Gross Domestic Product (GDP)	Percent	27.1	28.6	28.1	29.3	..
10.2 Exports of goods	Percent	263.2	290.5	267.9	238.8	..
10.3 Exports of services	Percent	64.0	65.8	64.1	62.1	..

(*) Balance of Payments items: 6.1 to 6.3 correspond to the "Credit" side (and are receipts for the country) while 8.2 to 8.4 correspond to the "Debit" side (and are expenditures in other countries).

BELARUS

Basic Indicators	Units	2002	2003	2004	2005	2006
INBOUND TOURISM						
Arrivals						
1.1 Visitors	('000)	..	..	..	..	5,276
1.2 Tourists (overnight visitors)	('000)	63	64	67	91	89
1.3 Same-day visitors	('000)	..	..	..	..	..
1.4 Cruise passengers	('000)	..	..	..	..	..
Arrivals by region						
2.1 Africa	('000)	..	..	..	..	..
2.2 Americas	('000)	3	4	6	5	4
2.3 Europe	('000)	57	58	59	82	81
2.4 East Asia and the Pacific	('000)	3	2	2	2	2
2.5 South Asia	('000)	..	..	..	1	1
2.6 Middle East	('000)	..	..	..	1	1
Arrivals by means of transport used						
3.1 Air	('000)	..	..	..	..	122
3.2 Rail	('000)	..	..	..	..	1,760
3.3 Road	('000)	..	..	..	..	3,286
3.4 Sea	('000)	..	..	..	..	..
Arrivals by purpose of visit						
4.1 Leisure, recreation and holidays	('000)	..	..	..	..	2,930
4.2 Business and professional	('000)	..	..	..	..	525
4.3 Other	('000)	..	..	..	..	1,821
Accommodation						
5.1 Overnight stays in hotels and similar establishments	('000)	496	538	575	597	688
5.2 Guests in hotels and similar establishments	('000)	208	226	236	246	272
5.3 Overnight stays in all types of accommodation establishments	('000)	..	..	..	..	..
5.4 Average length of stay of non-resident tourists in all accommodation establishments	Nights	..	..	..	..	..
6.1 **Tourism expenditure in the country**	US$ Mn	295	339	362	346	386
6.2 "Travel" (*)	US$ Mn	234	267	270	253	272
6.3 "Passenger transport" (*)	US$ Mn	61	72	92	93	114
DOMESTIC TOURISM						
Accommodation						
7.1 Overnight stays in hotels and similar establishments	('000)	2,491	2,753	2,926	3,306	3,649
7.2 Guests in hotels and similar establishments	('000)	866	991	1,030	1,084	1,171
7.3 Overnight stays in all types of accommodation establishments	('000)	..	..	..	..	..
7.4 Average length of stay of resident tourists in all accommodation establishments	Nights	..	..	..	..	..
OUTBOUND TOURISM						
8.1 **Departures**	('000)	1,436	1,108	515	572	525
8.2 **Tourism expenditure in other countries**	US$ Mn	593	510	588	672	823
8.3 "Travel" (*)	US$ Mn	559	473	538	604	735
8.4 "Passenger transport" (*)	US$ Mn	34	37	50	68	88
TOURISM INDUSTRIES						
Hotels and similar establishments						
9.1 Number of rooms	Units	12,534	12,724	12,894	12,946	13,292
9.2 Number of bed-places	Units	23,137	23,602	23,648	23,504	24,095
9.3 Occupancy rate	Percent	35.38	38.21	40.46	45.50	49.32
9.4 Average length of stay	Nights	2.78	2.70	2.77	2.93	3.00
RELATED INDICATORS						
Share of tourism expenditure (6.1) in:						
10.1 Gross Domestic Product (GDP)	Percent	2.0	1.9	1.6	1.2	1.0
10.2 Exports of goods	Percent	3.7	3.4	2.6	2.1	1.9
10.3 Exports of services	Percent	22.0	22.6	20.7	17.7	16.8

(*) Balance of Payments items: 6.1 to 6.3 correspond to the "Credit" side (and are receipts for the country) while 8.2 to 8.4 correspond to the "Debit" side (and are expenditures in other countries).

Basic Indicators	Units	2002	2003	2004	2005	2006
INBOUND TOURISM						
Arrivals						
1.1 Visitors	('000)	..	..	..	..	..
1.2 Tourists (overnight visitors)	('000)	6,720	6,690	6,710	6,747	6,995
1.3 Same-day visitors	('000)	..	..	..	..	..
1.4 Cruise passengers	('000)	..	..	..	..	..
Arrivals by region						
2.1 Africa	('000)	60	63	61	62	65
2.2 Americas	('000)	400	369	382	390	407
2.3 Europe	('000)	5,798	5,847	5,800	5,836	6,036
2.4 East Asia and the Pacific	('000)	348	294	318	298	305
2.5 South Asia	('000)	39	32	33	35	33
2.6 Middle East	('000)	18	18	18	20	21
Arrivals by means of transport used						
3.1 Air	('000)	7,102	7,505	7,709	8,027	..
3.2 Rail	('000)	..	..	..	..	..
3.3 Road	('000)	..	..	..	..	..
3.4 Sea	('000)	..	..	..	..	..
Arrivals by purpose of visit						
4.1 Leisure, recreation and holidays	('000)	4,183	4,330	4,352	4,381	4,503
4.2 Business and professional	('000)	2,400	2,284	2,333	2,366	2,492
4.3 Other	('000)	136	76	25	..	..
Accommodation						
5.1 Overnight stays in hotels and similar establishments	('000)	10,410	10,280	10,315	10,297	10,634
5.2 Guests in hotels and similar establishments	('000)	5,323	5,261	5,385	5,409	5,665
5.3 Overnight stays in all types of accommodation establishments	('000)	15,895	15,929	15,545	15,553	16,040
5.4 Average length of stay of non-resident tourists in all accommodation establishments	Nights	..	..	..	..	..
6.1 **Tourism expenditure in the country**	US$ Mn	7,598	8,848	10,089	10,881	11,556
6.2 "Travel" (*)	US$ Mn	6,935	8,193	9,208	9,845	10,242
6.3 "Passenger transport" (*)	US$ Mn	663	655	881	1,036	1,314
DOMESTIC TOURISM						
Accommodation						
7.1 Overnight stays in hotels and similar establishments	('000)	4,091	4,061	4,090	4,313	4,737
7.2 Guests in hotels and similar establishments	('000)	2,103	2,119	2,208	2,364	2,596
7.3 Overnight stays in all types of accommodation establishments	('000)	13,177	13,089	12,950	12,827	13,332
7.4 Average length of stay of resident tourists in all accommodation establishments	Nights	..	..	..	..	..
OUTBOUND TOURISM						
8.1 **Departures**	('000)	6,773	7,268	8,783	9,327	7,852
8.2 **Tourism expenditure in other countries**	US$ Mn	11,270	13,402	15,456	16,771	17,799
8.3 "Travel" (*)	US$ Mn	10,185	12,210	13,956	14,948	15,482
8.4 "Passenger transport" (*)	US$ Mn	1,085	1,192	1,500	1,823	2,317
TOURISM INDUSTRIES						
Hotels and similar establishments						
9.1 Number of rooms	Units	62,686	63,220	64,004	66,568	67,811
9.2 Number of bed-places	Units	161,510	163,688	169,613	168,443	172,883
9.3 Occupancy rate	Percent	..	..	..	..	..
9.4 Average length of stay	Nights	..	..	..	..	..
RELATED INDICATORS						
Share of tourism expenditure (6.1) in:						
10.1 Gross Domestic Product (GDP)	Percent	3.0	2.9	2.8	2.9	2.9
10.2 Exports of goods	Percent	4.5	4.3	4.1	4.1	4.1
10.3 Exports of services	Percent	20.1	19.8	19.1	19.4	19.4

(*) Balance of Payments items: 6.1 to 6.3 correspond to the "Credit" side (and are receipts for the country) while 8.2 to 8.4 correspond to the "Debit" side (and are expenditures in other countries).

BELIZE

Basic Indicators	Units	2002	2003	2004	2005	2006
INBOUND TOURISM						
Arrivals						
1.1 Visitors	('000)	694	999	1,329	1,037	903
1.2 Tourists (overnight visitors)	('000)	200	221	231	237	247
1.3 Same-day visitors	('000)	174	203	247	..	..
1.4 Cruise passengers	('000)	320	575	851	800	656
Arrivals by region						
2.1 Africa	('000)	..	..	..	..	..
2.2 Americas	('000)	154	175	185	190	199
2.3 Europe	('000)	29	34	33	33	34
2.4 East Asia and the Pacific	('000)	3	4	4	4	5
2.5 South Asia	('000)	..	..	..	..	..
2.6 Middle East	('000)	..	..	..	..	..
Arrivals by means of transport used						
3.1 Air	('000)	130	152	163	175	179
3.2 Rail	('000)	..	..	..	..	..
3.3 Road	('000)	62	60	60	54	60
3.4 Sea	('000)	8	8	8	8	8
Arrivals by purpose of visit						
4.1 Leisure, recreation and holidays	('000)	186	208	219	225	235
4.2 Business and professional	('000)	13	13	12	12	12
4.3 Other	('000)	..	..	..	..	..
Accommodation						
5.1 Overnight stays in hotels and similar establishments	('000)	536	..	..	..	..
5.2 Guests in hotels and similar establishments	('000)	..	..	..	..	..
5.3 Overnight stays in all types of accommodation establishments	('000)	..	..	..	..	..
5.4 Average length of stay of non-resident tourists in all accommodation establishments	Nights	7.60	6.80	6.80	..	..
6.1 **Tourism expenditure in the country**	US$ Mn	..	..	..	..	..
6.2 "Travel" (*)	US$ Mn	121	150	168	204	253
6.3 "Passenger transport" (*)	US$ Mn	..	..	..	..	..
DOMESTIC TOURISM						
Accommodation						
7.1 Overnight stays in hotels and similar establishments	('000)	..	..	..	..	..
7.2 Guests in hotels and similar establishments	('000)	..	..	..	..	..
7.3 Overnight stays in all types of accommodation establishments	('000)	80	..	..	..	..
7.4 Average length of stay of resident tourists in all accommodation establishments	Nights	..	..	..	..	..
OUTBOUND TOURISM						
8.1 **Departures**	('000)	..	..	..	..	..
8.2 **Tourism expenditure in other countries**	US$ Mn	48	50	47	45	43
8.3 "Travel" (*)	US$ Mn	44	46	43	42	41
8.4 "Passenger transport" (*)	US$ Mn	4	4	4	3	2
TOURISM INDUSTRIES						
Hotels and similar establishments						
9.1 Number of rooms	Units	4,705	5,050	5,139	5,593	5,789
9.2 Number of bed-places	Units	7,902	8,166	8,722	9,327	9,651
9.3 Occupancy rate	Percent	40.10	41.30	40.70	40.70	42.90
9.4 Average length of stay	Nights	7.60	6.80	6.80	..	..
RELATED INDICATORS						
Share of tourism expenditure (6.1) in: (**)						
10.1 Gross Domestic Product (GDP)	Percent	13.0	15.2	15.9	18.5	20.8
10.2 Exports of goods	Percent	39.0	47.5	54.7	63.4	59.4
10.3 Exports of services	Percent	68.8	70.8	71.5	69.6	71.3

(*) Balance of Payments items: 6.1 to 6.3 correspond to the "Credit" side (and are receipts for the country) while 8.2 to 8.4 correspond to the "Debit" side (and are expenditures in other countries).

(**) See Annex "Country notes".

Basic Indicators	Units	2002	2003	2004	2005	2006
INBOUND TOURISM						
Arrivals						
1.1 Visitors	('000)	853	850	845	960	975
1.2 Tourists (overnight visitors)	('000)	72	175	174	176	180
1.3 Same-day visitors	('000)	..	..	..	..	..
1.4 Cruise passengers	('000)	..	..	..	..	..
Arrivals by region						
2.1 Africa	('000)	49.4	148.6	147.5	140.2	152.0
2.2 Americas	('000)	1.3	0.5	0.4	0.5	1.0
2.3 Europe	('000)	21.1	25.4	25.2	31.5	22.3
2.4 East Asia and the Pacific	('000)	0.2	0.2	0.3	0.3	0.6
2.5 South Asia	('000)	0.1	0.1	0.1	3.0	3.5
2.6 Middle East	('000)	0.2	0.1	0.1	0.5	0.6
Arrivals by means of transport used						
3.1 Air	('000)	..	..	..	..	..
3.2 Rail	('000)	..	..	..	..	..
3.3 Road	('000)	..	..	..	..	..
3.4 Sea	('000)	..	..	..	..	..
Arrivals by purpose of visit						
4.1 Leisure, recreation and holidays	('000)	..	..	..	..	..
4.2 Business and professional	('000)	..	..	..	..	..
4.3 Other	('000)	..	..	..	..	..
Accommodation						
5.1 Overnight stays in hotels and similar establishments	('000)	..	..	..	..	..
5.2 Guests in hotels and similar establishments	('000)	..	..	..	..	..
5.3 Overnight stays in all types of accommodation establishments	('000)	144	219	215	348	321
5.4 Average length of stay of non-resident tourists in all accommodation establishments	Nights	..	..	..	..	..
6.1 **Tourism expenditure in the country**	US$ Mn	94.5	107.9	120.9	107.7	..
6.2 "Travel" (*)	US$ Mn	93	106	118	103	..
6.3 "Passenger transport" (*)	US$ Mn	1.5	1.9	2.9	4.7	..
DOMESTIC TOURISM						
Accommodation						
7.1 Overnight stays in hotels and similar establishments	('000)	..	..	..	..	..
7.2 Guests in hotels and similar establishments	('000)	..	..	..	..	..
7.3 Overnight stays in all types of accommodation establishments	('000)	..	..	..	..	138
7.4 Average length of stay of resident tourists in all accommodation establishments	Nights	..	..	..	..	..
OUTBOUND TOURISM						
8.1 **Departures**	('000)	..	..	..	..	..
8.2 **Tourism expenditure in other countries**	US$ Mn	49	53	59	58	..
8.3 "Travel" (*)	US$ Mn	20	21	29	27	..
8.4 "Passenger transport" (*)	US$ Mn	29	32	30	31	..
TOURISM INDUSTRIES						
Hotels and similar establishments						
9.1 Number of rooms	Units	..	..	..	..	6,942
9.2 Number of bed-places	Units	..	..	..	..	13,884
9.3 Occupancy rate	Percent	..	..	..	..	33.00
9.4 Average length of stay	Nights	..	..	..	..	2.55
RELATED INDICATORS						
Share of tourism expenditure (6.1) in:						
10.1 Gross Domestic Product (GDP)	Percent	3.4	3.0	3.0	2.5	..
10.2 Exports of goods	Percent	21.1	19.9	21.2	18.6	..
10.3 Exports of services	Percent	62.2	62.7	56.0	55.5	..

(*) Balance of Payments items: 6.1 to 6.3 correspond to the "Credit" side (and are receipts for the country) while 8.2 to 8.4 correspond to the "Debit" side (and are expenditures in other countries).

BERMUDA

Basic Indicators		Units	2002	2003	2004	2005	2006
INBOUND TOURISM							
Arrivals							
1.1	Visitors	('000)	484	483	478	517	635
1.2	Tourists (overnight visitors)	('000)	284	257	272	270	299
1.3	Same-day visitors	('000)	..	..	..	..	..
1.4	Cruise passengers	('000)	200	226	206	247	336
Arrivals by region							
2.1	Africa	('000)	..	..	..	..	..
2.2	Americas	('000)	244	222	236	233	255
2.3	Europe	('000)	31	26	26	27	32
2.4	East Asia and the Pacific	('000)	1	1	1	1	1
2.5	South Asia	('000)	..	..	..	..	..
2.6	Middle East	('000)	..	..	..	..	..
Arrivals by means of transport used							
3.1	Air	('000)	284	257	272	270	299
3.2	Rail	('000)	..	..	..	..	..
3.3	Road	('000)	..	..	..	..	..
3.4	Sea	('000)	200	226	206	247	336
Arrivals by purpose of visit							
4.1	Leisure, recreation and holidays	('000)	218	167	172	170	202
4.2	Business and professional	('000)	39	51	55	59	57
4.3	Other	('000)	26	39	44	41	40
Accommodation							
5.1	Overnight stays in hotels and similar establishments	('000)	..	..	..	..	..
5.2	Guests in hotels and similar establishments	('000)	220	196	206	207	227
5.3	Overnight stays in all types of accommodation establishments	('000)	1,822	1,598	1,733	1,729	1,931
5.4	Average length of stay of non-resident tourists in all accommodation establishments	Nights	6.42	6.43	6.38	6.40	6.50
6.1	**Tourism expenditure in the country** (**)	US$ Mn	378	348	426	429	508
6.2	"Travel" (*)	US$ Mn	..	..	..	..	..
6.3	"Passenger transport" (*)	US$ Mn	..	..	..	..	..
DOMESTIC TOURISM							
Accommodation							
7.1	Overnight stays in hotels and similar establishments	('000)	..	..	..	..	..
7.2	Guests in hotels and similar establishments	('000)	..	..	..	..	..
7.3	Overnight stays in all types of accommodation establishments	('000)	..	..	..	..	..
7.4	Average length of stay of resident tourists in all accommodation establishments	Nights	..	..	..	..	..
OUTBOUND TOURISM							
8.1	**Departures**	('000)	145	141	156	161	170
8.2	**Tourism expenditure in other countries** (**)	US$ Mn	243	248	217	239	277
8.3	"Travel" (*)	US$ Mn	..	..	..	..	..
8.4	"Passenger transport" (*)	US$ Mn	..	..	..	..	..
TOURISM INDUSTRIES							
Hotels and similar establishments							
9.1	Number of rooms	Units	3,251	3,100	2,921	3,067	3,011
9.2	Number of bed-places	Units	6,523	6,293	5,888	6,167	6,065
9.3	Occupancy rate	Percent	55.01	54.50	62.40	56.90	63.80
9.4	Average length of stay	Nights	6.50	6.20	6.40	6.40	6.50
RELATED INDICATORS							
Share of tourism expenditure (6.1) in:							
10.1	Gross Domestic Product (GDP)	Percent	..	..	..	..	..
10.2	Exports of goods	Percent	..	..	..	..	..
10.3	Exports of services	Percent	..	..	..	..	..

(*) Balance of Payments items: 6.1 to 6.3 correspond to the "Credit" side (and are receipts for the country) while 8.2 to 8.4 correspond to the "Debit" side (and are expenditures in other countries).

(**) See Annex "Country notes".

BHUTAN

Basic Indicators		Units	2002	2003	2004	2005	2006
	INBOUND TOURISM						
	Arrivals						
1.1	Visitors	('000)	..	..	..	..	..
1.2	Tourists (overnight visitors)	('000)	5.6	6.3	9.2	13.6	17.3
1.3	Same-day visitors	('000)	..	..	..	..	..
1.4	Cruise passengers	('000)	..	..	..	..	..
	Arrivals by region						
2.1	Africa	('000)	..	..	..	..	..
2.2	Americas	('000)	2.2	2.0	3.6	5.2	5.6
2.3	Europe	('000)	2.1	2.8	3.9	5.6	7.3
2.4	East Asia and the Pacific	('000)	1.3	1.4	1.7	2.8	4.3
2.5	South Asia	('000)	..	..	..	..	..
2.6	Middle East	('000)	..	..	..	..	..
	Arrivals by means of transport used						
3.1	Air	('000)	4.1	5.1	5.9	13.0	17.0
3.2	Rail	('000)	..	..	..	..	..
3.3	Road	('000)	1.5	1.1	3.4	0.6	0.3
3.4	Sea	('000)	..	..	..	..	..
	Arrivals by purpose of visit						
4.1	Leisure, recreation and holidays	('000)	5.3	6.3	9.2	13.6	17.3
4.2	Business and professional	('000)	..	..	..	..	..
4.3	Other	('000)	0.3	..	..	..	..
	Accommodation						
5.1	Overnight stays in hotels and similar establishments	('000)	47	49	74	74	..
5.2	Guests in hotels and similar establishments	('000)	..	..	..	..	..
5.3	Overnight stays in all types of accommodation establishments	('000)	..	..	..	..	..
5.4	Average length of stay of non-resident tourists in all accommodation establishments	Nights	7.00	7.00	8.00	8.00	8.00
6.1	**Tourism expenditure in the country** (**)	US$ Mn	8	8	13	19	24
6.2	"Travel" (*)	US$ Mn	..	..	..	..	..
6.3	"Passenger transport" (*)	US$ Mn	..	..	..	..	..
	DOMESTIC TOURISM						
	Accommodation						
7.1	Overnight stays in hotels and similar establishments	('000)	..	..	..	..	..
7.2	Guests in hotels and similar establishments	('000)	..	..	..	..	..
7.3	Overnight stays in all types of accommodation establishments	('000)	..	..	..	..	..
7.4	Average length of stay of resident tourists in all accommodation establishments	Nights	..	..	..	..	..
	OUTBOUND TOURISM						
8.1	**Departures**	('000)	..	..	..	..	..
8.2	**Tourism expenditure in other countries**	US$ Mn	..	..	..	..	..
8.3	"Travel" (*)	US$ Mn	..	..	..	..	..
8.4	"Passenger transport" (*)	US$ Mn	..	..	..	..	..
	TOURISM INDUSTRIES						
	Hotels and similar establishments						
9.1	Number of rooms	Units	1,239	1,239	1,239	1,436	1,532
9.2	Number of bed-places	Units	2,366	2,366	2,366	2,636	2,746
9.3	Occupancy rate	Percent	25.00	25.00	25.00	25.00	26.50
9.4	Average length of stay	Nights	8.00	8.00	8.00	8.50	8.00
	RELATED INDICATORS						
	Share of tourism expenditure (6.1) in:						
10.1	Gross Domestic Product (GDP)	Percent	..	..	..	..	..
10.2	Exports of goods	Percent	..	..	..	..	..
10.3	Exports of services	Percent	..	..	..	..	..

(*) Balance of Payments items: 6.1 to 6.3 correspond to the "Credit" side (and are receipts for the country) while 8.2 to 8.4 correspond to the "Debit" side (and are expenditures in other countries).

(**) See Annex "Country notes".

BOLIVIA

Basic Indicators	Units	2002	2003	2004	2005	2006
INBOUND TOURISM						
Arrivals						
1.1 Visitors	('000)	..	..	..	..	..
1.2 Tourists (overnight visitors)	('000)	334	427	480	524	515
1.3 Same-day visitors	('000)	..	..	..	..	
1.4 Cruise passengers	('000)	..	..	..	..	..
Arrivals by region						
2.1 Africa	('000)	1	1	1	2	..
2.2 Americas	('000)	217	210	227	250	..
2.3 Europe	('000)	146	141	143	142	..
2.4 East Asia and the Pacific	('000)	16	15	19	20	..
2.5 South Asia	('000)	..	..	..	..	..
2.6 Middle East	('000)	..	..	..	..	..
Arrivals by means of transport used						
3.1 Air	('000)	199	222	240	267	242
3.2 Rail	('000)	10	7	6	6	6
3.3 Road	('000)	123	197	232	250	266
3.4 Sea	('000)	2	2	3	1	1
Arrivals by purpose of visit						
4.1 Leisure, recreation and holidays	('000)	187	236	268	283	..
4.2 Business and professional	('000)	59	45	51	54	..
4.3 Other	('000)	88	139	158	167	..
Accommodation						
5.1 Overnight stays in hotels and similar establishments	('000)	969	1,006	1,030	1,099	964
5.2 Guests in hotels and similar establishments	('000)	380	367	391	413	471
5.3 Overnight stays in all types of accommodation establishments	('000)	..	..	..	..	..
5.4 Average length of stay of non-resident tourists in all accommodation establishments	Nights	2.55	2.74	2.64	2.66	..
6.1 **Tourism expenditure in the country**	US$ Mn	143	243	283	345	287
6.2 "Travel" (*)	US$ Mn	100	166	192	239	201
6.3 "Passenger transport" (*)	US$ Mn	43	77	91	106	86
DOMESTIC TOURISM						
Accommodation						
7.1 Overnight stays in hotels and similar establishments	('000)	1,322	1,404	1,523	1,644	1,447
7.2 Guests in hotels and similar establishments	('000)	742	775	871	933	1,107
7.3 Overnight stays in all types of accommodation establishments	('000)	..	..	..	..	..
7.4 Average length of stay of resident tourists in all accommodation establishments	Nights	1.78	1.81	1.75	1.76	..
OUTBOUND TOURISM						
8.1 **Departures**	('000)	217	304	346	386	466
8.2 **Tourism expenditure in other countries**	US$ Mn	114	197	232	257	328
8.3 "Travel" (*)	US$ Mn	80	138	164	186	226
8.4 "Passenger transport" (*)	US$ Mn	34	59	68	71	102
TOURISM INDUSTRIES						
Hotels and similar establishments						
9.1 Number of rooms	Units	18,463	19,800	20,862	21,999	21,791
9.2 Number of bed-places	Units	30,171	32,087	33,388	36,242	35,641
9.3 Occupancy rate	Percent	20.60	20.80	21.30	21.04	..
9.4 Average length of stay	Nights	2.04	2.11	2.02	2.04	..
RELATED INDICATORS						
Share of tourism expenditure (6.1) in:						
10.1 Gross Domestic Product (GDP)	Percent	1.8	3.0	3.2	3.7	2.6
10.2 Exports of goods	Percent	11.0	15.2	13.2	12.4	7.4
10.3 Exports of services	Percent	55.6	66.8	68.0	70.6	66.3

(*) Balance of Payments items: 6.1 to 6.3 correspond to the "Credit" side (and are receipts for the country) while 8.2 to 8.4 correspond to the "Debit" side (and are expenditures in other countries).

BONAIRE

Basic Indicators	Units	2002	2003	2004	2005	2006
INBOUND TOURISM						
Arrivals						
1.1 Visitors	('000)	94	107	116	103	126
1.2 Tourists (overnight visitors)	('000)	52	62	63	63	64
1.3 Same-day visitors	('000)	..	..	..	..	..
1.4 Cruise passengers	('000)	42	45	53	40	62
Arrivals by region						
2.1 Africa	('000)	..	..	..	..	..
2.2 Americas	('000)	34	33	34	32	35
2.3 Europe	('000)	18	29	28	30	28
2.4 East Asia and the Pacific	('000)	..	..	..	..	..
2.5 South Asia	('000)	..	..	..	..	..
2.6 Middle East	('000)	..	..	..	..	..
Arrivals by means of transport used						
3.1 Air	('000)	52	62	63	63	64
3.2 Rail	('000)	..	..	..	..	..
3.3 Road	('000)	..	..	..	..	..
3.4 Sea	('000)	42	45	53	40	62
Arrivals by purpose of visit						
4.1 Leisure, recreation and holidays	('000)	34	60	48	..	..
4.2 Business and professional	('000)	1	2	1	..	..
4.3 Other	('000)	16	3	13	..	..
Accommodation						
5.1 Overnight stays in hotels and similar establishments	('000)	340	415	419	428	435
5.2 Guests in hotels and similar establishments	('000)	..	..	..	..	..
5.3 Overnight stays in all types of accommodation establishments	('000)	486	574	578	587	621
5.4 Average length of stay of non-resident tourists in all accommodation establishments	Nights	9.30	9.23	9.15	9.66	9.77
6.1 **Tourism expenditure in the country**	US$ Mn	..	..	..	..	..
6.2 "Travel" (*)	US$ Mn	65	84	87	87	91
6.3 "Passenger transport" (*)	US$ Mn	..	..	..	..	..
DOMESTIC TOURISM						
Accommodation						
7.1 Overnight stays in hotels and similar establishments	('000)	..	..	..	..	..
7.2 Guests in hotels and similar establishments	('000)	..	..	..	..	..
7.3 Overnight stays in all types of accommodation establishments	('000)	..	..	..	..	..
7.4 Average length of stay of resident tourists in all accommodation establishments	Nights	..	..	..	..	..
OUTBOUND TOURISM						
8.1 **Departures**	('000)	..	..	..	..	..
8.2 **Tourism expenditure in other countries**	US$ Mn	..	..	..	..	..
8.3 "Travel" (*)	US$ Mn	2	3	6	5	5
8.4 "Passenger transport" (*)	US$ Mn	..	..	..	..	..
TOURISM INDUSTRIES						
Hotels and similar establishments						
9.1 Number of rooms	Units	1,070	1,699	1,175	..	..
9.2 Number of bed-places	Units	3,069	3,337	3,258	..	..
9.3 Occupancy rate	Percent	60.00	42.00	61.00	64.00	66.00
9.4 Average length of stay	Nights	9.33	9.23	9.15	..	..
RELATED INDICATORS						
Share of tourism expenditure (6.1) in:						
10.1 Gross Domestic Product (GDP)	Percent	..	..	..	..	..
10.2 Exports of goods	Percent	..	..	..	..	..
10.3 Exports of services	Percent	..	..	..	..	..

(*) Balance of Payments items: 6.1 to 6.3 correspond to the "Credit" side (and are receipts for the country) while 8.2 to 8.4 correspond to the "Debit" side (and are expenditures in other countries).

27

BOSNIA AND HERZEGOVINA

Basic Indicators	Units	2002	2003	2004	2005	2006
INBOUND TOURISM						
Arrivals						
1.1 Visitors	('000)	..	..	..	..	..
1.2 Tourists (overnight visitors)	('000)	160	165	190	217	256
1.3 Same-day visitors	('000)	..	..	..	..	..
1.4 Cruise passengers	('000)	..	..	..	..	..
Arrivals by region						
2.1 Africa	('000)	..	..	..	..	..
2.2 Americas	('000)	8	7	8	8	10
2.3 Europe	('000)	146	152	177	204	239
2.4 East Asia and the Pacific	('000)	1	2	2	2	3
2.5 South Asia	('000)	..	..	..	..	..
2.6 Middle East	('000)	..	..	..	..	..
Arrivals by means of transport used						
3.1 Air	('000)	..	..	..	..	..
3.2 Rail	('000)	..	..	..	..	..
3.3 Road	('000)	..	..	..	..	..
3.4 Sea	('000)	..	..	..	..	..
Arrivals by purpose of visit						
4.1 Leisure, recreation and holidays	('000)	..	..	..	..	..
4.2 Business and professional	('000)	..	..	..	..	..
4.3 Other	('000)	..	..	..	..	..
Accommodation						
5.1 Overnight stays in hotels and similar establishments	('000)					
5.2 Guests in hotels and similar establishments	('000)	..	..	..	..	..
5.3 Overnight stays in all types of accommodation establishments	('000)	392	419	460	485	594
5.4 Average length of stay of non-resident tourists in all accommodation establishments	Nights	..	..	..	..	..
6.1 **Tourism expenditure in the country**	US$ Mn	307	404	507	550	643
6.2 "Travel" (*)	US$ Mn	288	377	481	512	592
6.3 "Passenger transport" (*)	US$ Mn	19	27	26	38	51
DOMESTIC TOURISM						
Accommodation						
7.1 Overnight stays in hotels and similar establishments	('000)	..	..	..	..	..
7.2 Guests in hotels and similar establishments	('000)	..	..	..	..	..
7.3 Overnight stays in all types of accommodation establishments	('000)	496	494	511	533	583
7.4 Average length of stay of resident tourists in all accommodation establishments	Nights	..	..	..	..	..
OUTBOUND TOURISM						
8.1 **Departures**	('000)	..	..	..	..	..
8.2 **Tourism expenditure in other countries**	US$ Mn	112	145	162	158	198
8.3 "Travel" (*)	US$ Mn	85	106	117	122	158
8.4 "Passenger transport" (*)	US$ Mn	27	39	45	36	40
TOURISM INDUSTRIES						
Hotels and similar establishments						
9.1 Number of rooms	Units	7,280	7,731	8,353	8,687	9,030
9.2 Number of bed-places	Units	14,662	15,872	17,294	18,164	20,036
9.3 Occupancy rate	Percent	..	..	..	..	..
9.4 Average length of stay	Nights	..	..	..	..	..
RELATED INDICATORS						
Share of tourism expenditure (6.1) in:						
10.1 Gross Domestic Product (GDP)	Percent	5.0	5.2	5.4	5.5	5.7
10.2 Exports of goods	Percent	27.7	27.4	24.3	21.2	19.0
10.3 Exports of services	Percent	58.6	56.0	58.7	57.9	57.5

(*) Balance of Payments items: 6.1 to 6.3 correspond to the "Credit" side (and are receipts for the country) while 8.2 to 8.4 correspond to the "Debit" side (and are expenditures in other countries).

Basic Indicators	Units	2002	2003	2004	2005	2006
INBOUND TOURISM						
Arrivals						
1.1 Visitors	('000)	1,485	1,592	1,727	1,885	..
1.2 Tourists (overnight visitors)	('000)	1,274	1,406	1,523	1,675	..
1.3 Same-day visitors	('000)	211	187	204	210	..
1.4 Cruise passengers	('000)	..	..	..	..	..
Arrivals by region						
2.1 Africa	('000)	1,096	1,235	1,353	..	..
2.2 Americas	('000)	19	18	21	..	..
2.3 Europe	('000)	57	55	58	..	..
2.4 East Asia and the Pacific	('000)	12	12	12	..	..
2.5 South Asia	('000)	5	2	2	..	..
2.6 Middle East	('000)	..	..	..	..	..
Arrivals by means of transport used						
3.1 Air	('000)	95	71	66	..	..
3.2 Rail	('000)	1	1	1	..	..
3.3 Road	('000)	1,176	1,332	1,455	..	..
3.4 Sea	('000)	..	..	..	..	..
Arrivals by purpose of visit						
4.1 Leisure, recreation and holidays	('000)	178	231	248	..	..
4.2 Business and professional	('000)	123	106	80	..	..
4.3 Other	('000)	973	1,069	1,195	..	..
Accommodation						
5.1 Overnight stays in hotels and similar establishments	('000)	..	..	..	..	..
5.2 Guests in hotels and similar establishments	('000)	100	211	232	271	..
5.3 Overnight stays in all types of accommodation establishments	('000)	..	..	..	..	..
5.4 Average length of stay of non-resident tourists in all accommodation establishments	Nights	..	..	..	..	..
6.1 **Tourism expenditure in the country**	US$ Mn	324	459	582	561	539
6.2 "Travel" (*)	US$ Mn	319	457	581	560	537
6.3 "Passenger transport" (*)	US$ Mn	5	2	1	1	2
DOMESTIC TOURISM						
Accommodation						
7.1 Overnight stays in hotels and similar establishments	('000)	..	..	..	..	..
7.2 Guests in hotels and similar establishments	('000)	149	119	89	145	..
7.3 Overnight stays in all types of accommodation establishments	('000)	..	..	..	..	..
7.4 Average length of stay of resident tourists in all accommodation establishments	Nights	..	..	..	..	..
OUTBOUND TOURISM						
8.1 **Departures**	('000)	..	..	..	..	..
8.2 **Tourism expenditure in other countries**	US$ Mn	197	235	280	301	285
8.3 "Travel" (*)	US$ Mn	184	230	276	282	277
8.4 "Passenger transport" (*)	US$ Mn	13	5	4	19	8
TOURISM INDUSTRIES						
Hotels and similar establishments						
9.1 Number of rooms	Units	3,350	3,589	4,050	4,795	4,801
9.2 Number of bed-places	Units	6,450	6,646	7,800	8,040	8,468
9.3 Occupancy rate	Percent	24.10	30.50	35.50	41.50	..
9.4 Average length of stay	Nights	8.20	6.00	9.60	11.90	..
RELATED INDICATORS						
Share of tourism expenditure (6.1) in:						
10.1 Gross Domestic Product (GDP)	Percent	5.5	5.5	5.9	5.4	5.2
10.2 Exports of goods	Percent	14.0	15.2	15.7	12.6	11.9
10.3 Exports of services	Percent	66.1	71.4	74.6	65.7	69.9

(*) Balance of Payments items: 6.1 to 6.3 correspond to the "Credit" side (and are receipts for the country) while 8.2 to 8.4 correspond to the "Debit" side (and are expenditures in other countries).

BRAZIL

Basic Indicators		Units	2002	2003	2004	2005	2006
	INBOUND TOURISM						
	Arrivals						
1.1	Visitors	('000)	..	..	..	..	..
1.2	Tourists (overnight visitors)	('000)	3,785	4,133	4,794	5,358	5,019
1.3	Same-day visitors	('000)	..	..	..	..	..
1.4	Cruise passengers	('000)	..	..	..	..	..
	Arrivals by region						
2.1	Africa	('000)	40	52	65	76	84
2.2	Americas	('000)	2,206	2,397	2,703	2,998	2,703
2.3	Europe	('000)	1,415	1,544	1,860	2,097	1,997
2.4	East Asia and the Pacific	('000)	108	129	156	177	220
2.5	South Asia	('000)	..	..	..	..	..
2.6	Middle East	('000)	7	6	6	7	13
	Arrivals by means of transport used						
3.1	Air	('000)	2,815	3,083	3,569	3,938	3,680
3.2	Rail	('000)	..	..	..	..	..
3.3	Road	('000)	891	993	1,151	1,314	1,216
3.4	Sea	('000)	79	57	74	106	123
	Arrivals by purpose of visit						
4.1	Leisure, recreation and holidays	('000)	1,938	2,228	2,325	2,379	2,193
4.2	Business and professional	('000)	1,070	1,075	1,376	1,559	1,360
4.3	Other	('000)	776	831	1,093	1,420	1,466
	Accommodation						
5.1	Overnight stays in hotels and similar establishments	('000)	..	..	..	..	..
5.2	Guests in hotels and similar establishments	('000)	..	..	..	..	..
5.3	Overnight stays in all types of accommodation establishments	('000)	..	..	..	..	..
5.4	Average length of stay of non-resident tourists in all accommodation establishments	Nights	..	..	..	..	..
6.1	**Tourism expenditure in the country**	US$ Mn	2,142	2,673	3,389	4,168	4,577
6.2	"Travel" (*)	US$ Mn	1,998	2,479	3,222	3,861	4,316
6.3	"Passenger transport" (*)	US$ Mn	144	194	167	307	261
	DOMESTIC TOURISM						
	Accommodation						
7.1	Overnight stays in hotels and similar establishments	('000)	..	..	..	..	..
7.2	Guests in hotels and similar establishments	('000)	..	..	..	..	..
7.3	Overnight stays in all types of accommodation establishments	('000)	..	..	..	..	..
7.4	Average length of stay of resident tourists in all accommodation establishments	Nights	..	..	..	..	..
	OUTBOUND TOURISM						
8.1	**Departures**	('000)	2,338	3,225	3,701	4,667	4,825
8.2	**Tourism expenditure in other countries**	US$ Mn	2,929	2,874	3,752	5,905	7,501
8.3	"Travel" (*)	US$ Mn	2,396	2,261	2,871	4,720	5,764
8.4	"Passenger transport" (*)	US$ Mn	533	613	881	1,185	1,737
	TOURISM INDUSTRIES						
	Hotels and similar establishments						
9.1	Number of rooms	Units	..	..	..	..	..
9.2	Number of bed-places	Units	..	..	..	..	..
9.3	Occupancy rate	Percent	..	..	..	..	..
9.4	Average length of stay	Nights	..	..	..	..	..
	RELATED INDICATORS						
	Share of tourism expenditure (6.1) in:						
10.1	Gross Domestic Product (GDP)	Percent	0.4	0.5	0.5	0.5	0.4
10.2	Exports of goods	Percent	3.5	3.7	3.5	3.5	3.3
10.3	Exports of services	Percent	22.4	25.6	26.9	25.9	23.5

(*) Balance of Payments items: 6.1 to 6.3 correspond to the "Credit" side (and are receipts for the country) while 8.2 to 8.4 correspond to the "Debit" side (and are expenditures in other countries).

Basic Indicators	Units	2002	2003	2004	2005	2006
INBOUND TOURISM						
Arrivals						
1.1 Visitors	('000)	544	658	813	821	..
1.2 Tourists (overnight visitors)	('000)	282	318	304	337	356
1.3 Same-day visitors	('000)	32	40	42	34	..
1.4 Cruise passengers	('000)	230	300	467	449	444
Arrivals by region						
2.1 Africa	('000)	..	..	..	..	..
2.2 Americas	('000)	250	261	..	..	..
2.3 Europe	('000)	29	50	..	..	..
2.4 East Asia and the Pacific	('000)	..	..	..	..	..
2.5 South Asia	('000)	..	..	..	..	..
2.6 Middle East	('000)	..	..	..	..	..
Arrivals by means of transport used						
3.1 Air	('000)	135	153	220	205	..
3.2 Rail	('000)	..	..	..	..	..
3.3 Road	('000)	..	..	..	..	..
3.4 Sea	('000)	409	504	593	616	..
Arrivals by purpose of visit						
4.1 Leisure, recreation and holidays	('000)	271	287	293	..	..
4.2 Business and professional	('000)	6	6	5	..	..
4.3 Other	('000)	5	25	7	..	..
Accommodation						
5.1 Overnight stays in hotels and similar establishments	('000)	80	..	..	..	..
5.2 Guests in hotels and similar establishments	('000)	58	60	85	94	..
5.3 Overnight stays in all types of accommodation establishments	('000)	105	..	..	..	..
5.4 Average length of stay of non-resident tourists in all accommodation establishments	Nights	9.30	..	..	..	..
6.1 **Tourism expenditure in the country** (**)	US$ Mn	345	342	393	437	..
6.2 "Travel" (*)	US$ Mn	..	..	..	..	..
6.3 "Passenger transport" (*)	US$ Mn	..	..	..	..	..
DOMESTIC TOURISM						
Accommodation						
7.1 Overnight stays in hotels and similar establishments	('000)	..	..	..	..	..
7.2 Guests in hotels and similar establishments	('000)	..	..	..	..	..
7.3 Overnight stays in all types of accommodation establishments	('000)	..	..	..	..	..
7.4 Average length of stay of resident tourists in all accommodation establishments	Nights	..	..	..	..	..
OUTBOUND TOURISM						
8.1 **Departures**	('000)	..	..	..	..	..
8.2 **Tourism expenditure in other countries**	US$ Mn	..	..	..	..	..
8.3 "Travel" (*)	US$ Mn	..	..	..	..	..
8.4 "Passenger transport" (*)	US$ Mn	..	..	..	..	..
TOURISM INDUSTRIES						
Hotels and similar establishments						
9.1 Number of rooms	Units	2,661	2,661	2,760	2,722	..
9.2 Number of bed-places	Units	..	..	..	..	..
9.3 Occupancy rate	Percent	61.40	66.80	67.10	68.60	..
9.4 Average length of stay	Nights	9.00	10.00	11.00	9.00	..
RELATED INDICATORS						
Share of tourism expenditure (6.1) in:						
10.1 Gross Domestic Product (GDP)	Percent	..	..	..	..	..
10.2 Exports of goods	Percent	..	..	..	..	..
10.3 Exports of services	Percent	..	..	..	..	..

(*) Balance of Payments items: 6.1 to 6.3 correspond to the "Credit" side (and are receipts for the country) while 8.2 to 8.4 correspond to the "Debit" side (and are expenditures in other countries).

(**) See Annex "Country notes".

BRUNEI DARUSSALAM

Basic Indicators	Units	2002	2003	2004	2005	2006
INBOUND TOURISM						
Arrivals						
1.1 Visitors	('000)	..	..	..	815	836
1.2 Tourists (overnight visitors)	('000)	..	..	..	126	158
1.3 Same-day visitors	('000)	..	..	..	685	676
1.4 Cruise passengers	('000)	..	..	..	4	1
Arrivals by region						
2.1 Africa	('000)	..	..	..	..	..
2.2 Americas	('000)	..	..	..	3	4
2.3 Europe	('000)	..	..	..	14	21
2.4 East Asia and the Pacific	('000)	..	..	..	76	100
2.5 South Asia	('000)	..	..	..	..	..
2.6 Middle East	('000)	..	..	..	..	..
Arrivals by means of transport used						
3.1 Air	('000)	..	..	..	126	158
3.2 Rail	('000)	..	..	..	..	..
3.3 Road	('000)	..	..	..	..	..
3.4 Sea	('000)	..	..	..	..	..
Arrivals by purpose of visit						
4.1 Leisure, recreation and holidays	('000)	..	..	..	27	..
4.2 Business and professional	('000)	..	..	..	4	..
4.3 Other	('000)	..	..	..	784	..
Accommodation						
5.1 Overnight stays in hotels and similar establishments	('000)	..	..	..	..	..
5.2 Guests in hotels and similar establishments	('000)	141	151	197	300	..
5.3 Overnight stays in all types of accommodation establishments	('000)	..	..	..	..	..
5.4 Average length of stay of non-resident tourists in all accommodation establishments	Nights	..	..	..	..	..
6.1 **Tourism expenditure in the country**	US$ Mn	..	..	..	..	..
6.2 "Travel" (*)	US$ Mn	114	124	181	191	224
6.3 "Passenger transport" (*)	US$ Mn	..	..	..	..	..
DOMESTIC TOURISM						
Accommodation						
7.1 Overnight stays in hotels and similar establishments	('000)	..	..	..	..	..
7.2 Guests in hotels and similar establishments	('000)	..	..	..	..	..
7.3 Overnight stays in all types of accommodation establishments	('000)	..	..	..	..	..
7.4 Average length of stay of resident tourists in all accommodation establishments	Nights	..	..	..	..	..
OUTBOUND TOURISM						
8.1 **Departures**	('000)	..	..	..	..	..
8.2 **Tourism expenditure in other countries**	US$ Mn	..	..	..	..	..
8.3 "Travel" (*)	US$ Mn	398	468	382	374	408
8.4 "Passenger transport" (*)	US$ Mn	..	..	..	..	..
TOURISM INDUSTRIES						
Hotels and similar establishments						
9.1 Number of rooms	Units	2,142	2,311	2,311	2,371	2,548
9.2 Number of bed-places	Units	3,157	3,405	3,405	3,501	..
9.3 Occupancy rate	Percent	35.80	33.20	35.40	39.30	..
9.4 Average length of stay	Nights	..	..	..	..	..
RELATED INDICATORS						
Share of tourism expenditure (6.1) in: (**)						
10.1 Gross Domestic Product (GDP)	Percent	2.7	2.6	3.3	3.0	..
10.2 Exports of goods	Percent	3.1	2.8	3.6	3.1	2.9
10.3 Exports of services	Percent	26.7	28.4	33.3	31.0	30.1

(*) Balance of Payments items: 6.1 to 6.3 correspond to the "Credit" side (and are receipts for the country) while 8.2 to 8.4 correspond to the "Debit" side (and are expenditures in other countries).

(**) See Annex "Country notes".

Basic Indicators	Units	2002	2003	2004	2005	2006
INBOUND TOURISM						
Arrivals						
1.1 Visitors	('000)	5,563	6,241	6,982	7,282	7,499
1.2 Tourists (overnight visitors)	('000)	3,433	4,048	4,630	4,837	5,158
1.3 Same-day visitors	('000)	2,130	2,193	2,352	2,445	2,341
1.4 Cruise passengers	('000)	..	..	..	..	..
Arrivals by region						
2.1 Africa	('000)	4	4	3	3	3
2.2 Americas	('000)	47	55	68	77	85
2.3 Europe	('000)	5,426	6,088	6,807	7,088	7,287
2.4 East Asia and the Pacific	('000)	22	27	32	35	38
2.5 South Asia	('000)	9	12	12	11	13
2.6 Middle East	('000)	14	15	16	18	14
Arrivals by means of transport used						
3.1 Air	('000)	1,185	1,409	1,715	2,007	2,203
3.2 Rail	('000)	192	170	148	157	173
3.3 Road	('000)	4,082	4,542	4,963	4,940	4,954
3.4 Sea	('000)	104	120	156	178	169
Arrivals by purpose of visit						
4.1 Leisure, recreation and holidays	('000)	2,993	3,532	4,010	4,090	4,365
4.2 Business and professional	('000)	180	216	272	340	332
4.3 Other	('000)	2,390	2,493	2,699	2,852	2,802
Accommodation						
5.1 Overnight stays in hotels and similar establishments	('000)	6,985	8,987	10,139	11,471	11,776
5.2 Guests in hotels and similar establishments	('000)	1,030	1,376	1,668	1,909	2,023
5.3 Overnight stays in all types of accommodation establishments	('000)	7,055	9,142	10,304	11,624	11,960
5.4 Average length of stay of non-resident tourists in all accommodation establishments	Nights	8.50	8.60	4.20	4.20	4.10
6.1 **Tourism expenditure in the country**	US$ Mn	1,392	2,051	2,796	3,063	3,315
6.2 "Travel" (*)	US$ Mn	1,096	1,621	2,202	2,412	2,610
6.3 "Passenger transport" (*)	US$ Mn	296	430	594	651	705
DOMESTIC TOURISM						
Accommodation						
7.1 Overnight stays in hotels and similar establishments	('000)	2,982	3,058	3,423	3,957	4,342
7.2 Guests in hotels and similar establishments	('000)	1,355	1,431	1,503	1,721	1,921
7.3 Overnight stays in all types of accommodation establishments	('000)	3,231	3,379	3,857	4,447	5,467
7.4 Average length of stay of resident tourists in all accommodation establishments	Nights	..	..	..	..	..
OUTBOUND TOURISM						
8.1 **Departures**	('000)	3,188	3,403	3,882	4,235	4,180
8.2 **Tourism expenditure in other countries**	US$ Mn	1,018	1,467	1,935	1,858	2,092
8.3 "Travel" (*)	US$ Mn	717	1,033	1,363	1,309	1,474
8.4 "Passenger transport" (*)	US$ Mn	301	434	572	549	618
TOURISM INDUSTRIES						
Hotels and similar establishments						
9.1 Number of rooms	Units	..	..	..	..	..
9.2 Number of bed-places	Units	132,024	143,960	171,000	221,144	252,305
9.3 Occupancy rate	Percent	30.70	34.80	35.90	37.60	35.80
9.4 Average length of stay	Nights	4.20	4.30	4.30	4.30	4.10
RELATED INDICATORS						
Share of tourism expenditure (6.1) in:						
10.1 Gross Domestic Product (GDP)	Percent	8.9	10.3	11.3	11.3	10.5
10.2 Exports of goods	Percent	26.0	29.0	28.2	26.1	22.0
10.3 Exports of services	Percent	63.2	69.3	69.4	69.6	65.7

(*) Balance of Payments items: 6.1 to 6.3 correspond to the "Credit" side (and are receipts for the country) while 8.2 to 8.4 correspond to the "Debit" side (and are expenditures in other countries).

BURKINA FASO

Basic Indicators	Units	2002	2003	2004	2005	2006
INBOUND TOURISM						
Arrivals						
1.1 Visitors	('000)	..	..	..	..	
1.2 Tourists (overnight visitors)	('000)	150	163	222	245	264
1.3 Same-day visitors	('000)	..	..	..	..	
1.4 Cruise passengers	('000)	..	..	..	..	..
Arrivals by region						
2.1 Africa	('000)	55	65	96	101	108
2.2 Americas	('000)	10	10	13	15	16
2.3 Europe	('000)	73	77	100	113	123
2.4 East Asia and the Pacific	('000)	4	3	5	7	6
2.5 South Asia	('000)	..	..	..	..	
2.6 Middle East	('000)	1	1	2	2	2
Arrivals by means of transport used						
3.1 Air	('000)	..	..	..	..	
3.2 Rail	('000)	..	..	..	..	..
3.3 Road	('000)	..	..	..	..	
3.4 Sea	('000)	..	..	..	..	..
Arrivals by purpose of visit						
4.1 Leisure, recreation and holidays	('000)	54	63	71	50	65
4.2 Business and professional	('000)	111	115	165	225	233
4.3 Other	('000)	34	38	53	49	60
Accommodation						
5.1 Overnight stays in hotels and similar establishments	('000)	527	554	632	789	794
5.2 Guests in hotels and similar establishments	('000)	150	163	222	245	264
5.3 Overnight stays in all types of accommodation establishments	('000)	..	..		..	
5.4 Average length of stay of non-resident tourists in all accommodation establishments	Nights	3.22	3.05	2.50	2.90	3.00
6.1 **Tourism expenditure in the country**	US$ Mn	..	..	..	45.4	
6.2 "Travel" (*)	US$ Mn	..	..	40	45	..
6.3 "Passenger transport" (*)	US$ Mn	..	..	..	0.4	
DOMESTIC TOURISM						
Accommodation						
7.1 Overnight stays in hotels and similar establishments	('000)	112	119	135	173	204
7.2 Guests in hotels and similar establishments	('000)	48	54	68	80	95
7.3 Overnight stays in all types of accommodation establishments	('000)	..	..	..	..	
7.4 Average length of stay of resident tourists in all accommodation establishments	Nights	..	..	..	..	..
OUTBOUND TOURISM						
8.1 **Departures**	('000)	..		..		
8.2 **Tourism expenditure in other countries**	US$ Mn	..	..	..	53	..
8.3 "Travel" (*)	US$ Mn	..	..	39	46	
8.4 "Passenger transport" (*)	US$ Mn	..	..	..	7	..
TOURISM INDUSTRIES						
Hotels and similar establishments						
9.1 Number of rooms	Units	..	..	..	..	
9.2 Number of bed-places	Units	..	..	..	..	
9.3 Occupancy rate	Percent	59.93	59.10	63.95	69.00	64.79
9.4 Average length of stay	Nights	..	..	..	..	..
RELATED INDICATORS						
Share of tourism expenditure (6.1) in:						
10.1 Gross Domestic Product (GDP)	Percent	..	..	..	..	
10.2 Exports of goods	Percent	..	..	..	..	
10.3 Exports of services	Percent	..	..	..	..	

(*) Balance of Payments items: 6.1 to 6.3 correspond to the "Credit" side (and are receipts for the country) while 8.2 to 8.4 correspond to the "Debit" side (and are expenditures in other countries).

Basic Indicators	Units	2002	2003	2004	2005	2006
INBOUND TOURISM						
Arrivals						
1.1 Visitors	('000)	..	..	..	..	..
1.2 Tourists (overnight visitors)	('000)	74	74	133	148	201
1.3 Same-day visitors	('000)	..	..	..	..	..
1.4 Cruise passengers	('000)	..	..	..	..	..
Arrivals by region						
2.1 Africa	('000)	25	25	1	49	141
2.2 Americas	('000)	2	2	6	10	4
2.3 Europe	('000)	6	8	29	29	32
2.4 East Asia and the Pacific	('000)	1	1	5	4	10
2.5 South Asia	('000)	..	..	..	..	..
2.6 Middle East	('000)	..	..	..	..	..
Arrivals by means of transport used						
3.1 Air	('000)	18	17	39	49	50
3.2 Rail	('000)	..	..	..	..	..
3.3 Road	('000)	35	36	48	50	111
3.4 Sea	('000)	21	21	46	49	40
Arrivals by purpose of visit						
4.1 Leisure, recreation and holidays	('000)	17	18	38	49	66
4.2 Business and professional	('000)	22	22	45	49	64
4.3 Other	('000)	35	34	50	51	71
Accommodation						
5.1 Overnight stays in hotels and similar establishments	('000)	..	..	..	..	..
5.2 Guests in hotels and similar establishments	('000)	..	..	..	..	..
5.3 Overnight stays in all types of accommodation establishments	('000)	..	..	..	..	..
5.4 Average length of stay of non-resident tourists in all accommodation establishments	Nights	..	..	..	..	..
6.1 **Tourism expenditure in the country**	US$ Mn	1.6	1.2	1.8	1.9	1.6
6.2 "Travel" (*)	US$ Mn	1.1	0.7	1.2	1.5	1.3
6.3 "Passenger transport" (*)	US$ Mn	0.5	0.5	0.6	0.4	0.3
DOMESTIC TOURISM						
Accommodation						
7.1 Overnight stays in hotels and similar establishments	('000)	..	..	..	..	..
7.2 Guests in hotels and similar establishments	('000)	..	..	..	..	..
7.3 Overnight stays in all types of accommodation establishments	('000)	..	..	..	..	..
7.4 Average length of stay of resident tourists in all accommodation establishments	Nights	..	..	..	..	..
OUTBOUND TOURISM						
8.1 **Departures**	('000)	..	..	..	..	..
8.2 **Tourism expenditure in other countries**	US$ Mn	..	..	29	62	126
8.3 "Travel" (*)	US$ Mn	14	15	23	60	125
8.4 "Passenger transport" (*)	US$ Mn	..	..	6	2	1
TOURISM INDUSTRIES						
Hotels and similar establishments						
9.1 Number of rooms	Units	115	130	130	130	130
9.2 Number of bed-places	Units	1,270	1,420	1,420	1,420	1,420
9.3 Occupancy rate	Percent	..	..	..	..	..
9.4 Average length of stay	Nights	..	..	..	..	2.00
RELATED INDICATORS						
Share of tourism expenditure (6.1) in:						
10.1 Gross Domestic Product (GDP)	Percent	0.3	0.2	0.3	0.2	0.2
10.2 Exports of goods	Percent	5.2	3.2	3.8	3.3	2.7
10.3 Exports of services	Percent	20.0	17.1	11.3	5.4	4.6

(*) Balance of Payments items: 6.1 to 6.3 correspond to the "Credit" side (and are receipts for the country) while 8.2 to 8.4 correspond to the "Debit" side (and are expenditures in other countries).

CAMBODIA

Basic Indicators	Units	2002	2003	2004	2005	2006
INBOUND TOURISM						
Arrivals						
1.1 Visitors	('000)	..	..	..	..	..
1.2 Tourists (overnight visitors)	('000)	787	701	1,055	1,422	1,700
1.3 Same-day visitors	('000)	..	..	..	..	..
1.4 Cruise passengers	('000)	..	..	..	..	..
Arrivals by region						
2.1 Africa	('000)	..	..	..	..	..
2.2 Americas	('000)	113	89	122	152	159
2.3 Europe	('000)	219	183	243	310	314
2.4 East Asia and the Pacific	('000)	409	412	589	787	1,022
2.5 South Asia	('000)	4	5	7	8	9
2.6 Middle East	('000)	..	..	..	..	..
Arrivals by means of transport used						
3.1 Air	('000)	523	456	626	857	1,027
3.2 Rail	('000)	..	..	..	..	..
3.3 Road	('000)	264	226	336	445	525
3.4 Sea	('000)	..	19	25	32	40
Arrivals by purpose of visit						
4.1 Leisure, recreation and holidays	('000)	448	609	954	1,197	1,446
4.2 Business and professional	('000)	58	71	68	87	109
4.3 Other	('000)	17	21	33	138	145
Accommodation						
5.1 Overnight stays in hotels and similar establishments	('000)	..	..	..	..	..
5.2 Guests in hotels and similar establishments	('000)	..	..	..	..	..
5.3 Overnight stays in all types of accommodation establishments	('000)	..	..	..	..	..
5.4 Average length of stay of non-resident tourists in all accommodation establishments	Nights	5.80	5.50	6.30	6.30	6.50
6.1 **Tourism expenditure in the country**	US$ Mn	509	441	673	929	1,080
6.2 "Travel" (*)	US$ Mn	454	389	603	840	963
6.3 "Passenger transport" (*)	US$ Mn	55	52	70	89	117
DOMESTIC TOURISM						
Accommodation						
7.1 Overnight stays in hotels and similar establishments	('000)	..	..	..	..	..
7.2 Guests in hotels and similar establishments	('000)	..	..	..	..	..
7.3 Overnight stays in all types of accommodation establishments	('000)	..	..	..	..	..
7.4 Average length of stay of resident tourists in all accommodation establishments	Nights	..	..	..	..	..
OUTBOUND TOURISM						
8.1 **Departures**	('000)	45	60	239	427	
8.2 **Tourism expenditure in other countries**	US$ Mn	64	60	80	138	176
8.3 "Travel" (*)	US$ Mn	38	36	48	97	122
8.4 "Passenger transport" (*)	US$ Mn	26	24	32	41	54
TOURISM INDUSTRIES						
Hotels and similar establishments						
9.1 Number of rooms	Units	17,535	19,698	21,955	24,465	27,080
9.2 Number of bed-places	Units	29,195	33,486	37,323	41,600	46,036
9.3 Occupancy rate	Percent	50.00	50.00	52.00	52.00	54.79
9.4 Average length of stay	Nights	..	..	..	..	..
RELATED INDICATORS						
Share of tourism expenditure (6.1) in:						
10.1 Gross Domestic Product (GDP)	Percent	11.9	9.6	12.8	15.0	15.0
10.2 Exports of goods	Percent	28.8	21.1	26.0	31.9	29.2
10.3 Exports of services	Percent	84.3	80.5	83.6	83.1	83.3

(*) Balance of Payments items: 6.1 to 6.3 correspond to the "Credit" side (and are receipts for the country) while 8.2 to 8.4 correspond to the "Debit" side (and are expenditures in other countries).

CAMEROON

Basic Indicators		Units	2002	2003	2004	2005	2006
	INBOUND TOURISM						
	Arrivals						
1.1	Visitors	('000)	..	..	..	..	..
1.2	Tourists (overnight visitors)	('000)	226	..	190	176	..
1.3	Same-day visitors	('000)	..	..	..	..	..
1.4	Cruise passengers	('000)	..	..	..	..	..
	Arrivals by region						
2.1	Africa	('000)	105	..	80	89	..
2.2	Americas	('000)	14	..	12	10	..
2.3	Europe	('000)	99	..	83	68	..
2.4	East Asia and the Pacific	('000)	5	..	4	5	..
2.5	South Asia	('000)	..	..	..	..	..
2.6	Middle East	('000)	1	..	5	2	..
	Arrivals by means of transport used						
3.1	Air	('000)	..	..	..	..	..
3.2	Rail	('000)	..	..	..	..	..
3.3	Road	('000)	..	..	..	..	..
3.4	Sea	('000)	..	..	..	..	..
	Arrivals by purpose of visit						
4.1	Leisure, recreation and holidays	('000)	..	..	..	..	..
4.2	Business and professional	('000)	..	..	..	..	..
4.3	Other	('000)	..	..	..	..	..
	Accommodation						
5.1	Overnight stays in hotels and similar establishments	('000)	458	..	414	355	..
5.2	Guests in hotels and similar establishments	('000)	226	..	190	176	..
5.3	Overnight stays in all types of accommodation establishments	('000)	..	..	..	..	..
5.4	Average length of stay of non-resident tourists in all accommodation establishments	Nights	..	..	..	..	..
6.1	**Tourism expenditure in the country**	US$ Mn	124	266	212	..	..
6.2	"Travel" (*)	US$ Mn	62	182	158	..	..
6.3	"Passenger transport" (*)	US$ Mn	62	84	54	..	..
	DOMESTIC TOURISM						
	Accommodation						
7.1	Overnight stays in hotels and similar establishments	('000)	..	..	1,393	1,399	..
7.2	Guests in hotels and similar establishments	('000)	..	..	886	977	..
7.3	Overnight stays in all types of accommodation establishments	('000)	..	..	..	..	..
7.4	Average length of stay of resident tourists in all accommodation establishments	Nights	..	..	..	..	..
	OUTBOUND TOURISM						
8.1	**Departures**	('000)	..	..	..	..	..
8.2	**Tourism expenditure in other countries**	US$ Mn	205	272	394	..	..
8.3	"Travel" (*)	US$ Mn	171	171	323	..	..
8.4	"Passenger transport" (*)	US$ Mn	34	101	71	..	..
	TOURISM INDUSTRIES						
	Hotels and similar establishments						
9.1	Number of rooms	Units	..	..	..	22,112	..
9.2	Number of bed-places	Units	..	..	..	24,598	..
9.3	Occupancy rate	Percent	..	..	..	..	..
9.4	Average length of stay	Nights	..	..	..	..	..
	RELATED INDICATORS						
	Share of tourism expenditure (6.1) in:						
10.1	Gross Domestic Product (GDP)	Percent	1.1	2.0	1.3	..	..
10.2	Exports of goods	Percent	6.3	10.7	7.8	..	..
10.3	Exports of services	Percent	13.2	41.2	23.0	..	..

(*) Balance of Payments items: 6.1 to 6.3 correspond to the "Credit" side (and are receipts for the country) while 8.2 to 8.4 correspond to the "Debit" side (and are expenditures in other countries).

CANADA

Basic Indicators	Units	2002	2003	2004	2005	2006
INBOUND TOURISM						
Arrivals						
1.1 Visitors	('000)	44,896	38,903	38,845	36,160	33,390
1.2 Tourists (overnight visitors)	('000)	20,057	17,534	19,145	18,770	18,265
1.3 Same-day visitors	('000)	24,839	21,369	19,700	17,390	15,125
1.4 Cruise passengers	('000)	..	..	..	..	..
Arrivals by region						
2.1 Africa	('000)	54	52	58	62	72
2.2 Americas	('000)	16,576	14,589	15,518	14,867	14,372
2.3 Europe	('000)	2,095	1,873	2,202	2,397	2,360
2.4 East Asia and the Pacific	('000)	1,210	900	1,222	1,282	1,282
2.5 South Asia	('000)	79	80	96	110	119
2.6 Middle East	('000)	42	40	48	52	59
Arrivals by means of transport used						
3.1 Air	('000)	7,193	6,408	7,497	7,746	7,785
3.2 Rail	('000)	108	102	97	97	109
3.3 Road	('000)	12,226	10,398	10,837	10,221	9,617
3.4 Sea	('000)	531	626	714	706	754
Arrivals by purpose of visit						
4.1 Leisure, recreation and holidays	('000)	11,503	9,669	10,595	9,951	9,740
4.2 Business and professional	('000)	2,560	2,231	2,571	2,622	2,658
4.3 Other	('000)	5,901	5,519	5,865	6,038	5,728
Accommodation						
5.1 Overnight stays in hotels and similar establishments	('000)	..	..	..	..	..
5.2 Guests in hotels and similar establishments	('000)	..	..	..	..	..
5.3 Overnight stays in all types of accommodation establishments	('000)	122,150	107,698	123,426	125,656	120,703
5.4 Average length of stay of non-resident tourists in all accommodation establishments	Nights	..	..	..	..	..
6.1 **Tourism expenditure in the country**	US$ Mn	12,744	12,236	14,953	16,006	16,976
6.2 "Travel" (*)	US$ Mn	10,687	10,602	12,847	13,768	14,678
6.3 "Passenger transport" (*)	US$ Mn	2,057	1,634	2,106	2,238	2,298
DOMESTIC TOURISM						
Accommodation						
7.1 Overnight stays in hotels and similar establishments	('000)	59,217	53,882	55,312	..	..
7.2 Guests in hotels and similar establishments	('000)	..	..	..	..	..
7.3 Overnight stays in all types of accommodation establishments	('000)	308,046	278,468	284,093	..	..
7.4 Average length of stay of resident tourists in all accommodation establishments	Nights	..	..	..	..	..
OUTBOUND TOURISM						
8.1 **Departures**	('000)	17,705	17,739	19,595	21,099	22,732
8.2 **Tourism expenditure in other countries**	US$ Mn	14,257	16,309	19,657	22,891	25,994
8.3 "Travel" (*)	US$ Mn	11,722	13,337	15,914	18,174	20,538
8.4 "Passenger transport" (*)	US$ Mn	2,535	2,972	3,743	4,717	5,456
TOURISM INDUSTRIES						
Hotels and similar establishments						
9.1 Number of rooms	Units	..	363,628	377,771	..	..
9.2 Number of bed-places	Units	..	..	..	..	..
9.3 Occupancy rate	Percent	61.90	58.70	62.10	59.90	..
9.4 Average length of stay	Nights	..	..	..	..	..
RELATED INDICATORS						
Share of tourism expenditure (6.1) in:						
10.1 Gross Domestic Product (GDP)	Percent	1.8	1.4	1.5	1.4	1.4
10.2 Exports of goods	Percent	4.8	4.3	4.5	4.3	4.2
10.3 Exports of services	Percent	31.5	27.7	30.1	28.9	28.6

(*) Balance of Payments items: 6.1 to 6.3 correspond to the "Credit" side (and are receipts for the country) while 8.2 to 8.4 correspond to the "Debit" side (and are expenditures in other countries).

Basic Indicators	Units	2002	2003	2004	2005	2006
INBOUND TOURISM						
Arrivals						
1.1 Visitors	('000)	..	..	..	..	..
1.2 Tourists (overnight visitors)	('000)	126	150	157	198	242
1.3 Same-day visitors	('000)	..	..	..	..	..
1.4 Cruise passengers	('000)	..	..	..	..	..
Arrivals by region						
2.1 Africa	('000)	10	5	10	9	5
2.2 Americas	('000)	2	2	1	2	6
2.3 Europe	('000)	106	135	136	173	208
2.4 East Asia and the Pacific	('000)	..	..	..	..	..
2.5 South Asia	('000)	..	..	..	..	..
2.6 Middle East	('000)	..	..	..	..	..
Arrivals by means of transport used						
3.1 Air	('000)	..	..	..	..	..
3.2 Rail	('000)	..	..	..	..	..
3.3 Road	('000)	..	..	..	..	..
3.4 Sea	('000)	..	..	..	..	..
Arrivals by purpose of visit						
4.1 Leisure, recreation and holidays	('000)	..	..	..	..	..
4.2 Business and professional	('000)	..	..	..	..	..
4.3 Other	('000)	..	..	..	..	..
Accommodation						
5.1 Overnight stays in hotels and similar establishments	('000)	624	820	787	850	1,261
5.2 Guests in hotels and similar establishments	('000)	126	150	157	198	242
5.3 Overnight stays in all types of accommodation establishments	('000)	..	..	..	..	..
5.4 Average length of stay of non-resident tourists in all accommodation establishments	Nights	..	..	..	..	..
6.1 **Tourism expenditure in the country**	US$ Mn	100	135	153	177	286
6.2 "Travel" (*)	US$ Mn	65	87	99	122	215
6.3 "Passenger transport" (*)	US$ Mn	35	48	54	55	71
DOMESTIC TOURISM						
Accommodation						
7.1 Overnight stays in hotels and similar establishments	('000)	70	83	78	85	107
7.2 Guests in hotels and similar establishments	('000)	26	28	28	36	39
7.3 Overnight stays in all types of accommodation establishments	('000)	..	..	..	..	..
7.4 Average length of stay of resident tourists in all accommodation establishments	Nights	..	..	..	..	..
OUTBOUND TOURISM						
8.1 **Departures**	('000)	..	..	..	..	..
8.2 **Tourism expenditure in other countries**	US$ Mn	63	89	93	82	104
8.3 "Travel" (*)	US$ Mn	56	73	78	67	82
8.4 "Passenger transport" (*)	US$ Mn	7	16	15	15	22
TOURISM INDUSTRIES						
Hotels and similar establishments						
9.1 Number of rooms	Units	2,820	3,146	3,150	4,406	4,836
9.2 Number of bed-places	Units	5,159	5,715	5,804	8,278	8,828
9.3 Occupancy rate	Percent	41.16	44.16	40.89	39.85	44.34
9.4 Average length of stay	Nights	4.23	4.72	4.56	3.89	4.61
RELATED INDICATORS						
Share of tourism expenditure (6.1) in:						
10.1 Gross Domestic Product (GDP)	Percent	16.2	16.9	16.5	17.7	25.0
10.2 Exports of goods	Percent	238.1	254.7	268.4	198.9	234.4
10.3 Exports of services	Percent	65.4	66.8	64.0	63.9	72.0

(*) Balance of Payments items: 6.1 to 6.3 correspond to the "Credit" side (and are receipts for the country) while 8.2 to 8.4 correspond to the "Debit" side (and are expenditures in other countries).

CAYMAN ISLANDS

Basic Indicators		Units	2002	2003	2004	2005	2006
	INBOUND TOURISM						
	Arrivals						
1.1	Visitors	('000)	1,878	2,113	1,953	1,967	2,197
1.2	Tourists (overnight visitors)	('000)	303	294	260	168	267
1.3	Same-day visitors	('000)	..	..	..	..	..
1.4	Cruise passengers	('000)	1,575	1,819	1,693	1,799	1,930
	Arrivals by region						
2.1	Africa	('000)	..	..	..	..	..
2.2	Americas	('000)	282	272	242	153	247
2.3	Europe	('000)	19	19	16	13	18
2.4	East Asia and the Pacific	('000)	1	1	1	1	1
2.5	South Asia	('000)	..	..	..	..	..
2.6	Middle East	('000)	..	..	..	..	..
	Arrivals by means of transport used						
3.1	Air	('000)	303	294	260	168	267
3.2	Rail	('000)	..	..	..	..	..
3.3	Road	('000)	..	..	..	..	..
3.4	Sea	('000)	1,575	1,819	1,693	1,799	1,930
	Arrivals by purpose of visit						
4.1	Leisure, recreation and holidays	('000)	243	227	196	100	194
4.2	Business and professional	('000)	13	15	14	12	19
4.3	Other	('000)	47	52	50	56	54
	Accommodation						
5.1	Overnight stays in hotels and similar establishments	('000)			..	..	
5.2	Guests in hotels and similar establishments	('000)	..	..	190	96	157
5.3	Overnight stays in all types of accommodation establishments	('000)	..	..		..	
5.4	Average length of stay of non-resident tourists in all accommodation establishments	Nights	5.80	6.90	6.30	6.80	..
6.1	**Tourism expenditure in the country** (**)	US$ Mn	607	518	523	356	509
6.2	"Travel" (*)	US$ Mn	..	..	..	..	..
6.3	"Passenger transport" (*)	US$ Mn	..	..	..	..	..
	DOMESTIC TOURISM						
	Accommodation						
7.1	Overnight stays in hotels and similar establishments	('000)	..	..	..	..	..
7.2	Guests in hotels and similar establishments	('000)	..	..	..	..	..
7.3	Overnight stays in all types of accommodation establishments	('000)	..	..	..	..	..
7.4	Average length of stay of resident tourists in all accommodation establishments	Nights	..	..	..	..	..
	OUTBOUND TOURISM						
8.1	**Departures**	('000)	..		..	..	
8.2	**Tourism expenditure in other countries**	US$ Mn	..	..	..	..	..
8.3	"Travel" (*)	US$ Mn	..	..	..	..	..
8.4	"Passenger transport" (*)	US$ Mn	..	..	..	..	..
	TOURISM INDUSTRIES						
	Hotels and similar establishments						
9.1	Number of rooms	Units	5,238	5,108	..	2,954	3,907
9.2	Number of bed-places	Units	16,565	15,186	..	..	..
9.3	Occupancy rate	Percent	50.60	51.20	61.70	55.80	59.40
9.4	Average length of stay	Nights	4.80	4.70	4.90	4.90	4.50
	RELATED INDICATORS						
	Share of tourism expenditure (6.1) in:						
10.1	Gross Domestic Product (GDP)	Percent	..	..	..	..	..
10.2	Exports of goods	Percent	..	..	..	..	..
10.3	Exports of services	Percent	..	..	..	..	..

(*) Balance of Payments items: 6.1 to 6.3 correspond to the "Credit" side (and are receipts for the country) while 8.2 to 8.4 correspond to the "Debit" side (and are expenditures in other countries).

(**) See Annex "Country notes".

CENTRAL AFRICAN REPUBLIC

Basic Indicators	Units	2002	2003	2004	2005	2006
INBOUND TOURISM						
Arrivals						
1.1 Visitors	('000)	..	..	..	..	..
1.2 Tourists (overnight visitors)	('000)	2.9	5.7	8.2	12.0	13.8
1.3 Same-day visitors	('000)	..	..	..	..	..
1.4 Cruise passengers	('000)	..	..	..	..	..
Arrivals by region						
2.1 Africa	('000)	1.5	3.1	3.5	6.2	7.1
2.2 Americas	('000)	0.2	0.4	0.4	0.6	0.7
2.3 Europe	('000)	1.0	1.9	3.7	4.3	5.0
2.4 East Asia and the Pacific	('000)	0.2	0.3	0.3	0.4	0.4
2.5 South Asia	('000)	..	..	..	..	..
2.6 Middle East	('000)	..	..	0.2	0.4	0.5
Arrivals by means of transport used						
3.1 Air	('000)	2.9	5.7	8.2	12.0	13.7
3.2 Rail	('000)	..	..	..	..	..
3.3 Road	('000)	..	..	..	..	..
3.4 Sea	('000)	..	..	..	..	..
Arrivals by purpose of visit						
4.1 Leisure, recreation and holidays	('000)	0.1	0.7	1.0	..	1.9
4.2 Business and professional	('000)	1.6	1.7	2.5	..	5.6
4.3 Other	('000)	1.2	3.3	4.6	..	6.2
Accommodation						
5.1 Overnight stays in hotels and similar establishments	('000)	42	42	23	33	42
5.2 Guests in hotels and similar establishments	('000)	13	13	6	8	11
5.3 Overnight stays in all types of accommodation establishments	('000)	..	..	..	..	..
5.4 Average length of stay of non-resident tourists in all accommodation establishments	Nights	4.01	4.00	3.31	4.16	3.84
6.1 **Tourism expenditure in the country**	US$ Mn	3	4	4	..	..
6.2 "Travel" (*)	US$ Mn	..	..	..	..	..
6.3 "Passenger transport" (*)	US$ Mn	..	..	..	..	..
DOMESTIC TOURISM						
Accommodation						
7.1 Overnight stays in hotels and similar establishments	('000)	3	3	3	..	..
7.2 Guests in hotels and similar establishments	('000)	..	1	1	..	..
7.3 Overnight stays in all types of accommodation establishments	('000)	..	..	..	..	..
7.4 Average length of stay of resident tourists in all accommodation establishments	Nights	2.66	2.91	2.48	..	..
OUTBOUND TOURISM						
8.1 **Departures**	('000)	5	6	7	8	11
8.2 **Tourism expenditure in other countries**	US$ Mn	29	31	32	..	..
8.3 "Travel" (*)	US$ Mn	..	..	..	..	..
8.4 "Passenger transport" (*)	US$ Mn	..	..	..	..	..
TOURISM INDUSTRIES						
Hotels and similar establishments						
9.1 Number of rooms	Units	201	201	235	241	241
9.2 Number of bed-places	Units	..	..	..	355	355
9.3 Occupancy rate	Percent	42.78	40.27	34.03	41.00	49.00
9.4 Average length of stay	Nights	4.11	5.61	3.01	4.22	3.82
RELATED INDICATORS						
Share of tourism expenditure (6.1) in:						
10.1 Gross Domestic Product (GDP)	Percent	..	..	..	..	..
10.2 Exports of goods	Percent	..	..	..	..	..
10.3 Exports of services	Percent	..	..	..	..	..

(*) Balance of Payments items: 6.1 to 6.3 correspond to the "Credit" side (and are receipts for the country) while 8.2 to 8.4 correspond to the "Debit" side (and are expenditures in other countries).

CHAD

Basic Indicators	Units	2002	2003	2004	2005	2006
INBOUND TOURISM						
Arrivals						
1.1 Visitors	('000)	149	101	106	59	..
1.2 Tourists (overnight visitors)	('000)	32	21	26	29	..
1.3 Same-day visitors	('000)	..	..	..	..	..
1.4 Cruise passengers	('000)	..	..	..	..	
Arrivals by region						
2.1 Africa	('000)	8	5	6	7	..
2.2 Americas	('000)	6	4	6	6	..
2.3 Europe	('000)	15	10	13	15	..
2.4 East Asia and the Pacific	('000)	1	..	..	1	..
2.5 South Asia	('000)	..	..	..	..	..
2.6 Middle East	('000)	2	1	1	1	..
Arrivals by means of transport used						
3.1 Air	('000)	80	54	48	21	..
3.2 Rail	('000)	..	..	..	..	..
3.3 Road	('000)	40	27	21	9	..
3.4 Sea	('000)	..	..	..	..	..
Arrivals by purpose of visit						
4.1 Leisure, recreation and holidays	('000)	..	..	..	..	..
4.2 Business and professional	('000)	..	..	..	..	..
4.3 Other	('000)	..	..	..	..	..
Accommodation						
5.1 Overnight stays in hotels and similar establishments	('000)	107	60	76	64	..
5.2 Guests in hotels and similar establishments	('000)	32	21	26	29	..
5.3 Overnight stays in all types of accommodation establishments	('000)	..	..	..	..	..
5.4 Average length of stay of non-resident tourists in all accommodation establishments	Nights	3.00	3.00	3.00	3.00	..
6.1 **Tourism expenditure in the country**	US$ Mn	25	..	..	..	..
6.2 "Travel" (*)	US$ Mn	..	..	..	..	..
6.3 "Passenger transport" (*)	US$ Mn	..	..	..	..	..
DOMESTIC TOURISM						
Accommodation						
7.1 Overnight stays in hotels and similar establishments	('000)	5	4	5	4	..
7.2 Guests in hotels and similar establishments	('000)	..	..	..	..	..
7.3 Overnight stays in all types of accommodation establishments	('000)	..	..	..	..	..
7.4 Average length of stay of resident tourists in all accommodation establishments	Nights	..	..	..	..	..
OUTBOUND TOURISM						
8.1 **Departures**	('000)	23	..	..	..	..
8.2 **Tourism expenditure in other countries**	US$ Mn	80	..	..	..	..
8.3 "Travel" (*)	US$ Mn	..	..	..	..	..
8.4 "Passenger transport" (*)	US$ Mn	..	..	..	..	..
TOURISM INDUSTRIES						
Hotels and similar establishments						
9.1 Number of rooms	Units	904	835	835	922	..
9.2 Number of bed-places	Units	1,274	1,320	1,320	1,434	..
9.3 Occupancy rate	Percent	49.00	28.00	..	..	..
9.4 Average length of stay	Nights	..	3.00	3.00	3.00	..
RELATED INDICATORS						
Share of tourism expenditure (6.1) in:						
10.1 Gross Domestic Product (GDP)	Percent	..	..	..	..	..
10.2 Exports of goods	Percent	..	..	..	..	..
10.3 Exports of services	Percent	..	..	..	..	..

(*) Balance of Payments items: 6.1 to 6.3 correspond to the "Credit" side (and are receipts for the country) while 8.2 to 8.4 correspond to the "Debit" side (and are expenditures in other countries).

Basic Indicators	Units	2002	2003	2004	2005	2006
INBOUND TOURISM						
Arrivals						
1.1 Visitors	('000)	..	..	..	..	..
1.2 Tourists (overnight visitors)	('000)	1,412	1,614	1,785	2,027	2,253
1.3 Same-day visitors	('000)	..	448	856	901	866
1.4 Cruise passengers	('000)	..	..	..	..	..
Arrivals by region						
2.1 Africa	('000)	2	3	4	4	4
2.2 Americas	('000)	1,119	1,243	1,360	1,553	1,755
2.3 Europe	('000)	245	309	345	385	402
2.4 East Asia and the Pacific	('000)	41	54	70	75	84
2.5 South Asia	('000)	2	2	4	4	4
2.6 Middle East	('000)	1	1	1	1	2
Arrivals by means of transport used						
3.1 Air	('000)	606	708	760	855	912
3.2 Rail	('000)	1	2	3	3	2
3.3 Road	('000)	777	867	955	1,094	1,244
3.4 Sea	('000)	28	37	67	75	95
Arrivals by purpose of visit						
4.1 Leisure, recreation and holidays	('000)	886	1,054	1,109	1,193	1,330
4.2 Business and professional	('000)	250	229	272	322	442
4.3 Other	('000)	276	331	404	512	481
Accommodation						
5.1 Overnight stays in hotels and similar establishments	('000)	1,709	1,947	2,086	2,877	3,203
5.2 Guests in hotels and similar establishments	('000)	779	850	951	1,397	1,460
5.3 Overnight stays in all types of accommodation establishments	('000)	..	..	..	..	..
5.4 Average length of stay of non-resident tourists in all accommodation establishments	Nights	13.10	12.30	12.80	12.90	12.30
6.1 **Tourism expenditure in the country**	US$ Mn	1,221	1,309	1,571	1,652	1,816
6.2 "Travel" (*)	US$ Mn	898	883	1,095	1,109	1,214
6.3 "Passenger transport" (*)	US$ Mn	323	426	476	543	602
DOMESTIC TOURISM						
Accommodation						
7.1 Overnight stays in hotels and similar establishments	('000)	4,308	4,879	4,751	5,799	6,170
7.2 Guests in hotels and similar establishments	('000)	2,124	2,199	2,287	2,888	3,082
7.3 Overnight stays in all types of accommodation establishments	('000)	..	..	..	..	..
7.4 Average length of stay of resident tourists in all accommodation establishments	Nights	..	..	..	..	..
OUTBOUND TOURISM						
8.1 **Departures**	('000)	1,938	2,100	2,343	2,651	3,005
8.2 **Tourism expenditure in other countries**	US$ Mn	932	1,109	1,251	1,349	1,581
8.3 "Travel" (*)	US$ Mn	673	850	977	1,051	1,252
8.4 "Passenger transport" (*)	US$ Mn	259	259	274	298	329
TOURISM INDUSTRIES						
Hotels and similar establishments						
9.1 Number of rooms	Units	51,793	52,362	53,794	53,335	62,364
9.2 Number of bed-places	Units	117,315	117,905	127,085	131,634	137,187
9.3 Occupancy rate	Percent	31.00	32.50	32.20	34.10	35.90
9.4 Average length of stay	Nights	2.10	2.20	2.10	2.00	2.10
RELATED INDICATORS						
Share of tourism expenditure (6.1) in:						
10.1 Gross Domestic Product (GDP)	Percent	1.8	1.8	1.6	1.4	1.2
10.2 Exports of goods	Percent	6.7	6.0	4.8	4.0	3.1
10.3 Exports of services	Percent	27.8	25.8	26.0	23.5	24.2

(*) Balance of Payments items: 6.1 to 6.3 correspond to the "Credit" side (and are receipts for the country) while 8.2 to 8.4 correspond to the "Debit" side (and are expenditures in other countries).

CHINA

Basic Indicators	Units	2002	2003	2004	2005	2006
INBOUND TOURISM						
Arrivals						
1.1 Visitors	('000)	97,908	91,662	109,038	120,292	124,942
1.2 Tourists (overnight visitors)	('000)	36,803	32,970	41,761	46,809	49,913
1.3 Same-day visitors	('000)	..	..	..	..	..
1.4 Cruise passengers	('000)	..	..	..	..	..
Arrivals by region						
2.1 Africa	('000)	85	92	154	211	255
2.2 Americas	('000)	1,510	1,133	1,790	2,146	2,406
2.3 Europe	('000)	3,007	2,790	4,097	5,166	5,769
2.4 East Asia and the Pacific	('000)	92,866	87,214	102,394	112,053	115,700
2.5 South Asia	('000)	381	383	514	599	671
2.6 Middle East	('000)	52	47	84	111	136
Arrivals by means of transport used						
3.1 Air	('000)	10,343	8,080	12,617	14,736	16,500
3.2 Rail	('000)	1,252	1,110	1,470	1,610	1,661
3.3 Road	('000)	81,936	78,684	90,224	98,735	101,298
3.4 Sea	('000)	4,377	3,787	4,727	5,212	5,484
Arrivals by purpose of visit						
4.1 Leisure, recreation and holidays	('000)	5,560	4,307	7,412	9,345	11,332
4.2 Business and professional	('000)	3,220	2,902	3,861	4,598	5,548
4.3 Other	('000)	4,659	4,194	5,659	6,312	5,330
Accommodation						
5.1 Overnight stays in hotels and similar establishments	('000)	99,360	80,121	114,231	138,411	163,680
5.2 Guests in hotels and similar establishments	('000)	39,142	30,169	43,937	53,258	61,396
5.3 Overnight stays in all types of accommodation establishments	('000)	..	..	..	..	..
5.4 Average length of stay of non-resident tourists in all accommodation establishments	Nights	2.54	2.66	2.60	2.60	2.67
6.1 **Tourism expenditure in the country**	US$ Mn	21,742	18,707	27,755	31,842	37,132
6.2 "Travel" (*)	US$ Mn	20,385	17,406	25,739	29,296	33,949
6.3 "Passenger transport" (*)	US$ Mn	1,357	1,301	2,016	2,546	3,183
DOMESTIC TOURISM						
Accommodation						
7.1 Overnight stays in hotels and similar establishments	('000)	246,325	236,341	296,764	369,000	413,645
7.2 Guests in hotels and similar establishments	('000)	..	..	..	..	..
7.3 Overnight stays in all types of accommodation establishments	('000)	..	..	..	..	..
7.4 Average length of stay of resident tourists in all accommodation establishments	Nights	..	..	..	..	..
OUTBOUND TOURISM						
8.1 **Departures**	('000)	16,602	20,222	28,853	31,026	34,524
8.2 **Tourism expenditure in other countries**	US$ Mn	16,759	16,716	21,360	24,715	28,242
8.3 "Travel" (*)	US$ Mn	15,398	15,187	19,149	21,759	24,322
8.4 "Passenger transport" (*)	US$ Mn	1,361	1,529	2,211	2,956	3,920
TOURISM INDUSTRIES						
Hotels and similar establishments						
9.1 Number of rooms	Units	897,206	992,804	1,237,851	1,332,083	1,459,836
9.2 Number of bed-places	Units	1,729,460	1,887,740	2,366,638	2,571,664	2,785,481
9.3 Occupancy rate	Percent	60.15	56.14	60.62	60.96	61.03
9.4 Average length of stay	Nights	2.54	2.66	2.60	2.60	2.67
RELATED INDICATORS						
Share of tourism expenditure (6.1) in:						
10.1 Gross Domestic Product (GDP)	Percent	1.5	1.1	1.4	1.4	1.4
10.2 Exports of goods	Percent	6.7	4.3	4.7	4.2	3.8
10.3 Exports of services	Percent	54.7	40.0	44.5	42.8	40.4

(*) Balance of Payments items: 6.1 to 6.3 correspond to the "Credit" side (and are receipts for the country) while 8.2 to 8.4 correspond to the "Debit" side (and are expenditures in other countries).

COLOMBIA

Basic Indicators	Units	2002	2003	2004	2005	2006
INBOUND TOURISM						
Arrivals						
1.1 Visitors	('000)	567	625	791	933	1,053
1.2 Tourists (overnight visitors)	('000)	..	..	..	..	..
1.3 Same-day visitors	('000)	..	..	..	..	..
1.4 Cruise passengers	('000)	94	43	49	48	51
Arrivals by region						
2.1 Africa	('000)	1	1	1	1	2
2.2 Americas	('000)	428	484	618	730	825
2.3 Europe	('000)	118	125	156	183	204
2.4 East Asia and the Pacific	('000)	12	11	13	15	17
2.5 South Asia	('000)	1	1	1	2	2
2.6 Middle East	('000)	1	1	1	1	1
Arrivals by means of transport used						
3.1 Air	('000)	507	551	701	834	936
3.2 Rail	('000)	..	..	..	..	..
3.3 Road	('000)	58	72	88	97	116
3.4 Sea	('000)	2	2	2	2	1
Arrivals by purpose of visit						
4.1 Leisure, recreation and holidays	('000)	366	399	493	581	..
4.2 Business and professional	('000)	135	165	217	266	..
4.3 Other	('000)	66	61	81	86	..
Accommodation						
5.1 Overnight stays in hotels and similar establishments	('000)	..	..	..	..	..
5.2 Guests in hotels and similar establishments	('000)	..	..	..	..	..
5.3 Overnight stays in all types of accommodation establishments	('000)	..	..	..	..	..
5.4 Average length of stay of non-resident tourists in all accommodation establishments	Nights	..	..	..	..	..
6.1 **Tourism expenditure in the country**	US$ Mn	1,237	1,191	1,366	1,570	2,005
6.2 "Travel" (*)	US$ Mn	967	893	1,058	1,218	1,550
6.3 "Passenger transport" (*)	US$ Mn	270	298	308	352	455
DOMESTIC TOURISM						
Accommodation						
7.1 Overnight stays in hotels and similar establishments	('000)	..	..	..	..	..
7.2 Guests in hotels and similar establishments	('000)	..	..	..	..	..
7.3 Overnight stays in all types of accommodation establishments	('000)	..	..	..	..	..
7.4 Average length of stay of resident tourists in all accommodation establishments	Nights	..	..	..	..	..
OUTBOUND TOURISM						
8.1 **Departures**	('000)	1,277	1,177	1,405	1,553	1,767
8.2 **Tourism expenditure in other countries**	US$ Mn	1,355	1,349	1,466	1,562	1,796
8.3 "Travel" (*)	US$ Mn	1,075	1,062	1,108	1,127	1,329
8.4 "Passenger transport" (*)	US$ Mn	280	287	358	435	467
TOURISM INDUSTRIES						
Hotels and similar establishments						
9.1 Number of rooms	Units	55,755	60,005	66,576	71,247	..
9.2 Number of bed-places	Units	108,965	117,455	131,086	141,151	..
9.3 Occupancy rate	Percent	45.20	49.10	51.20	54.10	56.40
9.4 Average length of stay	Nights	..	..	..	..	..
RELATED INDICATORS						
Share of tourism expenditure (6.1) in:						
10.1 Gross Domestic Product (GDP)	Percent	1.5	1.5	1.4	1.3	1.5
10.2 Exports of goods	Percent	10.0	8.6	7.9	7.2	8.0
10.3 Exports of services	Percent	66.3	62.0	60.6	58.9	59.4

(*) Balance of Payments items: 6.1 to 6.3 correspond to the "Credit" side (and are receipts for the country) while 8.2 to 8.4 correspond to the "Debit" side (and are expenditures in other countries).

COMOROS

Basic Indicators		Units	2002	2003	2004	2005	2006
	INBOUND TOURISM						
	Arrivals						
1.1	Visitors	('000)	..	..	..	..	..
1.2	Tourists (overnight visitors)	('000)	18.9	20.6	23.3	25.9	28.5
1.3	Same-day visitors	('000)	..	..	..	..	..
1.4	Cruise passengers	('000)	..	..	..	..	..
	Arrivals by region						
2.1	Africa	('000)	8.7	5.6	6.3	8.8	6.1
2.2	Americas	('000)	..	..	..	..	..
2.3	Europe	('000)	9.5	8.0	10.6	9.6	9.5
2.4	East Asia and the Pacific	('000)	..	0.6	0.2	0.5	0.6
2.5	South Asia	('000)	..	..	..	..	..
2.6	Middle East	('000)	..	..	..	..	..
	Arrivals by means of transport used						
3.1	Air	('000)	18.9	14.2	17.6	19.6	17.1
3.2	Rail	('000)	..	..	..	..	..
3.3	Road	('000)	..	..	..	..	..
3.4	Sea	('000)	..	..	..	..	..
	Arrivals by purpose of visit						
4.1	Leisure, recreation and holidays	('000)	3.5	3.9	4.1	4.7	5.1
4.2	Business and professional	('000)	4.3	4.1	4.3	4.9	5.4
4.3	Other	('000)	11.1	12.5	14.9	16.3	18.0
	Accommodation						
5.1	Overnight stays in hotels and similar establishments	('000)	..	..	..	..	..
5.2	Guests in hotels and similar establishments	('000)	..	..	..	..	..
5.3	Overnight stays in all types of accommodation establishments	('000)	133	123	123	137	..
5.4	Average length of stay of non-resident tourists in all accommodation establishments	Nights	..	..	..	..	..
6.1	**Tourism expenditure in the country** (**)	US$ Mn	10.9	15.6	21.4	23.6	26.8
6.2	"Travel" (*)	US$ Mn	..	..	..	..	..
6.3	"Passenger transport" (*)	US$ Mn	..	..	..	..	..
	DOMESTIC TOURISM						
	Accommodation						
7.1	Overnight stays in hotels and similar establishments	('000)	..	..	..	..	..
7.2	Guests in hotels and similar establishments	('000)	..	..	..	..	..
7.3	Overnight stays in all types of accommodation establishments	('000)	..	..	..	..	..
7.4	Average length of stay of resident tourists in all accommodation establishments	Nights	..	..	..	..	..
	OUTBOUND TOURISM						
8.1	**Departures**	('000)	..	..	..	..	..
8.2	**Tourism expenditure in other countries** (**)	US$ Mn	..	7.9	9.4	9.6	10.8
8.3	"Travel" (*)	US$ Mn	..	..	..	..	..
8.4	"Passenger transport" (*)	US$ Mn	..	..	..	..	..
	TOURISM INDUSTRIES						
	Hotels and similar establishments						
9.1	Number of rooms	Units	376	375	375	328	328
9.2	Number of bed-places	Units	752	862	862	656	656
9.3	Occupancy rate	Percent	19.00	14.00	16.00	..	..
9.4	Average length of stay	Nights	7.00	7.00	7.00	7.00	7.00
	RELATED INDICATORS						
	Share of tourism expenditure (6.1) in:						
10.1	Gross Domestic Product (GDP)	Percent	..	..	..	..	..
10.2	Exports of goods	Percent	..	..	..	..	..
10.3	Exports of services	Percent	..	..	..	..	..

(*) Balance of Payments items: 6.1 to 6.3 correspond to the "Credit" side (and are receipts for the country) while 8.2 to 8.4 correspond to the "Debit" side (and are expenditures in other countries).

(**) See Annex "Country notes".

Basic Indicators		Units	2002	2003	2004	2005	2006
	INBOUND TOURISM						
	Arrivals						
1.1	Visitors	('000)	..	..	..	..	..
1.2	Tourists (overnight visitors)	('000)	73	78	83	88	92
1.3	Same-day visitors	('000)	..	..	..	..	..
1.4	Cruise passengers	('000)	..	..	..	..	..
	Arrivals by region						
2.1	Africa	('000)	..	..	..	..	..
2.2	Americas	('000)	11	11	8	6	8
2.3	Europe	('000)	20	22	20	18	18
2.4	East Asia and the Pacific	('000)	41	45	54	63	66
2.5	South Asia	('000)	..	..	..	..	..
2.6	Middle East	('000)	..	..	..	..	..
	Arrivals by means of transport used						
3.1	Air	('000)	..	..	..	..	..
3.2	Rail	('000)	..	..	..	..	..
3.3	Road	('000)	..	..	..	..	..
3.4	Sea	('000)	..	..	..	..	..
	Arrivals by purpose of visit						
4.1	Leisure, recreation and holidays	('000)	62	67	69	73	76
4.2	Business and professional	('000)	4	4	4	3	3
4.3	Other	('000)	7	7	10	12	13
	Accommodation						
5.1	Overnight stays in hotels and similar establishments	('000)	209	205	208	230	261
5.2	Guests in hotels and similar establishments	('000)	..	..	..	..	..
5.3	Overnight stays in all types of accommodation establishments	('000)	..	..	..	..	..
5.4	Average length of stay of non-resident tourists in all accommodation establishments	Nights	10.56	10.53	10.41	10.27	10.41
6.1	**Tourism expenditure in the country** (**)	US$ Mn	46	69	72	91	90
6.2	"Travel" (*)	US$ Mn	..	..	..	..	..
6.3	"Passenger transport" (*)	US$ Mn	..	..	..	..	..
	DOMESTIC TOURISM						
	Accommodation						
7.1	Overnight stays in hotels and similar establishments	('000)	..	..	..	..	..
7.2	Guests in hotels and similar establishments	('000)	..	..	..	..	..
7.3	Overnight stays in all types of accommodation establishments	('000)	..	..	..	..	..
7.4	Average length of stay of resident tourists in all accommodation establishments	Nights	..	..	..	..	..
	OUTBOUND TOURISM						
8.1	**Departures**	('000)	9	10	12	13	13
8.2	**Tourism expenditure in other countries**	US$ Mn	..	..	..	..	..
8.3	"Travel" (*)	US$ Mn	..	..	..	..	..
8.4	"Passenger transport" (*)	US$ Mn	..	..	..	..	..
	TOURISM INDUSTRIES						
	Hotels and similar establishments						
9.1	Number of rooms	Units	..	1,152	..	..	1,408
9.2	Number of bed-places	Units	..	..	..	..	3,554
9.3	Occupancy rate	Percent	63.10	60.50	55.40	61.40	74.80
9.4	Average length of stay	Nights	..	..	..	..	..
	RELATED INDICATORS						
	Share of tourism expenditure (6.1) in:						
10.1	Gross Domestic Product (GDP)	Percent	..	..	..	..	..
10.2	Exports of goods	Percent	..	..	..	..	..
10.3	Exports of services	Percent	..	..	..	..	..

(*) Balance of Payments items: 6.1 to 6.3 correspond to the "Credit" side (and are receipts for the country) while 8.2 to 8.4 correspond to the "Debit" side (and are expenditures in other countries).

(**) See Annex "Country notes".

COSTA RICA

Basic Indicators	Units	2002	2003	2004	2005	2006
INBOUND TOURISM						
Arrivals						
1.1 Visitors	('000)	1,335	1,514	1,771	1,959	2,071
1.2 Tourists (overnight visitors)	('000)	1,113	1,239	1,453	1,679	1,725
1.3 Same-day visitors	('000)	..	..	..	..	..
1.4 Cruise passengers	('000)	222	275	318	280	346
Arrivals by region						
2.1 Africa	('000)	1	1	1	1	1
2.2 Americas	('000)	928	1,018	1,214	1,412	1,457
2.3 Europe	('000)	164	198	215	242	243
2.4 East Asia and the Pacific	('000)	16	16	16	24	23
2.5 South Asia	('000)	..	..	..	..	..
2.6 Middle East	('000)	..	..	..	..	..
Arrivals by means of transport used						
3.1 Air	('000)	798	928	1,088	1,244	1,232
3.2 Rail	('000)	..	..	..	..	..
3.3 Road	('000)	309	299	355	427	487
3.4 Sea	('000)	6	12	10	9	6
Arrivals by purpose of visit						
4.1 Leisure, recreation and holidays	('000)	798	908	1,149	1,357	1,311
4.2 Business and professional	('000)	264	272	250	272	293
4.3 Other	('000)	51	58	54	50	121
Accommodation						
5.1 Overnight stays in hotels and similar establishments	('000)	..	..	..	..	..
5.2 Guests in hotels and similar establishments	('000)	..	..	..	..	..
5.3 Overnight stays in all types of accommodation establishments	('000)	..	..	..	..	..
5.4 Average length of stay of non-resident tourists in all accommodation establishments	Nights	11.00	11.10	11.30	10.50	12.50
6.1 **Tourism expenditure in the country**	US$ Mn	1,292	1,424	1,586	1,810	1,890
6.2 "Travel" (*)	US$ Mn	1,161	1,293	1,459	1,671	1,732
6.3 "Passenger transport" (*)	US$ Mn	131	131	127	139	158
DOMESTIC TOURISM						
Accommodation						
7.1 Overnight stays in hotels and similar establishments	('000)	..	..	..	..	..
7.2 Guests in hotels and similar establishments	('000)	..	..	..	..	..
7.3 Overnight stays in all types of accommodation establishments	('000)	..	..	..	..	..
7.4 Average length of stay of resident tourists in all accommodation establishments	Nights	..	..	..	..	..
OUTBOUND TOURISM						
8.1 **Departures**	('000)	364	373	425	487	485
8.2 **Tourism expenditure in other countries**	US$ Mn	430	434	481	556	577
8.3 "Travel" (*)	US$ Mn	345	353	406	470	485
8.4 "Passenger transport" (*)	US$ Mn	85	81	75	86	92
TOURISM INDUSTRIES						
Hotels and similar establishments						
9.1 Number of rooms	Units	33,126	35,003	36,299	38,737	40,811
9.2 Number of bed-places	Units	..	..	..	..	..
9.3 Occupancy rate	Percent	45.10	47.90	55.00	58.90	58.30
9.4 Average length of stay	Nights	..	..	..	..	..
RELATED INDICATORS						
Share of tourism expenditure (6.1) in:						
10.1 Gross Domestic Product (GDP)	Percent	7.7	8.1	8.5	9.1	8.5
10.2 Exports of goods	Percent	24.5	23.1	24.9	25.5	23.4
10.3 Exports of services	Percent	69.2	70.5	70.7	69.1	64.0

(*) Balance of Payments items: 6.1 to 6.3 correspond to the "Credit" side (and are receipts for the country) while 8.2 to 8.4 correspond to the "Debit" side (and are expenditures in other countries).

Basic Indicators	Units	2002	2003	2004	2005	2006
INBOUND TOURISM						
Arrivals						
1.1 Visitors	('000)	41,737	42,857	44,974	45,762	47,733
1.2 Tourists (overnight visitors)	('000)	6,944	7,409	7,912	8,467	8,659
1.3 Same-day visitors	('000)	..	..	..	..	..
1.4 Cruise passengers	('000)	..	..	..	..	..
Arrivals by region						
2.1 Africa	('000)	..	..	..	..	..
2.2 Americas	('000)	75	84	119	140	183
2.3 Europe	('000)	6,807	7,244	7,693	8,192	8,282
2.4 East Asia and the Pacific	('000)	36	43	58	83	133
2.5 South Asia	('000)	..	..	..	..	..
2.6 Middle East	('000)	..	..	..	..	..
Arrivals by means of transport used						
3.1 Air	('000)	887	1,006	1,202	1,566	1,825
3.2 Rail	('000)	312	335	327	302	312
3.3 Road	('000)	40,231	41,132	42,524	42,910	44,560
3.4 Sea	('000)	306	384	921	984	1,036
Arrivals by purpose of visit						
4.1 Leisure, recreation and holidays	('000)	..	..	..	..	..
4.2 Business and professional	('000)	..	..	..	..	..
4.3 Other	('000)	..	..	..	..	..
Accommodation						
5.1 Overnight stays in hotels and similar establishments	('000)	16,905	16,830	17,072	18,415	17,807
5.2 Guests in hotels and similar establishments	('000)	2,988	3,087	3,362	3,744	3,742
5.3 Overnight stays in all types of accommodation establishments	('000)	39,711	41,323	42,516	45,987	47,022
5.4 Average length of stay of non-resident tourists in all accommodation establishments	Nights	5.71	5.58	5.39	5.43	5.43
6.1 **Tourism expenditure in the country**	US$ Mn	3,952	6,513	6,945	7,625	8,296
6.2 "Travel" (*)	US$ Mn	3,811	6,310	6,727	7,370	7,990
6.3 "Passenger transport" (*)	US$ Mn	141	203	218	255	306
DOMESTIC TOURISM						
Accommodation						
7.1 Overnight stays in hotels and similar establishments	('000)	2,691	2,839	2,900	2,862	2,886
7.2 Guests in hotels and similar establishments	('000)	886	960	979	1,002	1,037
7.3 Overnight stays in all types of accommodation establishments	('000)	4,981	5,312	5,281	5,434	5,985
7.4 Average length of stay of resident tourists in all accommodation establishments	Nights	3.62	3.62	3.59	3.56	3.47
OUTBOUND TOURISM						
8.1 **Departures**	('000)	..	..	..	..	..
8.2 **Tourism expenditure in other countries**	US$ Mn	852	709	881	786	770
8.3 "Travel" (*)	US$ Mn	781	672	848	754	737
8.4 "Passenger transport" (*)	US$ Mn	71	37	33	32	33
TOURISM INDUSTRIES						
Hotels and similar establishments						
9.1 Number of rooms	Units	77,347	77,113	79,174	80,743	75,952
9.2 Number of bed-places	Units	187,947	193,538	199,033	203,464	163,168
9.3 Occupancy rate	Percent	25.49	27.84	27.49	28.65	34.75
9.4 Average length of stay	Nights	5.06	5.25	5.08	4.48	4.33
RELATED INDICATORS						
Share of tourism expenditure (6.1) in:						
10.1 Gross Domestic Product (GDP)	Percent	17.1	22.0	19.5	19.6	19.4
10.2 Exports of goods	Percent	79.0	103.2	84.6	85.1	78.2
10.3 Exports of services	Percent	70.8	76.0	74.1	76.9	76.8

(*) Balance of Payments items: 6.1 to 6.3 correspond to the "Credit" side (and are receipts for the country) while 8.2 to 8.4 correspond to the "Debit" side (and are expenditures in other countries).

CUBA

Basic Indicators		Units	2002	2003	2004	2005	2006
	INBOUND TOURISM						
	Arrivals						
1.1	Visitors	('000)	1,686	1,906	2,049	2,319	2,221
1.2	Tourists (overnight visitors)	('000)	1,656	1,847	2,017	2,261	2,150
1.3	Same-day visitors	('000)	30	59	32	58	71
1.4	Cruise passengers	('000)	6	20	5	17	30
	Arrivals by region						
2.1	Africa	('000)	6	7	6	7	7
2.2	Americas	('000)	788	917	1,026	1,216	1,149
2.3	Europe	('000)	859	942	977	1,048	1,013
2.4	East Asia and the Pacific	('000)	27	32	34	42	44
2.5	South Asia	('000)	4	6	4	5	5
2.6	Middle East	('000)	2	2	2	2	2
	Arrivals by means of transport used						
3.1	Air	('000)	1,656	1,847	2,017	2,261	2,150
3.2	Rail	('000)	..	..	..	..	..
3.3	Road	('000)	..	..	..	..	..
3.4	Sea	('000)	..	..	..	..	..
	Arrivals by purpose of visit						
4.1	Leisure, recreation and holidays	('000)	1,560	1,736	1,830	1,982	1,931
4.2	Business and professional	('000)	13	12	11	12	13
4.3	Other	('000)	83	99	176	267	206
	Accommodation						
5.1	Overnight stays in hotels and similar establishments	('000)	9,755	11,951	13,358	14,572	14,905
5.2	Guests in hotels and similar establishments	('000)	2,029	2,401	2,732	2,911	2,785
5.3	Overnight stays in all types of accommodation establishments	('000)	10,486	12,684	14,190	15,404	15,628
5.4	Average length of stay of non-resident tourists in all accommodation establishments	Nights	10.50	10.50	10.50	10.50	10.50
6.1	**Tourism expenditure in the country** (**)	US$ Mn	1,769	1,999	2,114	2,399	2,404
6.2	"Travel" (*)	US$ Mn	1,633	1,846	1,915	2,150	2,138
6.3	"Passenger transport" (*)	US$ Mn	136	153	199	249	266
	DOMESTIC TOURISM						
	Accommodation						
7.1	Overnight stays in hotels and similar establishments	('000)	3,263	3,142	2,529	2,548	3,256
7.2	Guests in hotels and similar establishments	('000)	..	..	..	..	..
7.3	Overnight stays in all types of accommodation establishments	('000)	7,046	6,988	6,421	6,931	7,720
7.4	Average length of stay of resident tourists in all accommodation establishments	Nights	..	..	..	..	..
	OUTBOUND TOURISM						
8.1	**Departures**	('000)	111	113	115	162	199
8.2	**Tourism expenditure in other countries**	US$ Mn	..	..	..	..	..
8.3	"Travel" (*)	US$ Mn	..	..	..	..	..
8.4	"Passenger transport" (*)	US$ Mn	..	..	..	..	..
	TOURISM INDUSTRIES						
	Hotels and similar establishments						
9.1	Number of rooms	Units	41,323	43,696	45,181	46,626	48,726
9.2	Number of bed-places	Units	81,086	84,200	85,605	87,252	90,097
9.3	Occupancy rate	Percent	59.70	61.80	63.50	63.60	60.70
9.4	Average length of stay	Nights	..	..	..	..	..
	RELATED INDICATORS						
	Share of tourism expenditure (6.1) in:						
10.1	Gross Domestic Product (GDP)	Percent	4.9	5.2	5.1	5.2	4.3
10.2	Exports of goods	Percent	124.4	119.6	96.6	120.3	87.1
10.3	Exports of services	Percent	..	..	..	..	..

(*) Balance of Payments items: 6.1 to 6.3 correspond to the "Credit" side (and are receipts for the country) while 8.2 to 8.4 correspond to the "Debit" side (and are expenditures in other countries).

(**) See Annex "Country notes".

Basic Indicators		Units	2002	2003	2004	2005	2006
	INBOUND TOURISM						
	Arrivals						
1.1	Visitors	('000)	545	508	452	510	572
1.2	Tourists (overnight visitors)	('000)	218	221	223	222	234
1.3	Same-day visitors	('000)	8	7	10	12	16
1.4	Cruise passengers	('000)	319	279	219	276	322
	Arrivals by region						
2.1	Africa	('000)	..	..	..	..	..
2.2	Americas	('000)	141	126	129	123	127
2.3	Europe	('000)	70	91	90	95	104
2.4	East Asia and the Pacific	('000)	..	..	..	..	..
2.5	South Asia	('000)	..	..	..	..	..
2.6	Middle East	('000)	..	..	..	..	..
	Arrivals by means of transport used						
3.1	Air	('000)	226	228	233	234	250
3.2	Rail	('000)	..	..	..	..	..
3.3	Road	('000)	..	..	..	..	..
3.4	Sea	('000)	319	279	219	276	322
	Arrivals by purpose of visit						
4.1	Leisure, recreation and holidays	('000)	170	183	191	198	213
4.2	Business and professional	('000)	31	24	21	15	15
4.3	Other	('000)	14	12	11	9	5
	Accommodation						
5.1	Overnight stays in hotels and similar establishments	('000)	677	754	782	842	..
5.2	Guests in hotels and similar establishments	('000)	119	127	129	135	139
5.3	Overnight stays in all types of accommodation establishments	('000)	1,815	1,919	1,920	1,958	2,156
5.4	Average length of stay of non-resident tourists in all accommodation establishments	Nights	8.35	8.63	8.59	8.82	9.20
6.1	**Tourism expenditure in the country** (**)	US$ Mn	290	286	296	284	..
6.2	"Travel" (*)	US$ Mn	..	..	..	..	..
6.3	"Passenger transport" (*)	US$ Mn	..	..	..	..	..
	DOMESTIC TOURISM						
	Accommodation						
7.1	Overnight stays in hotels and similar establishments	('000)	..	..	..	..	..
7.2	Guests in hotels and similar establishments	('000)	..	..	..	..	..
7.3	Overnight stays in all types of accommodation establishments	('000)	..	..	..	..	..
7.4	Average length of stay of resident tourists in all accommodation establishments	Nights	..	..	..	..	..
	OUTBOUND TOURISM						
8.1	**Departures**	('000)	..	..	..	..	..
8.2	**Tourism expenditure in other countries**	US$ Mn	..	..	..	..	..
8.3	"Travel" (*)	US$ Mn	..	..	..	..	..
8.4	"Passenger transport" (*)	US$ Mn	..	..	..	..	..
	TOURISM INDUSTRIES						
	Hotels and similar establishments						
9.1	Number of rooms	Units	3,422	3,474	3,557	3,647	..
9.2	Number of bed-places	Units	..	..	..	..	..
9.3	Occupancy rate	Percent	57.32	62.10	69.70	81.74	..
9.4	Average length of stay	Nights	8.38	8.56	8.59	8.82	9.20
	RELATED INDICATORS						
	Share of tourism expenditure (6.1) in:						
10.1	Gross Domestic Product (GDP)	Percent	..	..	..	..	..
10.2	Exports of goods	Percent	..	..	..	..	..
10.3	Exports of services	Percent	..	..	..	..	..

(*) Balance of Payments items: 6.1 to 6.3 correspond to the "Credit" side (and are receipts for the country) while 8.2 to 8.4 correspond to the "Debit" side (and are expenditures in other countries).

(**) See Annex "Country notes".

CYPRUS

Basic Indicators	Units	2002	2003	2004	2005	2006
INBOUND TOURISM						
Arrivals						
1.1 Visitors	('000)	2,495	2,416	2,478	2,657	2,629
1.2 Tourists (overnight visitors)	('000)	2,418	2,303	2,349	2,470	2,401
1.3 Same-day visitors	('000)	77	113	129	187	228
1.4 Cruise passengers	('000)	59	93	119	176	220
Arrivals by region						
2.1 Africa	('000)	7	7	5	7	7
2.2 Americas	('000)	27	23	23	29	26
2.3 Europe	('000)	2,324	2,207	2,263	2,375	2,308
2.4 East Asia and the Pacific	('000)	12	12	13	15	16
2.5 South Asia	('000)	3	3	2	3	4
2.6 Middle East	('000)	45	49	41	40	39
Arrivals by means of transport used						
3.1 Air	('000)	2,431	2,320	2,357	2,479	2,408
3.2 Rail	('000)	..	..	..	..	..
3.3 Road	('000)	..	..	..	..	..
3.4 Sea	('000)	64	96	121	178	221
Arrivals by purpose of visit						
4.1 Leisure, recreation and holidays	('000)	2,172	2,052	2,099	2,194	2,091
4.2 Business and professional	('000)	131	127	139	143	151
4.3 Other	('000)	115	124	111	133	159
Accommodation						
5.1 Overnight stays in hotels and similar establishments	('000)	15,235	13,424	13,554	13,899	13,227
5.2 Guests in hotels and similar establishments	('000)	2,034	1,818	1,725	1,750	1,761
5.3 Overnight stays in all types of accommodation establishments	('000)	15,289	13,490	13,637	14,006	13,310
5.4 Average length of stay of non-resident tourists in all accommodation establishments	Nights	7.52	7.42	7.91	7.94	7.52
6.1 **Tourism expenditure in the country**	US$ Mn	2,178	2,325	2,552	2,644	2,735
6.2 "Travel" (*)	US$ Mn	1,959	2,097	2,241	2,318	2,420
6.3 "Passenger transport" (*)	US$ Mn	219	228	311	326	315
DOMESTIC TOURISM						
Accommodation						
7.1 Overnight stays in hotels and similar establishments	('000)	868	957	1,069	1,040	1,114
7.2 Guests in hotels and similar establishments	('000)	376	400	446	449	509
7.3 Overnight stays in all types of accommodation establishments	('000)	870	968	1,081	1,052	1,128
7.4 Average length of stay of resident tourists in all accommodation establishments	Nights	2.31	2.38	2.42	2.31	2.18
OUTBOUND TOURISM						
8.1 **Departures**	('000)	645	629	743	781	789
8.2 **Tourism expenditure in other countries**	US$ Mn	582	700	907	1,001	1,047
8.3 "Travel" (*)	US$ Mn	512	611	811	932	982
8.4 "Passenger transport" (*)	US$ Mn	70	89	96	69	65
TOURISM INDUSTRIES						
Hotels and similar establishments						
9.1 Number of rooms	Units	44,523	44,892	45,535	45,202	44,404
9.2 Number of bed-places	Units	90,112	91,139	92,239	91,264	89,490
9.3 Occupancy rate	Percent	63.04	57.48	57.61	61.55	59.91
9.4 Average length of stay	Nights	6.70	6.48	6.73	6.79	6.32
RELATED INDICATORS						
Share of tourism expenditure (6.1) in:						
10.1 Gross Domestic Product (GDP)	Percent	20.8	17.7	16.6	15.8	15.0
10.2 Exports of goods	Percent	255.6	251.4	217.6	171.1	193.0
10.3 Exports of services	Percent	48.1	43.3	40.9	40.8	37.6

(*) Balance of Payments items: 6.1 to 6.3 correspond to the "Credit" side (and are receipts for the country) while 8.2 to 8.4 correspond to the "Debit" side (and are expenditures in other countries).

CZECH REPUBLIC

Basic Indicators	Units	2002	2003	2004	2005	2006
INBOUND TOURISM						
Arrivals						
1.1 Visitors	('000)	..	..	..	..	..
1.2 Tourists (overnight visitors)	('000)	4,743	5,076	6,061	6,336	6,435
1.3 Same-day visitors	('000)	..	..	..	..	..
1.4 Cruise passengers	('000)	..	..	..	..	..
Arrivals by region						
2.1 Africa	('000)	13	14	15	18	19
2.2 Americas	('000)	239	282	380	401	435
2.3 Europe	('000)	4,249	4,528	5,314	5,496	5,488
2.4 East Asia and the Pacific	('000)	242	251	352	421	493
2.5 South Asia	('000)	..	..	..	..	..
2.6 Middle East	('000)	..	..	..	..	..
Arrivals by means of transport used						
3.1 Air	('000)	..	..	..	..	..
3.2 Rail	('000)	..	..	..	..	..
3.3 Road	('000)	..	..	..	..	..
3.4 Sea	('000)	..	..	..	..	..
Arrivals by purpose of visit						
4.1 Leisure, recreation and holidays	('000)	..	..	..	..	..
4.2 Business and professional	('000)	..	..	..	..	..
4.3 Other	('000)	..	..	..	..	..
Accommodation						
5.1 Overnight stays in hotels and similar establishments	('000)	13,327	13,688	15,881	16,607	17,035
5.2 Guests in hotels and similar establishments	('000)	4,314	4,485	5,346	5,686	5,781
5.3 Overnight stays in all types of accommodation establishments	('000)	15,569	16,511	18,980	19,595	20,090
5.4 Average length of stay of non-resident tourists in all accommodation establishments	Nights	3.30	3.30	3.10	3.10	3.10
6.1 **Tourism expenditure in the country**	US$ Mn	3,376	4,069	4,931	5,618	5,844
6.2 "Travel" (*)	US$ Mn	2,964	3,566	4,187	4,659	5,026
6.3 "Passenger transport" (*)	US$ Mn	412	503	744	959	818
DOMESTIC TOURISM						
Accommodation						
7.1 Overnight stays in hotels and similar establishments	('000)	10,476	9,779	9,051	8,601	8,854
7.2 Guests in hotels and similar establishments	('000)	3,438	3,462	3,346	3,388	3,595
7.3 Overnight stays in all types of accommodation establishments	('000)	21,541	22,833	21,800	20,725	21,357
7.4 Average length of stay of resident tourists in all accommodation establishments	Nights	3.80	3.60	3.50	3.40	3.40
OUTBOUND TOURISM						
8.1 **Departures**	('000)	..	..	..	..	..
8.2 **Tourism expenditure in other countries**	US$ Mn	1,797	2,177	2,682	2,603	2,779
8.3 "Travel" (*)	US$ Mn	1,597	1,934	2,280	2,405	2,670
8.4 "Passenger transport" (*)	US$ Mn	200	243	402	198	109
TOURISM INDUSTRIES						
Hotels and similar establishments						
9.1 Number of rooms	Units	96,650	98,086	98,764	99,916	101,563
9.2 Number of bed-places	Units	223,392	226,770	229,689	232,211	236,104
9.3 Occupancy rate	Percent	39.70	35.40	37.00	35.80	35.80
9.4 Average length of stay	Nights	3.80	3.70	3.40	2.80	2.80
RELATED INDICATORS						
Share of tourism expenditure (6.1) in:						
10.1 Gross Domestic Product (GDP)	Percent	4.5	4.5	4.6	4.5	4.1
10.2 Exports of goods	Percent	8.8	8.4	7.3	7.2	6.1
10.3 Exports of services	Percent	47.7	52.2	51.1	47.8	43.8

(*) Balance of Payments items: 6.1 to 6.3 correspond to the "Credit" side (and are receipts for the country) while 8.2 to 8.4 correspond to the "Debit" side (and are expenditures in other countries).

DEMOCRATIC REPUBLIC OF THE CONGO

Basic Indicators	Units	2002	2003	2004	2005	2006
INBOUND TOURISM						
Arrivals						
1.1 Visitors	('000)	..	..	..	..	..
1.2 Tourists (overnight visitors)	('000)	28	35	36	61	55
1.3 Same-day visitors	('000)	20	20	..	..	..
1.4 Cruise passengers	('000)	..	..	..	..	..
Arrivals by region						
2.1 Africa	('000)	9	20	15	36	33
2.2 Americas	('000)	4	3	5	4	3
2.3 Europe	('000)	11	9	13	15	13
2.4 East Asia and the Pacific	('000)	4	3	4	6	6
2.5 South Asia	('000)	..	..	..	..	..
2.6 Middle East	('000)	..	..	..	..	..
Arrivals by means of transport used						
3.1 Air	('000)	28	35	36	39	41
3.2 Rail	('000)	..	..	..	..	..
3.3 Road	('000)	..	..	..	22	14
3.4 Sea	('000)	..	..	..	..	..
Arrivals by purpose of visit						
4.1 Leisure, recreation and holidays	('000)	2	2	7	8	10
4.2 Business and professional	('000)	3	21	22	42	35
4.3 Other	('000)	23	12	7	11	10
Accommodation						
5.1 Overnight stays in hotels and similar establishments	('000)	..	..	..	..	..
5.2 Guests in hotels and similar establishments	('000)	16	17	26	48	54
5.3 Overnight stays in all types of accommodation establishments	('000)	163	150	99	165	189
5.4 Average length of stay of non-resident tourists in all accommodation establishments	Nights	8.00	7.00	5.00	5.00	5.00
6.1 **Tourism expenditure in the country**	US$ Mn	..	..	..	..	..
6.2 "Travel" (*)	US$ Mn	..	..	..	..	..
6.3 "Passenger transport" (*)	US$ Mn	..	..	..	..	..
DOMESTIC TOURISM						
Accommodation						
7.1 Overnight stays in hotels and similar establishments	('000)	..	..	..	..	..
7.2 Guests in hotels and similar establishments	('000)	5	11	16	13	11
7.3 Overnight stays in all types of accommodation establishments	('000)	67	40	85	156	113
7.4 Average length of stay of resident tourists in all accommodation establishments	Nights	14.00	14.00	14.00	7.00	6.00
OUTBOUND TOURISM						
8.1 **Departures**	('000)	..	..	..	..	..
8.2 **Tourism expenditure in other countries**	US$ Mn	..	..	..	..	..
8.3 "Travel" (*)	US$ Mn	..	..	..	..	..
8.4 "Passenger transport" (*)	US$ Mn	..	..	..	..	..
TOURISM INDUSTRIES						
Hotels and similar establishments						
9.1 Number of rooms	Units	5,829	5,829	..	..	..
9.2 Number of bed-places	Units	10,000	10,000	..	..	..
9.3 Occupancy rate	Percent	50.00	50.00	..	..	..
9.4 Average length of stay	Nights	8.00	7.00	..	..	..
RELATED INDICATORS						
Share of tourism expenditure (6.1) in:						
10.1 Gross Domestic Product (GDP)	Percent	..	..	..	..	..
10.2 Exports of goods	Percent	..	..	..	..	..
10.3 Exports of services	Percent	..	..	..	..	..

(*) Balance of Payments items: 6.1 to 6.3 correspond to the "Credit" side (and are receipts for the country) while 8.2 to 8.4 correspond to the "Debit" side (and are expenditures in other countries).

Basic Indicators	Units	2002	2003	2004	2005	2006
INBOUND TOURISM						
Arrivals						
1.1 Visitors	('000)	..	21,119	22,054	22,448	22,396
1.2 Tourists (overnight visitors)	('000)	3,436	3,474	4,421	4,699	4,716
1.3 Same-day visitors	('000)	..	17,340	17,340	17,340	17,306
1.4 Cruise passengers	('000)	193	305	293	409	374
Arrivals by region						
2.1 Africa	('000)	..	..	..	..	..
2.2 Americas	('000)	80	78	126	147	186
2.3 Europe	('000)	3,221	3,253	4,065	4,357	4,364
2.4 East Asia and the Pacific	('000)	49	47	83	110	91
2.5 South Asia	('000)	..	..	..	..	..
2.6 Middle East	('000)	..	..	..	..	..
Arrivals by means of transport used						
3.1 Air	('000)	..	..	..	..	..
3.2 Rail	('000)	..	..	..	..	..
3.3 Road	('000)	..	..	..	..	..
3.4 Sea	('000)	..	..	..	..	..
Arrivals by purpose of visit						
4.1 Leisure, recreation and holidays	('000)	..	..	21,070	21,213	21,192
4.2 Business and professional	('000)	..	..	984	1,235	1,204
4.3 Other	('000)	..	..	..	..	..
Accommodation						
5.1 Overnight stays in hotels and similar establishments	('000)	4,735	4,730	4,984	5,015	4,955
5.2 Guests in hotels and similar establishments	('000)	1,379	1,385	1,970	2.230	2,216
5.3 Overnight stays in all types of accommodation establishments	('000)	25,663	26,152	24,925	23,012	23,371
5.4 Average length of stay of non-resident tourists in all accommodation establishments	Nights	..	..	..	5.00	5.00
6.1 **Tourism expenditure in the country**	US$ Mn	..	..	..	..	..
6.2 "Travel" (*)	US$ Mn	4,791	5,271	5,652	5,293	5,587
6.3 "Passenger transport" (*)	US$ Mn	..	..	..	..	..
DOMESTIC TOURISM						
Accommodation						
7.1 Overnight stays in hotels and similar establishments	('000)	5,250	5.104	5,404	5,806	6,194
7.2 Guests in hotels and similar establishments	('000)	2,172	2,112	2,805	3,348	3,533
7.3 Overnight stays in all types of accommodation establishments	('000)	20,953	21,678	21,534	21,914	24,000
7.4 Average length of stay of resident tourists in all accommodation establishments	Nights	..	..	3.00	3.00	2.00
OUTBOUND TOURISM						
8.1 **Departures**	('000)	4,935	5,564	4,630	5,469	6,142
8.2 **Tourism expenditure in other countries**	US$ Mn	..	..	..	..	..
8.3 "Travel" (*)	US$ Mn	5,838	6,659	7,279	6,850	7,428
8.4 "Passenger transport" (*)	US$ Mn	..	..	..	..	..
TOURISM INDUSTRIES						
Hotels and similar establishments						
9.1 Number of rooms	Units	41,194	41,729	43,163	42,834	43,446
9.2 Number of bed-places	Units	105,185	106,080	109,108	108,095	108,900
9.3 Occupancy rate	Percent	36.40	35.70	35.60	36.20	..
9.4 Average length of stay	Nights	..	..	..	..	..
RELATED INDICATORS						
Share of tourism expenditure (6.1) in: (**)						
10.1 Gross Domestic Product (GDP)	Percent	2.8	2.5	2.3	2.0	..
10.2 Exports of goods	Percent	8.6	8.2	7.5	6.4	..
10.3 Exports of services	Percent	18.0	16.6	15.6	12.1	..

(*) Balance of Payments items: 6.1 to 6.3 correspond to the "Credit" side (and are receipts for the country) while 8.2 to 8.4 correspond to the "Debit" side (and are expenditures in other countries).

(**) See Annex "Country notes".

DJIBOUTI

Basic Indicators	Units	2002	2003	2004	2005	2006
INBOUND TOURISM						
Arrivals						
1.1 Visitors	('000)	..	..	..	..	..
1.2 Tourists (overnight visitors)	('000)	22.5	23.2	26.3	30.2	39.5
1.3 Same-day visitors	('000)	..	..	..	..	..
1.4 Cruise passengers	('000)	..	..	..	..	..
Arrivals by region						
2.1 Africa	('000)	..	..	..	..	..
2.2 Americas	('000)	..	..	..	..	..
2.3 Europe	('000)	..	..	..	..	..
2.4 East Asia and the Pacific	('000)	..	..	..	..	..
2.5 South Asia	('000)	..	..	..	..	..
2.6 Middle East	('000)	..	..	..	..	..
Arrivals by means of transport used						
3.1 Air	('000)	..	..	..	..	..
3.2 Rail	('000)	..	..	..	..	..
3.3 Road	('000)	..	..	..	..	..
3.4 Sea	('000)	..	..	..	..	..
Arrivals by purpose of visit						
4.1 Leisure, recreation and holidays	('000)	..	..	..	..	..
4.2 Business and professional	('000)	..	..	..	..	..
4.3 Other	('000)	..	..	..	..	..
Accommodation						
5.1 Overnight stays in hotels and similar establishments	('000)	53.6	63.4	63.7	66.9	59.3
5.2 Guests in hotels and similar establishments	('000)	22.5	23.2	26.3	30.2	39.5
5.3 Overnight stays in all types of accommodation establishments	('000)	..	..	..	..	..
5.4 Average length of stay of non-resident tourists in all accommodation establishments	Nights	..	..	..	..	..
6.1 **Tourism expenditure in the country**	US$ Mn	..	..	..	..	..
6.2 "Travel" (*)	US$ Mn	8.9	6.9	6.8	7.1	9.2
6.3 "Passenger transport" (*)	US$ Mn	..	..	..	..	..
DOMESTIC TOURISM						
Accommodation						
7.1 Overnight stays in hotels and similar establishments	('000)	..	..	..	..	..
7.2 Guests in hotels and similar establishments	('000)	..	..	..	..	..
7.3 Overnight stays in all types of accommodation establishments	('000)	..	..	..	..	..
7.4 Average length of stay of resident tourists in all accommodation establishments	Nights	..	..	..	..	..
OUTBOUND TOURISM						
8.1 **Departures**	('000)	..	..	..	..	..
8.2 **Tourism expenditure in other countries**	US$ Mn	7.7	9.9	14.0	14.4	15.0
8.3 "Travel" (*)	US$ Mn	2.8	2.8	2.8	2.9	3.5
8.4 "Passenger transport" (*)	US$ Mn	4.9	7.1	11.2	11.5	11.5
TOURISM INDUSTRIES						
Hotels and similar establishments						
9.1 Number of rooms	Units	450	450	450	450	450
9.2 Number of bed-places	Units	675	675	675	675	675
9.3 Occupancy rate	Percent	31.10	47.20	38.70	40.70	35.90
9.4 Average length of stay	Nights	..	..	..	..	..
RELATED INDICATORS						
Share of tourism expenditure (6.1) in: (**)						
10.1 Gross Domestic Product (GDP)	Percent	1.5	1.1	1.0	1.0	1.2
10.2 Exports of goods	Percent	24.7	18.6	17.9	17.8	16.7
10.3 Exports of services	Percent	4.6	3.2	3.2	2.9	3.6

(*) Balance of Payments items: 6.1 to 6.3 correspond to the "Credit" side (and are receipts for the country) while 8.2 to 8.4 correspond to the "Debit" side (and are expenditures in other countries).

(**) See Annex "Country notes".

Basic Indicators	Units	2002	2003	2004	2005	2006
INBOUND TOURISM						
Arrivals						
1.1 Visitors	('000)	208	254	466	381	465
1.2 Tourists (overnight visitors)	('000)	69	73	80	79	84
1.3 Same-day visitors	('000)	1.7	3.9	2.6	0.7	0.9
1.4 Cruise passengers	('000)	137	177	384	302	380
Arrivals by region						
2.1 Africa	('000)	..	..	..	..	..
2.2 Americas	('000)	58	61	69	68	72
2.3 Europe	('000)	10	11	10	10	11
2.4 East Asia and the Pacific	('000)	0.5	0.5	0.4	0.5	0.5
2.5 South Asia	('000)	..	..	..	..	..
2.6 Middle East	('000)	..	..	..	..	..
Arrivals by means of transport used						
3.1 Air	('000)	49	52	56	59	62
3.2 Rail	('000)	..	..	..	..	..
3.3 Road	('000)	..	..	..	..	..
3.4 Sea	('000)	22	25	26	21	23
Arrivals by purpose of visit						
4.1 Leisure, recreation and holidays	('000)	56	60	66	66	70
4.2 Business and professional	('000)	13	13	14	13	14
4.3 Other	('000)	0.3	0.3	0.5	0.5	0.5
Accommodation						
5.1 Overnight stays in hotels and similar establishments	('000)	..	..	..	..	..
5.2 Guests in hotels and similar establishments	('000)	26	26	29	27	35
5.3 Overnight stays in all types of accommodation establishments	('000)	..	..	..	..	..
5.4 Average length of stay of non-resident tourists in all accommodation establishments	Nights	8.60	9.70	9.50	8.70	9.20
6.1 Tourism expenditure in the country	US$ Mn	..	..	..	..	..
6.2 "Travel" (*)	US$ Mn	46	52	61	56	68
6.3 "Passenger transport" (*)	US$ Mn	..	..	..	..	..
DOMESTIC TOURISM						
Accommodation						
7.1 Overnight stays in hotels and similar establishments	('000)	..	..	..	..	..
7.2 Guests in hotels and similar establishments	('000)	..	..	..	..	..
7.3 Overnight stays in all types of accommodation establishments	('000)	..	..	..	..	..
7.4 Average length of stay of resident tourists in all accommodation establishments	Nights	..	..	..	..	..
OUTBOUND TOURISM						
8.1 **Departures**	('000)	..	..	..	..	..
8.2 **Tourism expenditure in other countries**	US$ Mn	..	..	..	..	..
8.3 "Travel" (*)	US$ Mn	9	9	9	10	10
8.4 "Passenger transport" (*)	US$ Mn	..	..	..	..	..
TOURISM INDUSTRIES						
Hotels and similar establishments						
9.1 Number of rooms	Units	931	931	791	787	818
9.2 Number of bed-places	Units	..	..	..	..	..
9.3 Occupancy rate	Percent	..	..	..	..	..
9.4 Average length of stay	Nights	..	..	..	..	..
RELATED INDICATORS						
Share of tourism expenditure (6.1) in: (**)						
10.1 Gross Domestic Product (GDP)	Percent	18.3	20.2	22.5	19.7	22.7
10.2 Exports of goods	Percent	104.5	126.8	141.9	130.2	155.1
10.3 Exports of services	Percent	57.5	67.5	69.3	67.5	70.7

(*) Balance of Payments items: 6.1 to 6.3 correspond to the "Credit" side (and are receipts for the country) while 8.2 to 8.4 correspond to the "Debit" side (and are expenditures in other countries).

(**) See Annex "Country notes".

DOMINICAN REPUBLIC

Basic Indicators	Units	2002	2003	2004	2005	2006
INBOUND TOURISM						
Arrivals						
1.1 Visitors	('000)	3,058	3,680	3,907	3,981	4,268
1.2 Tourists (overnight visitors)	('000)	2,811	3,282	3,450	3,691	3,965
1.3 Same-day visitors	('000)	..	..	..	..	..
1.4 Cruise passengers	('000)	247	398	457	290	303
Arrivals by region						
2.1 Africa	('000)	..	..	..	..	..
2.2 Americas	('000)	1,261	1,504	1,597	1,711	1,948
2.3 Europe	('000)	1,031	1,251	1,271	1,372	1,389
2.4 East Asia and the Pacific	('000)	3	3	4	4	5
2.5 South Asia	('000)	..	..	..	..	..
2.6 Middle East	('000)	..	..	..	..	..
Arrivals by means of transport used						
3.1 Air	('000)	2,811	3,282	3,450	3,691	3,965
3.2 Rail	('000)	..	..	..	..	..
3.3 Road	('000)	..	..	..	..	..
3.4 Sea	('000)	247	398	457	290	303
Arrivals by purpose of visit						
4.1 Leisure, recreation and holidays	('000)	2,637	3,122	3,294	3,475	3,674
4.2 Business and professional	('000)	87	96	94	128	143
4.3 Other	('000)	69	64	62	88	148
Accommodation						
5.1 Overnight stays in hotels and similar establishments	('000)	22,318	23,920	23,795	28,411	31,247
5.2 Guests in hotels and similar establishments	('000)	..	..	..	..	..
5.3 Overnight stays in all types of accommodation establishments	('000)	..	..	..	..	..
5.4 Average length of stay of non-resident tourists in all accommodation establishments	Nights	9.65	9.32	8.97	9.20	9.30
6.1 **Tourism expenditure in the country**	US$ Mn	..	..	..	..	..
6.2 "Travel" (*)	US$ Mn	2,730	3,128	3,152	3,518	3,792
6.3 "Passenger transport" (*)	US$ Mn	..	..	..	..	..
DOMESTIC TOURISM						
Accommodation						
7.1 Overnight stays in hotels and similar establishments	('000)	..	..	..	..	..
7.2 Guests in hotels and similar establishments	('000)	..	..	..	..	..
7.3 Overnight stays in all types of accommodation establishments	('000)	..	..	..	..	..
7.4 Average length of stay of resident tourists in all accommodation establishments	Nights	..	..	..	..	..
OUTBOUND TOURISM						
8.1 **Departures**	('000)	332	321	368	419	420
8.2 **Tourism expenditure in other countries**	US$ Mn	429	408	448	511	499
8.3 "Travel" (*)	US$ Mn	295	272	310	352	333
8.4 "Passenger transport" (*)	US$ Mn	134	136	138	159	166
TOURISM INDUSTRIES						
Hotels and similar establishments						
9.1 Number of rooms	Units	54,730	56,378	58,932	59,870	63,206
9.2 Number of bed-places	Units	136,825	140,945	147,330	149,675	158,015
9.3 Occupancy rate	Percent	62.80	72.70	74.20	73.90	73.00
9.4 Average length of stay	Nights	9.65	9.32	8.97	9.20	9.30
RELATED INDICATORS						
Share of tourism expenditure (6.1) in: (**)						
10.1 Gross Domestic Product (GDP)	Percent	12.6	19.2	17.1	12.1	12.4
10.2 Exports of goods	Percent	52.9	57.2	53.1	57.2	58.9
10.3 Exports of services	Percent	88.9	90.2	90.0	89.9	89.8

(*) Balance of Payments items: 6.1 to 6.3 correspond to the "Credit" side (and are receipts for the country) while 8.2 to 8.4 correspond to the "Debit" side (and are expenditures in other countries).

(**) See Annex "Country notes".

58

Basic Indicators	Units	2002	2003	2004	2005	2006
INBOUND TOURISM						
Arrivals						
1.1 Visitors	('000)	683	761	819	860	841
1.2 Tourists (overnight visitors)	('000)	..	..	..	..	..
1.3 Same-day visitors	('000)	..	..	..	..	..
1.4 Cruise passengers	('000)	..	..	..	..	..
Arrivals by region						
2.1 Africa	('000)	2	2	2	2	1
2.2 Americas	('000)	550	617	662	691	642
2.3 Europe	('000)	113	124	133	147	145
2.4 East Asia and the Pacific	('000)	17	18	21	20	19
2.5 South Asia	('000)	..	..	..	..	..
2.6 Middle East	('000)	..	..	..	..	..
Arrivals by means of transport used						
3.1 Air	('000)	432	450	496	540	557
3.2 Rail	('000)	..	..	..	..	..
3.3 Road	('000)	245	306	315	315	279
3.4 Sea	('000)	6	5	8	5	4
Arrivals by purpose of visit						
4.1 Leisure, recreation and holidays	('000)	..	..	..	..	..
4.2 Business and professional	('000)	..	..	..	..	..
4.3 Other	('000)	..	..	..	..	..
Accommodation						
5.1 Overnight stays in hotels and similar establishments	('000)	..	..	..	..	..
5.2 Guests in hotels and similar establishments	('000)	..	..	..	..	..
5.3 Overnight stays in all types of accommodation establishments	('000)	..	..	..	..	..
5.4 Average length of stay of non-resident tourists in all accommodation establishments	Nights	..	..	..	..	..
6.1 **Tourism expenditure in the country**	US$ Mn	449	408	464	488	492
6.2 "Travel" (*)	US$ Mn	447	406	462	486	490
6.3 "Passenger transport" (*)	US$ Mn	2	2	2	2	2
DOMESTIC TOURISM						
Accommodation						
7.1 Overnight stays in hotels and similar establishments	('000)	..	..	..	..	..
7.2 Guests in hotels and similar establishments	('000)	..	..	..	..	..
7.3 Overnight stays in all types of accommodation establishments	('000)	..	..	..	..	..
7.4 Average length of stay of resident tourists in all accommodation establishments	Nights	..	..	..	..	..
OUTBOUND TOURISM						
8.1 **Departures**	('000)	627	613	603	664	733
8.2 **Tourism expenditure in other countries**	US$ Mn	507	500	577	644	706
8.3 "Travel" (*)	US$ Mn	364	354	391	429	466
8.4 "Passenger transport" (*)	US$ Mn	143	146	186	215	240
TOURISM INDUSTRIES						
Hotels and similar establishments						
9.1 Number of rooms	Units	36,766	38,237	38,029	41,342	44,046
9.2 Number of bed-places	Units	81,307	86,466	85,213	93,215	101,371
9.3 Occupancy rate	Percent	..	..	..	..	..
9.4 Average length of stay	Nights	..	..	..	..	..
RELATED INDICATORS						
Share of tourism expenditure (6.1) in:						
10.1 Gross Domestic Product (GDP)	Percent	1.8	1.4	1.4	1.3	1.2
10.2 Exports of goods	Percent	8.5	6.3	5.8	4.7	3.7
10.3 Exports of services	Percent	50.8	46.3	45.8	48.2	48.4

(*) Balance of Payments items: 6.1 to 6.3 correspond to the "Credit" side (and are receipts for the country) while 8.2 to 8.4 correspond to the "Debit" side (and are expenditures in other countries).

EGYPT

Basic Indicators		Units	2002	2003	2004	2005	2006
	INBOUND TOURISM						
	Arrivals						
1.1	Visitors	('000)	5,192	6,044	8,104	8,608	9,083
1.2	Tourists (overnight visitors)	('000)	4,906	5,746	7,795	8,244	8,646
1.3	Same-day visitors	('000)	286	298	309	363	437
1.4	Cruise passengers	('000)	..	..	..	..	..
	Arrivals by region						
2.1	Africa	('000)	161	183	245	264	302
2.2	Americas	('000)	171	188	257	298	341
2.3	Europe	('000)	3,584	4,204	5,920	6,047	6,260
2.4	East Asia and the Pacific	('000)	214	227	296	411	389
2.5	South Asia	('000)	46	51	63	73	81
2.6	Middle East	('000)	1,013	1,189	1,318	1,511	1,706
	Arrivals by means of transport used						
3.1	Air	('000)	4,280	4,841	6,577	6,713	7,610
3.2	Rail	('000)	..	..		..	..
3.3	Road	('000)	475	749	881	800	812
3.4	Sea	('000)	437	454	646	1,094	660
	Arrivals by purpose of visit						
4.1	Leisure, recreation and holidays	('000)	4,737	5,529	7,533	7,993	8,436
4.2	Business and professional	('000)	95	139	182	182	142
4.3	Other	('000)	74	78	80	69	68
	Accommodation						
5.1	Overnight stays in hotels and similar establishments	('000)	32,664	53,130	81,668	85,172	89,304
5.2	Guests in hotels and similar establishments	('000)	6,229	6,731	..	..	8,449
5.3	Overnight stays in all types of accommodation establishments	('000)	..	..	..	..	..
5.4	Average length of stay of non-resident tourists in all accommodation establishments	Nights	6.30	8.80	9.90	9.90	10.20
6.1	**Tourism expenditure in the country**	US$ Mn	4,133	4,704	6,328	7,206	8,133
6.2	"Travel" (*)	US$ Mn	3,764	4,584	6,125	6,851	7,591
6.3	"Passenger transport" (*)	US$ Mn	369	120	203	355	542
	DOMESTIC TOURISM						
	Accommodation						
7.1	Overnight stays in hotels and similar establishments	('000)	4,791	4,782	..	..	..
7.2	Guests in hotels and similar establishments	('000)	1,397	2,212	..	..	..
7.3	Overnight stays in all types of accommodation establishments	('000)	..	..		..	..
7.4	Average length of stay of resident tourists in all accommodation establishments	Nights	3.40	2.30	..	..	..
	OUTBOUND TOURISM						
8.1	**Departures**	('000)	3,330	3,644	5,210	5,307	4,531
8.2	**Tourism expenditure in other countries**	US$ Mn	1,309	1,465	1,543	1,932	2,156
8.3	"Travel" (*)	US$ Mn	1,266	1,321	1,257	1,629	1,784
8.4	"Passenger transport" (*)	US$ Mn	43	144	286	303	372
	TOURISM INDUSTRIES						
	Hotels and similar establishments						
9.1	Number of rooms	Units	132,109	136,510	148,039	170,776	177,613
9.2	Number of bed-places	Units	264,218	273,020	296,078	341,552	355,226
9.3	Occupancy rate	Percent	56.00	59.00	68.90	64.00	61.00
9.4	Average length of stay	Nights	6.30	8.80	10.70	10.40	10.20
	RELATED INDICATORS						
	Share of tourism expenditure (6.1) in:						
10.1	Gross Domestic Product (GDP)	Percent	4.7	5.7	8.0	8.0	7.6
10.2	Exports of goods	Percent	58.1	52.3	51.4	44.8	39.6
10.3	Exports of services	Percent	44.3	42.5	44.6	49.2	50.4

(*) Balance of Payments items: 6.1 to 6.3 correspond to the "Credit" side (and are receipts for the country) while 8.2 to 8.4 correspond to the "Debit" side (and are expenditures in other countries).

Basic Indicators		Units	2002	2003	2004	2005	2006
	INBOUND TOURISM						
	Arrivals						
1.1	Visitors	('000)	885	798	891	1,148	1,360
1.2	Tourists (overnight visitors)	('000)	798	720	812	969	1,138
1.3	Same-day visitors	('000)	87	78	79	179	222
1.4	Cruise passengers	('000)	..	..	..	..	..
	Arrivals by region						
2.1	Africa	('000)	..	..	..	1	1
2.2	Americas	('000)	733	682	775	934	1,104
2.3	Europe	('000)	22	30	28	26	25
2.4	East Asia and the Pacific	('000)	3	7	8	8	9
2.5	South Asia	('000)	..	..	..	..	..
2.6	Middle East	('000)	..	..	..	..	..
	Arrivals by means of transport used						
3.1	Air	('000)	253	262	310	341	342
3.2	Rail	('000)	..	..	..		
3.3	Road	('000)	541	457	501	627	795
3.4	Sea	('000)	5	1	1	1	1
	Arrivals by purpose of visit						
4.1	Leisure, recreation and holidays	('000)	780	181	205	321	335
4.2	Business and professional	('000)	4	156	175	157	293
4.3	Other	('000)	14	383	432	491	511
	Accommodation						
5.1	Overnight stays in hotels and similar establishments	('000)	3,193	3,600	4,058	5,816	8,310
5.2	Guests in hotels and similar establishments	('000)	407	381	426	577	699
5.3	Overnight stays in all types of accommodation establishments	('000)	..	..	..	..	..
5.4	Average length of stay of non-resident tourists in all accommodation establishments	Nights	4.00	5.00	5.00	6.00	7.30
6.1	**Tourism expenditure in the country** (**)	US$ Mn	521	664	748	838	1,175
6.2	"Travel" (*)	US$ Mn	245	383	453	543	871
6.3	"Passenger transport" (*)	US$ Mn	276	281	295	295	304
	DOMESTIC TOURISM						
	Accommodation						
7.1	Overnight stays in hotels and similar establishments	('000)	..	..	..	..	..
7.2	Guests in hotels and similar establishments	('000)	..	..	..	..	..
7.3	Overnight stays in all types of accommodation establishments	('000)	..	..	..	..	..
7.4	Average length of stay of resident tourists in all accommodation establishments	Nights	..	..	..	..	..
	OUTBOUND TOURISM						
8.1	**Departures**	('000)	1,001	940	1,218	1,397	1,382
8.2	**Tourism expenditure in other countries**	US$ Mn	266	311	373	429	601
8.3	"Travel" (*)	US$ Mn	191	230	292	347	518
8.4	"Passenger transport" (*)	US$ Mn	75	81	81	82	83
	TOURISM INDUSTRIES						
	Hotels and similar establishments						
9.1	Number of rooms	Units	5,152	4,501	4,766	5,757	6,518
9.2	Number of bed-places	Units	10,304	7,252	8,120	10,113	12,089
9.3	Occupancy rate	Percent	51.00	52.90	52.50	59.50	61.40
9.4	Average length of stay	Nights	4.00	5.00	5.00	6.00	7.30
	RELATED INDICATORS						
	Share of tourism expenditure (6.1) in:						
10.1	Gross Domestic Product (GDP)	Percent	3.6	4.4	4.7	4.9	6.4
10.2	Exports of goods	Percent	17.3	21.1	22.4	24.4	32.9
10.3	Exports of services	Percent	66.5	70.0	68.6	74.3	78.2

(*) Balance of Payments items: 6.1 to 6.3 correspond to the "Credit" side (and are receipts for the country) while 8.2 to 8.4 correspond to the "Debit" side (and are expenditures in other countries).

(**) See Annex "Country notes".

ERITREA

Basic Indicators		Units	2002	2003	2004	2005	2006
	INBOUND TOURISM						
	Arrivals						
1.1	Visitors	('000)	101	80	87	83	78
1.2	Tourists (overnight visitors)	('000)	..	..	..	..	..
1.3	Same-day visitors	('000)	..	..	..	..	..
1.4	Cruise passengers	('000)	..	..	..	..	..
	Arrivals by region						
2.1	Africa	('000)	8	3	5	3	4
2.2	Americas	('000)	2	2	3	2	1
2.3	Europe	('000)	8	8	10	8	6
2.4	East Asia and the Pacific	('000)	2	2	2	2	2
2.5	South Asia	('000)	3	3	2	3	3
2.6	Middle East	('000)	4	3	4	4	3
	Arrivals by means of transport used						
3.1	Air	('000)	51	49	51	45	35
3.2	Rail	('000)	..	..	..	..	..
3.3	Road	('000)	48	29	34	37	41
3.4	Sea	('000)	2	2	2	1	2
	Arrivals by purpose of visit						
4.1	Leisure, recreation and holidays	('000)	6	5	3	6	6
4.2	Business and professional	('000)	21	16	13	13	12
4.3	Other	('000)	74	59	71	65	60
	Accommodation						
5.1	Overnight stays in hotels and similar establishments	('000)	..	..	..	176	137
5.2	Guests in hotels and similar establishments	('000)	..	..	..	..	..
5.3	Overnight stays in all types of accommodation establishments	('000)	..	..	..	..	..
5.4	Average length of stay of non-resident tourists in all accommodation establishments	Nights	28.00	..	..	3.10	3.30
6.1	**Tourism expenditure in the country** (**)	US$ Mn	73	74	73	66	60
6.2	"Travel" (*)	US$ Mn	..	..	..	..	..
6.3	"Passenger transport" (*)	US$ Mn	..	..	..	..	..
	DOMESTIC TOURISM						
	Accommodation						
7.1	Overnight stays in hotels and similar establishments	('000)	..	..	..	669	672
7.2	Guests in hotels and similar establishments	('000)	..	..	..	..	..
7.3	Overnight stays in all types of accommodation establishments	('000)	..	..	..	..	..
7.4	Average length of stay of resident tourists in all accommodation establishments	Nights	..	..	..	1.40	1.30
	OUTBOUND TOURISM						
8.1	**Departures**	('000)	..				..
8.2	**Tourism expenditure in other countries**	US$ Mn	..	..	..	..	..
8.3	"Travel" (*)	US$ Mn	..	..	..	..	..
8.4	"Passenger transport" (*)	US$ Mn	..	..	..	..	..
	TOURISM INDUSTRIES						
	Hotels and similar establishments						
9.1	Number of rooms	Units	4,189	4,139	4,712	5,447	5,447
9.2	Number of bed-places	Units	8,912	8,794	9,445	10,720	10,720
9.3	Occupancy rate	Percent	56.00	52.12	54.37	43.00	43.00
9.4	Average length of stay	Nights	..	..	..	3.00	3.00
	RELATED INDICATORS						
	Share of tourism expenditure (6.1) in: (**)						
10.1	Gross Domestic Product (GDP)	Percent	..	..	..	..	..
10.2	Exports of goods	Percent	..	..	..	..	..
10.3	Exports of services	Percent	..	..	..	..	..

(*) Balance of Payments items: 6.1 to 6.3 correspond to the "Credit" side (and are receipts for the country) while 8.2 to 8.4 correspond to the "Debit" side (and are expenditures in other countries).

(**) See Annex "Country notes".

Basic Indicators	Units	2002	2003	2004	2005	2006
INBOUND TOURISM						
Arrivals						
1.1 Visitors	('000)	3,253	3,378	..	..	..
1.2 Tourists (overnight visitors)	('000)	1,362	1,462	1,750	1,917	1,940
1.3 Same-day visitors	('000)	1,773	1,741	..	..	..
1.4 Cruise passengers	('000)	118	175	206	295	313
Arrivals by region						
2.1 Africa	('000)	..	1	1	1	1
2.2 Americas	('000)	16	15	23	24	24
2.3 Europe	('000)	967	1,081	1,334	1,411	1,382
2.4 East Asia and the Pacific	('000)	7	11	13	15	18
2.5 South Asia	('000)	..	..	..	..	..
2.6 Middle East	('000)	..	..	..	..	..
Arrivals by means of transport used						
3.1 Air	('000)	161	185	..	..	..
3.2 Rail	('000)	35	37	..	..	..
3.3 Road	('000)	845	962	..	..	..
3.4 Sea	('000)	2,212	2,193	..	..	..
Arrivals by purpose of visit						
4.1 Leisure, recreation and holidays	('000)	..	..	..	..	..
4.2 Business and professional	('000)	..	..	..	..	..
4.3 Other	('000)	..	..	..	..	..
Accommodation						
5.1 Overnight stays in hotels and similar establishments	('000)	1,887	2,086	2,602	2,791	2,772
5.2 Guests in hotels and similar establishments	('000)	937	1,009	1,300	1,358	1,330
5.3 Overnight stays in all types of accommodation establishments	('000)	1,998	2,268	2,747	2,982	3,020
5.4 Average length of stay of non-resident tourists in all accommodation establishments	Nights	1.99	2.04	2.00	2.05	2.12
6.1 **Tourism expenditure in the country**	US$ Mn	737	883	1,111	1,207	1,372
6.2 "Travel" (*)	US$ Mn	555	671	887	948	1,035
6.3 "Passenger transport" (*)	US$ Mn	182	212	224	259	337
DOMESTIC TOURISM						
Accommodation						
7.1 Overnight stays in hotels and similar establishments	('000)	450	558	691	751	989
7.2 Guests in hotels and similar establishments	('000)	250	306	385	428	571
7.3 Overnight stays in all types of accommodation establishments	('000)	698	817	1,011	1,129	1,523
7.4 Average length of stay of resident tourists in all accommodation establishments	Nights	1.75	1.82	1.85	1.82	1.83
OUTBOUND TOURISM						
8.1 **Departures**	('000)	1,849	2,075	..	..	..
8.2 **Tourism expenditure in other countries**	US$ Mn	305	404	481	538	705
8.3 "Travel" (*)	US$ Mn	231	319	400	448	592
8.4 "Passenger transport" (*)	US$ Mn	74	85	81	90	113
TOURISM INDUSTRIES						
Hotels and similar establishments						
9.1 Number of rooms	Units	10,845	12,445	14,953	16,610	17,811
9.2 Number of bed-places	Units	22,849	27,487	32,899	38,088	40,850
9.3 Occupancy rate	Percent	45.00	47.00	47.00	48.00	47.00
9.4 Average length of stay	Nights	1.99	2.04	1.95	1.98	2.01
RELATED INDICATORS						
Share of tourism expenditure (6.1) in:						
10.1 Gross Domestic Product (GDP)	Percent	10.1	9.2	9.5	8.8	8.4
10.2 Exports of goods	Percent	21.0	19.2	18.6	15.5	14.2
10.3 Exports of services	Percent	43.2	39.7	39.3	38.2	39.3

(*) Balance of Payments items: 6.1 to 6.3 correspond to the "Credit" side (and are receipts for the country) while 8.2 to 8.4 correspond to the "Debit" side (and are expenditures in other countries).

ETHIOPIA

Basic Indicators		Units	2002	2003	2004	2005	2006
	INBOUND TOURISM						
	Arrivals						
1.1	Visitors	('000)	..	..	..	..	..
1.2	Tourists (overnight visitors)	('000)	156	180	184	227	290
1.3	Same-day visitors	('000)	..	..	..	..	..
1.4	Cruise passengers	('000)	..	..	..	..	..
	Arrivals by region						
2.1	Africa	('000)	60	82	66	86	90
2.2	Americas	('000)	19	27	34	41	61
2.3	Europe	('000)	34	44	48	57	76
2.4	East Asia and the Pacific	('000)	8	8	10	12	20
2.5	South Asia	('000)	4	4	5	7	8
2.6	Middle East	('000)	9	14	21	22	31
	Arrivals by means of transport used						
3.1	Air	('000)	132	163	173	193	290
3.2	Rail	('000)	18	17	..	..	..
3.3	Road	('000)	6	..	11	34	..
3.4	Sea	('000)	..	..	..	..	..
	Arrivals by purpose of visit						
4.1	Leisure, recreation and holidays	('000)	49	53	57	63	86
4.2	Business and professional	('000)	43	37	35	46	59
4.3	Other	('000)	64	90	92	118	145
	Accommodation						
5.1	Overnight stays in hotels and similar establishments	('000)	391	..	..	..	..
5.2	Guests in hotels and similar establishments	('000)	..	..	..	..	..
5.3	Overnight stays in all types of accommodation establishments	('000)	..	..	..	..	..
5.4	Average length of stay of non-resident tourists in all accommodation establishments	Nights	..	..	..	..	..
6.1	**Tourism expenditure in the country**	US$ Mn	261	336	458	533	639
6.2	"Travel" (*)	US$ Mn	72	114	174	168	162
6.3	"Passenger transport" (*)	US$ Mn	189	222	284	365	477
	DOMESTIC TOURISM						
	Accommodation						
7.1	Overnight stays in hotels and similar establishments	('000)	..	..	..	..	..
7.2	Guests in hotels and similar establishments	('000)	..	..	..	..	..
7.3	Overnight stays in all types of accommodation establishments	('000)	..	..	..	..	..
7.4	Average length of stay of resident tourists in all accommodation establishments	Nights	..	..	..	..	..
	OUTBOUND TOURISM						
8.1	**Departures**	('000)	..	..	..	..	..
8.2	**Tourism expenditure in other countries**	US$ Mn	55	63	59	..	..
8.3	"Travel" (*)	US$ Mn	45	50	58	77	97
8.4	"Passenger transport" (*)	US$ Mn	10	13	1	..	..
	TOURISM INDUSTRIES						
	Hotels and similar establishments						
9.1	Number of rooms	Units	2,979	3,497	..	3,387	9,836
9.2	Number of bed-places	Units	4,494	5,419	..	5,170	12,605
9.3	Occupancy rate	Percent	..	60.00	..	..	..
9.4	Average length of stay	Nights	..	3.00	..	..	..
	RELATED INDICATORS						
	Share of tourism expenditure (6.1) in:						
10.1	Gross Domestic Product (GDP)	Percent	3.5	4.2	4.8	4.7	4.8
10.2	Exports of goods	Percent	54.4	67.7	67.6	58.1	62.3
10.3	Exports of services	Percent	44.6	44.1	45.6	52.7	54.4

(*) Balance of Payments items: 6.1 to 6.3 correspond to the "Credit" side (and are receipts for the country) while 8.2 to 8.4 correspond to the "Debit" side (and are expenditures in other countries).

Basic Indicators	Units	2002	2003	2004	2005	2006
INBOUND TOURISM						
Arrivals						
1.1 Visitors	('000)	461	496	..	..	..
1.2 Tourists (overnight visitors)	('000)	398	431	499	550	545
1.3 Same-day visitors	('000)	57	45	..	..	..
1.4 Cruise passengers	('000)	6	13	8	..	..
Arrivals by region						
2.1 Africa	('000)	..	..	..	..	..
2.2 Americas	('000)	69	69	78	86	82
2.3 Europe	('000)	65	72	71	79	81
2.4 East Asia and the Pacific	('000)	262	288	352	384	382
2.5 South Asia	('000)	..	..	..	..	..
2.6 Middle East	('000)	..	..	..	..	..
Arrivals by means of transport used						
3.1 Air	('000)	390	422	..	..	..
3.2 Rail	('000)	..	..	..	..	..
3.3 Road	('000)	..	..	..	..	..
3.4 Sea	('000)	8	8	..	..	..
Arrivals by purpose of visit						
4.1 Leisure, recreation and holidays	('000)	306	332	428	470	467
4.2 Business and professional	('000)	31	33	36	39	39
4.3 Other	('000)	61	66	35	40	39
Accommodation						
5.1 Overnight stays in hotels and similar establishments	('000)	1,914	2,015	2,489	2,760	2,641
5.2 Guests in hotels and similar establishments	('000)	..	..	..	..	..
5.3 Overnight stays in all types of accommodation establishments	('000)	..	..	..	..	..
5.4 Average length of stay of non-resident tourists in all accommodation establishments	Nights	8.70	8.70	8.90	8.90	8.90
6.1 **Tourism expenditure in the country**	US$ Mn	379	490	585	676	636
6.2 "Travel" (*)	US$ Mn	255	340	420	439	433
6.3 "Passenger transport" (*)	US$ Mn	124	150	165	237	203
DOMESTIC TOURISM						
Accommodation						
7.1 Overnight stays in hotels and similar establishments	('000)	392	412	453	479	498
7.2 Guests in hotels and similar establishments	('000)	..	..	..	..	..
7.3 Overnight stays in all types of accommodation establishments	('000)	..	..	..	..	..
7.4 Average length of stay of resident tourists in all accommodation establishments	Nights	..	..	..	..	..
OUTBOUND TOURISM						
8.1 **Departures**	('000)	99	104	..	..	..
8.2 **Tourism expenditure in other countries**	US$ Mn	79	87	118	132	123
8.3 "Travel" (*)	US$ Mn	55	69	94	106	101
8.4 "Passenger transport" (*)	US$ Mn	24	18	24	26	22
TOURISM INDUSTRIES						
Hotels and similar establishments						
9.1 Number of rooms	Units	5,899	6,116	6,677	6,713	..
9.2 Number of bed-places	Units	14,559	14,206	15,680	16,536	..
9.3 Occupancy rate	Percent	55.60	55.90	61.30	64.40	64.10
9.4 Average length of stay	Nights	..	..	..	..	..
RELATED INDICATORS						
Share of tourism expenditure (6.1) in:						
10.1 Gross Domestic Product (GDP)	Percent	21.1	22.5	22.7	24.8	22.5
10.2 Exports of goods	Percent	78.3	72.2	89.6	96.8	89.2
10.3 Exports of services	Percent	75.5	79.8	85.0	83.5	82.2

(*) Balance of Payments items: 6.1 to 6.3 correspond to the "Credit" side (and are receipts for the country) while 8.2 to 8.4 correspond to the "Debit" side (and are expenditures in other countries).

FINLAND

Basic Indicators	Units	2002	2003	2004	2005	2006
INBOUND TOURISM						
Arrivals						
1.1 Visitors	('000)	4,687	4,527	4,854	5,038	5,345
1.2 Tourists (overnight visitors)	('000)	2,875	2,601	2,840	3,140	3,375
1.3 Same-day visitors	('000)	1,812	1,926	2,014	1,898	1,970
1.4 Cruise passengers	('000)	..	..	..	..	..
Arrivals by region						
2.1 Africa	('000)	7	9	6	12	13
2.2 Americas	('000)	182	151	159	160	167
2.3 Europe	('000)	4,245	4,157	4,417	4,581	4,891
2.4 East Asia and the Pacific	('000)	244	210	268	273	262
2.5 South Asia	('000)	5	..	4	8	8
2.6 Middle East	('000)	4	..	..	4	4
Arrivals by means of transport used						
3.1 Air	('000)	1,603	1,577	1,640	1,734	1,999
3.2 Rail	('000)	84	67	71	80	79
3.3 Road	('000)	1,638	1,596	1,694	1,686	1,674
3.4 Sea	('000)	1,362	1,287	1,449	1,538	1,593
Arrivals by purpose of visit						
4.1 Leisure, recreation and holidays	('000)	2,105	2,020	2,077	2,107	2,189
4.2 Business and professional	('000)	1,273	1,257	1,314	1,480	1,607
4.3 Other	('000)	1,309	1,250	1,463	1,451	1,549
Accommodation						
5.1 Overnight stays in hotels and similar establishments	('000)	3,721	3,758	3,758	3,887	4,354
5.2 Guests in hotels and similar establishments	('000)	1,796	1,814	1,820	1,828	2,045
5.3 Overnight stays in all types of accommodation establishments	('000)	4,290	4,331	4,383	4,499	5,036
5.4 Average length of stay of non-resident tourists in all accommodation establishments	Nights	2.10	2.12	2.10	2.16	2.16
6.1 **Tourism expenditure in the country**	US$ Mn	2,236	2,678	2,975	3,070	3,509
6.2 "Travel" (*)	US$ Mn	1,578	1,870	2,067	2,180	2,380
6.3 "Passenger transport" (*)	US$ Mn	658	808	908	890	1,129
DOMESTIC TOURISM						
Accommodation						
7.1 Overnight stays in hotels and similar establishments	('000)	9,552	9,671	10,032	10,388	10,676
7.2 Guests in hotels and similar establishments	('000)	5,327	5,415	5,736	5,948	6,203
7.3 Overnight stays in all types of accommodation establishments	('000)	11,703	11,751	12,243	12,760	13,165
7.4 Average length of stay of resident tourists in all accommodation establishments	Nights	1.83	1.82	1.79	1.82	1.80
OUTBOUND TOURISM						
8.1 **Departures**	('000)	5,857	5,585	5,798	5,902	5,756
8.2 **Tourism expenditure in other countries**	US$ Mn	2,438	2,954	3,383	3,622	4,094
8.3 "Travel" (*)	US$ Mn	2,006	2,433	2,821	3,057	3,424
8.4 "Passenger transport" (*)	US$ Mn	432	521	562	565	670
TOURISM INDUSTRIES						
Hotels and similar establishments						
9.1 Number of rooms	Units	54,916	55,767	53,537	53,335	54,452
9.2 Number of bed-places	Units	117,870	120,051	120,086	115,202	118,170
9.3 Occupancy rate	Percent	47.00	46.80	46.30	47.80	49.90
9.4 Average length of stay	Nights	1.90	1.89	1.83	1.84	1.82
RELATED INDICATORS						
Share of tourism expenditure (6.1) in:						
10.1 Gross Domestic Product (GDP)	Percent	1.7	1.6	1.6	1.6	1.7
10.2 Exports of goods	Percent	5.0	5.1	4.9	4.7	4.5
10.3 Exports of services	Percent	21.4	23.3	19.6	18.0	21.8

(*) Balance of Payments items: 6.1 to 6.3 correspond to the "Credit" side (and are receipts for the country) while 8.2 to 8.4 correspond to the "Debit" side (and are expenditures in other countries).

FRANCE

Basic Indicators	Units	2002	2003	2004	2005	2006
INBOUND TOURISM						
Arrivals						
1.1 Visitors	('000)	..	..	..	189,608	198,550
1.2 Tourists (overnight visitors)	('000)	77,012	75,048	75,121	75,908	79,083
1.3 Same-day visitors	('000)	..	..	..	113,700	119,467
1.4 Cruise passengers	('000)	..	..	..	..	..
Arrivals by region						
2.1 Africa	('000)	924	889	895	1,252	1,213
2.2 Americas	('000)	4,639	3,954	4,206	5,086	5,562
2.3 Europe	('000)	69,078	68,073	67,711	66,029	68,590
2.4 East Asia and the Pacific	('000)	2,080	1,890	2,058	3,192	3,338
2.5 South Asia	('000)	..	..	..	..	..
2.6 Middle East	('000)	249	210	237	349	380
Arrivals by means of transport used						
3.1 Air	('000)	..	..	..	16,295	17,718
3.2 Rail	('000)	..	..	..	4,335	4,880
3.3 Road	('000)	..	..	..	47,866	48,755
3.4 Sea	('000)	..	..	..	7,412	7,730
Arrivals by purpose of visit						
4.1 Leisure, recreation and holidays	('000)	..	..	..	53,404	55,810
4.2 Business and professional	('000)	..	..	..	9,125	9,543
4.3 Other	('000)	..	..	..	13,379	13,730
Accommodation						
5.1 Overnight stays in hotels and similar establishments	('000)	77,602	69,323	70,391	72,054	68,821
5.2 Guests in hotels and similar establishments	('000)	36,093	32,520	33,988	34,806	32,304
5.3 Overnight stays in all types of accommodation establishments	('000)	588,430	567,006	561,294	491,139	496,951
5.4 Average length of stay of non-resident tourists in all accommodation establishments	Nights	7.64	7.56	7.47	6.47	6.28
6.1 **Tourism expenditure in the country**	US$ Mn	38,110	43,406	52,607	52,153	54,033
6.2 "Travel" (*)	US$ Mn	32,437	36,619	44,895	43,942	46,499
6.3 "Passenger transport" (*)	US$ Mn	5,673	6,787	7,712	8,211	7,534
DOMESTIC TOURISM						
Accommodation						
7.1 Overnight stays in hotels and similar establishments	('000)	114,454	115,536	118,134	120,326	123,105
7.2 Guests in hotels and similar establishments	('000)	65,253	66,365	69,705	71,594	72,930
7.3 Overnight stays in all types of accommodation establishments	('000)	1,004,767	1,002,025	1,016,534	847,399	849,505
7.4 Average length of stay of resident tourists in all accommodation establishments	Nights	5.24	5.21	4.93	4.90	4.91
OUTBOUND TOURISM						
8.1 **Departures**	('000)	18,315	18,576	21,131	22,270	22,466
8.2 **Tourism expenditure in other countries**	US$ Mn	23,773	28,143	34,674	37,549	37,793
8.3 "Travel" (*)	US$ Mn	19,518	23,392	28,703	30,458	31,264
8.4 "Passenger transport" (*)	US$ Mn	4,255	4,751	5,971	7,091	6,529
TOURISM INDUSTRIES						
Hotels and similar establishments						
9.1 Number of rooms	Units	603,619	603,279	615,402	613,798	612,424
9.2 Number of bed-places	Units	1,207,238	1,206,558	1,230,804	1,227,596	1,224,848
9.3 Occupancy rate	Percent	60.30	58.40	58.60	59.10	60.40
9.4 Average length of stay	Nights	1.90	1.87	1.82	1.81	1.82
RELATED INDICATORS						
Share of tourism expenditure (6.1) in:						
10.1 Gross Domestic Product (GDP)	Percent	2.6	2.4	2.6	2.5	2.4
10.2 Exports of goods	Percent	12.4	12.0	12.5	11.9	11.2
10.3 Exports of services	Percent	44.2	43.9	46.7	43.9	45.6

(*) Balance of Payments items: 6.1 to 6.3 correspond to the "Credit" side (and are receipts for the country) while 8.2 to 8.4 correspond to the "Debit" side (and are expenditures in other countries).

FRENCH GUIANA

Basic Indicators	Units	2002	2003	2004	2005	2006
INBOUND TOURISM						
Arrivals						
1.1 Visitors	('000)	..	..	..	..	..
1.2 Tourists (overnight visitors)	('000)	65	..	..	95	
1.3 Same-day visitors	('000)	..	..	..	1.7	
1.4 Cruise passengers	('000)	..	..	..		
Arrivals by region						
2.1 Africa	('000)	..	..	..	..	..
2.2 Americas	('000)	18	..	..	..	
2.3 Europe	('000)	45	..	..	..	
2.4 East Asia and the Pacific	('000)	..	..	..	..	
2.5 South Asia	('000)	..	..	..	..	..
2.6 Middle East	('000)	..	..	..	..	
Arrivals by means of transport used						
3.1 Air	('000)	65	..	..		..
3.2 Rail	('000)	..	..	..	..	
3.3 Road	('000)	..	..	..	..	..
3.4 Sea	('000)	..	..	..	..	
Arrivals by purpose of visit						
4.1 Leisure, recreation and holidays	('000)	24	..	..		..
4.2 Business and professional	('000)	24	..	..		
4.3 Other	('000)	17	..	..		..
Accommodation						
5.1 Overnight stays in hotels and similar establishments	('000)	..	..		..	
5.2 Guests in hotels and similar establishments	('000)	..	..	..	..	
5.3 Overnight stays in all types of accommodation establishments	('000)	..	..	302	391	..
5.4 Average length of stay of non-resident tourists in all accommodation establishments	Nights	..	..	2.10	2.70	..
6.1 **Tourism expenditure in the country**	US$ Mn	45	..		45	..
6.2 "Travel" (*)	US$ Mn	..	..	..	..	..
6.3 "Passenger transport" (*)	US$ Mn	..	..	..	..	..
DOMESTIC TOURISM						
Accommodation						
7.1 Overnight stays in hotels and similar establishments	('000)	..	..	..	..	..
7.2 Guests in hotels and similar establishments	('000)	..	..	..	..	..
7.3 Overnight stays in all types of accommodation establishments	('000)	..	..	..	..	..
7.4 Average length of stay of resident tourists in all accommodation establishments	Nights	..	..	..	..	..
OUTBOUND TOURISM						
8.1 **Departures**	('000)	..		..		..
8.2 **Tourism expenditure in other countries**	US$ Mn	..	..	..	..	..
8.3 "Travel" (*)	US$ Mn	..	..	..	..	..
8.4 "Passenger transport" (*)	US$ Mn	..	..	..	..	..
TOURISM INDUSTRIES						
Hotels and similar establishments						
9.1 Number of rooms	Units	..	..	..	1,184	..
9.2 Number of bed-places	Units	..	..	..	..	
9.3 Occupancy rate	Percent	..	..	..	..	..
9.4 Average length of stay	Nights	..	..	..	..	..
RELATED INDICATORS						
Share of tourism expenditure (6.1) in:						
10.1 Gross Domestic Product (GDP)	Percent	..	..	..	..	..
10.2 Exports of goods	Percent	..	..	..	..	..
10.3 Exports of services	Percent	..	..	..	..	..

(*) Balance of Payments items: 6.1 to 6.3 correspond to the "Credit" side (and are receipts for the country) while 8.2 to 8.4 correspond to the "Debit" side (and are expenditures in other countries).

Basic Indicators	Units	2002	2003	2004	2005	2006
INBOUND TOURISM						
Arrivals						
1.1 Visitors	('000)	..	..	..	..	..
1.2 Tourists (overnight visitors)	('000)	189	213	212	208	222
1.3 Same-day visitors	('000)	..	..	..	..	..
1.4 Cruise passengers	('000)	..	..	..	..	..
Arrivals by region						
2.1 Africa	('000)	..	..	..	..	..
2.2 Americas	('000)	72	89	86	80	89
2.3 Europe	('000)	76	80	80	82	83
2.4 East Asia and the Pacific	('000)	40	42	45	46	48
2.5 South Asia	('000)	..	..	..	..	..
2.6 Middle East	('000)	..	..	..	..	..
Arrivals by means of transport used						
3.1 Air	('000)	189	213	212	208	222
3.2 Rail	('000)	..	..	..	..	..
3.3 Road	('000)	..	..	..	..	..
3.4 Sea	('000)	..	..	..	..	..
Arrivals by purpose of visit						
4.1 Leisure, recreation and holidays	('000)	166	187	191	190	203
4.2 Business and professional	('000)	12	14	13	13	14
4.3 Other	('000)	11	12	8	5	5
Accommodation						
5.1 Overnight stays in hotels and similar establishments	('000)	1,666	1,950	1,917	1,897	2,093
5.2 Guests in hotels and similar establishments	('000)	155	180	178	176	193
5.3 Overnight stays in all types of accommodation establishments	('000)	2,592	2,888	2,861	2,787	2,926
5.4 Average length of stay of non-resident tourists in all accommodation establishments	Nights	13.72	13.57	13.50	13.49	13.21
6.1 **Tourism expenditure in the country**	US$ Mn	471	651	737	751	785
6.2 "Travel" (*)	US$ Mn	372	480	523	522	558
6.3 "Passenger transport" (*)	US$ Mn	99	171	214	229	227
DOMESTIC TOURISM						
Accommodation						
7.1 Overnight stays in hotels and similar establishments	('000)	..	..	..	..	..
7.2 Guests in hotels and similar establishments	('000)	..	..	..	..	..
7.3 Overnight stays in all types of accommodation establishments	('000)	..	..	..	..	..
7.4 Average length of stay of resident tourists in all accommodation establishments	Nights	..	..	..	..	..
OUTBOUND TOURISM						
8.1 **Departures**	('000)	..	..	..	..	..
8.2 **Tourism expenditure in other countries**	US$ Mn	264	335	425	421	428
8.3 "Travel" (*)	US$ Mn	180	236	311	303	298
8.4 "Passenger transport" (*)	US$ Mn	84	99	114	118	130
TOURISM INDUSTRIES						
Hotels and similar establishments						
9.1 Number of rooms	Units	3,221	3,108	3,326	2,963	3,436
9.2 Number of bed-places	Units	..	..	..	..	..
9.3 Occupancy rate	Percent	59.12	58.50	57.90	65.60	62.70
9.4 Average length of stay	Nights	10.74	10.84	10.44	10.80	11.11
RELATED INDICATORS						
Share of tourism expenditure (6.1) in:						
10.1 Gross Domestic Product (GDP)	Percent	..	..	..	..	..
10.2 Exports of goods	Percent	285.5	436.9	411.7	354.2	398.5
10.3 Exports of services	Percent	61.6	68.2	71.7	70.1	71.2

(*) Balance of Payments items: 6.1 to 6.3 correspond to the "Credit" side (and are receipts for the country) while 8.2 to 8.4 correspond to the "Debit" side (and are expenditures in other countries).

GABON

Basic Indicators		Units	2002	2003	2004	2005	2006
	INBOUND TOURISM						
	Arrivals						
1.1	Visitors	('000)	269	234	..	..	..
1.2	Tourists (overnight visitors)	('000)	208	222	..	..	..
1.3	Same-day visitors	('000)	60	12	..	..	..
1.4	Cruise passengers	('000)	1	..	..	..	..
	Arrivals by region						
2.1	Africa	('000)	52	55	..	..	..
2.2	Americas	('000)	..	..	..	..	..
2.3	Europe	('000)	..	..	..	..	..
2.4	East Asia and the Pacific	('000)	..	..	..	..	..
2.5	South Asia	('000)	..	..	..	..	..
2.6	Middle East	('000)	..	..	..	..	..
	Arrivals by means of transport used						
3.1	Air	('000)	208	222	..	..	..
3.2	Rail	('000)	..	..	..	..	..
3.3	Road	('000)	..	..	..	..	..
3.4	Sea	('000)	..	..	..	..	..
	Arrivals by purpose of visit						
4.1	Leisure, recreation and holidays	('000)	..	..	..	..	..
4.2	Business and professional	('000)	..	..	..	..	..
4.3	Other	('000)	..	..	..	..	..
	Accommodation						
5.1	Overnight stays in hotels and similar establishments	('000)	250	..	..	..	..
5.2	Guests in hotels and similar establishments	('000)	..	..	..	..	..
5.3	Overnight stays in all types of accommodation establishments	('000)	..	..	..	..	..
5.4	Average length of stay of non-resident tourists in all accommodation establishments	Nights	..	..	..	..	..
6.1	**Tourism expenditure in the country**	US$ Mn	77	84	74	..	..
6.2	"Travel" (*)	US$ Mn	18	15	10	..	..
6.3	"Passenger transport" (*)	US$ Mn	59	69	64	..	..
	DOMESTIC TOURISM						
	Accommodation						
7.1	Overnight stays in hotels and similar establishments	('000)	..	..	..	..	..
7.2	Guests in hotels and similar establishments	('000)	..	..	..	..	..
7.3	Overnight stays in all types of accommodation establishments	('000)	..	..	..	..	..
7.4	Average length of stay of resident tourists in all accommodation establishments	Nights	..	..	..	..	..
	OUTBOUND TOURISM						
8.1	**Departures**	('000)	219	236	..	..	..
8.2	**Tourism expenditure in other countries**	US$ Mn	234	239	275	..	..
8.3	"Travel" (*)	US$ Mn	194	194	214	..	..
8.4	"Passenger transport" (*)	US$ Mn	40	45	61	..	..
	TOURISM INDUSTRIES						
	Hotels and similar establishments						
9.1	Number of rooms	Units	2,450	..	..	..	..
9.2	Number of bed-places	Units	..	..	..	..	..
9.3	Occupancy rate	Percent	70.00	..	..	..	..
9.4	Average length of stay	Nights	..	..	..	..	..
	RELATED INDICATORS						
	Share of tourism expenditure (6.1) in:						
10.1	Gross Domestic Product (GDP)	Percent	1.6	1.4	1.0	..	..
10.2	Exports of goods	Percent	3.0	2.6	1.8	..	..
10.3	Exports of services	Percent	89.5	48.8	47.4	..	..

(*) Balance of Payments items: 6.1 to 6.3 correspond to the "Credit" side (and are receipts for the country) while 8.2 to 8.4 correspond to the "Debit" side (and are expenditures in other countries).

Basic Indicators	Units	2002	2003	2004	2005	2006
INBOUND TOURISM						
Arrivals						
1.1 Visitors	('000)	..	..	..	460	613
1.2 Tourists (overnight visitors)	('000)	81	73	90	108	125
1.3 Same-day visitors	('000)	..	..	..	..	..
1.4 Cruise passengers	('000)	..	..	..	..	..
Arrivals by region						
2.1 Africa	('000)	1	5	1	11	18
2.2 Americas	('000)	1	1	3	1	2
2.3 Europe	('000)	77	64	82	86	91
2.4 East Asia and the Pacific	('000)	..	..	..	..	..
2.5 South Asia	('000)	..	..	..	..	..
2.6 Middle East	('000)	..	..	..	..	..
Arrivals by means of transport used						
3.1 Air	('000)	81	73	90	108	125
3.2 Rail	('000)	..	..	..	..	..
3.3 Road	('000)	..	..	..	347	486
3.4 Sea	('000)	..	..	..	5	3
Arrivals by purpose of visit						
4.1 Leisure, recreation and holidays	('000)	81	73	90	108	110
4.2 Business and professional	('000)	..	..	..	..	2
4.3 Other	('000)	..	..	..	..	13
Accommodation						
5.1 Overnight stays in hotels and similar establishments	('000)	..	..	..	..	..
5.2 Guests in hotels and similar establishments	('000)	..	..	..	..	..
5.3 Overnight stays in all types of accommodation establishments	('000)	..	..	..	..	..
5.4 Average length of stay of non-resident tourists in all accommodation establishments	Nights	..	..	..	..	..
6.1 **Tourism expenditure in the country**	US$ Mn	..	58	51	57	69
6.2 "Travel" (*)	US$ Mn	..	56	47	56	66
6.3 "Passenger transport" (*)	US$ Mn	..	2	4	1	3
DOMESTIC TOURISM						
Accommodation						
7.1 Overnight stays in hotels and similar establishments	('000)	..	..	..	..	..
7.2 Guests in hotels and similar establishments	('000)	..	..	..	..	..
7.3 Overnight stays in all types of accommodation establishments	('000)	..	..	..	..	..
7.4 Average length of stay of resident tourists in all accommodation establishments	Nights	..	..	..	..	..
OUTBOUND TOURISM						
8.1 **Departures**	('000)	..	..	..	387	..
8.2 **Tourism expenditure in other countries**	US$ Mn	..	8	6	7	8
8.3 "Travel" (*)	US$ Mn	..	4	4	5	6
8.4 "Passenger transport" (*)	US$ Mn	..	4	2	2	2
TOURISM INDUSTRIES						
Hotels and similar establishments						
9.1 Number of rooms	Units	..	..	..	3,066	3,992
9.2 Number of bed-places	Units	..	..	..	..	7,984
9.3 Occupancy rate	Percent	..	..	..	..	..
9.4 Average length of stay	Nights	12.90	12.90	..	..	14.00
RELATED INDICATORS						
Share of tourism expenditure (6.1) in:						
10.1 Gross Domestic Product (GDP)	Percent	..	15.8	12.7	12.4	13.5
10.2 Exports of goods	Percent	..	74.4	46.8	56.4	63.3
10.3 Exports of services	Percent	..	69.0	69.9	71.3	75.0

(*) Balance of Payments items: 6.1 to 6.3 correspond to the "Credit" side (and are receipts for the country) while 8.2 to 8.4 correspond to the "Debit" side (and are expenditures in other countries).

GEORGIA

Basic Indicators	Units	2002	2003	2004	2005	2006
INBOUND TOURISM						
Arrivals						
1.1 Visitors	('000)	298	313	368	560	983
1.2 Tourists (overnight visitors)	('000)	..	..	..	..	..
1.3 Same-day visitors	('000)	..	..	..	..	..
1.4 Cruise passengers	('000)	..	..	3	..	2
Arrivals by region						
2.1 Africa	('000)	1	..	1	..	1
2.2 Americas	('000)	7	9	11	15	19
2.3 Europe	('000)	275	289	343	533	936
2.4 East Asia and the Pacific	('000)	7	7	5	3	14
2.5 South Asia	('000)	6	7	7	7	10
2.6 Middle East	('000)	1	2	2	1	2
Arrivals by means of transport used						
3.1 Air	('000)	67	73	96	131	179
3.2 Rail	('000)	41	40	53	7	14
3.3 Road	('000)	150	155	184	422	731
3.4 Sea	('000)	40	45	34	..	59
Arrivals by purpose of visit						
4.1 Leisure, recreation and holidays	('000)	2	4	3	7	13
4.2 Business and professional	('000)	25	31	54	51	57
4.3 Other	('000)	2	4	3	5	12
Accommodation						
5.1 Overnight stays in hotels and similar establishments	('000)	..	..	..	..	..
5.2 Guests in hotels and similar establishments	('000)	29	39	61	63	82
5.3 Overnight stays in all types of accommodation establishments	('000)	..	..	..	..	..
5.4 Average length of stay of non-resident tourists in all accommodation establishments	Nights	7.80	..	..	..	..
6.1 **Tourism expenditure in the country**	US$ Mn	144	172	209	287	361
6.2 "Travel" (*)	US$ Mn	126	147	177	241	313
6.3 "Passenger transport" (*)	US$ Mn	18	25	32	46	48
DOMESTIC TOURISM						
Accommodation						
7.1 Overnight stays in hotels and similar establishments	('000)	..	..	..	..	..
7.2 Guests in hotels and similar establishments	('000)	41	44	56	89	134
7.3 Overnight stays in all types of accommodation establishments	('000)	..	..	..	..	..
7.4 Average length of stay of resident tourists in all accommodation establishments	Nights	..	..	..	..	..
OUTBOUND TOURISM						
8.1 **Departures**	('000)	317	..	..	..	..
8.2 **Tourism expenditure in other countries**	US$ Mn	189	170	196	237	257
8.3 "Travel" (*)	US$ Mn	149	130	147	169	167
8.4 "Passenger transport" (*)	US$ Mn	40	40	49	68	90
TOURISM INDUSTRIES						
Hotels and similar establishments						
9.1 Number of rooms	Units	9,550	9,614	9,680	6,757	10,022
9.2 Number of bed-places	Units	17,550	17,715	18,084	13,978	20,488
9.3 Occupancy rate	Percent	71.00	..	..	..	..
9.4 Average length of stay	Nights	..	..	..	..	..
RELATED INDICATORS						
Share of tourism expenditure (6.1) in:						
10.1 Gross Domestic Product (GDP)	Percent	4.2	4.3	4.1	4.5	4.8
10.2 Exports of goods	Percent	23.9	20.7	19.1	19.5	21.7
10.3 Exports of services	Percent	35.5	37.7	37.9	40.4	40.1

(*) Balance of Payments items: 6.1 to 6.3 correspond to the "Credit" side (and are receipts for the country) while 8.2 to 8.4 correspond to the "Debit" side (and are expenditures in other countries).

Basic Indicators	Units	2002	2003	2004	2005	2006
INBOUND TOURISM						
Arrivals						
1.1 Visitors	('000)	..	..	..	..	..
1.2 Tourists (overnight visitors)	('000)	17,969	18,399	20,137	21,500	23,569
1.3 Same-day visitors	('000)	..	..	..	..	..
1.4 Cruise passengers	('000)	..	..	..	..	..
Arrivals by region						
2.1 Africa	('000)	144	143	146	144	167
2.2 Americas	('000)	2,151	2,049	2,337	2,398	2,783
2.3 Europe	('000)	13,289	13,878	14,918	16,100	17,504
2.4 East Asia and the Pacific	('000)	1,716	1,605	1,931	2,001	2,176
2.5 South Asia	('000)	..	..	..	..	..
2.6 Middle East	('000)	128	143	160	185	202
Arrivals by means of transport used						
3.1 Air	('000)	46,906	49,866	57,194	61,997	65,667
3.2 Rail	('000)	..	..	..	..	..
3.3 Road	('000)	..	..	..	..	..
3.4 Sea	('000)	..	..	..	..	..
Arrivals by purpose of visit						
4.1 Leisure, recreation and holidays	('000)	..	..	..	..	..
4.2 Business and professional	('000)	..	..	..	..	..
4.3 Other	('000)	..	..	..	..	..
Accommodation						
5.1 Overnight stays in hotels and similar establishments	('000)	34,553	35,172	38,491	40,839	44,921
5.2 Guests in hotels and similar establishments	('000)	16,093	16,357	17,983	19,171	21,057
5.3 Overnight stays in all types of accommodation establishments	('000)	40,655	41,746	45,374	48,246	52,947
5.4 Average length of stay of non-resident tourists in all accommodation establishments	Nights	2.30	2.30	2.30	2.20	2.20
6.1 **Tourism expenditure in the country**	US$ Mn	26,690	30,104	35,569	38,220	42,792
6.2 "Travel" (*)	US$ Mn	19,278	23,125	27,613	29,121	32,846
6.3 "Passenger transport" (*)	US$ Mn	7,412	6,979	7,956	9,099	9,946
DOMESTIC TOURISM						
Accommodation						
7.1 Overnight stays in hotels and similar establishments	('000)	164,383	163,554	165,655	168,843	172,428
7.2 Guests in hotels and similar establishments	('000)	70,023	70,316	72,857	75,363	78,037
7.3 Overnight stays in all types of accommodation establishments	('000)	298,041	296,842	293,395	295,735	298,277
7.4 Average length of stay of resident tourists in all accommodation establishments	Nights	3.20	3.20	3.00	3.00	2.90
OUTBOUND TOURISM						
8.1 **Departures**	('000)	73,300	74,600	72,300	77,400	71,200
8.2 **Tourism expenditure in other countries**	US$ Mn	59,832	72,777	79,434	82,228	83,006
8.3 "Travel" (*)	US$ Mn	53,006	65,234	71,187	74,189	74,123
8.4 "Passenger transport" (*)	US$ Mn	6,826	7,543	8,247	8,039	8,883
TOURISM INDUSTRIES						
Hotels and similar establishments						
9.1 Number of rooms	Units	891,879	892,302	889,297	890,153	896,980
9.2 Number of bed-places	Units	1,671,117	1,672,151	1,667,919	1,678,284	1,690,932
9.3 Occupancy rate	Percent	33.20	33.50	34.20	35.00	35.90
9.4 Average length of stay	Nights	2.31	2.29	2.25	2.22	2.19
RELATED INDICATORS						
Share of tourism expenditure (6.1) in:						
10.1 Gross Domestic Product (GDP)	Percent	1.3	1.2	1.3	1.4	1.5
10.2 Exports of goods	Percent	4.4	4.0	3.9	3.9	3.8
10.3 Exports of services	Percent	25.9	24.6	24.6	24.5	24.7

(*) Balance of Payments items: 6.1 to 6.3 correspond to the "Credit" side (and are receipts for the country) while 8.2 to 8.4 correspond to the "Debit" side (and are expenditures in other countries).

GHANA

Basic Indicators		Units	2002	2003	2004	2005	2006
	INBOUND TOURISM						
	Arrivals						
1.1	Visitors	('000)	..	..	..	..	..
1.2	Tourists (overnight visitors)	('000)	483	531	584	429	
1.3	Same-day visitors	('000)	..	..	..	..	
1.4	Cruise passengers	('000)	..	..	..	..	..
	Arrivals by region						
2.1	Africa	('000)	164	181	199	173	..
2.2	Americas	('000)	41	45	49	63	..
2.3	Europe	('000)	120	132	145	101	..
2.4	East Asia and the Pacific	('000)	23	26	28	17	..
2.5	South Asia	('000)	..	..	..	..	..
2.6	Middle East	('000)	4	4	4	11	..
	Arrivals by means of transport used						
3.1	Air	('000)	..	..	..	..	..
3.2	Rail	('000)	..	..	..	..	..
3.3	Road	('000)	..	..	..	..	..
3.4	Sea	('000)	..	..	..	..	..
	Arrivals by purpose of visit						
4.1	Leisure, recreation and holidays	('000)	153	168	185	83	..
4.2	Business and professional	('000)	176	193	213	142	
4.3	Other	('000)	154	170	186	203	
	Accommodation						
5.1	Overnight stays in hotels and similar establishments	('000)	..	..	..	..	..
5.2	Guests in hotels and similar establishments	('000)	..	..	..	..	..
5.3	Overnight stays in all types of accommodation establishments	('000)	..	..	..	..	..
5.4	Average length of stay of non-resident tourists in all accommodation establishments	Nights	..	..	..	..	..
6.1	**Tourism expenditure in the country**	US$ Mn	383	441	495	867	910
6.2	"Travel" (*)	US$ Mn	358	414	466	836	861
6.3	"Passenger transport" (*)	US$ Mn	25	27	29	31	49
	DOMESTIC TOURISM						
	Accommodation						
7.1	Overnight stays in hotels and similar establishments	('000)	..	..	..	..	..
7.2	Guests in hotels and similar establishments	('000)	..	..	..	..	..
7.3	Overnight stays in all types of accommodation establishments	('000)	..	..	..	..	..
7.4	Average length of stay of resident tourists in all accommodation establishments	Nights	..	..	..	..	..
	OUTBOUND TOURISM						
8.1	**Departures**	('000)	..	..	..	..	..
8.2	**Tourism expenditure in other countries**	US$ Mn	184	216	270	472	575
8.3	"Travel" (*)	US$ Mn	119	138	186	303	345
8.4	"Passenger transport" (*)	US$ Mn	65	78	84	169	230
	TOURISM INDUSTRIES						
	Hotels and similar establishments						
9.1	Number of rooms	Units	16,180	17,352	18,079	18,632	..
9.2	Number of bed-places	Units	21,442	22,909	23,538	23,915	..
9.3	Occupancy rate	Percent	..	..	..	75.00	..
9.4	Average length of stay	Nights	..	..	..	..	..
	RELATED INDICATORS						
	Share of tourism expenditure (6.1) in:						
10.1	Gross Domestic Product (GDP)	Percent	6.2	5.8	5.6	8.1	7.1
10.2	Exports of goods	Percent	19.0	17.2	18.3	30.9	24.4
10.3	Exports of services	Percent	69.0	70.0	70.5	78.4	65.0

(*) Balance of Payments items: 6.1 to 6.3 correspond to the "Credit" side (and are receipts for the country) while 8.2 to 8.4 correspond to the "Debit" side (and are expenditures in other countries).

Basic Indicators		Units	2002	2003	2004	2005	2006
	INBOUND TOURISM						
	Arrivals						
1.1	Visitors	('000)	14,918	14,785	14,268	15,938	17,284
1.2	Tourists (overnight visitors)	('000)	14,180	13,969	13,313	14,765	16,039
1.3	Same-day visitors	('000)	..	..	..	..	..
1.4	Cruise passengers	('000)	738	815	955	1,173	1,245
	Arrivals by region						
2.1	Africa	('000)	22	19	23	23	30
2.2	Americas	('000)	217	219	236	417	513
2.3	Europe	('000)	13,630	13,459	12,766	13,996	15,104
2.4	East Asia and the Pacific	('000)	242	213	227	254	316
2.5	South Asia	('000)	4	4	5	4	..
2.6	Middle East	('000)	64	55	55	72	75
	Arrivals by means of transport used						
3.1	Air	('000)	10,438	10,417	9,974	10,915	11,509
3.2	Rail	('000)	89	95	92	104	79
3.3	Road	('000)	2,856	2,828	2,692	2,986	3,441
3.4	Sea	('000)	1,535	1,445	1,510	1,932	2,255
	Arrivals by purpose of visit						
4.1	Leisure, recreation and holidays	('000)	..	..	..	..	..
4.2	Business and professional	('000)	..	..	..	..	..
4.3	Other	('000)	..	..	..	..	..
	Accommodation						
5.1	Overnight stays in hotels and similar establishments	('000)	40,350	39,760	38,310	40,075	42,459
5.2	Guests in hotels and similar establishments	('000)	6,654	6,574	6,313	7,143	7,548
5.3	Overnight stays in all types of accommodation establishments	('000)	40,953	40,407	38,796	40,734	43,055
5.4	Average length of stay of non-resident tourists in all accommodation establishments	Nights	5.98	5.97	6.00	5.54	5.56
6.1	**Tourism expenditure in the country**	US$ Mn	10,005	10,842	12,809	13,453	14,495
6.2	"Travel" (*)	US$ Mn	9,909	10,766	12,715	13,334	14,402
6.3	"Passenger transport" (*)	US$ Mn	96	76	94	119	93
	DOMESTIC TOURISM						
	Accommodation						
7.1	Overnight stays in hotels and similar establishments	('000)	13,128	13,716	13,280	13,942	14,249
7.2	Guests in hotels and similar establishments	('000)	5,465	5,650	5,567	5,933	6,128
7.3	Overnight stays in all types of accommodation establishments	('000)	13,513	14,095	13,758	14,530	14,741
7.4	Average length of stay of resident tourists in all accommodation establishments	Nights	2.43	2.46	2.43	2.40	2.37
	OUTBOUND TOURISM						
8.1	**Departures**	('000)	..	..	..	..	..
8.2	**Tourism expenditure in other countries**	US$ Mn	2,453	2,439	2,880	3,045	3,004
8.3	"Travel" (*)	US$ Mn	2,436	2,431	2,872	3,039	2,997
8.4	"Passenger transport" (*)	US$ Mn	17	8	8	6	7
	TOURISM INDUSTRIES						
	Hotels and similar establishments						
9.1	Number of rooms	Units	330,348	339,540	351,891	358,721	364,179
9.2	Number of bed-places	Units	626,914	644,898	668,271	682,050	693,252
9.3	Occupancy rate	Percent	61.80	60.70	55.60	58.60	..
9.4	Average length of stay	Nights	..	..	..	..	..
	RELATED INDICATORS						
	Share of tourism expenditure (6.1) in:						
10.1	Gross Domestic Product (GDP)	Percent	7.4	6.2	6.1	6.0	5.9
10.2	Exports of goods	Percent	101.4	86.2	81.4	76.3	71.4
10.3	Exports of services	Percent	49.7	44.6	38.7	39.7	40.5

(*) Balance of Payments items: 6.1 to 6.3 correspond to the "Credit" side (and are receipts for the country) while 8.2 to 8.4 correspond to the "Debit" side (and are expenditures in other countries).

GRENADA

Basic Indicators	Units	2002	2003	2004	2005	2006
INBOUND TOURISM						
Arrivals						
1.1 Visitors	('000)	271	294	370	380	342
1.2 Tourists (overnight visitors)	('000)	132	142	134	99	119
1.3 Same-day visitors	('000)	4	5	6	6	5
1.4 Cruise passengers	('000)	135	147	230	275	219
Arrivals by region						
2.1 Africa	('000)	..	1	1	..	..
2.2 Americas	('000)	77	80	77	59	65
2.3 Europe	('000)	39	43	36	22	33
2.4 East Asia and the Pacific	('000)	1	1	1	1	2
2.5 South Asia	('000)	..	..	..	..	..
2.6 Middle East	('000)	..	..	..	..	..
Arrivals by means of transport used						
3.1 Air	('000)	121	134	128	94	114
3.2 Rail	('000)	..	..	..	..	..
3.3 Road	('000)	..	..	..	..	..
3.4 Sea	('000)	11	8	6	5	5
Arrivals by purpose of visit						
4.1 Leisure, recreation and holidays	('000)	85	90	71	49	59
4.2 Business and professional	('000)	19	22	31	19	19
4.3 Other	('000)	28	31	32	30	41
Accommodation						
5.1 Overnight stays in hotels and similar establishments	('000)	..	..	..	..	..
5.2 Guests in hotels and similar establishments	('000)	63	72	72	36	54
5.3 Overnight stays in all types of accommodation establishments	('000)	..	..	..	..	..
5.4 Average length of stay of non-resident tourists in all accommodation establishments	Nights	7.32	7.65	7.53	7.42	7.63
6.1 **Tourism expenditure in the country**	US$ Mn	..	..	..	..	..
6.2 "Travel" (*)	US$ Mn	91	104	83	71	93
6.3 "Passenger transport" (*)	US$ Mn	..	..	..	..	..
DOMESTIC TOURISM						
Accommodation						
7.1 Overnight stays in hotels and similar establishments	('000)	..	..	..	..	..
7.2 Guests in hotels and similar establishments	('000)	..	..	..	..	..
7.3 Overnight stays in all types of accommodation establishments	('000)	..	..	..	..	..
7.4 Average length of stay of resident tourists in all accommodation establishments	Nights	..	..	..	..	..
OUTBOUND TOURISM						
8.1 **Departures**	('000)	..	..	..	..	..
8.2 **Tourism expenditure in other countries**	US$ Mn	..	..	..	..	..
8.3 "Travel" (*)	US$ Mn	8	8	8	10	11
8.4 "Passenger transport" (*)	US$ Mn	..	..	..	..	..
TOURISM INDUSTRIES						
Hotels and similar establishments						
9.1 Number of rooms	Units	1,777	1,758	1,738	1,470	1,584
9.2 Number of bed-places	Units	3,590	3,844	3,892	2,326	3,139
9.3 Occupancy rate	Percent	71.00	..	..	..	..
9.4 Average length of stay	Nights	7.32	7.65	7.53	7.42	7.63
RELATED INDICATORS						
Share of tourism expenditure (6.1) in: (**)						
10.1 Gross Domestic Product (GDP)	Percent	22.3	23.4	19.0	15.0	17.9
10.2 Exports of goods	Percent	4882.9	4354.3	6072.7	5141.0	..
10.3 Exports of services	Percent	69.5	77.6	52.9	55.5	..

(*) Balance of Payments items: 6.1 to 6.3 correspond to the "Credit" side (and are receipts for the country) while 8.2 to 8.4 correspond to the "Debit" side (and are expenditures in other countries).

(**) See Annex "Country notes".

GUADELOUPE

Basic Indicators	Units	2002	2003	2004	2005	2006
INBOUND TOURISM						
Arrivals						
1.1 Visitors	('000)	..	569	560	445	..
1.2 Tourists (overnight visitors)	('000)	..	439	456	372	375
1.3 Same-day visitors	('000)	..	..	..	..	..
1.4 Cruise passengers	('000)	148	130	104	73	..
Arrivals by region						
2.1 Africa	('000)	..	..	..	..	..
2.2 Americas	('000)	..	..	..	..	..
2.3 Europe	('000)	..	..	..	370	..
2.4 East Asia and the Pacific	('000)	..	..	..	..	..
2.5 South Asia	('000)	..	..	..	..	..
2.6 Middle East	('000)	..	..	..	..	..
Arrivals by means of transport used						
3.1 Air	('000)	..	439	456	372	375
3.2 Rail	('000)	..	..	..	..	..
3.3 Road	('000)	..	..	..	..	..
3.4 Sea	('000)	148	130	104	73	..
Arrivals by purpose of visit						
4.1 Leisure, recreation and holidays	('000)	..	..	..	..	..
4.2 Business and professional	('000)	..	..	..	..	..
4.3 Other	('000)	..	..	..	..	..
Accommodation						
5.1 Overnight stays in hotels and similar establishments	('000)	..	1,534	1,736	..	..
5.2 Guests in hotels and similar establishments	('000)	..	439	456	..	..
5.3 Overnight stays in all types of accommodation establishments	('000)	..	..	..	..	..
5.4 Average length of stay of non-resident tourists in all accommodation establishments	Nights	..	..	..	..	..
6.1 **Tourism expenditure in the country**	US$ Mn	..	..	..	306	299
6.2 "Travel" (*)	US$ Mn	..	..	..	..	..
6.3 "Passenger transport" (*)	US$ Mn	..	..	..	..	..
DOMESTIC TOURISM						
Accommodation						
7.1 Overnight stays in hotels and similar establishments	('000)	..	..	..	..	..
7.2 Guests in hotels and similar establishments	('000)	..	..	..	..	..
7.3 Overnight stays in all types of accommodation establishments	('000)	..	..	..	..	..
7.4 Average length of stay of resident tourists in all accommodation establishments	Nights	..	..	..	..	..
OUTBOUND TOURISM						
8.1 **Departures**	('000)	..	..	..	..	..
8.2 **Tourism expenditure in other countries**	US$ Mn	..	..	..	..	..
8.3 "Travel" (*)	US$ Mn	..	..	..	..	..
8.4 "Passenger transport" (*)	US$ Mn	..	..	..	..	..
TOURISM INDUSTRIES						
Hotels and similar establishments						
9.1 Number of rooms	Units	7,433	7,603	4,416	3,506	..
9.2 Number of bed-places	Units	..	..	..	7,012	..
9.3 Occupancy rate	Percent	54.80	49.20	53.00	..	..
9.4 Average length of stay	Nights	..	3.50	3.90	3.50	..
RELATED INDICATORS						
Share of tourism expenditure (6.1) in:						
10.1 Gross Domestic Product (GDP)	Percent	..	..	..	..	..
10.2 Exports of goods	Percent	..	..	..	..	..
10.3 Exports of services	Percent	..	..	..	..	..

(*) Balance of Payments items: 6.1 to 6.3 correspond to the "Credit" side (and are receipts for the country) while 8.2 to 8.4 correspond to the "Debit" side (and are expenditures in other countries).

GUAM

Basic Indicators	Units	2002	2003	2004	2005	2006
INBOUND TOURISM						
Arrivals						
1.1 Visitors	('000)	..	..	..	..	..
1.2 Tourists (overnight visitors)	('000)	1,059	910	1,160	1,228	1,212
1.3 Same-day visitors	('000)	..	..	..	..	..
1.4 Cruise passengers	('000)	..	..	..	..	..
Arrivals by region						
2.1 Africa	('000)	..	..	..	..	..
2.2 Americas	('000)	43	..	47	46	45
2.3 Europe	('000)	1	..	2	2	1
2.4 East Asia and the Pacific	('000)	984	..	1,069	1,134	1,134
2.5 South Asia	('000)	..	..	..	..	..
2.6 Middle East	('000)	..	..	..	..	..
Arrivals by means of transport used						
3.1 Air	('000)	1,031	857	1,121	1,185	1,184
3.2 Rail	('000)	..	..	..	..	..
3.3 Road	('000)	..	..	..	..	..
3.4 Sea	('000)	28	52	39	43	28
Arrivals by purpose of visit						
4.1 Leisure, recreation and holidays	('000)	810	672	895	938	..
4.2 Business and professional	('000)	17	17	31	37	..
4.3 Other	('000)	196	162	195	210	..
Accommodation						
5.1 Overnight stays in hotels and similar establishments	('000)	..	..	..	..	..
5.2 Guests in hotels and similar establishments	('000)	..	..	..	..	..
5.3 Overnight stays in all types of accommodation establishments	('000)	..	..	..	..	..
5.4 Average length of stay of non-resident tourists in all accommodation establishments	Nights	..	..	..	..	..
6.1 **Tourism expenditure in the country**	US$ Mn	..	..	..	..	..
6.2 "Travel" (*)	US$ Mn	..	..	..	..	..
6.3 "Passenger transport" (*)	US$ Mn	..	..	..	..	..
DOMESTIC TOURISM						
Accommodation						
7.1 Overnight stays in hotels and similar establishments	('000)	..	..	..	..	..
7.2 Guests in hotels and similar establishments	('000)	..	..	..	..	..
7.3 Overnight stays in all types of accommodation establishments	('000)	..	..	..	..	..
7.4 Average length of stay of resident tourists in all accommodation establishments	Nights	..	..	..	..	..
OUTBOUND TOURISM						
8.1 **Departures**	('000)	..	..	..	..	..
8.2 **Tourism expenditure in other countries**	US$ Mn	..	..	..	..	..
8.3 "Travel" (*)	US$ Mn	..	..	..	..	..
8.4 "Passenger transport" (*)	US$ Mn	..	..	..	..	..
TOURISM INDUSTRIES						
Hotels and similar establishments						
9.1 Number of rooms	Units	8,451	8,915	8,555	9,236	8,075
9.2 Number of bed-places	Units	..	..	..	..	..
9.3 Occupancy rate	Percent	57.00	54.00	58.00	63.00	60.00
9.4 Average length of stay	Nights	..	..	..	..	..
RELATED INDICATORS						
Share of tourism expenditure (6.1) in:						
10.1 Gross Domestic Product (GDP)	Percent	..	..	..	..	..
10.2 Exports of goods	Percent	..	..	..	..	..
10.3 Exports of services	Percent	..	..	..	..	..

(*) Balance of Payments items: 6.1 to 6.3 correspond to the "Credit" side (and are receipts for the country) while 8.2 to 8.4 correspond to the "Debit" side (and are expenditures in other countries).

Basic Indicators		Units	2002	2003	2004	2005	2006
	INBOUND TOURISM						
	Arrivals						
1.1	Visitors	('000)	..	..	..	..	..
1.2	Tourists (overnight visitors)	('000)	884	880	1,182	1,316	1,502
1.3	Same-day visitors	('000)	..	..	..	..	..
1.4	Cruise passengers	('000)	..	..	..	..	..
	Arrivals by region						
2.1	Africa	('000)	..	..	..	..	..
2.2	Americas	('000)	712	704	1,007	1,148	1,325
2.3	Europe	('000)	145	151	150	140	147
2.4	East Asia and the Pacific	('000)	24	22	23	25	27
2.5	South Asia	('000)	..	..	..	..	..
2.6	Middle East	('000)	1	1	..	1	..
	Arrivals by means of transport used						
3.1	Air	('000)	403	402	434	480	497
3.2	Rail	('000)	..	..	..	..	..
3.3	Road	('000)	466	452	714	805	942
3.4	Sea	('000)	15	26	34	31	63
	Arrivals by purpose of visit						
4.1	Leisure, recreation and holidays	('000)	..	..	..	..	661
4.2	Business and professional	('000)	..	..	..	..	315
4.3	Other	('000)	..	..	..	..	526
	Accommodation						
5.1	Overnight stays in hotels and similar establishments	('000)					..
5.2	Guests in hotels and similar establishments	('000)	..	..	..	..	..
5.3	Overnight stays in all types of accommodation establishments	('000)	..	..	..	..	..
5.4	Average length of stay of non-resident tourists in all accommodation establishments	Nights	..	..	..	..	..
6.1	**Tourism expenditure in the country**	US$ Mn	647	646	806	883	1,008
6.2	"Travel" (*)	US$ Mn	620	621	776	846	969
6.3	"Passenger transport" (*)	US$ Mn	27	25	30	37	39
	DOMESTIC TOURISM						
	Accommodation						
7.1	Overnight stays in hotels and similar establishments	('000)	..	..	..	..	..
7.2	Guests in hotels and similar establishments	('000)	..	..	..	..	..
7.3	Overnight stays in all types of accommodation establishments	('000)	..	..	..	..	..
7.4	Average length of stay of resident tourists in all accommodation establishments	Nights	..	..	..	..	..
	OUTBOUND TOURISM						
8.1	**Departures**	('000)	629	658	854	982	1,055
8.2	**Tourism expenditure in other countries** (**)	US$ Mn	329	373	456	500	572
8.3	"Travel" (*)	US$ Mn	276	312	391	444	494
8.4	"Passenger transport" (*)	US$ Mn	53	61	65	56	78
	TOURISM INDUSTRIES						
	Hotels and similar establishments						
9.1	Number of rooms	Units	17,313	17,519	17,570	19,357	19,372
9.2	Number of bed-places	Units	44,421	44,579	44,883	51,955	50,904
9.3	Occupancy rate	Percent	..	47.95	49.86	44.54	46.18
9.4	Average length of stay	Nights	..	..	..	..	7.10
	RELATED INDICATORS						
	Share of tourism expenditure (6.1) in:						
10.1	Gross Domestic Product (GDP)	Percent	2.8	2.6	2.9	2.8	2.9
10.2	Exports of goods	Percent	23.0	21.1	23.2	16.4	16.7
10.3	Exports of services	Percent	56.5	61.0	68.4	71.8	72.3

(*) Balance of Payments items: 6.1 to 6.3 correspond to the "Credit" side (and are receipts for the country) while 8.2 to 8.4 correspond to the "Debit" side (and are expenditures in other countries).

(**) See Annex "Country notes".

GUINEA

Basic Indicators	Units	2002	2003	2004	2005	2006
INBOUND TOURISM						
Arrivals						
1.1 Visitors	('000)	..	..	..	..	46.6
1.2　Tourists (overnight visitors)	('000)	43.0	44.0	45.0	45.0	46.1
1.3　Same-day visitors	('000)	..	..	..	..	
1.4　Cruise passengers	('000)	..	..	..	..	0.5
Arrivals by region						
2.1 Africa	('000)	22	16	13	15	18
2.2 Americas	('000)	3	4	4	5	2
2.3 Europe	('000)	12	15	16	15	15
2.4 East Asia and the Pacific	('000)	2	2	2	3	3
2.5 South Asia	('000)	1	1	1	1	1
2.6 Middle East	('000)	2	1	1	1	1
Arrivals by means of transport used						
3.1 Air	('000)	40.6	44.0	42.0	45.0	46.1
3.2 Rail	('000)	..	..	..	..	..
3.3 Road	('000)	1.6	..	2.5	..	..
3.4 Sea	('000)	0.3	..	0.1	..	0.5
Arrivals by purpose of visit						
4.1 Leisure, recreation and holidays	('000)	5	5	7	5	8
4.2 Business and professional	('000)	20	20	19	20	20
4.3 Other	('000)	17	19	19	20	18
Accommodation						
5.1 Overnight stays in hotels and similar establishments	('000)	175	122	152	195	188
5.2 Guests in hotels and similar establishments	('000)	..	16	14	15	19
5.3 Overnight stays in all types of accommodation establishments	('000)	600	928	1,233	1,318	959
5.4 Average length of stay of non-resident tourists in all accommodation establishments	Nights	3.10	..	..	4.85	4.80
6.1 **Tourism expenditure in the country**	US$ Mn	..	32	..	..	..
6.2　"Travel" (*)	US$ Mn	43	31	30	..	70
6.3　"Passenger transport" (*)	US$ Mn	..	1	..	..	..
DOMESTIC TOURISM						
Accommodation						
7.1 Overnight stays in hotels and similar establishments	('000)	..	..	..	..	..
7.2 Guests in hotels and similar establishments	('000)	..	..	..	..	..
7.3 Overnight stays in all types of accommodation establishments	('000)	..	..	..	..	..
7.4 Average length of stay of resident tourists in all accommodation establishments	Nights	..	..	..	..	..
OUTBOUND TOURISM						
8.1 **Departures**	('000)	..	..	..	..	..
8.2 **Tourism expenditure in other countries**	US$ Mn	38	36	29	41	..
8.3　"Travel" (*)	US$ Mn	31	26	25	28	..
8.4　"Passenger transport" (*)	US$ Mn	7	10	4	13	..
TOURISM INDUSTRIES						
Hotels and similar establishments						
9.1 Number of rooms	Units	3,533	3,747	3,886	..	4,495
9.2 Number of bed-places	Units	..	4,518	4,658	..	5,394
9.3 Occupancy rate	Percent	70.00	..	..	..	..
9.4 Average length of stay	Nights	3.00	..	..	..	3.80
RELATED INDICATORS						
Share of tourism expenditure (6.1) in:						
10.1 Gross Domestic Product (GDP)	Percent	..	0.9	..	..	..
10.2 Exports of goods	Percent	..	5.3	..	..	..
10.3 Exports of services	Percent	..	23.9	..	..	..

(*) Balance of Payments items: 6.1 to 6.3 correspond to the "Credit" side (and are receipts for the country) while 8.2 to 8.4 correspond to the "Debit" side (and are expenditures in other countries).

(**) See Annex "Country notes".

GUINEA-BISSAU

Basic Indicators	Units	2002	2003	2004	2005	2006
INBOUND TOURISM						
Arrivals						
1.1 Visitors	('000)	..	..	..	..	..
1.2 Tourists (overnight visitors)	('000)	..	..	..	5.0	11.6
1.3 Same-day visitors	('000)	..	..	..	..	..
1.4 Cruise passengers	('000)	..	..	..	..	..
Arrivals by region						
2.1 Africa	('000)	..	..	..	1.2	2.7
2.2 Americas	('000)	..	..	..	0.5	2.0
2.3 Europe	('000)	..	..	..	3.1	5.1
2.4 East Asia and the Pacific	('000)	..	..	..	0.1	1.6
2.5 South Asia	('000)	..	..	..	0.1	0.2
2.6 Middle East	('000)	..	..	..	..	0.1
Arrivals by means of transport used						
3.1 Air	('000)	..	..	..	5.0	11.6
3.2 Rail	('000)	..	..	..	..	..
3.3 Road	('000)	..	..	..	..	..
3.4 Sea	('000)	..	..	..	..	..
Arrivals by purpose of visit						
4.1 Leisure, recreation and holidays	('000)	..	..	..	1.2	3.0
4.2 Business and professional	('000)	..	..	..	1.8	4.4
4.3 Other	('000)	..	..	..	2.0	4.2
Accommodation						
5.1 Overnight stays in hotels and similar establishments	('000)					..
5.2 Guests in hotels and similar establishments	('000)	..	..	..	..	..
5.3 Overnight stays in all types of accommodation establishments	('000)	..	..	..	..	..
5.4 Average length of stay of non-resident tourists in all accommodation establishments	Nights	..	..	..	..	..
6.1 **Tourism expenditure in the country**	US$ Mn	..	2.4	2.2	..	..
6.2 "Travel" (*)	US$ Mn	2.2	1.8	1.0	1.6	..
6.3 "Passenger transport" (*)	US$ Mn	..	0.6	1.2	..	..
DOMESTIC TOURISM						
Accommodation						
7.1 Overnight stays in hotels and similar establishments	('000)	..	..	..	..	..
7.2 Guests in hotels and similar establishments	('000)	..	..	..	..	..
7.3 Overnight stays in all types of accommodation establishments	('000)	..	..	..	..	..
7.4 Average length of stay of resident tourists in all accommodation establishments	Nights	..	..	..	..	..
OUTBOUND TOURISM						
8.1 **Departures**	('000)	..	..	..	..	..
8.2 **Tourism expenditure in other countries**	US$ Mn	10	21	22	18	..
8.3 "Travel" (*)	US$ Mn	5	13	13	10	..
8.4 "Passenger transport" (*)	US$ Mn	5	8	9	8	..
TOURISM INDUSTRIES						
Hotels and similar establishments						
9.1 Number of rooms	Units	..	..	3,533	..	..
9.2 Number of bed-places	Units	..	..	4,240	..	..
9.3 Occupancy rate	Percent	..	..	..	..	..
9.4 Average length of stay	Nights	..	..	..	..	..
RELATED INDICATORS						
Share of tourism expenditure (6.1) in:						
10.1 Gross Domestic Product (GDP)	Percent	..	1.0	0.8	..	..
10.2 Exports of goods	Percent	..	3.7	2.9	..	..
10.3 Exports of services	Percent	..	40.0	27.5	..	..

(*) Balance of Payments items: 6.1 to 6.3 correspond to the "Credit" side (and are receipts for the country) while 8.2 to 8.4 correspond to the "Debit" side (and are expenditures in other countries).

GUYANA

Basic Indicators	Units	2002	2003	2004	2005	2006
INBOUND TOURISM						
Arrivals						
1.1 Visitors	('000)	..	..	..	..	..
1.2 Tourists (overnight visitors)	('000)	104	101	122	117	113
1.3 Same-day visitors	('000)	..	..	..	..	..
1.4 Cruise passengers	('000)	..	..	..	..	..
Arrivals by region						
2.1 Africa	('000)	..	..	..	..	..
2.2 Americas	('000)	95	91	111	105	103
2.3 Europe	('000)	8	8	9	9	8
2.4 East Asia and the Pacific	('000)	..	..	..	..	..
2.5 South Asia	('000)	..	..	..	..	..
2.6 Middle East	('000)	..	..	..	..	..
Arrivals by means of transport used						
3.1 Air	('000)	104	101	122	117	113
3.2 Rail	('000)	..	..	..	..	..
3.3 Road	('000)	..	..	..	..	..
3.4 Sea	('000)	..	..	..	..	..
Arrivals by purpose of visit						
4.1 Leisure, recreation and holidays	('000)	..	..	..	..	..
4.2 Business and professional	('000)	..	..	..	..	..
4.3 Other	('000)	..	..	..	..	..
Accommodation						
5.1 Overnight stays in hotels and similar establishments	('000)	..	..	..	..	..
5.2 Guests in hotels and similar establishments	('000)	..	..	..	..	..
5.3 Overnight stays in all types of accommodation establishments	('000)	..	..	..	..	..
5.4 Average length of stay of non-resident tourists in all accommodation establishments	Nights	..	..	..	..	..
6.1 **Tourism expenditure in the country**	US$ Mn	53	28	29	37	40
6.2 "Travel" (*)	US$ Mn	49	26	27	35	37
6.3 "Passenger transport" (*)	US$ Mn	4	2	2	2	3
DOMESTIC TOURISM						
Accommodation						
7.1 Overnight stays in hotels and similar establishments	('000)	..	..	..	..	..
7.2 Guests in hotels and similar establishments	('000)	..	..	..	..	..
7.3 Overnight stays in all types of accommodation establishments	('000)	..	..	..	..	..
7.4 Average length of stay of resident tourists in all accommodation establishments	Nights	..	..	..	..	..
OUTBOUND TOURISM						
8.1 **Departures**	('000)	..	..	..	..	..
8.2 **Tourism expenditure in other countries**	US$ Mn	44	30	35	45	54
8.3 "Travel" (*)	US$ Mn	38	26	30	40	49
8.4 "Passenger transport" (*)	US$ Mn	6	4	5	5	5
TOURISM INDUSTRIES						
Hotels and similar establishments						
9.1 Number of rooms	Units	..	..	..	..	..
9.2 Number of bed-places	Units	..	..	..	..	..
9.3 Occupancy rate	Percent	..	..	..	..	..
9.4 Average length of stay	Nights	..	..	..	..	..
RELATED INDICATORS						
Share of tourism expenditure (6.1) in:						
10.1 Gross Domestic Product (GDP)	Percent	7.3	3.8	3.7	4.7	4.5
10.2 Exports of goods	Percent	10.8	5.5	5.0	6.8	6.7
10.3 Exports of services	Percent	30.8	17.8	18.0	25.0	27.0

(*) Balance of Payments items: 6.1 to 6.3 correspond to the "Credit" side (and are receipts for the country) while 8.2 to 8.4 correspond to the "Debit" side (and are expenditures in other countries).

82

HAITI

Basic Indicators	Units	2002	2003	2004	2005	2006
INBOUND TOURISM						
Arrivals						
1.1 Visitors	('000)	482	518	385	480	..
1.2 Tourists (overnight visitors)	('000)	140	136	96	112	..
1.3 Same-day visitors	('000)	..	..	..	..	..
1.4 Cruise passengers	('000)	342	382	289	368	..
Arrivals by region						
2.1 Africa	('000)	..	..	..	..	..
2.2 Americas	('000)	127	125	91	104	..
2.3 Europe	('000)	11	8	4	7	..
2.4 East Asia and the Pacific	('000)	..	..	..	..	..
2.5 South Asia	('000)	..	..	..	..	..
2.6 Middle East	('000)	..	..	..	..	..
Arrivals by means of transport used						
3.1 Air	('000)	140	136	96	112	..
3.2 Rail	('000)	..	..	..	..	..
3.3 Road	('000)	..	..	..	..	..
3.4 Sea	('000)	342	382	289	368	..
Arrivals by purpose of visit						
4.1 Leisure, recreation and holidays	('000)	..	..	..	..	..
4.2 Business and professional	('000)	..	..	..	..	..
4.3 Other	('000)	..	..	..	..	..
Accommodation						
5.1 Overnight stays in hotels and similar establishments	('000)	..	..	..	..	..
5.2 Guests in hotels and similar establishments	('000)	..	..	..	..	..
5.3 Overnight stays in all types of accommodation establishments	('000)	..	..	..	..	..
5.4 Average length of stay of non-resident tourists in all accommodation establishments	Nights	..	..	..	..	..
6.1 **Tourism expenditure in the country**	US$ Mn	..	..	..	..	..
6.2 "Travel" (*)	US$ Mn	108	96	87	80	135
6.3 "Passenger transport" (*)	US$ Mn	..	..	..	..	..
DOMESTIC TOURISM						
Accommodation						
7.1 Overnight stays in hotels and similar establishments	('000)	..	..	..	..	..
7.2 Guests in hotels and similar establishments	('000)	..	..	..	..	..
7.3 Overnight stays in all types of accommodation establishments	('000)	..	..	..	..	..
7.4 Average length of stay of resident tourists in all accommodation establishments	Nights	..	..	..	..	..
OUTBOUND TOURISM						
8.1 **Departures**	('000)	..	..	..	..	..
8.2 **Tourism expenditure in other countries**	US$ Mn	172	202	206	173	233
8.3 "Travel" (*)	US$ Mn	18	42	72	54	56
8.4 "Passenger transport" (*)	US$ Mn	154	160	134	119	177
TOURISM INDUSTRIES						
Hotels and similar establishments						
9.1 Number of rooms	Units	..	..	..	..	..
9.2 Number of bed-places	Units	..	..	..	..	..
9.3 Occupancy rate	Percent	..	..	..	..	..
9.4 Average length of stay	Nights	..	..	..	..	..
RELATED INDICATORS						
Share of tourism expenditure (6.1) in: (**)						
10.1 Gross Domestic Product (GDP)	Percent	3.1	3.2	2.2	1.8	2.7
10.2 Exports of goods	Percent	39.4	28.7	23.1	17.4	27.3
10.3 Exports of services	Percent	73.5	70.6	65.4	58.0	66.2

(*) Balance of Payments items: 6.1 to 6.3 correspond to the "Credit" side (and are receipts for the country) while 8.2 to 8.4 correspond to the "Debit" side (and are expenditures in other countries).

(**) See Annex "Country notes".

HONDURAS

Basic Indicators	Units	2002	2003	2004	2005	2006
INBOUND TOURISM						
Arrivals						
1.1 Visitors	('000)	788	887	1,026	1,118	1,136
1.2 Tourists (overnight visitors)	('000)	550	611	641	673	739
1.3 Same-day visitors	('000)	239	276	118	168	193
1.4 Cruise passengers	('000)	125	162	267	277	205
Arrivals by region						
2.1 Africa	('000)	0.3	0.2	0.3	0.2	0.3
2.2 Americas	('000)	493	557	585	610	666
2.3 Europe	('000)	49	45	48	53	60
2.4 East Asia and the Pacific	('000)	7	7	8	8	11
2.5 South Asia	('000)	0.2	0.3	0.3	0.3	0.4
2.6 Middle East	('000)	0.1	0.1	0.1	0.1	0.1
Arrivals by means of transport used						
3.1 Air	('000)	210	248	259	301	352
3.2 Rail	('000)	..	..	..	..	..
3.3 Road	('000)	320	344	362	348	361
3.4 Sea	('000)	20	19	20	23	26
Arrivals by purpose of visit						
4.1 Leisure, recreation and holidays	('000)	252	280	294	309	398
4.2 Business and professional	('000)	83	93	97	102	136
4.3 Other	('000)	214	238	250	262	205
Accommodation						
5.1 Overnight stays in hotels and similar establishments	('000)	..	..	..	..	..
5.2 Guests in hotels and similar establishments	('000)	..	..	..	..	..
5.3 Overnight stays in all types of accommodation establishments	('000)	..	..	..	..	..
5.4 Average length of stay of non-resident tourists in all accommodation establishments	Nights	10.60	9.70	12.50	10.80	9.10
6.1 **Tourism expenditure in the country**	US$ Mn	305	364	420	466	490
6.2 "Travel" (*)	US$ Mn	301	356	414	464	488
6.3 "Passenger transport" (*)	US$ Mn	4	8	6	2	2
DOMESTIC TOURISM						
Accommodation						
7.1 Overnight stays in hotels and similar establishments	('000)	..	..	..	..	..
7.2 Guests in hotels and similar establishments	('000)	..	..	..	..	..
7.3 Overnight stays in all types of accommodation establishments	('000)	..	..	..	..	..
7.4 Average length of stay of resident tourists in all accommodation establishments	Nights	..	..	..	..	..
OUTBOUND TOURISM						
8.1 **Departures**	('000)	279	277	295	296	308
8.2 **Tourism expenditure in other countries**	US$ Mn	187	271	307	327	353
8.3 "Travel" (*)	US$ Mn	149	211	245	262	283
8.4 "Passenger transport" (*)	US$ Mn	38	60	62	65	70
TOURISM INDUSTRIES						
Hotels and similar establishments						
9.1 Number of rooms	Units	17,178	18,590	19,519	20,453	21,015
9.2 Number of bed-places	Units	27,574	26,897	27,704	29,032	29,976
9.3 Occupancy rate	Percent	..	..	..	..	..
9.4 Average length of stay	Nights	10.60	9.70	12.50	10.80	9.10
RELATED INDICATORS						
Share of tourism expenditure (6.1) in:						
10.1 Gross Domestic Product (GDP)	Percent	4.7	5.3	5.6	5.6	5.3
10.2 Exports of goods	Percent	15.4	17.4	17.3	17.0	16.1
10.3 Exports of services	Percent	57.5	61.8	61.5	62.6	65.1

(*) Balance of Payments items: 6.1 to 6.3 correspond to the "Credit" side (and are receipts for the country) while 8.2 to 8.4 correspond to the "Debit" side (and are expenditures in other countries).

Basic Indicators		Units	2002	2003	2004	2005	2006
	INBOUND TOURISM						
	Arrivals						
1.1	Visitors	('000)	16,566	15,537	21,811	23,359	25,251
1.2	Tourists (overnight visitors)	('000)	10,689	9,676	13,655	14,773	15,821
1.3	Same-day visitors	('000)	5,865	5,857	8,147	8,567	9,410
1.4	Cruise passengers	('000)	13	4	9	19	20
	Arrivals by region						
2.1	Africa	('000)	92	99	146	206	218
2.2	Americas	('000)	1,347	926	1,400	1,565	1,631
2.3	Europe	('000)	1,135	822	1,202	1,472	1,635
2.4	East Asia and the Pacific	('000)	13,654	13,410	18,706	19,707	21,330
2.5	South Asia	('000)	303	255	326	363	375
2.6	Middle East	('000)	35	25	31	46	62
	Arrivals by means of transport used						
3.1	Air	('000)	6,891	4,981	7,015	7,803	8,625
3.2	Rail	('000)	..	..	..	..	..
3.3	Road	('000)	7,166	8,350	11,969	12,768	13,550
3.4	Sea	('000)	2,509	2,206	2,827	2,788	3,076
	Arrivals by purpose of visit						
4.1	Leisure, recreation and holidays	('000)	..	..	6,770	7,450	8,211
4.2	Business and professional	('000)	..	..	3,407	3,572	3,862
4.3	Other	('000)	..	..	3,477	3,751	3,748
	Accommodation						
5.1	Overnight stays in hotels and similar establishments	('000)	..	..	..	..	..
5.2	Guests in hotels and similar establishments	('000)	..	..	..	..	..
5.3	Overnight stays in all types of accommodation establishments	('000)	..	..	..	..	..
5.4	Average length of stay of non-resident tourists in all accommodation establishments	Nights	3.62	4.06	3.73	3.66	3.46
6.1	**Tourism expenditure in the country** (**)	US$ Mn	9,849	9,004	11,874	13,588	15,311
6.2	"Travel" (*)	US$ Mn	7,410	7,072	8,918	10,179	11,461
6.3	"Passenger transport" (*)	US$ Mn	2,439	1,932	2,956	3,409	3,850
	DOMESTIC TOURISM						
	Accommodation						
7.1	Overnight stays in hotels and similar establishments	('000)	..	..	..	..	..
7.2	Guests in hotels and similar establishments	('000)	..	..	..	..	..
7.3	Overnight stays in all types of accommodation establishments	('000)	..	..	..	..	..
7.4	Average length of stay of resident tourists in all accommodation establishments	Nights	..	..	..	..	..
	OUTBOUND TOURISM						
8.1	**Departures**	('000)	64,540	60,936	68,903	72,300	75,812
8.2	**Tourism expenditure in other countries**	US$ Mn	..	..	..	..	..
8.3	"Travel" (*)	US$ Mn	12,418	11,447	13,270	13,305	13,974
8.4	"Passenger transport" (*)	US$ Mn	..	..	..	..	..
	TOURISM INDUSTRIES						
	Hotels and similar establishments						
9.1	Number of rooms	Units	43,624	42,936	44,362	48,891	52,512
9.2	Number of bed-places	Units	..	..	..	..	..
9.3	Occupancy rate	Percent	84.00	70.00	88.00	86.00	87.00
9.4	Average length of stay	Nights	..	..	..	..	..
	RELATED INDICATORS						
	Share of tourism expenditure (6.1) in:						
10.1	Gross Domestic Product (GDP)	Percent	6.0	5.7	7.2	7.6	8.1
10.2	Exports of goods	Percent	4.9	4.0	4.6	4.7	4.8
10.3	Exports of services	Percent	22.1	19.3	21.5	21.3	21.1

(*) Balance of Payments items: 6.1 to 6.3 correspond to the "Credit" side (and are receipts for the country) while 8.2 to 8.4 correspond to the "Debit" side (and are expenditures in other countries).

(**) See Annex "Country notes".

HUNGARY

Basic Indicators		Units	2002	2003	2004	2005	2006
	INBOUND TOURISM						
	Arrivals						
1.1	Visitors	('000)	31,739	31,412	33,934	36,173	38,318
1.2	Tourists (overnight visitors)	('000)	..	..	12,212	9,979	9,259
1.3	Same-day visitors	('000)	..	..	21,722	26,194	29,059
1.4	Cruise passengers	('000)	..	..	518	428	232
	Arrivals by region						
2.1	Africa	('000)	6	6	12	10	8
2.2	Americas	('000)	170	174	202	218	245
2.3	Europe	('000)	2,689	2,627	2,861	2,986	2,828
2.4	East Asia and the Pacific	('000)	83	77	105	133	123
2.5	South Asia	('000)	..	..	..	..	..
2.6	Middle East	('000)	..	..	..	..	..
	Arrivals by means of transport used						
3.1	Air	('000)	1,302	1,353	2,282	2,084	2,110
3.2	Rail	('000)	1,746	1,611	1,549	1,516	1,653
3.3	Road	('000)	28,524	28,256	32,548	34,665	36,951
3.4	Sea	('000)	168	191	256	290	249
	Arrivals by purpose of visit						
4.1	Leisure, recreation and holidays	('000)	..	..	11,128	10,982	10,709
4.2	Business and professional	('000)	..	..	1,569	1,740	1,710
4.3	Other	('000)	..	..	21,237	23,451	25,899
	Accommodation						
5.1	Overnight stays in hotels and similar establishments	('000)	8,260	8,046	8,729	9,127	8,524
5.2	Guests in hotels and similar establishments	('000)	2,659	2,599	2,951	3,140	3,009
5.3	Overnight stays in all types of accommodation establishments	('000)	10,361	10,040	10,508	10,779	10,046
5.4	Average length of stay of non-resident tourists in all accommodation establishments	Nights	3.44	3.41	3.21	3.13	3.04
6.1	**Tourism expenditure in the country**	US$ Mn	3,774	4,119	4,129	4,717	4,943
6.2	"Travel" (*)	US$ Mn	3,728	4,061	4,034	4,120	4,254
6.3	"Passenger transport" (*)	US$ Mn	46	58	95	597	689
	DOMESTIC TOURISM						
	Accommodation						
7.1	Overnight stays in hotels and similar establishments	('000)	5,574	5,824	5,933	6,622	7,284
7.2	Guests in hotels and similar establishments	('000)	2,273	2,380	2,452	2,778	3,007
7.3	Overnight stays in all types of accommodation establishments	('000)	8,089	8,571	8,391	8,958	9,606
7.4	Average length of stay of resident tourists in all accommodation establishments	Nights	2.56	2.55	2.51	2.48	2.48
	OUTBOUND TOURISM						
8.1	**Departures**	('000)	12,966	14,283	17,558	18,622	17,612
8.2	**Tourism expenditure in other countries**	US$ Mn	2,211	2,700	2,909	2,826	2,568
8.3	"Travel" (*)	US$ Mn	2,133	2,594	2,848	2,382	2,126
8.4	"Passenger transport" (*)	US$ Mn	78	106	61	444	442
	TOURISM INDUSTRIES						
	Hotels and similar establishments						
9.1	Number of rooms	Units	62,415	64,091	64,263	66,066	66,873
9.2	Number of bed-places	Units	154,643	158,634	157,970	162,235	158,762
9.3	Occupancy rate	Percent	40.00	38.60	41.00	42.10	42.40
9.4	Average length of stay	Nights	2.81	2.79	2.71	2.66	2.63
	RELATED INDICATORS						
	Share of tourism expenditure (6.1) in:						
10.1	Gross Domestic Product (GDP)	Percent	5.7	4.9	4.0	4.3	4.4
10.2	Exports of goods	Percent	10.8	9.6	7.4	7.6	6.6
10.3	Exports of services	Percent	50.9	44.7	37.9	36.9	37.2

(*) Balance of Payments items: 6.1 to 6.3 correspond to the "Credit" side (and are receipts for the country) while 8.2 to 8.4 correspond to the "Debit" side (and are expenditures in other countries).

Basic Indicators	Units	2002	2003	2004	2005	2006
INBOUND TOURISM						
Arrivals						
1.1 Visitors	('000)	..	..	..	..	..
1.2 Tourists (overnight visitors)	('000)	705	771	836	871	971
1.3 Same-day visitors	('000)	..	..	..	..	..
1.4 Cruise passengers	('000)	30	31	45	55	55
Arrivals by region						
2.1 Africa	('000)	..	..	..	1	2
2.2 Americas	('000)	69	72	75	85	87
2.3 Europe	('000)	593	643	707	715	785
2.4 East Asia and the Pacific	('000)	7	9	11	30	33
2.5 South Asia	('000)	..	..	..	..	..
2.6 Middle East	('000)	..	..	..	..	..
Arrivals by means of transport used						
3.1 Air	('000)	278	309	349	361	399
3.2 Rail	('000)	..	..	..	..	..
3.3 Road	('000)	..	..	..	..	..
3.4 Sea	('000)	37	39	54	66	72
Arrivals by purpose of visit						
4.1 Leisure, recreation and holidays	('000)	..	..	..	..	..
4.2 Business and professional	('000)	..	..	..	..	..
4.3 Other	('000)	..	..	..	..	..
Accommodation						
5.1 Overnight stays in hotels and similar establishments	('000)	970	1,070	1,146	1,208	1,341
5.2 Guests in hotels and similar establishments	('000)	513	569	615	643	714
5.3 Overnight stays in all types of accommodation establishments	('000)	1,257	1,377	1,479	1,550	1,719
5.4 Average length of stay of non-resident tourists in all accommodation establishments	Nights	1.80	1.80	1.80	1.80	1.80
6.1 **Tourism expenditure in the country**	US$ Mn	415	486	558	630	663
6.2 "Travel" (*)	US$ Mn	256	319	370	408	439
6.3 "Passenger transport" (*)	US$ Mn	159	167	188	222	224
DOMESTIC TOURISM						
Accommodation						
7.1 Overnight stays in hotels and similar establishments	('000)	290	299	323	361	387
7.2 Guests in hotels and similar establishments	('000)	187	194	205	229	245
7.3 Overnight stays in all types of accommodation establishments	('000)	604	608	651	683	738
7.4 Average length of stay of resident tourists in all accommodation establishments	Nights	1.60	1.50	1.60	1.60	1.60
OUTBOUND TOURISM						
8.1 **Departures**	('000)	..	..	..	..	..
8.2 **Tourism expenditure in other countries**	US$ Mn	373	524	699	991	1,084
8.3 "Travel" (*)	US$ Mn	371	523	697	980	1,076
8.4 "Passenger transport" (*)	US$ Mn	2	1	2	11	8
TOURISM INDUSTRIES						
Hotels and similar establishments						
9.1 Number of rooms	Units	6,807	7,330	7,502	8,005	8,025
9.2 Number of bed-places	Units	14,009	14,948	15,517	16,639	16,849
9.3 Occupancy rate	Percent	44.30	42.30	43.30	45.00	47.00
9.4 Average length of stay	Nights	1.80	1.80	1.80	1.80	1.80
RELATED INDICATORS						
Share of tourism expenditure (6.1) in:						
10.1 Gross Domestic Product (GDP)	Percent	4.8	4.5	4.3	4.0	4.2
10.2 Exports of goods	Percent	18.5	20.4	19.3	20.3	19.1
10.3 Exports of services	Percent	37.1	35.3	34.4	30.9	36.2

(*) Balance of Payments items: 6.1 to 6.3 correspond to the "Credit" side (and are receipts for the country) while 8.2 to 8.4 correspond to the "Debit" side (and are expenditures in other countries).

INDIA

Basic Indicators	Units	2002	2003	2004	2005	2006
INBOUND TOURISM						
Arrivals						
1.1 Visitors	('000)	2,428	2,774	3,512	4,038	4,626
1.2 Tourists (overnight visitors)	('000)	2,384	2,726	3,457	3,919	4,447
1.3 Same-day visitors	('000)	..	..	..	..	..
1.4 Cruise passengers	('000)	44	48	55	119	179
Arrivals by region						
2.1 Africa	('000)	80	89	112	131	137
2.2 Americas	('000)	459	540	690	804	912
2.3 Europe	('000)	797	942	1,257	1,435	1,662
2.4 East Asia and the Pacific	('000)	328	393	512	585	702
2.5 South Asia	('000)	631	667	791	842	909
2.6 Middle East	('000)	66	69	80	86	98
Arrivals by means of transport used						
3.1 Air	('000)	1,953	2,265	2,960	3,390	3,873
3.2 Rail	('000)	..	..	..	..	..
3.3 Road	('000)	417	447	480	513	547
3.4 Sea	('000)	14	14	17	16	27
Arrivals by purpose of visit						
4.1 Leisure, recreation and holidays	('000)	2,272	2,538	3,357	3,785	4,358
4.2 Business and professional	('000)	112	188	100	133	89
4.3 Other	('000)	..	..	..	..	..
Accommodation						
5.1 Overnight stays in hotels and similar establishments	('000)					
5.2 Guests in hotels and similar establishments	('000)	..	..	..	..	..
5.3 Overnight stays in all types of accommodation establishments	('000)	..	..	..	..	..
5.4 Average length of stay of non-resident tourists in all accommodation establishments	Nights	..	..	..	..	..
6.1 **Tourism expenditure in the country**	US$ Mn	3,300	4,560	6,307	7,652	9,227
6.2 "Travel" (*)	US$ Mn	3,102	4,463	6,170	7,493	8,934
6.3 "Passenger transport" (*)	US$ Mn	198	97	137	159	293
DOMESTIC TOURISM						
Accommodation						
7.1 Overnight stays in hotels and similar establishments	('000)	..	..	..	..	..
7.2 Guests in hotels and similar establishments	('000)	..	..	..	..	..
7.3 Overnight stays in all types of accommodation establishments	('000)	..	..	..	..	..
7.4 Average length of stay of resident tourists in all accommodation establishments	Nights	..	..	..	..	..
OUTBOUND TOURISM						
8.1 **Departures**	('000)	4,940	5,351	6,213	7,185	8,340
8.2 **Tourism expenditure in other countries**	US$ Mn	4,350	4,385	5,783	7,798	9,296
8.3 "Travel" (*)	US$ Mn	2,988	3,585	4,816	6,013	7,352
8.4 "Passenger transport" (*)	US$ Mn	1,362	800	967	1,785	1,944
TOURISM INDUSTRIES						
Hotels and similar establishments						
9.1 Number of rooms	Units	85,481	91,720	97,770	67,613	75,502
9.2 Number of bed-places	Units	170,962	183,440	195,540	135,226	151,672
9.3 Occupancy rate	Percent	55.40	60.70	65.10	67.70	..
9.4 Average length of stay	Nights	..	..	..	..	..
RELATED INDICATORS						
Share of tourism expenditure (6.1) in:						
10.1 Gross Domestic Product (GDP)	Percent	0.6	0.8	0.9	0.9	1.0
10.2 Exports of goods	Percent	6.5	7.5	8.1	7.5	7.5
10.3 Exports of services	Percent	16.9	19.1	16.5	13.7	12.2

(*) Balance of Payments items: 6.1 to 6.3 correspond to the "Credit" side (and are receipts for the country) while 8.2 to 8.4 correspond to the "Debit" side (and are expenditures in other countries).

INDONESIA

Basic Indicators	Units	2002	2003	2004	2005	2006
INBOUND TOURISM						
Arrivals						
1.1 Visitors	('000)	..	..	..	..	..
1.2 Tourists (overnight visitors)	('000)	5,033	4,467	5,321	5,002	4,871
1.3 Same-day visitors	('000)	..	..	..	..	..
1.4 Cruise passengers	('000)	..	..	..	..	..
Arrivals by region						
2.1 Africa	('000)	37	30	36	27	23
2.2 Americas	('000)	222	176	210	210	185
2.3 Europe	('000)	808	606	721	798	730
2.4 East Asia and the Pacific	('000)	3,877	3,576	4,266	3,837	3,795
2.5 South Asia	('000)	52	48	54	69	83
2.6 Middle East	('000)	38	31	36	61	55
Arrivals by means of transport used						
3.1 Air	('000)	2,745	2,178	2,790	2,889	2,822
3.2 Rail	('000)	..	..	..	..	..
3.3 Road	('000)	32	27	22	31	30
3.4 Sea	('000)	2,256	2,262	2,509	2,082	2,019
Arrivals by purpose of visit						
4.1 Leisure, recreation and holidays	('000)	2,903	2,316	2,827	2,835	2,754
4.2 Business and professional	('000)	2,056	1,914	2,191	2,063	1,952
4.3 Other	('000)	74	237	303	104	166
Accommodation						
5.1 Overnight stays in hotels and similar establishments	('000)	..	..	..	..	..
5.2 Guests in hotels and similar establishments	('000)	3,947	3,380	4,248	3,883	3,621
5.3 Overnight stays in all types of accommodation establishments	('000)	..	..	..	..	..
5.4 Average length of stay of non-resident tourists in all accommodation establishments	Nights	3.09	2.99	3.04	2.90	3.20
6.1 **Tourism expenditure in the country**	US$ Mn	5,797	4,461	5,226	5,094	4,890
6.2 "Travel" (*)	US$ Mn	5,285	4,037	4,798	4,522	4,448
6.3 "Passenger transport" (*)	US$ Mn	512	424	428	572	442
DOMESTIC TOURISM						
Accommodation						
7.1 Overnight stays in hotels and similar establishments	('000)	..	..	..	..	..
7.2 Guests in hotels and similar establishments	('000)	9,861	10,582	11,682	11,610	11,659
7.3 Overnight stays in all types of accommodation establishments	('000)	..	..	..	..	..
7.4 Average length of stay of resident tourists in all accommodation establishments	Nights	1.72	1.71	1.68	1.70	1.86
OUTBOUND TOURISM						
8.1 **Departures**	('000)	..	3,491	3,941	4,106	4,341
8.2 **Tourism expenditure in other countries**	US$ Mn	5,042	4,427	4,569	4,740	5,028
8.3 "Travel" (*)	US$ Mn	3,289	3,082	3,507	3,584	3,600
8.4 "Passenger transport" (*)	US$ Mn	1,753	1,345	1,062	1,156	1,428
TOURISM INDUSTRIES						
Hotels and similar establishments						
9.1 Number of rooms	Units	259,741	263,014	272,939	280,433	285,530
9.2 Number of bed-places	Units	423,908	428,813	441,032	449,622	456,021
9.3 Occupancy rate	Percent	44.28	45.03	43.30	45.49	46.18
9.4 Average length of stay	Nights	2.07	1.99	2.00	1.99	2.17
RELATED INDICATORS						
Share of tourism expenditure (6.1) in:						
10.1 Gross Domestic Product (GDP)	Percent	3.0	1.9	2.0	1.8	1.3
10.2 Exports of goods	Percent	9.8	7.0	7.4	5.9	4.7
10.3 Exports of services	Percent	87.0	84.3	43.4	39.4	42.5

(*) Balance of Payments items: 6.1 to 6.3 correspond to the "Credit" side (and are receipts for the country) while 8.2 to 8.4 correspond to the "Debit" side (and are expenditures in other countries).

IRAN, ISLAMIC REPUBLIC OF

Basic Indicators		Units	2002	2003	2004	2005	2006
	INBOUND TOURISM						
	Arrivals						
1.1	Visitors	('000)	..	..	..	..	..
1.2	Tourists (overnight visitors)	('000)	1,585	1,546	1,659	..	..
1.3	Same-day visitors	('000)	..	..	..	..	..
1.4	Cruise passengers	('000)	..	..	..	..	..
	Arrivals by region						
2.1	Africa	('000)	..	..	..	..	..
2.2	Americas	('000)	..	..	..	..	..
2.3	Europe	('000)	..	..	..	..	..
2.4	East Asia and the Pacific	('000)	..	..	..	..	..
2.5	South Asia	('000)	..	..	..	..	..
2.6	Middle East	('000)	..	..	..	..	..
	Arrivals by means of transport used						
3.1	Air	('000)	429	..	545	..	..
3.2	Rail	('000)	..	..	..	..	..
3.3	Road	('000)	1,144	..	1,080	..	..
3.4	Sea	('000)	11	..	33	..	..
	Arrivals by purpose of visit						
4.1	Leisure, recreation and holidays	('000)	..	..	..	..	..
4.2	Business and professional	('000)	..	..	..	..	..
4.3	Other	('000)	..	..	..	..	..
	Accommodation						
5.1	Overnight stays in hotels and similar establishments	('000)	830	854	..	..	..
5.2	Guests in hotels and similar establishments	('000)	323	313	..	..	..
5.3	Overnight stays in all types of accommodation establishments	('000)	..	..	..	..	..
5.4	Average length of stay of non-resident tourists in all accommodation establishments	Nights	2.25	2.73	..	..	..
6.1	**Tourism expenditure in the country**	US$ Mn	1,607	1,266	1,305	1,364	1,513
6.2	"Travel" (*)	US$ Mn	1,357	1,033	1,044	1,069	1,194
6.3	"Passenger transport" (*)	US$ Mn	250	233	261	295	319
	DOMESTIC TOURISM						
	Accommodation						
7.1	Overnight stays in hotels and similar establishments	('000)	4,874	4,910	..	..	..
7.2	Guests in hotels and similar establishments	('000)	2,330	2,516	..	..	..
7.3	Overnight stays in all types of accommodation establishments	('000)	..	..	..	..	..
7.4	Average length of stay of resident tourists in all accommodation establishments	Nights	2.04	1.95	..	..	..
	OUTBOUND TOURISM						
8.1	**Departures**	('000)	2,921	..	..	..	..
8.2	**Tourism expenditure in other countries**	US$ Mn	3,990	4,120	4,402	4,560	5,004
8.3	"Travel" (*)	US$ Mn	3,750	3,842	4,093	4,202	4,597
8.4	"Passenger transport" (*)	US$ Mn	240	278	309	358	407
	TOURISM INDUSTRIES						
	Hotels and similar establishments						
9.1	Number of rooms	Units	24,199	27,148	32,360	..	..
9.2	Number of bed-places	Units	53,908	56,618	66,289	..	..
9.3	Occupancy rate	Percent	37.00	36.00	..	..	..
9.4	Average length of stay	Nights	2.16	2.04	..	..	..
	RELATED INDICATORS						
	Share of tourism expenditure (6.1) in:						
10.1	Gross Domestic Product (GDP)	Percent	1.4	0.9	0.8	0.7	0.7
10.2	Exports of goods	Percent	5.7	3.7	3.0	2.1	2.0
10.3	Exports of services	Percent	..	..	..	..	..

(*) Balance of Payments items: 6.1 to 6.3 correspond to the "Credit" side (and are receipts for the country) while 8.2 to 8.4 correspond to the "Debit" side (and are expenditures in other countries).

Basic Indicators	Units	2002	2003	2004	2005	2006
INBOUND TOURISM						
Arrivals						
1.1 Visitors	('000)	..	..	..	..	..
1.2 Tourists (overnight visitors)	('000)	6,476	6,764	6,953	7,333	8,001
1.3 Same-day visitors	('000)	305	334	349	367	424
1.4 Cruise passengers	('000)	..	..	..	..	..
Arrivals by region						
2.1 Africa	('000)	29	32	42	39	48
2.2 Americas	('000)	860	913	975	956	1,058
2.3 Europe	('000)	5,387	5,623	5,677	6,113	6,658
2.4 East Asia and the Pacific	('000)	201	196	259	226	237
2.5 South Asia	('000)	..	..	..	..	..
2.6 Middle East	('000)	..	..	..	..	..
Arrivals by means of transport used						
3.1 Air	('000)	4,439	4,819	4,980	5,546	6,304
3.2 Rail	('000)	..	..	..	..	..
3.3 Road	('000)	735	710	761	705	733
3.4 Sea	('000)	1,302	1,236	1,213	1,082	964
Arrivals by purpose of visit						
4.1 Leisure, recreation and holidays	('000)	3,665	3,726	3,803	3,832	4,177
4.2 Business and professional	('000)	838	815	890	910	1,026
4.3 Other	('000)	1,973	2,223	2,260	2,591	2,799
Accommodation						
5.1 Overnight stays in hotels and similar establishments	('000)	17,714	18,039	17,934	17,446	19,080
5.2 Guests in hotels and similar establishments	('000)	..	..	..	..	..
5.3 Overnight stays in all types of accommodation establishments	('000)	45,346	47,613	47,375	50,678	56,342
5.4 Average length of stay of non-resident tourists in all accommodation establishments	Nights	7.66	7.71	7.42	7.49	7.60
6.1 **Tourism expenditure in the country**	US$ Mn	4,228	5,206	6,075	6,780	7,664
6.2 "Travel" (*)	US$ Mn	3,097	3,862	4,375	4,782	5,369
6.3 "Passenger transport" (*)	US$ Mn	1,131	1,344	1,700	1,998	2,295
DOMESTIC TOURISM						
Accommodation						
7.1 Overnight stays in hotels and similar establishments	('000)	7,395	7,829	7,799	8,174	7,978
7.2 Guests in hotels and similar establishments	('000)	..	..	..	..	..
7.3 Overnight stays in all types of accommodation establishments	('000)	22,222	23,616	24,189	24,607	24,203
7.4 Average length of stay of resident tourists in all accommodation establishments	Nights	3.40	3.50	3.50	3.40	3.30
OUTBOUND TOURISM						
8.1 **Departures**	('000)	4,634	4,929	5,409	6,113	6,848
8.2 **Tourism expenditure in other countries**	US$ Mn	3,835	4,832	5,291	6,186	6,978
8.3 "Travel" (*)	US$ Mn	3,755	4,736	5,177	6,074	6,862
8.4 "Passenger transport" (*)	US$ Mn	80	96	114	112	116
TOURISM INDUSTRIES						
Hotels and similar establishments						
9.1 Number of rooms	Units	62,807	63,077	62,402	64,163	63,413
9.2 Number of bed-places	Units	145,641	146,920	145,299	149,617	148,819
9.3 Occupancy rate	Percent	59.00	60.00	60.00	62.00	64.00
9.4 Average length of stay	Nights	..	..	..	..	..
RELATED INDICATORS						
Share of tourism expenditure (6.1) in:						
10.1 Gross Domestic Product (GDP)	Percent	3.4	3.3	3.3	3.4	3.4
10.2 Exports of goods	Percent	5.0	5.9	6.1	6.6	7.3
10.3 Exports of services	Percent	14.1	12.4	11.5	11.3	11.1

(*) Balance of Payments items: 6.1 to 6.3 correspond to the "Credit" side (and are receipts for the country) while 8.2 to 8.4 correspond to the "Debit" side (and are expenditures in other countries).

ISRAEL

Basic Indicators		Units	2002	2003	2004	2005	2006
	INBOUND TOURISM						
	Arrivals						
1.1	Visitors	('000)	862.1	..	1,505.8	1,916	1,834
1.2	Tourists (overnight visitors)	('000)	861.9	1,063	1,505.6	1,903	1,825
1.3	Same-day visitors	('000)	..	..	..	..	..
1.4	Cruise passengers	('000)	0.3	..	0.2	13	9
	Arrivals by region						
2.1	Africa	('000)	29	30	40	41	54
2.2	Americas	('000)	261	348	487	603	607
2.3	Europe	('000)	484	598	857	1,107	1,016
2.4	East Asia and the Pacific	('000)	36	42	66	88	94
2.5	South Asia	('000)	11	10	15	23	23
2.6	Middle East	('000)	28	23	29	30	21
	Arrivals by means of transport used						
3.1	Air	('000)	778	972	1,339	1,653	1,568
3.2	Rail	('000)	..	..	..	..	..
3.3	Road	('000)	80	88	162	245	255
3.4	Sea	('000)	3	4	5	5	2
	Arrivals by purpose of visit						
4.1	Leisure, recreation and holidays	('000)	194	255	361	478	347
4.2	Business and professional	('000)	164	213	286	312	237
4.3	Other	('000)	504	595	858	1,113	1,241
	Accommodation						
5.1	Overnight stays in hotels and similar establishments	('000)	2,628	3,285	4,771	6,783	6,854
5.2	Guests in hotels and similar establishments	('000)	694	900	1,374	2,005	2,131
5.3	Overnight stays in all types of accommodation establishments	('000)	2,745	3,438	5,040	7,133	7,212
5.4	Average length of stay of non-resident tourists in all accommodation establishments	Nights	22.00	20.00	22.00	18.00	17.00
6.1	**Tourism expenditure in the country**	US$ Mn	2,426	2,473	2,863	3,358	3,319
6.2	"Travel" (*) (**)	US$ Mn	2,145	2,132	2,430	2,797	2,777
6.3	"Passenger transport" (*)	US$ Mn	281	341	433	561	542
	DOMESTIC TOURISM						
	Accommodation						
7.1	Overnight stays in hotels and similar establishments	('000)	11,978	11,810	12,202	12,304	12,454
7.2	Guests in hotels and similar establishments	('000)	5,134	5,060	5,180	5,154	5,178
7.3	Overnight stays in all types of accommodation establishments	('000)	14,025	13,855	14,230	14,413	14,651
7.4	Average length of stay of resident tourists in all accommodation establishments	Nights	..	..	..	..	..
	OUTBOUND TOURISM						
8.1	**Departures**	('000)	3,273	3,299	3,614	3,687	3,713
8.2	**Tourism expenditure in other countries**	US$ Mn	3,323	3,342	3,663	3,780	3,870
8.3	"Travel" (*)	US$ Mn	2,543	2,550	2,796	2,895	2,983
8.4	"Passenger transport" (*)	US$ Mn	780	792	867	885	887
	TOURISM INDUSTRIES						
	Hotels and similar establishments						
9.1	Number of rooms	Units	46,935	46,324	46,333	46,701	46,555
9.2	Number of bed-places	Units	114,737	114,042	114,792	114,766	114,462
9.3	Occupancy rate	Percent	38.80	39.70	44.20	49.90	49.60
9.4	Average length of stay	Nights	3.79	2.53	2.59	3.50	3.22
	RELATED INDICATORS						
	Share of tourism expenditure (6.1) in:						
10.1	Gross Domestic Product (GDP)	Percent	2.3	2.2	2.4	2.7	2.2
10.2	Exports of goods	Percent	8.8	8.2	7.8	8.4	7.6
10.3	Exports of services	Percent	20.4	18.5	17.9	19.2	17.2

(*) Balance of Payments items: 6.1 to 6.3 correspond to the "Credit" side (and are receipts for the country) while 8.2 to 8.4 correspond to the "Debit" side (and are expenditures in other countries).

(**) See Annex "Country notes".

Basic Indicators	Units	2002	2003	2004	2005	2006
INBOUND TOURISM						
Arrivals						
1.1 Visitors	('000)	63,561	63,026	58,480	59,230	66,353
1.2 Tourists (overnight visitors)	('000)	39,799	39,604	37,071	36,513	41,058
1.3 Same-day visitors	('000)	23,762	23,422	21,409	22,717	25,295
1.4 Cruise passengers	('000)	..	..	..	..	..
Arrivals by region						
2.1 Africa	('000)	179	122	206	251	254
2.2 Americas	('000)	2,065	1,680	2,988	3,250	3,579
2.3 Europe	('000)	36,001	36,584	32,522	31,571	35,594
2.4 East Asia and the Pacific	('000)	1,383	1,075	1,088	1,112	1,189
2.5 South Asia	('000)	89	67	135	115	190
2.6 Middle East	('000)	82	76	130	213	247
Arrivals by means of transport used						
3.1 Air	('000)	11,567	12,062	16,927	18,592	21,520
3.2 Rail	('000)	2,727	2,574	2,027	1,935	1,900
3.3 Road	('000)	46,354	45,457	37,504	36,577	41,032
3.4 Sea	('000)	2,913	2,932	2,022	2,126	1,901
Arrivals by purpose of visit						
4.1 Leisure, recreation and holidays	('000)	27,548	27,350	26,629	25,991	29,146
4.2 Business and professional	('000)	10,630	9,754	8,597	9,190	10,833
4.3 Other	('000)	25,383	25,922	23,253	24,048	26,374
Accommodation						
5.1 Overnight stays in hotels and similar establishments	('000)	97,837	93,935	97,175	102,312	107,859
5.2 Guests in hotels and similar establishments	('000)	29,340	28,174	29,916	30,943	33,513
5.3 Overnight stays in all types of accommodation establishments	('000)	145,560	139,653	141,169	148,501	156,861
5.4 Average length of stay of non-resident tourists in all accommodation establishments	Nights	..	3.99	3.84	3.89	3.81
6.1 Tourism expenditure in the country	US$ Mn	28,192	32,591	37,870	38,374	41,644
6.2 "Travel" (*)	US$ Mn	26,873	31,247	35,378	35,319	38,257
6.3 "Passenger transport" (*)	US$ Mn	1,319	1,344	2,492	3,055	3,387
DOMESTIC TOURISM						
Accommodation						
7.1 Overnight stays in hotels and similar establishments	('000)	133,295	135,217	136,845	138,123	140,397
7.2 Guests in hotels and similar establishments	('000)	38,011	39,155	40,767	41,276	42,521
7.3 Overnight stays in all types of accommodation establishments	('000)	199,687	204,760	204,447	206,754	209,903
7.4 Average length of stay of resident tourists in all accommodation establishments	Nights	..	4.29	4.15	4.12	4.05
OUTBOUND TOURISM						
8.1 **Departures**	('000)	25,126	26,817	23,349	24,796	25,697
8.2 **Tourism expenditure in other countries**	US$ Mn	19,636	23,731	24,064	26,771	27,437
8.3 "Travel" (*)	US$ Mn	16,924	20,589	20,460	22,370	23,152
8.4 "Passenger transport" (*)	US$ Mn	2,712	3,142	3,604	4,401	4,285
TOURISM INDUSTRIES						
Hotels and similar establishments						
9.1 Number of rooms	Units	986,326	999,722	1,011,773	1,020,478	1,034,710
9.2 Number of bed-places	Units	1,929,544	1,969,495	1,999,729	2,028,452	2,087,010
9.3 Occupancy rate	Percent	39.60	39.63	39.80	40.10	40.80
9.4 Average length of stay	Nights	4.21	4.16	4.02	4.02	3.94
RELATED INDICATORS						
Share of tourism expenditure (6.1) in:						
10.1 Gross Domestic Product (GDP)	Percent	2.3	2.2	2.2	2.2	2.3
10.2 Exports of goods	Percent	11.2	10.9	10.8	10.3	10.0
10.3 Exports of services	Percent	46.6	45.4	44.8	43.0	42.2

(*) Balance of Payments items: 6.1 to 6.3 correspond to the "Credit" side (and are receipts for the country) while 8.2 to 8.4 correspond to the "Debit" side (and are expenditures in other countries).

JAMAICA

Basic Indicators	Units	2002	2003	2004	2005	2006
INBOUND TOURISM						
Arrivals						
1.1 Visitors	('000)	2,131	2,483	2,515	2,615	3,016
1.2 Tourists (overnight visitors)	('000)	1,266	1,350	1,415	1,479	1,679
1.3 Same-day visitors	('000)	..	..	..	..	..
1.4 Cruise passengers	('000)	865	1,133	1,100	1,136	1,337
Arrivals by region						
2.1 Africa	('000)	1	1	1	1	1
2.2 Americas	('000)	1,076	1,120	1,162	1,234	1,411
2.3 Europe	('000)	180	219	243	235	257
2.4 East Asia and the Pacific	('000)	8	9	8	8	8
2.5 South Asia	('000)	1	1	1	..	1
2.6 Middle East	('000)	..	..	..	..	..
Arrivals by means of transport used						
3.1 Air	('000)	1,266	1,350	1,415	1,479	1,679
3.2 Rail	('000)	..	..	..	..	..
3.3 Road	('000)	..	..	..	..	..
3.4 Sea	('000)	..	..	..	..	..
Arrivals by purpose of visit						
4.1 Leisure, recreation and holidays	('000)	962	1,064	1,132	1,166	1,347
4.2 Business and professional	('000)	73	71	78	84	101
4.3 Other	('000)	231	215	205	228	231
Accommodation						
5.1 Overnight stays in hotels and similar establishments	('000)	5,544	5,687	6,076	6,967	7,812
5.2 Guests in hotels and similar establishments	('000)	852	887	932	995	1,125
5.3 Overnight stays in all types of accommodation establishments	('000)	12,038	12,844	13,134	13,608	15,465
5.4 Average length of stay of non-resident tourists in all accommodation establishments	Nights	10.20	10.20	9.90	9.80	9.80
6.1 **Tourism expenditure in the country**	US$ Mn	1,482	1,621	1,733	1,783	2,094
6.2 "Travel" (*)	US$ Mn	1,209	1,355	1,438	1,545	1,870
6.3 "Passenger transport" (*)	US$ Mn	273	266	295	238	224
DOMESTIC TOURISM						
Accommodation						
7.1 Overnight stays in hotels and similar establishments	('000)	..	..	..	..	..
7.2 Guests in hotels and similar establishments	('000)	..	..	..	..	..
7.3 Overnight stays in all types of accommodation establishments	('000)	..	..	..	..	..
7.4 Average length of stay of resident tourists in all accommodation establishments	Nights	..	..	..	..	..
OUTBOUND TOURISM						
8.1 **Departures**	('000)	..	..	..	..	..
8.2 **Tourism expenditure in other countries**	US$ Mn	274	269	318	290	315
8.3 "Travel" (*)	US$ Mn	258	252	286	249	273
8.4 "Passenger transport" (*)	US$ Mn	16	17	32	41	42
TOURISM INDUSTRIES						
Hotels and similar establishments						
9.1 Number of rooms	Units	20,425	20,827	21,322	22,528	23,104
9.2 Number of bed-places	Units	43,132	43,909	44,355	46,905	48,040
9.3 Occupancy rate	Percent	55.50	57.90	61.40	61.90	62.80
9.4 Average length of stay	Nights	6.40	6.40	6.50	6.90	6.90
RELATED INDICATORS						
Share of tourism expenditure (6.1) in:						
10.1 Gross Domestic Product (GDP)	Percent	17.2	19.6	19.5	18.3	19.9
10.2 Exports of goods	Percent	113.2	117.0	108.2	107.2	98.1
10.3 Exports of services	Percent	77.5	75.8	75.4	76.5	79.0

(*) Balance of Payments items: 6.1 to 6.3 correspond to the "Credit" side (and are receipts for the country) while 8.2 to 8.4 correspond to the "Debit" side (and are expenditures in other countries).

Basic Indicators	Units	2002	2003	2004	2005	2006
INBOUND TOURISM						
Arrivals						
1.1 Visitors	('000)	5,239	5,212	6,138	6,728	7,334
1.2 Tourists (overnight visitors)	('000)	..	..	..	..	..
1.3 Same-day visitors	('000)	..	..	..	..	..
1.4 Cruise passengers	('000)	..	..	..	..	..
Arrivals by region						
2.1 Africa	('000)	17	16	17	21	19
2.2 Americas	('000)	928	824	951	1,032	1,035
2.3 Europe	('000)	688	665	744	817	818
2.4 East Asia and the Pacific	('000)	3,528	3,625	4,338	4,761	5,362
2.5 South Asia	('000)	73	76	84	93	96
2.6 Middle East	('000)	3	3	3	3	3
Arrivals by means of transport used						
3.1 Air	('000)	5,496	5,428	6,399	7,022	7,607
3.2 Rail	('000)	..	..	..	..	..
3.3 Road	('000)	..	..	..	..	..
3.4 Sea	('000)	276	299	357	428	501
Arrivals by purpose of visit						
4.1 Leisure, recreation and holidays	('000)	3,095	3,055	3,840	4,369	4,981
4.2 Business and professional	('000)	1,287	1,281	1,383	1,477	1,523
4.3 Other	('000)	857	875	915	882	830
Accommodation						
5.1 Overnight stays in hotels and similar establishments	('000)					
5.2 Guests in hotels and similar establishments	('000)	..	..	..	..	..
5.3 Overnight stays in all types of accommodation establishments	('000)	..	..	..	..	..
5.4 Average length of stay of non-resident tourists in all accommodation establishments	Nights	8.30	8.50	8.10	8.00	7.20
6.1 **Tourism expenditure in the country**	US$ Mn	6,069	11,475	14,343	15,555	11,490
6.2 "Travel" (*)	US$ Mn	3,497	8,848	11,265	12,430	8,470
6.3 "Passenger transport" (*)	US$ Mn	2,572	2,627	3,078	3,125	3,020
DOMESTIC TOURISM						
Accommodation						
7.1 Overnight stays in hotels and similar establishments	('000)	286,000	269,000	255,000	..	..
7.2 Guests in hotels and similar establishments	('000)	..	..	..	..	..
7.3 Overnight stays in all types of accommodation establishments	('000)	..	..	..	..	..
7.4 Average length of stay of resident tourists in all accommodation establishments	Nights	..	..	..	..	..
OUTBOUND TOURISM						
8.1 **Departures**	('000)	16,523	13,296	16,831	17,404	17,535
8.2 **Tourism expenditure in other countries**	US$ Mn	34,977	36,505	48,175	48,102	37,659
8.3 "Travel" (*)	US$ Mn	26,656	28,958	38,252	37,565	26,876
8.4 "Passenger transport" (*)	US$ Mn	8,321	7,547	9,923	10,537	10,783
TOURISM INDUSTRIES						
Hotels and similar establishments						
9.1 Number of rooms	Units	1,564,689	1,562,867	1,551,876	1,548,449	..
9.2 Number of bed-places	Units	..	..	..	..	..
9.3 Occupancy rate	Percent	70.70	70.90	71.80	73.10	..
9.4 Average length of stay	Nights	..	..	..	..	..
RELATED INDICATORS						
Share of tourism expenditure (6.1) in:						
10.1 Gross Domestic Product (GDP)	Percent	0.2	0.3	0.3	0.3	0.3
10.2 Exports of goods	Percent	1.5	2.6	2.7	2.7	1.9
10.3 Exports of services	Percent	9.2	14.8	14.7	14.1	9.8

(*) Balance of Payments items: 6.1 to 6.3 correspond to the "Credit" side (and are receipts for the country) while 8.2 to 8.4 correspond to the "Debit" side (and are expenditures in other countries).

JORDAN

Basic Indicators	Units	2002	2003	2004	2005	2006
INBOUND TOURISM						
Arrivals						
1.1 Visitors	('000)	4,677	4,600	5,587	5,817	6,573
1.2 Tourists (overnight visitors)	('000)	2,384	2,353	2,853	2,987	3,225
1.3 Same-day visitors	('000)	2,293	2,247	2,734	2,831	3,348
1.4 Cruise passengers	('000)	4	3	9	26	41
Arrivals by region						
2.1 Africa	('000)	20	18	20	30	51
2.2 Americas	('000)	52	65	93	112	164
2.3 Europe	('000)	313	315	374	392	425
2.4 East Asia and the Pacific	('000)	43	44	60	64	83
2.5 South Asia	('000)	36	27	38	43	42
2.6 Middle East	('000)	1,498	1,465	1,781	1,829	1,880
Arrivals by means of transport used						
3.1 Air	('000)	948	1,028	1,407	1,449	1,885
3.2 Rail	('000)	2	2	2	1	1
3.3 Road	('000)	5,572	5,338	6,220	6,572	6,682
3.4 Sea	('000)	221	288	370	356	425
Arrivals by purpose of visit						
4.1 Leisure, recreation and holidays	('000)	..	..	..	..	..
4.2 Business and professional	('000)	..	..	..	..	..
4.3 Other	('000)	..	..	..	..	..
Accommodation						
5.1 Overnight stays in hotels and similar establishments	('000)	2,726	2,842	3,980	4,488	3,822
5.2 Guests in hotels and similar establishments	('000)	1,418	1,489	2,051	2,300	2,189
5.3 Overnight stays in all types of accommodation establishments	('000)	..	..	..	..	..
5.4 Average length of stay of non-resident tourists in all accommodation establishments	Nights	4.35	4.45	5.00	5.00	4.20
6.1 **Tourism expenditure in the country**	US$ Mn	1,254	1,266	1,621	1,759	2,008
6.2 "Travel" (*)	US$ Mn	1,048	1,062	1,330	1,441	1,642
6.3 "Passenger transport" (*)	US$ Mn	206	204	291	318	366
DOMESTIC TOURISM						
Accommodation						
7.1 Overnight stays in hotels and similar establishments	('000)	772	974	1,052	1,064	1,201
7.2 Guests in hotels and similar establishments	('000)	..	452	522	505	559
7.3 Overnight stays in all types of accommodation establishments	('000)	..	..	..	..	..
7.4 Average length of stay of resident tourists in all accommodation establishments	Nights	..	2.20	2.00	2.11	2.14
OUTBOUND TOURISM						
8.1 **Departures**	('000)	1,276	1,229	1,420	1,523	1,628
8.2 **Tourism expenditure in other countries**	US$ Mn	504	503	585	653	698
8.3 "Travel" (*)	US$ Mn	453	452	524	585	625
8.4 "Passenger transport" (*)	US$ Mn	51	51	61	68	73
TOURISM INDUSTRIES						
Hotels and similar establishments						
9.1 Number of rooms	Units	19,389	19,698	19,945	20,827	21,609
9.2 Number of bed-places	Units	37,289	37,859	38,658	40,480	42,029
9.3 Occupancy rate	Percent	32.00	34.20	45.20	48.00	40.70
9.4 Average length of stay	Nights	..	2.60	2.50	2.40	2.30
RELATED INDICATORS						
Share of tourism expenditure (6.1) in:						
10.1 Gross Domestic Product (GDP)	Percent	13.1	12.4	14.2	13.8	14.2
10.2 Exports of goods	Percent	45.3	41.1	41.7	40.9	38.6
10.3 Exports of services	Percent	70.4	72.4	78.2	75.4	80.7

(*) Balance of Payments items: 6.1 to 6.3 correspond to the "Credit" side (and are receipts for the country) while 8.2 to 8.4 correspond to the "Debit" side (and are expenditures in other countries).

Basic Indicators	Units	2002	2003	2004	2005	2006
INBOUND TOURISM						
Arrivals						
1.1 Visitors	('000)	3,678	3,237	4,291	4,365	4,707
1.2 Tourists (overnight visitors)	('000)	2,832	2,410	3,073	3,143	3,468
1.3 Same-day visitors	('000)	846	827	1,218	1,222	1,239
1.4 Cruise passengers	('000)	..	..	..	..	..
Arrivals by region						
2.1 Africa	('000)	1	1	2	2	5
2.2 Americas	('000)	25	23	32	31	32
2.3 Europe	('000)	3,569	3,114	4,126	4,194	4,487
2.4 East Asia and the Pacific	('000)	66	72	97	114	153
2.5 South Asia	('000)	12	18	21	19	22
2.6 Middle East	('000)	3	3	2	2	3
Arrivals by means of transport used						
3.1 Air	('000)	..	767	274	298	504
3.2 Rail	('000)	..	482	1,221	1,242	1,298
3.3 Road	('000)	..	1,988	2,766	2,813	2,891
3.4 Sea	('000)	..	..	30	12	14
Arrivals by purpose of visit						
4.1 Leisure, recreation and holidays	('000)	48	47	57	80	110
4.2 Business and professional	('000)	646	634	825	893	1,023
4.3 Other	('000)	2,984	2,556	3,409	3,392	3,574
Accommodation						
5.1 Overnight stays in hotels and similar establishments	('000)	173	198	220	261	331
5.2 Guests in hotels and similar establishments	('000)	..	..	..	..	..
5.3 Overnight stays in all types of accommodation establishments	('000)	..	..	..	..	..
5.4 Average length of stay of non-resident tourists in all accommodation establishments	Nights	..	3.00	3.00	3.00	3.00
6.1 **Tourism expenditure in the country**	US$ Mn	680	638	803	801	973
6.2 "Travel" (*)	US$ Mn	622	564	718	701	838
6.3 "Passenger transport" (*)	US$ Mn	58	74	85	100	135
DOMESTIC TOURISM						
Accommodation						
7.1 Overnight stays in hotels and similar establishments	('000)	601	689	815	963	1,140
7.2 Guests in hotels and similar establishments	('000)	..	..	..	..	..
7.3 Overnight stays in all types of accommodation establishments	('000)	..	..	..	..	..
7.4 Average length of stay of resident tourists in all accommodation establishments	Nights	..	..	..	..	..
OUTBOUND TOURISM						
8.1 **Departures**	('000)	2,274	2,374	3,915	3,004	3,688
8.2 **Tourism expenditure in other countries**	US$ Mn	863	783	997	940	1,060
8.3 "Travel" (*)	US$ Mn	757	669	844	753	821
8.4 "Passenger transport" (*)	US$ Mn	106	114	153	187	239
TOURISM INDUSTRIES						
Hotels and similar establishments						
9.1 Number of rooms	Units	9,838	11,104	12,196	15,515	18,838
9.2 Number of bed-places	Units	19,179	22,172	24,257	33,399	43,045
9.3 Occupancy rate	Percent	..	..	25.30	24.90	24.30
9.4 Average length of stay	Nights	..	..	..	..	..
RELATED INDICATORS						
Share of tourism expenditure (6.1) in:						
10.1 Gross Domestic Product (GDP)	Percent	2.8	2.1	1.9	1.4	1.3
10.2 Exports of goods	Percent	6.8	4.8	3.9	2.8	2.5
10.3 Exports of services	Percent	44.2	37.3	40.0	36.0	34.7

(*) Balance of Payments items: 6.1 to 6.3 correspond to the "Credit" side (and are receipts for the country) while 8.2 to 8.4 correspond to the "Debit" side (and are expenditures in other countries).

KENYA

Basic Indicators	Units	2002	2003	2004	2005	2006
INBOUND TOURISM						
Arrivals						
1.1 Visitors	('000)	1,001	1,146	1,359	1,675	1,840
1.2 Tourists (overnight visitors)	('000)	825	927	1,193	1,536	1,644
1.3 Same-day visitors	('000)	163	216	162	135	193
1.4 Cruise passengers	('000)	13	3	4	5	3
Arrivals by region						
2.1 Africa	('000)	549	632	827	999	1,035
2.2 Americas	('000)	49	57	70	94	111
2.3 Europe	('000)	324	367	381	474	568
2.4 East Asia and the Pacific	('000)	44	51	47	65	78
2.5 South Asia	('000)	24	27	19	21	25
2.6 Middle East	('000)	10	12	16	22	23
Arrivals by means of transport used						
3.1 Air	('000)	496	547	668	832	949
3.2 Rail	('000)	3.0	2.0	0.2	0.2	..
3.3 Road	('000)	489	594	686	838	886
3.4 Sea	('000)	13	3	4	5	6
Arrivals by purpose of visit						
4.1 Leisure, recreation and holidays	('000)	579	577	706	928	1,308
4.2 Business and professional	('000)	273	343	411	482	331
4.3 Other	('000)	149	226	242	266	201
Accommodation						
5.1 Overnight stays in hotels and similar establishments	('000)	2,766	1,890	5,060	6,832	7,515
5.2 Guests in hotels and similar establishments	('000)	..	..	..	..	..
5.3 Overnight stays in all types of accommodation establishments	('000)	..	..	..	..	..
5.4 Average length of stay of non-resident tourists in all accommodation establishments	Nights	10.00	14.00	14.00	14.00	11.00
6.1 **Tourism expenditure in the country**	US$ Mn	513	619	799	969	1,182
6.2 "Travel" (*)	US$ Mn	276	347	486	579	688
6.3 "Passenger transport" (*)	US$ Mn	237	272	313	390	494
DOMESTIC TOURISM						
Accommodation						
7.1 Overnight stays in hotels and similar establishments	('000)	656	771	780	840	798
7.2 Guests in hotels and similar establishments	('000)	..	..	..	..	..
7.3 Overnight stays in all types of accommodation establishments	('000)	..	..	..	..	..
7.4 Average length of stay of resident tourists in all accommodation establishments	Nights	5.00	5.00	5.00	5.00	5.00
OUTBOUND TOURISM						
8.1 **Departures**	('000)	..	..	..	..	..
8.2 **Tourism expenditure in other countries**	US$ Mn	..	..	..	..	..
8.3 "Travel" (*)	US$ Mn	126	127	108	124	178
8.4 "Passenger transport" (*)	US$ Mn	..	..	..	..	..
TOURISM INDUSTRIES						
Hotels and similar establishments						
9.1 Number of rooms	Units	10,638	15,320	19,660	20,037	22,140
9.2 Number of bed-places	Units	21,276	30,640	39,320	40,074	44,280
9.3 Occupancy rate	Percent	42.00	33.60	72.30	85.00	87.00
9.4 Average length of stay	Nights	8.50	8.40	14.00	14.00	11.00
RELATED INDICATORS						
Share of tourism expenditure (6.1) in:						
10.1 Gross Domestic Product (GDP)	Percent	4.0	4.2	4.9	5.0	5.6
10.2 Exports of goods	Percent	23.7	25.7	29.4	28.0	33.8
10.3 Exports of services	Percent	48.7	51.7	51.3	51.5	48.0

(*) Balance of Payments items: 6.1 to 6.3 correspond to the "Credit" side (and are receipts for the country) while 8.2 to 8.4 correspond to the "Debit" side (and are expenditures in other countries).

Basic Indicators	Units	2002	2003	2004	2005	2006
INBOUND TOURISM						
Arrivals						
1.1 Visitors	('000)	119.5	130.1	63.0	..	..
1.2 Tourists (overnight visitors)	('000)	4.9	4.9	3.6	3.0	4.4
1.3 Same-day visitors	('000)	..	..	..	..	..
1.4 Cruise passengers	('000)	114.6	125.2	59.4	..	..
Arrivals by region						
2.1 Africa	('000)	..	..	..	..	..
2.2 Americas	('000)	1.1	0.8	0.1	0.3	0.8
2.3 Europe	('000)	0.5	0.4	0.4	0.1	0.2
2.4 East Asia and the Pacific	('000)	2.7	2.9	2.5	2.2	2.7
2.5 South Asia	('000)	..	..	..	..	..
2.6 Middle East	('000)	..	..	..	..	..
Arrivals by means of transport used						
3.1 Air	('000)	4.9	4.9	3.6	3.0	4.4
3.2 Rail	('000)	..	..	..	..	..
3.3 Road	('000)	..	..	..	..	..
3.4 Sea	('000)	114.6	125.2	59.4	..	..
Arrivals by purpose of visit						
4.1 Leisure, recreation and holidays	('000)	0.2	0.2	0.1	0.3	0.2
4.2 Business and professional	('000)	1.6	1.6	1.6	1.7	0.9
4.3 Other	('000)	1.5	2.1	1.9	1.0	1.5
Accommodation						
5.1 Overnight stays in hotels and similar establishments	('000)	..	..	..	..	..
5.2 Guests in hotels and similar establishments	('000)	..	..	..	..	..
5.3 Overnight stays in all types of accommodation establishments	('000)	..	..	..	..	..
5.4 Average length of stay of non-resident tourists in all accommodation establishments	Nights	..	..	..	..	..
6.1 Tourism expenditure in the country	US$ Mn	..	..	..	..	..
6.2 "Travel" (*)	US$ Mn	..	..	..	..	..
6.3 "Passenger transport" (*)	US$ Mn	..	..	..	..	..
DOMESTIC TOURISM						
Accommodation						
7.1 Overnight stays in hotels and similar establishments	('000)	..	..	..	..	..
7.2 Guests in hotels and similar establishments	('000)	..	..	..	..	..
7.3 Overnight stays in all types of accommodation establishments	('000)	..	..	..	..	..
7.4 Average length of stay of resident tourists in all accommodation establishments	Nights	..	..	..	..	..
OUTBOUND TOURISM						
8.1 **Departures**	('000)	..	..	..	..	..
8.2 **Tourism expenditure in other countries**	US$ Mn	..	..	..	..	..
8.3 "Travel" (*)	US$ Mn	..	..	..	..	..
8.4 "Passenger transport" (*)	US$ Mn	..	..	..	..	..
TOURISM INDUSTRIES						
Hotels and similar establishments						
9.1 Number of rooms	Units	162	162	162	..	..
9.2 Number of bed-places	Units	..	..	..	..	..
9.3 Occupancy rate	Percent	..	..	..	..	..
9.4 Average length of stay	Nights	..	..	..	..	..
RELATED INDICATORS						
Share of tourism expenditure (6.1) in:						
10.1 Gross Domestic Product (GDP)	Percent	..	..	..	..	..
10.2 Exports of goods	Percent	..	..	..	..	..
10.3 Exports of services	Percent	..	..	..	..	..

(*) Balance of Payments items: 6.1 to 6.3 correspond to the "Credit" side (and are receipts for the country) while 8.2 to 8.4 correspond to the "Debit" side (and are expenditures in other countries).

KOREA, REPUBLIC OF

Basic Indicators		Units	2002	2003	2004	2005	2006
INBOUND TOURISM							
Arrivals							
1.1	Visitors	('000)	5,347	4,753	5,818	6,023	6,155
1.2	Tourists (overnight visitors)	('000)	..	..	..	..	..
1.3	Same-day visitors	('000)	..	..	..	..	..
1.4	Cruise passengers	('000)	..	..	..	..	..
Arrivals by region							
2.1	Africa	('000)	16	15	15	14	16
2.2	Americas	('000)	556	505	611	640	673
2.3	Europe	('000)	536	514	531	541	572
2.4	East Asia and the Pacific	('000)	3,829	3,335	4,253	4,442	4,557
2.5	South Asia	('000)	82	86	95	92	95
2.6	Middle East	('000)	11	8	11	13	15
Arrivals by means of transport used							
3.1	Air	('000)	4,067	3,536	4,529	4,776	5,116
3.2	Rail	('000)	..	..	..	..	..
3.3	Road	('000)	..	..	..	..	..
3.4	Sea	('000)	326	314	400	404	1,039
Arrivals by purpose of visit							
4.1	Leisure, recreation and holidays	('000)	3,844	3,217	4,185	4,347	4,365
4.2	Business and professional	('000)	225	231	267	304	348
4.3	Other	('000)	1,279	1,304	1,366	1,371	1,442
Accommodation							
5.1	Overnight stays in hotels and similar establishments	('000)	..	..	..	..	..
5.2	Guests in hotels and similar establishments	('000)	..	..	..	..	..
5.3	Overnight stays in all types of accommodation establishments	('000)	..	..	..	..	..
5.4	Average length of stay of non-resident tourists in all accommodation establishments	Nights	5.40	6.20	5.60	6.80	..
6.1	**Tourism expenditure in the country**	US$ Mn	7,621	7,005	8,226	8,290	8,069
6.2	"Travel" (*)	US$ Mn	5,936	5,358	6,069	5,806	5,322
6.3	"Passenger transport" (*)	US$ Mn	1,685	1,647	2,157	2,484	2,747
DOMESTIC TOURISM							
Accommodation							
7.1	Overnight stays in hotels and similar establishments	('000)	..	..	..	..	..
7.2	Guests in hotels and similar establishments	('000)	..	..	..	..	..
7.3	Overnight stays in all types of accommodation establishments	('000)	..	..	..	..	..
7.4	Average length of stay of resident tourists in all accommodation establishments	Nights	..	..	..	..	..
OUTBOUND TOURISM							
8.1	**Departures**	('000)	7,123	7,086	8,826	10,080	11,610
8.2	**Tourism expenditure in other countries** (**)	US$ Mn	11,440	11,063	13,507	16,924	20,386
8.3	"Travel" (*)	US$ Mn	10,465	10,103	12,350	15,406	18,241
8.4	"Passenger transport" (*)	US$ Mn	975	960	1,157	1,518	2,145
TOURISM INDUSTRIES							
Hotels and similar establishments							
9.1	Number of rooms	Units	54,086	56,196	59,135	58,950	60,596
9.2	Number of bed-places	Units	..	..	..	..	..
9.3	Occupancy rate	Percent	60.10	51.80	55.10	57.10	52.00
9.4	Average length of stay	Nights	..	..	..	..	..
RELATED INDICATORS							
Share of tourism expenditure (6.1) in:							
10.1	Gross Domestic Product (GDP)	Percent	1.4	1.2	1.2	1.0	0.9
10.2	Exports of goods	Percent	4.7	3.6	3.2	2.9	2.4
10.3	Exports of services	Percent	26.8	21.3	19.6	18.4	15.6

(*) Balance of Payments items: 6.1 to 6.3 correspond to the "Credit" side (and are receipts for the country) while 8.2 to 8.4 correspond to the "Debit" side (and are expenditures in other countries).

(**) See Annex "Country notes".

Basic Indicators	Units	2002	2003	2004	2005	2006
INBOUND TOURISM						
Arrivals						
1.1 Visitors	('000)	2,316	2,602	3,056	3,474	..
1.2 Tourists (overnight visitors)	('000)	96	94	91	104	178
1.3 Same-day visitors	('000)	..	..	..	..	..
1.4 Cruise passengers	('000)	..	..	..	..	
Arrivals by region						
2.1 Africa	('000)	24	26	29	..	..
2.2 Americas	('000)	50	103	115	..	..
2.3 Europe	('000)	81	94	126	..	..
2.4 East Asia and the Pacific	('000)	118	125	158	..	..
2.5 South Asia	('000)	648	746	856	..	..
2.6 Middle East	('000)	1,391	1,506	1,769	..	
Arrivals by means of transport used						
3.1 Air	('000)	1,139	1,272	1,525	1,657	..
3.2 Rail	('000)	..	..			..
3.3 Road	('000)	1,120	1,278	1,482	1,776	..
3.4 Sea	('000)	56	52	48	41	..
Arrivals by purpose of visit						
4.1 Leisure, recreation and holidays	('000)	7.6	7.1	1.2	..	..
4.2 Business and professional	('000)	33.7	17.9	2.3	..	..
4.3 Other	('000)	54.8	69.2	87.2	..	..
Accommodation						
5.1 Overnight stays in hotels and similar establishments	('000)	292	315	281	272	282
5.2 Guests in hotels and similar establishments	('000)	96	94	91	104	178
5.3 Overnight stays in all types of accommodation establishments	('000)	..	..	..	..	..
5.4 Average length of stay of non-resident tourists in all accommodation establishments	Nights	3.00	3.30	3.10	2.60	1.60
6.1 **Tourism expenditure in the country**	US$ Mn	320	328	412	410	470
6.2 "Travel" (*)	US$ Mn	117	118	178	165	205
6.3 "Passenger transport" (*)	US$ Mn	203	210	234	245	265
DOMESTIC TOURISM						
Accommodation						
7.1 Overnight stays in hotels and similar establishments	('000)	..	..	..	..	..
7.2 Guests in hotels and similar establishments	('000)	..	..		..	..
7.3 Overnight stays in all types of accommodation establishments	('000)	..	..	..	..	..
7.4 Average length of stay of resident tourists in all accommodation establishments	Nights	..	..	..	..	..
OUTBOUND TOURISM						
8.1 **Departures**	('000)	1,725	1,774	1,928	2,173	..
8.2 **Tourism expenditure in other countries**	US$ Mn	3,412	3,750	4,148	4,741	5,753
8.3 "Travel" (*)	US$ Mn	3,021	3,348	3,701	4,277	5,253
8.4 "Passenger transport" (*)	US$ Mn	391	402	447	464	500
TOURISM INDUSTRIES						
Hotels and similar establishments						
9.1 Number of rooms	Units	3,407	3,980	4,281	5,919	6,572
9.2 Number of bed-places	Units	3,870	5,063	5,064	9,847	11,387
9.3 Occupancy rate	Percent	..	..	..	..	..
9.4 Average length of stay	Nights	..	..	..	..	..
RELATED INDICATORS						
Share of tourism expenditure (6.1) in:						
10.1 Gross Domestic Product (GDP)	Percent	0.8	0.7	0.7	0.5	..
10.2 Exports of goods	Percent	2.1	1.5	1.4	0.9	0.8
10.3 Exports of services	Percent	19.4	10.4	11.0	8.7	6.7

(*) Balance of Payments items: 6.1 to 6.3 correspond to the "Credit" side (and are receipts for the country) while 8.2 to 8.4 correspond to the "Debit" side (and are expenditures in other countries).

KYRGYZSTAN

Basic Indicators	Units	2002	2003	2004	2005	2006
INBOUND TOURISM						
Arrivals						
1.1 Visitors	('000)	183	..	..	..	..
1.2 Tourists (overnight visitors)	('000)	140	342	398	315	766
1.3 Same-day visitors	('000)	..	..	..	..	..
1.4 Cruise passengers	('000)	..	..	..	..	..
Arrivals by region						
2.1 Africa	('000)	..	..	..	..	..
2.2 Americas	('000)	12	13	12	13	14
2.3 Europe	('000)	88	270	357	274	715
2.4 East Asia and the Pacific	('000)	11	14	17	22	26
2.5 South Asia	('000)	3	5	6	6	5
2.6 Middle East	('000)	..	..	..	..	..
Arrivals by means of transport used						
3.1 Air	('000)	40	47	59	65	56
3.2 Rail	('000)	73	71	86	90	129
3.3 Road	('000)	70	61	140	150	98
3.4 Sea	('000)	..	..	..	..	..
Arrivals by purpose of visit						
4.1 Leisure, recreation and holidays	('000)	..	..	..	..	..
4.2 Business and professional	('000)	..	..	..	..	..
4.3 Other	('000)	..	..	..	..	..
Accommodation						
5.1 Overnight stays in hotels and similar establishments	('000)	144	117	119	94	116
5.2 Guests in hotels and similar establishments	('000)	44	46	49	34	38
5.3 Overnight stays in all types of accommodation establishments	('000)	..	..	..	..	..
5.4 Average length of stay of non-resident tourists in all accommodation establishments	Nights	..	..	..	..	..
6.1 **Tourism expenditure in the country**	US$ Mn	48	62	92	94	189
6.2 "Travel" (*)	US$ Mn	36	48	76	73	167
6.3 "Passenger transport" (*)	US$ Mn	12	14	16	21	22
DOMESTIC TOURISM						
Accommodation						
7.1 Overnight stays in hotels and similar establishments	('000)	134	131	136	128	141
7.2 Guests in hotels and similar establishments	('000)	80	82	101	92	95
7.3 Overnight stays in all types of accommodation establishments	('000)	..	..	..	..	..
7.4 Average length of stay of resident tourists in all accommodation establishments	Nights	..	..	..	..	..
OUTBOUND TOURISM						
8.1 **Departures**	('000)	59	116	239	201	454
8.2 **Tourism expenditure in other countries**	US$ Mn	27	35	73	94	142
8.3 "Travel" (*)	US$ Mn	10	17	50	58	92
8.4 "Passenger transport" (*)	US$ Mn	17	18	23	36	50
TOURISM INDUSTRIES						
Hotels and similar establishments						
9.1 Number of rooms	Units	1,974	1,925	2,248	2,244	2,357
9.2 Number of bed-places	Units	3,498	3,409	4,022	4,472	7,383
9.3 Occupancy rate	Percent	..	..	..	..	..
9.4 Average length of stay	Nights	..	..	..	..	..
RELATED INDICATORS						
Share of tourism expenditure (6.1) in:						
10.1 Gross Domestic Product (GDP)	Percent	3.0	3.2	4.2	3.8	7.0
10.2 Exports of goods	Percent	9.6	10.5	12.6	13.7	23.3
10.3 Exports of services	Percent	33.8	39.2	43.8	36.7	50.5

(*) Balance of Payments items: 6.1 to 6.3 correspond to the "Credit" side (and are receipts for the country) while 8.2 to 8.4 correspond to the "Debit" side (and are expenditures in other countries).

LAO PEOPLE´S DEMOCRATIC REPUBLIC

Basic Indicators	Units	2002	2003	2004	2005	2006
INBOUND TOURISM						
Arrivals						
1.1 Visitors	('000)	736	636	895	1,095	1,215
1.2 Tourists (overnight visitors)	('000)	215	196	407	672	842
1.3 Same-day visitors	('000)	521	440	488	423	373
1.4 Cruise passengers	('000)	..	..	..	..	..
Arrivals by region						
2.1 Africa	('000)	..	..	..	..	..
2.2 Americas	('000)	47	39	47	60	61
2.3 Europe	('000)	107	97	116	134	144
2.4 East Asia and the Pacific	('000)	575	495	728	897	1,007
2.5 South Asia	('000)	4	3	2	2	2
2.6 Middle East	('000)	..	..	..	..	..
Arrivals by means of transport used						
3.1 Air	('000)	147	159	242	438	389
3.2 Rail	('000)	..	..	..	..	..
3.3 Road	('000)	589	477	653	657	826
3.4 Sea	('000)	..	..	..	..	..
Arrivals by purpose of visit						
4.1 Leisure, recreation and holidays	('000)	..	503	770	964	911
4.2 Business and professional	('000)	..	89	54	66	219
4.3 Other	('000)	..	44	71	65	85
Accommodation						
5.1 Overnight stays in hotels and similar establishments	('000)	..	..	..	..	..
5.2 Guests in hotels and similar establishments	('000)	..	..	..	..	..
5.3 Overnight stays in all types of accommodation establishments	('000)	..	..	..	..	..
5.4 Average length of stay of non-resident tourists in all accommodation establishments	Nights	4.30	4.00	4.30	4.50	4.50
6.1 **Tourism expenditure in the country**	US$ Mn	..	..	..	..	..
6.2 "Travel" (*)	US$ Mn	113	87	119	147	173
6.3 "Passenger transport" (*)	US$ Mn	..	..	..	..	..
DOMESTIC TOURISM						
Accommodation						
7.1 Overnight stays in hotels and similar establishments	('000)	..	..	..	..	..
7.2 Guests in hotels and similar establishments	('000)	..	..	..	..	..
7.3 Overnight stays in all types of accommodation establishments	('000)	..	..	..	..	..
7.4 Average length of stay of resident tourists in all accommodation establishments	Nights	..	..	..	..	..
OUTBOUND TOURISM						
8.1 **Departures**	('000)	..	..	..	..	..
8.2 **Tourism expenditure in other countries**	US$ Mn	..	..	..	..	..
8.3 "Travel" (*)	US$ Mn	..	..	..	..	..
8.4 "Passenger transport" (*)	US$ Mn	..	..	..	..	..
TOURISM INDUSTRIES						
Hotels and similar establishments						
9.1 Number of rooms	Units	8,625	12,289	13,666	15,828	17,633
9.2 Number of bed-places	Units	14,222	18,877	20,480	22,142	26,846
9.3 Occupancy rate	Percent	..	45.00	44.00	50.00	51.00
9.4 Average length of stay	Nights	..	..	..	..	..
RELATED INDICATORS						
Share of tourism expenditure (6.1) in: (**)						
10.1 Gross Domestic Product (GDP)	Percent	6.2	4.1	4.7	5.1	5.1
10.2 Exports of goods	Percent	..	..	..	..	..
10.3 Exports of services	Percent	..	..	..	..	..

(*) Balance of Payments items: 6.1 to 6.3 correspond to the "Credit" side (and are receipts for the country) while 8.2 to 8.4 correspond to the "Debit" side (and are expenditures in other countries).

(**) See Annex "Country notes".

LATVIA

Basic Indicators	Units	2002	2003	2004	2005	2006
INBOUND TOURISM						
Arrivals						
1.1 Visitors	('000)	2,297	2,524	3,127	3,791	4,649
1.2 Tourists (overnight visitors)	('000)	848	971	1,079	1,116	1,535
1.3 Same-day visitors	('000)	1,425	1,499	1,954	2,658	3,109
1.4 Cruise passengers	('000)	76	79	69	92	89
Arrivals by region						
2.1 Africa	('000)	..	..	1	..	1
2.2 Americas	('000)	24	22	32	22	20
2.3 Europe	('000)	2,218	2,429	2,985	3,739	4,601
2.4 East Asia and the Pacific	('000)	18	17	13	8	19
2.5 South Asia	('000)	1	1	1	2	1
2.6 Middle East	('000)	..	..	..	..	1
Arrivals by means of transport used						
3.1 Air	('000)	155	188	299	494	641
3.2 Rail	('000)	128	144	139	147	155
3.3 Road	('000)	1,840	2,004	2,481	2,939	3,622
3.4 Sea	('000)	174	188	208	210	231
Arrivals by purpose of visit						
4.1 Leisure, recreation and holidays	('000)	480	586	857	1,227	1,738
4.2 Business and professional	('000)	458	409	466	441	596
4.3 Other	('000)	1,335	1,475	1,710	2,106	2,310
Accommodation						
5.1 Overnight stays in hotels and similar establishments	('000)	853	963	1,158	1,507	1,745
5.2 Guests in hotels and similar establishments	('000)	352	402	520	680	746
5.3 Overnight stays in all types of accommodation establishments	('000)	871	983	1,201	1,613	1,872
5.4 Average length of stay of non-resident tourists in all accommodation establishments	Nights	2.41	2.37	2.20	2.21	2.29
6.1 **Tourism expenditure in the country**	US$ Mn	201	271	343	446	622
6.2 "Travel" (*)	US$ Mn	161	222	267	341	480
6.3 "Passenger transport" (*)	US$ Mn	40	49	76	105	142
DOMESTIC TOURISM						
Accommodation						
7.1 Overnight stays in hotels and similar establishments	('000)	674	669	717	796	855
7.2 Guests in hotels and similar establishments	('000)	225	257	287	354	418
7.3 Overnight stays in all types of accommodation establishments	('000)	821	825	865	1,022	1,241
7.4 Average length of stay of resident tourists in all accommodation establishments	Nights	2.69	2.39	2.43	2.41	2.42
OUTBOUND TOURISM						
8.1 **Departures**	('000)	2,306	2,286	2,457	2,959	3,151
8.2 **Tourism expenditure in other countries**	US$ Mn	267	365	428	655	788
8.3 "Travel" (*)	US$ Mn	230	328	377	584	704
8.4 "Passenger transport" (*)	US$ Mn	37	37	51	71	84
TOURISM INDUSTRIES						
Hotels and similar establishments						
9.1 Number of rooms	Units	7,198	7,618	8,826	9,219	9,706
9.2 Number of bed-places	Units	13,744	14,983	17,933	19,229	19,650
9.3 Occupancy rate	Percent	31.10	31.70	31.49	36.38	35.60
9.4 Average length of stay	Nights	2.50	2.48	2.32	2.23	2.23
RELATED INDICATORS						
Share of tourism expenditure (6.1) in:						
10.1 Gross Domestic Product (GDP)	Percent	2.2	2.4	2.5	2.8	3.1
10.2 Exports of goods	Percent	7.9	8.5	8.1	8.3	10.1
10.3 Exports of services	Percent	16.2	18.0	19.3	20.6	23.5

(*) Balance of Payments items: 6.1 to 6.3 correspond to the "Credit" side (and are receipts for the country) while 8.2 to 8.4 correspond to the "Debit" side (and are expenditures in other countries).

Basic indicators	Units	2002	2003	2004	2005	2006
INBOUND TOURISM						
Arrivals						
1.1 Visitors	('000)	..	..	..	..	..
1.2 Tourists (overnight visitors)	('000)	956	1,016	1,278	1,140	1,063
1.3 Same-day visitors	('000)	..	..	..	..	..
1.4 Cruise passengers	('000)	..	..	..	..	..
Arrivals by region						
2.1 Africa	('000)	37	39	45	31	39
2.2 Americas	('000)	108	120	152	137	130
2.3 Europe	('000)	251	267	337	317	269
2.4 East Asia and the Pacific	('000)	61	66	92	88	74
2.5 South Asia	('000)	96	102	128	129	115
2.6 Middle East	('000)	403	421	520	437	433
Arrivals by means of transport used						
3.1 Air	('000)	582	..	..	..	..
3.2 Rail	('000)	..	..	..	..	..
3.3 Road	('000)	374	..	..	..	..
3.4 Sea	('000)	1	..	..	..	..
Arrivals by purpose of visit						
4.1 Leisure, recreation and holidays	('000)	..	..	..	..	..
4.2 Business and professional	('000)	..	..	..	..	..
4.3 Other	('000)	..	..	..	..	..
Accommodation						
5.1 Overnight stays in hotels and similar establishments	('000)	653	1,180	1,484	1,133	1,150
5.2 Guests in hotels and similar establishments	('000)	..	..	..	..	..
5.3 Overnight stays in all types of accommodation establishments	('000)	..	..	..	..	..
5.4 Average length of stay of non-resident tourists in all accommodation establishments	Nights	2.63	2.58	2.65	2.49	2.46
6.1 **Tourism expenditure in the country**	US$ Mn	..	6,782	5,931	5,969	5,491
6.2 "Travel" (*)	US$ Mn	4,284	6,374	5,411	5,532	5,015
6.3 "Passenger transport" (*)	US$ Mn	..	408	520	437	476
DOMESTIC TOURISM						
Accommodation						
7.1 Overnight stays in hotels and similar establishments	('000)	..	..	..	..	..
7.2 Guests in hotels and similar establishments	('000)	..	..	..	..	..
7.3 Overnight stays in all types of accommodation establishments	('000)	..	..	..	..	..
7.4 Average length of stay of resident tourists in all accommodation establishments	Nights	..	..	..	..	..
OUTBOUND TOURISM						
8.1 **Departures**	('000)	..	..	..	..	..
8.2 **Tourism expenditure in other countries**	US$ Mn	..	3,319	3,719	3,565	3,783
8.3 "Travel" (*)	US$ Mn	2,683	2,943	3,170	2,908	3,006
8.4 "Passenger transport" (*)	US$ Mn	..	376	549	657	777
TOURISM INDUSTRIES						
Hotels and similar establishments						
9.1 Number of rooms	Units	17,601	16,202	16,171	16,735	16,680
9.2 Number of bed-places	Units	30,444	28,246	26,992	28,953	27,544
9.3 Occupancy rate	Percent	35.00	..	..	..	..
9.4 Average length of stay	Nights	..	..	..	..	..
RELATED INDICATORS						
Share of tourism expenditure (6.1) in:						
10.1 Gross Domestic Product (GDP)	Percent	..	34.3	27.6	27.7	24.2
10.2 Exports of goods	Percent	..	391.3	289.3	262.0	196.7
10.3 Exports of services	Percent	..	71.7	61.1	55.0	47.3

(*) Balance of Payments items: 6.1 to 6.3 correspond to the "Credit" side (and are receipts for the country) while 8.2 to 8.4 correspond to the "Debit" side (and are expenditures in other countries).

LESOTHO

Basic Indicators	Units	2002	2003	2004	2005	2006
INBOUND TOURISM						
Arrivals						
1.1 Visitors	('000)	287	329	304	304	357
1.2 Tourists (overnight visitors)	('000)	..	..	..	..	347
1.3 Same-day visitors	('000)	..	..	..	..	10
1.4 Cruise passengers	('000)	..	..	..	..	..
Arrivals by region						
2.1 Africa	('000)	278	303	290	289	330
2.2 Americas	('000)	1	3	1	1	3
2.3 Europe	('000)	6	13	8	8	20
2.4 East Asia and the Pacific	('000)	2	4	3	3	3
2.5 South Asia	('000)	..	..	..	..	..
2.6 Middle East	('000)	..	..	..	..	..
Arrivals by means of transport used						
3.1 Air	('000)	9	11	10	11	13
3.2 Rail	('000)	..	..	..	..	..
3.3 Road	('000)	279	318	294	293	344
3.4 Sea	('000)	..	..	..	..	..
Arrivals by purpose of visit						
4.1 Leisure, recreation and holidays	('000)	46	58	63	67	..
4.2 Business and professional	('000)	43	54	57	60	..
4.3 Other	('000)	198	217	183	177	..
Accommodation						
5.1 Overnight stays in hotels and similar establishments	('000)	..	..	..	..	..
5.2 Guests in hotels and similar establishments	('000)	..	..	..	..	..
5.3 Overnight stays in all types of accommodation establishments	('000)	..	..	..	..	..
5.4 Average length of stay of non-resident tourists in all accommodation establishments	Nights	..	..	..	..	..
6.1 **Tourism expenditure in the country**	US$ Mn	..	..	..	..	..
6.2 "Travel" (*)	US$ Mn	20	28	34	30	28
6.3 "Passenger transport" (*)	US$ Mn	..	..	..	..	..
DOMESTIC TOURISM						
Accommodation						
7.1 Overnight stays in hotels and similar establishments	('000)	..	..	..	..	..
7.2 Guests in hotels and similar establishments	('000)	..	..	..	..	..
7.3 Overnight stays in all types of accommodation establishments	('000)	..	..	..	..	..
7.4 Average length of stay of resident tourists in all accommodation establishments	Nights	..	..	..	..	..
OUTBOUND TOURISM						
8.1 **Departures**	('000)	..	..	..	..	..
8.2 **Tourism expenditure in other countries**	US$ Mn	16	30	37	36	22
8.3 "Travel" (*)	US$ Mn	14	26	30	27	19
8.4 "Passenger transport" (*)	US$ Mn	2	4	7	9	3
TOURISM INDUSTRIES						
Hotels and similar establishments						
9.1 Number of rooms	Units	..	..	1,492	1,209	1,770
9.2 Number of bed-places	Units	..	..	3,072	2,498	3,574
9.3 Occupancy rate	Percent	..	..	17.70	14.60	17.30
9.4 Average length of stay	Nights	..	..	..	..	2.40
RELATED INDICATORS						
Share of tourism expenditure (6.1) in: (**)						
10.1 Gross Domestic Product (GDP)	Percent	2.9	2.7	2.6	2.1	1.9
10.2 Exports of goods	Percent	5.6	5.9	4.8	4.6	4.0
10.3 Exports of services	Percent	57.1	56.0	53.1	53.6	46.7

(*) Balance of Payments items: 6.1 to 6.3 correspond to the "Credit" side (and are receipts for the country) while 8.2 to 8.4 correspond to the "Debit" side (and are expenditures in other countries).

(**) See Annex "Country notes".

Basic Indicators	Units	2002	2003	2004	2005	2006
INBOUND TOURISM						
Arrivals						
1.1 Visitors	('000)	858	958	999	..	..
1.2 Tourists (overnight visitors)	('000)	135	142	149	..	..
1.3 Same-day visitors	('000)	723	816	850	..	..
1.4 Cruise passengers	('000)	..	..	..	..	..
Arrivals by region						
2.1 Africa	('000)	439	458	483	..	..
2.2 Americas	('000)	2	2	2	..	..
2.3 Europe	('000)	36	42	46	..	..
2.4 East Asia and the Pacific	('000)	7	7	7	..	..
2.5 South Asia	('000)	4	4	4	..	..
2.6 Middle East	('000)	370	445	458	..	..
Arrivals by means of transport used						
3.1 Air	('000)	309	342	379	..	..
3.2 Rail	('000)	..	..	..	..	..
3.3 Road	('000)	531	591	658	..	..
3.4 Sea	('000)	18	19	20	..	..
Arrivals by purpose of visit						
4.1 Leisure, recreation and holidays	('000)	47	45	43	..	..
4.2 Business and professional	('000)	38	40	42	..	..
4.3 Other	('000)	50	57	64	..	..
Accommodation						
5.1 Overnight stays in hotels and similar establishments	('000)	453	477	502	..	..
5.2 Guests in hotels and similar establishments	('000)	..	..	..	..	..
5.3 Overnight stays in all types of accommodation establishments	('000)	..	..	..	..	..
5.4 Average length of stay of non-resident tourists in all accommodation establishments	Nights	7.00	7.00	7.00	..	..
6.1 **Tourism expenditure in the country**	US$ Mn	202	243	261	301	244
6.2 "Travel" (*)	US$ Mn	181	205	218	250	190
6.3 "Passenger transport" (*)	US$ Mn	21	38	43	51	54
DOMESTIC TOURISM						
Accommodation						
7.1 Overnight stays in hotels and similar establishments	('000)	..	..	..	..	..
7.2 Guests in hotels and similar establishments	('000)	..	..	..	..	..
7.3 Overnight stays in all types of accommodation establishments	('000)	972	968	964	..	..
7.4 Average length of stay of resident tourists in all accommodation establishments	Nights	..	..	..	..	..
OUTBOUND TOURISM						
8.1 **Departures**	('000)	..	..	..	..	..
8.2 **Tourism expenditure in other countries**	US$ Mn	654	689	789	920	915
8.3 "Travel" (*)	US$ Mn	586	557	603	680	668
8.4 "Passenger transport" (*)	US$ Mn	68	132	186	240	247
TOURISM INDUSTRIES						
Hotels and similar establishments						
9.1 Number of rooms	Units	12,405	12,405	12,704	..	..
9.2 Number of bed-places	Units	20,967	20,967	21,404	..	..
9.3 Occupancy rate	Percent	42.00	45.00	44.00	..	..
9.4 Average length of stay	Nights	..	..	..	..	..
RELATED INDICATORS						
Share of tourism expenditure (6.1) in:						
10.1 Gross Domestic Product (GDP)	Percent	1.1	1.0	0.9	0.7	0.5
10.2 Exports of goods	Percent	2.1	1.9	1.5	1.0	0.7
10.3 Exports of services	Percent	50.4	55.0	59.7	56.4	49.9

(*) Balance of Payments items: 6.1 to 6.3 correspond to the "Credit" side (and are receipts for the country) while 8.2 to 8.4 correspond to the "Debit" side (and are expenditures in other countries).

LIECHTENSTEIN

Basic Indicators	Units	2002	2003	2004	2005	2006
INBOUND TOURISM						
Arrivals						
1.1 Visitors	('000)	..	..	..	..	..
1.2 Tourists (overnight visitors)	('000)	48.7	49.0	48.5	49.8	54.9
1.3 Same-day visitors	('000)	..	..	..	..	..
1.4 Cruise passengers	('000)	..	..	..	..	..
Arrivals by region						
2.1 Africa	('000)	0.2	0.2	0.2	0.2	0.2
2.2 Americas	('000)	2.9	2.4	2.7	2.9	3.0
2.3 Europe	('000)	44.0	44.7	43.8	44.9	49.8
2.4 East Asia and the Pacific	('000)	1.7	1.6	1.7	1.6	1.7
2.5 South Asia	('000)	..	..	..	..	..
2.6 Middle East	('000)	..	..	..	..	..
Arrivals by means of transport used						
3.1 Air	('000)	..	..	..	..	..
3.2 Rail	('000)	..	..	..	..	..
3.3 Road	('000)	..	..	..	..	..
3.4 Sea	('000)	..	..	..	..	..
Arrivals by purpose of visit						
4.1 Leisure, recreation and holidays	('000)	..	..	..	..	..
4.2 Business and professional	('000)	..	..	..	..	..
4.3 Other	('000)	..	..	..	..	..
Accommodation						
5.1 Overnight stays in hotels and similar establishments	('000)	105.9	104.6	101.1	108.4	115.4
5.2 Guests in hotels and similar establishments	('000)	48.7	49.0	48.5	49.8	54.9
5.3 Overnight stays in all types of accommodation establishments	('000)	..	..	..	..	..
5.4 Average length of stay of non-resident tourists in all accommodation establishments	Nights	2.17	2.10	2.10	2.20	2.10
6.1 **Tourism expenditure in the country**	US$ Mn	..	..	..	..	..
6.2 "Travel" (*)	US$ Mn	..	..	..	..	..
6.3 "Passenger transport" (*)	US$ Mn	..	..	..	..	..
DOMESTIC TOURISM						
Accommodation						
7.1 Overnight stays in hotels and similar establishments	('000)	2.5	2.6	3.1	2.9	2.7
7.2 Guests in hotels and similar establishments	('000)	1.0	1.2	1.6	1.3	1.3
7.3 Overnight stays in all types of accommodation establishments	('000)	..	..	..	..	..
7.4 Average length of stay of resident tourists in all accommodation establishments	Nights	..	..	..	..	..
OUTBOUND TOURISM						
8.1 **Departures**	('000)	..	..	..	..	..
8.2 **Tourism expenditure in other countries**	US$ Mn	..	..	..	..	..
8.3 "Travel" (*)	US$ Mn	..	..	..	..	..
8.4 "Passenger transport" (*)	US$ Mn	..	..	..	..	..
TOURISM INDUSTRIES						
Hotels and similar establishments						
9.1 Number of rooms	Units	581	591	572	608	646
9.2 Number of bed-places	Units	1,112	1,160	1,176	1,188	1,263
9.3 Occupancy rate	Percent	26.70	25.30	24.20	25.60	25.60
9.4 Average length of stay	Nights	2.18	2.10	2.10	2.20	2.10
RELATED INDICATORS						
Share of tourism expenditure (6.1) in:						
10.1 Gross Domestic Product (GDP)	Percent	..	..	..	..	..
10.2 Exports of goods	Percent	..	..	..	..	..
10.3 Exports of services	Percent	..	..	..	..	..

(*) Balance of Payments items: 6.1 to 6.3 correspond to the "Credit" side (and are receipts for the country) while 8.2 to 8.4 correspond to the "Debit" side (and are expenditures in other countries).

Basic Indicators	Units	2002	2003	2004	2005	2006
INBOUND TOURISM						
Arrivals						
1.1 Visitors	('000)	3,999	3,635	..	..	..
1.2 Tourists (overnight visitors)	('000)	1,428	1,491	1,800	2,000	2,180
1.3 Same-day visitors	('000)	2,571	2,144	..	..	..
1.4 Cruise passengers	('000)	8	9	14	24	25
Arrivals by region						
2.1 Africa	('000)	..	..	1	1	1
2.2 Americas	('000)	16	16	22	24	26
2.3 Europe	('000)	358	400	538	623	694
2.4 East Asia and the Pacific	('000)	10	11	15	15	16
2.5 South Asia	('000)	..	..	..	..	..
2.6 Middle East	('000)	..	..	..	..	..
Arrivals by means of transport used						
3.1 Air	('000)	161	185	199	320	400
3.2 Rail	('000)	530	443	504	625	450
3.3 Road	('000)	699	808	1,032	960	1,160
3.4 Sea	('000)	38	55	66	95	170
Arrivals by purpose of visit						
4.1 Leisure, recreation and holidays	('000)	482	523	682	555	750
4.2 Business and professional	('000)	326	335	408	500	540
4.3 Other	('000)	620	632	710	945	890
Accommodation						
5.1 Overnight stays in hotels and similar establishments	('000)	719	766	1,131	1,334	1,451
5.2 Guests in hotels and similar establishments	('000)	343	385	530	623	692
5.3 Overnight stays in all types of accommodation establishments	('000)	1,145	1,170	1,526	1,762	1,906
5.4 Average length of stay of non-resident tourists in all accommodation establishments	Nights	2.90	2.70	2.59	2.59	2.52
6.1 **Tourism expenditure in the country**	US$ Mn	556	700	834	975	1,077
6.2 "Travel" (*)	US$ Mn	505	638	776	921	1,038
6.3 "Passenger transport" (*)	US$ Mn	51	62	58	54	39
DOMESTIC TOURISM						
Accommodation						
7.1 Overnight stays in hotels and similar establishments	('000)	331	342	511	728	934
7.2 Guests in hotels and similar establishments	('000)	156	175	258	347	463
7.3 Overnight stays in all types of accommodation establishments	('000)	1,886	1,845	2,169	2,489	2,774
7.4 Average length of stay of resident tourists in all accommodation establishments	Nights	5.30	4.50	4.10	3.86	3.61
OUTBOUND TOURISM						
8.1 **Departures**	('000)	3,584	3,502	..	..	..
8.2 **Tourism expenditure in other countries**	US$ Mn	334	476	643	757	931
8.3 "Travel" (*)	US$ Mn	326	471	636	744	909
8.4 "Passenger transport" (*)	US$ Mn	8	5	7	13	22
TOURISM INDUSTRIES						
Hotels and similar establishments						
9.1 Number of rooms	Units	6,179	7,384	9,465	10,134	10,843
9.2 Number of bed-places	Units	11,980	14,346	18,630	19,940	21,504
9.3 Occupancy rate	Percent	35.20	32.50	36.70	40.80	42.10
9.4 Average length of stay	Nights	2.13	1.98	2.10	2.15	2.06
RELATED INDICATORS						
Share of tourism expenditure (6.1) in:						
10.1 Gross Domestic Product (GDP)	Percent	3.9	3.8	3.7	3.8	3.6
10.2 Exports of goods	Percent	9.2	9.1	9.0	8.3	7.6
10.3 Exports of services	Percent	38.0	37.3	34.1	31.4	29.7

(*) Balance of Payments items: 6.1 to 6.3 correspond to the "Credit" side (and are receipts for the country) while 8.2 to 8.4 correspond to the "Debit" side (and are expenditures in other countries).

LUXEMBOURG

Basic Indicators	Units	2002	2003	2004	2005	2006
INBOUND TOURISM						
Arrivals						
1.1 Visitors	('000)	..	..	..	..	..
1.2 Tourists (overnight visitors)	('000)	885	867	878	913	908
1.3 Same-day visitors	('000)	..	..	..	..	..
1.4 Cruise passengers	('000)	..	..	..	..	..
Arrivals by region						
2.1 Africa	('000)	..	..	..	..	..
2.2 Americas	('000)	33	29	30	32	35
2.3 Europe	('000)	809	801	807	840	831
2.4 East Asia and the Pacific	('000)	..	..	..	..	..
2.5 South Asia	('000)	..	..	..	..	..
2.6 Middle East	('000)	..	..	..	..	..
Arrivals by means of transport used						
3.1 Air	('000)	..	..	..	..	..
3.2 Rail	('000)	..	..	..	..	..
3.3 Road	('000)	..	..	..	..	..
3.4 Sea	('000)	..	..	..	..	..
Arrivals by purpose of visit						
4.1 Leisure, recreation and holidays	('000)	..	..	..	..	..
4.2 Business and professional	('000)	..	..	..	..	..
4.3 Other	('000)	..	..	..	..	..
Accommodation						
5.1 Overnight stays in hotels and similar establishments	('000)	1,167	1,144	1,195	1,275	1,284
5.2 Guests in hotels and similar establishments	('000)	599	581	613	667	673
5.3 Overnight stays in all types of accommodation establishments	('000)	2,469	2,541	2,514	2,465	2,414
5.4 Average length of stay of non-resident tourists in all accommodation establishments	Nights	2.80	2.90	2.90	2.70	2.70
6.1 **Tourism expenditure in the country**	US$ Mn	2,547	3,149	3,880	..	..
6.2 "Travel" (*)	US$ Mn	2,406	2,994	3,650	3,614	3,626
6.3 "Passenger transport" (*)	US$ Mn	141	155	230	..	..
DOMESTIC TOURISM						
Accommodation						
7.1 Overnight stays in hotels and similar establishments	('000)	78	80	85	85	77
7.2 Guests in hotels and similar establishments	('000)	22	24	24	29	29
7.3 Overnight stays in all types of accommodation establishments	('000)	281	269	279	246	223
7.4 Average length of stay of resident tourists in all accommodation establishments	Nights	5.20	4.80	4.70	3.80	3.60
OUTBOUND TOURISM						
8.1 **Departures**	('000)	..	..	..	..	..
8.2 **Tourism expenditure in other countries**	US$ Mn	1,963	2,445	2,950	..	..
8.3 "Travel" (*)	US$ Mn	1,942	2,423	2,911	2,976	3,136
8.4 "Passenger transport" (*)	US$ Mn	21	22	39	..	..
TOURISM INDUSTRIES						
Hotels and similar establishments						
9.1 Number of rooms	Units	7,640	7,547	7,424	7,516	7,474
9.2 Number of bed-places	Units	14,545	14,620	14,237	..	..
9.3 Occupancy rate	Percent	25.60	25.10	28.20	29.50	29.90
9.4 Average length of stay	Nights	2.00	2.00	2.00	2.00	1.90
RELATED INDICATORS						
Share of tourism expenditure (6.1) in:						
10.1 Gross Domestic Product (GDP)	Percent	11.3	10.9	11.6	..	..
10.2 Exports of goods	Percent	26.7	28.8	28.7	..	..
10.3 Exports of services	Percent	12.6	12.5	11.5	..	..

(*) Balance of Payments items: 6.1 to 6.3 correspond to the "Credit" side (and are receipts for the country) while 8.2 to 8.4 correspond to the "Debit" side (and are expenditures in other countries).

Basic Indicators		Units	2002	2003	2004	2005	2006
	INBOUND TOURISM						
	Arrivals						
1.1	Visitors	('000)	11,531	11,888	16,673	18,711	21,998
1.2	Tourists (overnight visitors)	('000)	6,565	6,309	8,324	9,014	10,683
1.3	Same-day visitors	('000)	4,966	5,579	8,349	9,697	11,315
1.4	Cruise passengers	('000)	..	..	..	..	..
	Arrivals by region						
2.1	Africa	('000)	4	4	6	8	13
2.2	Americas	('000)	115	87	144	183	220
2.3	Europe	('000)	112	84	123	160	188
2.4	East Asia and the Pacific	('000)	11,280	11,693	16,372	18,325	21,530
2.5	South Asia	('000)	17	17	24	30	40
2.6	Middle East	('000)	1	1	2	3	4
	Arrivals by means of transport used						
3.1	Air	('000)	905	655	862	1,040	1,236
3.2	Rail	('000)		..			
3.3	Road	('000)	4,925	6,059	9,506	10,951	13,106
3.4	Sea	('000)	5,701	5,174	6,305	6,720	7,656
	Arrivals by purpose of visit						
4.1	Leisure, recreation and holidays	('000)	8,533	9,035	12,671	13,098	16,059
4.2	Business and professional	('000)	1,268	1,427	2,001	2,994	2,860
4.3	Other	('000)	1,730	1,426	2,001	2,619	3,080
	Accommodation						
5.1	Overnight stays in hotels and similar establishments	('000)	3,656	3,456	4,426	4,563	5,128
5.2	Guests in hotels and similar establishments	('000)	2,996	2,870	3,790	3,903	4,429
5.3	Overnight stays in all types of accommodation establishments	('000)	..	..	..	..	..
5.4	Average length of stay of non-resident tourists in all accommodation establishments	Nights	..	..	..	..	..
6.1	**Tourism expenditure in the country** (**)	US$ Mn	4,440	5,303	7,344	7,757	9,337
6.2	"Travel" (*)	US$ Mn	..	..	..	..	..
6.3	"Passenger transport" (*)	US$ Mn	..	..	..	..	..
	DOMESTIC TOURISM						
	Accommodation						
7.1	Overnight stays in hotels and similar establishments	('000)	218	240	226	281	338
7.2	Guests in hotels and similar establishments	('000)	159	173	166	218	253
7.3	Overnight stays in all types of accommodation establishments	('000)	..	..	..	..	..
7.4	Average length of stay of resident tourists in all accommodation establishments	Nights	..	..	1.44	1.30	1.40
	OUTBOUND TOURISM						
8.1	**Departures**	('000)	200	156	212	295	272
8.2	**Tourism expenditure in other countries**	US$ Mn	..	..	..	..	..
8.3	"Travel" (*)	US$ Mn	..	..	..	..	..
8.4	"Passenger transport" (*)	US$ Mn	..	..	..	..	..
	TOURISM INDUSTRIES						
	Hotels and similar establishments						
9.1	Number of rooms	Units	8,954	9,185	9,168	10,832	12,978
9.2	Number of bed-places	Units	18,628	19,117	18,591	21,460	26,851
9.3	Occupancy rate	Percent	67.13	64.27	75.55	70.93	72.25
9.4	Average length of stay	Nights	1.28	1.26	1.22	1.22	1.21
	RELATED INDICATORS						
	Share of tourism expenditure (6.1) in: (**)						
10.1	Gross Domestic Product (GDP)	Percent	..	..	..	..	..
10.2	Exports of goods	Percent	..	..	..	..	..
10.3	Exports of services	Percent	..	..	..	..	..

(*) Balance of Payments items: 6.1 to 6.3 correspond to the "Credit" side (and are receipts for the country) while 8.2 to 8.4 correspond to the "Debit" side (and are expenditures in other countries).

(**) See Annex "Country notes".

MADAGASCAR

Basic Indicators	Units	2002	2003	2004	2005	2006
INBOUND TOURISM						
Arrivals						
1.1 Visitors	('000)	..	..	..	..	..
1.2 Tourists (overnight visitors)	('000)	62	139	229	277	312
1.3 Same-day visitors	('000)	..	..	..	..	..
1.4 Cruise passengers	('000)	..	..	..	..	..
Arrivals by region						
2.1 Africa	('000)	6	22	39	52	59
2.2 Americas	('000)	2	4	9	14	16
2.3 Europe	('000)	43	99	176	203	228
2.4 East Asia and the Pacific	('000)	1	5	3	6	7
2.5 South Asia	('000)	..	..	..	..	..
2.6 Middle East	('000)	..	..	..	..	..
Arrivals by means of transport used						
3.1 Air	('000)	62	139	229	277	312
3.2 Rail	('000)	..	..	..	..	..
3.3 Road	('000)	..	..	..	..	..
3.4 Sea	('000)	..	..	..	..	..
Arrivals by purpose of visit						
4.1 Leisure, recreation and holidays	('000)	39	97	144	172	194
4.2 Business and professional	('000)	15	25	71	80	90
4.3 Other	('000)	8	18	14	25	28
Accommodation						
5.1 Overnight stays in hotels and similar establishments	('000)	555	2,088	3,536	5,221	5,299
5.2 Guests in hotels and similar establishments	('000)	..	..	..	..	..
5.3 Overnight stays in all types of accommodation establishments	('000)	..	..	..	..	..
5.4 Average length of stay of non-resident tourists in all accommodation establishments	Nights	9.00	15.00	16.00	20.00	17.00
6.1 **Tourism expenditure in the country**	US$ Mn	109	119	239	290	386
6.2 "Travel" (*)	US$ Mn	64	76	157	183	237
6.3 "Passenger transport" (*)	US$ Mn	45	43	82	107	149
DOMESTIC TOURISM						
Accommodation						
7.1 Overnight stays in hotels and similar establishments	('000)	..	..	..	..	..
7.2 Guests in hotels and similar establishments	('000)	..	..	..	..	..
7.3 Overnight stays in all types of accommodation establishments	('000)	..	..	..	..	..
7.4 Average length of stay of resident tourists in all accommodation establishments	Nights	..	..	..	..	..
OUTBOUND TOURISM						
8.1 **Departures**	('000)	..	..	..	..	..
8.2 **Tourism expenditure in other countries**	US$ Mn	192	67	108	80	..
8.3 "Travel" (*)	US$ Mn	160	64	93	74	86
8.4 "Passenger transport" (*)	US$ Mn	32	3	15	6	..
TOURISM INDUSTRIES						
Hotels and similar establishments						
9.1 Number of rooms	Units	8,780	9,325	10,230	10,879	11,872
9.2 Number of bed-places	Units	15,800	16,700	17,390	18,494	20,182
9.3 Occupancy rate	Percent	22.00	40.00	55.00	57.00	57.00
9.4 Average length of stay	Nights	2.00	4.00	4.00	4.00	4.00
RELATED INDICATORS						
Share of tourism expenditure (6.1) in:						
10.1 Gross Domestic Product (GDP)	Percent	2.5	2.2	5.5	5.8	7.0
10.2 Exports of goods	Percent	12.7	13.9	24.1	34.8	..
10.3 Exports of services	Percent	27.5	37.0	56.2	58.2	..

(*) Balance of Payments items: 6.1 to 6.3 correspond to the "Credit" side (and are receipts for the country) while 8.2 to 8.4 correspond to the "Debit" side (and are expenditures in other countries).

Basic Indicators	Units	2002	2003	2004	2005	2006
INBOUND TOURISM						
Arrivals						
1.1 Visitors	('000)	..	..	..	..	..
1.2 Tourists (overnight visitors)	('000)	383	424	427	438	..
1.3 Same-day visitors	('000)	..	..	..	..	..
1.4 Cruise passengers	('000)	..	..	..	..	..
Arrivals by region						
2.1 Africa	('000)	300	320	336	337	..
2.2 Americas	('000)	15	18	21	19	..
2.3 Europe	('000)	55	68	49	60	..
2.4 East Asia and the Pacific	('000)	6	10	11	9	..
2.5 South Asia	('000)	2	4	7	10	..
2.6 Middle East	('000)	..	..	..	..	..
Arrivals by means of transport used						
3.1 Air	('000)	94	114	114	106	..
3.2 Rail	('000)	12	9	4	8	..
3.3 Road	('000)	277	301	306	317	..
3.4 Sea	('000)	..	..	3	7	..
Arrivals by purpose of visit						
4.1 Leisure, recreation and holidays	('000)	101	112	95	114	..
4.2 Business and professional	('000)	206	209	208	227	..
4.3 Other	('000)	76	103	124	96	..
Accommodation						
5.1 Overnight stays in hotels and similar establishments	('000)	..	..	..	..	..
5.2 Guests in hotels and similar establishments	('000)	..	..	95	105	..
5.3 Overnight stays in all types of accommodation establishments	('000)	2,893	3,259	3,617	..	..
5.4 Average length of stay of non-resident tourists in all accommodation establishments	Nights	8.00	7.90	8.00	8.00	..
6.1 **Tourism expenditure in the country**	US$ Mn	45	35	36	43	43
6.2 "Travel" (*)	US$ Mn	33	23	24	24	24
6.3 "Passenger transport" (*)	US$ Mn	12	12	12	19	19
DOMESTIC TOURISM						
Accommodation						
7.1 Overnight stays in hotels and similar establishments	('000)	..	..	..	..	..
7.2 Guests in hotels and similar establishments	('000)	..	..	..	..	..
7.3 Overnight stays in all types of accommodation establishments	('000)	..	..	..	..	..
7.4 Average length of stay of resident tourists in all accommodation establishments	Nights	..	..	..	..	..
OUTBOUND TOURISM						
8.1 **Departures**	('000)	..	..	..	..	..
8.2 **Tourism expenditure in other countries**	US$ Mn	86	61	59	75	75
8.3 "Travel" (*)	US$ Mn	78	48	50	65	65
8.4 "Passenger transport" (*)	US$ Mn	8	13	9	10	10
TOURISM INDUSTRIES						
Hotels and similar establishments						
9.1 Number of rooms	Units	59,396	20,871	20,871	..	..
9.2 Number of bed-places	Units	63,585	113,874	113,874	..	..
9.3 Occupancy rate	Percent	27.00	33.00	40.00	54.00	..
9.4 Average length of stay	Nights	7.60	8.10	8.00	8.00	..
RELATED INDICATORS						
Share of tourism expenditure (6.1) in:						
10.1 Gross Domestic Product (GDP)	Percent	2.3	2.0	1.9	2.1	1.9
10.2 Exports of goods	Percent	10.7	..	..	..	..
10.3 Exports of services	Percent	91.8	..	..	..	..

(*) Balance of Payments items: 6.1 to 6.3 correspond to the "Credit" side (and are receipts for the country) while 8.2 to 8.4 correspond to the "Debit" side (and are expenditures in other countries).

MALAYSIA

Basic Indicators	Units	2002	2003	2004	2005	2006
INBOUND TOURISM						
Arrivals						
1.1 Visitors	('000)	20,756	16,293	24,432	24,209	25,298
1.2 Tourists (overnight visitors)	('000)	13,292	10,577	15,703	16,431	17,547
1.3 Same-day visitors	('000)	7,464	5,716	8,729	7,778	7,751
1.4 Cruise passengers	('000)	..	..	..	..	..
Arrivals by region						
2.1 Africa	('000)	148	134	137	128	157
2.2 Americas	('000)	283	270	272	275	312
2.3 Europe	('000)	637	456	540	618	673
2.4 East Asia and the Pacific	('000)	11,456	9,074	13,983	14,686	15,476
2.5 South Asia	('000)	244	209	249	321	390
2.6 Middle East	('000)	126	78	124	145	174
Arrivals by means of transport used						
3.1 Air	('000)	2,434	1,810	1,988	2,846	3,348
3.2 Rail	('000)	96	21	34	247	196
3.3 Road	('000)	9,869	7,989	12,299	11,878	12,169
3.4 Sea	('000)	245	265	330	449	523
Arrivals by purpose of visit						
4.1 Leisure, recreation and holidays	('000)	5,572	4,018	5,477	5,026	5,337
4.2 Business and professional	('000)	2,160	1,629	2,168	2,283	2,304
4.3 Other	('000)	4,912	4,438	7,006	7,335	8,595
Accommodation						
5.1 Overnight stays in hotels and similar establishments	('000)	..	..	..	..	..
5.2 Guests in hotels and similar establishments	('000)	15,615	13,239	20,009	21,448	22,457
5.3 Overnight stays in all types of accommodation establishments	('000)	..	..	..	..	..
5.4 Average length of stay of non-resident tourists in all accommodation establishments	Nights	..	..	..	..	..
6.1 **Tourism expenditure in the country**	US$ Mn	8,084	6,799	9,183	10,389	12,355
6.2 "Travel" (*)	US$ Mn	7,118	5,901	8,203	8,846	10,427
6.3 "Passenger transport" (*)	US$ Mn	966	898	980	1,543	1,928
DOMESTIC TOURISM						
Accommodation						
7.1 Overnight stays in hotels and similar establishments	('000)	..	..	..	..	..
7.2 Guests in hotels and similar establishments	('000)	16,458	18,335	27,885	29,926	31,900
7.3 Overnight stays in all types of accommodation establishments	('000)	..	..	..	..	..
7.4 Average length of stay of resident tourists in all accommodation establishments	Nights	..	..	..	..	..
OUTBOUND TOURISM						
8.1 **Departures**	('000)	29,866	32,201	30,761	..	..
8.2 **Tourism expenditure in other countries**	US$ Mn	3,330	3,401	3,822	4,339	4,847
8.3 "Travel" (*)	US$ Mn	2,618	2,846	3,178	3,711	4,020
8.4 "Passenger transport" (*)	US$ Mn	712	555	644	628	827
TOURISM INDUSTRIES						
Hotels and similar establishments						
9.1 Number of rooms	Units	137,196	144,380	151,135	155,356	157,251
9.2 Number of bed-places	Units	..	..	..	..	..
9.3 Occupancy rate	Percent	57.90	53.30	60.80	63.60	65.50
9.4 Average length of stay	Nights	..	..	..	..	..
RELATED INDICATORS						
Share of tourism expenditure (6.1) in:						
10.1 Gross Domestic Product (GDP)	Percent	8.5	6.5	7.8	7.9	8.3
10.2 Exports of goods	Percent	8.7	6.5	7.2	7.3	7.7
10.3 Exports of services	Percent	54.3	50.1	53.7	53.1	56.6

(*) Balance of Payments items: 6.1 to 6.3 correspond to the "Credit" side (and are receipts for the country) while 8.2 to 8.4 correspond to the "Debit" side (and are expenditures in other countries).

Basic Indicators	Units	2002	2003	2004	2005	2006
INBOUND TOURISM						
Arrivals						
1.1 Visitors	('000)	..	..	..	..	..
1.2 Tourists (overnight visitors)	('000)	485	564	617	395	602
1.3 Same-day visitors	('000)	..	..	..	..	..
1.4 Cruise passengers	('000)	3	4	4	4	3
Arrivals by region						
2.1 Africa	('000)	3	4	5	3	4
2.2 Americas	('000)	7	8	9	7	11
2.3 Europe	('000)	373	443	476	307	458
2.4 East Asia and the Pacific	('000)	77	84	100	56	102
2.5 South Asia	('000)	20	21	22	19	23
2.6 Middle East	('000)	3	4	5	2	4
Arrivals by means of transport used						
3.1 Air	('000)	485	564	617	395	602
3.2 Rail	('000)	..	..	..	..	..
3.3 Road	('000)	..	..	..	..	..
3.4 Sea	('000)	..	..	..	..	..
Arrivals by purpose of visit						
4.1 Leisure, recreation and holidays	('000)	485	564	617	395	602
4.2 Business and professional	('000)	..	..	..	..	..
4.3 Other	('000)	..	..	..	..	..
Accommodation						
5.1 Overnight stays in hotels and similar establishments	('000)	4,067	4,705	5,110	3,300	4,826
5.2 Guests in hotels and similar establishments	('000)	..	..	..	..	..
5.3 Overnight stays in all types of accommodation establishments	('000)	..	..	..	..	..
5.4 Average length of stay of non-resident tourists in all accommodation establishments	Nights	..	..	..	..	..
6.1 **Tourism expenditure in the country**	US$ Mn	..	..	..	..	..
6.2 "Travel" (*)	US$ Mn	337	402	471	287	434
6.3 "Passenger transport" (*)	US$ Mn	..	..	..	..	..
DOMESTIC TOURISM						
Accommodation						
7.1 Overnight stays in hotels and similar establishments	('000)	..	..	..	..	..
7.2 Guests in hotels and similar establishments	('000)	..	..	..	..	..
7.3 Overnight stays in all types of accommodation establishments	('000)	..	..	..	..	..
7.4 Average length of stay of resident tourists in all accommodation establishments	Nights	..	..	..	..	..
OUTBOUND TOURISM						
8.1 **Departures**	('000)	43	44	61	77	74
8.2 **Tourism expenditure in other countries**	US$ Mn	60	60	75	94	106
8.3 "Travel" (*)	US$ Mn	46	46	56	70	78
8.4 "Passenger transport" (*)	US$ Mn	14	14	19	24	28
TOURISM INDUSTRIES						
Hotels and similar establishments						
9.1 Number of rooms	Units	8,535	8,557	8,747	8,967	9,213
9.2 Number of bed-places	Units	17,070	17,114	17,494	17,934	18,425
9.3 Occupancy rate	Percent	68.98	77.23	83.93	64.39	81.39
9.4 Average length of stay	Nights	8.40	8.35	8.29	8.35	8.02
RELATED INDICATORS						
Share of tourism expenditure (6.1) in: (**)						
10.1 Gross Domestic Product (GDP)	Percent	52.6	58.1	60.7	38.0	47.4
10.2 Exports of goods	Percent	255.3	264.5	260.2	177.2	192.9
10.3 Exports of services	Percent	92.8	93.1	92.7	88.9	91.8

(*) Balance of Payments items: 6.1 to 6.3 correspond to the "Credit" side (and are receipts for the country) while 8.2 to 8.4 correspond to the "Debit" side (and are expenditures in other countries).

(**) See Annex "Country notes".

MALI

Basic Indicators	Units	2002	2003	2004	2005	2006
INBOUND TOURISM						
Arrivals						
1.1 Visitors	('000)	..	..	..	..	..
1.2 Tourists (overnight visitors)	('000)	96	110	113	143	153
1.3 Same-day visitors	('000)	..	..	..	..	..
1.4 Cruise passengers	('000)	..	..	..	..	..
Arrivals by region						
2.1 Africa	('000)	21	28	29	36	39
2.2 Americas	('000)	9	9	12	13	19
2.3 Europe	('000)	56	63	64	81	86
2.4 East Asia and the Pacific	('000)	1	1	3	2	2
2.5 South Asia	('000)	..	..	..	..	..
2.6 Middle East	('000)	3	3	2	1	1
Arrivals by means of transport used						
3.1 Air	('000)	96	110	113	143	153
3.2 Rail	('000)	..	..	..	..	..
3.3 Road	('000)	..	..	..	..	..
3.4 Sea	('000)	..	..	..	..	..
Arrivals by purpose of visit						
4.1 Leisure, recreation and holidays	('000)	..	..	..	..	..
4.2 Business and professional	('000)	..	..	..	..	..
4.3 Other	('000)	..	..	..	..	..
Accommodation						
5.1 Overnight stays in hotels and similar establishments	('000)	193	229	291	310	322
5.2 Guests in hotels and similar establishments	('000)	96	110	113	143	153
5.3 Overnight stays in all types of accommodation establishments	('000)	..	..	..	..	..
5.4 Average length of stay of non-resident tourists in all accommodation establishments	Nights	2.00	2.30	2.80	2.20	2.20
6.1 **Tourism expenditure in the country**	US$ Mn	105	136	142	149	..
6.2 "Travel" (*)	US$ Mn	104	128	140	148	167
6.3 "Passenger transport" (*)	US$ Mn	1	8	2	1	..
DOMESTIC TOURISM						
Accommodation						
7.1 Overnight stays in hotels and similar establishments	('000)	9	54	64	71	112
7.2 Guests in hotels and similar establishments	('000)	..	38	36	44	47
7.3 Overnight stays in all types of accommodation establishments	('000)	..	..	..	..	..
7.4 Average length of stay of resident tourists in all accommodation establishments	Nights	..	..	..	2.00	2.38
OUTBOUND TOURISM						
8.1 **Departures**	('000)	..	..	..	..	..
8.2 **Tourism expenditure in other countries**	US$ Mn	62	94	125	133	..
8.3 "Travel" (*)	US$ Mn	36	48	66	77	..
8.4 "Passenger transport" (*)	US$ Mn	26	46	59	56	..
TOURISM INDUSTRIES						
Hotels and similar establishments						
9.1 Number of rooms	Units	3,492	3,907	4,659	5,311	6,011
9.2 Number of bed-places	Units	5,349	5,066	5,546	7,521	9,016
9.3 Occupancy rate	Percent	36.50	38.00	40.00	40.00	40.00
9.4 Average length of stay	Nights	2.00	2.00	2.80	2.20	2.30
RELATED INDICATORS						
Share of tourism expenditure (6.1) in:						
10.1 Gross Domestic Product (GDP)	Percent	3.1	3.1	2.9	2.8	..
10.2 Exports of goods	Percent	12.0	14.7	14.5	13.5	..
10.3 Exports of services	Percent	62.1	60.7	58.9	54.4	..

(*) Balance of Payments items: 6.1 to 6.3 correspond to the "Credit" side (and are receipts for the country) while 8.2 to 8.4 correspond to the "Debit" side (and are expenditures in other countries).

Basic Indicators	Units	2002	2003	2004	2005	2006
INBOUND TOURISM						
Arrivals						
1.1 Visitors	('000)	1,483	1,516	1,448	1,491	1,532
1.2 Tourists (overnight visitors)	('000)	1,134	1,127	1,156	1,171	1,124
1.3 Same-day visitors	('000)	..	..	..	..	..
1.4 Cruise passengers	('000)	349	389	292	320	408
Arrivals by region						
2.1 Africa	('000)	9	..	..	..	..
2.2 Americas	('000)	27	21	19	18	17
2.3 Europe	('000)	1,040	940	983	990	940
2.4 East Asia and the Pacific	('000)	25	..	..	..	..
2.5 South Asia	('000)	2	..	..	..	..
2.6 Middle East	('000)	25	20	13	11	9
Arrivals by means of transport used						
3.1 Air	('000)	1,098	1,097	1,127	1,151	1,104
3.2 Rail	('000)	..	..	..	..	..
3.3 Road	('000)	..	..	..	..	..
3.4 Sea	('000)	35	29	29	20	20
Arrivals by purpose of visit						
4.1 Leisure, recreation and holidays	('000)	..	912	951	955	883
4.2 Business and professional	('000)	..	88	87	95	102
4.3 Other	('000)	..	89	89	101	119
Accommodation						
5.1 Overnight stays in hotels and similar establishments	('000)	7,021	7,712	7,725	7,603	7,377
5.2 Guests in hotels and similar establishments	('000)	797	863	904	906	868
5.3 Overnight stays in all types of accommodation establishments	('000)	10,599	11,115	10,973	10,933	10,503
5.4 Average length of stay of non-resident tourists in all accommodation establishments	Nights	9.30	10.20	9.70	9.50	9.50
6.1 **Tourism expenditure in the country**	US$ Mn	757	869	953	923	970
6.2 "Travel" (*)	US$ Mn	614	722	770	754	770
6.3 "Passenger transport" (*)	US$ Mn	143	147	183	169	200
DOMESTIC TOURISM						
Accommodation						
7.1 Overnight stays in hotels and similar establishments	('000)	..	..	..	..	..
7.2 Guests in hotels and similar establishments	('000)	..	..	..	..	..
7.3 Overnight stays in all types of accommodation establishments	('000)	..	..	..	..	..
7.4 Average length of stay of resident tourists in all accommodation establishments	Nights	..	..	..	..	..
OUTBOUND TOURISM						
8.1 **Departures**	('000)	157	174	203	225	257
8.2 **Tourism expenditure in other countries**	US$ Mn	180	238	292	311	363
8.3 "Travel" (*)	US$ Mn	154	215	256	268	321
8.4 "Passenger transport" (*)	US$ Mn	26	23	36	43	42
TOURISM INDUSTRIES						
Hotels and similar establishments						
9.1 Number of rooms	Units	..	..	..	..	..
9.2 Number of bed-places	Units	39,790	41,365	39,770	39,431	39,388
9.3 Occupancy rate	Percent	48.30	53.73	52.82	52.82	51.18
9.4 Average length of stay	Nights	8.80	9.00	9.50	8.40	8.40
RELATED INDICATORS						
Share of tourism expenditure (6.1) in:						
10.1 Gross Domestic Product (GDP)	Percent	18.2	17.9	17.9	16.6	.
10.2 Exports of goods	Percent	32.3	33.5	34.9	35.7	32.7
10.3 Exports of services	Percent	63.0	63.0	56.0	46.1	36.5

(*) Balance of Payments items: 6.1 to 6.3 correspond to the "Credit" side (and are receipts for the country) while 8.2 to 8.4 correspond to the "Debit" side (and are expenditures in other countries).

MARSHALL ISLANDS

Basic Indicators		Units	2002	2003	2004	2005	2006
	INBOUND TOURISM						
	Arrivals						
1.1	Visitors	('000)	..	..	..	..	..
1.2	Tourists (overnight visitors)	('000)	6.0	7.2	9.0	9.2	5.8
1.3	Same-day visitors	('000)	..	..	..	..	..
1.4	Cruise passengers	('000)	..	..	..	..	..
	Arrivals by region						
2.1	Africa	('000)	..	..	..	..	..
2.2	Americas	('000)	2.2	2.2	2.1	1.7	1.5
2.3	Europe	('000)	0.2	0.2	0.2	0.2	0.2
2.4	East Asia and the Pacific	('000)	3.4	4.4	4.5	5.6	3.9
2.5	South Asia	('000)	..	..	..	..	..
2.6	Middle East	('000)	..	..	..	..	..
	Arrivals by means of transport used						
3.1	Air	('000)	6.0	7.2	7.0	7.5	5.8
3.2	Rail	('000)	..	..	..	..	..
3.3	Road	('000)	..	..	..	..	..
3.4	Sea	('000)	..	..	2.0	1.7	..
	Arrivals by purpose of visit						
4.1	Leisure, recreation and holidays	('000)	1.4	1.4	2.7	2.7	1.3
4.2	Business and professional	('000)	2.2	2.2	3.0	3.1	2.0
4.3	Other	('000)	2.4	3.6	3.3	3.4	2.5
	Accommodation						
5.1	Overnight stays in hotels and similar establishments	('000)	..	..	..	..	..
5.2	Guests in hotels and similar establishments	('000)	..	..	..	..	..
5.3	Overnight stays in all types of accommodation establishments	('000)	37	40	38	41	37
5.4	Average length of stay of non-resident tourists in all accommodation establishments	Nights	6.09	5.61	4.17	4.50	6.33
6.1	**Tourism expenditure in the country** (**)	US$ Mn	3.4	4.0	5.0	5.7	6.6
6.2	"Travel" (*)	US$ Mn	..	..	..	..	..
6.3	"Passenger transport" (*)	US$ Mn	..	..	..	..	..
	DOMESTIC TOURISM						
	Accommodation						
7.1	Overnight stays in hotels and similar establishments	('000)	..	..	..	..	..
7.2	Guests in hotels and similar establishments	('000)	..	..	..	..	..
7.3	Overnight stays in all types of accommodation establishments	('000)	..	..	..	..	..
7.4	Average length of stay of resident tourists in all accommodation establishments	Nights	..	..	..	..	..
	OUTBOUND TOURISM						
8.1	**Departures**	('000)	..	..	..	..	..
8.2	**Tourism expenditure in other countries** (**)	US$ Mn	0.3	0.3	0.4	0.4	0.4
8.3	"Travel" (*)	US$ Mn	..	..	..	..	..
8.4	"Passenger transport" (*)	US$ Mn	..	..	..	..	..
	TOURISM INDUSTRIES						
	Hotels and similar establishments						
9.1	Number of rooms	Units	328	..	..	..	..
9.2	Number of bed-places	Units	..	..	..	..	..
9.3	Occupancy rate	Percent	..	..	..	..	..
9.4	Average length of stay	Nights	..	..	..	..	..
	RELATED INDICATORS						
	Share of tourism expenditure (6.1) in:						
10.1	Gross Domestic Product (GDP)	Percent	..	..	..	..	..
10.2	Exports of goods	Percent	..	..	..	..	..
10.3	Exports of services	Percent	..	..	..	..	..

(*) Balance of Payments items: 6.1 to 6.3 correspond to the "Credit" side (and are receipts for the country) while 8.2 to 8.4 correspond to the "Debit" side (and are expenditures in other countries).

(**) See Annex "Country notes".

Basic Indicators		Units	2002	2003	2004	2005	2006
	INBOUND TOURISM						
	Arrivals						
1.1	Visitors	('000)	654	722	630	577	599
1.2	Tourists (overnight visitors)	('000)	447	453	471	484	503
1.3	Same-day visitors	('000)	..	..	..	..	..
1.4	Cruise passengers	('000)	207	269	159	93	96
	Arrivals by region						
2.1	Africa	('000)	..	..	..	..	..
2.2	Americas	('000)	70	72	73	81	79
2.3	Europe	('000)	372	380	396	399	422
2.4	East Asia and the Pacific	('000)	..	..	..	..	..
2.5	South Asia	('000)	..	..	..	..	..
2.6	Middle East	('000)	..	..	..	..	..
	Arrivals by means of transport used						
3.1	Air	('000)	393	384	404	439	465
3.2	Rail	('000)	..	..	..	..	..
3.3	Road	('000)	..	..	..	..	..
3.4	Sea	('000)	54	70	67	45	38
	Arrivals by purpose of visit						
4.1	Leisure, recreation and holidays	('000)	390	384	393	374	424
4.2	Business and professional	('000)	44	53	61	79	58
4.3	Other	('000)	13	16	17	31	21
	Accommodation						
5.1	Overnight stays in hotels and similar establishments	('000)	1,991	1,693	1,705	1,924	1,707
5.2	Guests in hotels and similar establishments	('000)	198	187	192	216	204
5.3	Overnight stays in all types of accommodation establishments	('000)	6,022	6,136	6,770	6,496	6,965
5.4	Average length of stay of non-resident tourists in all accommodation establishments	Nights	13.50	13.50	14.40	13.40	13.80
6.1	**Tourism expenditure in the country** (**)	US$ Mn	237	247	291	280	306
6.2	"Travel" (*)	US$ Mn	..	..	..	..	..
6.3	"Passenger transport" (*)	US$ Mn	..	..	..	..	..
	DOMESTIC TOURISM						
	Accommodation						
7.1	Overnight stays in hotels and similar establishments	('000)	..	..	..	..	..
7.2	Guests in hotels and similar establishments	('000)	..	..	..	..	..
7.3	Overnight stays in all types of accommodation establishments	('000)	..	..	..	..	..
7.4	Average length of stay of resident tourists in all accommodation establishments	Nights	..	..	..	..	..
	OUTBOUND TOURISM						
8.1	**Departures**	('000)	..	..	..	..	..
8.2	**Tourism expenditure in other countries**	US$ Mn	..	..	..	..	..
8.3	"Travel" (*)	US$ Mn	..	..	..	..	..
8.4	"Passenger transport" (*)	US$ Mn	..	..	..	..	..
	TOURISM INDUSTRIES						
	Hotels and similar establishments						
9.1	Number of rooms	Units	6,766	6,766	6,153	6,153	6,153
9.2	Number of bed-places	Units	14,566	14,566	13,548	13,548	13,548
9.3	Occupancy rate	Percent	42.70	53.60	51.80	57.30	..
9.4	Average length of stay	Nights	10.00	9.00	9.00	8.50	..
	RELATED INDICATORS						
	Share of tourism expenditure (6.1) in:						
10.1	Gross Domestic Product (GDP)	Percent	..	..	..	..	..
10.2	Exports of goods	Percent	..	..	..	..	..
10.3	Exports of services	Percent	..	..	..	..	..

(*) Balance of Payments items: 6.1 to 6.3 correspond to the "Credit" side (and are receipts for the country) while 8.2 to 8.4 correspond to the "Debit" side (and are expenditures in other countries).

(**) See Annex "Country notes".

MAURITIUS

Basic Indicators	Units	2002	2003	2004	2005	2006
INBOUND TOURISM						
Arrivals						
1.1 Visitors	('000)	709	722	739	782	807
1.2 Tourists (overnight visitors)	('000)	682	702	719	761	788
1.3 Same-day visitors	('000)	9	11	11	11	11
1.4 Cruise passengers	('000)	18	9	9	9	8
Arrivals by region						
2.1 Africa	('000)	172	174	175	185	189
2.2 Americas	('000)	7	8	8	9	10
2.3 Europe	('000)	452	466	477	503	511
2.4 East Asia and the Pacific	('000)	25	22	27	29	34
2.5 South Asia	('000)	23	27	27	31	39
2.6 Middle East	('000)	2	5	4	4	5
Arrivals by means of transport used						
3.1 Air	('000)	668	690	708	748	775
3.2 Rail	('000)	..	..	..	..	..
3.3 Road	('000)	..	..	..	..	..
3.4 Sea	('000)	14	12	11	13	13
Arrivals by purpose of visit						
4.1 Leisure, recreation and holidays	('000)	620	636	654	692	713
4.2 Business and professional	('000)	29	31	30	30	32
4.3 Other	('000)	60	55	55	59	62
Accommodation						
5.1 Overnight stays in hotels and similar establishments	('000)	6,769	6,952	7,119	7,498	7,761
5.2 Guests in hotels and similar establishments	('000)	..	..	..	..	..
5.3 Overnight stays in all types of accommodation establishments	('000)	..	..	..	..	..
5.4 Average length of stay of non-resident tourists in all accommodation establishments	Nights	10.50	10.40	10.60	10.70	10.10
6.1 **Tourism expenditure in the country**	US$ Mn	829	960	1,156	1,189	1,302
6.2 "Travel" (*)	US$ Mn	612	697	856	871	1,005
6.3 "Passenger transport" (*)	US$ Mn	217	263	300	318	297
DOMESTIC TOURISM						
Accommodation						
7.1 Overnight stays in hotels and similar establishments	('000)	..	..	..	..	..
7.2 Guests in hotels and similar establishments	('000)	..	..	..	..	..
7.3 Overnight stays in all types of accommodation establishments	('000)	..	..	..	..	..
7.4 Average length of stay of resident tourists in all accommodation establishments	Nights	..	..	..	..	..
OUTBOUND TOURISM						
8.1 **Departures**	('000)	162	161	180	183	186
8.2 **Tourism expenditure in other countries**	US$ Mn	224	236	277	295	347
8.3 "Travel" (*)	US$ Mn	204	216	255	275	327
8.4 "Passenger transport" (*)	US$ Mn	20	20	22	20	20
TOURISM INDUSTRIES						
Hotels and similar establishments						
9.1 Number of rooms	Units	9,623	9,647	10,640	10,497	10,666
9.2 Number of bed-places	Units	19,597	19,727	21,355	21,072	21,403
9.3 Occupancy rate	Percent	67.00	63.00	63.00	63.00	66.00
9.4 Average length of stay	Nights	..	..	..	..	..
RELATED INDICATORS						
Share of tourism expenditure (6.1) in:						
10.1 Gross Domestic Product (GDP)	Percent	18.2	18.3	19.1	18.9	20.2
10.2 Exports of goods	Percent	46.0	50.6	58.0	55.6	55.8
10.3 Exports of services	Percent	72.1	75.0	79.4	73.5	77.9

(*) Balance of Payments items: 6.1 to 6.3 correspond to the "Credit" side (and are receipts for the country) while 8.2 to 8.4 correspond to the "Debit" side (and are expenditures in other countries).

Basic Indicators	Units	2002	2003	2004	2005	2006
INBOUND TOURISM						
Arrivals						
1.1 Visitors	('000)	100,153	92,330	99,250	103,146	97,701
1.2 Tourists (overnight visitors)	('000)	19,667	18,665	20,618	21,915	21,353
1.3 Same-day visitors	('000)	75,351	68,690	72,139	74,524	69,832
1.4 Cruise passengers	('000)	5,136	4,974	6,493	6,707	6,516
Arrivals by region						
2.1 Africa	('000)	..	..	..	..	..
2.2 Americas	('000)	19,133	18,155	19,706	18,983	18,652
2.3 Europe	('000)	479	443	..	1,149	1,310
2.4 East Asia and the Pacific	('000)	..	..	..	92	100
2.5 South Asia	('000)	..	..	..	..	..
2.6 Middle East	('000)	..	..	..	..	..
Arrivals by means of transport used						
3.1 Air	('000)	7,334	7,696	8,870	9,936	10,153
3.2 Rail	('000)	..	..	..	..	..
3.3 Road	('000)	12,333	10,969	11,748	11,979	11,199
3.4 Sea	('000)	..	..	..	..	..
Arrivals by purpose of visit						
4.1 Leisure, recreation and holidays	('000)	5,754	6,105	7,035	7,697	7,743
4.2 Business and professional	('000)	632	539	586	786	775
4.3 Other	('000)	13,280	12,021	12,998	13,432	12,835
Accommodation						
5.1 Overnight stays in hotels and similar establishments	('000)	25,291	26,011	30,227	33,623	30,236
5.2 Guests in hotels and similar establishments	('000)	7,869	8,556	9,972	10,691	9,689
5.3 Overnight stays in all types of accommodation establishments	('000)	..	..	..	..	..
5.4 Average length of stay of non-resident tourists in all accommodation establishments	Nights	10.28	10.32	10.14	9.93	9.93
6.1 **Tourism expenditure in the country**	US$ Mn	9,547	10,058	11,609	12,801	13,329
6.2 "Travel" (*)	US$ Mn	8,858	9,362	10,796	11,803	12,177
6.3 "Passenger transport" (*)	US$ Mn	689	696	813	998	1,152
DOMESTIC TOURISM						
Accommodation						
7.1 Overnight stays in hotels and similar establishments	('000)	57,174	58,715	64,355	64,607	64,124
7.2 Guests in hotels and similar establishments	('000)	29,939	31,128	34,454	34,547	35,192
7.3 Overnight stays in all types of accommodation establishments	('000)	..	..	..	..	..
7.4 Average length of stay of resident tourists in all accommodation establishments	Nights	..	..	..	..	..
OUTBOUND TOURISM						
8.1 **Departures**	('000)	11,948	11,044	12,494	13,305	14,002
8.2 **Tourism expenditure in other countries**	US$ Mn	7,087	7,252	8,034	8,951	9,387
8.3 "Travel" (*)	US$ Mn	6,060	6,253	6,959	7,600	8,108
8.4 "Passenger transport" (*)	US$ Mn	1,027	999	1,075	1,351	1,279
TOURISM INDUSTRIES						
Hotels and similar establishments						
9.1 Number of rooms	Units	469,488	496,292	515,904	535,639	556,399
9.2 Number of bed-places	Units	938,976	992,584	1,031,808	1,071,278	1,112,798
9.3 Occupancy rate	Percent	49.65	48.28	51.38	52.88	52.78
9.4 Average length of stay	Nights	3.21	3.04	3.03	3.15	3.12
RELATED INDICATORS						
Share of tourism expenditure (6.1) in:						
10.1 Gross Domestic Product (GDP)	Percent	1.5	1.6	1.7	1.7	1.6
10.2 Exports of goods	Percent	5.9	6.1	6.2	6.0	5.3
10.3 Exports of services	Percent	74.9	79.7	82.6	79.3	81.3

(*) Balance of Payments items: 6.1 to 6.3 correspond to the "Credit" side (and are receipts for the country) while 8.2 to 8.4 correspond to the "Debit" side (and are expenditures in other countries).

MICRONESIA (FEDERATED STATES OF)

Basic Indicators		Units	2002	2003	2004	2005	2006
	INBOUND TOURISM						
	Arrivals						
1.1	Visitors	('000)	..	..	..	..	..
1.2	Tourists (overnight visitors)	('000)	19.1	18.2	19.3	19.0	19.1
1.3	Same-day visitors	('000)	..	..		..	
1.4	Cruise passengers	('000)	..	..	..	..	
	Arrivals by region						
2.1	Africa	('000)	..	..	..	..	..
2.2	Americas	('000)	8.4	7.7	7.7	8.0	8.3
2.3	Europe	('000)	1.5	1.6	1.4	2.0	2.4
2.4	East Asia and the Pacific	('000)	9.0	8.9	10.0	8.9	8.4
2.5	South Asia	('000)	..	..		..	..
2.6	Middle East	('000)	..	..	..	..	..
	Arrivals by means of transport used						
3.1	Air	('000)	..	..	..	..	
3.2	Rail	('000)	..	..	..	..	
3.3	Road	('000)	..	..	..	..	
3.4	Sea	('000)	..	..	..	..	..
	Arrivals by purpose of visit						
4.1	Leisure, recreation and holidays	('000)	14.1	13.0	13.1	13.4	13.3
4.2	Business and professional	('000)	3.7	3.8	4.4	4.3	4.5
4.3	Other	('000)	1.3	1.4	1.8	1.2	1.3
	Accommodation						
5.1	Overnight stays in hotels and similar establishments	('000)	..	..	..		..
5.2	Guests in hotels and similar establishments	('000)	..	..	..	..	
5.3	Overnight stays in all types of accommodation establishments	('000)	..	..	..		
5.4	Average length of stay of non-resident tourists in all accommodation establishments	Nights	..	..	..	..	..
6.1	**Tourism expenditure in the country** (**)	US$ Mn	16.8	16.7	16.5	17.1	
6.2	"Travel" (*)	US$ Mn	..	..	..	..	..
6.3	"Passenger transport" (*)	US$ Mn	..	..	..	..	
	DOMESTIC TOURISM						
	Accommodation						
7.1	Overnight stays in hotels and similar establishments	('000)	..	..	..	..	..
7.2	Guests in hotels and similar establishments	('000)	..	..	..	..	..
7.3	Overnight stays in all types of accommodation establishments	('000)	..	..	..		..
7.4	Average length of stay of resident tourists in all accommodation establishments	Nights	..	..	..	..	..
	OUTBOUND TOURISM						
8.1	**Departures**	('000)	..	..	..		..
8.2	**Tourism expenditure in other countries** (**)	US$ Mn	5.3	5.6	5.4	5.7	..
8.3	"Travel" (*)	US$ Mn	..	..	..	..	..
8.4	"Passenger transport" (*)	US$ Mn	..	..	..	..	..
	TOURISM INDUSTRIES						
	Hotels and similar establishments						
9.1	Number of rooms	Units	..	..	..	..	..
9.2	Number of bed-places	Units	..	..	..	..	..
9.3	Occupancy rate	Percent	..	..	..	..	..
9.4	Average length of stay	Nights	..	..	..	..	..
	RELATED INDICATORS						
	Share of tourism expenditure (6.1) in:						
10.1	Gross Domestic Product (GDP)	Percent	..	..	..	..	..
10.2	Exports of goods	Percent	..	..	..	..	..
10.3	Exports of services	Percent	..	..	..	..	..

(*) Balance of Payments items: 6.1 to 6.3 correspond to the "Credit" side (and are receipts for the country) while 8.2 to 8.4 correspond to the "Debit" side (and are expenditures in other countries).

(**) See Annex "Country notes".

Basic Indicators	Units	2002	2003	2004	2005	2006
INBOUND TOURISM						
Arrivals						
1.1 Visitors	('000)	..	..	..	..	..
1.2 Tourists (overnight visitors)	('000)	263	235	250	286	313
1.3 Same-day visitors	('000)	..	..	..	..	..
1.4 Cruise passengers	('000)	56	80	125	133	180
Arrivals by region						
2.1 Africa	('000)	2	2	2	3	3
2.2 Americas	('000)	32	24	25	29	34
2.3 Europe	('000)	205	187	190	214	240
2.4 East Asia and the Pacific	('000)	12	10	13	12	11
2.5 South Asia	('000)	..	..	..	..	..
2.6 Middle East	('000)	4	3	3	3	4
Arrivals by means of transport used						
3.1 Air	('000)	169	151	168	196	222
3.2 Rail	('000)	..	..	..	..	..
3.3 Road	('000)	..	..	..	..	..
3.4 Sea	('000)	93	84	82	90	91
Arrivals by purpose of visit						
4.1 Leisure, recreation and holidays	('000)	183	178	192	219	244
4.2 Business and professional	('000)	79	57	59	67	69
4.3 Other	('000)	..	..	..	..	..
Accommodation						
5.1 Overnight stays in hotels and similar establishments	('000)	765	674	695	803	916
5.2 Guests in hotels and similar establishments	('000)	263	235	250	286	313
5.3 Overnight stays in all types of accommodation establishments	('000)	..	..	..	..	..
5.4 Average length of stay of non-resident tourists in all accommodation establishments	Nights	..	..	..	..	..
6.1 **Tourism expenditure in the country**	US$ Mn	..	..	..	..	..
6.2 "Travel" (*)	US$ Mn	..	..	..	..	..
6.3 "Passenger transport" (*)	US$ Mn	..	..	..	..	..
DOMESTIC TOURISM						
Accommodation						
7.1 Overnight stays in hotels and similar establishments	('000)	..	..	..	..	..
7.2 Guests in hotels and similar establishments	('000)	..	..	..	..	..
7.3 Overnight stays in all types of accommodation establishments	('000)	..	..	..	..	..
7.4 Average length of stay of resident tourists in all accommodation establishments	Nights	..	..	..	..	..
OUTBOUND TOURISM						
8.1 **Departures**	('000)	..	..	..	..	..
8.2 **Tourism expenditure in other countries**	US$ Mn	..	..	..	..	..
8.3 "Travel" (*)	US$ Mn	..	..	..	..	..
8.4 "Passenger transport" (*)	US$ Mn	..	..	..	..	..
TOURISM INDUSTRIES						
Hotels and similar establishments						
9.1 Number of rooms	Units	2,150	2,174	2,249	2,649	2,555
9.2 Number of bed-places	Units	3,513	3,232	3,737	5,312	5,288
9.3 Occupancy rate	Percent	63.75	59.04	58.02	58.39	58.77
9.4 Average length of stay	Nights	2.91	2.87	2.78	2.81	2.92
RELATED INDICATORS						
Share of tourism expenditure (6.1) in:						
10.1 Gross Domestic Product (GDP)	Percent	..	..	..	..	..
10.2 Exports of goods	Percent	..	..	..	..	..
10.3 Exports of services	Percent	..	..	..	..	..

(*) Balance of Payments items: 6.1 to 6.3 correspond to the "Credit" side (and are receipts for the country) while 8.2 to 8.4 correspond to the "Debit" side (and are expenditures in other countries).

MONGOLIA

Basic Indicators		Units	2002	2003	2004	2005	2006
	INBOUND TOURISM						
	Arrivals						
1.1	Visitors	('000)	235	205	305	345	390
1.2	Tourists (overnight visitors)	('000)	229	201	301	338	386
1.3	Same-day visitors	('000)	..	..	..	..	..
1.4	Cruise passengers	('000)	..	..	..	..	..
	Arrivals by region						
2.1	Africa	('000)	..	..	..	..	1
2.2	Americas	('000)	8	7	12	13	14
2.3	Europe	('000)	98	72	99	100	124
2.4	East Asia and the Pacific	('000)	122	121	188	223	246
2.5	South Asia	('000)	1	1	1	1	1
2.6	Middle East	('000)	..	..	..	..	..
	Arrivals by means of transport used						
3.1	Air	('000)	..	..	..	..	..
3.2	Rail	('000)	..	..	..	..	..
3.3	Road	('000)	..	..	..	..	..
3.4	Sea	('000)	..	..	..	..	..
	Arrivals by purpose of visit						
4.1	Leisure, recreation and holidays	('000)	51	21	64	65	128
4.2	Business and professional	('000)	28	39	73	86	80
4.3	Other	('000)	150	141	164	187	178
	Accommodation						
5.1	Overnight stays in hotels and similar establishments	('000)	..	..	..	..	..
5.2	Guests in hotels and similar establishments	('000)	..	..	..	..	..
5.3	Overnight stays in all types of accommodation establishments	('000)	..	..	..	..	..
5.4	Average length of stay of non-resident tourists in all accommodation establishments	Nights	..	..	..	..	..
6.1	**Tourism expenditure in the country**	US$ Mn	143	154	205	203	261
6.2	"Travel" (*)	US$ Mn	130	143	185	177	225
6.3	"Passenger transport" (*)	US$ Mn	13	11	20	26	36
	DOMESTIC TOURISM						
	Accommodation						
7.1	Overnight stays in hotels and similar establishments	('000)	..	..	..	..	..
7.2	Guests in hotels and similar establishments	('000)	..	..	..	..	..
7.3	Overnight stays in all types of accommodation establishments	('000)	..	..	..	..	..
7.4	Average length of stay of resident tourists in all accommodation establishments	Nights	..	..	..	..	..
	OUTBOUND TOURISM						
8.1	**Departures**	('000)	..	..	..	..	..
8.2	**Tourism expenditure in other countries**	US$ Mn	125	144	207	173	212
8.3	"Travel" (*)	US$ Mn	119	138	193	157	188
8.4	"Passenger transport" (*)	US$ Mn	6	6	14	16	24
	TOURISM INDUSTRIES						
	Hotels and similar establishments						
9.1	Number of rooms	Units	..	..	..	..	..
9.2	Number of bed-places	Units	..	..	..	..	..
9.3	Occupancy rate	Percent	..	..	..	..	..
9.4	Average length of stay	Nights	..	..	..	..	..
	RELATED INDICATORS						
	Share of tourism expenditure (6.1) in:						
10.1	Gross Domestic Product (GDP)	Percent	12.8	11.9	12.5	9.7	9.7
10.2	Exports of goods	Percent	27.3	24.6	23.5	19.0	16.9
10.3	Exports of services	Percent	77.7	74.0	60.7	49.0	53.7

(*) Balance of Payments items: 6.1 to 6.3 correspond to the "Credit" side (and are receipts for the country) while 8.2 to 8.4 correspond to the "Debit" side (and are expenditures in other countries).

Basic Indicators	Units	2002	2003	2004	2005	2006
INBOUND TOURISM						
Arrivals						
1.1 Visitors	('000)	..	..	..	..	..
1.2 Tourists (overnight visitors)	('000)	136	142	188	272	378
1.3 Same-day visitors	('000)	..	..	..	..	..
1.4 Cruise passengers	('000)	..	..	..	..	..
Arrivals by region						
2.1 Africa	('000)	..	..	..	..	..
2.2 Americas	('000)	3	3	3	4	7
2.3 Europe	('000)	129	135	180	260	360
2.4 East Asia and the Pacific	('000)	..	..	1	1	1
2.5 South Asia	('000)	..	..	..	..	..
2.6 Middle East	('000)	..	..	..	..	..
Arrivals by means of transport used						
3.1 Air	('000)	..	..	..	..	..
3.2 Rail	('000)	..	..	..	..	..
3.3 Road	('000)	..	..	..	..	..
3.4 Sea	('000)	..	..	..	..	..
Arrivals by purpose of visit						
4.1 Leisure, recreation and holidays	('000)	..	..	..	..	..
4.2 Business and professional	('000)	..	..	..	..	..
4.3 Other	('000)	..	..	..	..	..
Accommodation						
5.1 Overnight stays in hotels and similar establishments	('000)	717	688	917	1,031	1,452
5.2 Guests in hotels and similar establishments	('000)	114	115	150	190	269
5.3 Overnight stays in all types of accommodation establishments	('000)	912	916	1,224	1,584	2,196
5.4 Average length of stay of non-resident tourists in all accommodation establishments	Nights	..	..	..	..	..
6.1 **Tourism expenditure in the country**	US$ Mn	..	..	..	..	..
6.2 "Travel" (*)	US$ Mn	..	..	..	..	..
6.3 "Passenger transport" (*)	US$ Mn	..	..	..	..	..
DOMESTIC TOURISM						
Accommodation						
7.1 Overnight stays in hotels and similar establishments	('000)	1,370	1,314	1,552	1,505	1,200
7.2 Guests in hotels and similar establishments	('000)	174	165	196	197	169
7.3 Overnight stays in all types of accommodation establishments	('000)	2,778	3,061	3,337	3,628	3,740
7.4 Average length of stay of resident tourists in all accommodation establishments	Nights	..	..	..	..	..
OUTBOUND TOURISM						
8.1 **Departures**	('000)	..	..	..	..	..
8.2 **Tourism expenditure in other countries**	US$ Mn	..	..	..	..	..
8.3 "Travel" (*)	US$ Mn	..	..	..	..	..
8.4 "Passenger transport" (*)	US$ Mn	..	..	..	..	..
TOURISM INDUSTRIES						
Hotels and similar establishments						
9.1 Number of rooms	Units	..	..	..	..	..
9.2 Number of bed-places	Units	..	..	..	..	..
9.3 Occupancy rate	Percent	..	..	..	..	..
9.4 Average length of stay	Nights	..	..	..	..	..
RELATED INDICATORS						
Share of tourism expenditure (6.1) in:						
10.1 Gross Domestic Product (GDP)	Percent	..	..	..	..	..
10.2 Exports of goods	Percent	..	..	..	..	..
10.3 Exports of services	Percent	..	..	..	..	..

(*) Balance of Payments items: 6.1 to 6.3 correspond to the "Credit" side (and are receipts for the country) while 8.2 to 8.4 correspond to the "Debit" side (and are expenditures in other countries).

MONTSERRAT

Basic Indicators		Units	2002	2003	2004	2005	2006
	INBOUND TOURISM						
	Arrivals						
1.1	Visitors	('000)	15.0	13.6	15.2	13.1	9.5
1.2	Tourists (overnight visitors)	('000)	9.8	8.4	10.1	9.7	8.0
1.3	Same-day visitors	('000)	5.2	5.2	5.1	3.4	1.5
1.4	Cruise passengers	('000)	..	0.8	0.4	0.3	0.1
	Arrivals by region						
2.1	Africa	('000)	..	..	..	..	..
2.2	Americas	('000)	7.0	5.9	6.8	6.4	5.4
2.3	Europe	('000)	2.8	2.4	3.2	3.2	2.5
2.4	East Asia and the Pacific	('000)	..	..	..	..	..
2.5	South Asia	('000)	..	..	..	..	..
2.6	Middle East	('000)	..	..	..	..	..
	Arrivals by means of transport used						
3.1	Air	('000)	1.9	1.3	1.6	5.6	7.9
3.2	Rail	('000)	..	..	..	..	..
3.3	Road	('000)	..	..	..	..	..
3.4	Sea	('000)	7.9	7.1	8.5	4.1	0.1
	Arrivals by purpose of visit						
4.1	Leisure, recreation and holidays	('000)	4.1	4.2	4.9	3.6	4.3
4.2	Business and professional	('000)	1.5	1.4	1.8	1.9	1.3
4.3	Other	('000)	4.2	2.8	3.4	4.2	2.4
	Accommodation						
5.1	Overnight stays in hotels and similar establishments	('000)	..	..	..	..	..
5.2	Guests in hotels and similar establishments	('000)	2.0	1.4	1.9	2.5	2.3
5.3	Overnight stays in all types of accommodation establishments	('000)	..	..	..	..	..
5.4	Average length of stay of non-resident tourists in all accommodation establishments	Nights	..	..	..	..	..
6.1	**Tourism expenditure in the country**	US$ Mn	..	..	..	..	..
6.2	"Travel" (*)	US$ Mn	9	7	9	9	8
6.3	"Passenger transport" (*)	US$ Mn	..	..	..	..	..
	DOMESTIC TOURISM						
	Accommodation						
7.1	Overnight stays in hotels and similar establishments	('000)	..	..	..	..	..
7.2	Guests in hotels and similar establishments	('000)	..	..	..	..	..
7.3	Overnight stays in all types of accommodation establishments	('000)	..	..	..	..	..
7.4	Average length of stay of resident tourists in all accommodation establishments	Nights	..	..	..	..	..
	OUTBOUND TOURISM						
8.1	**Departures**	('000)	..	..	..	..	..
8.2	**Tourism expenditure in other countries**	US$ Mn	..	..	..	..	..
8.3	"Travel" (*)	US$ Mn	2	2	2	3	3
8.4	"Passenger transport" (*)	US$ Mn	..	..	..	..	..
	TOURISM INDUSTRIES						
	Hotels and similar establishments						
9.1	Number of rooms	Units	..	..	..	..	..
9.2	Number of bed-places	Units	..	..	..	..	..
9.3	Occupancy rate	Percent	..	..	..	..	..
9.4	Average length of stay	Nights	..	..	..	..	..
	RELATED INDICATORS						
	Share of tourism expenditure (6.1) in: (**)						
10.1	Gross Domestic Product (GDP)	Percent	..	..	..	..	..
10.2	Exports of goods	Percent	450.0	350.0	180.0	450.0	..
10.3	Exports of services	Percent	64.3	58.3	60.0	60.0	..

(*) Balance of Payments items: 6.1 to 6.3 correspond to the "Credit" side (and are receipts for the country) while 8.2 to 8.4 correspond to the "Debit" side (and are expenditures in other countries).

(**) See Annex "Country notes".

126

Basic Indicators	Units	2002	2003	2004	2005	2006
INBOUND TOURISM						
Arrivals						
1.1 Visitors	('000)	4,709	5,021	5,732	6,077	6,777
1.2 Tourists (overnight visitors)	('000)	4,453	4,761	5,477	5,843	6,558
1.3 Same-day visitors	('000)	..	..	..	..	..
1.4 Cruise passengers	('000)	255	260	256	233	218
Arrivals by region						
2.1 Africa	('000)	92	103	123	144	165
2.2 Americas	('000)	119	108	128	140	173
2.3 Europe	('000)	1,869	1,880	2,309	2,607	3,025
2.4 East Asia and the Pacific	('000)	44	42	49	52	65
2.5 South Asia	('000)	6	5	6	8	9
2.6 Middle East	('000)	86	79	84	91	106
Arrivals by means of transport used						
3.1 Air	('000)	2,095	2,139	2,548	2,986	3,549
3.2 Rail	('000)	..	..	..	..	..
3.3 Road	('000)	703	741	728	818	1,072
3.4 Sea	('000)	1,655	1,881	2,201	2,040	1,937
Arrivals by purpose of visit						
4.1 Leisure, recreation and holidays	('000)	2,330	2,394	2,849	3,145	3,620
4.2 Business and professional	('000)	106	110	130	143	164
4.3 Other	('000)	2,017	2,257	2,498	2,555	2,774
Accommodation						
5.1 Overnight stays in hotels and similar establishments	('000)	8,866	8,515	10,307	12,259	13,346
5.2 Guests in hotels and similar establishments	('000)	2,633	2,446	2,874	3,470	3,815
5.3 Overnight stays in all types of accommodation establishments	('000)	..	..	..	..	..
5.4 Average length of stay of non-resident tourists in all accommodation establishments	Nights	..	..	..	..	..
6.1 **Tourism expenditure in the country**	US$ Mn	3,157	3,802	4,540	5,426	6,899
6.2 "Travel" (*)	US$ Mn	2,646	3,221	3,922	4,610	5,984
6.3 "Passenger transport" (*)	US$ Mn	511	581	618	816	915
DOMESTIC TOURISM						
Accommodation						
7.1 Overnight stays in hotels and similar establishments	('000)	2,455	2,658	2,858	2,956	2,981
7.2 Guests in hotels and similar establishments	('000)	1,173	1,250	1,331	1,400	1,403
7.3 Overnight stays in all types of accommodation establishments	('000)	..	..	..	..	..
7.4 Average length of stay of resident tourists in all accommodation establishments	Nights	..	..	..	..	..
OUTBOUND TOURISM						
8.1 **Departures**	('000)	1,533	1,612	1,603	2,247	2,320
8.2 **Tourism expenditure in other countries**	US$ Mn	669	845	912	999	1,123
8.3 "Travel" (*)	US$ Mn	444	548	574	612	703
8.4 "Passenger transport" (*)	US$ Mn	225	297	338	387	420
TOURISM INDUSTRIES						
Hotels and similar establishments						
9.1 Number of rooms	Units	49,389	52,918	57,431	59,864	63,900
9.2 Number of bed-places	Units	102,097	109,615	119,248	124,270	133,230
9.3 Occupancy rate	Percent	42.00	39.00	43.00	47.00	49.00
9.4 Average length of stay	Nights	5.70	5.50	5.40	6.30	5.80
RELATED INDICATORS						
Share of tourism expenditure (6.1) in:						
10.1 Gross Domestic Product (GDP)	Percent	8.7	8.7	9.1	10.5	12.0
10.2 Exports of goods	Percent	40.3	43.3	45.8	50.8	57.9
10.3 Exports of services	Percent	72.4	69.4	67.7	67.0	70.1

(*) Balance of Payments items: 6.1 to 6.3 correspond to the "Credit" side (and are receipts for the country) while 8.2 to 8.4 correspond to the "Debit" side (and are expenditures in other countries).

MOZAMBIQUE

Basic Indicators	Units	2002	2003	2004	2005	2006
INBOUND TOURISM						
Arrivals						
1.1 Visitors	('000)	943	726	711	954	1,095
1.2　Tourists (overnight visitors)	('000)	541	441	470	578	664
1.3　Same-day visitors	('000)	402	285	241	376	431
1.4　Cruise passengers	('000)	..	..	..	..	..
Arrivals by region						
2.1 Africa	('000)	848	592	623	852	977
2.2 Americas	('000)	10	5	6	12	14
2.3 Europe	('000)	54	43	57	48	55
2.4 East Asia and the Pacific	('000)	6	..	..	8	9
2.5 South Asia	('000)	..	..	..	..	..
2.6 Middle East	('000)	..	..	..	..	..
Arrivals by means of transport used						
3.1 Air	('000)	55	70	116	156	175
3.2 Rail	('000)	..	..	..	..	..
3.3 Road	('000)	888	656	595	798	920
3.4 Sea	('000)	..	..	..	..	..
Arrivals by purpose of visit						
4.1 Leisure, recreation and holidays	('000)	222	141	131	175	214
4.2 Business and professional	('000)	210	187	254	275	310
4.3 Other	('000)	109	113	85	128	140
Accommodation						
5.1 Overnight stays in hotels and similar establishments	('000)	259	254	403	389	518
5.2 Guests in hotels and similar establishments	('000)	119	96	162	172	236
5.3 Overnight stays in all types of accommodation establishments	('000)	..	..	..	..	..
5.4 Average length of stay of non-resident tourists in all accommodation establishments	Nights	..	..	..	..	..
6.1 **Tourism expenditure in the country**	US$ Mn	65	106	96	138	145
6.2　"Travel" (*)	US$ Mn	63	98	95	130	140
6.3　"Passenger transport" (*)	US$ Mn	2	8	1	8	5
DOMESTIC TOURISM						
Accommodation						
7.1 Overnight stays in hotels and similar establishments	('000)	243	224	298	317	361
7.2 Guests in hotels and similar establishments	('000)	130	122	158	167	181
7.3 Overnight stays in all types of accommodation establishments	('000)	..	..	..	..	..
7.4 Average length of stay of resident tourists in all accommodation establishments	Nights	..	..	..	..	..
OUTBOUND TOURISM						
8.1 **Departures**	('000)	..	..	..	..	..
8.2 **Tourism expenditure in other countries**	US$ Mn	115	141	140	187	205
8.3　"Travel" (*)	US$ Mn	113	140	134	176	179
8.4　"Passenger transport" (*)	US$ Mn	2	1	6	11	26
TOURISM INDUSTRIES						
Hotels and similar establishments						
9.1 Number of rooms	Units	..	6,899	..	..	9,780
9.2 Number of bed-places	Units	12,292	13,601	13,807	14,827	15,740
9.3 Occupancy rate	Percent	19.00	13.90	..	..	..
9.4 Average length of stay	Nights	2.30	2.10	2.19	2.10	2.10
RELATED INDICATORS						
Share of tourism expenditure (6.1) in:						
10.1 Gross Domestic Product (GDP)	Percent	1.6	2.2	1.6	2.0	1.9
10.2 Exports of goods	Percent	8.0	10.2	6.4	7.9	6.1
10.3 Exports of services	Percent	19.2	34.9	37.5	40.4	37.6

(*) Balance of Payments items: 6.1 to 6.3 correspond to the "Credit" side (and are receipts for the country) while 8.2 to 8.4 correspond to the "Debit" side (and are expenditures in other countries).

Basic Indicators	Units	2002	2003	2004	2005	2006
INBOUND TOURISM						
Arrivals						
1.1 Visitors	('000)	487	597	657	660	630
1.2 Tourists (overnight visitors)	('000)	217	206	242	232	264
1.3 Same-day visitors	('000)	268	388	413	426	366
1.4 Cruise passengers	('000)	2	3	2	2	3
Arrivals by region						
2.1 Africa	('000)	..	..	..	..	1
2.2 Americas	('000)	18	16	20	21	23
2.3 Europe	('000)	65	60	65	68	81
2.4 East Asia and the Pacific	('000)	124	116	142	130	148
2.5 South Asia	('000)	7	12	12	11	9
2.6 Middle East	('000)	2	1	2	2	2
Arrivals by means of transport used						
3.1 Air	('000)	215	203	240	230	261
3.2 Rail	('000)	..	..	..	..	..
3.3 Road	('000)	270	391	415	428	366
3.4 Sea	('000)	2	3	2	2	3
Arrivals by purpose of visit						
4.1 Leisure, recreation and holidays	('000)	138	129	164	151	180
4.2 Business and professional	('000)	37	44	40	36	36
4.3 Other	('000)	312	423	453	473	414
Accommodation						
5.1 Overnight stays in hotels and similar establishments	('000)	1,521	1,416	1,679	1,626	1,845
5.2 Guests in hotels and similar establishments	('000)	..	..	..	..	..
5.3 Overnight stays in all types of accommodation establishments	('000)	..	..	..	..	..
5.4 Average length of stay of non-resident tourists in all accommodation establishments	Nights	7.00	7.50	7.00	7.00	7.00
6.1 **Tourism expenditure in the country**	US$ Mn	136	70	97	85	59
6.2 "Travel" (*)	US$ Mn	120	56	84	68	46
6.3 "Passenger transport" (*)	US$ Mn	16	14	13	17	13
DOMESTIC TOURISM						
Accommodation						
7.1 Overnight stays in hotels and similar establishments	('000)	..	..	..	..	601
7.2 Guests in hotels and similar establishments	('000)	..	..	..	..	..
7.3 Overnight stays in all types of accommodation establishments	('000)	..	..	..	..	822
7.4 Average length of stay of resident tourists in all accommodation establishments	Nights	..	..	..	..	2.00
OUTBOUND TOURISM						
8.1 **Departures**	('000)	..	..	..	..	..
8.2 **Tourism expenditure in other countries**	US$ Mn	34	36	32	34	40
8.3 "Travel" (*)	US$ Mn	29	32	29	31	37
8.4 "Passenger transport" (*)	US$ Mn	5	4	3	3	3
TOURISM INDUSTRIES						
Hotels and similar establishments						
9.1 Number of rooms	Units	15,848	17,039	18,985	19,040	19,506
9.2 Number of bed-places	Units	31,696	34,078	37,970	38,080	39,012
9.3 Occupancy rate	Percent	23.00	20.00	21.00	20.00	26.00
9.4 Average length of stay	Nights	4.00	4.00	4.00	4.00	4.00
RELATED INDICATORS						
Share of tourism expenditure (6.1) in:						
10.1 Gross Domestic Product (GDP)	Percent	..	..	..	..	..
10.2 Exports of goods	Percent	5.6	2.6	3.3	2.2	1.3
10.3 Exports of services	Percent	31.9	28.1	38.0	32.8	21.1

(*) Balance of Payments items: 6.1 to 6.3 correspond to the "Credit" side (and are receipts for the country) while 8.2 to 8.4 correspond to the "Debit" side (and are expenditures in other countries).

NAMIBIA

Basic Indicators	Units	2002	2003	2004	2005	2006
INBOUND TOURISM						
Arrivals						
1.1 Visitors	('000)	948	917	986	973	1,032
1.2 Tourists (overnight visitors)	('000)	757	695	..	778	833
1.3 Same-day visitors	('000)	42	44	..	78	127
1.4 Cruise passengers	('000)	..	..	..	..	..
Arrivals by region						
2.1 Africa	('000)	592	526	..	602	629
2.2 Americas	('000)	10	12	..	15	16
2.3 Europe	('000)	141	142	..	146	167
2.4 East Asia and the Pacific	('000)	3	4	..	5	5
2.5 South Asia	('000)	..	..	..	..	..
2.6 Middle East	('000)	..	..	..	..	..
Arrivals by means of transport used						
3.1 Air	('000)	183	167	167	185	217
3.2 Rail	('000)	3	4	..	2	2
3.3 Road	('000)	571	516	..	587	611
3.4 Sea	('000)	..	4	..	3	3
Arrivals by purpose of visit						
4.1 Leisure, recreation and holidays	('000)	430	299	..	322	406
4.2 Business and professional	('000)	53	98	..	101	102
4.3 Other	('000)	274	298	..	355	325
Accommodation						
5.1 Overnight stays in hotels and similar establishments	('000)	595	299	..	606	722
5.2 Guests in hotels and similar establishments	('000)	317	149	..	426	698
5.3 Overnight stays in all types of accommodation establishments	('000)	1,006	424	..	1,409	1,372
5.4 Average length of stay of non-resident tourists in all accommodation establishments	Nights	18.90	17.20	17.17	..	19.10
6.1 **Tourism expenditure in the country**	US$ Mn	251	383	426	363	473
6.2 "Travel" (*)	US$ Mn	218	333	405	349	381
6.3 "Passenger transport" (*)	US$ Mn	33	50	21	14	92
DOMESTIC TOURISM						
Accommodation						
7.1 Overnight stays in hotels and similar establishments	('000)	269	82	..	..	..
7.2 Guests in hotels and similar establishments	('000)	150	49	..	..	..
7.3 Overnight stays in all types of accommodation establishments	('000)	445	123	..	..	..
7.4 Average length of stay of resident tourists in all accommodation establishments	Nights	..	..	..	..	1.94
OUTBOUND TOURISM						
8.1 **Departures**	('000)	..	..	..	..	..
8.2 **Tourism expenditure in other countries**	US$ Mn	..	..	..	..	..
8.3 "Travel" (*)	US$ Mn	65	101	123	108	118
8.4 "Passenger transport" (*)	US$ Mn	..	..	..	..	..
TOURISM INDUSTRIES						
Hotels and similar establishments						
9.1 Number of rooms	Units	2,726	2,749	..	2,900	..
9.2 Number of bed-places	Units	5,674	6,091	..	7,240	..
9.3 Occupancy rate	Percent	59.10	43.30	..	39.00	59.60
9.4 Average length of stay	Nights	1.90	1.90	..	1.90	1.94
RELATED INDICATORS						
Share of tourism expenditure (6.1) in:						
10.1 Gross Domestic Product (GDP)	Percent	8.0	8.6	7.5	5.9	7.4
10.2 Exports of goods	Percent	23.4	30.3	23.3	17.5	17.9
10.3 Exports of services	Percent	92.3	92.5	89.7	87.7	89.4

(*) Balance of Payments items: 6.1 to 6.3 correspond to the "Credit" side (and are receipts for the country) while 8.2 to 8.4 correspond to the "Debit" side (and are expenditures in other countries).

Basic Indicators	Units	2002	2003	2004	2005	2006
INBOUND TOURISM						
Arrivals						
1.1 Visitors	('000)	..	..	..	..	..
1.2 Tourists (overnight visitors)	('000)	275	338	385	375	384
1.3 Same-day visitors	('000)	..	..	..	..	..
1.4 Cruise passengers	('000)	..	..	..	..	..
Arrivals by region						
2.1 Africa	('000)	1	2	1	1	2
2.2 Americas	('000)	25	25	30	26	28
2.3 Europe	('000)	96	111	131	112	107
2.4 East Asia and the Pacific	('000)	68	92	97	93	95
2.5 South Asia	('000)	84	108	125	139	137
2.6 Middle East	('000)	..	..	..	..	..
Arrivals by means of transport used						
3.1 Air	('000)	218	275	297	277	284
3.2 Rail	('000)	..	..	..	..	..
3.3 Road	('000)	57	63	88	98	100
3.4 Sea	('000)	..	..	..	..	..
Arrivals by purpose of visit						
4.1 Leisure, recreation and holidays	('000)	169	164	237	222	213
4.2 Business and professional	('000)	35	41	31	39	39
4.3 Other	('000)	71	133	117	115	132
Accommodation						
5.1 Overnight stays in hotels and similar establishments	('000)	..	..	..	..	..
5.2 Guests in hotels and similar establishments	('000)	..	..	..	..	..
5.3 Overnight stays in all types of accommodation establishments	('000)	..	..	..	..	..
5.4 Average length of stay of non-resident tourists in all accommodation establishments	Nights	7.92	9.60	13.51	9.09	10.20
6.1 **Tourism expenditure in the country**	US$ Mn	134	232	260	160	157
6.2 "Travel" (*)	US$ Mn	103	199	230	131	128
6.3 "Passenger transport" (*)	US$ Mn	31	33	30	29	29
DOMESTIC TOURISM						
Accommodation						
7.1 Overnight stays in hotels and similar establishments	('000)	..	..	..	..	..
7.2 Guests in hotels and similar establishments	('000)	..	..	..	..	..
7.3 Overnight stays in all types of accommodation establishments	('000)	..	..	..	..	..
7.4 Average length of stay of resident tourists in all accommodation establishments	Nights	..	..	..	..	..
OUTBOUND TOURISM						
8.1 **Departures**	('000)	238	258	286	373	415
8.2 **Tourism expenditure in other countries**	US$ Mn	108	119	205	221	261
8.3 "Travel" (*)	US$ Mn	69	81	154	163	185
8.4 "Passenger transport" (*)	US$ Mn	39	38	51	58	76
TOURISM INDUSTRIES						
Hotels and similar establishments						
9.1 Number of rooms	Units	19,667	20,063	20,624	20,801	12,253
9.2 Number of bed-places	Units	37,616	38,270	39,107	39,384	24,260
9.3 Occupancy rate	Percent	..	..	..	..	..
9.4 Average length of stay	Nights	..	..	..	..	..
RELATED INDICATORS						
Share of tourism expenditure (6.1) in:						
10.1 Gross Domestic Product (GDP)	Percent	2.4	4.0	3.9	2.2	1.9
10.2 Exports of goods	Percent	21.2	33.0	33.6	17.7	18.5
10.3 Exports of services	Percent	43.9	62.4	56.4	42.1	40.7

(*) Balance of Payments items: 6.1 to 6.3 correspond to the "Credit" side (and are receipts for the country) while 8.2 to 8.4 correspond to the "Debit" side (and are expenditures in other countries).

NETHERLANDS

Basic Indicators		Units	2002	2003	2004	2005	2006
	INBOUND TOURISM						
	Arrivals						
1.1	Visitors	('000)	..	..	..	..	..
1.2	Tourists (overnight visitors)	('000)	9,595	9,181	9,646	10,012	10,739
1.3	Same-day visitors	('000)	..	..	..	..	..
1.4	Cruise passengers	('000)	..	..	..	..	..
	Arrivals by region						
2.1	Africa	('000)	173	131	117	101	93
2.2	Americas	('000)	1,100	996	1,131	1,222	1,325
2.3	Europe	('000)	7,592	7,432	7,644	7,940	8,598
2.4	East Asia and the Pacific	('000)	731	622	754	749	723
2.5	South Asia	('000)	..	..	..	..	..
2.6	Middle East	('000)	..	..	..	..	..
	Arrivals by means of transport used						
3.1	Air	('000)	..	..	..	..	..
3.2	Rail	('000)	..	..	..	..	..
3.3	Road	('000)	..	..	..	..	..
3.4	Sea	('000)	..	..	..	..	..
	Arrivals by purpose of visit						
4.1	Leisure, recreation and holidays	('000)	..	..	..	..	..
4.2	Business and professional	('000)	..	..	..	..	..
4.3	Other	('000)	..	..	..	..	..
	Accommodation						
5.1	Overnight stays in hotels and similar establishments	('000)	14,922	13,798	14,616	15,143	15,976
5.2	Guests in hotels and similar establishments	('000)	7,433	6,931	7,601	8,081	8,567
5.3	Overnight stays in all types of accommodation establishments	('000)	26,368	25,342	25,385	25,210	26,887
5.4	Average length of stay of non-resident tourists in all accommodation establishments	Nights	2.70	2.80	2.60	2.50	2.50
6.1	**Tourism expenditure in the country**	US$ Mn	11,745	..	..	..	..
6.2	"Travel" (*)	US$ Mn	7,710	9,163	10,308	10,446	11,381
6.3	"Passenger transport" (*)	US$ Mn	4,035	..	..	..	..
	DOMESTIC TOURISM						
	Accommodation						
7.1	Overnight stays in hotels and similar establishments	('000)	13,593	13,384	13,761	14,375	15,783
7.2	Guests in hotels and similar establishments	('000)	7,515	7,379	7,911	8,301	9,463
7.3	Overnight stays in all types of accommodation establishments	('000)	56,004	55,864	55,518	54,951	57,057
7.4	Average length of stay of resident tourists in all accommodation establishments	Nights	..	..	..	..	..
	OUTBOUND TOURISM						
8.1	**Departures**	('000)	16,719	16,425	17,130	17,039	16,695
8.2	**Tourism expenditure in other countries**	US$ Mn	14,201	..	..	..	..
8.3	"Travel" (*)	US$ Mn	12,976	15,265	16,348	16,140	17,087
8.4	"Passenger transport" (*)	US$ Mn	1,225	..	..	..	..
	TOURISM INDUSTRIES						
	Hotels and similar establishments						
9.1	Number of rooms	Units	86,247	88,146	93,047	94,364	94,509
9.2	Number of bed-places	Units	177,435	180,158	189,835	192,215	192,067
9.3	Occupancy rate	Percent	45.50	42.80	42.10	42.10	45.30
9.4	Average length of stay	Nights	1.90	1.90	1.80	1.80	1.80
	RELATED INDICATORS						
	Share of tourism expenditure (6.1) in:						
10.1	Gross Domestic Product (GDP)	Percent	2.7	..	..	..	..
10.2	Exports of goods	Percent	5.6	..	..	..	..
10.3	Exports of services	Percent	20.9	..	..	..	..

(*) Balance of Payments items: 6.1 to 6.3 correspond to the "Credit" side (and are receipts for the country) while 8.2 to 8.4 correspond to the "Debit" side (and are expenditures in other countries).

Basic Indicators	Units	2002	2003	2004	2005	2006
INBOUND TOURISM						
Arrivals						
1.1 Visitors	('000)	158	166	177	182	219
1.2 Tourists (overnight visitors)	('000)	104	102	100	101	100
1.3 Same-day visitors	('000)	..	..	..	..	..
1.4 Cruise passengers	('000)	54	64	77	81	119
Arrivals by region						
2.1 Africa	('000)	1	..	1	1	1
2.2 Americas	('000)	2	2	2	2	2
2.3 Europe	('000)	33	32	30	30	32
2.4 East Asia and the Pacific	('000)	68	65	66	68	66
2.5 South Asia	('000)	..	..	..	..	..
2.6 Middle East	('000)	..	..	..	..	..
Arrivals by means of transport used						
3.1 Air	('000)	102	101	99	101	100
3.2 Rail	('000)	..	..	..	..	..
3.3 Road	('000)	..	..	..	..	..
3.4 Sea	('000)	2	1	1	..	..
Arrivals by purpose of visit						
4.1 Leisure, recreation and holidays	('000)	70	71	73	76	77
4.2 Business and professional	('000)	12	10	11	12	14
4.3 Other	('000)	22	21	16	13	9
Accommodation						
5.1 Overnight stays in hotels and similar establishments	('000)	352	343	369	350	379
5.2 Guests in hotels and similar establishments	('000)	82	75	79	77	85
5.3 Overnight stays in all types of accommodation establishments	('000)	..	..	..	..	..
5.4 Average length of stay of non-resident tourists in all accommodation establishments	Nights	16.30	15.60	16.20	16.80	19.10
6.1 **Tourism expenditure in the country**	US$ Mn	..	..	..	..	..
6.2 "Travel" (*)	US$ Mn	156	196	241	253	258
6.3 "Passenger transport" (*)	US$ Mn	..	..	..	..	..
DOMESTIC TOURISM						
Accommodation						
7.1 Overnight stays in hotels and similar establishments	('000)	129	156	167	193	233
7.2 Guests in hotels and similar establishments	('000)	54	59	63	69	82
7.3 Overnight stays in all types of accommodation establishments	('000)	..	..	..	..	..
7.4 Average length of stay of resident tourists in all accommodation establishments	Nights	..	..	..	..	..
OUTBOUND TOURISM						
8.1 **Departures**	('000)	72	78	89	96	100
8.2 **Tourism expenditure in other countries**	US$ Mn	..	..	..	..	..
8.3 "Travel" (*)	US$ Mn	104	128	167	171	186
8.4 "Passenger transport" (*)	US$ Mn	..	..	..	..	..
TOURISM INDUSTRIES						
Hotels and similar establishments						
9.1 Number of rooms	Units	2,140	2,149	2,295	2,245	..
9.2 Number of bed-places	Units	..	..	..	..	..
9.3 Occupancy rate	Percent	57.10	59.70	59.60	61.30	61.90
9.4 Average length of stay	Nights	4.00	4.40	4.50	4.40	3.70
RELATED INDICATORS						
Share of tourism expenditure (6.1) in: (**)						
10.1 Gross Domestic Product (GDP)	Percent	..	..	..	..	..
10.2 Exports of goods	Percent	33.8	25.0	23.9	23.2	21.6
10.3 Exports of services	Percent	44.7	45.7	49.5	52.4	46.6

(*) Balance of Payments items: 6.1 to 6.3 correspond to the "Credit" side (and are receipts for the country) while 8.2 to 8.4 correspond to the "Debit" side (and are expenditures in other countries).

(**) See Annex "Country notes".

NEW ZEALAND

Basic Indicators		Units	2002	2003	2004	2005	2006
	INBOUND TOURISM						
	Arrivals						
1.1	Visitors	('000)	2,045	2,104	2,334	2,366	2,409
1.2	Tourists (overnight visitors)	('000)	..	..	..	..	..
1.3	Same-day visitors	('000)	..	..	..	..	..
1.4	Cruise passengers	('000)	19	18	9	13	19
	Arrivals by region						
2.1	Africa	('000)	21	19	19	20	21
2.2	Americas	('000)	261	266	276	276	294
2.3	Europe	('000)	423	461	489	521	516
2.4	East Asia and the Pacific	('000)	1,240	1,272	1,468	1,484	1,512
2.5	South Asia	('000)	19	17	18	20	23
2.6	Middle East	('000)	6	7	8	9	10
	Arrivals by means of transport used						
3.1	Air	('000)	2,022	2,083	2,322	2,349	2,387
3.2	Rail	('000)	..	..	..	..	..
3.3	Road	('000)	..	..	..	..	..
3.4	Sea	('000)	23	21	12	17	22
	Arrivals by purpose of visit						
4.1	Leisure, recreation and holidays	('000)	1,074	1,083	1,190	1,192	1,195
4.2	Business and professional	('000)	252	262	303	319	328
4.3	Other	('000)	719	759	841	855	886
	Accommodation						
5.1	Overnight stays in hotels and similar establishments	('000)	..	..	..	..	..
5.2	Guests in hotels and similar establishments	('000)	..	..	..	..	..
5.3	Overnight stays in all types of accommodation establishments	('000)	11,426	11,653	12,838	13,408	13,120
5.4	Average length of stay of non-resident tourists in all accommodation establishments	Nights	..	..	..	..	..
6.1	**Tourism expenditure in the country**	US$ Mn	..	..	..	..	..
6.2	"Travel" (*)	US$ Mn	3,077	4,028	4,782	4,873	4,563
6.3	"Passenger transport" (*)	US$ Mn	..	..	..	..	..
	DOMESTIC TOURISM						
	Accommodation						
7.1	Overnight stays in hotels and similar establishments	('000)	..	..	..	..	..
7.2	Guests in hotels and similar establishments	('000)	..	..	..	..	..
7.3	Overnight stays in all types of accommodation establishments	('000)	17,493	17,924	18,111	18,103	18,585
7.4	Average length of stay of resident tourists in all accommodation establishments	Nights	..	..	..	..	..
	OUTBOUND TOURISM						
8.1	**Departures**	('000)	1,293	1,374	1,733	1,872	1,861
8.2	**Tourism expenditure in other countries**	US$ Mn	..	..	..	..	..
8.3	"Travel" (*)	US$ Mn	1,386	1,649	2,217	2,657	2,526
8.4	"Passenger transport" (*)	US$ Mn	..	..	..	..	..
	TOURISM INDUSTRIES						
	Hotels and similar establishments						
9.1	Number of rooms	Units	19,841	20,072	20,482	21,498	22,084
9.2	Number of bed-places	Units	..	..	..	..	..
9.3	Occupancy rate	Percent	54.24	54.28	56.07	54.15	53.34
9.4	Average length of stay	Nights	1.82	1.82	1.80	1.80	1.81
	RELATED INDICATORS						
	Share of tourism expenditure (6.1) in: (**)						
10.1	Gross Domestic Product (GDP)	Percent	5.1	5.0	4.9	4.5	4.4
10.2	Exports of goods	Percent	21.2	24.0	23.4	22.2	20.3
10.3	Exports of services	Percent	57.8	60.2	60.5	58.7	58.0

(*) Balance of Payments items: 6.1 to 6.3 correspond to the "Credit" side (and are receipts for the country) while 8.2 to 8.4 correspond to the "Debit" side (and are expenditures in other countries).

(**) See Annex "Country notes".

Basic Indicators	Units	2002	2003	2004	2005	2006
INBOUND TOURISM						
Arrivals						
1.1 Visitors	('000)	579	646	735	804	898
1.2 Tourists (overnight visitors)	('000)	472	526	615	712	773
1.3 Same-day visitors	('000)	102	110	113	79	110
1.4 Cruise passengers	('000)	5	10	7	13	15
Arrivals by region						
2.1 Africa	('000)	..	..	1	1	1
2.2 Americas	('000)	417	464	553	619	660
2.3 Europe	('000)	45	49	53	59	65
2.4 East Asia and the Pacific	('000)	9	11	8	11	16
2.5 South Asia	('000)	1	1	..	2	2
2.6 Middle East	('000)	..	..	..	..	..
Arrivals by means of transport used						
3.1 Air	('000)	164	180	204	235	264
3.2 Rail	('000)	..	..	..	..	..
3.3 Road	('000)	291	324	397	451	480
3.4 Sea	('000)	17	21	13	26	29
Arrivals by purpose of visit						
4.1 Leisure, recreation and holidays	('000)	200	182	361	504	569
4.2 Business and professional	('000)	261	322	176	138	129
4.3 Other	('000)	11	22	77	70	75
Accommodation						
5.1 Overnight stays in hotels and similar establishments	('000)	340	319	441	422	366
5.2 Guests in hotels and similar establishments	('000)	100	148	207	174	203
5.3 Overnight stays in all types of accommodation establishments	('000)	423	412	527	523	427
5.4 Average length of stay of non-resident tourists in all accommodation establishments	Nights	3.30	2.30	2.20	2.40	1.90
6.1 **Tourism expenditure in the country**	US$ Mn	138	164	196	210	237
6.2 "Travel" (*)	US$ Mn	135	160	192	206	231
6.3 "Passenger transport" (*)	US$ Mn	3	4	4	4	6
DOMESTIC TOURISM						
Accommodation						
7.1 Overnight stays in hotels and similar establishments	('000)	101	102	118	130	245
7.2 Guests in hotels and similar establishments	('000)	73	74	61	71	87
7.3 Overnight stays in all types of accommodation establishments	('000)	169	241	220	205	322
7.4 Average length of stay of resident tourists in all accommodation establishments	Nights	1.70	2.00	1.90	1.70	2.30
OUTBOUND TOURISM						
8.1 **Departures**	('000)	532	562	701	740	788
8.2 **Tourism expenditure in other countries**	US$ Mn	125	139	154	162	177
8.3 "Travel" (*)	US$ Mn	69	75	89	91	97
8.4 "Passenger transport" (*)	US$ Mn	56	64	65	71	80
TOURISM INDUSTRIES						
Hotels and similar establishments						
9.1 Number of rooms	Units	4,225	4,418	4,795	5,335	5,889
9.2 Number of bed-places	Units	7,134	7,669	7,946	9,036	9,787
9.3 Occupancy rate	Percent	..	..	..	..	..
9.4 Average length of stay	Nights	2.60	2.20	2.10	2.20	2.00
RELATED INDICATORS						
Share of tourism expenditure (6.1) in:						
10.1 Gross Domestic Product (GDP)	Percent	3.4	4.0	4.4	4.3	4.4
10.2 Exports of goods	Percent	15.1	15.5	14.3	12.7	12.0
10.3 Exports of services	Percent	61.3	63.6	68.5	68.2	69.3

(*) Balance of Payments items: 6.1 to 6.3 correspond to the "Credit" side (and are receipts for the country) while 8.2 to 8.4 correspond to the "Debit" side (and are expenditures in other countries).

NIGER

Basic Indicators	Units	2002	2003	2004	2005	2006
INBOUND TOURISM						
Arrivals						
1.1 Visitors	('000)	..	..	..	..	..
1.2 Tourists (overnight visitors)	('000)	39	55	57	60	60
1.3 Same-day visitors	('000)	..	..	..	..	..
1.4 Cruise passengers	('000)	..	..	..	..	..
Arrivals by region						
2.1 Africa	('000)	26	37	38	36	36
2.2 Americas	('000)	2	2	2	4	4
2.3 Europe	('000)	10	14	15	17	17
2.4 East Asia and the Pacific	('000)	1	1	2	3	3
2.5 South Asia	('000)	..	..	..	..	..
2.6 Middle East	('000)	..	..	..	..	..
Arrivals by means of transport used						
3.1 Air	('000)	39	50	54	58	60
3.2 Rail	('000)	..	..	..	..	..
3.3 Road	('000)	..	..	..	..	..
3.4 Sea	('000)	..	..	..	..	..
Arrivals by purpose of visit						
4.1 Leisure, recreation and holidays	('000)	7	9	10	14	14
4.2 Business and professional	('000)	21	29	31	28	31
4.3 Other	('000)	11	17	16	18	15
Accommodation						
5.1 Overnight stays in hotels and similar establishments	('000)	101	121	124	140	147
5.2 Guests in hotels and similar establishments	('000)	..	..	..	..	..
5.3 Overnight stays in all types of accommodation establishments	('000)	114	132	139	146	154
5.4 Average length of stay of non-resident tourists in all accommodation establishments	Nights	7.00	8.00	8.00	8.00	8.00
6.1 **Tourism expenditure in the country**	US$ Mn	20.2	28.5	32.3	43.9	..
6.2 "Travel" (*)	US$ Mn	20	28	31	43	35
6.3 "Passenger transport" (*)	US$ Mn	0.2	0.5	1.3	0.9	..
DOMESTIC TOURISM						
Accommodation						
7.1 Overnight stays in hotels and similar establishments	('000)	37	25	15	18	19
7.2 Guests in hotels and similar establishments	('000)	13	11	8	8	9
7.3 Overnight stays in all types of accommodation establishments	('000)	..	..	..	..	..
7.4 Average length of stay of resident tourists in all accommodation establishments	Nights	5.00	5.00	5.00	5.00	5.00
OUTBOUND TOURISM						
8.1 **Departures**	('000)	..	..	..	..	..
8.2 **Tourism expenditure in other countries**	US$ Mn	29	39	42	42	54
8.3 "Travel" (*)	US$ Mn	17	22	22	30	31
8.4 "Passenger transport" (*)	US$ Mn	12	17	20	12	23
TOURISM INDUSTRIES						
Hotels and similar establishments						
9.1 Number of rooms	Units	1,420	1,472	1,741	1,873	1,919
9.2 Number of bed-places	Units	2,528	2,629	3,061	3,209	3,246
9.3 Occupancy rate	Percent	37.00	44.00	45.00	46.00	48.00
9.4 Average length of stay	Nights	5.00	7.00	7.00	7.00	7.00
RELATED INDICATORS						
Share of tourism expenditure (6.1) in:						
10.1 Gross Domestic Product (GDP)	Percent	0.9	1.0	1.1	1.3	..
10.2 Exports of goods	Percent	7.2	8.1	7.4	9.2	..
10.3 Exports of services	Percent	39.6	45.2	34.7	49.9	..

(*) Balance of Payments items: 6.1 to 6.3 correspond to the "Credit" side (and are receipts for the country) while 8.2 to 8.4 correspond to the "Debit" side (and are expenditures in other countries).

Basic Indicators	Units	2002	2003	2004	2005	2006
INBOUND TOURISM						
Arrivals						
1.1 Visitors	('000)	2,046	2,253	2,646	2,778	3,056
1.2 Tourists (overnight visitors)	('000)	887	924	962	1,010	1,111
1.3 Same-day visitors	('000)	..	..	..	..	..
1.4 Cruise passengers	('000)	..	..	..	..	..
Arrivals by region						
2.1 Africa	('000)	1,451	1,554	1,825	1,916	2,108
2.2 Americas	('000)	80	94	111	117	129
2.3 Europe	('000)	317	373	438	460	506
2.4 East Asia and the Pacific	('000)	111	130	153	161	177
2.5 South Asia	('000)	45	53	62	65	72
2.6 Middle East	('000)	35	41	48	50	55
Arrivals by means of transport used						
3.1 Air	('000)	1,924	2,116	2,493	2,618	2,879
3.2 Rail	('000)	..	..	..	..	..
3.3 Road	('000)	99	112	125	131	144
3.4 Sea	('000)	22	25	28	29	32
Arrivals by purpose of visit						
4.1 Leisure, recreation and holidays	('000)	293	304	315	331	1,222
4.2 Business and professional	('000)	445	464	483	507	1,527
4.3 Other	('000)	149	156	164	172	306
Accommodation						
5.1 Overnight stays in hotels and similar establishments	('000)	..	..	..	..	..
5.2 Guests in hotels and similar establishments	('000)	..	..	..	..	..
5.3 Overnight stays in all types of accommodation establishments	('000)	..	..	..	..	..
5.4 Average length of stay of non-resident tourists in all accommodation establishments	Nights	..	..	..	..	..
6.1 **Tourism expenditure in the country**	US$ Mn	256	58	49	46	51
6.2 "Travel" (*)	US$ Mn	139	30	21	18	21
6.3 "Passenger transport" (*)	US$ Mn	117	28	28	28	30
DOMESTIC TOURISM						
Accommodation						
7.1 Overnight stays in hotels and similar establishments	('000)	..	..	..	..	..
7.2 Guests in hotels and similar establishments	('000)	..	..	..	..	..
7.3 Overnight stays in all types of accommodation establishments	('000)	..	..	..	..	..
7.4 Average length of stay of resident tourists in all accommodation establishments	Nights	..	..	..	..	..
OUTBOUND TOURISM						
8.1 **Departures**	('000)	..	..	..	..	..
8.2 **Tourism expenditure in other countries**	US$ Mn	910	2,076	1,469	1,385	2,078
8.3 "Travel" (*)	US$ Mn	881	1,795	1,161	1,109	1,664
8.4 "Passenger transport" (*)	US$ Mn	29	281	308	276	414
TOURISM INDUSTRIES						
Hotels and similar establishments						
9.1 Number of rooms	Units	..	..	..	..	..
9.2 Number of bed-places	Units	30,699	37,528	37,738	38,870	42,757
9.3 Occupancy rate	Percent	79.30	82.50	85.60	81.20	87.54
9.4 Average length of stay	Nights	..	..	..	..	..
RELATED INDICATORS						
Share of tourism expenditure (6.1) in:						
10.1 Gross Domestic Product (GDP)	Percent	0.5	0.1	0.1	0.0	..
10.2 Exports of goods	Percent	1.6	0.2	0.1	0.1	1.3
10.3 Exports of services	Percent	10.1	1.7	1.5	1.1	1.6

(*) Balance of Payments items: 6.1 to 6.3 correspond to the "Credit" side (and are receipts for the country) while 8.2 to 8.4 correspond to the "Debit" side (and are expenditures in other countries).

NIUE

Basic Indicators	Units	2002	2003	2004	2005	2006
INBOUND TOURISM						
Arrivals						
1.1 Visitors	('000)	..	..	..	..	..
1.2 Tourists (overnight visitors)	('000)	2.1	2.7	2.6	2.8	3.0
1.3 Same-day visitors	('000)	..	..	..	..	..
1.4 Cruise passengers	('000)	..	..	..	..	..
Arrivals by region						
2.1 Africa	('000)	..	..	..	..	..
2.2 Americas	('000)	0.3	0.2	0.1	0.2	0.2
2.3 Europe	('000)	0.3	0.2	0.2	0.3	0.2
2.4 East Asia and the Pacific	('000)	1.4	2.2	2.2	2.3	2.6
2.5 South Asia	('000)	..	..	..	..	..
2.6 Middle East	('000)	..	..	..	..	..
Arrivals by means of transport used						
3.1 Air	('000)	2.1	2.7	2.6	2.8	3.0
3.2 Rail	('000)	..	..	..	..	..
3.3 Road	('000)	..	..	..	..	..
3.4 Sea	('000)	..	..	..	..	..
Arrivals by purpose of visit						
4.1 Leisure, recreation and holidays	('000)	1.2	1.4	0.7	1.2	1.5
4.2 Business and professional	('000)	0.4	0.4	0.8	0.7	0.4
4.3 Other	('000)	0.5	0.9	1.0	0.9	1.1
Accommodation						
5.1 Overnight stays in hotels and similar establishments	('000)	..	..	..	..	..
5.2 Guests in hotels and similar establishments	('000)	..	..	..	..	..
5.3 Overnight stays in all types of accommodation establishments	('000)	..	..	..	..	..
5.4 Average length of stay of non-resident tourists in all accommodation establishments	Nights	..	..	..	..	..
6.1 **Tourism expenditure in the country**	US$ Mn	..	1.3	1.0	1.2	0.9
6.2 "Travel" (*)	US$ Mn	..	..	..	..	..
6.3 "Passenger transport" (*)	US$ Mn	..	..	..	..	..
DOMESTIC TOURISM						
Accommodation						
7.1 Overnight stays in hotels and similar establishments	('000)	..	..	..	..	..
7.2 Guests in hotels and similar establishments	('000)	..	..	..	..	..
7.3 Overnight stays in all types of accommodation establishments	('000)	..	..	..	..	..
7.4 Average length of stay of resident tourists in all accommodation establishments	Nights	..	..	..	..	..
OUTBOUND TOURISM						
8.1 **Departures**	('000)	1.1	1.4	1.5	1.6	1.8
8.2 **Tourism expenditure in other countries**	US$ Mn	..	..	..	..	..
8.3 "Travel" (*)	US$ Mn	..	..	..	..	..
8.4 "Passenger transport" (*)	US$ Mn	..	..	..	..	..
TOURISM INDUSTRIES						
Hotels and similar establishments						
9.1 Number of rooms	Units	50	50	42	58	54
9.2 Number of bed-places	Units	106	106	52	110	89
9.3 Occupancy rate	Percent	..	..	..	..	..
9.4 Average length of stay	Nights	7.00	7.00	7.00	7.00	7.00
RELATED INDICATORS						
Share of tourism expenditure (6.1) in:						
10.1 Gross Domestic Product (GDP)	Percent	..	..	..	..	..
10.2 Exports of goods	Percent	..	..	..	..	..
10.3 Exports of services	Percent	..	..	..	..	..

(*) Balance of Payments items: 6.1 to 6.3 correspond to the "Credit" side (and are receipts for the country) while 8.2 to 8.4 correspond to the "Debit" side (and are expenditures in other countries).

NORTHERN MARIANA ISLANDS

Basic Indicators	Units	2002	2003	2004	2005	2006
INBOUND TOURISM						
Arrivals						
1.1 Visitors	('000)	476	459	536	507	436
1.2 Tourists (overnight visitors)	('000)	466	452	525	498	429
1.3 Same-day visitors	('000)	..	..	..	..	..
1.4 Cruise passengers	('000)	10	7	11	9	7
Arrivals by region						
2.1 Africa	('000)	..	..	..	..	..
2.2 Americas	('000)	36	35	37	38	33
2.3 Europe	('000)	1	..	1	1	2
2.4 East Asia and the Pacific	('000)	437	423	495	465	399
2.5 South Asia	('000)	..	..	..	..	..
2.6 Middle East	('000)	..	..	..	..	..
Arrivals by means of transport used						
3.1 Air	('000)	466	452	525	498	429
3.2 Rail	('000)	..	..	..	..	..
3.3 Road	('000)	..	..	..	..	..
3.4 Sea	('000)	10	7	11	9	7
Arrivals by purpose of visit						
4.1 Leisure, recreation and holidays	('000)	476	459	536	507	436
4.2 Business and professional	('000)	..	..	..	..	..
4.3 Other	('000)	..	..	..	..	..
Accommodation						
5.1 Overnight stays in hotels and similar establishments	('000)	..	..	..	..	..
5.2 Guests in hotels and similar establishments	('000)	..	..	..	..	..
5.3 Overnight stays in all types of accommodation establishments	('000)	..	..	..	..	..
5.4 Average length of stay of non-resident tourists in all accommodation establishments	Nights	..	..	..	..	..
6.1 **Tourism expenditure in the country**	US$ Mn	..	..	..	..	..
6.2 "Travel" (*)	US$ Mn	..	..	..	..	..
6.3 "Passenger transport" (*)	US$ Mn	..	..	..	..	..
DOMESTIC TOURISM						
Accommodation						
7.1 Overnight stays in hotels and similar establishments	('000)	..	..	..	..	..
7.2 Guests in hotels and similar establishments	('000)	..	..	..	..	..
7.3 Overnight stays in all types of accommodation establishments	('000)	..	..	..	..	..
7.4 Average length of stay of resident tourists in all accommodation establishments	Nights	..	..	..	..	..
OUTBOUND TOURISM						
8.1 **Departures**	('000)	..	..	..	..	..
8.2 **Tourism expenditure in other countries**	US$ Mn	..	..	..	..	..
8.3 "Travel" (*)	US$ Mn	..	..	..	..	..
8.4 "Passenger transport" (*)	US$ Mn	..	..	..	..	..
TOURISM INDUSTRIES						
Hotels and similar establishments						
9.1 Number of rooms	Units	4,419	4,231	4,192	4,122	4,003
9.2 Number of bed-places	Units					
9.3 Occupancy rate	Percent	63.36	64.88	71.75	70.16	63.57
9.4 Average length of stay	Nights	..	..	..	..	..
RELATED INDICATORS						
Share of tourism expenditure (6.1) in:						
10.1 Gross Domestic Product (GDP)	Percent	..	..	..	..	..
10.2 Exports of goods	Percent	..	..	..	..	..
10.3 Exports of services	Percent	..	..	..	..	..

(*) Balance of Payments items: 6.1 to 6.3 correspond to the "Credit" side (and are receipts for the country) while 8.2 to 8.4 correspond to the "Debit" side (and are expenditures in other countries).

NORWAY

Basic Indicators	Units	2002	2003	2004	2005	2006
INBOUND TOURISM						
Arrivals						
1.1 Visitors	('000)	5,247	5,446	6,035	6,538	7,044
1.2 Tourists (overnight visitors)	('000)	3,111	3,269	3,628	3,824	3,945
1.3 Same-day visitors	('000)	1,222	1,163	1,200	1,270	1,299
1.4 Cruise passengers	('000)	914	1,014	1,207	1,444	1,800
Arrivals by region						
2.1 Africa	('000)	..	..	..	..	..
2.2 Americas	('000)	126	144	176	146	163
2.3 Europe	('000)	2,865	3,009	3,307	3,508	3,591
2.4 East Asia and the Pacific	('000)	35	35	35	41	37
2.5 South Asia	('000)	..	..	..	..	..
2.6 Middle East	('000)	..	..	..	..	..
Arrivals by means of transport used						
3.1 Air	('000)	1,011	1,170	1,414	1,588	1,721
3.2 Rail	('000)	83	79	123	80	83
3.3 Road	('000)	1,327	1,322	1,398	1,447	1,447
3.4 Sea	('000)	690	698	694	709	694
Arrivals by purpose of visit						
4.1 Leisure, recreation and holidays	('000)	2,373	2,520	2,780	2,913	3,004
4.2 Business and professional	('000)	738	749	848	911	940
4.3 Other	('000)	..	..	..	..	..
Accommodation						
5.1 Overnight stays in hotels and similar establishments	('000)	4,706	4,375	4,596	4,761	4,914
5.2 Guests in hotels and similar establishments	('000)	2,561	2,439	2,556	2,656	2,841
5.3 Overnight stays in all types of accommodation establishments	('000)	7,275	6,956	7,442	7,651	7,944
5.4 Average length of stay of non-resident tourists in all accommodation establishments	Nights	..	..	..	..	..
6.1 **Tourism expenditure in the country**	US$ Mn	2,581	2,989	3,531	3,959	4,251
6.2 "Travel" (*)	US$ Mn	2,179	2,500	2,980	3,332	3,613
6.3 "Passenger transport" (*)	US$ Mn	402	489	551	627	638
DOMESTIC TOURISM						
Accommodation						
7.1 Overnight stays in hotels and similar establishments	('000)	11,482	11,262	11,764	12,349	12,859
7.2 Guests in hotels and similar establishments	('000)	7,029	6,998	7,319	7,736	8,122
7.3 Overnight stays in all types of accommodation establishments	('000)	17,109	16,853	17,832	18,628	19,567
7.4 Average length of stay of resident tourists in all accommodation establishments	Nights	..	..	..	..	..
OUTBOUND TOURISM						
8.1 **Departures**	('000)	2,629	2,588	2,916	3,122	3,193
8.2 **Tourism expenditure in other countries**	US$ Mn	5,610	7,089	8,894	..	12,072
8.3 "Travel" (*)	US$ Mn	5,189	6,716	8,489	10,182	11,586
8.4 "Passenger transport" (*)	US$ Mn	421	373	405	..	486
TOURISM INDUSTRIES						
Hotels and similar establishments						
9.1 Number of rooms	Units	66,728	67,113	66,373	67,522	69,477
9.2 Number of bed-places	Units	143,635	143,799	141,096	143,568	151,252
9.3 Occupancy rate	Percent	36.30	35.50	37.00	38.10	..
9.4 Average length of stay	Nights	1.69	1.66	1.66	1.65	1.62
RELATED INDICATORS						
Share of tourism expenditure (6.1) in:						
10.1 Gross Domestic Product (GDP)	Percent	1.4	1.3	1.4	1.3	1.4
10.2 Exports of goods	Percent	4.3	4.4	4.2	3.8	3.5
10.3 Exports of services	Percent	13.2	13.8	14.0	13.5	12.8

(*) Balance of Payments items: 6.1 to 6.3 correspond to the "Credit" side (and are receipts for the country) while 8.2 to 8.4 correspond to the "Debit" side (and are expenditures in other countries).

Basic Indicators	Units	2002	2003	2004	2005	2006
INBOUND TOURISM						
Arrivals						
1.1 Visitors	('000)	1,112	1,210	1,407	..	..
1.2 Tourists (overnight visitors)	('000)	817	1,039	1,195	..	..
1.3 Same-day visitors	('000)	295	171	212	..	..
1.4 Cruise passengers	('000)	..	..	..	..	..
Arrivals by region						
2.1 Africa	('000)	17	19	28	15	15
2.2 Americas	('000)	36	36	40	18	48
2.3 Europe	('000)	197	164	281	404	578
2.4 East Asia and the Pacific	('000)	66	51	55	56	83
2.5 South Asia	('000)	85	102	131	141	133
2.6 Middle East	('000)	193	205	249	241	231
Arrivals by means of transport used						
3.1 Air	('000)	..	..	..	..	..
3.2 Rail	('000)	..	..	..	..	..
3.3 Road	('000)	..	..	..	..	..
3.4 Sea	('000)	..	..	..	..	..
Arrivals by purpose of visit						
4.1 Leisure, recreation and holidays	('000)	392	349	491	..	..
4.2 Business and professional	('000)	164	213	298	..	..
4.3 Other	('000)	556	648	618	..	..
Accommodation						
5.1 Overnight stays in hotels and similar establishments	('000)	739	777	995	1,392	1,705
5.2 Guests in hotels and similar establishments	('000)	643	630	908	989	1,306
5.3 Overnight stays in all types of accommodation establishments	('000)	3,965	..	..	..	..
5.4 Average length of stay of non-resident tourists in all accommodation establishments	Nights	4.90	..	..	..	..
6.1 **Tourism expenditure in the country**	US$ Mn	539	546	604	599	743
6.2 "Travel" (*)	US$ Mn	393	385	414	401	538
6.3 "Passenger transport" (*)	US$ Mn	146	161	190	198	205
DOMESTIC TOURISM						
Accommodation						
7.1 Overnight stays in hotels and similar establishments	('000)	221	301	326	357	418
7.2 Guests in hotels and similar establishments	('000)	219	257	293	320	349
7.3 Overnight stays in all types of accommodation establishments	('000)	..	..	..	..	..
7.4 Average length of stay of resident tourists in all accommodation establishments	Nights	..	..	..	..	..
OUTBOUND TOURISM						
8.1 **Departures**	('000)	2,060	..	..	..	..
8.2 **Tourism expenditure in other countries**	US$ Mn	702	752	795	838	868
8.3 "Travel" (*)	US$ Mn	530	578	616	643	686
8.4 "Passenger transport" (*)	US$ Mn	172	174	179	195	182
TOURISM INDUSTRIES						
Hotels and similar establishments						
9.1 Number of rooms	Units	6,078	6,473	7,045	8,132	8,539
9.2 Number of bed-places	Units	9,208	9,809	10,919	12,575	13,380
9.3 Occupancy rate	Percent	41.00	39.00	43.00	47.00	46.10
9.4 Average length of stay	Nights	..	..	..	..	..
RELATED INDICATORS						
Share of tourism expenditure (6.1) in:						
10.1 Gross Domestic Product (GDP)	Percent	2.7	2.5	2.5	..	..
10.2 Exports of goods	Percent	4.8	4.7	4.5	3.2	3.4
10.3 Exports of services	Percent	88.9	84.7	83.2	80.8	81.4

(*) Balance of Payments items: 6.1 to 6.3 correspond to the "Credit" side (and are receipts for the country) while 8.2 to 8.4 correspond to the "Debit" side (and are expenditures in other countries).

PAKISTAN

Basic Indicators		Units	2002	2003	2004	2005	2006
	INBOUND TOURISM						
	Arrivals						
1.1	Visitors	('000)	..	..	..	..	..
1.2	Tourists (overnight visitors)	('000)	498	501	648	798	898
1.3	Same-day visitors	('000)	..	..	..	..	..
1.4	Cruise passengers	('000)	..	..	..	..	..
	Arrivals by region						
2.1	Africa	('000)	12	12	13	15	19
2.2	Americas	('000)	88	86	103	147	161
2.3	Europe	('000)	215	193	281	357	394
2.4	East Asia and the Pacific	('000)	44	44	60	84	99
2.5	South Asia	('000)	116	147	160	159	182
2.6	Middle East	('000)	22	20	28	32	38
	Arrivals by means of transport used						
3.1	Air	('000)	408	385	536	682	763
3.2	Rail	('000)	..	..	..	34	37
3.3	Road	('000)	90	116	112	82	98
3.4	Sea	('000)	..	..	..	..	..
	Arrivals by purpose of visit						
4.1	Leisure, recreation and holidays	('000)	76	77	99	122	137
4.2	Business and professional	('000)	127	127	165	203	228
4.3	Other	('000)	295	297	384	473	533
	Accommodation						
5.1	Overnight stays in hotels and similar establishments	('000)	1,135	1,603	2,789	2,213	..
5.2	Guests in hotels and similar establishments	('000)	1,016	1,457	2,361	2,206	..
5.3	Overnight stays in all types of accommodation establishments	('000)	..	..	..	..	..
5.4	Average length of stay of non-resident tourists in all accommodation establishments	Nights	24.00	24.00	24.00	24.00	..
6.1	**Tourism expenditure in the country**	US$ Mn	562	620	765	828	899
6.2	"Travel" (*)	US$ Mn	97	122	179	182	255
6.3	"Passenger transport" (*)	US$ Mn	465	498	586	646	644
	DOMESTIC TOURISM						
	Accommodation						
7.1	Overnight stays in hotels and similar establishments	('000)	11,500	12,520	12,935	13,173	..
7.2	Guests in hotels and similar establishments	('000)	8,679	9,883	9,598	9,947	..
7.3	Overnight stays in all types of accommodation establishments	('000)	..	..	..	..	..
7.4	Average length of stay of resident tourists in all accommodation establishments	Nights	..	..	..	..	..
	OUTBOUND TOURISM						
8.1	**Departures**	('000)	..	..	..	..	..
8.2	**Tourism expenditure in other countries**	US$ Mn	491	1,163	1,612	1,753	2,029
8.3	"Travel" (*)	US$ Mn	255	925	1,268	1,280	1,545
8.4	"Passenger transport" (*)	US$ Mn	236	238	344	473	484
	TOURISM INDUSTRIES						
	Hotels and similar establishments						
9.1	Number of rooms	Units	35,883	36,451	37,391	38,183	41,146
9.2	Number of bed-places	Units	54,725	54,677	56,087	57,275	61,719
9.3	Occupancy rate	Percent	55.00	55.00	58.00	64.00	..
9.4	Average length of stay	Nights	1.27	1.23	1.28	1.27	..
	RELATED INDICATORS						
	Share of tourism expenditure (6.1) in:						
10.1	Gross Domestic Product (GDP)	Percent	0.8	0.8	0.8	0.7	0.7
10.2	Exports of goods	Percent	5.7	5.2	5.8	5.4	5.3
10.3	Exports of services	Percent	23.1	20.9	27.8	22.5	25.6

(*) Balance of Payments items: 6.1 to 6.3 correspond to the "Credit" side (and are receipts for the country) while 8.2 to 8.4 correspond to the "Debit" side (and are expenditures in other countries).

Basic Indicators		Units	2002	2003	2004	2005	2006
	INBOUND TOURISM						
	Arrivals						
1.1	Visitors	('000)	..	..	..	..	..
1.2	Tourists (overnight visitors)	('000)	59	68	95	86	86
1.3	Same-day visitors	('000)	..	..	..	..	..
1.4	Cruise passengers	('000)	..	..	..	..	..
	Arrivals by region						
2.1	Africa	('000)	..	..	..	..	..
2.2	Americas	('000)	5	5	7	6	7
2.3	Europe	('000)	1	1	2	2	2
2.4	East Asia and the Pacific	('000)	52	61	84	76	76
2.5	South Asia	('000)	..	..	..	..	..
2.6	Middle East	('000)	..	..	..	..	..
	Arrivals by means of transport used						
3.1	Air	('000)	59	68	95	86	86
3.2	Rail	('000)	..	..	..	..	..
3.3	Road	('000)	..	..	..	..	..
3.4	Sea	('000)	..	..	..	..	..
	Arrivals by purpose of visit						
4.1	Leisure, recreation and holidays	('000)	50	60	83	76	78
4.2	Business and professional	('000)	3	3	4	4	4
4.3	Other	('000)	5	5	7	6	4
	Accommodation						
5.1	Overnight stays in hotels and similar establishments	('000)	..	..	..	..	..
5.2	Guests in hotels and similar establishments	('000)	..	..	..	..	..
5.3	Overnight stays in all types of accommodation establishments	('000)	..	..	..	..	..
5.4	Average length of stay of non-resident tourists in all accommodation establishments	Nights	..	..	..	..	..
6.1	**Tourism expenditure in the country** (**)	US$ Mn	57	76	97	97	90
6.2	"Travel" (*)	US$ Mn	..	..	..	..	..
6.3	"Passenger transport" (*)	US$ Mn	..	..	..	..	..
	DOMESTIC TOURISM						
	Accommodation						
7.1	Overnight stays in hotels and similar establishments	('000)	..	..	..	..	..
7.2	Guests in hotels and similar establishments	('000)	..	..	..	..	..
7.3	Overnight stays in all types of accommodation establishments	('000)	..	..	..	..	..
7.4	Average length of stay of resident tourists in all accommodation establishments	Nights	..	..	..	..	..
	OUTBOUND TOURISM						
8.1	**Departures**	('000)	..	..	..	..	..
8.2	**Tourism expenditure in other countries** (**)	US$ Mn	1.2	1.0	1.5	1.5	1.4
8.3	"Travel" (*)	US$ Mn	..	..	..	..	..
8.4	"Passenger transport" (*)	US$ Mn	..	..	..	..	..
	TOURISM INDUSTRIES						
	Hotels and similar establishments						
9.1	Number of rooms	Units	967	959	959	..	..
9.2	Number of bed-places	Units	..	..	..	..	..
9.3	Occupancy rate	Percent	..	..	..	..	..
9.4	Average length of stay	Nights	7.00	7.00	6.00	..	..
	RELATED INDICATORS						
	Share of tourism expenditure (6.1) in:						
10.1	Gross Domestic Product (GDP)	Percent	..	..	..	..	..
10.2	Exports of goods	Percent	..	..	..	..	..
10.3	Exports of services	Percent	..	..	..	..	..

(*) Balance of Payments items: 6.1 to 6.3 correspond to the "Credit" side (and are receipts for the country) while 8.2 to 8.4 correspond to the "Debit" side (and are expenditures in other countries).

(**) See Annex "Country notes".

PALESTINE

Basic Indicators		Units	2002	2003	2004	2005	2006
INBOUND TOURISM							
Arrivals							
1.1	Visitors	('000)	..	..	..	..	..
1.2	Tourists (overnight visitors)	('000)	33	37	56	88	123
1.3	Same-day visitors	('000)	..	..	..	..	..
1.4	Cruise passengers	('000)	..	..	..	..	..
Arrivals by region							
2.1	Africa	('000)	1	1	1	1	2
2.2	Americas	('000)	6	6	11	14	19
2.3	Europe	('000)	18	24	35	55	83
2.4	East Asia and the Pacific	('000)	6	5	8	16	17
2.5	South Asia	('000)	..	..	..	..	..
2.6	Middle East	('000)	1	1	1	2	2
Arrivals by means of transport used							
3.1	Air	('000)	..	..	..	..	..
3.2	Rail	('000)	..	..	..	..	..
3.3	Road	('000)	..	..	..	..	..
3.4	Sea	('000)	..	..	..	..	..
Arrivals by purpose of visit							
4.1	Leisure, recreation and holidays	('000)	..	..	..	..	..
4.2	Business and professional	('000)	..	..	..	..	..
4.3	Other	('000)	..	..	..	..	..
Accommodation							
5.1	Overnight stays in hotels and similar establishments	('000)	103	113	164	251	331
5.2	Guests in hotels and similar establishments	('000)	33	37	56	88	123
5.3	Overnight stays in all types of accommodation establishments	('000)	..	..	..	..	..
5.4	Average length of stay of non-resident tourists in all accommodation establishments	Nights	..	..	..	..	..
6.1	**Tourism expenditure in the country**	US$ Mn	..	..	..	..	..
6.2	"Travel" (*)	US$ Mn	33	107	56	121	..
6.3	"Passenger transport" (*)	US$ Mn	..	..	..	..	..
DOMESTIC TOURISM							
Accommodation							
7.1	Overnight stays in hotels and similar establishments	('000)	66	86	104	99	52
7.2	Guests in hotels and similar establishments	('000)	18	26	44	44	29
7.3	Overnight stays in all types of accommodation establishments	('000)	..	..	..	..	..
7.4	Average length of stay of resident tourists in all accommodation establishments	Nights	3.70	3.30	2.40	2.30	1.80
OUTBOUND TOURISM							
8.1	**Departures**	('000)	..	..	..	..	..
8.2	**Tourism expenditure in other countries**	US$ Mn	..	..	..	..	..
8.3	"Travel" (*)	US$ Mn	388	317	286	265	..
8.4	"Passenger transport" (*)	US$ Mn	..	..	..	..	..
TOURISM INDUSTRIES							
Hotels and similar establishments							
9.1	Number of rooms	Units	3,098	3,050	3,299	3,648	3,897
9.2	Number of bed-places	Units	6,473	6,620	7,218	7,732	8,429
9.3	Occupancy rate	Percent	10.10	11.70	13.50	15.50	15.80
9.4	Average length of stay	Nights	3.30	3.20	2.50	2.70	2.50
RELATED INDICATORS							
Share of tourism expenditure (6.1) in: (**)							
10.1	Gross Domestic Product (GDP)	Percent	1.2	3.4	1.6	3.0	..
10.2	Exports of goods	Percent	9.0	27.9	13.7	29.4	..
10.3	Exports of services	Percent	17.2	50.0	30.9	45.7	..

(*) Balance of Payments items: 6.1 to 6.3 correspond to the "Credit" side (and are receipts for the country) while 8.2 to 8.4 correspond to the "Debit" side (and are expenditures in other countries).

(**) See Annex "Country notes".

Basic Indicators	Units	2002	2003	2004	2005	2006
INBOUND TOURISM						
Arrivals						
1.1 Visitors	('000)	800	897	1,004	1,070	1,215
1.2 Tourists (overnight visitors)	('000)	534	566	621	702	843
1.3 Same-day visitors	('000)	267	331	383	368	372
1.4 Cruise passengers	('000)	160	224	290	255	256
Arrivals by region						
2.1 Africa	('000)	..	..	..	..	..
2.2 Americas	('000)	376	411	439	507	620
2.3 Europe	('000)	38	43	45	52	63
2.4 East Asia and the Pacific	('000)	12	14	14	16	20
2.5 South Asia	('000)	..	..	..	..	..
2.6 Middle East	('000)	..	..	..	..	..
Arrivals by means of transport used						
3.1 Air	('000)	409	450	476	546	671
3.2 Rail	('000)	..	..	..	..	..
3.3 Road	('000)	73	65	71	81	97
3.4 Sea	('000)	15	10	23	21	21
Arrivals by purpose of visit						
4.1 Leisure, recreation and holidays	('000)	230	246	260	299	373
4.2 Business and professional	('000)	141	164	174	199	245
4.3 Other	('000)	38	40	42	48	53
Accommodation						
5.1 Overnight stays in hotels and similar establishments	('000)	1,028	1,059	1,165	1,453	1,795
5.2 Guests in hotels and similar establishments	('000)	..	..	..	..	..
5.3 Overnight stays in all types of accommodation establishments	('000)	..	..	..	..	..
5.4 Average length of stay of non-resident tourists in all accommodation establishments	Nights	10.40	10.50	9.43	10.40	9.98
6.1 **Tourism expenditure in the country**	US$ Mn	710	804	903	1,108	1,450
6.2 "Travel" (*)	US$ Mn	513	585	651	780	960
6.3 "Passenger transport" (*)	US$ Mn	197	219	252	328	490
DOMESTIC TOURISM						
Accommodation						
7.1 Overnight stays in hotels and similar establishments	('000)	..	..	..	..	..
7.2 Guests in hotels and similar establishments	('000)	..	..	..	..	..
7.3 Overnight stays in all types of accommodation establishments	('000)	..	..	..	..	..
7.4 Average length of stay of resident tourists in all accommodation establishments	Nights	..	..	..	..	..
OUTBOUND TOURISM						
8.1 **Departures**	('000)	200	227	256	285	284
8.2 **Tourism expenditure in other countries**	US$ Mn	252	267	294	388	403
8.3 "Travel" (*)	US$ Mn	179	208	239	271	271
8.4 "Passenger transport" (*)	US$ Mn	73	59	55	117	132
TOURISM INDUSTRIES						
Hotels and similar establishments						
9.1 Number of rooms	Units	14,302	14,488	14,898	15,700	15,838
9.2 Number of bed-places	Units	27,981	28,434	29,523	31,400	31,676
9.3 Occupancy rate	Percent	37.97	44.34	44.07	48.63	53.70
9.4 Average length of stay	Nights	2.08	2.10	2.20	2.22	2.40
RELATED INDICATORS						
Share of tourism expenditure (6.1) in:						
10.1 Gross Domestic Product (GDP)	Percent	5.8	6.2	6.4	7.2	8.5
10.2 Exports of goods	Percent	13.4	15.9	14.9	15.4	15.4
10.3 Exports of services	Percent	31.2	32.0	32.4	35.3	35.3

(*) Balance of Payments items: 6.1 to 6.3 correspond to the "Credit" side (and are receipts for the country) while 8.2 to 8.4 correspond to the "Debit" side (and are expenditures in other countries).

PAPUA NEW GUINEA

Basic Indicators	Units	2002	2003	2004	2005	2006
INBOUND TOURISM						
Arrivals						
1.1 Visitors	('000)	..	..	..	..	..
1.2 Tourists (overnight visitors)	('000)	54	56	59	69	78
1.3 Same-day visitors	('000)	..	..	..	..	..
1.4 Cruise passengers	('000)	..	..	..	..	..
Arrivals by region						
2.1 Africa	('000)	..	..	..	..	1
2.2 Americas	('000)	7	5	5	6	7
2.3 Europe	('000)	5	4	5	4	5
2.4 East Asia and the Pacific	('000)	39	46	48	58	63
2.5 South Asia	('000)	2	1	1	1	1
2.6 Middle East	('000)	..	..	..	..	..
Arrivals by means of transport used						
3.1 Air	('000)	54	56	59	69	78
3.2 Rail	('000)	..	..	..	..	..
3.3 Road	('000)	..	..	..	..	..
3.4 Sea	('000)	..	..	..	..	..
Arrivals by purpose of visit						
4.1 Leisure, recreation and holidays	('000)	15	15	17	18	23
4.2 Business and professional	('000)	33	35	37	45	50
4.3 Other	('000)	5	6	5	6	5
Accommodation						
5.1 Overnight stays in hotels and similar establishments	('000)					
5.2 Guests in hotels and similar establishments	('000)	..	..	..	..	..
5.3 Overnight stays in all types of accommodation establishments	('000)	..	..	..	..	..
5.4 Average length of stay of non-resident tourists in all accommodation establishments	Nights	..	..	..	..	..
6.1 **Tourism expenditure in the country**	US$ Mn	..	..	5.9	3.7	..
6.2 "Travel" (*)	US$ Mn	2.8	4.0	5.8	3.6	..
6.3 "Passenger transport" (*)	US$ Mn	..	..	0.1	0.1	..
DOMESTIC TOURISM						
Accommodation						
7.1 Overnight stays in hotels and similar establishments	('000)	..	..	..	..	..
7.2 Guests in hotels and similar establishments	('000)	..	..	..	..	..
7.3 Overnight stays in all types of accommodation establishments	('000)	..	..	..	..	..
7.4 Average length of stay of resident tourists in all accommodation establishments	Nights	..	..	..	..	..
OUTBOUND TOURISM						
8.1 **Departures**	('000)	92	..	..	..	..
8.2 **Tourism expenditure in other countries**	US$ Mn	..	..	71.9	56.2	..
8.3 "Travel" (*)	US$ Mn	59.5	51.9	71.2	55.6	..
8.4 "Passenger transport" (*)	US$ Mn	..	..	0.7	0.6	..
TOURISM INDUSTRIES						
Hotels and similar establishments						
9.1 Number of rooms	Units	2,824	2,830	..	..	..
9.2 Number of bed-places	Units	4,234	4,306	..	..	..
9.3 Occupancy rate	Percent	..	..	..	..	..
9.4 Average length of stay	Nights	..	..	..	..	..
RELATED INDICATORS						
Share of tourism expenditure (6.1) in:						
10.1 Gross Domestic Product (GDP)	Percent	..	..	0.2	0.1	..
10.2 Exports of goods	Percent	..	..	0.2	0.1	..
10.3 Exports of services	Percent	..	..	2.9	1.2	..

(*) Balance of Payments items: 6.1 to 6.3 correspond to the "Credit" side (and are receipts for the country) while 8.2 to 8.4 correspond to the "Debit" side (and are expenditures in other countries).

146

Basic Indicators	Units	2002	2003	2004	2005	2006
INBOUND TOURISM						
Arrivals						
1.1 Visitors	('000)	3,194	2,859	2,589	2,648	2,830
1.2 Tourists (overnight visitors)	('000)	250	268	309	341	388
1.3 Same-day visitors	('000)	2,944	2,591	2,280	2,307	2,442
1.4 Cruise passengers	('000)	..	..	..	..	..
Arrivals by region						
2.1 Africa	('000)	..	..	..	..	..
2.2 Americas	('000)	232	248	284	312	349
2.3 Europe	('000)	14	15	20	23	31
2.4 East Asia and the Pacific	('000)	5	4	5	5	8
2.5 South Asia	('000)	..	..	..	..	..
2.6 Middle East	('000)	..	..	..	..	..
Arrivals by means of transport used						
3.1 Air	('000)	68	68	85	99	102
3.2 Rail	('000)	..	..			
3.3 Road	('000)	176	195	217	232	276
3.4 Sea	('000)	6	5	8	10	10
Arrivals by purpose of visit						
4.1 Leisure, recreation and holidays	('000)	121	129	149	164	186
4.2 Business and professional	('000)	27	29	33	37	43
4.3 Other	('000)	102	110	127	140	159
Accommodation						
5.1 Overnight stays in hotels and similar establishments	('000)	219	..	..	..	..
5.2 Guests in hotels and similar establishments	('000)	88	..	..	..	..
5.3 Overnight stays in all types of accommodation establishments	('000)	..	..	..	..	..
5.4 Average length of stay of non-resident tourists in all accommodation establishments	Nights	2.50	2.50	2.50	2.50	2.50
6.1 **Tourism expenditure in the country**	US$ Mn	76	81	87	96	111
6.2 "Travel" (*)	US$ Mn	62	64	70	78	91
6.3 "Passenger transport" (*)	US$ Mn	14	17	17	18	20
DOMESTIC TOURISM						
Accommodation						
7.1 Overnight stays in hotels and similar establishments	('000)	..	..	..	..	..
7.2 Guests in hotels and similar establishments	('000)	..	..	..	..	..
7.3 Overnight stays in all types of accommodation establishments	('000)	..	..	..	..	..
7.4 Average length of stay of resident tourists in all accommodation establishments	Nights	..	..	..	..	..
OUTBOUND TOURISM						
8.1 **Departures**	('000)	141	153	170	188	210
8.2 **Tourism expenditure in other countries**	US$ Mn	117	115	121	130	143
8.3 "Travel" (*)	US$ Mn	65	67	71	79	91
8.4 "Passenger transport" (*)	US$ Mn	52	48	50	51	52
TOURISM INDUSTRIES						
Hotels and similar establishments						
9.1 Number of rooms	Units	4,800	4,816	4,899	5,058	5,355
9.2 Number of bed-places	Units	10,597	10,483	10,565	10,939	11,532
9.3 Occupancy rate	Percent	36.00	38.00	40.00	44.00	45.00
9.4 Average length of stay	Nights	2.50	2.50	2.50	2.50	2.50
RELATED INDICATORS						
Share of tourism expenditure (6.1) in:						
10.1 Gross Domestic Product (GDP)	Percent	1.6	1.8	1.3	1.3	1.2
10.2 Exports of goods	Percent	4.1	3.7	3.0	2.9	2.3
10.3 Exports of services	Percent	13.4	14.1	13.9	13.9	13.8

(*) Balance of Payments items: 6.1 to 6.3 correspond to the "Credit" side (and are receipts for the country) while 8.2 to 8.4 correspond to the "Debit" side (and are expenditures in other countries).

PERU

Basic Indicators		Units	2002	2003	2004	2005	2006
	INBOUND TOURISM						
	Arrivals						
1.1	Visitors	('000)	..	..	..	..	..
1.2	Tourists (overnight visitors)	('000)	998	1,070	1,277	1,487	1,635
1.3	Same-day visitors	('000)	..	..	..	..	..
1.4	Cruise passengers	('000)	4	4	7	8	16
	Arrivals by region						
2.1	Africa	('000)	2	2	3	3	3
2.2	Americas	('000)	714	762	929	1,066	1,190
2.3	Europe	('000)	236	252	281	340	354
2.4	East Asia and the Pacific	('000)	44	50	62	74	82
2.5	South Asia	('000)	1	1	1	2	2
2.6	Middle East	('000)	..	..	..	..	..
	Arrivals by means of transport used						
3.1	Air	('000)	589	618	736	875	894
3.2	Rail	('000)	..	..	..	..	..
3.3	Road	('000)	402	445	533	604	725
3.4	Sea	('000)	7	7	7	8	16
	Arrivals by purpose of visit						
4.1	Leisure, recreation and holidays	('000)	906	971	1,197	1,394	1,533
4.2	Business and professional	('000)	37	39	35	41	45
4.3	Other	('000)	55	59	44	52	57
	Accommodation						
5.1	Overnight stays in hotels and similar establishments	('000)	2,802	3,870	4,495	5,024	5,367
5.2	Guests in hotels and similar establishments	('000)	1,434	2,051	2,376	2,709	2,793
5.3	Overnight stays in all types of accommodation establishments	('000)	..	..	..	..	..
5.4	Average length of stay of non-resident tourists in all accommodation establishments	Nights	10.80	10.20	10.80	10.60	..
6.1	**Tourism expenditure in the country**	US$ Mn	836	1,023	1,232	1,438	1,586
6.2	"Travel" (*)	US$ Mn	787	963	1,142	1,308	1,381
6.3	"Passenger transport" (*)	US$ Mn	49	60	90	130	205
	DOMESTIC TOURISM						
	Accommodation						
7.1	Overnight stays in hotels and similar establishments	('000)	13,643	14,872	15,230	17,178	18,406
7.2	Guests in hotels and similar establishments	('000)	10,529	12,078	12,345	13,943	14,156
7.3	Overnight stays in all types of accommodation establishments	('000)	..	..	..	..	..
7.4	Average length of stay of resident tourists in all accommodation establishments	Nights	..	..	..	..	..
	OUTBOUND TOURISM						
8.1	**Departures**	('000)	1,232	1,392	1,635	1,841	1,857
8.2	**Tourism expenditure in other countries**	US$ Mn	806	847	852	970	1,005
8.3	"Travel" (*)	US$ Mn	606	641	643	752	760
8.4	"Passenger transport" (*)	US$ Mn	200	206	209	218	245
	TOURISM INDUSTRIES						
	Hotels and similar establishments						
9.1	Number of rooms	Units	121,591	125,242	130,811	136,605	142,791
9.2	Number of bed-places	Units	209,918	218,602	228,658	238,979	249,582
9.3	Occupancy rate	Percent	24.44	24.08	24.26	25.20	..
9.4	Average length of stay	Nights	1.37	1.32	1.34	1.34	1.40
	RELATED INDICATORS						
	Share of tourism expenditure (6.1) in:						
10.1	Gross Domestic Product (GDP)	Percent	1.5	1.7	1.8	1.8	1.7
10.2	Exports of goods	Percent	10.8	11.3	9.6	8.3	6.7
10.3	Exports of services	Percent	57.5	59.6	61.8	62.8	64.7

(*) Balance of Payments items: 6.1 to 6.3 correspond to the "Credit" side (and are receipts for the country) while 8.2 to 8.4 correspond to the "Debit" side (and are expenditures in other countries).

Basic Indicators	Units	2002	2003	2004	2005	2006
INBOUND TOURISM						
Arrivals						
1.1 Visitors	('000)	..	..	..	..	..
1.2 Tourists (overnight visitors)	('000)	1,933	1,907	2,291	2,623	2,843
1.3 Same-day visitors	('000)	..	..	..	..	..
1.4 Cruise passengers	('000)	5	5	8	2	4
Arrivals by region						
2.1 Africa	('000)	1	1	2	2	2
2.2 Americas	('000)	454	444	546	605	652
2.3 Europe	('000)	184	177	212	246	264
2.4 East Asia and the Pacific	('000)	1,154	1,129	1,359	1,565	1,691
2.5 South Asia	('000)	21	22	25	28	32
2.6 Middle East	('000)	19	17	21	25	28
Arrivals by means of transport used						
3.1 Air	('000)	1,905	1,880	2,260	2,586	2,807
3.2 Rail	('000)	..	..	..	..	..
3.3 Road	('000)	..	..	..	..	..
3.4 Sea	('000)	28	27	31	37	36
Arrivals by purpose of visit						
4.1 Leisure, recreation and holidays	('000)	833	815	1,020	1,174	1,319
4.2 Business and professional	('000)	336	308	344	366	409
4.3 Other	('000)	736	757	896	1,047	1,079
Accommodation						
5.1 Overnight stays in hotels and similar establishments	('000)	11,878	12,212	12,503	12,842	14,200
5.2 Guests in hotels and similar establishments	('000)	758	742	836	955	1,013
5.3 Overnight stays in all types of accommodation establishments	('000)	..	..	..	..	..
5.4 Average length of stay of non-resident tourists in all accommodation establishments	Nights	9.12	9.17	9.11	8.41	11.23
6.1 **Tourism expenditure in the country**	US$ Mn	2,018	1,821	2,390	2,755	4,019
6.2 "Travel" (*)	US$ Mn	1,761	1,544	2,017	2,265	3,501
6.3 "Passenger transport" (*)	US$ Mn	257	277	373	490	518
DOMESTIC TOURISM						
Accommodation						
7.1 Overnight stays in hotels and similar establishments	('000)	..	..	..	..	..
7.2 Guests in hotels and similar establishments	('000)	..	..	..	..	..
7.3 Overnight stays in all types of accommodation establishments	('000)	..	..	..	..	..
7.4 Average length of stay of resident tourists in all accommodation establishments	Nights	..	..	..	..	..
OUTBOUND TOURISM						
8.1 **Departures**	('000)	1,969	1,803	1,920	2,144	..
8.2 **Tourism expenditure in other countries**	US$ Mn	1,874	1,649	1,526	1,547	1,558
8.3 "Travel" (*)	US$ Mn	1,626	1,413	1,275	1,279	1,232
8.4 "Passenger transport" (*)	US$ Mn	248	236	251	268	326
TOURISM INDUSTRIES						
Hotels and similar establishments						
9.1 Number of rooms	Units	37,944	21,409	29,489	29,757	30,272
9.2 Number of bed-places	Units	75,958	42,818	57,978	59,514	60,544
9.3 Occupancy rate	Percent	59.92	60.10	68.15	71.71	71.95
9.4 Average length of stay	Nights	2.63	2.63	2.73	2.58	2.56
RELATED INDICATORS						
Share of tourism expenditure (6.1) in:						
10.1 Gross Domestic Product (GDP)	Percent	2.6	2.3	2.8	2.8	3.4
10.2 Exports of goods	Percent	5.9	5.2	6.2	6.8	8.6
10.3 Exports of services	Percent	58.9	53.7	59.1	60.9	62.3

(*) Balance of Payments items: 6.1 to 6.3 correspond to the "Credit" side (and are receipts for the country) while 8.2 to 8.4 correspond to the "Debit" side (and are expenditures in other countries).

POLAND

Basic Indicators	Units	2002	2003	2004	2005	2006
INBOUND TOURISM						
Arrivals						
1.1 Visitors	('000)	50,735	52,130	61,918	64,606	65,115
1.2 Tourists (overnight visitors)	('000)	13,980	13,720	14,290	15,200	15,670
1.3 Same-day visitors	('000)	36,755	38,410	47,628	49,406	49,445
1.4 Cruise passengers	('000)	..	..	..	..	..
Arrivals by region						
2.1 Africa	('000)	9	10	11	13	15
2.2 Americas	('000)	272	294	345	439	466
2.3 Europe	('000)	50,315	51,691	61,386	63,927	64,367
2.4 East Asia and the Pacific	('000)	87	89	123	163	194
2.5 South Asia	('000)	9	9	12	13	15
2.6 Middle East	('000)	6	6	6	8	8
Arrivals by means of transport used						
3.1 Air	('000)	1,126	1,182	1,539	2,004	2,432
3.2 Rail	('000)	1,921	1,879	1,854	1,606	1,669
3.3 Road	('000)	46,255	47,442	57,666	60,591	60,646
3.4 Sea	('000)	1,433	1,627	859	404	368
Arrivals by purpose of visit						
4.1 Leisure, recreation and holidays	('000)	3,430	3,920	3,080	3,680	3,210
4.2 Business and professional	('000)	4,050	4,100	3,945	4,240	4,240
4.3 Other	('000)	6,500	5,700	7,265	7,280	8,220
Accommodation						
5.1 Overnight stays in hotels and similar establishments	('000)	4,999	5,450	6,876	7,869	7,911
5.2 Guests in hotels and similar establishments	('000)	2,536	2,701	3,385	3,723	3,738
5.3 Overnight stays in all types of accommodation establishments	('000)	7,085	7,828	9,313	10,542	10,555
5.4 Average length of stay of non-resident tourists in all accommodation establishments	Nights	3.90	4.10	4.60	4.40	3.40
6.1 **Tourism expenditure in the country**	US$ Mn	4,971	4,733	6,499	7,128	8,122
6.2 "Travel" (*)	US$ Mn	4,314	4,069	5,833	6,274	7,239
6.3 "Passenger transport" (*)	US$ Mn	657	664	666	854	883
DOMESTIC TOURISM						
Accommodation						
7.1 Overnight stays in hotels and similar establishments	('000)	8,382	8,813	11,572	12,464	13,910
7.2 Guests in hotels and similar establishments	('000)	4,580	4,834	6,273	6,805	7,564
7.3 Overnight stays in all types of accommodation establishments	('000)	37,127	37,520	37,344	38,076	40,680
7.4 Average length of stay of resident tourists in all accommodation establishments	Nights	3.37	3.32	3.16	3.10	3.08
OUTBOUND TOURISM						
8.1 **Departures**	('000)	45,043	38,730	37,226	40,841	44,696
8.2 **Tourism expenditure in other countries**	US$ Mn	3,364	3,002	4,157	4,687	6,190
8.3 "Travel" (*)	US$ Mn	3,202	2,801	3,841	4,341	5,760
8.4 "Passenger transport" (*)	US$ Mn	162	201	316	346	430
TOURISM INDUSTRIES						
Hotels and similar establishments						
9.1 Number of rooms	Units	65,658	68,588	83,007	84,865	88,409
9.2 Number of bed-places	Units	127,559	134,323	165,311	169,609	178,056
9.3 Occupancy rate	Percent	35.70	35.67	32.20	40.50	42.20
9.4 Average length of stay	Nights	1.88	1.89	1.91	1.93	1.93
RELATED INDICATORS						
Share of tourism expenditure (6.1) in:						
10.1 Gross Domestic Product (GDP)	Percent	2.5	2.2	2.6	2.4	2.4
10.2 Exports of goods	Percent	10.6	7.8	7.9	7.4	6.9
10.3 Exports of services	Percent	49.5	42.4	48.2	43.8	39.5

(*) Balance of Payments items: 6.1 to 6.3 correspond to the "Credit" side (and are receipts for the country) while 8.2 to 8.4 correspond to the "Debit" side (and are expenditures in other countries).

Basic Indicators	Units	2002	2003	2004	2005	2006
INBOUND TOURISM						
Arrivals						
1.1 Visitors	('000)	27,194	27,532	21,165	21,172	22,588
1.2 Tourists (overnight visitors)	('000)	11,644	11,707	10,639	10,612	11,282
1.3 Same-day visitors	('000)	15,389	15,535	10,526	10,561	11,306
1.4 Cruise passengers	('000)	161	290	..	..	..
Arrivals by region						
2.1 Africa	('000)	..	..	..	..	..
2.2 Americas	('000)	464	481	367	413	499
2.3 Europe	('000)	10,849	10,888	9,343	9,271	9,831
2.4 East Asia and the Pacific	('000)	44	40	43	37	32
2.5 South Asia	('000)	..	..	132	159	204
2.6 Middle East	('000)	..	..	..	..	..
Arrivals by means of transport used						
3.1 Air	('000)	5,073	5,162	5,938	6,137	6,734
3.2 Rail	('000)	90	92	..	..	..
3.3 Road	('000)	21,845	21,961	15,225	15,036	15,854
3.4 Sea	('000)	187	317	..	..	..
Arrivals by purpose of visit						
4.1 Leisure, recreation and holidays	('000)	..	..	15,394	15,328	16,393
4.2 Business and professional	('000)	..	..	3,272	3,308	3,555
4.3 Other	('000)	..	..	2,499	2,536	2,640
Accommodation						
5.1 Overnight stays in hotels and similar establishments	('000)	23,563	23,215	23,002	23,873	25,216
5.2 Guests in hotels and similar establishments	('000)	5,060	4,906	5,201	5,355	6,511
5.3 Overnight stays in all types of accommodation establishments	('000)	25,119	24,870	24,617	25,388	26,842
5.4 Average length of stay of non-resident tourists in all accommodation establishments	Nights	4.70	4.60	4.35	4.40	3.85
6.1 **Tourism expenditure in the country**	US$ Mn	6,595	7,634	8,863	9,009	10,036
6.2 "Travel" (*)	US$ Mn	5,798	6,622	7,672	7,676	8,388
6.3 "Passenger transport" (*)	US$ Mn	797	1,012	1,191	1,333	1,648
DOMESTIC TOURISM						
Accommodation						
7.1 Overnight stays in hotels and similar establishments	('000)	10,646	10,661	11,139	11,648	12,350
7.2 Guests in hotels and similar establishments	('000)	4,674	4,714	4,934	5,274	5,866
7.3 Overnight stays in all types of accommodation establishments	('000)	16,692	16,713	17,105	17,877	18,948
7.4 Average length of stay of resident tourists in all accommodation establishments	Nights	..	..	..	2.10	2.10
OUTBOUND TOURISM						
8.1 **Departures**	('000)	..	..	17,141	18,110	18,378
8.2 **Tourism expenditure in other countries**	US$ Mn	2,631	2,982	3,369	3,744	4,050
8.3 "Travel" (*)	US$ Mn	2,125	2,409	2,763	3,050	3,298
8.4 "Passenger transport" (*)	US$ Mn	506	573	606	694	752
TOURISM INDUSTRIES						
Hotels and similar establishments						
9.1 Number of rooms	Units	105,805	108,367	112,659	116,123	117,565
9.2 Number of bed-places	Units	239,903	245,778	253,927	263,814	264,037
9.3 Occupancy rate	Percent	39.30	38.00	38.60	46.60	48.30
9.4 Average length of stay	Nights	3.50	3.30	3.10	3.10	3.00
RELATED INDICATORS						
Share of tourism expenditure (6.1) in:						
10.1 Gross Domestic Product (GDP)	Percent	5.2	4.9	5.0	4.9	5.2
10.2 Exports of goods	Percent	25.4	23.8	24.0	23.6	23.0
10.3 Exports of services	Percent	63.7	61.8	60.3	59.3	56.4

(*) Balance of Payments items: 6.1 to 6.3 correspond to the "Credit" side (and are receipts for the country) while 8.2 to 8.4 correspond to the "Debit" side (and are expenditures in other countries).

PUERTO RICO

Basic Indicators		Units	2002	2003	2004	2005	2006
	INBOUND TOURISM						
	Arrivals						
1.1	Visitors	('000)	4,364	4,402	4,889	5,073	5,022
1.2	Tourists (overnight visitors)	('000)	3,087	3,238	3,541	3,686	3,722
1.3	Same-day visitors	('000)	1	..	..	..	..
1.4	Cruise passengers	('000)	1,276	1,164	1,348	1,387	1,300
	Arrivals by region						
2.1	Africa	('000)	..	..	..	..	..
2.2	Americas	('000)	2,230	2,471	2,754	2,847	2,930
2.3	Europe	('000)	..	..	..	..	..
2.4	East Asia and the Pacific	('000)	..	..	..	..	..
2.5	South Asia	('000)	..	..	..	..	..
2.6	Middle East	('000)	..	..	..	..	..
	Arrivals by means of transport used						
3.1	Air	('000)	3,087	3,238	3,541	3,686	3,722
3.2	Rail	('000)	..	..	..	..	..
3.3	Road	('000)	..	..	..	..	..
3.4	Sea	('000)	1,276	1,164	1,348	1,387	1,300
	Arrivals by purpose of visit						
4.1	Leisure, recreation and holidays	('000)	..	..	..	..	..
4.2	Business and professional	('000)	..	..	..	..	..
4.3	Other	('000)	..	..	..	..	..
	Accommodation						
5.1	Overnight stays in hotels and similar establishments	('000)	2,505	2,718	2,835	2,928	3,021
5.2	Guests in hotels and similar establishments	('000)	1,204	1,305	1,371	1,440	1,497
5.3	Overnight stays in all types of accommodation establishments	('000)	..	..	..	..	..
5.4	Average length of stay of non-resident tourists in all accommodation establishments	Nights	2.50	2.60	2.60	2.60	2.60
6.1	**Tourism expenditure in the country** (**)	US$ Mn	2,486	2,677	3,024	3,239	3,369
6.2	"Travel" (*)	US$ Mn	..	..	..	..	..
6.3	"Passenger transport" (*)	US$ Mn	..	..	..	..	..
	DOMESTIC TOURISM						
	Accommodation						
7.1	Overnight stays in hotels and similar establishments	('000)	..	..	..	..	..
7.2	Guests in hotels and similar establishments	('000)	617	660	638	658	654
7.3	Overnight stays in all types of accommodation establishments	('000)	..	..	..	..	..
7.4	Average length of stay of resident tourists in all accommodation establishments	Nights	..	..	..	..	..
	OUTBOUND TOURISM						
8.1	**Departures**	('000)	1,227	1,272	1,361	1,410	1,468
8.2	**Tourism expenditure in other countries** (**)	US$ Mn	1,319	1,420	1,584	1,663	1,752
8.3	"Travel" (*)	US$ Mn	928	985	1,085	1,143	1,205
8.4	"Passenger transport" (*)	US$ Mn	391	435	499	520	547
	TOURISM INDUSTRIES						
	Hotels and similar establishments						
9.1	Number of rooms	Units	12,768	12,788	12,864	13,459	16,564
9.2	Number of bed-places	Units	..	..	..	..	..
9.3	Occupancy rate	Percent	61.80	64.90	68.90	67.70	67.90
9.4	Average length of stay	Nights	2.70	2.60	2.60	2.63	2.60
	RELATED INDICATORS						
	Share of tourism expenditure (6.1) in:						
10.1	Gross Domestic Product (GDP)	Percent	3.5	3.6	3.8	3.9	3.9
10.2	Exports of goods	Percent	5.0	4.8	5.1	5.4	5.3
10.3	Exports of services	Percent	40.0	42.2	43.7	38.8	38.8

(*) Balance of Payments items: 6.1 to 6.3 correspond to the "Credit" side (and are receipts for the country) while 8.2 to 8.4 correspond to the "Debit" side (and are expenditures in other countries).

(**) See Annex "Country notes".

Basic Indicators		Units	2002	2003	2004	2005	2006
	INBOUND TOURISM						
	Arrivals						
1.1	Visitors	('000)	..	..	..	..	..
1.2	Tourists (overnight visitors)	('000)	587	557	732	913	946
1.3	Same-day visitors	('000)	..	..	..	..	..
1.4	Cruise passengers	('000)	..	..	..	..	..
	Arrivals by region						
2.1	Africa	('000)	..	..	..	..	..
2.2	Americas	('000)	..	..	..	..	..
2.3	Europe	('000)	103	89	196	233	201
2.4	East Asia and the Pacific	('000)	108	127	146	159	181
2.5	South Asia	('000)	..	..	..	..	..
2.6	Middle East	('000)	312	283	295	365	414
	Arrivals by means of transport used						
3.1	Air	('000)	..	..	..	..	..
3.2	Rail	('000)	..	..	..	..	..
3.3	Road	('000)	..	..	..	..	..
3.4	Sea	('000)	..	..	..	..	..
	Arrivals by purpose of visit						
4.1	Leisure, recreation and holidays	('000)	..	..	..	..	240
4.2	Business and professional	('000)	..	..	..	..	722
4.3	Other	('000)	..	..	..	..	..
	Accommodation						
5.1	Overnight stays in hotels and similar establishments	('000)	698	848	983	1,024	1,147
5.2	Guests in hotels and similar establishments	('000)	587	557	732	913	946
5.3	Overnight stays in all types of accommodation establishments	('000)	..	..	..	..	..
5.4	Average length of stay of non-resident tourists in all accommodation establishments	Nights	1.20	1.50	1.30	1.10	1.20
6.1	**Tourism expenditure in the country**	US$ Mn	..	..	..	..	..
6.2	"Travel" (*)	US$ Mn	285	369	498	760	374
6.3	"Passenger transport" (*)	US$ Mn	..	..	..	..	..
	DOMESTIC TOURISM						
	Accommodation						
7.1	Overnight stays in hotels and similar establishments	('000)	..	..	..	..	..
7.2	Guests in hotels and similar establishments	('000)	..	..	..	..	..
7.3	Overnight stays in all types of accommodation establishments	('000)	..	..	..	..	..
7.4	Average length of stay of resident tourists in all accommodation establishments	Nights	..	..	..	..	..
	OUTBOUND TOURISM						
8.1	**Departures**	('000)					
8.2	**Tourism expenditure in other countries**	US$ Mn	..	..	..	..	..
8.3	"Travel" (*)	US$ Mn	423	471	691	1,759	3,993
8.4	"Passenger transport" (*)	US$ Mn	..	..	..	..	..
	TOURISM INDUSTRIES						
	Hotels and similar establishments						
9.1	Number of rooms	Units	3,225	3,858	3,792	4,180	6,871
9.2	Number of bed-places	Units	4,889	5,266	5,414	5,810	10,002
9.3	Occupancy rate	Percent	39.00	44.00	50.00	74.90	74.50
9.4	Average length of stay	Nights	..	..	..	..	..
	RELATED INDICATORS						
	Share of tourism expenditure (6.1) in:						
10.1	Gross Domestic Product (GDP)	Percent	..	..	..	..	..
10.2	Exports of goods	Percent	..	..	..	..	..
10.3	Exports of services	Percent	..	..	..	..	..

(*) Balance of Payments items: 6.1 to 6.3 correspond to the "Credit" side (and are receipts for the country) while 8.2 to 8.4 correspond to the "Debit" side (and are expenditures in other countries).

(**) See Annex "Country notes".

REPUBLIC OF MOLDOVA

Basic Indicators	Units	2002	2003	2004	2005	2006
INBOUND TOURISM						
Arrivals						
1.1 Visitors	('000)	20	24	26	25	14
1.2 Tourists (overnight visitors)	('000)	18	21	24	23	13
1.3 Same-day visitors	('000)	2	3	2	2	1
1.4 Cruise passengers	('000)	..	..	..	..	..
Arrivals by region						
2.1 Africa	('000)	..	..	..	..	..
2.2 Americas	('000)	1.8	2.6	2.6	3.2	1.1
2.3 Europe	('000)	17.6	20.2	22.7	21.2	12.7
2.4 East Asia and the Pacific	('000)	0.4	0.3	0.3	0.3	0.2
2.5 South Asia	('000)	..	..	..	..	..
2.6 Middle East	('000)	0.3	0.5	0.4	0.4	0.1
Arrivals by means of transport used						
3.1 Air	('000)	..	..	..	..	..
3.2 Rail	('000)	..	..	..	..	..
3.3 Road	('000)	..	..	..	..	..
3.4 Sea	('000)	..	..	..	..	..
Arrivals by purpose of visit						
4.1 Leisure, recreation and holidays	('000)	8.0	9.9	11.8	7.8	6.2
4.2 Business and professional	('000)	11.5	13.0	13.0	16.4	7.4
4.3 Other	('000)	0.6	0.7	1.2	0.9	0.6
Accommodation						
5.1 Overnight stays in hotels and similar establishments	('000)	76	84	153	170	202
5.2 Guests in hotels and similar establishments	('000)	..	..	68	66	62
5.3 Overnight stays in all types of accommodation establishments	('000)	..	..	174	187	214
5.4 Average length of stay of non-resident tourists in all accommodation establishments	Nights	..	..	2.50	2.80	3.40
6.1 **Tourism expenditure in the country**	US$ Mn	72	79	112	138	145
6.2 "Travel" (*)	US$ Mn	50	54	91	103	112
6.3 "Passenger transport" (*)	US$ Mn	22	25	21	35	33
DOMESTIC TOURISM						
Accommodation						
7.1 Overnight stays in hotels and similar establishments	('000)	..	..	251	264	282
7.2 Guests in hotels and similar establishments	('000)	..	..	99	104	107
7.3 Overnight stays in all types of accommodation establishments	('000)	316	400	1,313	1,432	1,539
7.4 Average length of stay of resident tourists in all accommodation establishments	Nights	..	..	6.00	6.10	6.20
OUTBOUND TOURISM						
8.1 **Departures**	('000)	52	67	68	57	68
8.2 **Tourism expenditure in other countries**	US$ Mn	109	118	135	170	220
8.3 "Travel" (*)	US$ Mn	95	99	113	141	187
8.4 "Passenger transport" (*)	US$ Mn	14	19	22	29	33
TOURISM INDUSTRIES						
Hotels and similar establishments						
9.1 Number of rooms	Units	2,806	2,565	2,576	2,475	2,457
9.2 Number of bed-places	Units	5,484	4,651	4,850	4,581	4,519
9.3 Occupancy rate	Percent	14.00	22.10	25.20	26.60	30.90
9.4 Average length of stay	Nights	..	..	2.40	2.60	2.90
RELATED INDICATORS						
Share of tourism expenditure (6.1) in:						
10.1 Gross Domestic Product (GDP)	Percent	4.3	4.0	4.3	4.6	4.4
10.2 Exports of goods	Percent	10.9	9.8	11.3	12.5	13.8
10.3 Exports of services	Percent	33.2	31.6	33.7	34.6	29.7

(*) Balance of Payments items: 6.1 to 6.3 correspond to the "Credit" side (and are receipts for the country) while 8.2 to 8.4 correspond to the "Debit" side (and are expenditures in other countries).

Basic Indicators	Units		2002	2003	2004	2005	2006
INBOUND TOURISM							
Arrivals							
1.1 Visitors	('000)		..	..	..	..	..
1.2 Tourists (overnight visitors)	('000)		426	432	430	409	279
1.3 Same-day visitors	('000)		..	..	..	..	..
1.4 Cruise passengers	('000)		..	..	..	..	..
Arrivals by region							
2.1 Africa	('000)		..	..	..	..	..
2.2 Americas	('000)		..	..	..	..	..
2.3 Europe	('000)		357	367	370	344	224
2.4 East Asia and the Pacific	('000)		..	..	..	..	..
2.5 South Asia	('000)		..	..	..	..	..
2.6 Middle East	('000)		..	..	..	..	..
Arrivals by means of transport used							
3.1 Air	('000)		421	427	426	404	275
3.2 Rail	('000)		..	..	..	..	..
3.3 Road	('000)		..	..	..	..	..
3.4 Sea	('000)		5	5	4	5	4
Arrivals by purpose of visit							
4.1 Leisure, recreation and holidays	('000)		206	209	183	162	80
4.2 Business and professional	('000)		45	44	52	47	47
4.3 Other	('000)		175	179	195	200	152
Accommodation							
5.1 Overnight stays in hotels and similar establishments	('000)		1,087	..	1,154	1,112	761
5.2 Guests in hotels and similar establishments	('000)		198	209	193	180	98
5.3 Overnight stays in all types of accommodation establishments	('000)		..	..	..	..	..
5.4 Average length of stay of non-resident tourists in all accommodation establishments	Nights		16.40	16.50	16.40	17.00	18.20
6.1 **Tourism expenditure in the country**	(**) US$ Mn		329	413	448	442	308
6.2 "Travel" (*)	US$ Mn		..	..	..	..	..
6.3 "Passenger transport" (*)	US$ Mn		..	..	..	..	..
DOMESTIC TOURISM							
Accommodation							
7.1 Overnight stays in hotels and similar establishments	('000)		..	..	..	..	..
7.2 Guests in hotels and similar establishments	('000)		..	..	..	..	..
7.3 Overnight stays in all types of accommodation establishments	('000)		..	..	..	..	..
7.4 Average length of stay of resident tourists in all accommodation establishments	Nights		..	..	..	..	..
OUTBOUND TOURISM							
8.1 **Departures**	('000)		319	333	385	395	409
8.2 **Tourism expenditure in other countries**	US$ Mn		..	..	..	..	..
8.3 "Travel" (*)	US$ Mn		..	..	..	..	..
8.4 "Passenger transport" (*)	US$ Mn		..	..	..	..	..
TOURISM INDUSTRIES							
Hotels and similar establishments							
9.1 Number of rooms	Units		2,850	2,910	2,904	2,930	2,982
9.2 Number of bed-places	Units		5,700	5,820	5,808	5,860	5,964
9.3 Occupancy rate	Percent		64.00	..	58.30	60.03	..
9.4 Average length of stay	Nights		7.00	6.90	6.80	6.90	7.00
RELATED INDICATORS							
Share of tourism expenditure (6.1) in:							
10.1 Gross Domestic Product (GDP)	Percent		..	..	..	..	..
10.2 Exports of goods	Percent		..	..	..	..	..
10.3 Exports of services	Percent		..	..	..	..	..

(*) Balance of Payments items: 6.1 to 6.3 correspond to the "Credit" side (and are receipts for the country) while 8.2 to 8.4 correspond to the "Debit" side (and are expenditures in other countries).

(**) See Annex "Country notes".

ROMANIA

Basic Indicators		Units	2002	2003	2004	2005	2006
	INBOUND TOURISM						
	Arrivals						
1.1	Visitors	('000)	4,794	5,595	6,600	5,839	6,037
1.2	Tourists (overnight visitors)	('000)	..	..	..	..	..
1.3	Same-day visitors	('000)	..	..	..	..	..
1.4	Cruise passengers	('000)	..	..	..	..	..
	Arrivals by region						
2.1	Africa	('000)	5	5	7	7	9
2.2	Americas	('000)	102	115	139	154	172
2.3	Europe	('000)	4,604	5,392	6,361	5,580	5,752
2.4	East Asia and the Pacific	('000)	42	42	49	57	62
2.5	South Asia	('000)	12	13	15	16	16
2.6	Middle East	('000)	27	27	28	24	25
	Arrivals by means of transport used						
3.1	Air	('000)	689	752	704	919	1,122
3.2	Rail	('000)	374	347	308	305	316
3.3	Road	('000)	3,594	4,343	5,401	4,429	4,390
3.4	Sea	('000)	137	152	186	187	209
	Arrivals by purpose of visit						
4.1	Leisure, recreation and holidays	('000)	..	..	..	..	..
4.2	Business and professional	('000)	..	..	..	..	..
4.3	Other	('000)	..	..	..	..	..
	Accommodation						
5.1	Overnight stays in hotels and similar establishments	('000)	2,471	2,688	3,211	3,377	3,169
5.2	Guests in hotels and similar establishments	('000)	982	1,086	1,332	1,407	1,363
5.3	Overnight stays in all types of accommodation establishments	('000)	2,534	2,766	3,333	3,464	3,242
5.4	Average length of stay of non-resident tourists in all accommodation establishments	Nights	2.50	2.50	2.50	2.40	2.30
6.1	**Tourism expenditure in the country**	US$ Mn	400	523	607	1,325	1,676
6.2	"Travel" (*)	US$ Mn	335	449	503	1,052	1,308
6.3	"Passenger transport" (*)	US$ Mn	65	74	104	273	368
	DOMESTIC TOURISM						
	Accommodation						
7.1	Overnight stays in hotels and similar establishments	('000)	13,369	13,867	13,980	14,094	14,929
7.2	Guests in hotels and similar establishments	('000)	3,505	3,636	3,963	4,139	4,604
7.3	Overnight stays in all types of accommodation establishments	('000)	14,743	15,079	15,168	14,909	15,750
7.4	Average length of stay of resident tourists in all accommodation establishments	Nights	3.80	3.80	3.50	3.40	3.20
	OUTBOUND TOURISM						
8.1	**Departures**	('000)	5,757	6,497	6,972	7,140	8,906
8.2	**Tourism expenditure in other countries**	US$ Mn	448	572	672	1,073	1,459
8.3	"Travel" (*)	US$ Mn	396	479	539	925	1,310
8.4	"Passenger transport" (*)	US$ Mn	52	93	133	148	149
	TOURISM INDUSTRIES						
	Hotels and similar establishments						
9.1	Number of rooms	Units	95,062	97,320	101,574	105,787	111,805
9.2	Number of bed-places	Units	197,320	201,636	207,810	216,499	228,126
9.3	Occupancy rate	Percent	34.00	34.60	34.30	33.40	33.60
9.4	Average length of stay	Nights	3.60	3.50	3.25	3.20	3.18
	RELATED INDICATORS						
	Share of tourism expenditure (6.1) in:						
10.1	Gross Domestic Product (GDP)	Percent	0.9	0.9	0.8	1.3	1.4
10.2	Exports of goods	Percent	2.9	3.0	2.6	4.8	5.2
10.3	Exports of services	Percent	17.0	17.3	16.8	26.1	23.8

(*) Balance of Payments items: 6.1 to 6.3 correspond to the "Credit" side (and are receipts for the country) while 8.2 to 8.4 correspond to the "Debit" side (and are expenditures in other countries).

Basic Indicators	Units	2002	2003	2004	2005	2006
INBOUND TOURISM						
Arrivals						
1.1 Visitors	('000)	23,309	22,521	22,064	22,201	22,486
1.2 Tourists (overnight visitors)	('000)	21,279	20,443	19,892	19,940	..
1.3 Same-day visitors	('000)	524	485	547	498	..
1.4 Cruise passengers	('000)	153	213	280	333	573
Arrivals by region						
2.1 Africa	('000)	31	29	29	27	28
2.2 Americas	('000)	343	421	477	457	533
2.3 Europe	('000)	21,097	20,237	19,607	19,691	19,873
2.4 East Asia and the Pacific	('000)	1,150	1,107	1,314	1,315	1,346
2.5 South Asia	('000)	58	59	63	68	72
2.6 Middle East	('000)	28	32	32	33	33
Arrivals by means of transport used						
3.1 Air	('000)	3,140	3,475	4,090	4,135	4,426
3.2 Rail	('000)	8,086	7,676	7,277	6,899	7,188
3.3 Road	('000)	11,138	10,447	9,544	10,020	9,765
3.4 Sea	('000)	945	923	1,153	1,147	1,107
Arrivals by purpose of visit						
4.1 Leisure, recreation and holidays	('000)	3,106	3,152	2,861	2,385	2,433
4.2 Business and professional	('000)	3,014	2,568	2,723	3,226	3,233
4.3 Other	('000)	17,189	16,801	16,480	16,588	16,819
Accommodation						
5.1 Overnight stays in hotels and similar establishments	('000)	10,564	10,036	10,687	10,696	12,637
5.2 Guests in hotels and similar establishments	('000)	3,231	3,101	3,275	3,438	4,416
5.3 Overnight stays in all types of accommodation establishments	('000)	11,357	10,858	11,516	11,643	13,738
5.4 Average length of stay of non-resident tourists in all accommodation establishments	Nights	..	..	4.38	4.63	5.20
6.1 **Tourism expenditure in the country**	US$ Mn	5,428	5,879	7,262	7,806	9,720
6.2 "Travel" (*)	US$ Mn	4,167	4,502	5,530	5,870	7,628
6.3 "Passenger transport" (*)	US$ Mn	1,261	1,377	1,732	1,936	2,092
DOMESTIC TOURISM						
Accommodation						
7.1 Overnight stays in hotels and similar establishments	('000)	35,343	35,499	35,549	40,730	82,630
7.2 Guests in hotels and similar establishments	('000)	13,678	13,539	13,741	14,909	30,246
7.3 Overnight stays in all types of accommodation establishments	('000)	146,890	140,160	143,039	155,201	172,041
7.4 Average length of stay of resident tourists in all accommodation establishments	Nights	11.20	10.80	11.00	9.00	11.52
OUTBOUND TOURISM						
8.1 **Departures**	('000)	20,428	20,572	24,507	28,416	29,107
8.2 **Tourism expenditure in other countries**	US$ Mn	11,713	13,427	16,082	18,425	19,601
8.3 "Travel" (*)	US$ Mn	11,284	12,880	15,285	17,434	18,235
8.4 "Passenger transport" (*)	US$ Mn	429	547	797	991	1,366
TOURISM INDUSTRIES						
Hotels and similar establishments						
9.1 Number of rooms	Units	178,300	177,200	178,600	199,010	208,309
9.2 Number of bed-places	Units	343,339	364,017	344,400	414,086	430,970
9.3 Occupancy rate	Percent	37.00	34.00	37.00	34.00	35.00
9.4 Average length of stay	Nights	..	..	5.00	4.81	5.30
RELATED INDICATORS						
Share of tourism expenditure (6.1) in:						
10.1 Gross Domestic Product (GDP)	Percent	1.6	1.4	1.2	1.0	1.0
10.2 Exports of goods	Percent	5.1	4.3	4.0	3.2	3.2
10.3 Exports of services	Percent	39.9	36.2	35.3	31.3	31.4

(*) Balance of Payments items: 6.1 to 6.3 correspond to the "Credit" side (and are receipts for the country) while 8.2 to 8.4 correspond to the "Debit" side (and are expenditures in other countries).

SABA

Basic Indicators		Units	2002	2003	2004	2005	2006
	INBOUND TOURISM						
	Arrivals						
1.1	Visitors	('000)	21.5	20.5	23.2	24.9	22.9
1.2	Tourists (overnight visitors)	('000)	10.8	10.3	11.0	11.5	11.0
1.3	Same-day visitors	('000)	10.7	10.2	12.2	13.4	11.9
1.4	Cruise passengers	('000)	..	..	..	..	
	Arrivals by region						
2.1	Africa	('000)	..	..	..	..	..
2.2	Americas	('000)	4.4	4.1	4.8	4.9	..
2.3	Europe	('000)	4.6	4.7	5.0	5.5	..
2.4	East Asia and the Pacific	('000)	..	..	..	..	..
2.5	South Asia	('000)	..	..	..	..	..
2.6	Middle East	('000)	..	..	..	..	..
	Arrivals by means of transport used						
3.1	Air	('000)	7.9	6.8	7.3	7.4	6.9
3.2	Rail	('000)	..	..	..	..	..
3.3	Road	('000)	..	..	..	..	..
3.4	Sea	('000)	2.9	3.5	3.7	4.1	4.1
	Arrivals by purpose of visit						
4.1	Leisure, recreation and holidays	('000)	..	..	..	..	..
4.2	Business and professional	('000)	..	..	..	..	..
4.3	Other	('000)	..	..	..	..	..
	Accommodation						
5.1	Overnight stays in hotels and similar establishments	('000)					
5.2	Guests in hotels and similar establishments	('000)	..	..	..	..	
5.3	Overnight stays in all types of accommodation establishments	('000)	..	..	..	..	
5.4	Average length of stay of non-resident tourists in all accommodation establishments	Nights	..	..	..	..	..
6.1	**Tourism expenditure in the country**	US$ Mn	..	..	..	..	
6.2	"Travel" (*)	US$ Mn	..	..	..	..	
6.3	"Passenger transport" (*)	US$ Mn	..	..	..	..	
	DOMESTIC TOURISM						
	Accommodation						
7.1	Overnight stays in hotels and similar establishments	('000)	..	..	..	..	
7.2	Guests in hotels and similar establishments	('000)	..	..	..	..	..
7.3	Overnight stays in all types of accommodation establishments	('000)	..	..	..	..	..
7.4	Average length of stay of resident tourists in all accommodation establishments	Nights	..	..	..	..	..
	OUTBOUND TOURISM						
8.1	**Departures**	('000)	..	..	..	..	
8.2	**Tourism expenditure in other countries**	US$ Mn	..	..	..	..	
8.3	"Travel" (*)	US$ Mn	..	..	..	..	..
8.4	"Passenger transport" (*)	US$ Mn	..	..	..	..	..
	TOURISM INDUSTRIES						
	Hotels and similar establishments						
9.1	Number of rooms	Units	..	..	..	..	..
9.2	Number of bed-places	Units	..	..	..	..	..
9.3	Occupancy rate	Percent	..	..	..	..	..
9.4	Average length of stay	Nights	..	..	..	..	..
	RELATED INDICATORS						
	Share of tourism expenditure (6.1) in:						
10.1	Gross Domestic Product (GDP)	Percent	..	..	..	..	..
10.2	Exports of goods	Percent	..	..	..	..	..
10.3	Exports of services	Percent	..	..	..	..	..

(*) Balance of Payments items: 6.1 to 6.3 correspond to the "Credit" side (and are receipts for the country) while 8.2 to 8.4 correspond to the "Debit" side (and are expenditures in other countries).

Basic Indicators	Units	2002	2003	2004	2005	2006
INBOUND TOURISM						
Arrivals						
1.1 Visitors	('000)	..	..	..	..	..
1.2 Tourists (overnight visitors)	('000)	9.8	10.5	11.1	10.4	9.6
1.3 Same-day visitors	('000)	..	..	..	..	..
1.4 Cruise passengers	('000)	..	..	..	..	..
Arrivals by region						
2.1 Africa	('000)	..	..	..	..	..
2.2 Americas	('000)	3.4	3.5	3.7	3.5	3.2
2.3 Europe	('000)	4.6	5.3	5.5	5.4	4.9
2.4 East Asia and the Pacific	('000)	..	..	..	..	..
2.5 South Asia	('000)	..	..	..	..	..
2.6 Middle East	('000)	..	..	..	..	..
Arrivals by means of transport used						
3.1 Air	('000)	..	..	..	..	..
3.2 Rail	('000)	..	..	..	..	..
3.3 Road	('000)	..	..	..	..	..
3.4 Sea	('000)	..	..	..	..	..
Arrivals by purpose of visit						
4.1 Leisure, recreation and holidays	('000)	..	..	..	..	..
4.2 Business and professional	('000)	..	..	..	..	..
4.3 Other	('000)	..	..	..	..	..
Accommodation						
5.1 Overnight stays in hotels and similar establishments	('000)	..	..	..	..	..
5.2 Guests in hotels and similar establishments	('000)	..	..	..	..	..
5.3 Overnight stays in all types of accommodation establishments	('000)	..	..	..	..	..
5.4 Average length of stay of non-resident tourists in all accommodation establishments	Nights	..	..	..	..	..
6.1 **Tourism expenditure in the country**	US$ Mn	..	..	..	..	..
6.2 "Travel" (*)	US$ Mn	..	..	..	..	..
6.3 "Passenger transport" (*)	US$ Mn	..	..	..	..	..
DOMESTIC TOURISM						
Accommodation						
7.1 Overnight stays in hotels and similar establishments	('000)	..	..	..	..	..
7.2 Guests in hotels and similar establishments	('000)	..	..	..	..	..
7.3 Overnight stays in all types of accommodation establishments	('000)	..	..	..	..	..
7.4 Average length of stay of resident tourists in all accommodation establishments	Nights	..	..	..	..	..
OUTBOUND TOURISM						
8.1 **Departures**	('000)	..	..	..	..	..
8.2 **Tourism expenditure in other countries**	US$ Mn	..	..	..	..	..
8.3 "Travel" (*)	US$ Mn	..	..	..	..	..
8.4 "Passenger transport" (*)	US$ Mn	..	..	..	..	..
TOURISM INDUSTRIES						
Hotels and similar establishments						
9.1 Number of rooms	Units	..	..	..	..	..
9.2 Number of bed-places	Units	..	..	..	..	..
9.3 Occupancy rate	Percent	..	..	..	..	..
9.4 Average length of stay	Nights	..	..	..	..	..
RELATED INDICATORS						
Share of tourism expenditure (6.1) in:						
10.1 Gross Domestic Product (GDP)	Percent	..	..	..	..	..
10.2 Exports of goods	Percent	..	..	..	..	..
10.3 Exports of services	Percent	..	..	..	..	..

(*) Balance of Payments items: 6.1 to 6.3 correspond to the "Credit" side (and are receipts for the country) while 8.2 to 8.4 correspond to the "Debit" side (and are expenditures in other countries).

SAINT KITTS AND NEVIS

Basic Indicators	Units	2002	2003	2004	2005	2006
INBOUND TOURISM						
Arrivals						
1.1 Visitors	('000)	240	241	376	347	339
1.2 Tourists (overnight visitors)	('000)	69	91	118	128	133
1.3 Same-day visitors	('000)	4	4	3	4	3
1.4 Cruise passengers	('000)	167	146	255	215	203
Arrivals by region						
2.1 Africa	('000)	..	..	..	..	..
2.2 Americas	('000)	60	..	103	112	119
2.3 Europe	('000)	..	..	13	12	12
2.4 East Asia and the Pacific	('000)	..	..	..	..	..
2.5 South Asia	('000)	..	..	..	..	..
2.6 Middle East	('000)	..	..	..	..	..
Arrivals by means of transport used						
3.1 Air	('000)	73	95	121	132	136
3.2 Rail	('000)	..	..	..	..	..
3.3 Road	('000)	..	..	..	..	..
3.4 Sea	('000)	167	146	255	215	203
Arrivals by purpose of visit						
4.1 Leisure, recreation and holidays	('000)	..	..	..	..	..
4.2 Business and professional	('000)	..	..	..	..	..
4.3 Other	('000)	..	..	..	..	..
Accommodation						
5.1 Overnight stays in hotels and similar establishments	('000)	..	..	..	..	..
5.2 Guests in hotels and similar establishments	('000)	..	..	..	..	..
5.3 Overnight stays in all types of accommodation establishments	('000)	..	..	..	..	..
5.4 Average length of stay of non-resident tourists in all accommodation establishments	Nights	..	..	..	..	..
6.1 **Tourism expenditure in the country**	US$ Mn	..	..	..	..	..
6.2 "Travel" (*)	US$ Mn	57	75	103	115	116
6.3 "Passenger transport" (*)	US$ Mn	..	..	..	..	..
DOMESTIC TOURISM						
Accommodation						
7.1 Overnight stays in hotels and similar establishments	('000)	..	..	..	..	..
7.2 Guests in hotels and similar establishments	('000)	..	..	..	..	..
7.3 Overnight stays in all types of accommodation establishments	('000)	..	..	..	..	..
7.4 Average length of stay of resident tourists in all accommodation establishments	Nights	..	..	..	..	..
OUTBOUND TOURISM						
8.1 **Departures**	('000)	..	..	..	..	..
8.2 **Tourism expenditure in other countries**	US$ Mn	..	..	..	..	..
8.3 "Travel" (*)	US$ Mn	8	8	10	10	12
8.4 "Passenger transport" (*)	US$ Mn	..	..	..	..	..
TOURISM INDUSTRIES						
Hotels and similar establishments						
9.1 Number of rooms	Units	1,438	1,611	1,550	1,859	1,859
9.2 Number of bed-places	Units	2,182	2,361	..	..	..
9.3 Occupancy rate	Percent	..	..	..	..	..
9.4 Average length of stay	Nights	..	..	..	..	..
RELATED INDICATORS						
Share of tourism expenditure (6.1) in: (**)						
10.1 Gross Domestic Product (GDP)	Percent	16.2	20.5	25.4	25.4	23.8
10.2 Exports of goods	Percent	90.5	131.6	180.7	198.3	..
10.3 Exports of services	Percent	63.3	69.4	76.3	80.4	..

(*) Balance of Payments items: 6.1 to 6.3 correspond to the "Credit" side (and are receipts for the country) while 8.2 to 8.4 correspond to the "Debit" side (and are expenditures in other countries).

(**) See Annex "Country notes".

Basic Indicators	Units	2002	2003	2004	2005	2006
INBOUND TOURISM						
Arrivals						
1.1 Visitors	('000)	648	683	791	720	670
1.2 Tourists (overnight visitors)	('000)	253	277	298	318	303
1.3 Same-day visitors	('000)	8	13	11	8	7
1.4 Cruise passengers	('000)	387	393	481	394	360
Arrivals by region						
2.1 Africa	('000)	..	..	..	..	..
2.2 Americas	('000)	175	183	197	215	213
2.3 Europe	('000)	76	90	97	102	86
2.4 East Asia and the Pacific	('000)	..	..	..	..	..
2.5 South Asia	('000)	..	..	..	..	..
2.6 Middle East	('000)	..	..	..	..	..
Arrivals by means of transport used						
3.1 Air	('000)	..	..	..	..	..
3.2 Rail	('000)	..	..	..	..	..
3.3 Road	('000)	..	..	..	..	..
3.4 Sea	('000)	..	..	..	..	..
Arrivals by purpose of visit						
4.1 Leisure, recreation and holidays	('000)	..	243	268	292	..
4.2 Business and professional	('000)	..	13	12	16	..
4.3 Other	('000)	..	21	18	10	..
Accommodation						
5.1 Overnight stays in hotels and similar establishments	('000)	..	..	..	..	..
5.2 Guests in hotels and similar establishments	('000)	230	245	263	285	..
5.3 Overnight stays in all types of accommodation establishments	('000)	..	..	..	..	..
5.4 Average length of stay of non-resident tourists in all accommodation establishments	Nights	..	..	..	..	..
6.1 **Tourism expenditure in the country**	US$ Mn	..	..	..	..	..
6.2 "Travel" (*)	US$ Mn	207	282	326	356	347
6.3 "Passenger transport" (*)	US$ Mn	..	..	..	..	..
DOMESTIC TOURISM						
Accommodation						
7.1 Overnight stays in hotels and similar establishments	('000)	..	..	..	..	..
7.2 Guests in hotels and similar establishments	('000)	..	..	..	..	..
7.3 Overnight stays in all types of accommodation establishments	('000)	..	..	..	..	..
7.4 Average length of stay of resident tourists in all accommodation establishments	Nights	..	..	..	..	..
OUTBOUND TOURISM						
8.1 **Departures**	('000)	..	..	..	..	..
8.2 **Tourism expenditure in other countries**	US$ Mn	..	..	..	..	..
8.3 "Travel" (*)	US$ Mn	34	36	37	39	43
8.4 "Passenger transport" (*)	US$ Mn	..	..	..	..	..
TOURISM INDUSTRIES						
Hotels and similar establishments						
9.1 Number of rooms	Units	4,428	3,749	3,974	4,511	..
9.2 Number of bed-places	Units	8,236	6,748	7,153	8,120	..
9.3 Occupancy rate	Percent	56.10	62.70	61.90	68.70	64.90
9.4 Average length of stay	Nights	9.99	10.00	9.30	9.40	9.30
RELATED INDICATORS						
Share of tourism expenditure (6.1) in: (**)						
10.1 Gross Domestic Product (GDP)	Percent	30.4	39.4	42.6	43.2	38.3
10.2 Exports of goods	Percent	300.0	391.7	299.1	515.9	..
10.3 Exports of services	Percent	82.8	88.7	88.8	91.3	..

(*) Balance of Payments items: 6.1 to 6.3 correspond to the "Credit" side (and are receipts for the country) while 8.2 to 8.4 correspond to the "Debit" side (and are expenditures in other countries).

(**) See Annex "Country notes".

SAINT MAARTEN

Basic Indicators	Units	2002	2003	2004	2005	2006
INBOUND TOURISM						
Arrivals						
1.1 Visitors	('000)	1,436	1,600	1,823	1,956	1,906
1.2 Tourists (overnight visitors)	('000)	381	428	475	468	468
1.3 Same-day visitors	('000)	..	..	..	..	..
1.4 Cruise passengers	('000)	1,055	1,172	1,348	1,488	1,438
Arrivals by region						
2.1 Africa	('000)	..	..	..	..	..
2.2 Americas	('000)	260	301	338	332	328
2.3 Europe	('000)	87	88	96	94	97
2.4 East Asia and the Pacific	('000)	..	..	..	..	..
2.5 South Asia	('000)	..	..	..	..	..
2.6 Middle East	('000)	..	..	..	..	..
Arrivals by means of transport used						
3.1 Air	('000)	381	428	475	468	468
3.2 Rail	('000)	..	..	..	..	..
3.3 Road	('000)	..	..	..	..	..
3.4 Sea	('000)	1,055	1,172	1,348	1,488	1,438
Arrivals by purpose of visit						
4.1 Leisure, recreation and holidays	('000)	..	..	..	..	..
4.2 Business and professional	('000)	..	..	..	..	..
4.3 Other	('000)	..	..	..	..	..
Accommodation						
5.1 Overnight stays in hotels and similar establishments	('000)	..	..	..	..	..
5.2 Guests in hotels and similar establishments	('000)	..	..	..	.	..
5.3 Overnight stays in all types of accommodation establishments	('000)	..	..	..	..	..
5.4 Average length of stay of non-resident tourists in all accommodation establishments	Nights	..	..	..	..	..
6.1 **Tourism expenditure in the country**	US$ Mn	..	..	..	..	..
6.2 "Travel" (*)	US$ Mn	489	538	626	659	652
6.3 "Passenger transport" (*)	US$ Mn	..	..	..	..	..
DOMESTIC TOURISM						
Accommodation						
7.1 Overnight stays in hotels and similar establishments	('000)	..	..	..	..	..
7.2 Guests in hotels and similar establishments	('000)	..	..	..	..	..
7.3 Overnight stays in all types of accommodation establishments	('000)	..	..	..	..	..
7.4 Average length of stay of resident tourists in all accommodation establishments	Nights	..	..	..	..	..
OUTBOUND TOURISM						
8.1 **Departures**	('000)	..	..	..	..	..
8.2 **Tourism expenditure in other countries**	US$ Mn	..	..	..	..	..
8.3 "Travel" (*)	US$ Mn	140	144	80	94	86
8.4 "Passenger transport" (*)	US$ Mn	..	..	..	..	..
TOURISM INDUSTRIES						
Hotels and similar establishments						
9.1 Number of rooms	Units	3,532	..	..	..	..
9.2 Number of bed-places	Units	6,358	..	..	..	..
9.3 Occupancy rate	Percent	56.70	56.20	..	..	..
9.4 Average length of stay	Nights	..	..	..	..	..
RELATED INDICATORS						
Share of tourism expenditure (6.1) in:						
10.1 Gross Domestic Product (GDP)	Percent	..	..	..	..	..
10.2 Exports of goods	Percent	..	..	..	..	..
10.3 Exports of services	Percent	..	..	..	..	..

(*) Balance of Payments items: 6.1 to 6.3 correspond to the "Credit" side (and are receipts for the country) while 8.2 to 8.4 correspond to the "Debit" side (and are expenditures in other countries).

Basic Indicators	Units	2002	2003	2004	2005	2006
INBOUND TOURISM						
Arrivals						
1.1 Visitors	('000)	247	242	262	256	306
1.2 Tourists (overnight visitors)	('000)	78	79	87	96	97
1.3 Same-day visitors	('000)	13	14	13	9	9
1.4 Cruise passengers	('000)	157	149	162	152	200
Arrivals by region						
2.1 Africa	('000)	..	..	..	..	..
2.2 Americas	('000)	58	60	67	74	74
2.3 Europe	('000)	18	17	19	20	22
2.4 East Asia and the Pacific	('000)	..	..	..	..	..
2.5 South Asia	('000)	..	..	..	..	..
2.6 Middle East	('000)	..	..	..	..	..
Arrivals by means of transport used						
3.1 Air	('000)	90	92	100	104	106
3.2 Rail	('000)	..	..	..	..	..
3.3 Road	('000)	..	..	..	..	..
3.4 Sea	('000)	157	149	162	152	200
Arrivals by purpose of visit						
4.1 Leisure, recreation and holidays	('000)	61	63	63	68	80
4.2 Business and professional	('000)	13	14	17	21	17
4.3 Other	('000)	4	2	7	7	1
Accommodation						
5.1 Overnight stays in hotels and similar establishments	('000)	..	..	..	..	..
5.2 Guests in hotels and similar establishments	('000)	28	26	28	31	31
5.3 Overnight stays in all types of accommodation establishments	('000)	..	..	..	..	..
5.4 Average length of stay of non-resident tourists in all accommodation establishments	Nights	11.90	7.20	12.50	..	..
6.1 **Tourism expenditure in the country**	US$ Mn	..	..	..	..	..
6.2 "Travel" (*)	US$ Mn	91	91	96	104	113
6.3 "Passenger transport" (*)	US$ Mn	..	..	..	..	..
DOMESTIC TOURISM						
Accommodation						
7.1 Overnight stays in hotels and similar establishments	('000)	..	..	..	..	..
7.2 Guests in hotels and similar establishments	('000)	..	..	..	..	..
7.3 Overnight stays in all types of accommodation establishments	('000)	..	..	..	..	..
7.4 Average length of stay of resident tourists in all accommodation establishments	Nights	..	..	..	..	..
OUTBOUND TOURISM						
8.1 **Departures**	('000)	..	..	..	..	..
8.2 **Tourism expenditure in other countries**	US$ Mn	..	..	..	..	..
8.3 "Travel" (*)	US$ Mn	10	13	14	15	15
8.4 "Passenger transport" (*)	US$ Mn	..	..	..	..	..
TOURISM INDUSTRIES						
Hotels and similar establishments						
9.1 Number of rooms	Units	1,689	1,680	1,785	1,692	1,778
9.2 Number of bed-places	Units	3,378	3,360	3,570	3,384	3,556
9.3 Occupancy rate	Percent	..	..	..	..	..
9.4 Average length of stay	Nights	..	..	..	..	..
RELATED INDICATORS						
Share of tourism expenditure (6.1) in: (**)						
10.1 Gross Domestic Product (GDP)	Percent	24.9	23.8	23.5	24.2	24.2
10.2 Exports of goods	Percent	222.0	227.5	246.2	241.9	..
10.3 Exports of services	Percent	66.4	68.4	66.2	66.2	..

(*) Balance of Payments items: 6.1 to 6.3 correspond to the "Credit" side (and are receipts for the country) while 8.2 to 8.4 correspond to the "Debit" side (and are expenditures in other countries).

(**) See Annex "Country notes".

SAMOA

Basic Indicators		Units	2002	2003	2004	2005	2006
	INBOUND TOURISM						
	Arrivals						
1.1	Visitors	('000)	..	..	..	..	..
1.2	Tourists (overnight visitors)	('000)	89	92	98	102	116
1.3	Same-day visitors	('000)	..	..	..	..	..
1.4	Cruise passengers	('000)	..	..	..	..	..
	Arrivals by region						
2.1	Africa	('000)	..	..	..	..	..
2.2	Americas	('000)	9	9	8	10	9
2.3	Europe	('000)	5	5	5	5	5
2.4	East Asia and the Pacific	('000)	75	78	85	87	101
2.5	South Asia	('000)	..	..	..	..	..
2.6	Middle East	('000)	..	..	..	..	..
	Arrivals by means of transport used						
3.1	Air	('000)	86	89	94	99	112
3.2	Rail	('000)	..	..	..	..	..
3.3	Road	('000)	..	..	..	..	..
3.4	Sea	('000)	3	3	4	3	3
	Arrivals by purpose of visit						
4.1	Leisure, recreation and holidays	('000)	29	30	30	34	43
4.2	Business and professional	('000)	10	10	11	10	12
4.3	Other	('000)	50	52	57	58	61
	Accommodation						
5.1	Overnight stays in hotels and similar establishments	('000)	..	..	..	..	..
5.2	Guests in hotels and similar establishments	('000)	..	..	..	..	40
5.3	Overnight stays in all types of accommodation establishments	('000)	..	..	..	..	..
5.4	Average length of stay of non-resident tourists in all accommodation establishments	Nights	..	..	..	..	..
6.1	**Tourism expenditure in the country**	US$ Mn	..	..	70	78	91
6.2	"Travel" (*)	US$ Mn	45	54	69	77	90
6.3	"Passenger transport" (*)	US$ Mn	..	..	1	1	1
	DOMESTIC TOURISM						
	Accommodation						
7.1	Overnight stays in hotels and similar establishments	('000)	..	..	..	..	..
7.2	Guests in hotels and similar establishments	('000)	..	..	..	..	..
7.3	Overnight stays in all types of accommodation establishments	('000)	..	..	..	..	..
7.4	Average length of stay of resident tourists in all accommodation establishments	Nights	..	..	..	..	..
	OUTBOUND TOURISM						
8.1	**Departures**	('000)	53	51	54	52	..
8.2	**Tourism expenditure in other countries**	US$ Mn	..	..	12	13	16
8.3	"Travel" (*)	US$ Mn	..	..	5	9	6
8.4	"Passenger transport" (*)	US$ Mn	..	..	7	4	10
	TOURISM INDUSTRIES						
	Hotels and similar establishments						
9.1	Number of rooms	Units	850	939	..	..	..
9.2	Number of bed-places	Units	1,945	2,131	..	..	..
9.3	Occupancy rate	Percent	..	..	..	..	..
9.4	Average length of stay	Nights	..	..	..	..	..
	RELATED INDICATORS						
	Share of tourism expenditure (6.1) in:						
10.1	Gross Domestic Product (GDP)	Percent	..	..	19.6	19.3	21.6
10.2	Exports of goods	Percent	..	..	583.3	650.0	910.0
10.3	Exports of services	Percent	..	..	73.7	69.6	67.9

(*) Balance of Payments items: 6.1 to 6.3 correspond to the "Credit" side (and are receipts for the country) while 8.2 to 8.4 correspond to the "Debit" side (and are expenditures in other countries).

Basic Indicators	Units	2002	2003	2004	2005	2006
INBOUND TOURISM						
Arrivals						
1.1 Visitors	('000)	3,102	2,882	2,812	2,107	2,136
1.2 Tourists (overnight visitors)	('000)	46	41	42	50	50
1.3 Same-day visitors	('000)	..	..	..	2,057	2,086
1.4 Cruise passengers	('000)	..	..	..	..	..
Arrivals by region						
2.1 Africa	('000)	..	..	..	..	..
2.2 Americas	('000)	..	..	..	17	22
2.3 Europe	('000)	..	..	..	2,035	2,076
2.4 East Asia and the Pacific	('000)	..	..	..	53	36
2.5 South Asia	('000)	..	..	..	..	..
2.6 Middle East	('000)	..	..	..	..	..
Arrivals by means of transport used						
3.1 Air	('000)	..	..	..	..	..
3.2 Rail	('000)	..	..	..	..	..
3.3 Road	('000)	3,102	2,882	2,812	2,107	2,136
3.4 Sea	('000)	..	..	..	..	..
Arrivals by purpose of visit						
4.1 Leisure, recreation and holidays	('000)	..	..	..	738	880
4.2 Business and professional	('000)	..	..	..	695	700
4.3 Other	('000)	..	..	..	674	556
Accommodation						
5.1 Overnight stays in hotels and similar establishments	('000)	69	64	68	80	80
5.2 Guests in hotels and similar establishments	('000)	46	41	42	50	50
5.3 Overnight stays in all types of accommodation establishments	('000)	..	..	..	..	..
5.4 Average length of stay of non-resident tourists in all accommodation establishments	Nights	..	..	1.64	1.61	1.61
6.1 **Tourism expenditure in the country**	US$ Mn	..	..	..	..	..
6.2 "Travel" (*)	US$ Mn	..	..	..	..	..
6.3 "Passenger transport" (*)	US$ Mn	..	..	..	..	..
DOMESTIC TOURISM						
Accommodation						
7.1 Overnight stays in hotels and similar establishments	('000)	..	..	..	..	..
7.2 Guests in hotels and similar establishments	('000)	..	..	..	..	..
7.3 Overnight stays in all types of accommodation establishments	('000)	..	..	..	..	..
7.4 Average length of stay of resident tourists in all accommodation establishments	Nights	..	..	..	..	..
OUTBOUND TOURISM						
8.1 **Departures**	('000)	..	..	..	..	..
8.2 **Tourism expenditure in other countries**	US$ Mn	..	..	..	..	..
8.3 "Travel" (*)	US$ Mn	..	..	..	..	..
8.4 "Passenger transport" (*)	US$ Mn	..	..	..	..	..
TOURISM INDUSTRIES						
Hotels and similar establishments						
9.1 Number of rooms	Units	500	683	685	718	806
9.2 Number of bed-places	Units	1,180	1,549	1,549	1,593	1,816
9.3 Occupancy rate	Percent	..	..	..	54.10	55.00
9.4 Average length of stay	Nights	1.51	1.57	1.63	1.61	1.61
RELATED INDICATORS						
Share of tourism expenditure (6.1) in:						
10.1 Gross Domestic Product (GDP)	Percent	..	..	..	..	..
10.2 Exports of goods	Percent	..	..	..	..	..
10.3 Exports of services	Percent	..	..	..	..	..

(*) Balance of Payments items: 6.1 to 6.3 correspond to the "Credit" side (and are receipts for the country) while 8.2 to 8.4 correspond to the "Debit" side (and are expenditures in other countries).

SAO TOME AND PRINCIPE

Basic Indicators	Units	2002	2003	2004	2005	2006
INBOUND TOURISM						
Arrivals						
1.1 Visitors	('000)	..	..	..	..	..
1.2 Tourists (overnight visitors)	('000)	9.2	10.0	10.6	15.8	12.3
1.3 Same-day visitors	('000)	..	..	..	..	..
1.4 Cruise passengers	('000)	..	..	..	..	..
Arrivals by region						
2.1 Africa	('000)	1.9	2.6	2.1	4.4	2.8
2.2 Americas	('000)	0.3	0.6	0.7	0.6	0.5
2.3 Europe	('000)	5.4	6.7	6.8	10.3	7.6
2.4 East Asia and the Pacific	('000)	..	..	..	0.2	..
2.5 South Asia	('000)	..	..	..	..	..
2.6 Middle East	('000)	..	..	..	..	..
Arrivals by means of transport used						
3.1 Air	('000)	9.2	10.0	10.6	15.8	11.9
3.2 Rail	('000)	..	..	..	..	..
3.3 Road	('000)	..	..	..	..	..
3.4 Sea	('000)	..	..	..	..	0.4
Arrivals by purpose of visit						
4.1 Leisure, recreation and holidays	('000)	..	..	..	9.3	6.7
4.2 Business and professional	('000)	..	..	..	1.1	0.6
4.3 Other	('000)	..	..	..	5.4	5.0
Accommodation						
5.1 Overnight stays in hotels and similar establishments	('000)	..	..	..	..	..
5.2 Guests in hotels and similar establishments	('000)	..	..	..	..	..
5.3 Overnight stays in all types of accommodation establishments	('000)	..	..	..	..	..
5.4 Average length of stay of non-resident tourists in all accommodation establishments	Nights	..	..	..	..	..
6.1 **Tourism expenditure in the country**	US$ Mn	..	..	..	..	..
6.2 "Travel" (*)	US$ Mn	10.1	10.6	12.8	13.6	..
6.3 "Passenger transport" (*)	US$ Mn	..	..	..	..	..
DOMESTIC TOURISM						
Accommodation						
7.1 Overnight stays in hotels and similar establishments	('000)	..	..	..	..	..
7.2 Guests in hotels and similar establishments	('000)	..	..	..	..	..
7.3 Overnight stays in all types of accommodation establishments	('000)	..	..	..	..	..
7.4 Average length of stay of resident tourists in all accommodation establishments	Nights	..	..	..	..	..
OUTBOUND TOURISM						
8.1 **Departures**	('000)	..	..	..	..	..
8.2 **Tourism expenditure in other countries**	US$ Mn	1.9	..	..	..	..
8.3 "Travel" (*)	US$ Mn	0.6	..	..	..	..
8.4 "Passenger transport" (*)	US$ Mn	1.3	..	..	..	..
TOURISM INDUSTRIES						
Hotels and similar establishments						
9.1 Number of rooms	Units	257	273	..	..	..
9.2 Number of bed-places	Units	448	492	..	..	..
9.3 Occupancy rate	Percent	..	..	..	..	..
9.4 Average length of stay	Nights	..	..	..	..	..
RELATED INDICATORS						
Share of tourism expenditure (6.1) in: (**)						
10.1 Gross Domestic Product (GDP)	Percent	11.0	10.7	12.0	12.0	..
10.2 Exports of goods	Percent	202.0	151.4	320.0	453.3	..
10.3 Exports of services	Percent	77.7	75.7	75.3	75.6	..

(*) Balance of Payments items: 6.1 to 6.3 correspond to the "Credit" side (and are receipts for the country) while 8.2 to 8.4 correspond to the "Debit" side (and are expenditures in other countries).

(**) See Annex "Country notes".

Basic Indicators		Units	2002	2003	2004	2005	2006
	INBOUND TOURISM						
	Arrivals						
1.1	Visitors	('000)	..	..	11,083	10,417	10,962
1.2	Tourists (overnight visitors)	('000)	7,511	7,332	8,599	8,037	8,620
1.3	Same-day visitors	('000)	..	..	2,484	2,380	2,342
1.4	Cruise passengers	('000)	..	..	..	..	..
	Arrivals by region						
2.1	Africa	('000)	607	525	675	436	489
2.2	Americas	('000)	52	46	53	70	66
2.3	Europe	('000)	339	334	424	340	485
2.4	East Asia and the Pacific	('000)	660	612	753	439	595
2.5	South Asia	('000)	1,619	1,869	1,933	1,142	1,469
2.6	Middle East	('000)	4,213	3,924	4,752	5,607	5,516
	Arrivals by means of transport used						
3.1	Air	('000)	..	..	4,194	4,287	4,857
3.2	Rail	('000)	..	..	..	..	..
3.3	Road	('000)	..	..	3,824	3,301	3,493
3.4	Sea	('000)	..	..	581	488	270
	Arrivals by purpose of visit						
4.1	Leisure, recreation and holidays	('000)	..	..	433	397	566
4.2	Business and professional	('000)	..	..	2,381	1,951	1,603
4.3	Other	('000)	..	..	5,785	5,689	6,451
	Accommodation						
5.1	Overnight stays in hotels and similar establishments	('000)	..	..	58,982	70,339	98,978
5.2	Guests in hotels and similar establishments	('000)	..	..	6,799	6,310	7,228
5.3	Overnight stays in all types of accommodation establishments	('000)	..	..	111,810	91,359	112,383
5.4	Average length of stay of non-resident tourists in all accommodation establishments	Nights	..	..	13.12	10.70	14.00
6.1	**Tourism expenditure in the country** (**)	US$ Mn	..	3,418	6,916	5,626	5,391
6.2	"Travel" (*)	US$ Mn	..	..	6,486	5,149	4,955
6.3	"Passenger transport" (*)	US$ Mn	..	..	430	477	436
	DOMESTIC TOURISM						
	Accommodation						
7.1	Overnight stays in hotels and similar establishments	('000)	..	..	117,162	108,236	99,858
7.2	Guests in hotels and similar establishments	('000)	..	..	19,954	17,031	15,894
7.3	Overnight stays in all types of accommodation establishments	('000)	334,100	284,900	216,870	196,737	183,527
7.4	Average length of stay of resident tourists in all accommodation establishments	Nights	..	5.90	6.10	6.50	6.50
	OUTBOUND TOURISM						
8.1	**Departures**	('000)	7,896	4,104	3,811	4,403	2,000
8.2	**Tourism expenditure in other countries** (**)	US$ Mn	7,370	4,165	4,600	4,178	2,316
8.3	"Travel" (*)	US$ Mn	..	..	4,428	3,975	1,804
8.4	"Passenger transport" (*)	US$ Mn	..	..	172	203	512
	TOURISM INDUSTRIES						
	Hotels and similar establishments						
9.1	Number of rooms	Units	81,197	81,197	148,932	156,921	167,736
9.2	Number of bed-places	Units	..	..	300,167	316,145	337,775
9.3	Occupancy rate	Percent	..	42.00	50.60	51.30	51.00
9.4	Average length of stay	Nights	..	2.70	2.27	2.23	1.93
	RELATED INDICATORS						
	Share of tourism expenditure (6.1) in:						
10.1	Gross Domestic Product (GDP)	Percent	..	..	..	..	..
10.2	Exports of goods	Percent	..	..	..	..	..
10.3	Exports of services	Percent	..	..	..	..	..

(*) Balance of Payments items: 6.1 to 6.3 correspond to the "Credit" side (and are receipts for the country) while 8.2 to 8.4 correspond to the "Debit" side (and are expenditures in other countries).

(**) See Annex "Country notes".

SENEGAL

Basic Indicators	Units	2002	2003	2004	2005	2006
INBOUND TOURISM						
Arrivals						
1.1 Visitors	('000)	..	502	677	779	876
1.2 Tourists (overnight visitors)	('000)	427	495	667	769	866
1.3 Same-day visitors	('000)	..	..			
1.4 Cruise passengers	('000)	7	7	10	9	10
Arrivals by region						
2.1 Africa	('000)	86	86	209	265	430
2.2 Americas	('000)	10	10	25	26	26
2.3 Europe	('000)	323	252	349	393	324
2.4 East Asia and the Pacific	('000)	2	2	..	..	..
2.5 South Asia	('000)	..	..	..	..	..
2.6 Middle East	('000)	1	1	..	..	..
Arrivals by means of transport used						
3.1 Air	('000)	..	..	523	564	522
3.2 Rail	('000)	..	..	..	..	..
3.3 Road	('000)	..	..	144	206	344
3.4 Sea	('000)	..	..	10	9	10
Arrivals by purpose of visit						
4.1 Leisure, recreation and holidays	('000)	..	..	..	..	..
4.2 Business and professional	('000)	..	..	..	..	..
4.3 Other	('000)	..	..	..	..	..
Accommodation						
5.1 Overnight stays in hotels and similar establishments	('000)	1,569	1,451	1,349	1,397	1,426
5.2 Guests in hotels and similar establishments	('000)	427	354	363	387	406
5.3 Overnight stays in all types of accommodation establishments	('000)	..	..	..	..	..
5.4 Average length of stay of non-resident tourists in all accommodation establishments	Nights	3.70	4.10	3.50	3.40	3.50
6.1 **Tourism expenditure in the country**	US$ Mn	210	269	287	334	..
6.2 "Travel" (*)	US$ Mn	190	209	212	242	
6.3 "Passenger transport" (*)	US$ Mn	20	60	75	92	..
DOMESTIC TOURISM						
Accommodation						
7.1 Overnight stays in hotels and similar establishments	('000)	133	156	159	198	177
7.2 Guests in hotels and similar establishments	('000)	61	65	71	81	72
7.3 Overnight stays in all types of accommodation establishments	('000)	..	..	..	..	..
7.4 Average length of stay of resident tourists in all accommodation establishments	Nights	..	..	..	..	..
OUTBOUND TOURISM						
8.1 **Departures**	('000)	..	..	..	..	..
8.2 **Tourism expenditure in other countries**	US$ Mn	112	129	138	144	..
8.3 "Travel" (*)	US$ Mn	43	55	57	65	..
8.4 "Passenger transport" (*)	US$ Mn	69	74	81	79	..
TOURISM INDUSTRIES						
Hotels and similar establishments						
9.1 Number of rooms	Units	11,280	11,539	12,101	15,842	15,842
9.2 Number of bed-places	Units	19,729	20,437	21,741	31,229	31,229
9.3 Occupancy rate	Percent	38.60	37.10	34.00	34.40	34.80
9.4 Average length of stay	Nights	3.70	4.10	3.50	3.40	3.50
RELATED INDICATORS						
Share of tourism expenditure (6.1) in:						
10.1 Gross Domestic Product (GDP)	Percent	4.2	4.2	3.8	4.1	..
10.2 Exports of goods	Percent	19.7	21.4	19.0	..	..
10.3 Exports of services	Percent	46.1	47.3	42.8	..	..

(*) Balance of Payments items: 6.1 to 6.3 correspond to the "Credit" side (and are receipts for the country) while 8.2 to 8.4 correspond to the "Debit" side (and are expenditures in other countries).

Basic Indicators		Units	2002	2003	2004	2005	2006
INBOUND TOURISM							
Arrivals							
1.1	Visitors	('000)	..	..	..	..	..
1.2	Tourists (overnight visitors)	('000)	312	339	392	453	469
1.3	Same-day visitors	('000)	..	..	..	..	..
1.4	Cruise passengers	('000)	..	..	..	..	..
Arrivals by region							
2.1	Africa	('000)	..	..	..	..	
2.2	Americas	('000)	12	14	13	16	17
2.3	Europe	('000)	288	313	363	419	435
2.4	East Asia and the Pacific	('000)	3	4	5	6	6
2.5	South Asia	('000)	..	..	..	..	..
2.6	Middle East	('000)	..	..	..	..	..
Arrivals by means of transport used							
3.1	Air	('000)	..	..	..	..	..
3.2	Rail	('000)	..	..	..	..	..
3.3	Road	('000)	..	..	..	..	..
3.4	Sea	('000)	..	..	..	..	..
Arrivals by purpose of visit							
4.1	Leisure, recreation and holidays	('000)	..	..	..	..	..
4.2	Business and professional	('000)	..	..	..	..	..
4.3	Other	('000)	..	..	..	..	..
Accommodation							
5.1	Overnight stays in hotels and similar establishments	('000)	687	736	798	933	949
5.2	Guests in hotels and similar establishments	('000)	294	321	374	434	448
5.3	Overnight stays in all types of accommodation establishments	('000)	738	792	851	992	1,015
5.4	Average length of stay of non-resident tourists in all accommodation establishments	Nights	2.37	2.34	2.17	2.19	2.16
6.1	**Tourism expenditure in the country** (**)	US$ Mn	77	159	220	308	398
6.2	"Travel" (*)	US$ Mn	..	..	..	..	..
6.3	"Passenger transport" (*)	US$ Mn	..	..	..	..	..
DOMESTIC TOURISM							
Accommodation							
7.1	Overnight stays in hotels and similar establishments	('000)	3,748	3,336	3,362	3,198	3,120
7.2	Guests in hotels and similar establishments	('000)	1,305	1,121	1,113	1,079	1,058
7.3	Overnight stays in all types of accommodation establishments	('000)	6,468	5,893	5,792	5,508	5,577
7.4	Average length of stay of resident tourists in all accommodation establishments	Nights	3.41	3.55	3.67	3.59	3.63
OUTBOUND TOURISM							
8.1	**Departures**	('000)	..	..	..	..	..
8.2	**Tourism expenditure in other countries** (**)	US$ Mn	105	144	208	260	322
8.3	"Travel" (*)	US$ Mn	..	..	..	..	..
8.4	"Passenger transport" (*)	US$ Mn	..	..	..	..	..
TOURISM INDUSTRIES							
Hotels and similar establishments							
9.1	Number of rooms	Units	21,909	21,417	21,999	22,236	22,631
9.2	Number of bed-places	Units	46,932	46,393	47,987	48,360	49,145
9.3	Occupancy rate	Percent	25.89	24.05	23.68	23.40	22.69
9.4	Average length of stay	Nights	2.77	2.82	2.80	2.73	2.70
RELATED INDICATORS							
Share of tourism expenditure (6.1) in:							
10.1	Gross Domestic Product (GDP)	Percent	..	..	..	..	..
10.2	Exports of goods	Percent	..	..	..	..	..
10.3	Exports of services	Percent	..	..	..	..	..

(*) Balance of Payments items: 6.1 to 6.3 correspond to the "Credit" side (and are receipts for the country) while 8.2 to 8.4 correspond to the "Debit" side (and are expenditures in other countries).

(**) See Annex "Country notes".

SEYCHELLES

Basic Indicators		Units	2002	2003	2004	2005	2006
	INBOUND TOURISM						
	Arrivals						
1.1	Visitors	('000)	135	127	126	135	151
1.2	Tourists (overnight visitors)	('000)	132	122	121	129	141
1.3	Same-day visitors	('000)	..	..	..	..	..
1.4	Cruise passengers	('000)	3	5	5	6	10
	Arrivals by region						
2.1	Africa	('000)	14	14	13	12	13
2.2	Americas	('000)	4	3	4	4	3
2.3	Europe	('000)	108	100	99	104	114
2.4	East Asia and the Pacific	('000)	3	2	2	3	3
2.5	South Asia	('000)	2	1	1	2	2
2.6	Middle East	('000)	2	2	2	4	5
	Arrivals by means of transport used						
3.1	Air	('000)	129	119	117	125	137
3.2	Rail	('000)	..	..	..	..	..
3.3	Road	('000)	..	..	..	..	..
3.4	Sea	('000)	3	3	4	4	4
	Arrivals by purpose of visit						
4.1	Leisure, recreation and holidays	('000)	117	110	108	116	128
4.2	Business and professional	('000)	7	6	7	7	7
4.3	Other	('000)	8	6	6	6	6
	Accommodation						
5.1	Overnight stays in hotels and similar establishments	('000)	883	825	798	822	926
5.2	Guests in hotels and similar establishments	('000)	..	..	..	104	114
5.3	Overnight stays in all types of accommodation establishments	('000)	1,336	1,233	1,208	1,248	1,378
5.4	Average length of stay of non-resident tourists in all accommodation establishments	Nights	10.10	10.10	10.00	9.70	9.80
6.1	**Tourism expenditure in the country**	US$ Mn	247	258	256	269	323
6.2	"Travel" (*)	US$ Mn	164	171	172	192	228
6.3	"Passenger transport" (*)	US$ Mn	83	87	84	77	95
	DOMESTIC TOURISM						
	Accommodation						
7.1	Overnight stays in hotels and similar establishments	('000)	14	8	10	..	..
7.2	Guests in hotels and similar establishments	('000)	..	..	..	..	..
7.3	Overnight stays in all types of accommodation establishments	('000)	..	..	..	..	..
7.4	Average length of stay of resident tourists in all accommodation establishments	Nights	..	..	..	..	..
	OUTBOUND TOURISM						
8.1	**Departures**	('000)	53	50	48	52	55
8.2	**Tourism expenditure in other countries**	US$ Mn	53	54	53	59	56
8.3	"Travel" (*)	US$ Mn	33	36	34	39	36
8.4	"Passenger transport" (*)	US$ Mn	20	18	19	20	20
	TOURISM INDUSTRIES						
	Hotels and similar establishments						
9.1	Number of rooms	Units	2,358	2,435	2,477	..	..
9.2	Number of bed-places	Units	4,780	4,930	5,030	4,920	5,140
9.3	Occupancy rate	Percent	51.00	51.00	44.00	46.00	49.00
9.4	Average length of stay	Nights	..	..	..	..	..
	RELATED INDICATORS						
	Share of tourism expenditure (6.1) in:						
10.1	Gross Domestic Product (GDP)	Percent	35.4	36.5	36.6	37.2	43.1
10.2	Exports of goods	Percent	104.2	90.2	85.0	76.6	76.4
10.3	Exports of services	Percent	78.9	78.2	78.3	72.9	74.9

(*) Balance of Payments items: 6.1 to 6.3 correspond to the "Credit" side (and are receipts for the country) while 8.2 to 8.4 correspond to the "Debit" side (and are expenditures in other countries).

170

Basic Indicators	Units	2002	2003	2004	2005	2006
INBOUND TOURISM						
Arrivals						
1.1 Visitors	('000)	..	..	..	..	..
1.2 Tourists (overnight visitors)	('000)	28	38	44	40	34
1.3 Same-day visitors	('000)	..	..	..	..	..
1.4 Cruise passengers	('000)	..	..	..	..	..
Arrivals by region						
2.1 Africa	('000)	13	23	24	22	10
2.2 Americas	('000)	4	5	5	5	7
2.3 Europe	('000)	7	6	9	10	10
2.4 East Asia and the Pacific	('000)	2	2	2	2	5
2.5 South Asia	('000)	..	..	..	..	..
2.6 Middle East	('000)	2	2	3	1	2
Arrivals by means of transport used						
3.1 Air	('000)	28	38	44	40	34
3.2 Rail	('000)	..	..	..	..	..
3.3 Road	('000)	..	..	..	..	..
3.4 Sea	('000)	..	..	..	..	..
Arrivals by purpose of visit						
4.1 Leisure, recreation and holidays	('000)	5	8	7	5	3
4.2 Business and professional	('000)	11	20	15	14	13
4.3 Other	('000)	12	9	22	21	18
Accommodation						
5.1 Overnight stays in hotels and similar establishments	('000)	142	191	218	280	236
5.2 Guests in hotels and similar establishments	('000)	..	..	..	..	..
5.3 Overnight stays in all types of accommodation establishments	('000)	..	..	..	..	..
5.4 Average length of stay of non-resident tourists in all accommodation establishments	Nights	2.43	3.16	2.80	7.00	7.30
6.1 **Tourism expenditure in the country**	US$ Mn	..	..	..	..	..
6.2 "Travel" (*)	US$ Mn	38	60	58	64	23
6.3 "Passenger transport" (*)	US$ Mn	..	..	..	..	..
DOMESTIC TOURISM						
Accommodation						
7.1 Overnight stays in hotels and similar establishments	('000)	..	..	..	..	..
7.2 Guests in hotels and similar establishments	('000)	..	..	..	..	..
7.3 Overnight stays in all types of accommodation establishments	('000)	..	..	..	..	..
7.4 Average length of stay of resident tourists in all accommodation establishments	Nights	..	..	..	..	..
OUTBOUND TOURISM						
8.1 **Departures**	('000)	27	13	28	63	67
8.2 **Tourism expenditure in other countries**	US$ Mn	39.1	37.8	30.3	33.6	15.0
8.3 "Travel" (*)	US$ Mn	39	37	30	32	12
8.4 "Passenger transport" (*)	US$ Mn	0.1	0.8	0.3	1.6	3.0
TOURISM INDUSTRIES						
Hotels and similar establishments						
9.1 Number of rooms	Units	869	1,457	1,622	2,012	2,156
9.2 Number of bed-places	Units	993	1,718	2,331	2,519	2,642
9.3 Occupancy rate	Percent	14.00	13.00	12.00	11.00	23.00
9.4 Average length of stay	Nights	5.00	5.00	5.00	7.00	7.00
RELATED INDICATORS						
Share of tourism expenditure (6.1) in: (**)						
10.1 Gross Domestic Product (GDP)	Percent	4.1	6.1	5.4	5.3	1.6
10.2 Exports of goods	Percent	63.3	54.1	37.7	34.8	8.4
10.3 Exports of services	Percent	100.0	90.9	95.1	82.1	57.5

(*) Balance of Payments items: 6.1 to 6.3 correspond to the "Credit" side (and are receipts for the country) while 8.2 to 8.4 correspond to the "Debit" side (and are expenditures in other countries).

(**) See Annex "Country notes".

SINGAPORE

Basic Indicators	Units	2002	2003	2004	2005	2006
INBOUND TOURISM						
Arrivals						
1.1 Visitors	('000)	7,567	6,127	8,329	8,943	9,751
1.2 Tourists (overnight visitors)	('000)	5,855	4,703	6,553	7,080	7,588
1.3 Same-day visitors	('000)	1,712	1,424	1,776	1,863	2,163
1.4 Cruise passengers	('000)	..	..	..	..	..
Arrivals by region						
2.1 Africa	('000)	70	56	71	79	87
2.2 Americas	('000)	416	315	422	470	510
2.3 Europe	('000)	1,112	885	1,081	1,136	1,220
2.4 East Asia and the Pacific	('000)	5,426	4,426	6,073	6,445	7,012
2.5 South Asia	('000)	490	415	626	751	850
2.6 Middle East	('000)	47	30	55	56	66
Arrivals by means of transport used						
3.1 Air	('000)	5,394	4,232	5,728	6,267	6,757
3.2 Rail	('000)					
3.3 Road	('000)	997	867	1,269	1,312	1,423
3.4 Sea	('000)	1,177	1,028	1,332	1,364	1,571
Arrivals by purpose of visit						
4.1 Leisure, recreation and holidays	('000)	3,548	2,713	2,832	2,683	3,608
4.2 Business and professional	('000)	1,567	1,299	2,165	2,415	2,925
4.3 Other	('000)	2,452	2,115	3,331	3,845	3,218
Accommodation						
5.1 Overnight stays in hotels and similar establishments	('000)	..	..	..	..	..
5.2 Guests in hotels and similar establishments	('000)	4,483	3,473	4,914	5,276	5,948
5.3 Overnight stays in all types of accommodation establishments	('000)	..	..	..	..	..
5.4 Average length of stay of non-resident tourists in all accommodation establishments	Nights	3.08	3.18	3.21	3.38	3.38
6.1 Tourism expenditure in the country	US$ Mn	..	..	..	..	..
6.2 "Travel" (*)	US$ Mn	4,428	3,783	5,226	5,903	7,069
6.3 "Passenger transport" (*)	US$ Mn	..	..	..	..	..
DOMESTIC TOURISM						
Accommodation						
7.1 Overnight stays in hotels and similar establishments	('000)	..	..	..	..	..
7.2 Guests in hotels and similar establishments	('000)	..	..	..	..	..
7.3 Overnight stays in all types of accommodation establishments	('000)	..	..	..	..	..
7.4 Average length of stay of resident tourists in all accommodation establishments	Nights	..	..	..	..	..
OUTBOUND TOURISM						
8.1 Departures	('000)	4,399	4,221	5,165	5,159	5,533
8.2 Tourism expenditure in other countries	US$ Mn	..	..	..	..	..
8.3 "Travel" (*)	US$ Mn	7,861	7,916	9,242	9,947	10,384
8.4 "Passenger transport" (*)	US$ Mn	..	..	..	..	..
TOURISM INDUSTRIES						
Hotels and similar establishments						
9.1 Number of rooms	Units	35,989	35,930	36,765	36,861	37,198
9.2 Number of bed-places	Units	..	..	..	..	..
9.3 Occupancy rate	Percent	74.40	67.20	80.60	83.80	85.20
9.4 Average length of stay	Nights	2.62	2.70	..	..	..
RELATED INDICATORS						
Share of tourism expenditure (6.1) in: (**)						
10.1 Gross Domestic Product (GDP)	Percent	5.0	4.1	4.9	5.1	5.3
10.2 Exports of goods	Percent	3.1	2.3	2.6	2.5	2.6
10.3 Exports of services	Percent	15.0	10.4	11.2	11.2	12.0

(*) Balance of Payments items: 6.1 to 6.3 correspond to the "Credit" side (and are receipts for the country) while 8.2 to 8.4 correspond to the "Debit" side (and are expenditures in other countries).

(**) See Annex "Country notes".

Basic Indicators	Units	2002	2003	2004	2005	2006
INBOUND TOURISM						
Arrivals						
1.1 Visitors	('000)	26,450	24,985	26,415	29,396	30,592
1.2 Tourists (overnight visitors)	('000)	1,399	1,387	1,401	1,515	1,612
1.3 Same-day visitors	('000)	..	..	..	..	..
1.4 Cruise passengers	('000)	..	..	..	..	..
Arrivals by region						
2.1 Africa	('000)	3	3	2	2	3
2.2 Americas	('000)	33	34	39	42	39
2.3 Europe	('000)	1,326	1,316	1,317	1,413	1,499
2.4 East Asia and the Pacific	('000)	34	32	42	56	69
2.5 South Asia	('000)	1	1	..	1	..
2.6 Middle East	('000)	..	..	..	..	..
Arrivals by means of transport used						
3.1 Air	('000)	7	9	14	16	17
3.2 Rail	('000)	55	56	57	54	62
3.3 Road	('000)	11,566	11,407	12,535	13,807	14,436
3.4 Sea	('000)	3	3	4	3	3
Arrivals by purpose of visit						
4.1 Leisure, recreation and holidays	('000)	..	..	..	..	..
4.2 Business and professional	('000)	..	..	..	..	..
4.3 Other	('000)	..	..	..	..	..
Accommodation						
5.1 Overnight stays in hotels and similar establishments	('000)	4,050	3,989	3,820	4,055	4,362
5.2 Guests in hotels and similar establishments	('000)	1,154	1,151	1,188	1,307	1,407
5.3 Overnight stays in all types of accommodation establishments	('000)	5,043	4,964	4,675	4,872	5,134
5.4 Average length of stay of non-resident tourists in all accommodation establishments	Nights	3.60	3.60	3.30	3.20	3.20
6.1 **Tourism expenditure in the country**	US$ Mn	742	876	932	..	..
6.2 "Travel" (*)	US$ Mn	736	865	901	1,210	1,513
6.3 "Passenger transport" (*)	US$ Mn	6	11	31	..	..
DOMESTIC TOURISM						
Accommodation						
7.1 Overnight stays in hotels and similar establishments	('000)	4,917	4,789	4,148	3,978	3,936
7.2 Guests in hotels and similar establishments	('000)	1,591	1,530	1,439	1,495	1,521
7.3 Overnight stays in all types of accommodation establishments	('000)	7,263	7,095	6,074	5,861	6,004
7.4 Average length of stay of resident tourists in all accommodation establishments	Nights	3.50	3.60	3.30	3.10	3.00
OUTBOUND TOURISM						
8.1 **Departures**	('000)	17,617	18,298	20,380	22,405	22,688
8.2 **Tourism expenditure in other countries**	US$ Mn	506	662	903	..	..
8.3 "Travel" (*)	US$ Mn	442	573	745	846	1,055
8.4 "Passenger transport" (*)	US$ Mn	64	89	158	..	..
TOURISM INDUSTRIES						
Hotels and similar establishments						
9.1 Number of rooms	Units	34,619	35,853	35,544	35,688	35,948
9.2 Number of bed-places	Units	87,554	90,773	90,004	90,093	91,036
9.3 Occupancy rate	Percent	40.00	38.70	34.70	35.00	35.70
9.4 Average length of stay	Nights	3.20	3.20	2.90	2.80	2.80
RELATED INDICATORS						
Share of tourism expenditure (6.1) in:						
10.1 Gross Domestic Product (GDP)	Percent	3.0	2.7	2.2	..	..
10.2 Exports of goods	Percent	5.1	4.0	3.4	..	..
10.3 Exports of services	Percent	26.4	26.6	25.0	..	..

(*) Balance of Payments items: 6.1 to 6.3 correspond to the "Credit" side (and are receipts for the country) while 8.2 to 8.4 correspond to the "Debit" side (and are expenditures in other countries).

SLOVENIA

Basic Indicators		Units	2002	2003	2004	2005	2006
	INBOUND TOURISM						
	Arrivals						
1.1	Visitors	('000)	60,031	59,388	63,013	60,230	58,274
1.2	Tourists (overnight visitors)	('000)	1,302	1,373	1,499	1,555	1,617
1.3	Same-day visitors	('000)	..	..	..	..	..
1.4	Cruise passengers	('000)	..	..	..	..	..
	Arrivals by region						
2.1	Africa	('000)				2	1
2.2	Americas	('000)	36	36	46	59	67
2.3	Europe	('000)	1,236	1,308	1,411	1,454	1,496
2.4	East Asia and the Pacific	('000)	17	17	24	40	52
2.5	South Asia	('000)	..	..	..	..	..
2.6	Middle East	('000)	..	..	..	..	..
	Arrivals by means of transport used						
3.1	Air	('000)	241	264	288	298	310
3.2	Rail	('000)	25	41	45	47	48
3.3	Road	('000)	1,034	1,067	1,165	1,208	1,256
3.4	Sea	('000)	2	1	1	2	2
	Arrivals by purpose of visit						
4.1	Leisure, recreation and holidays	('000)	799	894	976	1,012	1,052
4.2	Business and professional	('000)	228	273	298	309	322
4.3	Other	('000)	275	206	225	233	242
	Accommodation						
5.1	Overnight stays in hotels and similar establishments	('000)	3,049	3,166	3,258	3,322	3,401
5.2	Guests in hotels and similar establishments	('000)	1,006	1,053	1,125	1,192	1,247
5.3	Overnight stays in all types of accommodation establishments	('000)	4,021	4,175	4,363	4,399	4,489
5.4	Average length of stay of non-resident tourists in all accommodation establishments	Nights	3.09	3.04	2.91	2.80	2.78
6.1	**Tourism expenditure in the country**	US$ Mn	1,152	1,427	1,725	1,894	1,911
6.2	"Travel" (*)	US$ Mn	1,086	1,342	1,624	1,795	1,797
6.3	"Passenger transport" (*)	US$ Mn	66	85	101	99	114
	DOMESTIC TOURISM						
	Accommodation						
7.1	Overnight stays in hotels and similar establishments	('000)	1,714	1,725	1,707	1,653	1,746
7.2	Guests in hotels and similar establishments	('000)	463	463	467	459	484
7.3	Overnight stays in all types of accommodation establishments	('000)	3,300	3,327	3,226	3,173	3,233
7.4	Average length of stay of resident tourists in all accommodation establishments	Nights	3.84	3.81	3.83	3.80	3.61
	OUTBOUND TOURISM						
8.1	**Departures**	('000)	2,127	2,114	2,800	2,660	2,680
8.2	**Tourism expenditure in other countries**	US$ Mn	647	805	937	1,019	1,058
8.3	"Travel" (*)	US$ Mn	608	753	868	950	974
8.4	"Passenger transport" (*)	US$ Mn	39	52	69	69	84
	TOURISM INDUSTRIES						
	Hotels and similar establishments						
9.1	Number of rooms	Units	15,056	15,534	15,785	15,811	16,402
9.2	Number of bed-places	Units	30,715	31,997	32,652	33,151	34,415
9.3	Occupancy rate	Percent	47.39	47.60	47.98	47.56	47.58
9.4	Average length of stay	Nights	3.24	3.23	3.12	3.01	2.97
	RELATED INDICATORS						
	Share of tourism expenditure (6.1) in:						
10.1	Gross Domestic Product (GDP)	Percent	5.2	5.1	5.3	5.5	5.1
10.2	Exports of goods	Percent	11.0	11.0	10.7	10.4	8.9
10.3	Exports of services	Percent	49.7	51.1	49.9	47.6	44.0

(*) Balance of Payments items: 6.1 to 6.3 correspond to the "Credit" side (and are receipts for the country) while 8.2 to 8.4 correspond to the "Debit" side (and are expenditures in other countries).

SOLOMON ISLANDS

Basic Indicators	Units	2002	2003	2004	2005	2006
INBOUND TOURISM						
Arrivals						
1.1 Visitors	('000)	..	..	..	..	..
1.2 Tourists (overnight visitors)	('000)	..	6.6	..	9.4	11.5
1.3 Same-day visitors	('000)	..	..	..	..	..
1.4 Cruise passengers	('000)	..	..	..	..	..
Arrivals by region						
2.1 Africa	('000)	..	..	..	..	..
2.2 Americas	('000)	..	0.6	..	0.6	0.9
2.3 Europe	('000)	..	0.5	..	0.5	0.7
2.4 East Asia and the Pacific	('000)	..	5.4	..	8.1	9.8
2.5 South Asia	('000)	..	..	..	..	..
2.6 Middle East	('000)	..	..	..	..	..
Arrivals by means of transport used						
3.1 Air	('000)	..	..	..	..	..
3.2 Rail	('000)	..	..	..	..	..
3.3 Road	('000)	..	..	..	..	..
3.4 Sea	('000)	..	..	..	..	..
Arrivals by purpose of visit						
4.1 Leisure, recreation and holidays	('000)	..	2.1	..	..	3.1
4.2 Business and professional	('000)	..	3.0	..	..	5.4
4.3 Other	('000)	..	1.5	..	..	3.0
Accommodation						
5.1 Overnight stays in hotels and similar establishments	('000)	..	..	..	..	..
5.2 Guests in hotels and similar establishments	('000)	..	..	..	..	..
5.3 Overnight stays in all types of accommodation establishments	('000)	..	..	..	..	..
5.4 Average length of stay of non-resident tourists in all accommodation establishments	Nights	..	..	..	..	..
6.1 **Tourism expenditure in the country**	US$ Mn	1.1	2.1	4	7	8
6.2 "Travel" (*)	US$ Mn	1	2	4	2	2
6.3 "Passenger transport" (*)	US$ Mn	0.1	0.1	0.02	5	6
DOMESTIC TOURISM						
Accommodation						
7.1 Overnight stays in hotels and similar establishments	('000)	..	..	..	..	..
7.2 Guests in hotels and similar establishments	('000)	..	..	..	..	..
7.3 Overnight stays in all types of accommodation establishments	('000)	..	..	..	..	..
7.4 Average length of stay of resident tourists in all accommodation establishments	Nights	..	..	..	..	..
OUTBOUND TOURISM						
8.1 **Departures**	('000)	..	..	..	..	..
8.2 **Tourism expenditure in other countries**	US$ Mn	9	6	12	11	15
8.3 "Travel" (*)	US$ Mn	6	4	9	5	8
8.4 "Passenger transport" (*)	US$ Mn	3	2	3	6	7
TOURISM INDUSTRIES						
Hotels and similar establishments						
9.1 Number of rooms	Units	..	..	..	..	..
9.2 Number of bed-places	Units	..	..	..	..	..
9.3 Occupancy rate	Percent	..	..	..	..	..
9.4 Average length of stay	Nights	..	..	..	..	..
RELATED INDICATORS						
Share of tourism expenditure (6.1) in:						
10.1 Gross Domestic Product (GDP)	Percent	0.5	0.9	1.5	2.3	2.4
10.2 Exports of goods	Percent	3.3	3.1	4.7	6.7	6.6
10.3 Exports of services	Percent	6.9	8.4	13.0	17.1	13.3

(*) Balance of Payments items: 6.1 to 6.3 correspond to the "Credit" side (and are receipts for the country) while 8.2 to 8.4 correspond to the "Debit" side (and are expenditures in other countries).

SOUTH AFRICA

Basic Indicators	Units	2002	2003	2004	2005	2006
INBOUND TOURISM						
Arrivals						
1.1 Visitors	('000)	6,550	6,640	6,815	7,518	8,509
1.2 Tourists (overnight visitors)	('000)	6,430	6,505	6,678	7,369	8,396
1.3 Same-day visitors	('000)	..	..	..	..	..
1.4 Cruise passengers	('000)	..	..	..	..	..
Arrivals by region						
2.1 Africa	('000)	4,453	4,450	4,638	5,370	6,281
2.2 Americas	('000)	255	262	291	322	358
2.3 Europe	('000)	1,213	1,275	1,249	1,269	1,341
2.4 East Asia and the Pacific	('000)	229	225	239	239	258
2.5 South Asia	('000)	34	41	36	36	44
2.6 Middle East	('000)	15	15	16	17	20
Arrivals by means of transport used						
3.1 Air	('000)	1,885	1,980	2,025	2,127	2,318
3.2 Rail	('000)	6	4	6	450	2
3.3 Road	('000)	4,640	4,651	4,781	4,938	6,183
3.4 Sea	('000)	18	5	3	3	7
Arrivals by purpose of visit						
4.1 Leisure, recreation and holidays	('000)	5,596	5,853	6,081	6,812	7,859
4.2 Business and professional	('000)	540	406	361	335	324
4.3 Other	('000)	294	246	236	222	213
Accommodation						
5.1 Overnight stays in hotels and similar establishments	('000)	..	..	..	..	..
5.2 Guests in hotels and similar establishments	('000)	..	..	..	..	..
5.3 Overnight stays in all types of accommodation establishments	('000)	..	..	..	..	..
5.4 Average length of stay of non-resident tourists in all accommodation establishments	Nights	..	..	..	..	..
6.1 **Tourism expenditure in the country**	US$ Mn	3,695	6,533	7,380	8,448	8,967
6.2 "Travel" (*)	US$ Mn	2,923	5,571	6,322	7,335	7,876
6.3 "Passenger transport" (*)	US$ Mn	772	962	1,058	1,113	1,091
DOMESTIC TOURISM						
Accommodation						
7.1 Overnight stays in hotels and similar establishments	('000)	..	..	..	..	..
7.2 Guests in hotels and similar establishments	('000)	..	..	..	..	..
7.3 Overnight stays in all types of accommodation establishments	('000)	..	..	..	..	..
7.4 Average length of stay of resident tourists in all accommodation establishments	Nights	..	..	..	..	..
OUTBOUND TOURISM						
8.1 **Departures**	('000)	3,794	..	..	..	
8.2 **Tourism expenditure in other countries**	US$ Mn	2,251	3,654	4,237	4,811	5,230
8.3 "Travel" (*)	US$ Mn	1,811	2,889	3,157	3,373	3,384
8.4 "Passenger transport" (*)	US$ Mn	440	765	1,080	1,438	1,846
TOURISM INDUSTRIES						
Hotels and similar establishments						
9.1 Number of rooms	Units	52,257	52,329	53,075	55,300	54,850
9.2 Number of bed-places	Units	110,133	110,479	105,691	..	..
9.3 Occupancy rate	Percent	56.90	57.70	51.20	53.60	56.30
9.4 Average length of stay	Nights	..	..	..	8.40	8.20
RELATED INDICATORS						
Share of tourism expenditure (6.1) in:						
10.1 Gross Domestic Product (GDP)	Percent	3.3	3.9	3.4	3.5	3.5
10.2 Exports of goods	Percent	11.6	16.9	15.3	15.3	14.1
10.3 Exports of services	Percent	74.1	78.7	76.2	75.7	74.6

(*) Balance of Payments items: 6.1 to 6.3 correspond to the "Credit" side (and are receipts for the country) while 8.2 to 8.4 correspond to the "Debit" side (and are expenditures in other countries).

Basic Indicators	Units	2002	2003	2004	2005	2006
INBOUND TOURISM						
Arrivals						
1.1 Visitors	('000)	80,024	82,326	85,981	92,563	95,935
1.2 Tourists (overnight visitors)	('000)	52,327	50,854	52,430	55,914	58,190
1.3 Same-day visitors	('000)	27,697	31,472	33,551	36,649	37,745
1.4 Cruise passengers	('000)	..	..	..	..	..
Arrivals by region						
2.1 Africa	('000)	..	..	..	..	..
2.2 Americas	('000)	2,080	1,894	2,079	2,233	2,384
2.3 Europe	('000)	49,304	47,835	49,239	52,190	54,362
2.4 East Asia and the Pacific	('000)	241	237	151	181	257
2.5 South Asia	('000)	..	..	..	..	..
2.6 Middle East	('000)	..	..	..	..	..
Arrivals by means of transport used						
3.1 Air	('000)	34,947	36,923	38,524	40,730	42,445
3.2 Rail	('000)	458	292	298	290	281
3.3 Road	('000)	13,872	12,118	12,097	13,121	13,819
3.4 Sea	('000)	3,050	1,521	1,511	1,772	1,646
Arrivals by purpose of visit						
4.1 Leisure, recreation and holidays	('000)	43,253	40,393	41,377	43,898	46,022
4.2 Business and professional	('000)	4,091	5,686	5,286	5,940	6,084
4.3 Other	('000)	4,983	4,775	5,767	6,075	6,085
Accommodation						
5.1 Overnight stays in hotels and similar establishments	('000)	135,836	136,865	134,654	138,762	151,940
5.2 Guests in hotels and similar establishments	('000)	26,611	27,249	27,620	29,029	34,412
5.3 Overnight stays in all types of accommodation establishments	('000)	220,707	217,852	209,081	209,518	224,067
5.4 Average length of stay of non-resident tourists in all accommodation establishments	Nights	5.10	5.02	4.88	4.78	5.20
6.1 **Tourism expenditure in the country**	US$ Mn	35,468	43,863	49,996	53,066	57,537
6.2 "Travel" (*)	US$ Mn	31,880	39,634	45,067	47,789	51,292
6.3 "Passenger transport" (*)	US$ Mn	3,588	4,229	4,929	5,277	6,245
DOMESTIC TOURISM						
Accommodation						
7.1 Overnight stays in hotels and similar establishments	('000)	86,718	91,295	100,044	106,875	115,088
7.2 Guests in hotels and similar establishments	('000)	33,258	35,283	39,211	41,600	47,444
7.3 Overnight stays in all types of accommodation establishments	('000)	118,179	124,689	135,188	143,874	154,836
7.4 Average length of stay of resident tourists in all accommodation establishments	Nights	2.61	2.59	2.55	2.57	2.73
OUTBOUND TOURISM						
8.1 **Departures**	('000)	3,871	4,094	5,121	10,508	10,676
8.2 **Tourism expenditure in other countries**	US$ Mn	9,366	11,330	14,864	18,441	20,348
8.3 "Travel" (*)	US$ Mn	7,295	9,071	12,153	15,046	16,697
8.4 "Passenger transport" (*)	US$ Mn	2,071	2,259	2,711	3,395	3,651
TOURISM INDUSTRIES						
Hotels and similar establishments						
9.1 Number of rooms	Units	713,481	740,890	766,952	797,354	810,591
9.2 Number of bed-places	Units	1,395,383	1,451,922	1,511,592	1,578,629	1,615,284
9.3 Occupancy rate	Percent	55.27	54.47	53.47	54.24	56.43
9.4 Average length of stay	Nights	3.72	3.65	3.51	3.48	3.25
RELATED INDICATORS						
Share of tourism expenditure (6.1) in:						
10.1 Gross Domestic Product (GDP)	Percent	5.2	5.0	4.8	4.7	4.7
10.2 Exports of goods	Percent	27.9	27.8	27.0	27.0	26.6
10.3 Exports of services	Percent	58.9	59.0	58.1	56.1	54.1

(*) Balance of Payments items: 6.1 to 6.3 correspond to the "Credit" side (and are receipts for the country) while 8.2 to 8.4 correspond to the "Debit" side (and are expenditures in other countries).

SRI LANKA

Basic Indicators		Units	2002	2003	2004	2005	2006
	INBOUND TOURISM						
	Arrivals						
1.1	Visitors	('000)	457	583	681	669	689
1.2	Tourists (overnight visitors)	('000)	393	501	566	549	560
1.3	Same-day visitors	('000)	64	82	115	120	129
1.4	Cruise passengers	('000)	..	..	..	..	..
	Arrivals by region						
2.1	Africa	('000)	2	2	2	2	3
2.2	Americas	('000)	20	26	31	47	36
2.3	Europe	('000)	208	266	299	236	243
2.4	East Asia and the Pacific	('000)	66	84	91	100	98
2.5	South Asia	('000)	90	116	133	153	169
2.6	Middle East	('000)	6	7	10	10	10
	Arrivals by means of transport used						
3.1	Air	('000)	393	500	566	549	559
3.2	Rail	('000)	..	..	..	..	..
3.3	Road	('000)	..	..	..	..	..
3.4	Sea	('000)	..	0.2	0.2	0.3	0.4
	Arrivals by purpose of visit						
4.1	Leisure, recreation and holidays	('000)	336	404	443	382	377
4.2	Business and professional	('000)	42	56	74	105	116
4.3	Other	('000)	15	41	49	62	66
	Accommodation						
5.1	Overnight stays in hotels and similar establishments	('000)	3,180	4,184	4,744	3,249	3,815
5.2	Guests in hotels and similar establishments	('000)	..	..	..	..	..
5.3	Overnight stays in all types of accommodation establishments	('000)	3,989	5,093	5,742	4,754	5,794
5.4	Average length of stay of non-resident tourists in all accommodation establishments	Nights	10.10	10.20	10.10	8.70	10.40
6.1	**Tourism expenditure in the country**	US$ Mn	594	709	808	729	733
6.2	"Travel" (*)	US$ Mn	363	441	513	429	410
6.3	"Passenger transport" (*)	US$ Mn	231	268	295	300	323
	DOMESTIC TOURISM						
	Accommodation						
7.1	Overnight stays in hotels and similar establishments	('000)	1,243	1,327	1,381	1,292	1,302
7.2	Guests in hotels and similar establishments	('000)	..	..	..	..	..
7.3	Overnight stays in all types of accommodation establishments	('000)	..	..	..	..	..
7.4	Average length of stay of resident tourists in all accommodation establishments	Nights	..	..	..	..	..
	OUTBOUND TOURISM						
8.1	**Departures**	('000)	533	561	680	727	757
8.2	**Tourism expenditure in other countries**	US$ Mn	438	462	499	552	666
8.3	"Travel" (*)	US$ Mn	263	279	296	314	373
8.4	"Passenger transport" (*)	US$ Mn	175	183	203	238	293
	TOURISM INDUSTRIES						
	Hotels and similar establishments						
9.1	Number of rooms	Units	16,318	16,973	17,640	17,124	19,207
9.2	Number of bed-places	Units	30,218	31,331	32,578	31,277	35,349
9.3	Occupancy rate	Percent	43.10	53.20	59.30	45.40	47.80
9.4	Average length of stay	Nights	..	..	..	..	..
	RELATED INDICATORS						
	Share of tourism expenditure (6.1) in:						
10.1	Gross Domestic Product (GDP)	Percent	3.6	3.9	4.0	3.1	2.7
10.2	Exports of goods	Percent	12.6	13.8	14.0	11.5	10.6
10.3	Exports of services	Percent	46.8	50.2	52.9	47.3	45.1

(*) Balance of Payments items: 6.1 to 6.3 correspond to the "Credit" side (and are receipts for the country) while 8.2 to 8.4 correspond to the "Debit" side (and are expenditures in other countries).

Basic Indicators		Units	2002	2003	2004	2005	2006
INBOUND TOURISM							
Arrivals							
1.1	Visitors	('000)	..	..	..	..	..
1.2	Tourists (overnight visitors)	('000)	52	52	61	246	328
1.3	Same-day visitors	('000)	..	..	..	..	..
1.4	Cruise passengers	('000)	..	..	..	..	..
Arrivals by region							
2.1	Africa	('000)	7	7	9	59	51
2.2	Americas	('000)	..	..	..	21	12
2.3	Europe	('000)	12	14	17	56	44
2.4	East Asia and the Pacific	('000)	13	14	17	109	222
2.5	South Asia	('000)	..	..	..	..	..
2.6	Middle East	('000)	..	..	..	..	..
Arrivals by means of transport used							
3.1	Air	('000)	42	40	51	197	318
3.2	Rail	('000)	..	..	..	..	..
3.3	Road	('000)	3	3	3	12	3
3.4	Sea	('000)	7	8	8	37	7
Arrivals by purpose of visit							
4.1	Leisure, recreation and holidays	('000)	..	..	..	13	..
4.2	Business and professional	('000)	..	..	..	61	..
4.3	Other	('000)	..	..	..	172	..
Accommodation							
5.1	Overnight stays in hotels and similar establishments	('000)	..	..	..	..	..
5.2	Guests in hotels and similar establishments	('000)	..	..	..	..	..
5.3	Overnight stays in all types of accommodation establishments	('000)	..	..	..	..	..
5.4	Average length of stay of non-resident tourists in all accommodation establishments	Nights	..	..	..	..	..
6.1	**Tourism expenditure in the country** (**)	US$ Mn	..	..	..	..	..
6.2	"Travel" (*)	US$ Mn	108	17	21	89	126
6.3	"Passenger transport" (*)	US$ Mn	..	..	..	..	..
DOMESTIC TOURISM							
Accommodation							
7.1	Overnight stays in hotels and similar establishments	('000)	..	..	..	..	..
7.2	Guests in hotels and similar establishments	('000)	..	..	..	..	..
7.3	Overnight stays in all types of accommodation establishments	('000)	..	..	..	..	..
7.4	Average length of stay of resident tourists in all accommodation establishments	Nights	..	..	..	..	..
OUTBOUND TOURISM							
8.1	**Departures**	('000)	..	..	..	..	..
8.2	**Tourism expenditure in other countries**	US$ Mn	..	..	..	..	..
8.3	"Travel" (*)	US$ Mn	91	119	176	667	1,403
8.4	"Passenger transport" (*)	US$ Mn	..	..	..	..	..
TOURISM INDUSTRIES							
Hotels and similar establishments							
9.1	Number of rooms	Units	..	..	4,200	4,200	4,746
9.2	Number of bed-places	Units	..	..	10,102	10,102	21,661
9.3	Occupancy rate	Percent	..	..	79.10	..	..
9.4	Average length of stay	Nights	..	..	8.00	8.00	8.00
RELATED INDICATORS							
Share of tourism expenditure (6.1) in: (**)							
10.1	Gross Domestic Product (GDP)	Percent	0.7	0.1	0.1	0.3	0.3
10.2	Exports of goods	Percent	5.5	0.7	0.6	1.8	2.2
10.3	Exports of services	Percent	81.8	47.2	47.7	78.1	61.2

(*) Balance of Payments items: 6.1 to 6.3 correspond to the "Credit" side (and are receipts for the country) while 8.2 to 8.4 correspond to the "Debit" side (and are expenditures in other countries).

(**) See Annex "Country notes".

SURINAME

Basic Indicators	Units	2002	2003	2004	2005	2006
INBOUND TOURISM						
Arrivals						
1.1 Visitors	('000)	..	100	..	..	..
1.2 Tourists (overnight visitors)	('000)	60	82	138	160	
1.3 Same-day visitors	('000)	..		..	..	..
1.4 Cruise passengers	('000)	..	17		..	..
Arrivals by region						
2.1 Africa	('000)	..	..	..	..	..
2.2 Americas	('000)	4	7	45	56	
2.3 Europe	('000)	54	74	87	95	
2.4 East Asia and the Pacific	('000)	1	1	..	3	
2.5 South Asia	('000)	..	..	..	..	
2.6 Middle East	('000)	..	..	..	..	..
Arrivals by means of transport used						
3.1 Air	('000)	60	82	75	122	
3.2 Rail	('000)	..	..	..	..	..
3.3 Road	('000)	..	..	..	..	
3.4 Sea	('000)	..	17	16	38	..
Arrivals by purpose of visit						
4.1 Leisure, recreation and holidays	('000)	48	61	32	43	
4.2 Business and professional	('000)	3	12	14	16	..
4.3 Other	('000)	9	9	91	101	
Accommodation						
5.1 Overnight stays in hotels and similar establishments	('000)					
5.2 Guests in hotels and similar establishments	('000)	7	27	42	..	
5.3 Overnight stays in all types of accommodation establishments	('000)	..	..	..		
5.4 Average length of stay of non-resident tourists in all accommodation establishments	Nights	..	..	..	..	..
6.1 **Tourism expenditure in the country**	US$ Mn	17	18	52	96	109
6.2 "Travel" (*)	US$ Mn	3	4	17	45	95
6.3 "Passenger transport" (*)	US$ Mn	14	14	35	51	14
DOMESTIC TOURISM						
Accommodation						
7.1 Overnight stays in hotels and similar establishments	('000)	..	..	..	..	..
7.2 Guests in hotels and similar establishments	('000)	..	..	..	..	..
7.3 Overnight stays in all types of accommodation establishments	('000)	..	..	..	..	..
7.4 Average length of stay of resident tourists in all accommodation establishments	Nights	..	..	..	..	..
OUTBOUND TOURISM						
8.1 **Departures**	('000)	..	..	..	..	..
8.2 **Tourism expenditure in other countries**	US$ Mn	54	68	85	94	33
8.3 "Travel" (*)	US$ Mn	10	6	14	17	18
8.4 "Passenger transport" (*)	US$ Mn	44	62	71	77	15
TOURISM INDUSTRIES						
Hotels and similar establishments						
9.1 Number of rooms	Units	2,014	2,160	4,271	4,575	
9.2 Number of bed-places	Units	..	..	..	..	..
9.3 Occupancy rate	Percent	..	..	..	..	..
9.4 Average length of stay	Nights	..	..	..	..	..
RELATED INDICATORS						
Share of tourism expenditure (6.1) in:						
10.1 Gross Domestic Product (GDP)	Percent	1.8	1.8	4.5	7.1	6.8
10.2 Exports of goods	Percent	4.6	3.7	6.6	7.9	9.3
10.3 Exports of services	Percent	43.6	30.5	36.9	47.1	46.6

(*) Balance of Payments items: 6.1 to 6.3 correspond to the "Credit" side (and are receipts for the country) while 8.2 to 8.4 correspond to the "Debit" side (and are expenditures in other countries).

Basic Indicators	Units	2002	2003	2004	2005	2006
INBOUND TOURISM						
Arrivals						
1.1 Visitors	('000)	1,371	1,543	..	1,182	1,200
1.2 Tourists (overnight visitors)	('000)	256	461	459	839	873
1.3 Same-day visitors	('000)	..	..	..	130	173
1.4 Cruise passengers	('000)	..	..	..	..	..
Arrivals by region						
2.1 Africa	('000)	173	110	152	1,043	1,056
2.2 Americas	('000)	10	11	5	17	19
2.3 Europe	('000)	40	88	111	108	110
2.4 East Asia and the Pacific	('000)	5	2	3	10	10
2.5 South Asia	('000)	..	..	..	4	5
2.6 Middle East	('000)	..	..	..	..	..
Arrivals by means of transport used						
3.1 Air	('000)	14	17	..	22	22
3.2 Rail	('000)			..		
3.3 Road	('000)	1,357	1,526	..	1,160	1,178
3.4 Sea	('000)	..	..	..	..	..
Arrivals by purpose of visit						
4.1 Leisure, recreation and holidays	('000)	125	170	168	705	661
4.2 Business and professional	('000)	109	122	121	168	174
4.3 Other	('000)	22	169	170	309	365
Accommodation						
5.1 Overnight stays in hotels and similar establishments	('000)	..	..	..	..	..
5.2 Guests in hotels and similar establishments	('000)	256	219	352	312	316
5.3 Overnight stays in all types of accommodation establishments	('000)	..	..	..	..	..
5.4 Average length of stay of non-resident tourists in all accommodation establishments	Nights	0.83	1.00	0.83	1.25	1.00
6.1 **Tourism expenditure in the country**	US$ Mn	45.0	70.0	75.1	78.3	74.1
6.2 "Travel" (*)	US$ Mn	43	70	75	78	74
6.3 "Passenger transport" (*)	US$ Mn	2.0	0.0	0.1	0.3	0.1
DOMESTIC TOURISM						
Accommodation						
7.1 Overnight stays in hotels and similar establishments	('000)	76	136	..	39	54
7.2 Guests in hotels and similar establishments	('000)	..	..	..	..	..
7.3 Overnight stays in all types of accommodation establishments	('000)	..	..	..	..	..
7.4 Average length of stay of resident tourists in all accommodation establishments	Nights	..	..	..	..	1.00
OUTBOUND TOURISM						
8.1 **Departures**	('000)	..	..	..	1,082	1,072
8.2 **Tourism expenditure in other countries**	US$ Mn	27	23	54	60	53
8.3 "Travel" (*)	US$ Mn	26	22	48	49	48
8.4 "Passenger transport" (*)	US$ Mn	1	1	6	11	5
TOURISM INDUSTRIES						
Hotels and similar establishments						
9.1 Number of rooms	Units	1,153	1,339	1,307	1,244	1,250
9.2 Number of bed-places	Units	2,283	2,436	2,490	2,377	2,520
9.3 Occupancy rate	Percent	33.30	33.60	..	38.64	49.84
9.4 Average length of stay	Nights	0.83	1.00	..	2.00	1.00
RELATED INDICATORS						
Share of tourism expenditure (6.1) in:						
10.1 Gross Domestic Product (GDP)	Percent	3.8	3.7	3.2	3.0	2.8
10.2 Exports of goods	Percent	4.2	4.2	4.2	4.0	3.8
10.3 Exports of services	Percent	48.4	34.2	30.0	27.6	26.2

(*) Balance of Payments items: 6.1 to 6.3 correspond to the "Credit" side (and are receipts for the country) while 8.2 to 8.4 correspond to the "Debit" side (and are expenditures in other countries).

SWEDEN

Basic Indicators	Units	2002	2003	2004	2005	2006
INBOUND TOURISM						
Arrivals						
1.1 Visitors	('000)	14,271	..	..	..	..
1.2 Tourists (overnight visitors)	('000)	7,458	7,627	..	..	..
1.3 Same-day visitors	('000)	6,813	..	..	..	..
1.4 Cruise passengers	('000)	..	..	..	..	..
Arrivals by region						
2.1 Africa	('000)	42	46	..	..	..
2.2 Americas	('000)	413	467	..	..	..
2.3 Europe	('000)	6,656	6,696	..	..	..
2.4 East Asia and the Pacific	('000)	348	380	..	..	..
2.5 South Asia	('000)	..	..	..	..	..
2.6 Middle East	('000)	..	..	..	..	..
Arrivals by means of transport used						
3.1 Air	('000)	2,700	..	..	..	..
3.2 Rail	('000)	485	..	..	..	..
3.3 Road	('000)	1,715	..	..	..	..
3.4 Sea	('000)	2,558	..	..	..	..
Arrivals by purpose of visit						
4.1 Leisure, recreation and holidays	('000)	3,495	3,536	..	..	..
4.2 Business and professional	('000)	2,414	2,518	..	..	..
4.3 Other	('000)	1,548	1,573	..	..	..
Accommodation						
5.1 Overnight stays in hotels and similar establishments	('000)	4,868	4,833	5,061	5,382	5,606
5.2 Guests in hotels and similar establishments	('000)	2,577	2,552	2,610	2,736	2,867
5.3 Overnight stays in all types of accommodation establishments	('000)	9,768	9,715	9,724	10,078	10,952
5.4 Average length of stay of non-resident tourists in all accommodation establishments	Nights	2.28	2.28	2.08	2.06	2.33
6.1 **Tourism expenditure in the country**	US$ Mn	5,671	6,548	7,686	8,580	10,437
6.2 "Travel" (*)	US$ Mn	4,710	5,304	6,198	7,385	9,133
6.3 "Passenger transport" (*)	US$ Mn	961	1,244	1,488	1,195	1,304
DOMESTIC TOURISM						
Accommodation						
7.1 Overnight stays in hotels and similar establishments	('000)	16,143	16,235	16,465	17,517	18,606
7.2 Guests in hotels and similar establishments	('000)	10,375	10,359	10,509	11,096	11,866
7.3 Overnight stays in all types of accommodation establishments	('000)	33,128	34,339	32,942	34,862	36,754
7.4 Average length of stay of resident tourists in all accommodation establishments	Nights	2.22	2.23	2.04	1.97	2.17
OUTBOUND TOURISM						
8.1 **Departures**	('000)	12,888	12,649	13,967	12,603	12,591
8.2 **Tourism expenditure in other countries**	US$ Mn	8,221	9,375	11,088	11,844	12,844
8.3 "Travel" (*)	US$ Mn	7,301	8,296	10,165	10,771	11,543
8.4 "Passenger transport" (*)	US$ Mn	920	1,079	923	1,073	1,301
TOURISM INDUSTRIES						
Hotels and similar establishments						
9.1 Number of rooms	Units	95,125	96,372	98,888	100,155	101,651
9.2 Number of bed-places	Units	180,804	184,771	189,988	197,470	201,316
9.3 Occupancy rate	Percent	35.20	34.30	34.30	35.00	36.10
9.4 Average length of stay	Nights	..	..	..	..	..
RELATED INDICATORS						
Share of tourism expenditure (6.1) in:						
10.1 Gross Domestic Product (GDP)	Percent	2.3	2.2	2.2	2.4	2.7
10.2 Exports of goods	Percent	6.7	6.4	6.2	6.5	7.0
10.3 Exports of services	Percent	23.6	21.4	19.7	20.0	20.7

(*) Balance of Payments items: 6.1 to 6.3 correspond to the "Credit" side (and are receipts for the country) while 8.2 to 8.4 correspond to the "Debit" side (and are expenditures in other countries).

Basic Indicators	Units	2002	2003	2004	2005	2006
INBOUND TOURISM						
Arrivals						
1.1 Visitors	('000)	..	..	..	..	..
1.2 Tourists (overnight visitors)	('000)	6,868	6,530	..	7,229	7,863
1.3 Same-day visitors	('000)	..	..	..	..	..
1.4 Cruise passengers	('000)	..	..	..	..	..
Arrivals by region						
2.1 Africa	('000)	74	73	..	78	85
2.2 Americas	('000)	871	757	..	830	934
2.3 Europe	('000)	4,906	4,821	..	5,305	5,747
2.4 East Asia and the Pacific	('000)	865	727	..	847	896
2.5 South Asia	('000)	80	85	..	93	115
2.6 Middle East	('000)	70	67	..	76	85
Arrivals by means of transport used						
3.1 Air	('000)	..	..	..	..	..
3.2 Rail	('000)	..	..	..	..	..
3.3 Road	('000)	..	..	..	..	..
3.4 Sea	('000)	..	..	..	..	..
Arrivals by purpose of visit						
4.1 Leisure, recreation and holidays	('000)	..	..	..	..	..
4.2 Business and professional	('000)	..	..	..	..	..
4.3 Other	('000)	..	..	..	..	..
Accommodation						
5.1 Overnight stays in hotels and similar establishments	('000)	17,768	16,964	17,247	18,321	19,644
5.2 Guests in hotels and similar establishments	('000)	6,868	6,530	..	7,229	7,863
5.3 Overnight stays in all types of accommodation establishments	('000)	29,641	28,569	..	..	..
5.4 Average length of stay of non-resident tourists in all accommodation establishments	Nights	..	..	..	..	2.50
6.1 **Tourism expenditure in the country**	US$ Mn	9,117	10,496	11,409	11,991	12,755
6.2 "Travel" (*)	US$ Mn	7,260	8,617	9,600	10,095	10,640
6.3 "Passenger transport" (*)	US$ Mn	1,857	1,879	1,809	1,896	2,115
DOMESTIC TOURISM						
Accommodation						
7.1 Overnight stays in hotels and similar establishments	('000)	14,196	14,236	13,837	14,622	15,204
7.2 Guests in hotels and similar establishments	('000)	6,190	6,195	..	6,574	6,948
7.3 Overnight stays in all types of accommodation establishments	('000)	36,254	36,392	35,360	..	..
7.4 Average length of stay of resident tourists in all accommodation establishments	Nights	..	..	..	2.20	2.20
OUTBOUND TOURISM						
8.1 **Departures**	('000)	11,427	..	..	..	..
8.2 **Tourism expenditure in other countries**	US$ Mn	7,210	8,614	9,924	10,634	11,866
8.3 "Travel" (*)	US$ Mn	5,537	6,883	8,104	8,837	9,919
8.4 "Passenger transport" (*)	US$ Mn	1,673	1,731	1,820	1,797	1,947
TOURISM INDUSTRIES						
Hotels and similar establishments						
9.1 Number of rooms	Units	139,943	139,969	..	127,410	127,527
9.2 Number of bed-places	Units	259,004	258,726	..	239,150	240,430
9.3 Occupancy rate	Percent	40.10	38.70	..	39.70	41.70
9.4 Average length of stay	Nights	2.40	2.50	..	2.40	2.40
RELATED INDICATORS						
Share of tourism expenditure (6.1) in:						
10.1 Gross Domestic Product (GDP)	Percent	3.3	3.3	3.2	3.3	3.4
10.2 Exports of goods	Percent	8.7	8.8	8.0	7.9	7.6
10.3 Exports of services	Percent	30.8	30.3	27.2	25.4	24.5

(*) Balance of Payments items: 6.1 to 6.3 correspond to the "Credit" side (and are receipts for the country) while 8.2 to 8.4 correspond to the "Debit" side (and are expenditures in other countries).

SYRIAN ARAB REPUBLIC

Basic Indicators		Units	2002	2003	2004	2005	2006
	INBOUND TOURISM						
	Arrivals						
1.1	Visitors	('000)	4,273	4,388	6,154	5,838	6,009
1.2	Tourists (overnight visitors)	('000)	2,186	2,085	3,033	3,368	4,422
1.3	Same-day visitors	('000)	2,087	2,303	3,121	2,470	1,587
1.4	Cruise passengers	('000)	..	..	..	..	..
	Arrivals by region						
2.1	Africa	('000)	71	73	90	93	81
2.2	Americas	('000)	45	44	58	58	59
2.3	Europe	('000)	646	652	933	947	710
2.4	East Asia and the Pacific	('000)	28	26	37	35	35
2.5	South Asia	('000)	340	228	218	269	290
2.6	Middle East	('000)	3,094	3,325	4,761	4,370	4,734
	Arrivals by means of transport used						
3.1	Air	('000)	501	443	579	604	686
3.2	Rail	('000)	..	..	..	..	..
3.3	Road	('000)	3,766	3,941	5,566	5,219	5,313
3.4	Sea	('000)	6	5	8	15	11
	Arrivals by purpose of visit						
4.1	Leisure, recreation and holidays	('000)	2,361	2,426	3,401	3,227	2,512
4.2	Business and professional	('000)	398	408	573	543	481
4.3	Other	('000)	1,514	1,554	2,180	2,068	3,017
	Accommodation						
5.1	Overnight stays in hotels and similar establishments	('000)	1,941	5,775	7,995	8,803	9,788
5.2	Guests in hotels and similar establishments	('000)	847	863	1,232	1,380	1,754
5.3	Overnight stays in all types of accommodation establishments	('000)	..	20,700	27,930	30,948	48,482
5.4	Average length of stay of non-resident tourists in all accommodation establishments	Nights	10.40	10.40	10.00	9.18	10.90
6.1	**Tourism expenditure in the country**	US$ Mn	..	877	1,883	2,035	2,113
6.2	"Travel" (*)	US$ Mn	970	773	1,800	1,944	2,025
6.3	"Passenger transport" (*)	US$ Mn	..	104	83	91	88
	DOMESTIC TOURISM						
	Accommodation						
7.1	Overnight stays in hotels and similar establishments	('000)	1,053	1,052	981	964	1,013
7.2	Guests in hotels and similar establishments	('000)	688	679	661	649	650
7.3	Overnight stays in all types of accommodation establishments	('000)	..	..	..	..	..
7.4	Average length of stay of resident tourists in all accommodation establishments	Nights	..	..	..	..	..
	OUTBOUND TOURISM						
8.1	**Departures**	('000)	3,299	3,997	4,309	4,564	4,042
8.2	**Tourism expenditure in other countries**	US$ Mn	..	734	688	584	585
8.3	"Travel" (*)	US$ Mn	760	700	650	550	540
8.4	"Passenger transport" (*)	US$ Mn	..	34	38	34	45
	TOURISM INDUSTRIES						
	Hotels and similar establishments						
9.1	Number of rooms	Units	16,042	16,966	17,267	18,798	20,110
9.2	Number of bed-places	Units	35,253	38,928	39,985	43,262	45,523
9.3	Occupancy rate	Percent	..	..	60.00	64.00	65.00
9.4	Average length of stay	Nights	..	..	..	..	..
	RELATED INDICATORS						
	Share of tourism expenditure (6.1) in:						
10.1	Gross Domestic Product (GDP)	Percent	..	3.5	7.4	6.8	5.8
10.2	Exports of goods	Percent	..	13.4	24.9	22.6	19.8
10.3	Exports of services	Percent	..	58.1	68.9	66.8	69.3

(*) Balance of Payments items: 6.1 to 6.3 correspond to the "Credit" side (and are receipts for the country) while 8.2 to 8.4 correspond to the "Debit" side (and are expenditures in other countries).

TAIWAN (PROVINCE OF CHINA)

Basic Indicators	Units	2002	2003	2004	2005	2006
INBOUND TOURISM						
Arrivals						
1.1 Visitors	('000)	2,978	2,248	2,950	3,378	3,520
1.2 Tourists (overnight visitors)	('000)	..	..	..	..	..
1.3 Same-day visitors	('000)	..	..	..	..	..
1.4 Cruise passengers	('000)	..	..	..	..	..
Arrivals by region						
2.1 Africa	('000)	9	7	10	9	9
2.2 Americas	('000)	406	312	441	453	457
2.3 Europe	('000)	147	118	164	172	172
2.4 East Asia and the Pacific	('000)	1,762	1,349	1,782	2,131	2,185
2.5 South Asia	('000)	14	12	16	17	18
2.6 Middle East	('000)	10	8	13	13	13
Arrivals by means of transport used						
3.1 Air	('000)	2,954	2,228	2,916	3,341	3,450
3.2 Rail	('000)	..	..	..	..	..
3.3 Road	('000)	..	..	..	..	..
3.4 Sea	('000)	24	20	35	37	70
Arrivals by purpose of visit						
4.1 Leisure, recreation and holidays	('000)	1,029	695	1,032	1,382	1,510
4.2 Business and professional	('000)	933	779	1,001	1,033	1,041
4.3 Other	('000)	1,016	774	917	963	969
Accommodation						
5.1 Overnight stays in hotels and similar establishments	('000)	..	..	..	..	..
5.2 Guests in hotels and similar establishments	('000)	..	..	..	..	..
5.3 Overnight stays in all types of accommodation establishments	('000)	16,856	14,461	18,838	20,593	21,157
5.4 Average length of stay of non-resident tourists in all accommodation establishments	Nights	7.54	7.97	7.61	7.10	6.92
6.1 **Tourism expenditure in the country**	US$ Mn	5,077	3,578	4,670	5,740	5,956
6.2 "Travel" (*)	US$ Mn	4,583	2,977	4,054	4,977	5,136
6.3 "Passenger transport" (*)	US$ Mn	494	601	616	763	820
DOMESTIC TOURISM						
Accommodation						
7.1 Overnight stays in hotels and similar establishments	('000)	..	..	..	..	..
7.2 Guests in hotels and similar establishments	('000)	..	..	..	..	..
7.3 Overnight stays in all types of accommodation establishments	('000)	..	..	..	..	..
7.4 Average length of stay of resident tourists in all accommodation establishments	Nights	..	..	..	..	..
OUTBOUND TOURISM						
8.1 **Departures**	('000)	7,319	5,923	7,781	8,208	8,671
8.2 **Tourism expenditure in other countries**	US$ Mn	8,229	7,402	9,376	10,047	10,406
8.3 "Travel" (*)	US$ Mn	6,956	6,480	8,170	8,682	8,746
8.4 "Passenger transport" (*)	US$ Mn	1,273	922	1,206	1,365	1,660
TOURISM INDUSTRIES						
Hotels and similar establishments						
9.1 Number of rooms	Units	21,763	21,896	21,744	21,434	21,095
9.2 Number of bed-places	Units	..	..	..	..	..
9.3 Occupancy rate	Percent	61.30	56.43	65.59	72.00	69.20
9.4 Average length of stay	Nights	..	..	..	..	..
RELATED INDICATORS						
Share of tourism expenditure (6.1) in:						
10.1 Gross Domestic Product (GDP)	Percent	..	..	..	..	..
10.2 Exports of goods	Percent	3.8	2.4	2.6	2.9	2.7
10.3 Exports of services	Percent	23.5	15.4	18.1	22.2	20.3

(*) Balance of Payments items: 6.1 to 6.3 correspond to the "Credit" side (and are receipts for the country) while 8.2 to 8.4 correspond to the "Debit" side (and are expenditures in other countries).

THAILAND

Basic Indicators	Units	2002	2003	2004	2005	2006
INBOUND TOURISM						
Arrivals						
1.1 Visitors	('000)	..	..	..	..	..
1.2 Tourists (overnight visitors)	('000)	10,873	10,082	11,737	11,567	13,822
1.3 Same-day visitors	('000)	..	..	..	..	..
1.4 Cruise passengers	('000)	..	..	..	..	..
Arrivals by region						
2.1 Africa	('000)	89	67	83	73	96
2.2 Americas	('000)	640	577	693	740	825
2.3 Europe	('000)	2,550	2,321	2,706	2,779	3,439
2.4 East Asia and the Pacific	('000)	6,955	6,510	7,501	7,195	8,569
2.5 South Asia	('000)	414	411	495	552	654
2.6 Middle East	('000)	151	118	173	179	239
Arrivals by means of transport used						
3.1 Air	('000)	8,955	8,164	9,803	9,544	11,495
3.2 Rail	('000)	..	..	..	..	..
3.3 Road	('000)	1,693	1,738	1,688	1,781	2,024
3.4 Sea	('000)	225	180	247	242	303
Arrivals by purpose of visit						
4.1 Leisure, recreation and holidays	('000)	9,639	8,792	10,165	9,458	11,387
4.2 Business and professional	('000)	972	985	1,174	1,545	1,976
4.3 Other	('000)	188	227	312	514	458
Accommodation						
5.1 Overnight stays in hotels and similar establishments	('000)	..	81,931	94,666	..	..
5.2 Guests in hotels and similar establishments	('000)	..	..	11,338	10,654	12,819
5.3 Overnight stays in all types of accommodation establishments	('000)	..	..	..	..	..
5.4 Average length of stay of non-resident tourists in all accommodation establishments	Nights	7.98	8.19	8.13	8.20	8.62
6.1 **Tourism expenditure in the country**	US$ Mn	10,388	10,456	13,054	12,102	15,653
6.2 "Travel" (*)	US$ Mn	7,901	7,856	10,043	9,577	12,432
6.3 "Passenger transport" (*)	US$ Mn	2,487	2,600	3,011	2,525	3,221
DOMESTIC TOURISM						
Accommodation						
7.1 Overnight stays in hotels and similar establishments	('000)	..	..	..	..	..
7.2 Guests in hotels and similar establishments	('000)	..	..	..	..	..
7.3 Overnight stays in all types of accommodation establishments	('000)	..	..	..	..	..
7.4 Average length of stay of resident tourists in all accommodation establishments	Nights	..	..	..	..	..
OUTBOUND TOURISM						
8.1 **Departures**	('000)	2,250	2,152	2,709	3,047	3,382
8.2 **Tourism expenditure in other countries**	US$ Mn	3,888	3,538	5,343	4,917	6,140
8.3 "Travel" (*)	US$ Mn	3,303	2,921	4,514	3,800	4,632
8.4 "Passenger transport" (*)	US$ Mn	585	617	829	1,117	1,508
TOURISM INDUSTRIES						
Hotels and similar establishments						
9.1 Number of rooms	Units	335,421	348,094	357,922	376,214	..
9.2 Number of bed-places	Units	..	..	..	..	..
9.3 Occupancy rate	Percent	..	..	52.57	..	..
9.4 Average length of stay	Nights	..	..	..	..	..
RELATED INDICATORS						
Share of tourism expenditure (6.1) in:						
10.1 Gross Domestic Product (GDP)	Percent	8.2	7.3	8.1	6.9	7.6
10.2 Exports of goods	Percent	15.7	13.4	13.7	11.1	12.2
10.3 Exports of services	Percent	67.5	66.2	68.6	60.0	64.9

(*) Balance of Payments items: 6.1 to 6.3 correspond to the "Credit" side (and are receipts for the country) while 8.2 to 8.4 correspond to the "Debit" side (and are expenditures in other countries).

THE FORMER YUGOSLAV REPUBLIC OF MACEDONIA

Basic Indicators	Units	2002	2003	2004	2005	2006
INBOUND TOURISM						
Arrivals						
1.1 Visitors	('000)	2,079	2,183	2,594	3,246	3,369
1.2 Tourists (overnight visitors)	('000)	123	158	165	197	202
1.3 Same-day visitors	('000)	..	..	..	..	..
1.4 Cruise passengers	('000)	..	..	..	..	..
Arrivals by region						
2.1 Africa	('000)	..	..	..	..	..
2.2 Americas	('000)	8	8	8	8	9
2.3 Europe	('000)	111	143	151	183	187
2.4 East Asia and the Pacific	('000)	2	2	2	3	3
2.5 South Asia	('000)	..	..	..	..	..
2.6 Middle East	('000)	..	..	..	..	..
Arrivals by means of transport used						
3.1 Air	('000)	116	104	105	129	120
3.2 Rail	('000)	41	42	41	44	53
3.3 Road	('000)	1,922	2,036	2,448	3,073	3,196
3.4 Sea	('000)	..	..	..	..	..
Arrivals by purpose of visit						
4.1 Leisure, recreation and holidays	('000)	..	..	..	..	..
4.2 Business and professional	('000)	..	..	..	..	..
4.3 Other	('000)	..	..	..	..	..
Accommodation						
5.1 Overnight stays in hotels and similar establishments	('000)	249	321	329	391	392
5.2 Guests in hotels and similar establishments	('000)	115	149	154	181	185
5.3 Overnight stays in all types of accommodation establishments	('000)	275	346	361	443	443
5.4 Average length of stay of non-resident tourists in all accommodation establishments	Nights	2.20	2.20	2.20	2.30	2.20
6.1 Tourism expenditure in the country	US$ Mn	55	65	77	92	156
6.2 "Travel" (*)	US$ Mn	39	57	72	84	129
6.3 "Passenger transport" (*)	US$ Mn	16	8	5	8	27
DOMESTIC TOURISM						
Accommodation						
7.1 Overnight stays in hotels and similar establishments	('000)	366	347	289	275	267
7.2 Guests in hotels and similar establishments	('000)	154	146	128	128	121
7.3 Overnight stays in all types of accommodation establishments	('000)	1,576	1,661	1,505	1,527	1,475
7.4 Average length of stay of resident tourists in all accommodation establishments	Nights	4.90	5.10	5.00	4.90	5.00
OUTBOUND TOURISM						
8.1 Departures	('000)	..	..	..	..	..
8.2 Tourism expenditure in other countries	US$ Mn	61	71	83	94	110
8.3 "Travel" (*)	US$ Mn	45	48	54	60	71
8.4 "Passenger transport" (*)	US$ Mn	16	23	29	34	39
TOURISM INDUSTRIES						
Hotels and similar establishments						
9.1 Number of rooms	Units	6,813	6,825	6,918	6,883	7,043
9.2 Number of bed-places	Units	16,488	16,297	16,479	16,407	16,773
9.3 Occupancy rate	Percent	10.20	11.20	10.30	11.10	10.80
9.4 Average length of stay	Nights	4.20	4.20	4.00	3.90	3.80
RELATED INDICATORS						
Share of tourism expenditure (6.1) in:						
10.1 Gross Domestic Product (GDP)	Percent	1.5	1.4	1.4	1.6	2.5
10.2 Exports of goods	Percent	4.9	4.8	4.6	4.5	6.5
10.3 Exports of services	Percent	21.7	19.9	18.9	19.5	26.0

(*) Balance of Payments items: 6.1 to 6.3 correspond to the "Credit" side (and are receipts for the country) while 8.2 to 8.4 correspond to the "Debit" side (and are expenditures in other countries).

TOGO

Basic Indicators	Units	2002	2003	2004	2005	2006
INBOUND TOURISM						
Arrivals						
1.1 Visitors	('000)	..	..	..	..	..
1.2 Tourists (overnight visitors)	('000)	58	61	83	81	94
1.3 Same-day visitors	('000)	..	..	..	..	..
1.4 Cruise passengers	('000)	..	..	..	..	..
Arrivals by region						
2.1 Africa	('000)	29	31	44	46	53
2.2 Americas	('000)	2	2	3	3	3
2.3 Europe	('000)	24	24	30	27	33
2.4 East Asia and the Pacific	('000)	1	1	3	3	3
2.5 South Asia	('000)	..	..	..	..	..
2.6 Middle East	('000)	2	1	3	2	2
Arrivals by means of transport used						
3.1 Air	('000)	..	..	..	..	..
3.2 Rail	('000)	..	..	..	..	..
3.3 Road	('000)	..	..	..	..	..
3.4 Sea	('000)	..	..	..	..	..
Arrivals by purpose of visit						
4.1 Leisure, recreation and holidays	('000)	..	..	..	..	..
4.2 Business and professional	('000)	..	..	..	..	..
4.3 Other	('000)	..	..	..	..	..
Accommodation						
5.1 Overnight stays in hotels and similar establishments	('000)	117	136	183	157	209
5.2 Guests in hotels and similar establishments	('000)	58	61	83	81	94
5.3 Overnight stays in all types of accommodation establishments	('000)	..	..	..	..	..
5.4 Average length of stay of non-resident tourists in all accommodation establishments	Nights	..	..	..	..	2.20
6.1 **Tourism expenditure in the country**	US$ Mn	16	26	25	27	26
6.2 "Travel" (*)	US$ Mn	13	15	19	20	10
6.3 "Passenger transport" (*)	US$ Mn	3	11	6	7	16
DOMESTIC TOURISM						
Accommodation						
7.1 Overnight stays in hotels and similar establishments	('000)	20	18	29	25	15
7.2 Guests in hotels and similar establishments	('000)	..	10	14	12	8
7.3 Overnight stays in all types of accommodation establishments	('000)	..	..	..	..	..
7.4 Average length of stay of resident tourists in all accommodation establishments	Nights	..	..	..	..	1.90
OUTBOUND TOURISM						
8.1 **Departures**	('000)	..	..	..	..	..
8.2 **Tourism expenditure in other countries**	US$ Mn	26	37	38	42	24
8.3 "Travel" (*)	US$ Mn	5	7	8	8	3
8.4 "Passenger transport" (*)	US$ Mn	21	30	30	34	21
TOURISM INDUSTRIES						
Hotels and similar establishments						
9.1 Number of rooms	Units	4,365	4,480	4,728	4,944	5,201
9.2 Number of bed-places	Units	6,546	6,720	7,216	7,636	7,803
9.3 Occupancy rate	Percent	13.70	10.70	10.11	9.30	10.70
9.4 Average length of stay	Nights	2.00	2.10	2.10	1.90	2.10
RELATED INDICATORS						
Share of tourism expenditure (6.1) in:						
10.1 Gross Domestic Product (GDP)	Percent	1.1	1.5	1.2	1.3	2.2
10.2 Exports of goods	Percent	3.8	4.3	4.2	4.1	6.5
10.3 Exports of services	Percent	17.8	27.4	16.7	15.3	23.0

(*) Balance of Payments items: 6.1 to 6.3 correspond to the "Credit" side (and are receipts for the country) while 8.2 to 8.4 correspond to the "Debit" side (and are expenditures in other countries).

Basic Indicators	Units	2002	2003	2004	2005	2006
INBOUND TOURISM						
Arrivals						
1.1 Visitors	('000)	45	51	51	60	54
1.2　Tourists (overnight visitors)	('000)	37	40	41	42	39
1.3　Same-day visitors	('000)	..	..	..	..	..
1.4　Cruise passengers	('000)	8	11	10	18	15
Arrivals by region						
2.1 Africa	('000)	..	..	..	..	..
2.2 Americas	('000)	8	8	8	8	6
2.3 Europe	('000)	4	4	3	3	3
2.4 East Asia and the Pacific	('000)	24	28	29	30	30
2.5 South Asia	('000)	..	..	..	..	..
2.6 Middle East	('000)	..	..	..	..	..
Arrivals by means of transport used						
3.1 Air	('000)	37	40	41	42	39
3.2 Rail	('000)	..	..	..	..	..
3.3 Road	('000)	..	..	..	..	..
3.4 Sea	('000)	8	11	10	18	15
Arrivals by purpose of visit						
4.1 Leisure, recreation and holidays	('000)	16	16	..	..	..
4.2 Business and professional	('000)	1	3	..	..	..
4.3 Other	('000)	20	20	..	..	..
Accommodation						
5.1 Overnight stays in hotels and similar establishments	('000)	..	..	..	..	..
5.2 Guests in hotels and similar establishments	('000)	..	..	..	..	..
5.3 Overnight stays in all types of accommodation establishments	('000)	..	..	..	..	..
5.4 Average length of stay of non-resident tourists in all accommodation establishments	Nights	..	..	..	..	..
6.1 **Tourism expenditure in the country**	US$ Mn	..	..	..	..	..
6.2　"Travel" (*)	US$ Mn	6	10	13	15	16
6.3　"Passenger transport" (*)	US$ Mn	..	..	..	..	..
DOMESTIC TOURISM						
Accommodation						
7.1 Overnight stays in hotels and similar establishments	('000)	..	..	..	..	..
7.2 Guests in hotels and similar establishments	('000)	..	..	..	..	..
7.3 Overnight stays in all types of accommodation establishments	('000)	..	..	..	..	..
7.4 Average length of stay of resident tourists in all accommodation establishments	Nights	..	..	..	..	..
OUTBOUND TOURISM						
8.1 **Departures**	('000)	..	..	..	..	..
8.2 **Tourism expenditure in other countries**	US$ Mn	..	..	..	..	..
8.3　"Travel" (*)	US$ Mn	3	3	6	4	8
8.4　"Passenger transport" (*)	US$ Mn	..	..	..	..	..
TOURISM INDUSTRIES						
Hotels and similar establishments						
9.1 Number of rooms	Units	..	..	..	..	..
9.2 Number of bed-places	Units	..	..	..	..	..
9.3 Occupancy rate	Percent	..	..	..	..	..
9.4 Average length of stay	Nights	..	..	..	..	..
RELATED INDICATORS						
Share of tourism expenditure (6.1) in: (**)						
10.1 Gross Domestic Product (GDP)	Percent	4.2	6.1	6.9	7.0	7.2
10.2 Exports of goods	Percent	33.3	47.6	68.4	83.3	160.0
10.3 Exports of services	Percent	26.1	38.5	48.1	40.5	51.6

(*) Balance of Payments items: 6.1 to 6.3 correspond to the "Credit" side (and are receipts for the country) while 8.2 to 8.4 correspond to the "Debit" side (and are expenditures in other countries).

(**) See Annex "Country notes".

TRINIDAD AND TOBAGO

Basic Indicators	Units	2002	2003	2004	2005	2006
INBOUND TOURISM						
Arrivals						
1.1 Visitors	('000)	444	465	497	530	543
1.2 Tourists (overnight visitors)	('000)	384	409	443	463	457
1.3 Same-day visitors	('000)	..	..	..	..	
1.4 Cruise passengers	('000)	60	56	54	67	86
Arrivals by region						
2.1 Africa	('000)	1	1	1	1	1
2.2 Americas	('000)	308	324	347	365	365
2.3 Europe	('000)	71	79	90	91	84
2.4 East Asia and the Pacific	('000)	3	3	3	3	4
2.5 South Asia	('000)	1	1	1	2	2
2.6 Middle East	('000)	..	..	..	..	..
Arrivals by means of transport used						
3.1 Air	('000)	384	409	443	463	457
3.2 Rail	('000)	..	..	..	..	..
3.3 Road	('000)	..	..	..	..	..
3.4 Sea	('000)	60	56	54	67	86
Arrivals by purpose of visit						
4.1 Leisure, recreation and holidays	('000)	250	281	299	313	293
4.2 Business and professional	('000)	72	79	86	89	92
4.3 Other	('000)	62	49	58	61	72
Accommodation						
5.1 Overnight stays in hotels and similar establishments	('000)	..	..	..	..	..
5.2 Guests in hotels and similar establishments	('000)	..	..	..	..	..
5.3 Overnight stays in all types of accommodation establishments	('000)	..	..	..	..	..
5.4 Average length of stay of non-resident tourists in all accommodation establishments	Nights	16.90	14.40	14.40	14.30	14.80
6.1 **Tourism expenditure in the country**	US$ Mn	402	437	568	593	357
6.2 "Travel" (*)	US$ Mn	242	249	341	453	177
6.3 "Passenger transport" (*)	US$ Mn	160	188	227	140	180
DOMESTIC TOURISM						
Accommodation						
7.1 Overnight stays in hotels and similar establishments	('000)	..	..	..	..	..
7.2 Guests in hotels and similar establishments	('000)	..	..	..	..	..
7.3 Overnight stays in all types of accommodation establishments	('000)	..	..	..	..	..
7.4 Average length of stay of resident tourists in all accommodation establishments	Nights	..	..	..	..	..
OUTBOUND TOURISM						
8.1 **Departures**	('000)	..	..	..	..	..
8.2 **Tourism expenditure in other countries**	US$ Mn	208	143	141	234	147
8.3 "Travel" (*)	US$ Mn	186	107	96	180	82
8.4 "Passenger transport" (*)	US$ Mn	22	36	45	54	65
TOURISM INDUSTRIES						
Hotels and similar establishments						
9.1 Number of rooms	Units	4,387	5,378	6,007	5,929	6,048
9.2 Number of bed-places	Units	..	..	..	..	..
9.3 Occupancy rate	Percent	41.00	..	..	..	..
9.4 Average length of stay	Nights	..	..	..	..	..
RELATED INDICATORS						
Share of tourism expenditure (6.1) in:						
10.1 Gross Domestic Product (GDP)	Percent	4.5	4.1	4.7	3.7	1.8
10.2 Exports of goods	Percent	10.3	8.4	8.9	6.1	3.0
10.3 Exports of services	Percent	63.1	63.8	66.7	66.1	..

(*) Balance of Payments items: 6.1 to 6.3 correspond to the "Credit" side (and are receipts for the country) while 8.2 to 8.4 correspond to the "Debit" side (and are expenditures in other countries).

Basic Indicators		Units	2002	2003	2004	2005	2006
	INBOUND TOURISM						
	Arrivals						
1.1	Visitors	('000)	5,322	5,492	6,419	6,975	7,176
1.2	Tourists (overnight visitors)	('000)	5,064	5,114	5,998	6,378	6,550
1.3	Same-day visitors	('000)	..	..	..	..	..
1.4	Cruise passengers	('000)	258	378	421	597	626
	Arrivals by region						
2.1	Africa	('000)	786	872	985	993	1,010
2.2	Americas	('000)	22	23	30	35	34
2.3	Europe	('000)	2,919	2,840	3,482	3,869	3,956
2.4	East Asia and the Pacific	('000)	7	9	11	14	15
2.5	South Asia	('000)	..	..	..	..	..
2.6	Middle East	('000)	1,311	1,356	1,472	1,440	1,507
	Arrivals by means of transport used						
3.1	Air	('000)	3,066	2,992	3,664	4,053	4,144
3.2	Rail	('000)	..	..	..	..	..
3.3	Road	('000)	1,920	2,033	2,250	2,232	2,305
3.4	Sea	('000)	78	89	84	94	101
	Arrivals by purpose of visit						
4.1	Leisure, recreation and holidays	('000)	..	..	..	..	..
4.2	Business and professional	('000)	..	..	..	..	..
4.3	Other	('000)	..	..	..	..	..
	Accommodation						
5.1	Overnight stays in hotels and similar establishments	('000)	25,897	25,301	30,665	33,587	34,086
5.2	Guests in hotels and similar establishments	('000)	4,245	4,064	4,900	5,442	5,415
5.3	Overnight stays in all types of accommodation establishments	('000)	..	..	..	..	..
5.4	Average length of stay of non-resident tourists in all accommodation establishments	Nights	5.10	4.90	5.10	5.30	5.20
6.1	**Tourism expenditure in the country**	US$ Mn	1,831	1,935	2,432	2,800	2,999
6.2	"Travel" (*)	US$ Mn	1,523	1,583	1,970	2,143	2,275
6.3	"Passenger transport" (*)	US$ Mn	308	352	462	657	724
	DOMESTIC TOURISM						
	Accommodation						
7.1	Overnight stays in hotels and similar establishments	('000)	2,621	2,809	2,822	2,723	2,754
7.2	Guests in hotels and similar establishments	('000)	1,191	1,225	1,242	1,224	1,251
7.3	Overnight stays in all types of accommodation establishments	('000)	..	..	..	..	..
7.4	Average length of stay of resident tourists in all accommodation establishments	Nights	2.30	2.30	2.30	2.20	2.20
	OUTBOUND TOURISM						
8.1	**Departures**	('000)	1,939	2,274	2,312	2,241	2,302
8.2	**Tourism expenditure in other countries**	US$ Mn	303	355	427	452	498
8.3	"Travel" (*)	US$ Mn	260	300	340	374	410
8.4	"Passenger transport" (*)	US$ Mn	43	55	87	78	88
	TOURISM INDUSTRIES						
	Hotels and similar establishments						
9.1	Number of rooms	Units	107,159	111,009	113,076	114,919	115,919
9.2	Number of bed-places	Units	214,319	222,018	226,153	229,837	231,838
9.3	Occupancy rate	Percent	44.00	42.00	48.70	51.50	51.50
9.4	Average length of stay	Nights	6.10	6.20	6.30	6.20	6.30
	RELATED INDICATORS						
	Share of tourism expenditure (6.1) in:						
10.1	Gross Domestic Product (GDP)	Percent	8.7	7.7	8.6	9.8	9.9
10.2	Exports of goods	Percent	26.7	24.1	25.1	26.7	26.1
10.3	Exports of services	Percent	68.3	65.9	67.0	69.6	69.8

(*) Balance of Payments items: 6.1 to 6.3 correspond to the "Credit" side (and are receipts for the country) while 8.2 to 8.4 correspond to the "Debit" side (and are expenditures in other countries).

TURKEY

Basic Indicators		Units	2002	2003	2004	2005	2006
	INBOUND TOURISM						
	Arrivals						
1.1	Visitors	('000)	13,256	14,030	17,517	21,125	19,820
1.2	Tourists (overnight visitors)	('000)	12,790	13,341	16,826	20,273	18,916
1.3	Same-day visitors	('000)	466	689	691	852	903
1.4	Cruise passengers	('000)	..	..	..	..	..
	Arrivals by region						
2.1	Africa	('000)	131	119	131	154	153
2.2	Americas	('000)	254	213	283	391	459
2.3	Europe	('000)	11,359	11,872	14,946	17,663	16,269
2.4	East Asia and the Pacific	('000)	281	242	288	422	471
2.5	South Asia	('000)	451	522	661	995	917
2.6	Middle East	('000)	304	359	498	626	630
	Arrivals by means of transport used						
3.1	Air	('000)	9,990	10,080	12,575	14,980	14,085
3.2	Rail	('000)	55	63	73	80	72
3.3	Road	('000)	2,465	2,894	3,717	4,745	4,206
3.4	Sea	('000)	745	992	1,152	1,320	1,457
	Arrivals by purpose of visit						
4.1	Leisure, recreation and holidays	('000)	10,049	10,512	13,310	15,769	13,698
4.2	Business and professional	('000)	1,381	1,543	1,897	1,972	2,316
4.3	Other	('000)	1,492	1,647	1,996	2,782	3,262
	Accommodation						
5.1	Overnight stays in hotels and similar establishments	('000)	43,225	40,819	49,614	55,996	46,588
5.2	Guests in hotels and similar establishments	('000)	9,859	8,983	10,962	12,937	11,883
5.3	Overnight stays in all types of accommodation establishments	('000)	43,312	40,866	49,728	56,108	46,640
5.4	Average length of stay of non-resident tourists in all accommodation establishments	Nights	4.39	4.54	4.53	4.33	3.92
6.1	**Tourism expenditure in the country**	US$ Mn	..	..	..	19,720	18,520
6.2	"Travel" (*)	US$ Mn	11,901	13,203	15,888	18,152	16,853
6.3	"Passenger transport" (*)	US$ Mn	..	..	..	1,568	1,667
	DOMESTIC TOURISM						
	Accommodation						
7.1	Overnight stays in hotels and similar establishments	('000)	15,152	16,199	18,341	18,807	21,476
7.2	Guests in hotels and similar establishments	('000)	7,908	8,423	9,720	10,454	11,566
7.3	Overnight stays in all types of accommodation establishments	('000)	15,202	16,234	18,357	18,819	21,503
7.4	Average length of stay of resident tourists in all accommodation establishments	Nights	1.92	1.93	1.89	1.80	1.86
	OUTBOUND TOURISM						
8.1	**Departures**	('000)	5,131	5,928	7,299	8,246	8,275
8.2	**Tourism expenditure in other countries**	US$ Mn	..	..	..	3,210	3,155
8.3	"Travel" (*)	US$ Mn	1,880	2,113	2,524	2,872	2,743
8.4	"Passenger transport" (*)	US$ Mn	..	..	..	338	412
	TOURISM INDUSTRIES						
	Hotels and similar establishments						
9.1	Number of rooms	Units	189,528	201,510	217,066	230,605	241,702
9.2	Number of bed-places	Units	393,718	418,177	452,424	481,704	507,210
9.3	Occupancy rate	Percent	48.68	46.90	50.07	52.38	47.26
9.4	Average length of stay	Nights	3.29	3.28	3.29	3.20	2.90
	RELATED INDICATORS						
	Share of tourism expenditure (6.1) in: (**)						
10.1	Gross Domestic Product (GDP)	Percent	6.5	5.5	5.2	5.4	4.6
10.2	Exports of goods	Percent	29.7	25.8	23.7	25.6	20.1
10.3	Exports of services	Percent	84.7	73.3	69.2	74.0	75.4

(*) Balance of Payments items: 6.1 to 6.3 correspond to the "Credit" side (and are receipts for the country) while 8.2 to 8.4 correspond to the "Debit" side (and are expenditures in other countries).

(**) See Annex "Country notes".

Basic Indicators	Units	2002	2003	2004	2005	2006
INBOUND TOURISM						
Arrivals						
1.1 Visitors	('000)	..	..	..	..	..
1.2 Tourists (overnight visitors)	('000)	10.8	8.2	14.8	11.6	
1.3 Same-day visitors	('000)	..	..	..	..	
1.4 Cruise passengers	('000)	..	..	..	..	
Arrivals by region						
2.1 Africa	('000)	..	..	..	..	..
2.2 Americas	('000)	0.2	0.2	0.4	0.4	
2.3 Europe	('000)	2.3	1.9	3.9	3.3	..
2.4 East Asia and the Pacific	('000)	0.5	0.5	1.1	0.8	
2.5 South Asia	('000)	7.6	5.6	9.4	7.2	..
2.6 Middle East	('000)	..	..	..	..	
Arrivals by means of transport used						
3.1 Air	('000)	4.8	2.7	3.8	2.7	..
3.2 Rail	('000)	..	..			
3.3 Road	('000)	6.0	5.5	11.0	8.9	..
3.4 Sea	('000)	..	..	..	..	
Arrivals by purpose of visit						
4.1 Leisure, recreation and holidays	('000)	5.0	1.2	2.9	9.0	..
4.2 Business and professional	('000)	..	0.6	1.4	1.3	
4.3 Other	('000)	5.8	6.4	10.5	1.3	
Accommodation						
5.1 Overnight stays in hotels and similar establishments	('000)	..	..	..	..	..
5.2 Guests in hotels and similar establishments	('000)	..	..	..	..	..
5.3 Overnight stays in all types of accommodation establishments	('000)	..	..	..	..	..
5.4 Average length of stay of non-resident tourists in all accommodation establishments	Nights	6.00	6.00	6.00	6.00	..
6.1 **Tourism expenditure in the country**	US$ Mn	..	..	..	..	..
6.2 "Travel" (*)	US$ Mn	..	..	..	..	..
6.3 "Passenger transport" (*)	US$ Mn	..	..	..	..	..
DOMESTIC TOURISM						
Accommodation						
7.1 Overnight stays in hotels and similar establishments	('000)	..	..	..	..	..
7.2 Guests in hotels and similar establishments	('000)	..	..	..	..	..
7.3 Overnight stays in all types of accommodation establishments	('000)	..	..	..	..	..
7.4 Average length of stay of resident tourists in all accommodation establishments	Nights	..	..	..	..	..
OUTBOUND TOURISM						
8.1 **Departures**	('000)	79	34	32	33	..
8.2 **Tourism expenditure in other countries**	US$ Mn	..	..	..	..	..
8.3 "Travel" (*)	US$ Mn	..	..	..	..	..
8.4 "Passenger transport" (*)	US$ Mn	..	..	..	..	..
TOURISM INDUSTRIES						
Hotels and similar establishments						
9.1 Number of rooms	Units	970	970	970	..	..
9.2 Number of bed-places	Units	1,675	1,675	1,675	..	..
9.3 Occupancy rate	Percent	12.00	10.00	19.00	..	..
9.4 Average length of stay	Nights	7.00	8.00	8.00		
RELATED INDICATORS						
Share of tourism expenditure (6.1) in:						
10.1 Gross Domestic Product (GDP)	Percent	..	..	..	..	..
10.2 Exports of goods	Percent	..	..	..	..	..
10.3 Exports of services	Percent	..	..	..	..	..

(*) Balance of Payments items: 6.1 to 6.3 correspond to the "Credit" side (and are receipts for the country) while 8.2 to 8.4 correspond to the "Debit" side (and are expenditures in other countries).

TURKS AND CAICOS ISLANDS

Basic Indicators		Units	2002	2003	2004	2005	2006
INBOUND TOURISM							
Arrivals							
1.1	Visitors	('000)	..	..	..	..	..
1.2	Tourists (overnight visitors)	('000)	155	164	173	176	248
1.3	Same-day visitors	('000)	..	..	..	..	..
1.4	Cruise passengers	('000)	..	..	..	..	..
Arrivals by region							
2.1	Africa	('000)	..	..	..	..	..
2.2	Americas	('000)	140	149	149	157	221
2.3	Europe	('000)	11	13	14	18	25
2.4	East Asia and the Pacific	('000)	..	..	..	..	..
2.5	South Asia	('000)	..	..	..	..	..
2.6	Middle East	('000)	..	..	..	..	..
Arrivals by means of transport used							
3.1	Air	('000)	154	158	..	..	..
3.2	Rail	('000)	..	..	..	..	..
3.3	Road	('000)	..	..	..	..	..
3.4	Sea	('000)	3	..	..	..	..
Arrivals by purpose of visit							
4.1	Leisure, recreation and holidays	('000)	90	96	..	..	..
4.2	Business and professional	('000)	47	59	..	..	..
4.3	Other	('000)	18	9	..	..	..
Accommodation							
5.1	Overnight stays in hotels and similar establishments	('000)	..	..	..	..	..
5.2	Guests in hotels and similar establishments	('000)	..	..	..	..	..
5.3	Overnight stays in all types of accommodation establishments	('000)	1,172	..	..	..	..
5.4	Average length of stay of non-resident tourists in all accommodation establishments	Nights	6.46	6.46	6.75	..	7.00
6.1	**Tourism expenditure in the country** (**)	US$ Mn	292	..	..	..	..
6.2	"Travel" (*)	US$ Mn	..	..	..	..	..
6.3	"Passenger transport" (*)	US$ Mn	..	..	..	..	..
DOMESTIC TOURISM							
Accommodation							
7.1	Overnight stays in hotels and similar establishments	('000)	..	..	..	..	..
7.2	Guests in hotels and similar establishments	('000)	..	..	..	..	..
7.3	Overnight stays in all types of accommodation establishments	('000)	..	..	..	..	..
7.4	Average length of stay of resident tourists in all accommodation establishments	Nights	..	..	..	..	..
OUTBOUND TOURISM							
8.1	**Departures**	('000)	..	..	..	..	..
8.2	**Tourism expenditure in other countries**	US$ Mn	..	..	..	..	..
8.3	"Travel" (*)	US$ Mn	..	..	..	..	..
8.4	"Passenger transport" (*)	US$ Mn	..	..	..	..	..
TOURISM INDUSTRIES							
Hotels and similar establishments							
9.1	Number of rooms	Units	2,155	2,155	2,190	2,227	2,799
9.2	Number of bed-places	Units	..	..	..	..	..
9.3	Occupancy rate	Percent	73.00	..	..	..	..
9.4	Average length of stay	Nights	..	..	..	..	..
RELATED INDICATORS							
Share of tourism expenditure (6.1) in:							
10.1	Gross Domestic Product (GDP)	Percent	..	..	..	..	..
10.2	Exports of goods	Percent	..	..	..	..	..
10.3	Exports of services	Percent	..	..	..	..	..

(*) Balance of Payments items: 6.1 to 6.3 correspond to the "Credit" side (and are receipts for the country) while 8.2 to 8.4 correspond to the "Debit" side (and are expenditures in other countries).

(**) See Annex "Country notes".

TUVALU

Basic Indicators	Units	2002	2003	2004	2005	2006
INBOUND TOURISM						
Arrivals						
1.1 Visitors	('000)	..	..	..	..	..
1.2 Tourists (overnight visitors)	('000)	1.3	1.4	1.3	1.1	1.1
1.3 Same-day visitors	('000)	..	..	..	..	..
1.4 Cruise passengers	('000)	..	..	..	..	..
Arrivals by region						
2.1 Africa	('000)	..	..	..	..	..
2.2 Americas	('000)	0.1	0.1	0.1	0.1	0.1
2.3 Europe	('000)	0.1	0.1	0.1	0.1	0.1
2.4 East Asia and the Pacific	('000)	1.1	1.1	1.0	0.8	0.9
2.5 South Asia	('000)	..	..	..	..	..
2.6 Middle East	('000)	..	..	..	..	..
Arrivals by means of transport used						
3.1 Air	('000)	..	1.1	1.1	0.9	..
3.2 Rail	('000)	..	..	..	..	..
3.3 Road	('000)	..	..	..	..	..
3.4 Sea	('000)	..	0.3	0.2	0.2	..
Arrivals by purpose of visit						
4.1 Leisure, recreation and holidays	('000)	0.2	0.2	0.2	0.2	0.2
4.2 Business and professional	('000)	0.3	0.3	0.9	0.6	0.2
4.3 Other	('000)	0.8	0.9	0.2	0.3	0.8
Accommodation						
5.1 Overnight stays in hotels and similar establishments	('000)	..	..	..	..	..
5.2 Guests in hotels and similar establishments	('000)	..	..	..	..	..
5.3 Overnight stays in all types of accommodation establishments	('000)	..	..	..	..	..
5.4 Average length of stay of non-resident tourists in all accommodation establishments	Nights	..	..	..	..	..
6.1 **Tourism expenditure in the country**	US$ Mn	..	..	..	..	..
6.2 "Travel" (*)	US$ Mn	..	..	..	..	..
6.3 "Passenger transport" (*)	US$ Mn	..	..	..	..	..
DOMESTIC TOURISM						
Accommodation						
7.1 Overnight stays in hotels and similar establishments	('000)	..	..	..	..	..
7.2 Guests in hotels and similar establishments	('000)	..	..	..	..	..
7.3 Overnight stays in all types of accommodation establishments	('000)	..	..	..	..	..
7.4 Average length of stay of resident tourists in all accommodation establishments	Nights	..	..	..	..	..
OUTBOUND TOURISM						
8.1 **Departures**	('000)	2.7	2.6	2.3	2.2	..
8.2 **Tourism expenditure in other countries**	US$ Mn	..	..	..	..	..
8.3 "Travel" (*)	US$ Mn	..	..	..	..	..
8.4 "Passenger transport" (*)	US$ Mn	..	..	..	..	..
TOURISM INDUSTRIES						
Hotels and similar establishments						
9.1 Number of rooms	Units	..	..	..	..	..
9.2 Number of bed-places	Units	..	..	..	..	..
9.3 Occupancy rate	Percent	..	..	..	..	..
9.4 Average length of stay	Nights	..	..	..	..	..
RELATED INDICATORS						
Share of tourism expenditure (6.1) in:						
10.1 Gross Domestic Product (GDP)	Percent	..	..	..	..	..
10.2 Exports of goods	Percent	..	..	..	..	..
10.3 Exports of services	Percent	..	..	..	..	..

(*) Balance of Payments items: 6.1 to 6.3 correspond to the "Credit" side (and are receipts for the country) while 8.2 to 8.4 correspond to the "Debit" side (and are expenditures in other countries).

UGANDA

Basic Indicators		Units	2002	2003	2004	2005	2006
	INBOUND TOURISM						
	Arrivals						
1.1	Visitors	('000)	..	..	..	..	..
1.2	Tourists (overnight visitors)	('000)	254	305	512	468	539
1.3	Same-day visitors	('000)	..	..	..	..	..
1.4	Cruise passengers	('000)	..	..	..	..	..
	Arrivals by region						
2.1	Africa	('000)	192	233	406	337	397
2.2	Americas	('000)	15	16	23	29	36
2.3	Europe	('000)	34	39	49	62	71
2.4	East Asia and the Pacific	('000)	4	5	8	10	12
2.5	South Asia	('000)	6	8	12	14	14
2.6	Middle East	('000)	2	2	3	4	4
	Arrivals by means of transport used						
3.1	Air	('000)	86	97	131	172	200
3.2	Rail	('000)	..	..	..	..	..
3.3	Road	('000)	168	208	381	296	339
3.4	Sea	('000)	..	..	..	..	..
	Arrivals by purpose of visit						
4.1	Leisure, recreation and holidays	('000)	69	76	86	9	30
4.2	Business and professional	('000)	59	67	81	31	72
4.3	Other	('000)	126	162	345	428	436
	Accommodation						
5.1	Overnight stays in hotels and similar establishments	('000)	..	..	..	..	..
5.2	Guests in hotels and similar establishments	('000)	..	..	..	..	..
5.3	Overnight stays in all types of accommodation establishments	('000)	1,016	..	..	..	..
5.4	Average length of stay of non-resident tourists in all accommodation establishments	Nights	..	..	..	..	..
6.1	**Tourism expenditure in the country**	US$ Mn	194	185	257	383	356
6.2	"Travel" (*)	US$ Mn	171	184	256	381	355
6.3	"Passenger transport" (*)	US$ Mn	23	1	1	2	1
	DOMESTIC TOURISM						
	Accommodation						
7.1	Overnight stays in hotels and similar establishments	('000)	..	..	..	..	..
7.2	Guests in hotels and similar establishments	('000)	..	..	..	..	..
7.3	Overnight stays in all types of accommodation establishments	('000)	..	..	..	..	..
7.4	Average length of stay of resident tourists in all accommodation establishments	Nights	..	..	..	..	..
	OUTBOUND TOURISM						
8.1	**Departures**	('000)	184	189	231	189	254
8.2	**Tourism expenditure in other countries**	US$ Mn	..	..	136	133	210
8.3	"Travel" (*)	US$ Mn	..	..	133	129	137
8.4	"Passenger transport" (*)	US$ Mn	2	2	3	4	73
	TOURISM INDUSTRIES						
	Hotels and similar establishments						
9.1	Number of rooms	Units	19,385	..	..	..	..
9.2	Number of bed-places	Units	29,295	..	..	..	..
9.3	Occupancy rate	Percent	..	..	..	..	..
9.4	Average length of stay	Nights	..	..	..	..	..
	RELATED INDICATORS						
	Share of tourism expenditure (6.1) in:						
10.1	Gross Domestic Product (GDP)	Percent	3.3	3.0	3.8	4.4	3.8
10.2	Exports of goods	Percent	40.3	32.9	36.2	44.3	35.5
10.3	Exports of services	Percent	86.2	69.5	71.8	75.4	72.7

(*) Balance of Payments items: 6.1 to 6.3 correspond to the "Credit" side (and are receipts for the country) while 8.2 to 8.4 correspond to the "Debit" side (and are expenditures in other countries).

Basic Indicators	Units	2002	2003	2004	2005	2006
INBOUND TOURISM						
Arrivals						
1.1 Visitors	('000)	12,793	15,161	18,583	20,489	21,714
1.2 Tourists (overnight visitors)	('000)	10,517	12,514	15,629	17,631	18,900
1.3 Same-day visitors	('000)	2,215	2,556	2,918	2,823	2,776
1.4 Cruise passengers	('000)	61	91	36	35	38
Arrivals by region						
2.1 Africa	('000)	5	12	7	7	11
2.2 Americas	('000)	53	83	99	96	141
2.3 Europe	('000)	10,409	12,345	15,450	17,442	18,655
2.4 East Asia and the Pacific	('000)	22	26	32	35	41
2.5 South Asia	('000)	10	14	13	15	14
2.6 Middle East	('000)	15	19	20	26	22
Arrivals by means of transport used						
3.1 Air	('000)	665	675	844	952	1,058
3.2 Rail	('000)	7,684	7,230	9,035	6,697	6,704
3.3 Road	('000)	4,137	4,309	5,375	9,752	10,892
3.4 Sea	('000)	307	300	375	229	246
Arrivals by purpose of visit						
4.1 Leisure, recreation and holidays	('000)	613	728	844	922	977
4.2 Business and professional	('000)	1,786	2,122	2,734	2,868	3,040
4.3 Other	('000)	10,393	12,310	15,005	16,698	17,697
Accommodation						
5.1 Overnight stays in hotels and similar establishments	('000)	1,453	1,420	1,380	1,395	..
5.2 Guests in hotels and similar establishments	('000)	..	..	..	..	..
5.3 Overnight stays in all types of accommodation establishments	('000)	4,757	4,479	4,188	3,895	..
5.4 Average length of stay of non-resident tourists in all accommodation establishments	Nights	5.00	4.80	4.00	3.80	..
6.1 **Tourism expenditure in the country**	US$ Mn	1,001	1,204	2,931	3,542	4,018
6.2 "Travel" (*)	US$ Mn	788	935	2,560	3,125	3,485
6.3 "Passenger transport" (*)	US$ Mn	213	269	371	417	533
DOMESTIC TOURISM						
Accommodation						
7.1 Overnight stays in hotels and similar establishments	('000)	8,398	8,411	8,486	8,554	..
7.2 Guests in hotels and similar establishments	('000)	..	..	..	..	..
7.3 Overnight stays in all types of accommodation establishments	('000)	38,951	38,100	38,098	37,336	..
7.4 Average length of stay of resident tourists in all accommodation establishments	Nights	..	..	..	..	..
OUTBOUND TOURISM						
8.1 **Departures**	('000)	14,729	14,795	15,588	16,454	16,875
8.2 **Tourism expenditure in other countries**	US$ Mn	794	953	2,660	3,078	3,202
8.3 "Travel" (*)	US$ Mn	657	789	2,463	2,805	2,834
8.4 "Passenger transport" (*)	US$ Mn	137	164	197	273	368
TOURISM INDUSTRIES						
Hotels and similar establishments						
9.1 Number of rooms	Units	35,139	32,572	32,623	33,388	..
9.2 Number of bed-places	Units	90,289	86,243	84,259	86,803	..
9.3 Occupancy rate	Percent	26.00	30.00	31.00	33.00	..
9.4 Average length of stay	Nights	2.60	2.60	2.60	2.60	..
RELATED INDICATORS						
Share of tourism expenditure (6.1) in:						
10.1 Gross Domestic Product (GDP)	Percent	2.4	2.4	4.5	4.1	3.8
10.2 Exports of goods	Percent	5.4	5.1	8.8	10.1	10.3
10.3 Exports of services	Percent	21.4	23.1	37.3	37.9	35.6

(*) Balance of Payments items: 6.1 to 6.3 correspond to the "Credit" side (and are receipts for the country) while 8.2 to 8.4 correspond to the "Debit" side (and are expenditures in other countries).

UNITED ARAB EMIRATES

Basic Indicators		Units	2002	2003	2004	2005	2006
INBOUND TOURISM							
Arrivals							
1.1	Visitors	('000)	..	..	..	..	..
1.2	Tourists (overnight visitors)	('000)	5,445	5,871	6,195	7,126	
1.3	Same-day visitors	('000)	..	..	..	..	..
1.4	Cruise passengers	('000)	..	..	..	..	..
Arrivals by region							
2.1	Africa	('000)	311	307	315	..	..
2.2	Americas	('000)	239	254	286	432	..
2.3	Europe	('000)	1,468	1,585	2,008	2,395	..
2.4	East Asia and the Pacific	('000)	395	428	445	..	..
2.5	South Asia	('000)	807	922	909	..	..
2.6	Middle East	('000)	1,557	1,583	1,545	..	..
Arrivals by means of transport used							
3.1	Air	('000)	..	..	..	..	..
3.2	Rail	('000)	..	..	..	..	..
3.3	Road	('000)	..	..	..	..	..
3.4	Sea	('000)	..	..	..	..	..
Arrivals by purpose of visit							
4.1	Leisure, recreation and holidays	('000)	..	..	..	..	..
4.2	Business and professional	('000)	..	..	..	..	..
4.3	Other	('000)	..	..	..	..	..
Accommodation							
5.1	Overnight stays in hotels and similar establishments	('000)	12,360	14,192	16,345	18,326	..
5.2	Guests in hotels and similar establishments	('000)	5,445	5,871	6,195	7,126	..
5.3	Overnight stays in all types of accommodation establishments	('000)	..	..	..	..	..
5.4	Average length of stay of non-resident tourists in all accommodation establishments	Nights	..	..	..	..	..
6.1	**Tourism expenditure in the country** (**)	US$ Mn	1,332	1,438	1,593	3,218	4,972
6.2	"Travel" (*)	US$ Mn	..	..	..	..	..
6.3	"Passenger transport" (*)	US$ Mn	..	..	..	..	..
DOMESTIC TOURISM							
Accommodation							
7.1	Overnight stays in hotels and similar establishments	('000)	..	..	..	..	..
7.2	Guests in hotels and similar establishments	('000)	..	..	..	..	..
7.3	Overnight stays in all types of accommodation establishments	('000)	..	..	..	..	..
7.4	Average length of stay of resident tourists in all accommodation establishments	Nights	..	..	..	..	..
OUTBOUND TOURISM							
8.1	**Departures**	('000)	..	..	..	..	..
8.2	**Tourism expenditure in other countries** (**)	US$ Mn	3,651	3,956	4,472	6,186	8,827
8.3	"Travel" (*)	US$ Mn	..	..	..	..	..
8.4	"Passenger transport" (*)	US$ Mn	..	..	..	..	..
TOURISM INDUSTRIES							
Hotels and similar establishments							
9.1	Number of rooms	Units	34,536	38,402	37,674	41,272	..
9.2	Number of bed-places	Units	56,142	60,572	60,129	65,995	..
9.3	Occupancy rate	Percent	67.20	68.00	77.00	81.00	..
9.4	Average length of stay	Nights	2.00	2.00	3.00	3.00	..
RELATED INDICATORS							
Share of tourism expenditure (6.1) in:							
10.1	Gross Domestic Product (GDP)	Percent	..	..	..	..	..
10.2	Exports of goods	Percent	..	..	..	..	..
10.3	Exports of services	Percent	..	..	..	..	..

(*) Balance of Payments items: 6.1 to 6.3 correspond to the "Credit" side (and are receipts for the country) while 8.2 to 8.4 correspond to the "Debit" side (and are expenditures in other countries).

(**) See Annex "Country notes".

Basic Indicators	Units	2002	2003	2004	2005	2006
INBOUND TOURISM						
Arrivals						
1.1 Visitors	('000)	24,180	24,715	27,755	29,970	32,713
1.2 Tourists (overnight visitors)	('000)	22,307	22,787	25,678	28,039	30,654
1.3 Same-day visitors	('000)	1,873	1,928	2,077	1,931	2,059
1.4 Cruise passengers	('000)	..	..	..	..	..
Arrivals by region						
2.1 Africa	('000)	631	569	639	654	701
2.2 Americas	('000)	4,619	4,326	4,692	4,597	5,167
2.3 Europe	('000)	16,409	17,371	19,582	21,742	23,541
2.4 East Asia and the Pacific	('000)	1,854	1,809	2,086	2,190	2,310
2.5 South Asia	('000)	308	294	371	407	521
2.6 Middle East	('000)	360	346	384	380	472
Arrivals by means of transport used						
3.1 Air	('000)	17,098	17,635	20,002	22,023	24,588
3.2 Rail	('000)	2,677	2,711	2,983	3,252	3,267
3.3 Road	('000)	..	..	..	..	..
3.4 Sea	('000)	4,405	4,369	4,770	4,697	4,858
Arrivals by purpose of visit						
4.1 Leisure, recreation and holidays	('000)	7,735	7,973	9,275	9,693	10,566
4.2 Business and professional	('000)	7,840	7,590	8,055	8,820	9,717
4.3 Other	('000)	8,605	9,152	10,425	11,459	12,430
Accommodation						
5.1 Overnight stays in hotels and similar establishments	('000)	48,377	49,003	53,789	58,909	63,023
5.2 Guests in hotels and similar establishments	('000)	14,176	14,397	13,172	17,009	18,322
5.3 Overnight stays in all types of accommodation establishments	('000)	199,285	203,432	227,406	247,587	273,417
5.4 Average length of stay of non-resident tourists in all accommodation establishments	Nights	8.20	8.20	8.20	8.30	8.40
6.1 **Tourism expenditure in the country**	US$ Mn	27,819	30,736	37,166	39,569	43,041
6.2 "Travel" (*)	US$ Mn	20,549	22,668	28,202	30,573	33,888
6.3 "Passenger transport" (*)	US$ Mn	7,270	8,068	8,964	8,996	9,153
DOMESTIC TOURISM						
Accommodation						
7.1 Overnight stays in hotels and similar establishments	('000)	130,560	118,480	106,510	117,926	102,010
7.2 Guests in hotels and similar establishments	('000)	57,680	52,020	48,100	52,611	46,783
7.3 Overnight stays in all types of accommodation establishments	('000)	531,940	490,540	408,950	442,300	400,100
7.4 Average length of stay of resident tourists in all accommodation establishments	Nights	..	..	..	..	..
OUTBOUND TOURISM						
8.1 **Departures**	('000)	59,377	61,424	64,194	66,494	69,536
8.2 **Tourism expenditure in other countries**	US$ Mn	51,125	58,627	69,463	73,672	78,325
8.3 "Travel" (*)	US$ Mn	41,744	47,853	56,444	59,532	63,319
8.4 "Passenger transport" (*)	US$ Mn	9,381	10,774	13,019	14,140	15,006
TOURISM INDUSTRIES						
Hotels and similar establishments						
9.1 Number of rooms	Units	591,342	599,882	606,881	518,028	593,086
9.2 Number of bed-places	Units	1,188,075	1,203,701	1,223,047	1,062,342	1,201,736
9.3 Occupancy rate	Percent	44.00	44.00	45.00	44.00	47.00
9.4 Average length of stay	Nights	..	..	..	..	..
RELATED INDICATORS						
Share of tourism expenditure (6.1) in:						
10.1 Gross Domestic Product (GDP)	Percent	1.8	1.7	1.7	1.8	1.8
10.2 Exports of goods	Percent	9.9	10.0	10.6	10.3	9.6
10.3 Exports of services	Percent	20.6	19.4	18.8	18.9	18.7

(*) Balance of Payments items: 6.1 to 6.3 correspond to the "Credit" side (and are receipts for the country) while 8.2 to 8.4 correspond to the "Debit" side (and are expenditures in other countries).

UNITED REPUBLIC OF TANZANIA

Basic Indicators		Units	2002	2003	2004	2005	2006
	INBOUND TOURISM						
	Arrivals						
1.1	Visitors	('000)	575	576	583	613	644
1.2	Tourists (overnight visitors)	('000)	550	552	566	590	622
1.3	Same-day visitors	('000)	25	24	17	23	22
1.4	Cruise passengers	('000)	..	..	..	..	..
	Arrivals by region						
2.1	Africa	('000)	250	268	256	276	293
2.2	Americas	('000)	59	50	53	62	71
2.3	Europe	('000)	192	191	222	220	229
2.4	East Asia and the Pacific	('000)	30	27	23	25	28
2.5	South Asia	('000)	28	27	17	20	15
2.6	Middle East	('000)	17	14	12	11	7
	Arrivals by means of transport used						
3.1	Air	('000)	316	320	257	331	359
3.2	Rail	('000)	25	16	5	6	5
3.3	Road	('000)	214	215	297	266	266
3.4	Sea	('000)	20	25	24	10	14
	Arrivals by purpose of visit						
4.1	Leisure, recreation and holidays	('000)	358	337	429	467	524
4.2	Business and professional	('000)	115	133	83	85	71
4.3	Other	('000)	102	106	71	61	49
	Accommodation						
5.1	Overnight stays in hotels and similar establishments	('000)	..	..	..	..	..
5.2	Guests in hotels and similar establishments	('000)	..	..	..	..	..
5.3	Overnight stays in all types of accommodation establishments	('000)	4,459	5,500	5,525	6,130	7,729
5.4	Average length of stay of non-resident tourists in all accommodation establishments	Nights	..	..	..	..	..
6.1	**Tourism expenditure in the country**	US$ Mn	639	654	762	835	950
6.2	"Travel" (*)	US$ Mn	635	647	746	824	914
6.3	"Passenger transport" (*)	US$ Mn	4	7	16	11	36
	DOMESTIC TOURISM						
	Accommodation						
7.1	Overnight stays in hotels and similar establishments	('000)	..	..	..	..	..
7.2	Guests in hotels and similar establishments	('000)	..	..	..	..	..
7.3	Overnight stays in all types of accommodation establishments	('000)	3,971	4,100	4,100	4,500	..
7.4	Average length of stay of resident tourists in all accommodation establishments	Nights	..	..	..	..	..
	OUTBOUND TOURISM						
8.1	**Departures**	('000)	..	..	..	..	
8.2	**Tourism expenditure in other countries**	US$ Mn	361	375	470	577	571
8.3	"Travel" (*)	US$ Mn	337	353	445	554	534
8.4	"Passenger transport" (*)	US$ Mn	24	22	25	23	37
	TOURISM INDUSTRIES						
	Hotels and similar establishments						
9.1	Number of rooms	Units	25,300	30,600	30,840	31,365	..
9.2	Number of bed-places	Units	45,500	55,500	55,932	56,562	..
9.3	Occupancy rate	Percent	51.00	47.00	47.00	48.00	..
9.4	Average length of stay	Nights	11.00	11.00	11.00	12.00	12.00
	RELATED INDICATORS						
	Share of tourism expenditure (6.1) in:						
10.1	Gross Domestic Product (GDP)	Percent	6.5	6.4	6.7	6.6	7.4
10.2	Exports of goods	Percent	65.2	53.8	51.7	49.8	55.1
10.3	Exports of services	Percent	69.5	69.0	67.2	65.8	64.1

(*) Balance of Payments items: 6.1 to 6.3 correspond to the "Credit" side (and are receipts for the country) while 8.2 to 8.4 correspond to the "Debit" side (and are expenditures in other countries).

UNITED STATES

Basic Indicators		Units	2002	2003	2004	2005	2006
INBOUND TOURISM							
Arrivals							
1.1	Visitors	('000)	..	..	..	..	..
1.2	Tourists (overnight visitors)	('000)	43,581	41,218	46,086	49,206	50,978
1.3	Same-day visitors	('000)	..	..	..	..	..
1.4	Cruise passengers	('000)	..	..	..	..	..
Arrivals by region							
2.1	Africa	('000)	241	236	240	252	252
2.2	Americas	('000)	28,036	26,368	29,196	31,178	33,129
2.3	Europe	('000)	8,964	8,982	10,056	10,702	10,531
2.4	East Asia and the Pacific	('000)	5,889	5,192	6,087	6,518	6,428
2.5	South Asia	('000)	324	330	370	411	474
2.6	Middle East	('000)	127	110	137	144	164
Arrivals by means of transport used							
3.1	Air	('000)	24,185	23,076	25,824	27,685	..
3.2	Rail	('000)	..	..	..	..	..
3.3	Road	('000)	18,954	17,759	19,844	21,105	..
3.4	Sea	('000)	386	376	418	419	
Arrivals by purpose of visit							
4.1	Leisure, recreation and holidays	('000)	8,182	8,094	9,592	10,232	..
4.2	Business and professional	('000)	5,792	5,011	5,202	5,637	..
4.3	Other	('000)	5,142	4,921	5,528	5,810	..
Accommodation							
5.1	Overnight stays in hotels and similar establishments	('000)	..	..	..	..	..
5.2	Guests in hotels and similar establishments	('000)	14,911	13,898	16,034	16,975	..
5.3	Overnight stays in all types of accommodation establishments	('000)	..	..	..	..	..
5.4	Average length of stay of non-resident tourists in all accommodation establishments	Nights	..	..	..	..	..
6.1	**Tourism expenditure in the country**	US$ Mn	101,798	99,207	113,387	123,093	128,922
6.2	"Travel" (*)	US$ Mn	84,752	83,316	94,537	102,124	106,736
6.3	"Passenger transport" (*)	US$ Mn	17,046	15,891	18,850	20,969	22,186
DOMESTIC TOURISM							
Accommodation							
7.1	Overnight stays in hotels and similar establishments	('000)	..	..	..	..	..
7.2	Guests in hotels and similar establishments	('000)	..	..	..	..	..
7.3	Overnight stays in all types of accommodation establishments	('000)	..	..	..	..	..
7.4	Average length of stay of resident tourists in all accommodation establishments	Nights	..	..	..	..	..
OUTBOUND TOURISM							
8.1	**Departures**	('000)	58,066	56,250	61,809	63,503	63,662
8.2	**Tourism expenditure in other countries**	US$ Mn	81,707	81,924	94,345	99,439	104,310
8.3	"Travel" (*)	US$ Mn	61,738	60,935	69,627	73,290	76,807
8.4	"Passenger transport" (*)	US$ Mn	19,969	20,989	24,718	26,149	27,503
TOURISM INDUSTRIES							
Hotels and similar establishments							
9.1	Number of rooms	Units	4,397,534	4,415,696	4,411,908	4,402,466	4,389,443
9.2	Number of bed-places	Units	..	..	..	..	..
9.3	Occupancy rate	Percent	59.10	61.10	61.30	63.10	63.30
9.4	Average length of stay	Nights	..	..	..	..	..
RELATED INDICATORS							
Share of tourism expenditure (6.1) in:							
10.1	Gross Domestic Product (GDP)	Percent	1.0	0.9	1.0	1.0	1.0
10.2	Exports of goods	Percent	14.8	13.8	14.0	13.7	12.6
10.3	Exports of services	Percent	35.3	33.0	32.7	32.0	30.8

(*) Balance of Payments items: 6.1 to 6.3 correspond to the "Credit" side (and are receipts for the country) while 8.2 to 8.4 correspond to the "Debit" side (and are expenditures in other countries).

(**) See Annex "Country notes".

UNITED STATES VIRGIN ISLANDS

Basic Indicators		Units	2002	2003	2004	2005	2006
INBOUND TOURISM							
Arrivals							
1.1	Visitors	('000)	2,337	2,395	2,620	2,605	2,575
1.2	Tourists (overnight visitors)	('000)	520	538	544	582	570
1.3	Same-day visitors	('000)	78	83	111	110	101
1.4	Cruise passengers	('000)	1,739	1,774	1,965	1,913	1,904
Arrivals by region							
2.1	Africa	('000)	1	..	..	..	..
2.2	Americas	('000)	494	531	561	569	649
2.3	Europe	('000)	6	8	16	19	15
2.4	East Asia and the Pacific	('000)	..	..	..	..	..
2.5	South Asia	('000)	..	..	..	..	..
2.6	Middle East	('000)	..	..	..	..	..
Arrivals by means of transport used							
3.1	Air	('000)	598	621	655	692	671
3.2	Rail	('000)	..	..	..	..	..
3.3	Road	('000)	..	..	..	..	..
3.4	Sea	('000)	1,739	1,774	1,965	1,913	1,904
Arrivals by purpose of visit							
4.1	Leisure, recreation and holidays	('000)	..	..	..	..	..
4.2	Business and professional	('000)	..	..	..	..	..
4.3	Other	('000)	..	..	..	..	..
Accommodation							
5.1	Overnight stays in hotels and similar establishments	('000)	..	..	..	..	..
5.2	Guests in hotels and similar establishments	('000)	586	623	604	618	701
5.3	Overnight stays in all types of accommodation establishments	('000)	1,057	1,052	1,096	1,094	1,041
5.4	Average length of stay of non-resident tourists in all accommodation establishments	Nights	..	..	..	..	..
6.1	**Tourism expenditure in the country** (**)	US$ Mn	1,195	1,257	1,356	1,491	1,466
6.2	"Travel" (*)	US$ Mn	..	..	..	..	..
6.3	"Passenger transport" (*)	US$ Mn	..	..	..	..	..
DOMESTIC TOURISM							
Accommodation							
7.1	Overnight stays in hotels and similar establishments	('000)	..	..	..	..	..
7.2	Guests in hotels and similar establishments	('000)	65	68	69	80	103
7.3	Overnight stays in all types of accommodation establishments	('000)	..	..	..	..	..
7.4	Average length of stay of resident tourists in all accommodation establishments	Nights	..	..	..	..	..
OUTBOUND TOURISM							
8.1	**Departures**	('000)	..	..	..	..	..
8.2	**Tourism expenditure in other countries**	US$ Mn	..	..	..	..	..
8.3	"Travel" (*)	US$ Mn	..	..	..	..	..
8.4	"Passenger transport" (*)	US$ Mn	..	..	..	..	..
TOURISM INDUSTRIES							
Hotels and similar establishments							
9.1	Number of rooms	Units	5,138	5,045	4,959	4,762	4,817
9.2	Number of bed-places	Units	..	..	..	..	..
9.3	Occupancy rate	Percent	56.60	57.20	61.30	63.80	60.10
9.4	Average length of stay	Nights	4.40	4.40	4.30	4.30	4.30
RELATED INDICATORS							
Share of tourism expenditure (6.1) in:							
10.1	Gross Domestic Product (GDP)	Percent	..	..	..	..	..
10.2	Exports of goods	Percent	..	..	..	..	..
10.3	Exports of services	Percent	..	..	..	..	..

(*) Balance of Payments items: 6.1 to 6.3 correspond to the "Credit" side (and are receipts for the country) while 8.2 to 8.4 correspond to the "Debit" side (and are expenditures in other countries).

(**) See Annex "Country notes".

Basic Indicators	Units	2002	2003	2004	2005	2006
INBOUND TOURISM						
Arrivals						
1.1 Visitors	('000)	1,354	1,508	1,871	1,917	1,824
1.2 Tourists (overnight visitors)	('000)	1,258	1,420	1,756	1,808	1,749
1.3 Same-day visitors	('000)	95	88	115	109	75
1.4 Cruise passengers	('000)	..	..	..	..	..
Arrivals by region						
2.1 Africa	('000)	..	..	..	..	..
2.2 Americas	('000)	1,031	1,160	1,458	1,498	1,403
2.3 Europe	('000)	56	73	97	120	124
2.4 East Asia and the Pacific	('000)	6	6	7	12	13
2.5 South Asia	('000)	..	..	..	..	..
2.6 Middle East	('000)	..	..	..	..	..
Arrivals by means of transport used						
3.1 Air	('000)	299	314	380	406	419
3.2 Rail	('000)	..	..	..	..	6
3.3 Road	('000)	586	649	801	819	624
3.4 Sea	('000)	469	537	691	692	775
Arrivals by purpose of visit						
4.1 Leisure, recreation and holidays	('000)	783	948	1,230	1,249	1,180
4.2 Business and professional	('000)	94	91	128	137	140
4.3 Other	('000)	477	469	513	531	504
Accommodation						
5.1 Overnight stays in hotels and similar establishments	('000)	1,486	1,903	2,673	2,620	2,791
5.2 Guests in hotels and similar establishments	('000)	322	411	557	608	625
5.3 Overnight stays in all types of accommodation establishments	('000)	2,927	3,531	2,938	2,925	3,020
5.4 Average length of stay of non-resident tourists in all accommodation establishments	Nights	7.40	7.10	6.35	4.51	4.51
6.1 **Tourism expenditure in the country**	US$ Mn	409	419	591	699	706
6.2 "Travel" (*)	US$ Mn	351	345	494	594	597
6.3 "Passenger transport" (*)	US$ Mn	58	74	97	105	109
DOMESTIC TOURISM						
Accommodation						
7.1 Overnight stays in hotels and similar establishments	('000)	..	..	..	..	..
7.2 Guests in hotels and similar establishments	('000)	..	..	..	..	..
7.3 Overnight stays in all types of accommodation establishments	('000)	..	..	..	..	..
7.4 Average length of stay of resident tourists in all accommodation establishments	Nights	..	..	..	..	..
OUTBOUND TOURISM						
8.1 **Departures**	('000)	530	495	569	658	666
8.2 **Tourism expenditure in other countries**	US$ Mn	243	236	267	331	306
8.3 "Travel" (*)	US$ Mn	178	169	194	252	213
8.4 "Passenger transport" (*)	US$ Mn	65	67	73	79	93
TOURISM INDUSTRIES						
Hotels and similar establishments						
9.1 Number of rooms	Units	18,060	18,160	19,151	14,729	14,350
9.2 Number of bed-places	Units	41,559	41,759	43,726	26,222	29,604
9.3 Occupancy rate	Percent	..	..	..	..	..
9.4 Average length of stay	Nights	4.40	4.60	4.78	4.31	4.31
RELATED INDICATORS						
Share of tourism expenditure (6.1) in:						
10.1 Gross Domestic Product (GDP)	Percent	3.3	3.7	4.5	4.2	3.7
10.2 Exports of goods	Percent	21.3	18.4	18.8	18.5	16.1
10.3 Exports of services	Percent	54.2	52.2	53.1	53.3	55.0

(*) Balance of Payments items: 6.1 to 6.3 correspond to the "Credit" side (and are receipts for the country) while 8.2 to 8.4 correspond to the "Debit" side (and are expenditures in other countries).

UZBEKISTAN

Basic Indicators		Units	2002	2003	2004	2005	2006
INBOUND TOURISM							
Arrivals							
1.1	Visitors	('000)	..	..	..	..	..
1.2	Tourists (overnight visitors)	('000)	332	231	262	242	281
1.3	Same-day visitors	('000)	..	..	..	..	..
1.4	Cruise passengers	('000)	..	..	..		
Arrivals by region							
2.1	Africa	('000)	1	1	1	..	..
2.2	Americas	('000)	4	2	12	..	..
2.3	Europe	('000)	100	51	69	..	..
2.4	East Asia and the Pacific	('000)	195	145	140	..	..
2.5	South Asia	('000)	8	8	10	..	..
2.6	Middle East	('000)	24	24	30	..	..
Arrivals by means of transport used							
3.1	Air	('000)	296	220	235	217	252
3.2	Rail	('000)	15	10	25	23	27
3.3	Road	('000)	1	1	2	2	2
3.4	Sea	('000)	..	..	..	..	..
Arrivals by purpose of visit							
4.1	Leisure, recreation and holidays	('000)	43	21	34	38	53
4.2	Business and professional	('000)	73	22	37	48	80
4.3	Other	('000)	215	188	190	156	148
Accommodation							
5.1	Overnight stays in hotels and similar establishments	('000)	672	457	487	448	533
5.2	Guests in hotels and similar establishments	('000)	..	..	..	..	..
5.3	Overnight stays in all types of accommodation establishments	('000)	1,069	935	964	840	976
5.4	Average length of stay of non-resident tourists in all accommodation establishments	Nights	3.10	3.10	3.70	2.30	2.20
6.1	**Tourism expenditure in the country** (**)	US$ Mn	68	48	57	..	..
6.2	"Travel" (*)	US$ Mn	22	24	28	28	43
6.3	"Passenger transport" (*)	US$ Mn	46	24	29	..	..
DOMESTIC TOURISM							
Accommodation							
7.1	Overnight stays in hotels and similar establishments	('000)	588	484	667	321	560
7.2	Guests in hotels and similar establishments	('000)	..	..	..	..	..
7.3	Overnight stays in all types of accommodation establishments	('000)	1,497	1,255	1,438	1,312	1,767
7.4	Average length of stay of resident tourists in all accommodation establishments	Nights	..	..	..	..	..
OUTBOUND TOURISM							
8.1	**Departures**	('000)	264	400	455	572	893
8.2	**Tourism expenditure in other countries**	US$ Mn	..	..	..	..	..
8.3	"Travel" (*)	US$ Mn	..	..	..	..	..
8.4	"Passenger transport" (*)	US$ Mn	..	..	..	..	..
TOURISM INDUSTRIES							
Hotels and similar establishments							
9.1	Number of rooms	Units	7,332	7,332	7,332	8,598	9,240
9.2	Number of bed-places	Units	15,670	15,670	15,670	17,152	16,985
9.3	Occupancy rate	Percent	35.20	31.00	31.00	..	..
9.4	Average length of stay	Nights	3.10	3.10	3.70	2.30	2.20
RELATED INDICATORS							
Share of tourism expenditure (6.1) in:							
10.1	Gross Domestic Product (GDP)	Percent	0.7	0.5	0.5	0.4	..
10.2	Exports of goods	Percent	..	..	..	..	..
10.3	Exports of services	Percent	..	..	..	..	..

(*) Balance of Payments items: 6.1 to 6.3 correspond to the "Credit" side (and are receipts for the country) while 8.2 to 8.4 correspond to the "Debit" side (and are expenditures in other countries).

(**) See Annex "Country notes".

Basic Indicators	Units	2002	2003	2004	2005	2006
INBOUND TOURISM						
Arrivals						
1.1 Visitors	('000)	99	102	99	126	154
1.2 Tourists (overnight visitors)	('000)	49	50	61	62	68
1.3 Same-day visitors	('000)	..	..	..	..	..
1.4 Cruise passengers	('000)	50	52	38	64	86
Arrivals by region						
2.1 Africa	('000)	..	..	..	..	..
2.2 Americas	('000)	1	2	2	2	2
2.3 Europe	('000)	3	3	3	3	4
2.4 East Asia and the Pacific	('000)	44	45	55	56	61
2.5 South Asia	('000)	..	..	..	..	..
2.6 Middle East	('000)	..	..	..	..	..
Arrivals by means of transport used						
3.1 Air	('000)	49	50	61	62	68
3.2 Rail	('000)	..	..	..	..	..
3.3 Road	('000)	..	..	..	..	..
3.4 Sea	('000)	50	52	38	64	86
Arrivals by purpose of visit						
4.1 Leisure, recreation and holidays	('000)	39	39	47	48	53
4.2 Business and professional	('000)	6	7	8	8	9
4.3 Other	('000)	4	4	6	6	6
Accommodation						
5.1 Overnight stays in hotels and similar establishments	('000)	334	316	352	..	..
5.2 Guests in hotels and similar establishments	('000)	172	158	179	..	..
5.3 Overnight stays in all types of accommodation establishments	('000)	..	..	..	..	..
5.4 Average length of stay of non-resident tourists in all accommodation establishments	Nights	7.50	9.50	9.10	9.70	9.80
6.1 **Tourism expenditure in the country**	US$ Mn	72	83	93	104	109
6.2 "Travel" (*)	US$ Mn	54	64	75	85	92
6.3 "Passenger transport" (*)	US$ Mn	18	19	18	19	17
DOMESTIC TOURISM						
Accommodation						
7.1 Overnight stays in hotels and similar establishments	('000)	..	..	..	..	..
7.2 Guests in hotels and similar establishments	('000)	..	..	..	..	..
7.3 Overnight stays in all types of accommodation establishments	('000)	..	..	..	..	..
7.4 Average length of stay of resident tourists in all accommodation establishments	Nights	..	..	..	..	..
OUTBOUND TOURISM						
8.1 **Departures**	('000)	11	12	13	14	15
8.2 **Tourism expenditure in other countries**	US$ Mn	11	14	15	13	11
8.3 "Travel" (*)	US$ Mn	9	12	13	11	9
8.4 "Passenger transport" (*)	US$ Mn	2	2	2	2	2
TOURISM INDUSTRIES						
Hotels and similar establishments						
9.1 Number of rooms	Units	993	895	874	886	924
9.2 Number of bed-places	Units	2,662	2,370	2,064	2,382	2,466
9.3 Occupancy rate	Percent	44.20	46.50	51.90	52.30	51.60
9.4 Average length of stay	Nights	7.50	9.50	9.10	9.70	9.80
RELATED INDICATORS						
Share of tourism expenditure (6.1) in:						
10.1 Gross Domestic Product (GDP)	Percent	30.6	29.6	28.2	28.3	28.1
10.2 Exports of goods	Percent	360.0	307.4	244.7	273.7	286.8
10.3 Exports of services	Percent	76.6	74.8	76.2	74.8	74.7

(*) Balance of Payments items: 6.1 to 6.3 correspond to the "Credit" side (and are receipts for the country) while 8.2 to 8.4 correspond to the "Debit" side (and are expenditures in other countries).

VENEZUELA

Basic Indicators		Units	2002	2003	2004	2005	2006
	INBOUND TOURISM						
	Arrivals						
1.1	Visitors	('000)	590	435	618	841	911
1.2	Tourists (overnight visitors)	('000)	432	337	486	706	748
1.3	Same-day visitors	('000)	158	98	..	..	..
1.4	Cruise passengers	('000)	..	..	132	135	163
	Arrivals by region						
2.1	Africa	('000)	1	..	1	1	1
2.2	Americas	('000)	185	154	218	374	412
2.3	Europe	('000)	237	175	258	296	298
2.4	East Asia and the Pacific	('000)	4	3	4	16	17
2.5	South Asia	('000)	..	..	..	2	2
2.6	Middle East	('000)	..	..	..	10	10
	Arrivals by means of transport used						
3.1	Air	('000)	409	335	484	704	723
3.2	Rail	('000)	..	..	..	..	
3.3	Road	('000)	21	..	..	..	23
3.4	Sea	('000)	2	2	2	2	2
	Arrivals by purpose of visit						
4.1	Leisure, recreation and holidays	('000)	124	82	167	173	310
4.2	Business and professional	('000)	230	169	185	273	169
4.3	Other	('000)	78	86	135	260	269
	Accommodation						
5.1	Overnight stays in hotels and similar establishments	('000)	4,694	4,023	..	..	..
5.2	Guests in hotels and similar establishments	('000)	..	..	300	435	360
5.3	Overnight stays in all types of accommodation establishments	('000)	9,126	9,819	..	..	..
5.4	Average length of stay of non-resident tourists in all accommodation establishments	Nights	14.78	14.80	15.60	16.65	18.13
6.1	**Tourism expenditure in the country**	US$ Mn	484	378	554	722	843
6.2	"Travel" (*)	US$ Mn	434	331	502	650	768
6.3	"Passenger transport" (*)	US$ Mn	50	47	52	72	75
	DOMESTIC TOURISM						
	Accommodation						
7.1	Overnight stays in hotels and similar establishments	('000)	..	..	..	..	..
7.2	Guests in hotels and similar establishments	('000)	..	..	..	..	..
7.3	Overnight stays in all types of accommodation establishments	('000)	..	..	..	..	..
7.4	Average length of stay of resident tourists in all accommodation establishments	Nights	..	..	4.04	4.38	4.65
	OUTBOUND TOURISM						
8.1	**Departures**	('000)	881	832	816	1,067	1,095
8.2	**Tourism expenditure in other countries**	US$ Mn	1,546	1,311	1,604	1,843	1,807
8.3	"Travel" (*)	US$ Mn	981	859	1,077	1,276	1,229
8.4	"Passenger transport" (*)	US$ Mn	565	452	527	567	578
	TOURISM INDUSTRIES						
	Hotels and similar establishments						
9.1	Number of rooms	Units	80,022	82,366	84,607	68,819	74,976
9.2	Number of bed-places	Units	174,447	180,556	187,753	157,112	172,433
9.3	Occupancy rate	Percent	..	..	55.94	..	78.93
9.4	Average length of stay	Nights	..	..	..	..	..
	RELATED INDICATORS						
	Share of tourism expenditure (6.1) in:						
10.1	Gross Domestic Product (GDP)	Percent	0.5	0.5	0.5	0.5	0.5
10.2	Exports of goods	Percent	1.8	1.4	1.4	1.3	1.3
10.3	Exports of services	Percent	47.8	43.1	49.7	53.8	53.6

(*) Balance of Payments items: 6.1 to 6.3 correspond to the "Credit" side (and are receipts for the country) while 8.2 to 8.4 correspond to the "Debit" side (and are expenditures in other countries).

Basic Indicators		Units	2002	2003	2004	2005	2006
	INBOUND TOURISM						
	Arrivals						
1.1	Visitors	('000)	2,628	2,429	2,928	3,468	3,583
1.2	Tourists (overnight visitors)	('000)	..	..	..	..	..
1.3	Same-day visitors	('000)	..	..	..	..	..
1.4	Cruise passengers	('000)	309	241	263	200	224
	Arrivals by region						
2.1	Africa	('000)	..	..	..	..	..
2.2	Americas	('000)	304	259	326	397	459
2.3	Europe	('000)	343	294	355	426	481
2.4	East Asia and the Pacific	('000)	1,695	1,670	2,008	2,365	2,361
2.5	South Asia	('000)	..	..	..	..	
2.6	Middle East	('000)	..	..	..	..	..
	Arrivals by means of transport used						
3.1	Air	('000)	1,540	1,395	1,822	2,335	2,702
3.2	Rail	('000)	..	..	..	..	..
3.3	Road	('000)	779	793	843	932	657
3.4	Sea	('000)	309	241	263	200	224
	Arrivals by purpose of visit						
4.1	Leisure, recreation and holidays	('000)	1,460	1,239	1,584	2,042	2,069
4.2	Business and professional	('000)	446	468	522	493	976
4.3	Other	('000)	722	722	822	933	939
	Accommodation						
5.1	Overnight stays in hotels and similar establishments	('000)	..	..	..	..	..
5.2	Guests in hotels and similar establishments	('000)	..	..	..	..	..
5.3	Overnight stays in all types of accommodation establishments	('000)	..	..	..	..	..
5.4	Average length of stay of non-resident tourists in all accommodation establishments	Nights	..	..	..	..	..
6.1	**Tourism expenditure in the country** (**)	US$ Mn	..	1,400	1,700	1,880	3,200
6.2	"Travel" (*)	US$ Mn	..	..	..	..	..
6.3	"Passenger transport" (*)	US$ Mn	..	..	..	..	..
	DOMESTIC TOURISM						
	Accommodation						
7.1	Overnight stays in hotels and similar establishments	('000)	..	..	..	..	..
7.2	Guests in hotels and similar establishments	('000)	..	..	..	..	..
7.3	Overnight stays in all types of accommodation establishments	('000)	..	..	..	..	..
7.4	Average length of stay of resident tourists in all accommodation establishments	Nights	..	..	..	..	..
	OUTBOUND TOURISM						
8.1	**Departures**	('000)	..	..	..	..	..
8.2	**Tourism expenditure in other countries**	US$ Mn	..	..	..	..	..
8.3	"Travel" (*)	US$ Mn	..	..	..	..	..
8.4	"Passenger transport" (*)	US$ Mn	..	..	..	..	..
	TOURISM INDUSTRIES						
	Hotels and similar establishments						
9.1	Number of rooms	Units	..	..	122,114	130,000	142,585
9.2	Number of bed-places	Units	..	..	..	..	
9.3	Occupancy rate	Percent	..	..	..		51.95
9.4	Average length of stay	Nights	..	..	7.70	..	..
	RELATED INDICATORS						
	Share of tourism expenditure (6.1) in:						
10.1	Gross Domestic Product (GDP)	Percent	..	..	..	..	..
10.2	Exports of goods	Percent	..	..	..	..	..
10.3	Exports of services	Percent	..	..	..	..	..

(*) Balance of Payments items: 6.1 to 6.3 correspond to the "Credit" side (and are receipts for the country) while 8.2 to 8.4 correspond to the "Debit" side (and are expenditures in other countries).

(**) See Annex "Country notes".

YEMEN

Basic Indicators		Units	2002	2003	2004	2005	2006
	INBOUND TOURISM						
	Arrivals						
1.1	Visitors	('000)	..	..	..	..	..
1.2	Tourists (overnight visitors)	('000)	98	155	274	336	382
1.3	Same-day visitors	('000)	..	..	..	..	..
1.4	Cruise passengers	('000)	..	..	..	..	..
	Arrivals by region						
2.1	Africa	('000)	3	9	11	13	13
2.2	Americas	('000)	4	13	17	18	19
2.3	Europe	('000)	16	13	29	26	33
2.4	East Asia and the Pacific	('000)	11	16	23	24	19
2.5	South Asia	('000)	..	..	19	16	21
2.6	Middle East	('000)	63	103	176	240	278
	Arrivals by means of transport used						
3.1	Air	('000)	..	..	..	..	..
3.2	Rail	('000)	..	..	..	..	..
3.3	Road	('000)	..	..	..	..	..
3.4	Sea	('000)	..	..	..	..	..
	Arrivals by purpose of visit						
4.1	Leisure, recreation and holidays	('000)	..	..	..	..	..
4.2	Business and professional	('000)	..	..	..	..	..
4.3	Other	('000)	..	..	..	..	..
	Accommodation						
5.1	Overnight stays in hotels and similar establishments	('000)	588	928	1,642	2,017	2,294
5.2	Guests in hotels and similar establishments	('000)	98	155	274	336	382
5.3	Overnight stays in all types of accommodation establishments	('000)	..	..	..	..	..
5.4	Average length of stay of non-resident tourists in all accommodation establishments	Nights	6.00	6.00	6.00	6.00	6.00
6.1	**Tourism expenditure in the country**	US$ Mn	..	..	..	..	..
6.2	"Travel" (*)	US$ Mn	38	139	139	181	181
6.3	"Passenger transport" (*)	US$ Mn	..	..	..	..	..
	DOMESTIC TOURISM						
	Accommodation						
7.1	Overnight stays in hotels and similar establishments	('000)	1,289	3,359	..	4,172	..
7.2	Guests in hotels and similar establishments	('000)	692	597	..	..	..
7.3	Overnight stays in all types of accommodation establishments	('000)	..	..	..	..	..
7.4	Average length of stay of resident tourists in all accommodation establishments	Nights	..	..	..	..	..
	OUTBOUND TOURISM						
8.1	**Departures**	('000)	..	..	..	..	..
8.2	**Tourism expenditure in other countries**	US$ Mn	135	134	183	224	225
8.3	"Travel" (*)	US$ Mn	78	77	126	167	162
8.4	"Passenger transport" (*)	US$ Mn	57	57	57	57	63
	TOURISM INDUSTRIES						
	Hotels and similar establishments						
9.1	Number of rooms	Units	13,301	13,280	12,890	15,265	22,163
9.2	Number of bed-places	Units	31,269	33,816	30,142	34,844	50,381
9.3	Occupancy rate	Percent	..	..	..	..	..
9.4	Average length of stay	Nights	..	..	..	..	..
	RELATED INDICATORS						
	Share of tourism expenditure (6.1) in: (**)						
10.1	Gross Domestic Product (GDP)	Percent	0.4	1.3	1.0	1.1	0.9
10.2	Exports of goods	Percent	1.0	3.5	3.0	2.8	2.5
10.3	Exports of services	Percent	22.9	43.7	37.6	48.7	31.9

(*) Balance of Payments items: 6.1 to 6.3 correspond to the "Credit" side (and are receipts for the country) while 8.2 to 8.4 correspond to the "Debit" side (and are expenditures in other countries).

(**) See Annex "Country notes".

Basic Indicators		Units	2002	2003	2004	2005	2006
	INBOUND TOURISM						
	Arrivals						
1.1	Visitors	('000)	..	..	..	..	..
1.2	Tourists (overnight visitors)	('000)	565	413	515	669	757
1.3	Same-day visitors	('000)	..	..	..	..	..
1.4	Cruise passengers	('000)	..	..	..	..	..
	Arrivals by region						
2.1	Africa	('000)	364	298	367	461	510
2.2	Americas	('000)	34	23	29	38	52
2.3	Europe	('000)	130	71	92	122	143
2.4	East Asia and the Pacific	('000)	34	17	23	40	38
2.5	South Asia	('000)	3	3	4	9	13
2.6	Middle East	('000)	..	..	..	..	..
	Arrivals by means of transport used						
3.1	Air	('000)	71	104	137	164	227
3.2	Rail	('000)	..	..	..	..	..
3.3	Road	('000)	494	309	378	504	530
3.4	Sea	('000)	..	..	..	..	..
	Arrivals by purpose of visit						
4.1	Leisure, recreation and holidays	('000)	152	144	195	206	242
4.2	Business and professional	('000)	248	156	160	253	290
4.3	Other	('000)	165	113	160	210	224
	Accommodation						
5.1	Overnight stays in hotels and similar establishments	('000)	..	..	..	..	..
5.2	Guests in hotels and similar establishments	('000)	..	..	..	..	..
5.3	Overnight stays in all types of accommodation establishments	('000)	..	..	..	..	..
5.4	Average length of stay of non-resident tourists in all accommodation establishments	Nights	8.00	6.00	6.00	6.00	6.00
6.1	**Tourism expenditure in the country**	US$ Mn	..	..	..	..	..
6.2	"Travel" (*)	US$ Mn	64	88	92	98	110
6.3	"Passenger transport" (*)	US$ Mn	..	..	..	..	..
	DOMESTIC TOURISM						
	Accommodation						
7.1	Overnight stays in hotels and similar establishments	('000)	217	241	267	289	310
7.2	Guests in hotels and similar establishments	('000)	..	..	..	..	..
7.3	Overnight stays in all types of accommodation establishments	('000)	..	..	..	..	..
7.4	Average length of stay of resident tourists in all accommodation establishments	Nights	..	..	..	..	..
	OUTBOUND TOURISM						
8.1	**Departures**	('000)	..	..	..	..	..
8.2	**Tourism expenditure in other countries**	US$ Mn	109	115	68	79	96
8.3	"Travel" (*)	US$ Mn	47	49	37	43	53
8.4	"Passenger transport" (*)	US$ Mn	62	66	31	36	43
	TOURISM INDUSTRIES						
	Hotels and similar establishments						
9.1	Number of rooms	Units	5,060	5,202	5,360	5,521	5,667
9.2	Number of bed-places	Units	8,601	8,774	9,115	9,417	9,960
9.3	Occupancy rate	Percent	50.40	53.20	55.20	57.20	61.00
9.4	Average length of stay	Nights	..	..	..	..	..
	RELATED INDICATORS						
	Share of tourism expenditure (6.1) in: (**)						
10.1	Gross Domestic Product (GDP)	Percent	1.7	2.0	1.7	1.3	1.0
10.2	Exports of goods	Percent	6.9	8.1	5.0	4.4	2.9
10.3	Exports of services	Percent	55.7	53.3	39.7	36.0	36.1

(*) Balance of Payments items: 6.1 to 6.3 correspond to the "Credit" side (and are receipts for the country) while 8.2 to 8.4 correspond to the "Debit" side (and are expenditures in other countries).

(**) See Annex "Country notes".

ZIMBABWE

Basic Indicators		Units	2002	2003	2004	2005	2006
	INBOUND TOURISM						
	Arrivals						
1.1	Visitors	('000)	2,041	2,256	1,854	1,559	2,287
1.2	Tourists (overnight visitors)	('000)	..	..	..	..	..
1.3	Same-day visitors	('000)	..	..	..	..	..
1.4	Cruise passengers	('000)	..	..	..	..	..
	Arrivals by region						
2.1	Africa	('000)	1,760	1,942	1,523	1,356	2,083
2.2	Americas	('000)	65	61	75	44	45
2.3	Europe	('000)	150	170	156	113	97
2.4	East Asia and the Pacific	('000)	66	68	90	39	54
2.5	South Asia	('000)	..	12	6	5	4
2.6	Middle East	('000)	..	2	4	2	4
	Arrivals by means of transport used						
3.1	Air	('000)	340	340	330	327	275
3.2	Rail	('000)	..	..	..	..	..
3.3	Road	('000)	1,738	2,016	1,524	1,231	2,012
3.4	Sea	('000)	..	..	..	..	..
	Arrivals by purpose of visit						
4.1	Leisure, recreation and holidays	('000)	..	..	964	970	1,850
4.2	Business and professional	('000)	..	..	593	265	393
4.3	Other	('000)	..	..	297	323	44
	Accommodation						
5.1	Overnight stays in hotels and similar establishments	('000)	..	..	..	..	..
5.2	Guests in hotels and similar establishments	('000)	..	..	..	..	..
5.3	Overnight stays in all types of accommodation establishments	('000)	..	..	..	..	..
5.4	Average length of stay of non-resident tourists in all accommodation establishments	Nights	..	3.00	4.00	3.00	3.00
6.1	**Tourism expenditure in the country** (**)	US$ Mn	76	61	194	99	338
6.2	"Travel" (*)	US$ Mn	..	..	..	..	..
6.3	"Passenger transport" (*)	US$ Mn	..	..	..	..	..
	DOMESTIC TOURISM						
	Accommodation						
7.1	Overnight stays in hotels and similar establishments	('000)	..	..	..	..	..
7.2	Guests in hotels and similar establishments	('000)	..	..	..	..	..
7.3	Overnight stays in all types of accommodation establishments	('000)	..	..	..	..	..
7.4	Average length of stay of resident tourists in all accommodation establishments	Nights	..	..	..	..	..
	OUTBOUND TOURISM						
8.1	**Departures**	('000)	..	..	..	..	..
8.2	**Tourism expenditure in other countries**	US$ Mn	..	..	..	..	..
8.3	"Travel" (*)	US$ Mn	..	..	..	..	..
8.4	"Passenger transport" (*)	US$ Mn	..	..	..	..	..
	TOURISM INDUSTRIES						
	Hotels and similar establishments						
9.1	Number of rooms	Units	5,766	5,766	5,766	5,657	6,022
9.2	Number of bed-places	Units	12,053	12,053	12,053	11,282	11,578
9.3	Occupancy rate	Percent	36.00	38.50	30.00	34.00	22.70
9.4	Average length of stay	Nights	3.00	3.00	4.00	3.00	3.00
	RELATED INDICATORS						
	Share of tourism expenditure (6.1) in:						
10.1	Gross Domestic Product (GDP)	Percent	..	..	..	..	..
10.2	Exports of goods	Percent	..	..	..	..	..
10.3	Exports of services	Percent	..	..	..	..	..

(*) Balance of Payments items: 6.1 to 6.3 correspond to the "Credit" side (and are receipts for the country) while 8.2 to 8.4 correspond to the "Debit" side (and are expenditures in other countries).

(**) See Annex "Country notes".

Annexes

- ➢ Basic references
- ➢ Country notes
- ➢ IMF notes

BASIC REFERENCES

INBOUND TOURISM

Arrivals

When a person visits the same country several times a year, each visit by the same person is counted as a separate arrival. If a person visits several countries during the course of a single trip, his/her arrival in each country is recorded separately. Consequently, arrivals are not necessarily equal to the number of different persons travelling.

Arrivals data correspond to *international visitors* to the economic territory of the country of reference and include both tourists and same-day non-resident visitors.

Data may be obtained from different sources: border statistics derived from administrative records (police, immigration, traffic counts, and other types of controls), border surveys and registrations at accommodation establishments.

Arrivals by region

The aggregate of basic indicators (2.1) to (2.6) does not always correspond to the total of the basic indicators (1.1) or (1.2), due to the exclusion by some countries of "nationals residing abroad" and of "arrivals from other countries of the world".

Accommodation

Overnight stays refers to the number of nights spent by non-resident tourists in accommodation establishments (*guests*). If one person travels to a country and spends five nights there, that makes five tourist overnight stays (or person-nights).

Average length of stay refers to the average number of nights spent by non-resident guests in the country.

Expenditure

Expenditure associated with tourism activity of visitors has been traditionally identified with the travel item of the Balance of Payments (BOP): in the case of inbound tourism, those expenditures associated with non-resident visitors are registered as "credits" in the BOP and refers to "travel receipts".

The new conceptual framework approved by the United Nations Statistical Commission in relation to the measurement of tourism macroeconomic activity (the so-called Tourism Satellite Account) considers that "tourism industries and products" includes transport of passengers. Consequently, a better estimate of tourism-related expenditures by resident and non-resident visitors in an international scenario would be, in terms of the BOP, the value of the travel item plus that of the passenger transport item.

Nevertheless, users should be aware that BOP estimates include, in addition to expenditures associated with visitors, those related to other types of individuals.

The data published should allow international comparability and therefore correspond to those published by the International Monetary Fund (IMF) (and provided by the Central Banks); in the case of a significant difference with data provided to UNWTO by National Tourism Administrations (NTAs), the NTAs data will be given separately in Annex "Country notes".

DOMESTIC TOURISM

Indicators are the same as for Accommodation in Inbound Tourism but referred to resident tourists.

OUTBOUND TOURISM

Departures data correspond to tourists and same-day resident visitors outside the economic territory of the country of reference. As in the case of arrivals, departures are not necessarily equal to the number of different persons travelling.

Indicators on expenditure are equivalent to those for Inbound Tourism but registered as "debits" in the BOP's *travel* and *passenger transport* items.

The data published are also provided by IMF and the same previous warning is applicable.

TOURISM INDUSTRIES

Hotels and similar establishments

The number of *rooms* and *bed-places* refers to the capacity in hotels and similar establishments for providing temporary accommodation to visitors.

Occupancy rate refers to the relationship between available capacity and the extent to which it is used. This rate may refer either to use of rooms or of beds. Occupancy rate is based on the number of overnight stays of both resident and non-resident tourists.

Average length of stay refers to both resident and non-resident overnight stays.

For additional references, visit
http://www.unwto.org/statistics/basic_references/index-en.htm

COUNTRY NOTES

ALBANIA

(1.1,2.2-4.3) Visitors and other travellers; (1.2,5.2,7.2) Arrivals in hotels only; (1.2,5.1-5.4,7.1-74,9.1-9.4/2004-2006) Quarterly survey: hotels with 5 rooms or more; (4.3) Transit.
Sources: (1.1-5.4,7.1-7.4,9.1-9.4) Institute of Statistics - INSTAT; (6.1-6.3,8.2-8.4) International Monetary Fund.

ALGERIA

(1.1,3.1-3.4) Including nationals residing abroad:
2002   736,915
2003   861,373
2004   865,157
2005 1,001,884
2006 1,159,224
(2.1-2.6,4.1,4.2) Excluding nationals residing abroad; (6.1,8.2) The expenditure figures are those provided by the country to UNWTO, which do not appear in the International Monetary Fund data used in the preparation of this edition of the Compendium.
Sources: "Ministère de l'Aménagement du Territoire, de l'Environnement et du Tourisme" and "Office National des Statistiques".

AMERICAN SAMOA

(1.2,2.4,4.1-4.3) Including Western Samoa; (4.3) Visit friends, relatives.
Source: American Samoa Government - Department of Commerce - Statistics Division.

ANDORRA

Source: "Ministerio de Turismo y Medio Ambiente".

ANGOLA

(5.1,5.2,7.1,7.2) Hotels only.
Sources: (1.2-5.3,7.1-7.3,9.1-9.4) "Ministério de Hotelaria e Turismo - Gabinete de Estudos, Planeamento e Estatística"; (6.1-6.3,8.2-8.4) International Monetary Fund.

ANGUILLA

(1.1,3.1-4.3) Arrivals of non-resident visitors at national borders; (1.2,2.2,2.3) Arrivals of non-resident tourists at national borders; excluding nationals residing abroad; (4.3) Same-day visitors (excursionists); (9.1) Hotels, guest houses, apartments/villas; (9.3) Rooms; January-May; (10.2,10.3) This section includes only the "travel" item because the "passenger transport" item was not included in the data provided by the International Monetary Fund for the preparation of this edition of the Compendium.
Sources: (1.1-5.4,9.1-9.4) Statistical Department - Ministry of Finance; (6.2,8.3) International Monetary Fund.

ANTIGUA AND BARBUDA

(1.1) Excluding yacht passenger arrivals; (2.2,2.3,3.1,4.1-4.3) Air arrivals; excluding nationals residing abroad; (3.4) Cruise passengers only; (10.1-10.3) This section includes only the "travel" item because the "passenger transport" item was not included in the data provided by the International Monetary Fund for the preparation of this edition of the Compendium.
Sources: (1.1-5.4,9.1) Ministry of Tourism; (6.2,8.3) International Monetary Fund.

ARGENTINA

Starting 2004, as a result of the importance of the "Survey on International Tourism", the estimates of the series of the "Travel" item of the Balance of Payments were modified. For this reason, the data are not rigorously comparable with those of previous years.
Note 2005-2006: Provisional data.
Sources: (1.2-5.4,7.1,7.2,8.1,9.1-9.3) "Dirección de Estudios de Mercado y Estadística - Secretaría de Turismo de la Nación"; (6.1-6.3,8.2-8.4) International Monetary Fund.

ARMENIA

Sources: (1.2-5.4,7.1-7.4,8.1,9.1-9.4) Tourism Department - Ministry of Trade and Economic Development; (6.1-6.3,8.2-8.4) International Monetary Fund.

ARUBA

(1.2,2.2-4.3) Arrivals of non-resident tourists at national borders; (5.4) Non-resident tourists staying in hotels and similar establishments; (9.3) Rooms.
Sources: (1.1-5.4,9.1-9.3) Aruba Tourism Authority; (6.1-6.3,8.2-8.4) International Monetary Fund.

COUNTRY NOTES

AUSTRALIA

(1.1) Excluding nationals residing abroad and crew members; (1.2,1.3) Arrivals by air; (2.1-4.3) Arrivals of non-resident visitors at national borders; (9.1,9.2/2002-2004) Hotels, motels, guests houses and serviced apartments with 15 rooms or more; (9.1,9.2/2005/2006) Hotels, motels, guests houses and serviced apartments with 5 rooms or more; (9.3) Rooms.
Sources: (1.1-4.3,8.1,9.1-9.4) Australian Bureau of Statistics; (6.1-6.3,8.2-8.4) International Monetary Fund.

AUSTRIA

(1.2-2.6) Non-resident tourists staying in all types of accommodation establishments; (5.1,5.2,7.1,7.2) Including holiday villages; (5.3,7.3) Excluding private accommodation; (8.1) From 2003, new methodology. Including leisure and business trips abroad with at least one overnight stay; (9.1) Hotels only; (9.2) Hotels and holiday villages; (9.3) Based on summer season; (9.4) Average length of stay in hotels and similar establishments; including holiday villages.
Sources: (1.2-5.4,7.1-7.4,8.1,9.1-9.4) Department for Tourism and Historic Objects - Federal Ministry of Economics and Labour; (6.1-6.3,8.2-8.4) International Monetary Fund.

AZERBAIJAN

Sources: (1.2-5.2,7.1,7.2,8.1,9.1,9.2) Ministry of Culture and Tourism; (6.1-6.3,8.2-8.4) International Monetary Fund.

BAHAMAS

(1.2,2.1-2.6,4.1-4.3) Arrivals of non-resident tourists at national borders; (5.2) Arrivals in hotels only; (9.1,9.2) Hotels, apartments, cottages and villas - Licensed properties only; (9.3) Rooms.
Sources: (1.1-5.4,9.1-9.4) Bahamas Ministry of Tourism; (6.1-6.3,8.2-8.4) International Monetary Fund.

BAHRAIN

(1.1,2.1-4.3) Arrivals of non-resident visitors at national borders; excluding nationals residing abroad; (3.1) Arrivals at Bahrain International Airport; (3.3) Arrivals through King Fahad Causeway; (3.4) Arrivals at Mina Salman Port; (5.1,9.1,9.2) Classified hotels only.
Sources: (1.1-5.4,9.1-9.3) Tourism Affairs - Ministry of Information; (6.1-6.3,8.2-8.4) International Monetary Fund.

BANGLADESH

Sources: (1.2-5.4,8.1,9.1-9.3) Bangladesh Parjatan Corporation; (6.1-6.3,8.2-8.4) International Monetary Fund.

BARBADOS

(1.2,2.1-4.3) Arrivals of non-resident tourists at national borders; (9.1,9.2) Hotels, apartment hotels, apartments and cottages, guest houses; (9.3) Rooms.
Note 2006: Provisional data.
Sources: (1.1-5.4,9.1-9.4) Barbados Tourism Authority; (6.1-6.3,8.2-8.4) International Monetary Fund.

BELARUS

(1.2,2.2-2.6) Organized tourism.
Sources: (1.1,3.1-3.3,4.1-4.3) State Committee of Frontier Troops; (1.2,2.2-2.6,5.1,5.2,7.1,7.2,8.1,9.1-9.4) Ministry of Statistics and Analysis; (6.1-6.3,8.2-8.4) International Monetary Fund.

BELGIUM

(1.2,2.1-2.6,4.1-4.3) Non-resident tourists staying in all types of accommodation establishments; (5.1,5.2,7.1,7.2) Hotels only; (9.1,9.2) Hotels and holiday villages.
Sources: (1.2-5.3,7.1-7.3,8.1,9.1,9.2) "Institut National de Statistique"; (6.1-6.3,8.2-8.4) International Monetary Fund.

BELIZE

(1.3) In transit and border permits; (2.2-4.2) Arrivals of non-resident tourists at national borders; (10.1-10.3) This section includes only the "travel" item because the "passenger transport" item was not included in the data provided by the International Monetary Fund for the preparation of this edition of the Compendium.
Sources: (1.1-5.4,7.3,9.1-9.4) Belize Tourist Board; (6.2,8.2-8.4) International Monetary Fund.

BENIN

1.2,2.1-2.6) Arrivals of non-resident tourists at national borders.
Note 2003-2006: Estimates.

Sources: (1.1-5.3,7.3,9.1-9.4) "Direction du développement touristique - Ministère de la culture, de l'artisanat et du tourisme"; (6.1-6.3,8.2-8.4) International Monetary Fund.

BERMUDA

(1.1) Excluding nationals residing abroad; (1.2,2.2-2.4,4.1-4.3) Air arrivals; (5.3) Including overnight stays at private houses; (6.1,8.2) The expenditure figures are those provided by the country to UNWTO, which do not appear in the International Monetary Fund data used in the preparation of this edition of the Compendium; (9.3) Rooms.
Source: Bermuda Department of Tourism.

BHUTAN

(6.1) The expenditure figures are those provided by the country to UNWTO, which do not appear in the International Monetary Fund data used in the preparation of this edition of the Compendium.
Source: Department of Tourism - Royal Government of Bhutan.

BOLIVIA

(1.2) Arrivals of non-resident tourists at national borders; (2.1-2.4) Non-resident tourists staying in hotels and similar establishments; (3.4) Arrivals by lake; (4.1-4.3) Data based on surveys; (5.1-5.4,7.1-7.4,9.1,9.2) Department capitals only; (9.3) Bed-places (hotels); (9.4) Days, hotels and similar establishments, inbound tourism.
Note 2003-2006: Provisional data.
Sources: (1.2-5.4,7.1-7.4,8.1,9.1-9.4) "Viceministerio de Turismo - Ministerio de Producción y Microempresa"; (6.1-6.3,8.2-8.4) International Monetary Fund.

BONAIRE

Sources: (1.1-5.4,9.1-9.4) Tourism Corporation of Bonaire (TCB); (6.2,8.3) Central Bank of the Netherlands Antilles.

BOSNIA AND HERZEGOVINA

(1.2,2.2-2.4) Non-resident tourists staying in all types of accommodation establishments; (2.5,2.6) Less than 500 arrivals; (9.1,9.2) Excluding the Republic Srpska.
Sources: (1.2-5.3,7.3,9.1,9.2) Agency for Statistics of Bosnia and Herzegovina; (6.1-6.3,8.2-8.4) International Monetary Fund.

BOTSWANA

Sources: (1.1-5.2,7.2,9.1-9.4) Department of Tourism - Ministry of Environment, Wildlife and Tourism; (6.1-6.3,8.2-8.4) International Monetary Fund.

BRAZIL

(1.2-4.3) Including nationals residing abroad; (3.4) Including arrivals by river.
Note 2006: Estimates.
Sources: (1.2-4.3,8.1) "Instituto Brasileiro de Turismo (EMBRATUR)"; (6.1-6.3,8.2-8.4) International Monetary Fund.

BRITISH VIRGIN ISLANDS

(1.1-9.4/2004/2005) Estimates; (6.1) The expenditure figures are those provided by the country to UNWTO, which do not appear in the International Monetary Fund data used in the preparation of this edition of the Compendium; (9.3) Rooms.
Source: The Development Planning Unit - Ministry of Finance.

BRUNEI DARUSSALAM

(1.2,2.2-2.4,3.1) Air arrivals; (10.1-10.3) This section includes only the "travel" item because the "passenger transport" item was not included in the data provided by the International Monetary Fund for the preparation of this edition of the Compendium.
Sources: (1.1-5.2,9.1-9.3) Brunei Tourism - Ministry of Industry and Primary Resources; (6.2,8.3) International Monetary Fund.

BULGARIA

(1.3) Transit visitors; (3.4) Sea and inland waterways; (5.1,5.3,5.4,7.1,7.3,9.2-9.4) Covers mainly former Stateowned and Public Sector in accommodation. Considerable part of the private sector (more than 70% in 1998) is not included in the data; (9.2) Hotels only; (9.3) Bed-places in hotels.
Sources: (1.1-5.4,7.1-7.3,8.1,9.2-9.4) National Statistical Institute - State Agency for Tourism; (6.1-6.3,8.2-8.4) International Monetary Fund.

BURKINA FASO

(1.2,2.1-2.6,5.2) Non-resident tourists staying in hotels and similar establishments; (4.1-4.3) Including domestic tourism; (9.3) Rooms.
Sources: (1.2-5.4,7.1,7.2,9.3) "Service de l'analyse statistique et de la Coopération touristique - Ministère de la Culture, des Arts et du Tourisme"; (6.1-6.3,8.2-8.4) "Banque Centrale des Etats de l'Afrique de l'Ouest".

BURUNDI

(1.2-4.3) Arrivals of non-resident tourists at national borders; including nationals residing abroad; (3.4) Arrivals by lake.
Sources: (1.2-4.3,9.1,9.2) "Office National du Tourisme"; (6.1-6.3,8.2-8.4) International Monetary Fund.

CAMBODIA

(1.2) International tourist arrivals by all means of transport; (2.2-2.5,3.1-3.4/2004-2006) Excluding arrivals in the Phreah Vihear Province: 2004: 67,843; 2005: 88,615; 2006: 108,691; (3.3/2002) Arrivals by land and boat; (3.4) Arrivals by boat; (4.1-4.3/2002) Arrivals by air; (4.1/2002) Including arrivals at Siem Reap Airport by direct-flights: 202,791; (4.3/2005/2006) Including arrivals in the Phreah Vihear Province; (5.4) Days.
Sources: (1.2-5.4,8.1,9.1-9.3) Ministry of Tourism; (6.1-6.3,8.2-8.4) International Monetary Fund.

CAMEROON

(1.2,2.1-2.6,5.2) Non-resident tourists staying in hotels and similar establishments.
Sources: (1.2-5.2,7.1,7.2,9.1,9.2) "Ministère du Tourisme"; (6.1-6.3,8.2-8.4) International Monetary Fund.

CANADA

(1.1,1.3) Data based on customs counts and adjusted using questionnaire surveys; (1.2,2.1-4.3) Arrivals of non-resident tourists at national borders; (4.2) Including convention; (8.1) Person-trips (one or more nights).
Note 2006: Provisional data.
Sources: (1.1-4.3,5.3,7.1,7.3,8.1,9.1,9.3) Canadian Tourism Commission and Statistics Canada; (6.1-6.3,8.2-8.4) International Monetary Fund.

CAPE VERDE

(1.2,2.1-2.3) Non-resident tourists staying in hotels and similar establishments.
Sources: (1.2,2.1-2.3,5.1,5.2,7.1,7.2,9.1-9.4) "Instituto Nacional de Estatística" and "Ministério da Economia, Crescimento e Competitividade"; (6.1-6.3,8.2-8.4) International Monetary Fund.

CAYMAN ISLANDS

(1.2,2.2-2.4,4.1-4.3) Arrivals by air; (5.4,9.4) Days; (6.1) The expenditure figures are those provided by the country to UNWTO, which do not appear in the International Monetary Fund data used in the preparation of this edition of the Compendium. Including expenditure by cruise passengers; (5.2,9.1,9.2) Hotels and apartments; (9.3) Hotels (rooms).
Source: Cayman Islands Department of Tourism.

CENTRAL AFRICAN REPUBLIC

(1.2,2.1-2.6,4.1-4.3) Arrivals by air to Bangui only.
Note 2006: Estimates.
Sources: (1.2-5.4,7.1-7.4,8.1,9.1-9.4) (6.1,8.2/2003/2004) "Ministère du Développement du Tourisme et de l'Artisanat"; (6.1,8.2/2002) "Banque des Etats de l'Afrique Centrale (B.E.A.C.)".

CHAD

(1.2,2.1-2.6,5.2) Non-resident tourists staying in hotels and similar establishments; (9.3) Rooms.
Sources: (1.1-5.4,7.1,8.1,9.1-9.4) "Direction des Études et de la Programmation - Ministère du Développement Touristique"; (6.1,8.2) "Banque des Etats de l'Afrique Centrale (B.E.A.C.)".

CHILE

(5.1,5.2,7.1,7.2) Figures for 2005 are not comparable with those of previous years due to a revision of the National Census of Tourism Accommodation Establishments.
Sources: (1.2-5.4,7.1,7.2,8.1,9.1-9.4) "Servicio Nacional de Turismo - SERNATUR"; (6.1-6.3,8.2-8.4) International Monetary Fund.

CHINA

(1.1,2.1-2.6,3.1-3.4) Including ethnic Chinese arriving from "Hong Kong, China", "Macao, China", "Taiwan (Province of China)" and overseas Chinese, of which most same-day visitors are from "Hong Kong, China" and "Macao, China"; (4.1-4.3) Excluding ethnic Chinese arriving from "Hong Kong, China", "Macao, China", "Taiwan (Province of China)" and overseas Chinese; (7.1,9.1,9.2) Only refer to the star-rated hotels; (8.1) Including air crew members and other servicemen; (9.3) Rooms; (9.4) Inbound tourism only.
Sources: (1.1-5.4,7.1,8.1,9.1-9.4) National Tourism Administration; (6.1-6.3,8.2-8.4) International Monetary Fund.

COLOMBIA

1.1,2.1-2.6,3.1-3.4,4.1-4.3) Arrivals of non-resident visitors at national borders. Excluding cruise passengers; (9.3) Rooms.
Note 2006: Provisional data.
Sources: (1.1-4.3,8.1) "Dirección de Extranjería - Departamento Administrativo de Seguridad (DAS)"; (6.1-6.3,8.2-8.4) International Monetary Fund; (9.1-9.3) "Dirección de Turismo - Ministerio de Comercio, Industria y Turismo, Asociación Hotelera de Colombia (COTELCO)".

COMOROS

(6.1,8.2) The expenditure figures are those provided by the country to UNWTO, which do not appear in the International Monetary Fund data used in the preparation of this edition of the Compendium.
Sources: "Direction Nationale de la Promotion du Tourisme et de l'Hôtellerie - Ministère du Transport, Tourisme, Postes et Télécommunications" and "Banque centrale des Comores".

COOK ISLANDS

(1.2,2.2-2.4,4.1-4.3) Air and sea arrivals; (6.1) The expenditure figures are those provided by the country to UNWTO, which do not appear in the International Monetary Fund data used in the preparation of this edition of the Compendium; (9.3) Rooms.
Note 2006: Provisional data.
Source: Cook Islands Tourism Corporation and Cook Islands Statistics Office.

COSTA RICA

(4.1) Pleasure trips and visits to relatives; (5.4) In the central area of the country; (9.3) "Five category" establishments in San José Metropolitan Area (survey).
Sources: (1.1-5.4,8.1,9.1,9.3) "Instituto Costarricense de Turismo"; (6.1-6.3,8.2-8.4) International Monetary Fund.

CROATIA

(1.2,2.2-2.4) Non-resident tourists staying in all types of accommodation establishments; including arrivals in ports of nautical tourism; (3.1-3.4) Arrivals of non-resident visitors at national borders; (3.4/2004) Since 2004 a new methodology and new coverage have been applied and data are not comparable to previous years; (5.3,7.3) Including nights in ports of nautical tourism; (9.4) Internal tourism (domestic and inbound) in all accommodation facilities (including ports of nautical tourism).
Sources: (1.1-5.4,7.1-7.4,9.1-9.4) Central Bureau of Statistics; (6.1-6.3,8.2-8.4) International Monetary Fund.

CUBA

(1.1,2.1-2.6) Arrivals of non-resident visitors at national borders; (1.2,4.1-4.3) Air arrivals; (1.3) Including cruise passengers; (5.1,7.1,9.1,9.2) Hotels, motels & apart-hotels; (5.3,7.3) Hotels, motels, apart-hotels, camping/caravaning and other; (6.1-6.3) The expenditure figures are those provided by the country to UNWTO, which do not appear in the International Monetary Fund data used in the preparation of this edition of the Compendium; (8.1) Including only tours authorized by the "Instituto de Turismo"; (9.3) Rooms.
Source: "Oficina Nacional de Estadísticas".

CURAÇAO

(1.2,1.3,2.2,2.3,3.1,4.1-4.3) Arrivals by air; (3.4) Cruise ship arrivals; (4.1-4.3) Differences in overall totals due to incompletion of items on the E/D card by visitors; (6.1) The expenditure figures are those provided by the country to UNWTO, which do not appear in the International Monetary Fund data used in the preparation of this edition of the Compendium; (9.1) Hotels, guest houses, apartments; (9.3) Rooms.
Source: Curaçao Tourist Board.

CYPRUS

(1.2,2.1-2.6) Arrivals of non-resident tourists at national borders; (1.3) Including transit & cruise passengers; (3.4) Including transit passengers; (5.4) Data extracted from the Tourist Expenditure (Departures) Survey and concerns stay in any type of accommodation; (9.3) Bed-places; (9.4) From 2000 onwards, average length of stay calculations are based on guest nights and arrivals at hotels and similar establishments.
Sources: (1.1-5.4,7.1-7.4,8.1,9.1-9.4) Cyprus Tourism Organization; (6.1-6.3,8.2-8.4) International Monetary Fund.

CZECH REPUBLIC

(1.2,2.1-2.4) Non-resident tourists staying in all types of accommodation establishments.
Sources: (1.2-5.4,7.1-7.4,9.1-9.4) Department of Conception and International Cooperation in Tourism - Ministry for Regional Development; (6.1-6.3,8.2-8.4) International Monetary Fund.

DEMOCRATIC REPUBLIC OF THE CONGO

(1.2,2.1-2.4,4.1-4.3/2002-2004) Arrivals by air only; (9.1) Registered hotels.
Note 2005-2006: Provisional data.
Source: "Office National du Tourisme".

DENMARK

(1.2,2.2-2.4) Non-resident tourists staying in all types of accommodation establishments; (1.2-5.3,7.1-7.3,8.1) New methodology from 2004; (5.2,7.2) Hotels only; (9.1-9.3) Only hotels and holiday dwellings with 40 beds or more; (9.3) Bed-places; (10.1-10.3) This section includes only the "travel" item because the "passenger transport" item was not included in the data provided by the International Monetary Fund for the preparation of this edition of the Compendium.
Sources: (1.1-5.4,7.1-7.4,8.1,9.1-9.3) Statistics Denmark; (6.2,8.3) International Monetary Fund.

DJIBOUTI

(1.2) Non-resident tourists staying in hotels; (9.3) Rooms; (10.1-10.3) This section includes only the "travel" item because the "passenger transport" item was not included in the data provided by the International Monetary Fund for the preparation of this edition of the Compendium.
Sources: (1.2,5.1,5.2,9.1-9.3) "Office national du tourisme"; (6.2,8.2-8.4) International Monetary Fund.

DOMINICA

(1.2,2.2-2.4,4.1-4.3) Arrivals of non-resident tourists at national borders; (3.1,3.4) Arrivals of non-resident visitors at national borders; excluding cruise ships; (5.4) Days; (10.1-10.3) This section includes only the "travel" item because the "passenger transport" item was not included in the data provided by the International Monetary Fund for the preparation of this edition of the Compendium.
Sources: (1.1-5.4,9.1) Central Statistical Office - Ministry of Finance; (6.2,8.3) International Monetary Fund.

DOMINICAN REPUBLIC

(1.2) Arrivals by air only; including nationals residing abroad; (1.4) All arrivals by sea; (2.2-2.4) Arrivals by air; excluding nationals residing abroad; (2.2-2.4,4.1-4.3/2002) Excluding the passengers at Herrera airport; (4.1-4.3) Arrivals by air only; including nationals residing abroad; (9.1,9.2) Hotels; (9.3) Rooms; (10.1-10.3) This section includes only the "travel" item because the "passenger transport" item was not included in the data provided by the International Monetary Fund for the preparation of this edition of the Compendium.
Note 2006: Provisional data.
Sources: (1.1-5.4,8.1,9.1-9.4) "Secretaría de Estado de Turismo"; (6.2,8.2-8.4) International Monetary Fund.

ECUADOR

(1.1) Excluding nationals residing abroad.
Sources: (1.1-3.4,8.1,9.1,9.2) "Ministerio de Turismo"; (6.1-6.3,8.2-8.4) International Monetary Fund.

EGYPT

(1.1,2.1-3.4) Arrivals of non-resident visitors at national borders; (4.1-4.3) Arrivals of non-resident tourists at national borders; (7.1) Hotels only. Main regions only, namely: Cairo, Giza, South Sinai, Red Sea, Luxor, Aswan, Alexandria; (8.1) Travel for tourism and non-tourism purposes (more than 50% for work purpose); (9.3) Rooms.
Sources: (1.1-5.4,7.1-7.4,8.1,9.1-9.4) Ministry of Tourism; (6.1-6.3,8.2-8.4) International Monetary Fund.

EL SALVADOR

(1.2,2.1-4.3) Arrivals of non-resident tourists at national borders; (6.1) The country provides UNWTO with aggregate expenditure figures that differ significantly from the International Monetary Fund data used in the preparation of this edition of the Compendium. The country figures are as follows (US$ million):
2002: 342
2003: 373
2004: 425
2005: 644
2006: 862
This tourism expenditure is obtained based on research carried out jointly with the Central Reserve Bank of El Salvador and the Salvadorian Tourism Corporation aimed at identifying the basic profile of an international tourist visiting El Salvador.

(9.3) Bed-places.
Sources: (1.1-5.4,8.1,9.1-9.4) "Corporación Salvadoreña de Turismo (CORSATUR) - Ministerio de Turismo"; (6.1-6.3,8.2-8.4) International Monetary Fund.

ERITREA

(1.1) Including nationals residing abroad; (2.1-2.6) Excluding nationals residing abroad; (5.1,7.1) Only hotels and similar establishments in the three major towns: Asmara, Karen and Massawa; (6.1) The expenditure figures used were the ones provided by the country to UNWTO, as this data series is more complete than that provided by the International Monetary Fund (IMF) for the preparation of this Compendium; (9.1,9.2/2002-2004) Only major towns of Eritrea; (9.1,9.2/2005) All hotels and similar establishments in Eritrea; (10.1-10.3) It was not possible to complete this section because the "travel" and "passenger transport" items were not included in the data provided by the International Monetary Fund for the preparation of this edition of the Compendium.
Source: Ministry of Tourism.

ESTONIA

(1.1,3.1-3.4) Arrivals of non-resident visitors at national borders; (1.1-1.3,3.1-3.4,8.1/2004) Starting from 2004, border statistics are not collected any more; (1.2/2004-2006) Calculated on the basis of accommodation statistics and "Foreign Visitor Survey" carried out by the Statistical Office of Estonia; (2.1-2.4) Non-resident tourists staying in all types of accommodation establishments; (9.1-9.4) Including the data of health resorts providing accommodation service.
Sources: (1.1-5.4,7.1-7.4,8.1,9.1-9.4) Estonian Tourist Board / Enterprise Estonia; (6.1-6.3,8.2-8.4) International Monetary Fund.

ETHIOPIA

(1.2) Arrivals through all ports of entry; including nationals residing abroad; (2.1-2.6,3.1-3.3,4.1-4.3) Arrivals through all ports of entry; (9.1,9.2/2002/2003/2005) Excluding unclassified hotels; (9.3) Bed-places; (9.4) Ethiopian Fiscal Year.
Sources: (1.2-5.1,9.1-9.4) Ethiopian Tourism Commission; (6.1-6.3,8.2-8.4) International Monetary Fund.

FIJI

(1.2,2.2-4.3) Arrivals of non-resident tourists at national borders; excluding nationals residing abroad; (1.2-4.3,5.4/2004-2006) Provisional data; (5.4) Days; (9.3) Rooms.
Sources: (1.1-5.4,7.1,8.1,9.1-9.3) Fiji Islands Bureau of Statistics; (6.1-6.3,8.2-8.4) International Monetary Fund.

FINLAND

(1.1,2.1-4.3) Arrivals of non-resident visitors at national borders. Border Survey; (1.2) Arrivals of non-resident tourists at national borders; (5.1-5.3,7.1-7.3) Due to a change in the methodology, data for 2004 are not comparable to previous years; (8.1) Overnight trips abroad, including cruises abroad with overnight on board only.
Sources: (1.1-5.4,7.1-7.4,8.1,9.1-9.4) Tourism Statistics - Statistics Finland; (6.1-6.3,8.2-8.4) International Monetary Fund.

FRANCE

(1.1-4.3,5.3) Estimates based on surveys at national borders (1996-2004); (1.1-4.3,5.3,5.4/2005) Break in the series, data not comparable with previous years; (4.1) Holidays and visits to friends, relatives; (4.2) Business, pleasure; (4.3) Transit and other purposes; (5.1,5.2,7.1,7.2,9.1-9.4) 2002/2003: only hotels 0 to 4 stars. 2004-2006: including unclassified hotels. 2006: renewal of the survey, data not comparable with previous years; (5.3,7.3) All types of accommodation; (5.4) Inbound average length of stay; (7.1-7.4/2005/2006) Resident population aged 15 years and above; (9.3) Net room occupancy rate.
2005: Revised data; 2006: Provisional data.
Sources: (1.2-5.4,7.1-7.4,8.1,9.1-9.4) "Bureau des études, des statistiques et des comptes économiques - Direction du Tourisme"; (6.2,8.3) International Monetary Fund; (6.3,8.4) "Banque de France".

FRENCH GUIANA

(1.2,6.1/2005) 2005 survey at Cayenne-Rochambeau airport on departure.
Sources: "Comité du Tourisme de la Guyane" and "INSEE Guyane".

FRENCH POLYNESIA

(1.2,2.2-4.3) Arrivals of non-resident tourists at national borders; excluding nationals residing abroad; (5.2) Hotels only; (5.4,9.4) Days; (9.1) Hotels only; at 31st December of each year; (9.3) Rooms in hotels.
Sources: (1.2-5.4,9.1-9.4) "Service du Tourisme"; (6.1-6.3,8.2-8.4) International Monetary Fund.

GABON

(1.2,2.1,3.1) Arrivals of non-resident tourists at Libreville airport.

COUNTRY NOTES

Sources: (1.1-5.1,8.1,9.1,9.3) "Centre Gabonais de Promotion Touristique (GABONTOUR)"; (6.1-6.3,8.2-8.4) International Monetary Fund.

GAMBIA

(1.2,2.1-2.3,3.1,4.1-4.3) Charter tourists only.
Sources: (1.1-4.3,8.1,9.1-9.4) Gambia Tourism Authority; (6.1-6.3,8.2-8.4) International Monetary Fund.

GEORGIA

(4.1-4.3) Arrivals in hotels only.
Sources: (1.1-4.3,8.1) Department of Tourism and Resorts - Ministry of Economic Development; (5.2,7.2,9.1,9.2) State Department for Statistics - Ministry of Economic Development; (6.1-6.3,8.2-8.4) International Monetary Fund.

GERMANY

(1.2,2.1-2.6) Non-resident tourists staying in all types of accommodation establishments; (9.3) Bed-places; (9.4) Inbound tourism in hotels and similar establishments.
Sources: (1.2-5.4,7.1-7.4,8.1,9.1-9.4) "Statistiches Bundesamt"; (6.1-6.3,8.2-8.4) International Monetary Fund.

GHANA

(1.2) Including nationals residing abroad; (2.1-2.6) Excluding nationals residing abroad.
Sources: (1.2-4.3,9.1-9.3) Ghana Tourist Board and Ministry of Tourism and Modernisation of the Capital City; (6.1-6.3,8.2-8.4) International Monetary Fund.

GREECE

(1.1,3.1-3.4) Arrivals of non-resident visitors at national borders; (1.2,2.1-2.6) Arrivals of non-resident tourists at national borders; information based on administrative data; (3.4) Including cruise passengers.
Sources: (1.1-5.4,7.1-7.4,9.3) National Statistical Service; (6.1-6.3,8.2-8.4) International Monetary Fund; (9.1,9.2) Hellenic Chamber of Hotels.

GRENADA

(1.2,2.1-4.3) Arrivals of non-resident tourists at national borders; (9.1,9.2) Hotels, cottages/apartments and guest houses; (9.3) Rooms; (10.1-10.3) This section includes only the "travel" item because the "passenger transport" item was not included in the data provided by the International Monetary Fund for the preparation of this edition of the Compendium.
Sources: (1.1-5.4,9.1-9.4) Grenada Board of Tourism; (6.2,8.3) International Monetary Fund.

GUADELOUPE

(1.2) Arrivals by air; excluding the north islands (Saint Martin and Saint Barthelemy); (1.2/2003/2004) Non-resident tourists staying in hotels only; (1.2,2.3,3.1/2005) Data based on a survey conducted at Guadeloupe airport; (5.2) Hotels only; (9.1) Hotels; (9.3) Rooms.
Source: "Comité du Tourisme des Îles de la Guadeloupe".

GUAM

(1.2) Air and sea arrivals; (2.2-2.4) Air arrivals only; (4.1-4.3) Civilian air arrivals only; (9.1) Rooms available.
Source: Guam Visitors Bureau.

GUATEMALA

(8.2) The country provides UNWTO with aggregate expenditure figures that differ significantly from the International Monetary Fund data. The country figures are as follows:
2002: 517
2003: 601
2004: 735
2005: 754
2006: 789
Sources: (1.2-4.3,8.1,9.1-9.4) "Instituto Guatemalteco de Turismo - INGUAT"; (6.1-6.3,8.2-8.4) International Monetary Fund.

GUINEA

(1.2,2.1-2.6,4.1-4.3/2003/2005/2006) Arrivals by air at Conakry airport; (5.2) Hotels only; (6.2) The expenditure figures used were the ones provided by the country to UNWTO, as this data series is more complete than that provided by the International Monetary Fund (IMF) for the preparation of this Compendium.

Sources: (1.2-5.4,6.2,9.1-9.4) "Division Observatoire du Tourisme - Ministère du Tourisme, de l'Hôtellerie et de l'Artisanat"; (6.3,8.2-8.4) International Monetary Fund.

GUINEA BISSAU

(1.2,2.1-2.6,4.1-4.3) Arrivals at "Osvaldo Vieira" Airport.
Sources: (1.2-4.3) "Ministério do Turismo e do Ordenamento do Território"; (6.1-6.3,8.2-8.4) International Monetary Fund.

GUYANA

(1.2,2.2,2.3,3.1) Arrivals to Timehri airport only.
Sources: (1.2-3.1) Guyana Tourism Authority; (6.1-6.3,8.2-8.4) International Monetary Fund.

HAITI

(10.1-10.3) This section includes only the "travel" item because the "passenger transport" item was not included in the data provided by the International Monetary Fund for the preparation of this edition of the Compendium.
Sources: (1.1-3.4) "Ministère du Tourisme"; (6.2,8.2-8.4) International Monetary Fund.

HONDURAS

(1.2,2.1-4.3) Arrivals of non-resident tourists at national borders.
Sources: (1.1-5.4,8.1,9.1-9.4) "Instituto Hondureño de Turismo" (6.1-6.3,8.2-8.4) International Monetary Fund.

HONG KONG, CHINA

(6.1-6.3) The expenditure figures used were the ones provided by the country to UNWTO, as this data series is more complete than that provided by the International Monetary Fund (IMF) for the preparation of this Compendium (Source: HKTB Visitors Survey); (8.1) Including Hong Kong residents to Macao and Mainland China; (9.1) Hotels (high/medium tariffs) and hostels/guest houses; (9.3) Rooms.
Sources: (1.1-8.1,9.1,9.3) Hong Kong Tourism Board; (8.3) Census and Statistics Department.

HUNGARY

(1.1/2002/2003) (3.1-3.4) Departures of non-resident visitors; (1.1-1.4,4.1-4.3/2004) New series; (2.1-2.4) Non-resident tourists staying in all types of accommodation establishments; (3.4) By river; (9.3) Rooms, July-June.
Sources: (1.1-5.4,7.1-7.4,8.1,9.1-9.4) Hungarian Central statistical Office; (6.1-6.3,8.2-8.4) International Monetary Fund.

ICELAND

(1.2,2.1-2.4) Non-resident tourists staying in all types of accommodation establishments; (3.1,3.4) Arrivals of non-resident tourists at the Icelandic borders.
Note: Due to the introduction of Schengen in March 2001, the data collection on arrivals and departures at the Icelandic borders was changed. From 2002 this data collection is done by the Icelandic Tourist Board.
Sources: (1.2-2.4,5.1-5.4,7.1-7.4,9.1-9.4) "Hagstofa Íslands Statistics Iceland"; (3.1,3.4) Icelandic Tourist Board; (6.1-6.3,8.2-8.4) International Monetary Fund.

INDIA

(1.2,2.1-4.2) Arrivals of non-resident tourists at national borders; excluding nationals residing abroad; (4.1) Including other purposes; (8.1) Departures of nationals only, irrespective of purpose; (9.1,9.2) In classified hotels; (9.3) Rooms.
Sources: (1.1-4.2,8.1,9.1-9.3) Market Research Division - Government of India; (6.1-6.3,8.2-8.4) International Monetary Fund.

Short Note on Revision of Methodology for estimation of month-wise Foreign Exchange Earnings (FEE) from Tourism in India

1.   The Reserve Bank of India (RBI), the central bank of India, compiles the official estimates of Foreign Exchange Earnings (FEE) from Tourism on a quarterly basis as a part of Balance of Payment (BOP) statistics. The preliminary quarterly estimate, released with a time lag of 3 months, generally gets revised two times – and is termed as partially revised (PR) estimate – before being finally revised. In order to prepare the monthly estimates of FEE from tourism with a lag of not more than one week, the Ministry of Tourism (MOT) had developed a methodology. The main inputs in this methodology were –norms of FEE per visitor from Bangladesh and Pakistan; ratio of total FEE from tourism and foreign tourist arrivals (FTAs) from countries other than Bangladesh and Pakistan; the total number of FTAs in the month for which FEE estimates need to be compiled; and the wholesale price index (WPI). This method had two major deficiencies. Firstly, the norms of FEE per visitor from Bangladesh and Pakistan were based on very old figures. Secondly, the ratio of total FEE from tourism per visitor from countries other than Bangladesh and Pakistan, which was derived from the FEE data of RBI, was not updated on a continuous basis using the latest available final figures. These deficiencies resulted in MOT estimates being substantially lower than the RBI estimates, and this underestimation increased from 9% in 2000 to 26% in 2003 and further to 36% in 2006.

2.   To ensure the minimum possible variation with the final estimates of FEE from tourism provided by the RBI, the methodology used by MOT was revised from December 2007. The basic steps involved in the revised methodology are as follow:

(i)   Latest quarterly partially revised estimate of FEE from tourism available from the RBI is apportioned by using the monthly figures of FTAs in that quarter to obtain the monthly estimates of the FEE.

(ii)   The ratio of FEE and FTAs for the last month of the quarter mentioned in step (i) is inflated using the Consumer Price Index number for Urban Non-Manual Employees (CPI-UNME) to have the ratio for the latest month for which FEE estimates are being prepared.

(iii)   The ratio mentioned in step (ii) is multiplied by the number of FTAs for the month to get the estimate of FEE in Indian Rupee (INR) terms for that month.   Such estimates are termed as advance estimates.

(iv)   Foreign exchange rate available from the RBI is used to convert the FEE estimate in INR terms to US $ terms.

(v)   As soon as the partially revised estimate of FEE for a more recent quarter becomes available from the RBI, the same is used for working out the monthly estimates for subsequent months.

3.   Advance estimates of FEE for a year will be revised twice in a year when the partially revised estimates for different quarters of that year become available from the RBI. These revised figures will be further revised to obtain the final figures when the finally revised estimates for all the quarters of the year become available from the RBI.

4.   Based on the new methodology, MOT's estimates of FEE from tourism have been revised for the years from 2000 onwards. The adoption of the new methodology has reduced the variation in MOT's advance estimates and RBI figures to the level of about 5% in place of the earlier divergence of up to 40%. A comparison of the estimates of FEE on the basis of the new and the earlier methodologies is given below.

| | | | (US $ million) |
Year	New Methodology	Earlier Methodology	% Variation
(1)	(2)	(3)	(4)
2000	3460	3168	9.2%
2001	3198	3042	5.1%
2002	3103	2923	6.2%
2003	4463	3533	26.3%
2004	6170	4769	29.4%
2005	7493 *	5731	30.7%
2006	8934 *	6569	36.0%
2007	11956 #	8255	44.8%

* Revised Estimates, # Advance Estimates

5.   As the new methodology will be using continuously the latest quarterly partially revised figures of FEE available from the RBI, the divergence between the estimates of MOT and RBI is likely to be minimal in future also.

6.   Details of the methodology are available on the website of Ministry of Tourism, Government of India (www.tourism.gov.in).

INDONESIA

(5.2,5.4,7.2,7.4,9.3,9.4) Classified hotels only; (9.1,9.2) All forms of commercial accommodation; (9.3) Rooms.
Sources: (1.2-5.4,7.2,7.4,8.1,9.1-9.4) Ministry of Culture and Tourism and BPS Statistics Indonesia; (6.1-6.3,8.2-8.4) International Monetary Fund.

IRAN, ISLAMIC REPUBLIC OF

(3.3) Including rail; (5.2,7.2) Hotels only; (9.1,9.2) Hotels only, 21 March-20 March; (9.3) Estimates (Bed-places).
Sources: (1.2-5.4,7.1-7.4,8.1,9.1-9.4) Iran Cultural Heritage and Tourism Organization (ICHTO); (6.1-6.3,8.2-8.4) Central Bank of Islamic Republic of Iran.

IRELAND

(1.2,2.3,3.3,4.1-4.3,5.4) Including tourists from North Ireland; (3.3) Including rail; (8.1) Including same-day visitors; (9.1) Excluding hostels; (9.3) Rooms, hotels only.
Sources: (1.2-5.4,7.1-7.4,8.1,9.1-9.3) Fáilte Ireland; (6.1-6.3,8.2-8.4) International Monetary Fund.

ISRAEL

(1.1) Arrivals of non-resident visitors at national borders; excluding nationals residing abroad; (1.2,2.1-4.3) Arrivals of non-resident tourists at national borders; excluding nationals residing abroad; (3.3) Including tourists' reentry after a visit of up to 7 days in Sinai; (3.4) Including US Navy personnel on courtesy visits; (4.3) Including visit friends and relatives and pilgrimage; (5.1) Tourist hotels and aparthotels; (6.2) Including the expenditures of foreign workers in Israel (US$ Million):
2002: 1,125
2003:   997
2004:   904
2005:   847
2006:   909
(9.3) Bed-occupancy in hotels and similar establishments open; (9.4) Inbound tourism in tourist hotels.
Sources: (1.1-5.4,7.1-7.3,8.1,9.1-9.4) Ministry of Tourism; (6.1-6.3,8.2-8.4) International Monetary Fund.

ITALY

(1.1,3.1-4.3) Arrivals of non-resident visitors at national borders; excluding seasonal and border workers; (1.1-4.3,8.1) Border survey of the "Ufficio Italiano dei Cambi"; (1.2,2.1-2.6) Arrivals of non-resident tourists at national borders; excluding seasonal and border workers; (1.3) Including cruise passengers; (5.1,5.2) Hotels only; (8.1) Number of resident tourists (overnight visitors) abroad; (9.3) Bed-places.
Sources: (1.1-4.3,8.1) "Ufficio Italiano dei Cambi"; (5.1-5.4,7.1-7.4,9.1-9.4) "Statistiche sul Turismo - Istituto Nazionale di Statistica (ISTAT)"; (6.1-6.3,8.2-8.4) International Monetary Fund.

JAMAICA

(1.2,2.1-4.3) Arrivals of non-resident tourists by air; including nationals residing abroad; E/D cards; (5.3) Data obtained by multiplying the average length of stay by number of stopovers of each country of origin; (5.4) Intended length of stay; (9.3) Rooms; (9.4) Hotel nights only.
Sources: (1.1-5.4,9.1-9.4) Jamaica Tourist Board; (6.1-6.3,8.2-8.4) International Monetary Fund.

JAPAN

(1.1,2.1-2.6,4.1-4.3) Arrivals of non-resident visitors at national borders; excluding nationals residing abroad; (3.1,3.4) Arrivals of non-resident visitors at national borders; including foreign residents in Japan; (5.4) Days; (6.2,8.3/2003) The calculation method has been changed since January 2003; (6.2,8.3/2006) The calculation method has been changed since January 2006; (7.1,9.1/2005) Data are not available from 2005; (9.1) Government registered and unregistered hotels and "ryokans" (inns); (9.3) Occupancy rate of major government registered hotels (rooms); (9.3/2006) Data are not available from 2006.
Sources: (1.1-5.4,7.1,8.1,9.1,9.3) Japan National Tourist Organization; (6.1-6.3,8.2-8.4) International Monetary Fund.

JORDAN

(1.1-1.3) Including nationals residing abroad; (2.1-2.6) Arrivals of non-resident tourists at national borders; excluding nationals residing abroad; (3.1-3.4) Arrivals of resident and non resident visitors; (5.4) For organized tours only; (9.3) Rooms.
Sources: (1.1-5.4,7.1-7.4,8.1,9.1-9.4) Ministry of Tourism and Antiquities; (6.1-6.3,8.2-8.4) International Monetary Fund.

KAZAKHSTAN

(2.1-2.6,3.1-4.3) Arrivals of non-resident visitors at national borders.
Sources: (1.1-5.4,7.1,8.1,9.1-9.3) Agency of Statistics of the Republic of Kazakhstan; (6.1-6.3,8.2-8.4) International Monetary Fund.

KENYA

(1.1,2.1-4.3) Arrivals of non-resident visitors from all border entry points; excluding nationals residing abroad; (9.3) Bed-places; (9.4) Days.
Sources: (1.1-5.4,7.1,7.4,9.1-9.4) Kenya Tourist Board; (6.1-6.3,8.3) International Monetary Fund.

KIRIBATI

(1.2,2.2-2.4,3.1) Air arrivals. 2002/2003/2006: Tarawa and Christmas Island. 2004/2005: Tarawa only; (4.1-4.3) Air arrivals. Tarawa only.
Source: Kiribati National Tourism Office, Ministry of Communication, Transport and Tourism Development.

KOREA, REPUBLIC OF

(1.1) Including nationals residing abroad and crew members; (2.1-2.6) Excluding nationals residing abroad; (3.1,3.4/2002-2005) Excluding overseas Koreans and crew members; (8.2) The country provides UNWTO with aggregate expenditure figures that differ significantly from the International Monetary Fund data used in the preparation of this edition of the Compendium (excluding expenses of students studying overseas). The country figures are as follows:

2002: 9,038
2003: 8,248
2004: 9,856
2005: 12,025
2006: 14,336
(9.1) Hotels only; (9.3) Rooms.
Sources: (1.1-5.4,8.1,9.1,9.3) Ministry of Culture and Tourism; (6.1-6.3,8.2-8.4) International Monetary Fund.

KUWAIT

(1.1,2.1-2.6,3.1-3.4) Arrivals of non-resident visitors at national borders; (1.2,4.1-4.3) Non-resident tourists staying in hotels and similar establishments.
Sources: (1.1-5.4,8.1,9.1,9.2) Ministry of Planning; (6.1-6.3,8.2-8.4) International Monetary Fund.

KYRGYZSTAN

(1.2,2.2-2.5,8.1/2003-2006) New data source: Department of Customs Control.
Sources: (1.1-5.2,7.1,7.2,8.1,9.1,9.2) National Statistical Committee; (6.1-6.3,8.2-8.4) International Monetary Fund.

LAO PEOPLE'S DEMOCRATIC REPUBLIC

(1.2) Arrivals of non-resident tourists at national borders; (2.2-2.5,3.1,3.3,4.1-4.3) Arrivals of non-resident visitors at national borders; (5.4) Days; (10.1-10.3) This section includes only the "travel" item because the "passenger transport" item was not included in the data provided by the International Monetary Fund for the preparation of this edition of the Compendium.
Source: National Tourism Authority.

LATVIA

(1.1,3.1-3.4) Arrivals of non-resident visitors at national border. Data by State Border Guard. (1.2-1.4,2.1-2.6,4.1-4.3) Non-resident departures. Survey of persons crossing the state border; (1.3) Including cruise passengers; (4.3) Including visit friends and relatives and health treatment; (5.3,7.3) Overnight stays in all collective accommodation establishments; (5.4) Average length of stay of overnight non-resident visitors; survey of persons crossing the state border; (8.1) Data by State Border Guard; (9.3) Bed-places.
Sources: (1.1-5.4,7.1-7.4,8.1,9.1-9.4) Transport and Tourism Statistics Section - Central Statistical Bureau; (6.1-6.3,8.2-8.4) International Monetary Fund.

LEBANON

(1.2) Excluding Syrian nationals.
Sources: (1.2-5.4,9.1-9.3) "Ministère du Tourisme"; (6.1-6.3,8.2-8.4) International Monetary Fund.

LESOTHO

(1.1,2.1-4.3) Arrivals of non-resident visitors at national borders; (10.1-10.3) This section includes only the "travel" item because the "passenger transport" item was not included in the data provided by the International Monetary Fund for the preparation of this edition of the Compendium.
Sources: (1.1-4.3,9.1-9.4) Lesotho Tourism Development Corporation; (6.2,8.2-8.4) International Monetary Fund.

LIBYAN ARAB JAMAHIRIYA

(1.1,2.1-2.6) Including all travellers (visitors and other travellers not defined as visitors by UNWTO); (3.1-3.4) Arrivals of non-resident visitors at national borders; (4.1-4.3) Arrivals of non-resident tourists at national borders.
Note 2002-2004: Preliminary data.
Sources: (1.1-5.4,7.3,9.1-9.3) General People's Committee for Tourism; (6.1-6.3,8.2-8.4) International Monetary Fund.

LIECHTENSTEIN

(1.2,2.1-2.4) Non-resident tourists staying in hotels and similar establishments; (9.3) Bed-places.
Source: "Liechtenstein Tourismus".

LITHUANIA

(2.1-2.4) Non-resident tourists staying in all types of accommodation establishments; (3.1-3.4,4.1-4.3) Arrivals of non-resident tourists at national borders; (5.1,5.2,7.1,7.2,9.1,9.2) Hotels and motels; (9.3) Rooms.
Sources: (1.1-5.4,7.1-7.4,8.1,9.1-9.4) Lithuanian State Department of Tourism; (6.1-6.3,8.2-8.4) International Monetary Fund.

LUXEMBOURG

(1.2,2.2,2.3) Non-resident tourists staying in all types of accommodation establishments; including youth hostels, tourist private accommodation and others; (5.1,7.1) Nights in hotels, inns and guest houses; (5.3,7.3) Including tourist private accommodation and others; (9.3) Rooms.
Sources: (1.2-5.4,7.1-7.4,9.1-9.4) "Office National du Tourisme" and "STATEC"; (6.1-6.3,8.2-8.4) International Monetary Fund.

MACAO, CHINA

(1.1,2.1-4.3) Arrivals of non-resident visitors at national borders; (1.1-1.3,2.4,3.1-3.4) Including ethnic Chinese arriving from "Hong Kong, China"; (1.2,1.3) Estimates; (3.1) Including entrees by helicopter; (6.1) The expenditure figures used were the ones provided by the country to UNWTO, as this data series is more complete than that provided by the International Monetary Fund (IMF) for the preparation of this Compendium. Including gambling receipts; (8.1) Package tours; (9.1,9.2) Hotels, guest houses and pousadas (inns); (9.3) Rooms; (10.1-10.3) It was not possible to complete this section because the "travel" and "passenger transport" items were not included in the data provided by the International Monetary Fund for the preparation of this edition of the Compendium.
Source: Macau Government Tourist Office and Statistics and Census Service.

MADAGASCAR

(1.2,2.1-2.4,3.1,4.1-4.3) Arrivals of non-resident tourists by air; (9.3) Rooms.
Sources: (1.2-5.4,9.1-9.4) "Ministère des Transports et du Tourisme"; (6.1-6.3,8.2-8.4) International Monetary Fund.

MALAWI

(1.2-4.3) Departures; (5.3/2004) Provisional data; (9.3) Bed-places.
Sources: (1.2-5.4,9.1-9.4) Ministry of Information and Tourism; (6.1-6.3,8.2-8.4) Reserve Bank of Malawi.

MALAYSIA

(1.2,2.1-2.6) Arrivals of non-resident tourists at national borders; including Singapore residents crossing the frontier by road through Johore Causeway; (3.1-3.4,4.1-4.3) Peninsular Malaysia only; (8.1) Outgoing Peninsular Malaysians, including departures via Johore Causeway by road; (9.1) Hotels with 10 rooms and above; (9.3) Rooms.
Sources: (1.1-5.2,7.2,8.1,9.1,9.3) Tourism Malaysia; (6.1-6.3,8.2-8.4) International Monetary Fund.

MALDIVES

(1.2,2.1-2.6) Air arrivals; (5.1,9.1-9.4) Tourist resorts and hotels; (9.4) Days; (10.1-10.3) This section includes only the "travel" item because the "passenger transport" item was not included in the data provided by the International Monetary Fund for the preparation of this edition of the Compendium.
Sources: (1.2-5.1,8.1,9.1-9.4) Ministry of Tourism; (6.2,8.2-8.4) International Monetary Fund.

MALI

(1.2) Arrivals by air; (2.1-2.6) Non-resident tourists staying in hotels and similar establishments; (9.3) Rooms.
Sources: (1.2-5.4,7.1-7.4,9.1-9.4) "Office malien du tourisme et de l'hôtellerie (O.MA.T.HO)"; (6.1-6.3,8.2-8.4) International Monetary Fund.

MALTA

(1.2,2.1-2.6,3.1,3.4/2002/2003) Arrivals of non-resident tourists at national borders; (1.2,2.2-2.6,3.1,3.4/2004-2006) Departures by air and by sea; (4.1-4.3,5.1-5.3/2003-2006) Tourist departures by air; (8.1/2002-2004) By air only; (9.3) Bed-places.
Sources: (1.1-5.4,8.1,9.2-9.4) Malta Tourism Authority and National Statistics Office; (6.1-6.3,8.2-8.4) International Monetary Fund.

MARSHALL ISLANDS

(1.2,2.2-2.4,4.1-4.3/2002/2003/2006) Air arrivals; (1.2,2.2-2.4,4.1-4.3/2004/2005) Air and sea arrivals; (6.1,8.2) The expenditure figures are those provided by the country to UNWTO, which do not appear in the International Monetary Fund data used in the preparation of this edition of the Compendium. Fiscal years (October 1 to September 30).
Source: Marshall Islands Visitors Authority.

MARTINIQUE

(1.2,2.2,2.3,4.1-4.3) Arrivals of non-resident tourists at national borders; (6.1) The expenditure figures are those provided by the country to UNWTO, which do not appear in the International Monetary Fund data used in the preparation of this edition of the Compendium; (9.1) Hotels and holiday villages (Club Méditerranée); (9.3) Rooms in hotels and similar establishments.
Source: "Comité Martiniquais du Tourisme".

MAURITIUS

(1.2,2.1-3.4) Arrivals of non-resident tourists at national borders; (4.1-4.3) Arrivals of non-resident visitors at national borders; (5.4) Large hotels; (9.3) Rooms.
Sources: (1.1-5.4,8.1,9.1-9.3) Ministry of Tourism and Leisure; (6.1-6.3,8.2-8.4) International Monetary Fund.

MEXICO

(1.2,2.2-4.3) Arrivals of non-resident tourists at national borders; including nationals residing abroad; (1.3) Including visitors of the US border zone with a length of stay under 24 hours; (2.2/2004) United States and Canada only; (2.2,2.3/2002-2004) Data compiled by country of residence; (2.2-2.4/2005/2006) Data compiled by nationality; (2.4/2005/2006) Japan and Republic of Korea only; (3.3) Including rail; (5.1) Selected tourism resorts; (5.2,7.2) Hotels only; (9.3) Rooms; (9.4) Foreign tourism only. 2006: Preliminary data.
Sources: (1.1-5.4,7.1,7.2,8.1,9.1-9.4) "Secretaría de Turismo de México (SECTUR)"; (6.1-6.3,8.2-8.4) International Monetary Fund.

MICRONESIA (FEDERATED STATES OF)

(1.2,2.2-2.4,4.1-4.3) Arrivals in the States of Kosrae, Chuuk, Pohnpei and Yap; excluding FSM citizens; (6.1,8.2) The expenditure figures are those provided by the country to UNWTO, which do not appear in the International Monetary Fund data used in the preparation of this edition of the Compendium. Fiscal years (October 1 to September 30).
Source: Department of Economic Affairs.

MONACO

(1.2,2.1-4.2) Non-resident tourists staying in hotels and similar establishments.
Source: "Direction du Tourisme et des Congrès".

MONGOLIA

(1.2,2.1-2.5,4.1-4.3) Arrivals of non-resident tourists at national borders. Excluding diplomats and foreign residents in Mongolia.
Sources: (1.1-4.3) Tourism Department - Ministry of Road, Transport and Tourism; (6.1-6.3,8.2-8.4) International Monetary Fund.

MONTENEGRO

(1.2,2.2-2.4) Non-resident tourists staying in all types of accommodation establishments.
Source: MONSTAT - Statistical Office of the Republic of Montenegro.

MONTSERRAT

(10.2,10.3) This section includes only the "travel" item because the "passenger transport" item was not included in the data provided by the International Monetary Fund for the preparation of this edition of the Compendium.
Sources: (1.1-5.2) Statistics Department Montserrat; (6.2,8.3) International Monetary Fund.

MOROCCO

(1.2,3.1-4.3) Arrivals of non-resident tourists at national borders; including nationals residing abroad; (2.1-2.6) Arrivals of non-resident tourists at national borders; excluding nationals residing abroad; (5.1,5.2,7.1,7.2,9.1-9.3) Classified hotels, holiday villages and tourist residences; (9.3) Rooms; (9.4) Foreign tourists.
Sources: (1.1-5.2,7.1,7.2,8.1,9.1-9.4) "Ministère du tourisme"; (6.1-6.3,8.2-8.4) International Monetary Fund.

MOZAMBIQUE

Sources: (1.1-4.3,9.1-9.4) Ministry of Tourism; (5.1,5.2,7.1,7.2) "Instituto Nacional de Estatística"; (6.1-6.3,8.2-8.4) International Monetary Fund.

MYANMAR

(1.2,2.2-2.6) Including tourist arrivals through border entry points to Yangon; (4.1-4.3) Arrivals of non-resident visitors at national borders; (5.1,9.4) State-run hotels and similar establishments only; (9.1,9.2) State-run hotels and private registered guest houses; (9.3) Rooms.
Sources: (1.1-5.4,9.1-9.4) Ministry of Hotels and Tourism; (6.1-6.3,8.2-8.4) International Monetary Fund.

NAMIBIA

(2.1-4.3) Arrivals of non-resident tourists at national borders; (2.2) United States only; (2.4) Australia only; (9.3) Bed-places.
Sources: (1.1-5.4,7.1-7.4,9.1-9.4) Ministry of Environment and Tourism; (6.1-6.3,8.3) International Monetary Fund.

COUNTRY NOTES

NEPAL

(1.2) Including arrivals from India; (3.3) Land; (9.1,9.2) Hotels in Kathmandu and in the interior of the country; (9.1,9.2/2006) Excluding hotels under construction.
Sources: (1.2-5.4,8.1,9.1,9.2) Nepal Tourism Board; (6.1-6.3,8.2-8.4) International Monetary Fund.

NETHERLANDS

(1.2-2.4) Non-resident tourists staying in all types of accommodation establishments; (5.1,7.1) Hotels and boarding houses; (8.1) Holiday departures of nationals; (8.1/2002) New survey; (9.2) Hotels; (9.3) Bed-places; (9.4) All types of accommodation establishments.
Sources: (1.2-5.4,7.1-7.3,8.1,9.1-9.4) Statistics Netherlands; (6.1-6.3,8.2-8.4) International Monetary Fund.

NEW CALEDONIA

(1.2,2.1-4.3) Including nationals residing abroad; (4.1) Holidays and visit relatives; (4.2) Business only; (5.1,5.2,7.1,7.2) Hotels in Noumea only; (8.1) Returning residents; (9.3) Rooms in Noumea; (9.4) Days, hotels in Noumea; (10.2,10.3) This section includes only the "travel" item because the "passenger transport" item was not included in the data provided by the International Monetary Fund for the preparation of this edition of the Compendium.
Sources: (1.1-5.4,7.1,7.2,8.1,9.1-9.4) "Institut de la Statistique et des Études Économiques (ISEE)"; (6.2,8.3) International Monetary Fund.

NEW ZEALAND

(1.1,3.1-4.3) Arrivals of non-resident visitors at national borders; including nationals residing abroad; (2.1-2.6) Arrivals of non-resident visitors at national borders; excluding nationals residing abroad; (5.3,7.3) Estimated from total guest nights in commercial accommodation establishments with an annual turnover at least NZ$30,000, based on average percentage of international and domestic guests in Jan, Apr, Jul and Oct; (8.1) Short-term departures of NZ residents (calendar year); (9.1) Refer to "staying units" capacity in hotels, motels and hosted guest houses; (10.1-10.3) This section includes only the "travel" item because the "passenger transport" item was not included in the data provided by the International Monetary Fund for the preparation of this edition of the Compendium.
Sources: (1.1-5.3,7.3,8.1,9.1-9.4) Ministry of Tourism; (6.2,8.3) International Monetary Fund.

NICARAGUA

(1.2,2.1-4.3) Arrivals of non-resident tourists at national borders; (1.2/2002-2004) (2.1-2.5) Excluding nationals residing abroad; (1.2/2005/2006) Including nationals residing abroad; (5.1,7.1) Main accommodation establishments in the country (7); (5.3,7.3) Total number of establishments in the country; (9.1,9.2) Hotels and similar establishments classified in higher categories; (9.4) All types of accommodation establishments, inbound tourism.
Note 2006: (1.1-4.3,8.1) Preliminary estimates.
Sources: (1.1-5.4,7.1-7.4,8.1,9.1-9.4) "Instituto Nicaragüense de Turismo (INTUR)"; (6.1-6.3,8.2-8.4) International Monetary Fund.

NIGER

(5.4,7.4,9.4) Days.
Sources: (1.2-5.4,7.1,7.2,9.1-9.4) (6.2,8.2-8.4/2006) "Ministère du Tourisme et de l'Artisanat"; (6.1-6.3,8.2-8.4/2002-2005) International Monetary Fund.

NIGERIA

(1.1,2.1-2.6,3.1-3.4) (4.1-4.3/2006) Arrivals of non-resident visitors at national borders; (1.2,4.1-4.3) Arrivals of non-resident tourists at national borders.
Sources: (1.1-4.3,9.2,9.3) Nigerian Tourism Development Corporation; (6.1-6.3,8.2-8.4) International Monetary Fund.

NIUE

(1.2) Arrivals by air; including Niueans residing usually in New Zealand; (8.1) Returning residents.
Source: Statistics Niue.

NORTHERN MARIANA ISLANDS

(1.1,2.2-2.4) Arrivals of non-resident visitors at national borders; (1.2) Arrivals by air; (2.2) Including Guam; (9.1) Covers 68 per cent of the total hotel room inventory.
Source: Marianas Visitors Authority.

COUNTRY NOTES

NORWAY

(1.1-4.2) Figures are based on "The Guest survey" carried out by "Institute of Transport Economics"; (2.2-4.2) Arrivals of non-resident tourists at national borders; (2.2) United States only; (2.4) Japan only; (5.1) Nights in registered establishments; (5.1,9.1,9.2) Figures for hotels and similar establishments relate to establishments with 20 or more beds the whole year; (8.1) Holiday trips; (9.3) Bed-places.
Sources: (1.1-5.3,7.1-7.3,8.1,9.1-9.4) Statistics Norway and Institute of Transport Economics; (6.1-6.3,8.2-8.4) International Monetary Fund.

OMAN

(1.1-1.3,4.1-4.3,5.3,5.4) Inbound Tourism Survey; (2.1-2.6) Non-resident tourists staying in hotels and similar establishments; (4.1-4.3) Arrivals of non-resident visitors at national borders; (8.1) Outbound Tourism Survey; including same-day visitors; (9.3) Rooms.
Sources: (1.1-1.3,4.1-4.3,5.3,5.4,8.1) Ministry of National Economy and Ministry of Commerce and Industry; (2.1-2.6,5.1,5.2,7.1,7.2,9.1-9.3) Directorate General of Tourism - Ministry of Tourism; (6.1-6.3,8.2-8.4) International Monetary Fund.

PAKISTAN

(5.4) Days.
Sources: (1.2-5.4,7.1,7.2,9.1-9.4) Pakistan Tourism Development Corporation - Ministry of Tourism; (6.1-6.3,8.2-8.4) International Monetary Fund.

PALAU

(1.2-4.3) Air arrivals (Palau International Airport); (6.1,8.2) The expenditure figures are those provided by the country to UNWTO, which do not appear in the International Monetary Fund data used in the preparation of this edition of the Compendium. Fiscal years.
Source: Office of Planning and Statistics, Bureau of Budget and Planning - Ministry of Finance.

PALESTINE

(1.2,2.1-2.6) Non-resident tourists staying in hotels; (5.1,5.2,7.1,7.2) Hotels only; (10.1-10.3) This section includes only the "travel" item because the "passenger transport" item was not included in the data provided by the International Monetary Fund for the preparation of this edition of the Compendium.
Sources: (1.2-5.2,7.1-7.4,9.1-9.4) Palestinian Central Bureau of Statistics; (6.2,8.3) International Monetary Fund; (6.2,8.3,10-1-10.3) West Bank and Gaza.

PANAMA

(1.1) Arrivals of non-resident visitors, Tocúmen International Airport (TIA), Paso Canoa frontier (PCF) and the ports of Cristóbal and Balboa (PCB); (2.2-2.4) Arrivals of non-resident visitors, TIA; (3.1-3.4) Arrivals of non-resident tourists, TIA, PCF and PCB; excluding arrivals to other ports of entry (non specified):
2002: 34,996
2003: 39,870
2004: 51,295
2005: 53,818
2006: 53,638
(4.1-4.3) Arrivals of non-resident tourists, TIA; (5.1) Hotels in Panama City; (9.1,9.2) Rooms/bed-places recorded for international tourism; (9.3) Rooms.
Sources: (1.1-5.4,8.1,9.1-9.4) "Instituto Panameño de Turismo"; (6.1-6.3,8.2-8.4) International Monetary Fund.

PAPUA NEW GUINEA

Sources: (1.2-4.3,8.1,9.1,9.2) Papua New Guinea Tourism Promotion Authority; (6.1-6.3,8.2-8.4) International Monetary Fund.

PARAGUAY

(1.1-3.4,8.1) E/D cards in the "Silvio Petirossi" airport and passenger counts at the national border crossings - National Police and SENATUR; (1.2,2.2-4.3) Excluding nationals residing abroad and crew members; (3.4) River; (9.3) Bed-places.
Sources: (1.1-5.4,8.1,9.1-9.4) "Secretaría Nacional de Turismo - SENATUR"; (6.1-6.3,8.2-8.4) International Monetary Fund.

PERU

(1.2) Including overnight cruise passengers; (1.2,2.1-2.5) From 2002, new estimated series including tourists with identity document other than a passport; (1.4) Overnight cruise passengers; (3.4) Includes the arrivals by river and lake.
Note 2003-2006: Preliminary estimates.
Sources: (1.2-4.3,8.1) "Dirección General de Migraciones y Naturalización (DIGEMIN)"; (5.1-5.4,7.1,7.2,9.1-9.4) "Ministerio de Comercio Exterior y Turismo (MINCETUR)"; (6.1-6.3,8.2-8.4) International Monetary Fund.

COUNTRY NOTES

PHILIPPINES

(1.2,3.1-4.3) Arrivals of non-resident tourists at national borders; including nationals residing abroad; (2.1-2.6) Arrivals of non-resident tourists at national borders; excluding nationals residing abroad; (4.1-4.3) Air arrivals; (8.1) Including overseas contract workers; (9.1,9.2) Classified hotels only; (9.3,9.4) Classified hotels in Metro Manila.
Sources: (1.2-5.4,8.1,9.1-9.4) Department of Tourism; (6.1-6.3,8.2-8.4) International Monetary Fund.

POLAND

(1.1,2.1-3.4) Arrivals of non-resident visitors at national borders; (4.1-4.3) Arrivals of non-resident tourists at national borders, based on surveys by the Institute of Tourism; (5.4) Both collective and private accommodation establishments, based on surveys by the Institute of Tourism; (8.1) Outbound trips registered at frontiers; (9.3) Rooms.
Sources: (1.1-5.4,7.1-7.4,8.1,9.1-9.4) Institute of Tourism; (6.1-6.3,8.2-8.4) International Monetary Fund.

PORTUGAL

(1.1-4.3) Due to a change in the methodology, from 2004 the data are not comparable with those of previous years; (1.1,3.1-3.4,4.1-4.3) Arrivals of non-resident visitors at national borders; (1.1-3.4/2002/2003) Excluding nationals residing abroad; (1.1-4.3/2004-2006) Including national residing abroad; (1.2,2.2-2.5) Arrivals of non-resident tourists at national borders; (1.4) Including transit sea passengers; (5.1-5.4,7.1-7.4,9.1-9.4) Since 2002, new methodology; (5.1-5.4,7.1-7.4/2006) Provisional data; (9.3) Bed-places; (9.4) All types of accommodation establishments.
Sources: (1.1-5.4,7.1-7.4,8.1,9.1-9.4) "Direcçao-Geral do Turismo (DGT)"; (6.1-6.3,8.2-8.4) International Monetary Fund.

PUERTO RICO

(1.2) Arrivals of non-resident tourists by air; (2.2) United States Virgin Islands and the United States only; (5.1,5.4) Including residents and non-residents; (6.1,8.2-8.4) The expenditure figures are those provided by the country to UNWTO, which do not appear in the International Monetary Fund data used in the preparation of this edition of the Compendium; (9.1) Rooms classified by the "Compañía de Turismo" of Puerto Rico; (9.1/2006) Including 2,927 unclassified rooms; (9.3) Rooms; including rooms occupied by residents of Puerto Rico.
Data: Fiscal years (July-June).
Source: (1.1-3.4,6.1,8.1,8.2-8.4,10.1-10.3) "Junta de Planificación de Puerto Rico"; (5.1,5.2,5.4,7.2,9.1,9.3,9.4) "Compañía de Turismo de Puerto Rico".

QATAR

(1.2-5.4,9.1-9.3) Hotels only; (6.2,8.3) The expenditure figures are those provided by the country to UNWTO, which do not appear in the International Monetary Fund data used in the preparation of this edition of the Compendium; (6.2,8.3/2006) Preliminary estimates; (9.3) Bed-places.
Sources: (1.2-5.4,9.1-9.3) The Planning Council - Statistics Department and Qatar Tourism Authority; (6.2,8.3) Qatar Central Bank.

REPUBLIC OF MOLDOVA

(1.1-4.3,8.1) (5.1,7.3/2002/2003) Visitors who enjoyed the services of the economic agents officially registered under tourism activity and accommodation.
Note: Excluding the left side of the river Nistru and the municipality of Bender.
Sources: (1.1-5.4,7.1-7.4,8.1,9.1-9.4) National Bureau of Statistics; (6.1-6.3,8.2-8.4) International Monetary Fund.

REUNION

(5.4) Days; (6.1) The expenditure figures are those provided by the country to UNWTO, which do not appear in the International Monetary Fund data used in the preparation of this edition of the Compendium.
Sources: "Institut National de la Statistique et des Études Économique - INSEE" and "Comité du Tourisme de la Réunion".

ROMANIA

Sources: (1.1-5.4,7.1-7.4,8.1,9.1-9.4) National Authority for Tourism - Ministry of Transports, Constructions and Tourism; (6.1-6.3,8.2-8.4) International Monetary Fund.

RUSSIAN FEDERATION

(1.1,2.1-4.3) Arrivals of non-resident visitors at national borders; (9.1,9.2) Accommodation in hotels and other tourist establishments.
Sources: (1.1-5.4,7.1-7.4,8.1,9.1-9.4) Russian Federal Agency for Tourism; (6.1-6.3,8.2-8.4) International Monetary Fund.

SABA

(1.3) Mainly from St. Maarten.

Sources: Saba Tourist Bureau, Caribbean Tourism Organization and Central Bank of the Netherlands Antilles.

SAINT EUSTATIUS

(1.2,2.2,2.3) Excluding Netherlands Antillean residents.
Source: Central Bank of the Netherlands Antilles.

SAINT KITTS AND NEVIS

(1.2,2.2) Arrivals of non-resident tourists by air; (1.4,3.4) Yacht and cruise ship arrivals; (10.1-10.3) This section includes only the "travel" item because the "passenger transport" item was not included in the data provided by the International Monetary Fund for the preparation of this edition of the Compendium.
Sources: (1.1-3.4,9.1,9.2) Statistics Department - Ministry of Sustainable Development; (6.2,8.3) International Monetary Fund.

SAINT LUCIA

(1.1) Excluding yacht passenger arrivals; (1.2,2.2-4.3) Arrivals of non-resident tourists at national borders; excluding nationals residing abroad; (9.3) Rooms; (10.1-10.3) This section includes only the "travel" item because the "passenger transport" item was not included in the data provided by the International Monetary Fund for the preparation of this edition of the Compendium.
Sources: (1.1-5.2,9.1-9.4) Saint Lucia Tourist Board; (6.2,8.3) International Monetary Fund.

SAINT MAARTEN

(1.2,2.2,2.3) By air; including arrivals to Saint Maarten (the French side of the island); (3.1) Arrivals at Juliana Airport (including visitors destined to Saint Maarten, French side); (6.2,8.3) Including the estimates for Saba and Saint Eustatius; (9.1,9.2) Hotels, guest houses and apartments.
Sources: (1.1-3.4,9.1-9.3) St. Maarten Tourist Bureau; (6.2,8.3) Central Bank of the Netherlands Antilles.

SAINT VINCENT AND THE GRENADINES

(1.2,2.2-2.3,4.1-4.3) Arrivals of non-resident tourists by air; (3.4) Including cruise ship and yacht passengers; (9.1) Hotels, apartments, cottages, villas and guest houses; (10.1-10.3) This section includes only the "travel" item because the "passenger transport" item was not included in the data provided by the International Monetary Fund for the preparation of this edition of the Compendium.
Sources: (1.1-5.4,9.1,9.2) Ministry of Tourism and Culture; (6.2,8.3) International Monetary Fund.

SAMOA

Sources: (1.2-4.3,9.1,9.2) (6.2/2002/2003) Samoa Tourism Authority and Statistical Services Division (Ministry of Finance); (6.1-6.3,8.2-8.4/2004-2006) International Monetary Fund.

SAN MARINO

(1.1) Including Italian visitors; (1.2) Non-resident tourists staying in hotels and similar establishments; including Italian tourists; (9.1,9.2) Hotels only.
Note: New methodology from 2005.
Source: "Segreteria di Stato per il Turismo, lo Sport, le Telecomunicazioni, i Trasporti e la Cooperazione Economica".

SAO TOME AND PRINCIPE

(10.1-10.3) This section includes only the "travel" item because the "passenger transport" item was not included in the data provided by the International Monetary Fund for the preparation of this edition of the Compendium.
Sources: (1.2-4.3) "Direcçao do Turismo e Hotelaria"; (6.2,8.2-8.4/2002) International Monetary Fund; (6.2/2003-2005) "Banco Central".

SAUDI ARABIA

(9.1/2002/2003) Hotels only; (6.1-6.3,8.2-8.4) The expenditure figures are those provided by the country to UNWTO, which do not appear in the International Monetary Fund data used in the preparation of this edition of the Compendium.
Source: The Supreme Commission for Tourism.

SENEGAL

(1.2/2002) (2.1-2.6/2002/2003) Non-resident tourists staying in hotels and similar establishments; (1.2/2003-2006) (2.1-2.3/2004-2006) Arrivals of non-resident tourists at national borders; (5.1,5.2,7.1,7.2,9.1,9.2) Hotels and holiday villages; (9.3) Bed-places.
Sources: (1.1-5.4,7.1,7.2,9.1-9.4) "Ministère du Tourisme et des Transports Aériens"; (6.1-6.3,8.2-8.4) International Monetary Fund.

SERBIA

(1.2,2.2-2.4) Non-resident tourists staying in all types of accommodation establishments; (6.1,8.2) The expenditure figures are those provided by the country to UNWTO, which do not appear in the International Monetary Fund data used in the preparation of this edition of the Compendium.
Source: Statistical Office of the Republic of Serbia.

SEYCHELLES

(1.2,2.1-4.3) Arrivals of non-resident tourists at national borders; (5.4) Nights based on departures; (9.1,9.2) Hotels and guest houses; (9.3) Bed-places.
Sources: (1.1-5.4,7.1,8.1,9.1-9.3) National Statistics Bureau; (6.1-6.3,8.2-8.4) International Monetary Fund.

SIERRA LEONE

(1.2,2.1-2.6,4.1-4.3) Arrivals by air; (9.1,9.2) Hotels only; (10.1-10.3) This section includes only the "travel" item because the "passenger transport" item was not included in the data provided by the International Monetary Fund for the preparation of this edition of the Compendium.
Sources: (1.2-5.4,8.1,9.1-9.4) National Tourist Board; (6.2,8.2-8.4) International Monetary Fund.

SINGAPORE

(1.1) Excluding arrivals of Malaysian citizens by land; including same-day visitors; (5.4,9.4) Days; (9.1) Hotels (gazetted and non-gazetted); (9.3) Rooms; classified hotels only; (10.1-10.3) This section includes only the "travel" item because the "passenger transport" item was not included in the data provided by the International Monetary Fund for the preparation of this edition of the Compendium.
Sources: (1.1-5.4,8.1,9.1-9.4) Singapore Tourism Board; (6.2,8.3) International Monetary Fund.

SLOVAKIA

(1.2,2.1-2.5) Non-resident tourists staying in all types of accommodation establishments.
Sources: (1.1-5.4,7.1-7.4,8.1,9.1-9.4) Department of Tourism - Ministry of Economy and Statistical Office; (6.1-6.3,8.2-8.4/2002/2003) International Monetary Fund.

SLOVENIA

(1.1) Including all categories of travellers irrespective of purpose of visit; (1.2,2.1-2.4) Non-resident tourists staying in all types of accommodation establishments; (3.1-3.4,4.1-4.3) Non-resident tourists staying in all types of accommodation establishments; data from 3 yearly survey on foreign tourists in Slovenia in Summer; (8.1) Quarterly survey on travels of domestic population.
Sources: (1.1-5.4,7.1-7.4,8.1,9.1-9.4) Statistical Office - Information Society and Tourism Statistics; (6.1-6.3,8.2-8.4) International Monetary Fund.

SOLOMON ISLANDS

(1.2,2.2-2.4/2005) Without 1st quarter.
Sources: (1.2,2.2-2.4) Solomon Islands National Statistics Office; (6.1-6.3,8.2-8.4) International Monetary Fund.

SOUTH AFRICA

(1.1,3.1-3.4) Excluding nationals residing abroad. Including arrivals by purpose of holiday, business, study, work, transit, border traffic and contract workers; (1.2,2.1-2.6,4.1-4.3) Arrivals of non-resident tourists at national borders; excluding arrivals by work and contract workers; (9.1) Figures for 2002 and 2003 are based on the 'Hotel: Trading statistics' survey which was discontinued in March 2004. This survey was replaced by the current 'Tourist accommodation' survey in September 2004. Figures for 2004, 2005 and 2006 are based on the 'Tourist accommodation' survey and are not comparable with the discontinued 'Hotels: Trading statistics' survey figures. Figures for 2004 and 2005 have been revised due to backcasting based on the 2006 sample for the 'Tourist accommodation' survey; (9.1,9.3) Figures for 2006 are preliminary estimates; (9.3) Rooms (hotels).
Sources: (1.1-4.3,8.1,9.1-9.3) Statistics South Africa and South African Tourism; (6.1-6.3,8.2-8.4) International Monetary Fund.

SPAIN

(1.1) Arrivals of non-resident visitors at national borders; including nationals residing abroad; (2.2-4.3) Arrivals of non-resident tourists at national borders; including nationals residing abroad; (2.4) Japan only; (5.1,7.1) Nights in hotels and "hostales" (accommodation establishments providing limited services); (5.3,7.3) Nights in hotels, "hostales", camping sites, tourism apartments and rural dwellings; (5.4,7.4,9.1-9.4) Hotels and "hostales" only; (8.1) Since 2005 a new methodology has been applied and data are not comparable to previous years; (9.3) Bed-places.
Sources: (1.1-4.3,8.1) "Instituto de Estudios Turísticos"; (5.1-5.4,7.1-7.4,9.1-9.4) "Instituto Nacional de Estadística"; (6.1-6.3,8.2-8.4) International Monetary Fund.

COUNTRY NOTES

SRI LANKA

(1.2,2.1-4.3) Arrivals of non-resident tourists at national borders; excluding nationals residing abroad; (9.1,9.2) Hotels, motels, inns, guest houses and apart-hotels; (9.3) Rooms.
Sources: (1.1-5.4,7.1,8.1,9.1-9.3) Sri Lanka Tourist Board; (6.1-6.3,8.2-8.4) International Monetary Fund.

SUDAN

(1.2-4.3/2005/2006) Arrivals of non-resident tourists at national borders; including nationals residing abroad; (6.1) The country provides UNWTO with aggregate expenditure figures that differ significantly from the International Monetary Fund data used in the preparation of this edition of the Compendium. The country figures are as follows:
2002: 62
2003: 63
2004: 68
2005: 316
2006: 409
(10.1-10.3) This section includes only the "travel" item because the "passenger transport" item was not included in the data provided by the International Monetary Fund for the preparation of this edition of the Compendium.
Sources: (1.2-4.3,9.1-9.4) Ministry of Tourism and Wildlife; (6.2,8.3) International Monetary Fund.

SURINAME

(1.2,2.2-2.4,4.1-4.3,5.2/2002/2003) (3.1) (5.2/2004) Arrivals at Zanderij Airport; (1.2,2.2-2.4,4.1-4.3/2004/2005) Arrivals at Zanderij Airport, Zorg en Hoop Airport, Albina and Nickerie; (1.4/2003) (3.4) Arrivals via Nw. Nickerie Harbour.
Sources: (1.1-1.4,2.2-2.4,4.1-4.3,5.2/2002/2003) (3.1,3.4/2002-2004) General Bureau of Statistics (ABS); (1.2,2.2-2.4,4.1-4.3,5.2/2004/2005) (3.1,3.4/2005) (9.1) Suriname Tourism Foundation; (6.1-6.3,8.2-8.4) International Monetary Fund.

SWAZILAND

(1.1) (2.1-2.5,4.4-4.3/2005/2006) (3.1,3.3) Arrivals of non-resident visitors at national borders; (1.2,4.1-4.3/2002) (2.1-2.4/2002-2004) (5.2) Arrivals in hotels only; (9.3) Bed-places.
Sources: (1.1-5.4,7.1,7.4,8.1,9.1-9.4) Swaziland Tourism Authority and Ministry of Tourism, Environment and Communications; (6.1-6.3,8.2-8.4) International Monetary Fund.

SWEDEN

(1.1-4.3) Data according to IBIS-Survey (Incoming Visitors to Sweden) during the years 2001 to 2003, (no data collected before 2001 or after 2003). Source: Swedish Tourist Authority and Statistics Sweden; (1.2,2.1-4.3) Arrivals of non-resident tourists at national borders; (3.2) Data includes rail and others; (5.1,7.1,9.1,9.2) Hotels only; (9.3) Bed-places.
Sources: (1.1-5.4,7.1-7.4,8.1,9.1-9.3) NUTEK - The Swedish Agency for Economic and Regional Growth; (6.1-6.3,8.2-8.4) International Monetary Fund.

SWITZERLAND

(1.2,2.1-2.6,5.1,5.2,7.1,7.2,9.1,9.2/2002-2004) Hotels, motels and inns; (1.2,2.1-2.6,5.1,5.2,7.1,7.2,9.1-9.4/2005/2006) Hotels and health establishments; (9.3) Net occupancy rates (bed-places available).
Sources: (1.2-5.3,7.1-7.3,8.1,9.1-9.4) Swiss Federal Statistical Office; (6.1-6.3,8.2-8.4) International Monetary Fund.

SYRIAN ARAB REPUBLIC

(1.1,2.1-4.3) Arrivals of non-resident visitors at national borders; excluding arrivals of nationals residing abroad; (9.3) Rooms.
Sources: (1.1-5.4,7.1,7.2,8.1,9.1-9.4) Ministry of Tourism - Data source: the survey of the incoming tourism in 2002 and 2004; (6.1-6.3,8.2-8.4) International Monetary Fund.

TAIWAN (PROVINCE OF CHINA)

(1.1) Including nationals residing abroad; (2.1-2.6) Excluding nationals residing abroad.
Sources: (1.1-5.4,8.1,9.1,9.3) Planning Division Tourism Bureau - Ministry of Transportation and Communication; (6.1-6.3,8.2-8.4) International Monetary Fund.

THAILAND

(1.2,3.1-3.4/2002-2005) Including arrivals of nationals residing abroad; (1.2,3.1-3.4/2006) (2.1-2.6,4.1-4.3) Excluding arrivals of nationals residing abroad; (3.3) Including rail; (5.4) Days; (9.3) In main tourist destinations only.
Sources: (1.2-5.4,8.1,9.1,9.3) Tourism Authority of Thailand (TAT); (6.1-6.3,8.2-8.4) International Monetary Fund.

THE FORMER YUGOSLAV REPUBLIC OF MACEDONIA

(1.2,2.2-2.4) Non-resident tourists staying in all types of accommodation establishments; (3.1-3.3) Arrivals of non-resident visitors at national borders; (9.4) Average length of stay in all accommodation establishments.
Sources: (1.1-5.4,7.1-7.4,9.1-9.4) State Statistical Office; (6.1-6.3,8.2-8.4) International Monetary Fund.

TOGO

(1.2) Non-resident tourists staying in hotels and similar establishments; (9.3) Rooms.
Sources: (1.2-5.4,7.1-7.4,9.1-9.4) "Ministère de l'Environnement, du Tourisme et des Ressources Forestières"; (6.1-6.3,8.2-8.4) International Monetary Fund.

TONGA

(1.2,2.2-2.4,4.1-4.3) Arrivals by air; (10.1-10.3) This section includes only the "travel" item because the "passenger transport" item was not included in the data provided by the International Monetary Fund for the preparation of this edition of the Compendium.
Sources: (1.1-4.3) Tonga Visitors Bureau; (6.2,8.3) International Monetary Fund.

TRINIDAD AND TOBAGO

(1.2,2.1-2.5,4.1-4.3) Arrivals by air; (4.1) Including visit friends and relatives.
Sources: (1.1-5.4,9.1,9.3) Central Statistical Office - Ministry of Planning and Development; (6.1-6.3,8.2-8.4) International Monetary Fund.

TUNISIA

(1.2,2.1-3.4) Arrivals of non-resident tourists at national borders; excluding nationals residing abroad; (9.1,9.2) Classified and unclassified hotels, boarding houses and holiday villages; (9.3) Bed-places.
Sources: (1.1-5.4,7.1-7.4,8.1,9.1-9.4) "Ministère du Tourisme - Office National du Tourisme" and "Institut National de la Statistique"; (6.1-6.3,8.2-8.4) International Monetary Fund.

TURKEY

(1.1,3.1-3.4) Arrivals of non-resident visitors at national borders; (1.3) Sea arrivals (excluding one land border from 1989); (2.1-2.6) Arrivals of non-resident tourists at national borders; (3.4) Including cruise passengers; (4.1-4.3) Departures of non-resident visitors; (5.3) Survey in accommodation establishments licensed by Ministry of Tourism; (5.3,7.3) Including camping sites; (6.2) Including expenditure of the nationals residing abroad; (9.3,9.4) Classified hotels; excluding camping sites; (9.3) Bed-places; (10.1-10.3/2002-2004) This section includes only the "travel" item because the "passenger transport" item was not included in the data provided by the International Monetary Fund for the preparation of this edition of the Compendium.
Sources: (1.1-3.4,5.1-5.4,7.1-7.4,8.1,9.1-9.4) (6.2/2002) Ministry of Culture and Tourism; (4.1-4.3) Departing Visitors Survey - Turkish Statistical Institute (TURKSTAT); (6.1-6.3/2003-2006) (8.2-8.4) International Monetary Fund.

TURKMENISTAN

Source: State Committee for Tourism and Sport.

TURKS AND CAICOS ISLANDS

(6.1) The expenditure figures are those provided by the country to UNWTO, which do not appear in the International Monetary Fund data used in the preparation of this edition of the Compendium.
Source: Turks and Caicos Tourist Board.

TUVALU

Source: Central Statistics Division - Ministry of Finance, Economic Planning and Industry.

UGANDA

Sources: (1.2-5.3,8.1,9.1,9.2) Ministry of Tourism, Trade an Industry and Uganda Bureau of Statistics; (6.1-6.3,8.2-8.4) International Monetary Fund.

UKRAINE

(2.1-2.6) Arrivals of non-resident tourists at national borders; (3.1-3.4/2002) Arrivals of non-resident visitors at national borders; (3.1-3.4/2003-2006) Arrivals of non-resident tourists at national borders; (4.1-4.3) Arrivals of non-resident visitors at national borders.
Sources: (1.1-5.4,7.1,7.3,8.1,9.1-9.4) State Tourism Administration; (6.1-6.3,8.2-8.4) International Monetary Fund.

COUNTRY NOTES

UNITED ARAB EMIRATES

(1.2) Arrivals in hotels only. Including domestic tourism and nationals residing abroad; (2.1-2.6) Arrivals in hotels only. Excluding domestic tourism and nationals residing abroad; (5.1) Nights in hotels only. Including domestic tourism and nationals residing abroad; (6.1,8.2) The expenditure figures are those provided by the country to UNWTO, which do not appear in the International Monetary Fund data used in the preparation of this edition of the Compendium; (9.1,9.2) Hotels only; (9.3) Rooms rented.
Source: Ministry of Economy and Planning - Planning Sector.

UNITED KINGDOM

(3.2) Tunnel; (5.4) Days; (9.3) Bed-places (England only).
Sources: (1.1-4.3,5.3,5.4,7.3,8.1,9.3) VisitBritain; (5.1,5.2,7.1,7.2,9.1,9.2) EUROSTAT (New Cronos); (6.1-6.3,8.2-8.4) International Monetary Fund.

UNITED REPUBLIC OF TANZANIA

Sources: (1.1-5.3,7.3,9.1-9.4) Tourism Division - Ministry of Natural Resources and Tourism and National Bureau of Statistics; (6.1-6.3,8.2-8.4) International Monetary Fund.

UNITED STATES

(1.2,2.2) Including Mexicans staying one or more nights in the US; (3.1-3.4) Preliminary estimates; (3.3) Including a very small percentage (0.2%) of travelers for whom transportation mode is not known; (4.1-4.3) Main trip purpose; (4.1-4.3,5.2) Overseas only; excluding Mexico (data are not available); (6.2,8.3) The country provides UNWTO with expenditure figures that differ significantly from the International Monetary Fund data used in the preparation of this edition of the Compendium. The country figures are as follows:

	6.2	8.3
2002:	66,605	58,715
2003:	64,359	57,447
2004:	74,546	65,750
2005:	81,799	68,970
2006:	85,694	72,029

(8.1) Including Americans staying one or more nights in Mexico.
Sources: (1.2-5.2,8.1) Office of Travel and Tourism Industries; (6.1-6.3,8.2-8.4) International Monetary Fund; (9.1,9.3) American Hotel & Lodging Association (AHLA).

UNITED STATES VIRGIN ISLANDS

(2.1-2.4) Non-resident tourists staying in hotels and similar establishments; (3.1) Visitor air arrivals; excluding resident arrivals and inter-island traffic but including same-day visitors; (3.4) Cruise passengers; (5.3) Including domestic tourist nights (about 40% of total); (6.1) The expenditure figures are those provided by the country to UNWTO, which do not appear in the International Monetary Fund data used in the preparation of this edition of the Compendium; (9.1,9.3) Hotel units and condominium or villa units; (9.3) Rooms.
2006: Provisional data.
Source: Bureau of Economic Research.

URUGUAY

(1.1,4.1-4.3) Including nationals residing abroad; (2.2-3.4) Excluding nationals residing abroad; (3.3) Including rail; (5.4) Days; (9.1,9.2/2005/2006) Excluding unclassified hotels.
Sources: (1.1-5.4,8.1,9.1-9.4) "Ministerio de Turismo y Deporte"; (6.1-6.3,8.2-8.4) International Monetary Fund.

UZBEKISTAN

(6.1-6.3) The expenditure figures are those provided by the country to UNWTO, which do not appear in the International Monetary Fund data used in the preparation of this edition of the Compendium.
Source: National Company "Uzbektourism".

VANUATU

(5.4) Days; (9.3) Rooms.
Sources: (1.1-5.4,8.1,9.1-9.4) Vanuatu National Statistics Office; (6.1-6.3,8.2-8.4) International Monetary Fund.

VENEZUELA

(1.2,2.1-4.3) Arrivals of non-resident tourists at national borders; (9.1,9.2/2002-2004) Hotels and Paradores/Pousadas; (9.1,9.2/2005/2006) Hotels only.
Sources: (1.1-5.4,7.4,8.1,9.1-9.3) "Ministerio del Poder Popular para el Turismo"; (6.1-6.3,8.2-8.4) International Monetary Fund.

VIET NAM

(1.1) Including nationals residing abroad; (1.4,3.4) Including cruise and sea passengers; (2.2-4.3) Arrivals of non-resident visitors at national borders; (6.1) The expenditure figures are those provided by the country to UNWTO, which do not appear in the International Monetary Fund data used in the preparation of this edition of the Compendium.
Source: Viet Nam National Administration of Tourism.

YEMEN

(1.2,2.1-2.6,5.2) Non-resident tourists staying in hotels and similar establishments; (10.1-10.3) This section includes only the "travel" item because the "passenger transport" item was not included in the data provided by the International Monetary Fund for the preparation of this edition of the Compendium.
Sources: (1.2-5.4,7.1,7.2,9.1,9.2) Ministry of Tourism; (6.2,8.2-8.4) International Monetary Fund.

ZAMBIA

(5.4) Days; (9.3) Rooms; (10.1-10.3) This section includes only the "travel" item because the "passenger transport" item was not included in the data provided by the International Monetary Fund for the preparation of this edition of the Compendium.
Note 2002: Provisional data.
Sources: (1.2-5.4,7.1,9.1-9.3) Ministry of Tourism, Environment and Natural Resources; (6.2,8.2-8.4) International Monetary Fund.

ZIMBABWE

(2.1-2.6,3.1,3.3,4.1-4.3) Arrivals of non-resident visitors at national borders; (3.1,3.3/2002/2003) Including persons in transit; (6.1) The expenditure figures are those provided by the country to UNWTO, which do not appear in the International Monetary Fund data used in the preparation of this edition of the Compendium; (9.1,9.2) Graded hotels only; (9.3) Bed-places.
Source: Zimbabwe Tourism Authority - ZTA.

NOTES DES PAYS

AFRIQUE DU SUD

(1.1,3.1-3.4) À l'exclusion des nationaux résidant à l'étranger. Y compris les arrivées par motif de vacances, affaires, études, travail, transit, trafic frontalier et travailleurs contractuels; (1.2,2.1-2.6,4.1-4.3) Arrivées de touristes non résidents aux frontières nationales; à l'exclusion des arrivées par travail et les travailleurs contractuels; (9.1) Les chiffres de 2002 et de 2003 sont tirés de l'enquête sur les statistiques de l'activité hôtelière. Cette enquête, supprimée en mars 2004, était remplacée en septembre de la même année par l'enquête sur l'hébergement touristique. Les chiffres de 2004, 2005 et 2006, tirés de cette dernière, ne sont pas comparables avec ceux de l'ancienne enquête sur les statistiques de l'activité hôtelière. Les chiffres de 2004 et de 2005 ont été revus par extrapolation rétrospective sur la base de l'échantillon de 2006 de l'enquête sur l'hébergement touristique; (9.1,9.3) Les chiffres de 2006 sont de premières estimations. (9.3) Chambres (hôtels).
Sources: (1.1-4.3,8.1,9.1-9.3) "Statistics South Africa" et "South African Tourism"; (6.1-6.3,8.2-8.4) Fonds monétaire international.

ALBANIE

(1.1,2.2-4.3) Visiteurs et autres voyageurs; (1.2,5.2,7.2) Arrivées dans les hôtels seulement; 5.4,7.1-74,9.1-9.4/2004-2006) Enquête trimestrielle: hôtels avec 5 chambres ou plus; (4.3) Transit.
Sources: (1.1-5.4,7.1-7.4,9.1-9.4) "Institute of Statistics - INSTAT"; (6.1-6.3,8.2-8.4) Fonds monétaire international.

ALGERIE

(1.1,3.1-3.4) Y compris les nationaux résidant à l'étranger:

2002   736.915
2003   861.373
2004   865.157
2005   1.001.884
2006   1.159.224

(2.1-2.6,4.1,4.2) À l'exclusion des nationaux résidant à l'étranger; (6.1,8.2) Les chiffres de dépense sont ceux que le pays a fournis à l'OMT mais ils ne figurent pas dans les données du Fonds monétaire international qui ont servi à la préparation de la présente édition du Compendium.
Sources: Ministère de l'Aménagement du Territoire, de l'Environnement et du Tourisme et Office National des Statistiques.

ALLEMAGNE

(1.2,2.1-2.6) Touristes non résidents dans tous types d'établissements d'hébergement; (9.3) Places-lit; (9.4) Tourisme récepteur, hôtels et établissements assimilés.
Sources: (1.2-5.4,7.1-7.4,8.1,9.1-9.4) "Statistiches Bundesamt"; (6.1-6.3,8.2-8.4) Fonds monétaire international.

ANDORRE

Source: "Ministerio de Turismo y Medio Ambiente".

ANGOLA

(5.1,5.2,7.1,7.2) Hôtels uniquement.
Sources: (1.2-5.3,7.1-7.3,9.1-9.4) "Ministério de Hotelaria e Turismo - Gabinete de Estudos, Planeamento e Estatística"; (6.1-6.3,8.2-8.4) Fonds monétaire international.

ANGUILLA

(1.1,3.1-4.3) Arrivées de visiteurs non résidents aux frontières nationales; (1.2,2.2,2.3) Arrivées de touristes non résidents aux frontières nationales; à l'exclusion des nationaux résidant à l'étranger; (4.3) Visiteurs de la journée (excursionnistes); (9.1) Hôtels, pensions de famille, appartements/ villas; (9.3) Chambres; janvier-mai; (10.2,10.3) Cette section comprend uniquement le poste « voyages » parce que le poste « transport de passagers » ne figure pas dans les données du Fonds monétaire international qui ont servi à la préparation de la présente édition du Compendium.
Sources: (1.1-5.4,9.1-9.4) "Statistical Department - Ministry of Finance"; (6.2,8.3) Fonds monétaire international.

ANTIGUA-ET-BARBUDA

(1.1) À l'exclusion des arrivées de passagers en yacht; (2.2,2.3,3.1,4.1-4.3) Arrivées par voie aérienne; á l'exclusion des nationaux résidant à l'étranger; (3.4) Passagers en croisière uniquement; (10.1-10.3) Cette section comprend uniquement le poste « voyages » parce que le poste « transport de passagers » ne figure pas dans les données du Fonds monétaire international qui ont servi à la préparation de la présente édition du Compendium.
Sources: (1.1-5.4,9.1) "Ministry of Tourism"; (6.2,8.3) Fonds monétaire international.

NOTES DES PAYS

ARABIE SAOUDITE

(9.1/2002/2003) Hôtels seulement; (6.1-6.3,8.2-8.4) Les chiffres de dépense sont ceux que le pays a fournis à l'OMT mais ils ne figurent pas dans les données du Fonds monétaire international qui ont servi à la préparation de la présente édition du Compendium.
Source: "The Supreme Commission for Tourism".

ARGENTINE

À partir de 2004, vu l'importance de l'« Enquête sur le tourisme international », des modifications ont été apportées aux estimations de la série du poste « Voyages » de la balance des paiements. C'est la raison pour laquelle les données ne sont pas rigoureusement comparables avec celles des années précédentes.
Note 2005-2006: Données provisoires.
Sources: (1.2-5.4,7.1,7.2,8.1,9.1-9.3) "Dirección de Estudios de Mercado y Estadística - Secretaría de Turismo de la Nación"; (6.1-6.3,8.2-8.4) Fonds monétaire international.

ARMENIE

Sources: (1.2-5.4,7.1-7.4,8.1,9.1-9.4) "Tourism Department - Ministry of Trade and Economic Development"; (6.1-6.3,8.2-8.4) Fonds monétaire international.

ARUBA

(1.2,2.2-4.3) Arrivées de touristes non résidents aux frontières nationales; (5.4) Touristes non résidents dans les hôtels et établissements assimilés; (9.3) Chambres.
Sources: (1.1-5.4,9.1-9.3) "Aruba Tourism Authority"; (6.1-6.3,8.2-8.4) Fonds monétaire international.

AUSTRALIE

(1.1) À l'exclusion des nationaux résidant à l'étranger et membres des équipages; (1.2,1.3) Arrivées par voie aérienne; (2.1-4.3) Arrivées de visiteurs non résidents aux frontières nationales; (9.1,9.2/2002-2004) Hôtels, motels, pensions de famille et appartements avec services hôteliers avec 15 chambres ou plus; (9.1,9.2/2005/2006) Hôtels, motels, pensions de famille et appartements avec services hôteliers avec 5 chambres ou plus; (9.3) Chambres.
Sources: (1.1-4.3,8.1,9.1-9.4) "Australian Bureau of Statistics"; (6.1-6.3,8.2-8.4) Fonds monétaire international.

AUTRICHE

(1.2-2.6) Touristes non résidents dans tous types d'établissements d'hébergement; (5.1,5.2,7.1,7.2) Villages de vacances compris; (5.3,7.3) À l'exclusion de l'hébergement privé; (8.1) À partir de 2003, nouvelle méthodologie. Y compris voyages à l'étranger pour vacances et affaires avec au moins une nuitée; (9.1) Uniquement hôtels; (9.2) Hôtels et villages de vacances; (9.3) Sur la base de la saison d'été; (9.4) Durée moyenne du séjour dans les hôtels et établissements assimilés; villages de vacances compris.
Sources: (1.2-5.4,7.1-7.4,8.1,9.1-9.4) "Department for Tourism and Historic Objects - Federal Ministry of Economics and Labour"; (6.1-6.3,8.2-8.4) Fonds monétaire international.

AZERBAIDJAN

Sources: (1.2-5.2,7.1,7.2,8.1,9.1,9.2) "Ministry of Culture and Tourism"; (6.1-6.3,8.2-8.4) Fonds monétaire international.

BAHAMAS

(1.2,2.1-2.6,4.1-4.3) Arrivées de touristes non résidents aux frontières nationales; (5.2) Arrivées dans les hôtels seulement; (9.1,9.2) Hôtels, appartements, bungalows et villas - Etablissements homologués uniquement; (9.3) Chambres.
Sources: (1.1-5.4,9.1-9.4) "Bahamas Ministry of Tourism"; (6.1-6.3,8.2-8.4) Fonds monétaire international.

BAHREIN

(1.1,2.1-4.3) Arrivées de visiteurs non résidents aux frontières nationales; à l'exclusion des nationaux résidant à l'étranger; (3.1) Arrivées à l'aéroport international de Bahreïn; (3.3) Arrivées à travers le "King Fahad Causeway"; (3.4) Arrivées au port Mina Salman; (5.1,9.1,9.2) Hôtels homologués seulement.
Sources: (1.1-5.4,9.1-9.3) "Tourism Affairs - Ministry of Information"; (6.1-6.3,8.2-8.4) Fonds monétaire international.

BANGLADESH

Sources: (1.2-5.4,8.1,9.1-9.3) "Bangladesh Parjatan Corporation"; (6.1-6.3,8.2-8.4) Fonds monétaire international.

BARBADE

(1.2,2.1-4.3) Arrivées de touristes non résidents aux frontières nationales; (9.1,9.2) Hôtels, hôtels-appartements, appartements et bungalows, pensions de famille; (9.3) Chambres.
Note 2006: Données provisoires.
Sources: (1.1-5.4,9.1-9.4) "Barbados Tourism Authority"; (6.1-6.3,8.2-8.4) Fonds monétaire international.

BELARUS

(1.2,2.2-2.6) Tourisme organisé.
Sources: (1.1,3.1-3.3,4.1-4.3) "State Committee of Frontier Troops"; (1.2,2.2-2.6,5.1,5.2,7.1,7.2,8.1,9.1-9.4) "Ministry of Statistics and Analysis"; (6.1-6.3,8.2-8.4) Fonds monétaire international.

BELGIQUE

(1.2,2.1-2.6,4.1-4.3) Touristes non résidents dans tous types d'établissements d'hébergement; (5.1,5.2,7.1,7.2) Hôtels uniquement; (9.1,9.2) Hôtels et villages de vacances.
Sources: (1.2-5.3,7.1-7.3,8.1,9.1,9.2) Institut National de Statistique; (6.1-6.3,8.2-8.4) Fonds monétaire international.

BELIZE

(1.3) Passagers en transit et passages aux frontières; (2.2-4.2) Arrivées de touristes non résidents aux frontières nationales; (10.1-10.3) Cette section comprend uniquement le poste « voyages » parce que le poste « transport de passagers » ne figure pas dans les données du Fonds monétaire international qui ont servi à la préparation de la présente édition du Compendium.
Sources: (1.1-5.4,7.3,9.1-9.4) "Belize Tourist Board"; (6.2,8.2-8.4) Fonds monétaire international.

BENIN

(1.2,2.1-2.6) Arrivées de touristes non résidents aux frontières nationales.
Note 2003-2006: Estimations.
Sources: (1.1-5.3,7.3,9.1-9.4) Direction du développement touristique - Ministère de la culture, de l'artisanat et du tourisme; (6.1-6.3,8.2-8.4) Fonds monétaire international.

BERMUDES

(1.1) À l'exclusion des nationaux résidant à l'étranger; (1.2,2.2-2.4,4.1-4.3) Arrivées par voie aérienne; (5.3) Y compris les nuitées dans les résidences particulières; (6.1,8.2) Les chiffres de dépense sont ceux que le pays a fournis à l'OMT mais ils ne figurent pas dans les données du Fonds monétaire international qui ont servi à la préparation de la présente édition du Compendium; (9.3) Chambres.
Source: "Bermuda Department of Tourism".

BHOUTAN

(6.1) Les chiffres de dépense sont ceux que le pays a fournis à l'OMT mais ils ne figurent pas dans les données du Fonds monétaire international qui ont servi à la préparation de la présente édition du Compendium.
Source: "Department of Tourism - Royal Government of Bhutan".

BOLIVIE

(1.2) Arrivées de touristes non résidents aux frontières nationales; (2.1-2.4) Touristes non résidents dans les hôtels et établissements assimilés; (3.4) Arrivées par voie lacustre; (4.1-4.3) Données tirées d'enquêtes; (5.1-5.4,7.1-7.4,9.1,9.2) Capitales de département seulement; (9.3) Places-lit (hôtels); (9.4) Jours, hôtels et établissements assimilés, tourisme récepteur.
Note 2003-2006: Données provisoires.
Sources: (1.2-5.4,7.1-7.4,8.1,9.1-9.4) "Viceministerio de Turismo - Ministerio de Producción y Microempresa"; (6.1-6.3,8.2-8.4) Fonds monétaire international.

BONAIRE

Sources: (1.1-5.4,9.1-9.4) "Tourism Corporation of Bonaire (TCB)"; (6.2,8.3) "Central Bank of the Netherlands Antilles".

BOSNIE-HERZEGOVINE

(1.2,2.2-2.4) Touristes non résidents dans tous types d'établissements d'hébergement; (2.5,2.6) Moins de 500 arrivées; (9.1,9.2) À l'exclusion de la République Srpska.
Sources: (1.2-5.3,7.3,9.1,9.2) "Agency for Statistics of Bosnia and Herzegovina"; (6.1-6.3,8.2-8.4) Fonds monétaire international.

NOTES DES PAYS

BOTSWANA

Sources: (1.1-5.2,7.2,9.1-9.4) "Department of Tourism - Ministry of Environment, Wildlife and Tourism"; (6.1-6.3,8.2-8.4) Fonds monétaire international.

BRESIL

(1.2-4.3) Y compris les nationaux résidant à l'étranger; (3.4) Y compris les arrivées par voie fluviale.
Note 2006: Estimations.
Sources: (1.2-4.3,8.1) "Instituto Brasileiro de Turismo (EMBRATUR)"; (6.1-6.3,8.2-8.4) Fonds monétaire international.

BRUNEI DARUSSALAM

(1.2,2.2-2.4,3.1) Arrivées par voie aérienne; (10.1-10.3) Cette section comprend uniquement le poste « voyages » parce que le poste « transport de passagers » ne figure pas dans les données du Fonds monétaire international qui ont servi à la préparation de la présente édition du Compendium.
Sources: (1.1-5.2,9.1-9.3) "Brunei Tourism - Ministry of Industry and Primary Resources"; (6.2,8.3) Fonds monétaire international.

BULGARIE

(1.3) Visiteurs en transit; (3.4) Mer et voies d'eau intérieures; (5.1,5.3,5.4,7.1,7.3,9.2-9.4) Couvre principalement l'ancien hébergement du secteur public et celui propriété de l'Etat. Une partie considérable du secteur privé (plus de 70 pour cent en 1998) n'est pas inclus dans ces données; (9.2) Hôtels uniquement; (9.3) Places-lit dans les hôtels.
Sources: (1.1-5.4,7.1-7.3,8.1,9.2-9.4) "National Statistical Institute - State Agency for Tourism"; (6.1-6.3,8.2-8.4) Fonds monétaire international.

BURKINA FASO

(1.2,2.1-2.6,5.2) Touristes non résidents dans les hôtels et établissements assimilés; (4.1-4.3) Y compris le tourisme interne; (9.3) Chambres.
Sources: (1.2-5.4,7.1,7.2,9.3) Service de l'analyse statistique et de la Coopération touristique - Ministère de la Culture, des Arts et du Tourisme; (6.1-6.3,8.2-8.4) Banque Centrale des Etats de l'Afrique de l'Ouest.

BURUNDI

(1.2-4.3) Arrivées de touristes non résidents aux frontières nationales; y compris les nationaux résidant à l'étranger; (3.4) Arrivées par voie lacustre.
Sources: (1.2-4.3,9.1,9.2) Office National du Tourisme; (6.1-6.3,8.2-8.4) Fonds monétaire international.

CAMBODGE

(1.2) Arrivées de touristes internationaux par tous moyens de transport; (2.2-2.5,3.1-3.4/2004-2006) À l'exclusion des arrivées dans la région "Phreah Vihear": 2004: 67.843; 2005: 88.615; 2006: 108.691; (3.3/2002) Arrivées par terre ou par navire; (3.4) Arrivées par navire; (4.1-4.3/2002) Arrivées par voie aérienne; (4.1/2002) Y compris les arrivées à l'aéroport de Siem Reap en vols directs: 202.791; (4.3/2005/2006) Y compris les arrivées dans la région "Phreah Vihear"; (5.4) Jours.
Sources: (1.2-5.4,8.1,9.1-9.3) "Ministry of Tourism"; (6.1-6.3,8.2-8.4) Fonds monétaire international.

CAMEROUN

(1.2,2.1-2.6,5.2) Touristes non résidents dans les hôtels et établissements assimilés.
Sources: (1.2-5.2,7.1,7.2,9.1,9.2) Ministère du Tourisme; (6.1-6.3,8.2-8.4) Fonds monétaire international.

CANADA

(1.1,1.3) Données élaborées à partir des inventaires douaniers et ajustées en fonction des résultats d'enquêtes; (1.2,2.1-4.3) Arrivées de touristes non résidents aux frontières nationales; (4.2) Y compris congrès; (8.1) Voyages- personnes (une/plusieurs nuits).
Note 2006: Données provisoires.
Sources: (1.1-4.3,5.3,7.1,7.3,8.1) "Canadian Tourism Commission" et "Statistics Canada"; (6.1-6.3,8.2-8.4) Fonds monétaire international.

CAP-VERT

(1.2,2.1-2.3) Touristes non résidents dans les hôtels et établissements assimilés.
Sources: (1.2,2.1-2.3,5.1,5.2,7.1,7.2,9.1-9.4) "Instituto Nacional de Estatística" et "Ministério da Economia, Crescimento e Competitividade"; (6.1-6.3,8.2-8.4) Fonds monétaire international.

CHILI

(5.1,5.2,7.1,7.2) Les chiffres de 2005 ne sont pas comparables à ceux des années précédentes en raison de la mise à jour du recensement national des établissements d'hébergement touristique.
Sources: (1.2-5.4,7.1,7.2,8.1,9.1-9.4) "Servicio Nacional de Turismo - SERNATUR"; (6.1-6.3,8.2-8.4) Fonds monétaire international.

CHINE

(1.1,2.1-2.6,3.1-3.4) Y compris les arrivées de personnes d'origine ethnique chinoise en provenance de "Hong-Kong, Chine", "Macao, Chine", "Taïwan (Province de Chine)" et chinois de l'étranger, la plupart visiteurs de la journée (excursionnistes) en provenance de "Hong-Kong, Chine" et de "Macao, Chine"; (4.1-4.3) À l'exclusion des arrivées de personnes d'origine chinoise de souche en provenance de "Hong-Kong, Chine", "Macao, Chine", "Taïwan (Province de Chine)" et chinois de l'étranger; (7.1,9.1,9.2) Ne concernent que les hôtels classés par étoiles; (8.1) Y compris les membres des équipages et autres membres des forces armées; (9.3) Chambres; (9.4) Tourisme récepteur uniquement.
Sources: (1.1-5.4,7.1,8.1,9.1-9.4) "National Tourism Administration"; (6.1-6.3,8.2-8.4) Fonds monétaire international.

CHYPRE

(1.2,2.1-2.6) Arrivées de touristes non résidents aux frontières nationales; (1.3) Y compris les passagers en croisière/transit; (3.4) Y compris les passagers en croisière; (5.4) Ces données extraites de l'enquête sur les dépenses des touristes (départs), concernent les séjours dans tous les types d'hébergement; (9.3) Places-lit; (9.4) À partir de 2000, la durée moyenne du séjour est calculée sur la base des nuitées et des arrivées de clients dans les hôtels et établissements assimilés.
Sources: (1.1-5.4,7.1-7.4,8.1,9.1-9.4) "Cyprus Tourism Organization"; (6.1-6.3,8.2-8.4) Fonds monétaire international.

COLOMBIE

(1.1,2.1-2.6,3.1-3.4,4.1-4.3) Arrivées de visiteurs non résidents aux frontières nationales. À l'exclusion des passagers en croisière; (9.3) Chambres.
Note 2006: Données provisoires.
Sources: (1.1-4.3,8.1) "Dirección de Extranjería - Departamento Administrativo de Seguridad (DAS)"; (6.1-6.3,8.2-8.4) Fonds monétaire international; (9.1-9.3) "Dirección de Turismo - Ministerio de Comercio, Industria y Turismo, Asociación Hotelera de Colombia (COTELCO)".

COMORES

(6.1,8.2) Les chiffres de dépense sont ceux que le pays a fournis à l'OMT mais ils ne figurent pas dans les données du Fonds monétaire international qui ont servi à la préparation de la présente édition du Compendium.
Sources: Direction Nationale de la Promotion du Tourisme et de l'Hôtellerie - Ministère du Transport, Tourisme, Postes et Télécommunications et Banque centrale des Comores.

COREE, REPUBLIQUE DE

(1.1) Y compris les nationaux résidant à l'étranger et membres des équipages; (2.1-2.6) À l'exclusion des nationaux résidant à l'étranger; (3.1,3.4/2002-2005) À l'exclusion des nationaux résidant à l'étranger et membres des équipages; (8.2) Pour la dépense, le pays fournit à l'OMT des niveaux d'agrégation qui diffèrent de façon significative des données du Fonds monétaire international utilisées pour la préparation de la présente édition du Compendium (à l'exclusion des dépenses des étudiants qui font des études à l'étranger). Les données du pays sont les suivantes :
2002:   9.038
2003:   8.248
2004:   9.856
2005: 12.025
2006: 14.336
(9.1) Hôtels seulement; (9.3) Chambres.
Sources: (1.1-5.4,8.1,9.1,9.3) "Ministry of Culture and Tourism"; (6.1-6.3,8.2-8.4) Fonds monétaire international.

COSTA RICA

(4.1) Voyages d'agrément et visites aux parents; (5.4) Dans la zone centrale du pays; (9.3) Etablissements de catégorie "5 étoiles" dans la zone métropolitaine de San José (enquête).
Sources: (1.1-5.4,8.1,9.1,9.3) "Instituto Costarricense de Turismo"; (6.1-6.3,8.2-8.4) Fonds monétaire international.

CROATIE

(1.2,2.2-2.4) Touristes non résidents dans tous types d'établissements d'hébergement; y compris les arrivées dans des ports à tourisme nautique; (3.1-3.4) Arrivées de visiteurs non résidents aux frontières nationales; (3.4/2004) Depuis 2004, une nouvelle méthodologie et une nouvelle couverture ont été appliquées. L'information n'est donc pas comparable à celle des années précédentes; (5.3,7.3) Y compris les nuitées dans des ports à tourisme nautique; (9.4) Tourisme intérieur (interne et récepteur) dans l'ensemble des moyens d'hébergement (y compris les ports à tourisme nautique).

NOTES DES PAYS

Sources: (1.1-5.4,7.1-7.4,9.1-9.4) "Central Bureau of Statistics"; (6.1-6.3,8.2-8.4) Fonds monétaire international.

CUBA

(1.1,2.1-2.6) Arrivées de visiteurs non résidents aux frontières nationales; (1.2,4.1-4.3) Arrivées par voie aérienne; (1.3) Y compris les passagers en croisière; (5.1,7.1,9.1,9.2) Hôtels, motels et apart-hôtels; (5.3,7.3) Hôtels, motels, apart-hôtels, terrains de camping/caravaning et autres; (6.1-6.3) Les chiffres de dépense sont ceux que le pays a fournis à l'OMT mais ils ne figurent pas dans les données du Fonds monétaire international qui ont servi à la préparation de la présente édition du Compendium; (8.1) Comprend seulement circuits contrôlés par l'Instituto de Turismo; (9.3) Chambres.
Source: "Oficina Nacional de Estadísticas".

CURAÇAO

(1.2,1.3,2.2,2.3,3.1,4.1-4.3) Arrivées par voie aérienne; (3.4) Arrivées de passagers en croisière; (4.1-4.3) Les différences entre les totaux globaux sont dues au caractère incomplet des cartes d'embarquement et de débarquement remplies par les visiteurs; (6.1) Les chiffres de dépense sont ceux que le pays a fournis à l'OMT mais ils ne figurent pas dans les données du Fonds monétaire international qui ont servi à la préparation de la présente édition du Compendium; (9.1) Hôtels, pensions de famille, appartements; (9.3) Chambres.
Source: "Curaçao Tourist Board".

DANEMARK

(1.2,2.2-2.4) Touristes non résidents dans tous types d'établissements d'hébergement; (1.2-5.3,7.1-7.3,8.1) Nouvelle méthodologie à partir de 2004; (5.2,7.2) Hôtels uniquement; (9.1-9.3) Hôtels et logements pour vacances avec 40 lits et plus seulement; (9.3) Places-lit; (10.1-10.3) Cette section comprend uniquement le poste « voyages » parce que le poste « transport de passagers » ne figure pas dans les données du Fonds monétaire international qui ont servi à la préparation de la présente édition du Compendium.
Sources: (1.1-5.4,7.1-7.4,8.1,9.1-9.3) "Statistics Denmark"; (6.2,8.3) Fonds monétaire international.

DJIBOUTI

(1.2) Touristes non résidents dans les hôtels; (9.3) Chambres; (10.1-10.3) Cette section comprend uniquement le poste « voyages » parce que le poste « transport de passagers » ne figure pas dans les données du Fonds monétaire international qui ont servi à la préparation de la présente édition du Compendium.
Sources: (1.2,5.1,5.2,9.1-9.3) Office national du tourisme; (6.2,8.2-8.4) Fonds monétaire international.

DOMINIQUE

(1.2,2.2-2.4,4.1-4.3) Arrivées de touristes non résidents aux frontières nationales; (3.1,3.4) Arrivées de visiteurs non résidents aux frontières nationales; à l'exclusion des passagers en croisière; (5.4) Jours; (10.1-10.3) Cette section comprend uniquement le poste « voyages » parce que le poste « transport de passagers » ne figure pas dans les données du Fonds monétaire international qui ont servi à la préparation de la présente édition du Compendium.
Sources: (1.1-5.4,9.1) "Central Statistical Office - Ministry of Finance"; (6.2,8.3) Fonds monétaire international.

EGYPTE

(1.1,2.1-3.4) Arrivées de visiteurs non résidents aux frontières nationales; (4.1-4.3) Arrivées de touristes non résidents aux frontières nationales; (7.1) Hôtels seulement dans les principales régions: le Caire, Giza, le Sud du Sinaï, la Mer Rouge, Luxor, Aswan, Alexandrie; (8.1) Voyages à des fins de tourisme et de non-tourisme (plus de 50 % des départs ont lieu pour des motifs de travail); (9.3) Chambres.
Sources: (1.1-5.4,7.1-7.4,8.1,9.1-9.4) "Ministry of Tourism"; (6.1-6.3,8.2-8.4) Fonds monétaire international.

EL SALVADOR

(1.2,2.1-4.3) Arrivées de touristes non résidents aux frontières nationales; (6.1) Pour la dépense, le pays fournit à l'OMT des niveaux d'agrégation qui diffèrent de façon significative des données du Fonds monétaire international utilisées pour la préparation de la présente édition du Compendium. Les données du pays sont les suivantes (millions $E.U.) :
2002: 342
2003: 373
2004: 425
2005: 644
2006: 862
Cette dépense touristique est obtenue à partir d'études communes menées avec le "Banco Central de Reserva" d'El Salvador et la "Corporación Salvadoreña de Turismo" pour préciser le profil de base du touriste international qui visite ce pays.
(9.3) Places-lit.
Sources: (1.1-5.4,8.1,9.1-9.4) "Corporación Salvadoreña de Turismo (CORSATUR) - Ministerio de Turismo"; (6.1-6.3,8.2-8.4) Fonds monétaire international.

EMIRATS ARABES UNIS

(1.2) Arrivées dans les hôtels seulement. Y compris le tourisme interne et les nationaux résidant à l'étranger; (2.1-2.6) Arrivées dans les hôtels seulement. À l'exclusion du tourisme interne et des nationaux résidant à l'étranger; (5.1) Nuitées dans les hôtels seulement. Y compris le tourisme interne et les nationaux résidant à l'étranger; (6.1,8.2) Les chiffres de dépense sont ceux que le pays a fournis à l'OMT mais ils ne figurent pas dans les données du Fonds monétaire international qui ont servi à la préparation de la présente édition du Compendium; (9.1,9.2) Hôtels seulement; (9.3) Chambres louées.
Source: "Ministry of Economy and Planning - Planning Sector".

EQUATEUR

(1.1) À l'exclusion des nationaux résidant à l'étranger.
Sources: (1.1-3.4,8.1,9.1,9.2) "Ministerio de Turismo"; (6.1-6.3,8.2-8.4) Fonds monétaire international.

ERYTHREE

(1.1) Y compris les nationaux résidant à l'étranger; (2.1-2.6) À l'exclusion des nationaux résidant à l'étranger; (5.1,7.1) Uniquement hôtels et établissements assimilés dans les trois villes principales: Asmara, Karen et Massawa; (6.1) Les données de dépense sont celles que le pays a fournies à l'OMT car il s'agit d'une série plus complète que celle obtenue du Fonds monétaire international (FMI) pour la préparation de la présente édition du Compendium; (9.1,9.2/2002-2004) Uniquement dans les villes principales d'Erythrée; (9.1,9.2/2005) Tous les hôtels et établissements assimilés en Erythrée; (10.1-10.3) Cette section n'a pas pu être remplie parce que les postes « voyages » et « transport de passagers » ne figurent pas dans les données du Fonds monétaire international qui ont servi à la préparation de la présente édition du Compendium.
Source: "Ministry of Tourism".

ESPAGNE

(1.1) Arrivées de visiteurs non résidents aux frontières nationales; y compris les nationaux résidant à l'étranger; (2.2-4.3) Arrivées de touristes non résidents aux frontières nationales; y compris les nationaux résidant à l'étranger; (2.4) Japon seulement; (5.1,7.1) Nuitées dans les hôtels et les "hostales" (établissements d'hébergement offrant des services limités); (5.3,7.3) Nuitées dans les hôtels, "hostales", terrains de camping, appartements touristiques et logements ruraux; (5.4,7.4,9.1-9.4) Hôtels et "hostales" seulement; (8.1) Nouvelle méthodoligie à partir de 2005. L'information n'est donc pas comparable à celle des années précédentes; (9.3) Places-lit.
Sources: (1.1-4.3,8.1) "Instituto de Estudios Turísticos"; (5.1-5.4,7.1-7.4,9.1-9.4) "Instituto Nacional de Estadística"; (6.1-6.3,8.2-8.4) Fonds monétaire international.

ESTONIE

(1.1,3.1-3.4) Arrivées de visiteurs non résidents aux frontières nationales; (1.1-1.3,3.1-3.4,8.1/2004) À partir de 2004, les statistiques de frontière ne sont plus collectées; (1.2/2004-2006) Calculé sur la base des statistiques d'hébergement et de la "Foreign Visitor Survey" menée par la "Statistical Office of Estonia"; (2.1-2.4) Touristes non résidents dans tous types d'établissements d'hébergement; (9.1-9.4) Y compris les données des stations thermales et climatiques assurant l'hébergement.
Sources: (1.1-5.4,7.1-7.4,8.1,9.1-9.4) "Estonian Tourist Board / Enterprise Estonia"; (6.1-6.3,8.2-8.4) Fonds monétaire international.

ETATS-UNIS

(1.2,2.2) Y compris les Mexicains passant une nuit ou plus aux Etats-Unis; (3.1-3.4) Estimations préliminaires; (3.3) Y compris un très petit pourcentage (0.2%) de voyageurs dont on ne connaît pas le mode de transport utilisé; (4.1-4.3,5.2) Outre-mer uniquement; à l'exclusion du Mexique (les données ne sont pas disponibles); (6.2,8.3) Pour la dépense, le pays fournit à l'OMT des données qui diffèrent de façon significative des données du Fonds monétaire international utilisées pour la préparation de la présente édition du Compendium. Les données du pays sont les suivantes :

	6.2	8.3
2002:	66.605	58.715
2003:	64.359	57.447
2004:	74.546	65.750
2005:	81.799	68.970
2006:	85.694	72.029

(8.1) Y compris les Américains passant une nuit ou plus au Mexique.
Sources: (1.2-5.2,8.1) "Office of Travel and Tourism Industries"; (6.1-6.3,8.2-8.4) Fonds monétaire international; (9.1,9.3) "American Hotel & Lodging Association (AHLA)".

ETHIOPIE

(1.2) Arrivées à travers tous les ports d'entrée; y compris les nationaux résidant à l'étranger; (2.1-2.6,3.1-3.3,4.1-4.3) Arrivées à travers tous les ports d'entrée; (9.1,9.2/2002/2003/2005) À l'exclusion des hôtels non-homologués; (9.3) Places-lit; (9.4) Années fiscales éthiopiennes.
Sources: (1.2-5.1,9.1-9.4) "Ethiopian Tourism Commission"; (6.1-6.3,8.2-8.4) Fonds monétaire international.

EX-REPUBLIQUE YOUGOSLAVE DE MACEDOINE

(1.2,2.2-2.4) Touristes non résidents dans tous types d'établissements d'hébergement; (3.1-3.3) Arrivées de visiteurs non résidents aux frontières nationales; (9.4) Durée moyenne du séjour dans tous les établissements d'hébergement.
Sources: (1.1-5.4,7.1-7.4,9.1-9.4) "State Statistical Office"; (6.1-6.3,8.2-8.4) Fonds monétaire international.

FEDERATION DE RUSSIE

(1.1,2.1-4.3) Arrivées de visiteurs non résidents aux frontières nationales; (9.1,9.2) Hébergement dans les hôtels et autres établissements touristiques.
Sources: (1.1-5.4,7.1-7.4,8.1,9.1-9.4) "Russian Federal Agency for Tourism"; (6.1-6.3,8.2-8.4) Fonds monétaire international.

FIDJI

(1.2,2.2-4.3) Arrivées de touristes non résidents aux frontières nationales; à l'exclusion des nationaux résidant à l'étranger; (1.2-4.3,5.4,/2004-2006) Données provisoires; (5.4) Jours; (9.3) Chambres.
Sources: (1.1-5.4,7.1,8.1,9.1-9.3) "Fiji Islands Bureau of Statistics"(6.1-6.3,8.2-8.4) Fonds monétaire international.

FINLANDE

(1.1,2.1-4.3) Arrivées de visiteurs non résidents aux frontières nationales. Enquête aux frontières; (1.2) Arrivées de touristes non résidents aux frontières nationales; (5.1-5.3,7.1-7.3) Dû à un changement dans la méthodologie, l'information n'est pas comparable à celle des années précédentes; (8.1) Voyages à l'étranger, croisières avec nuitées à bord comprises.
Sources: (1.1-5.4,7.1-7.4,8.1,9.1-9.4) "Tourism Statistics - Statistics Finland"; (6.1-6.3,8.2-8.4) Fonds monétaire international.

FRANCE

(1.1-4.3,5.3) Estimations à partir d'enquêtes aux frontières (1996-2004); (1.1-4.3,5.3,5.4/2005) Rupture de série, données non comparables aux années antérieures; (4.1) Vacances et visites à des parents, amis; (4.2) Affaires, plaisir; (4.3) Transit et autres motifs; (5.1,5.2,7.1,7.2,9.1-9.4) 2002/2003: uniquement hôtels 0 à 4 étoiles. 2004-2006: y compris hôtels non homologués. 2006: rénovation de l'enquête, données non comparables aux années antérieures; (5.3,7.3) Tous modes d'hébergement; (5.4) Durée moyenne du séjour récepteur; (7.1-7.4/2005/2006) Population résidente de 15 ans et plus; (9.3) Taux net des chambres. 2005: Données révisées; 2006: Données provisoires.
Sources: (1.2-5.4,7.1-7.4,8.1,9.1-9.4) Bureau des études, des statistiques et des comptes économiques - Direction du Tourisme; (6.2,8.3) Fonds monétaire international; (6.3,8.4) Banque de France.

GABON

(1.2,2.1,3.1) Arrivées de touristes non résidents à l'aéroport de Libreville.
Sources: (1.1-5.1,8.1,9.1,9.3) Centre Gabonais de Promotion Touristique (GABONTOUR); (6.1-6.3,8.2-8.4) Fonds monétaire international.

GAMBIE

(1.2,2.1-2.3,3.1,4.1-4.3) Arrivées en vols à la demande seulement.
Sources: (1.1-4.3,8.1,9.1-9.4) "Gambia Tourism Authority"; (6.1-6.3,8.2-8.4) Fonds monétaire international.

GEORGIE

(4.1-4.3) Arrivées dans les hôtels seulement.
Sources: (1.1-4.3,8.1) "Department of Tourism and Resorts - Ministry of Economic Development"; (5.2,7.2,9.1,9.2) "State Department for Statistics - Ministry of Economic Development"; (6.1-6.3,8.2-8.4) Fonds monétaire international.

GHANA

(1.2) Y compris les nationaux résidant à l'étranger; (2.1-2.6) À l'exclusion des nationaux résidant à l'étranger.
Sources: (1.2-4.3,9.1-9.3) "Ghana Tourist Board" et "Ministry of Tourism and Modernisation of the Capital City"; (6.1-6.3,8.2-8.4) Fonds monétaire international.

GRECE

(1.1,3.1-3.4) Arrivées de visiteurs non résidents aux frontières nationales; (1.2,2.1-2.6) Arrivées de touristes non résidents aux frontières nationales; information tirée de données administratives; (3.4) Y compris les passagers en croisière.
Sources: (1.1-5.4,7.1-7.4,9.3) "National Statistical Service"; (6.1-6.3,8.2-8.4) Fonds monétaire international; (9.1,9.2) "Hellenic Chamber of Hotels".

GRENADE

(1.2,2.1-4.3) Arrivées de touristes non résidents aux frontières nationales; (9.1,9.2) Hôtels, bungalows/ appartements et pensions de famille; (9.3) Chambres; (10.1-10.3) Cette section comprend uniquement le poste « voyages » parce que le poste « transport de passagers » ne figure pas dans les données du Fonds monétaire international qui ont servi à la préparation de la présente édition du Compendium.
Sources: (1.1-5.4,9.1-9.4) "Grenada Board of Tourism"; (6.2,8.3) Fonds monétaire international.

GUADELOUPE

(1.2) Arrivées par voie aérienne; À l'exclusion des îles du nord (Saint Martin et Saint Barthélemy); (1.2/2003/2004) Touristes non résidents dans les hôtels seulement; (1.2,2.3,3.1/2005) Données tirées d'une enquête réalisée à l'aéroport de Guadeloupe; (5.2) Hôtels seulement; (9.1) Hôtels; (9.3) Chambres.
Source: Comité du Tourisme des Îles de la Guadeloupe.

GUAM

(1.2) Arrivées par voies aérienne et maritime; (2.2-2.4) Arrivées par voie aérienne uniquement; (4.1-4.3) Uniquement arrivées de civils par voie aérienne; (9.1) Chambres disponibles.
Source: "Guam Visitors Bureau".

GUATEMALA

(8.2) Pour la dépense, le pays fournit à l'OMT des niveaux d'agrégation qui diffèrent de façon significative des données du Fonds monétaire international. Les données du pays sont les suivantes :
2002: 517
2003: 601
2004: 735
2005: 754
2006: 789
Sources: (1.2-4.3,8.1,9.1-9.4) "Instituto Guatemalteco de Turismo - INGUAT"; (6.1-6.3,8.2-8.4) Fonds monétaire international.

GUINEE

(1.2,2.1-2.6,4.1-4.3/2003/2005/2006) Arrivées par voie aérienne à l'aéroport de Conakry; (5.2) Hôtels seulement; (6.2) Les données de dépense sont celles que le pays a fournies à l'OMT car il s'agit d'une série plus complète que celle obtenue du Fonds monétaire international (FMI) pour la préparation de la présente édition du Compendium.
Sources: (1.2-5.4,6.2,9.1-9.4) Division Observatoire du Tourisme - Ministère du Tourisme, de l'Hôtellerie et de l'Artisanat; (6.3,8.2-8.4) Fonds monétaire international.

GUINEE-BISSAU

(1.2,2.1-2.6,4.1-4.3) Arrivées à l'aéroport "Osvaldo Vieira".
Sources: (1.2-4.3) "Ministério do Turismo e do Ordenamento do Território"; (6.1-6.3,8.2-8.4) Fonds monétaire international.

GUYANE

(1.2,2.2,2.3,3.1) Arrivées à l'aéroport de Timehri seulement.
Sources: (1.2-3.1) "Guyana Tourism Authority"; (6.1-6.3,8.2-8.4) Fonds monétaire international.

GUYANE FRANÇAISE

(1.2,6.1/2005) Enquête 2005 au départ de l'aéroport de Cayenne-Rochambeau.
Sources: Comité du Tourisme de la Guyane et INSEE Guyane.

HAITI

(10.1-10.3) Cette section comprend uniquement le poste « voyages » parce que le poste « transport de passagers » ne figure pas dans les données du Fonds monétaire international qui ont servi à la préparation de la présente édition du Compendium.
Sources: (1.1-3.4) Ministère du Tourisme; (6.2,8.2-8.4) Fonds monétaire international.

HONDURAS

(1.2,2.1-4.3) Arrivées de touristes non résidents aux frontières nationales.
Sources: (1.1-5.4,8.1,9.1-9.4) "Instituto Hondureño de Turismo" (6.1-6.3,8.2-8.4) Fonds monétaire international.

NOTES DES PAYS

HONG-KONG, CHINE

(6.1-6.3) Les données de dépense sont celles que le pays a fournies à l'OMT car il s'agit d'une série plus complète que celle obtenue du Fonds monétaire international (FMI) pour la préparation de la présente édition du Compendium. (Source: "HKTB Visitors Survey"); (8.1) À l'inclusion des résidents de Hong-Kong voyageant à Macao et Chine; (9.1) Hôtels (tarifs élevés/moyens) et auberges/ pensions de famille; (9.3) Chambres.
Sources: (1.1-8.1,9.1,9.3) "Hong Kong Tourism Board"; (8.3) "Census and Statistics Department".

HUNGARY

(1.1/2002/2003) (3.1-3.4) Départs de visiteurs non résidents; (1.1-1.4,4.1-4.3/2004) Nouvelle série; (2.1-2.4) Touristes non résidents dans tous types d'établissements d'hébergement; (3.4) Voie fluviale; (9.3) Chambres, juillet-juin.
Sources: (1.1-5.4,7.1-7.4,8.1,9.1-9.4) "Hungarian Central statistical Office"; (6.1-6.3,8.2-8.4) Fonds monétaire international.

ILES CAIMANES

(1.2,2.2-2.4,4.1-4.3) Arrivées par voie aérienne; (5.4,9.4) Jours; (6.1) Les chiffres de dépense sont ceux que le pays a fournis à l'OMT mais ils ne figurent pas dans les données du Fonds monétaire international qui ont servi à la préparation de la présente édition du Compendium. Y compris les dépenses des passagers en croisière; (5.2,9.1,9.2) Hôtels et appartements; (9.3) Hôtels (chambres).
Source: "Cayman Islands Department of Tourism".

ILES COOK

(1.2,2.2-2.4,4.1-4.3) Arrivées par voies aérienne et maritime; (6.1) Les chiffres de dépense sont ceux que le pays a fournis à l'OMT mais ils ne figurent pas dans les données du Fonds monétaire international qui ont servi à la préparation de la présente édition du Compendium; (9.3) Chambres.
Note 2006: Données provisoires.
Source: "Cook Islands Tourism Corporation" et "Cook Islands Statistics Office".

ILES MARIANNES SEPTENTRIONALES

(1.1,2.2-2.4) Arrivées de visiteurs non résidents aux frontières nationales; (1.2) Arrivées par voie aérienne; (2.2) Y compris Guam; (9.1) Couvre 68 pour cent du nombre total de chambres recensées.
Source: "Marianas Visitors Authority".

ILES MARSHALL

(1.2,2.2-2.4,4.1-4.3/2002/2003/2006) Arrivées par voie aérienne; (1.2,2.2-2.4,4.1-4.3/2004/2005) Arrivées par voies aérienne et maritime; (6.1,8.2) Les chiffres de dépense sont ceux que le pays a fournis à l'OMT mais ils ne figurent pas dans les données du Fonds monétaire international qui ont servi à la préparation de la présente édition du Compendium. Années fiscales (1 octobre - 30 septembre).
Source: "Marshall Islands Visitors Authority".

ILES SALOMON

(1.2,2.2-2.4/2005) À l'exclusion du 1er trimestre.
Sources: (1.2,2.2-2.4) "Solomon Islands National Statistics Office"; (6.1-6.3,8.2-8.4) Fonds monétaire international.

ILES TURQUES ET CAIQUES

(6.1) Les chiffres de dépense sont ceux que le pays a fournis à l'OMT mais ils ne figurent pas dans les données du Fonds monétaire international qui ont servi à la préparation de la présente édition du Compendium.
Source: "Turks and Caicos Tourist Board".

ILES VIERGES AMERICAINES

(2.1-2.4) Touristes non résidents dans les hôtels et établissements assimilés; (3.1) Arrivées de visiteurs par voie aérienne; à l'exclusion des arrivées de résidents et le trafic entre les îles, mais compris les visiteurs de la journée (excursionnistes); (3.4) Passagers en croisière; (5.3) Y compris celles de touristes nationaux (environ 40 pour cent de l'ensemble); (6.1) Les chiffres de dépense sont ceux que le pays a fournis à l'OMT mais ils ne figurent pas dans les données du Fonds monétaire international qui ont servi à la préparation de la présente édition du Compendium; (9.1,9.3) Hôtels et condominiums ou villas; (9.3) Chambres.
2006: Données provisoires.
Source: "Bureau of Economic Research".

ILES VIERGES BRITANNIQUES

(1.1-9.4/2004/2005) Estimations; (6.1) Les chiffres de dépense sont ceux que le pays a fournis à l'OMT mais ils ne figurent pas dans les données du Fonds monétaire international qui ont servi à la préparation de la présente édition du Compendium; (9.3) Chambres.
Source: "The Development Planning Unit - Ministry of Finance".

INDE

(1.2,2.1-4.2) Arrivées de touristes non résidents aux frontières nationales; à l'exclusion des nationaux résidant à l'étranger; (4.1) Y compris autres motifs; (8.1) Départs de nationaux seulement, pour tous motifs de visite; (9.1,9.2) Hôtels homologués; (9.3) Chambres.
Sources: (1.1-4.2,8.1,9.1-9.3) "Market Research Division - Government of India"; (6.1-6.3,8.2-8.4) Fonds monétaire international.

Brève note sur la révision de la méthode d'estimation des rentrées de devises étrangères (RDE) mensuelles du tourisme en Inde

1.   La *Reserve Bank of India* (RBI), banque centrale de l'Inde, établit les estimations officielles des rentrées de devises étrangères (RDE) du tourisme sur une base trimestrielle dans le cadre des statistiques de la balance des paiements (BP). L'estimation trimestrielle préliminaire, publiée avec un décalage de trois mois, est généralement révisée à deux reprises – et qualifiée d'estimation partiellement révisée (PR) – avant sa dernière révision. Afin de préparer les estimations mensuelles des RDE du tourisme dans un délai ne dépassant pas une semaine, le ministère du Tourisme (MT) a mis au point une méthode. Les principaux apports utilisés pour cette méthode étaient les normes relatives aux RDE par visiteur en provenance du Bangladesh et du Pakistan, le rapport entre les RDE totales du tourisme et les arrivées de touristes étrangers (ATE) en provenance de pays autres que le Bangladesh et le Pakistan, le nombre total d'ATE du mois pour lequel il faut établir les estimations de RDE et enfin l'indice des prix de gros (IPG). Cette méthode présentait deux grandes imperfections. Premièrement, les normes relatives aux RDE par visiteur en provenance du Bangladesh et du Pakistan reposaient sur des chiffres très anciens. Deuxièmement, le rapport entre les RDE totales du tourisme et les ATE de pays autres que le Bangladesh et le Pakistan, obtenu à partir des données sur les RDE de la RBI, ne faisait pas l'objet d'une mise à jour permanente utilisant les derniers chiffres définitifs disponibles. Ces imperfections avaient pour résultat que les estimations du MT étaient nettement inférieures aux estimations de la RBI. Cette sous-estimation, de 9 % en 2000, était passée à 26 % en 2003 et elle avait encore augmenté jusqu'à 36% en 2006.

2.   Pour réduire autant que possible au minimum la différence avec les estimations définitives des RDE du tourisme que fournit la RBI, la méthode employée par le MT a été revue à partir de décembre 2007. Les phases essentielles de cette méthode revue sont les suivantes :

i)   La dernière estimation trimestrielle partiellement révisée des RDE du tourisme transmise par la RBI est ventilée à l'aide des chiffres mensuels des ATE du trimestre en question pour obtenir les estimations mensuelles des RDE.

ii)   Le rapport entre les RDE et les ATE pour le dernier mois du trimestre visé à la phase i) est gonflé en se servant de l'indice des prix à la consommation pour les salariés non manuels urbains (IPC-SNMU) afin d'obtenir le rapport pour le dernier mois pour lequel l'estimation des RDE est préparée.

iii)   Le rapport mentionné à la phase ii) est multiplié par le nombre d'ATE du mois en question afin d'obtenir l'estimation des RDE en roupies indiennes (INR) pour ce mois. Cette estimation est dite estimation préalable.

iv)   Le cours du change qu'indique la RBI sert à convertir en dollars des États-Unis l'estimation des RDE exprimée en INR.

v)   Dès que la RBI transmet l'estimation partiellement révisée des RDE pour un trimestre plus récent, celle-ci sert à établir les estimations mensuelles pour les mois ultérieurs.

3.   Les estimations préalables des RDE d'une année seront revues deux fois dans l'année lorsque la RBI publiera les estimations partiellement révisées pour ses différents trimestres. Ces chiffres revus le seront encore une fois pour obtenir les chiffres définitifs lorsque la RBI publiera les estimations définitivement révisées pour tous les trimestres de l'année en question.

4.   Sur la base de cette nouvelle méthode, les estimations du MT concernant les RDE du tourisme ont été revues pour toutes les années à partir de 2000. L'adoption de la nouvelle méthode a ramené la différence entre les estimations préalables du MT et les chiffres de la RBI à un niveau d'environ 5 % alors qu'auparavant la divergence avait atteint 40 %. Le tableau ci-dessous compare les estimations des RDE selon les nouvelle et ancienne méthodes.

			(millions de $EU)
Année	Nouvelle méthode	Méthode précédente	Variation (%)
(1)	(2)	(3)	(4)
2000	3 460	3 168	9,2 %
2001	3 198	3 042	5,1 %
2002	3 103	2 923	6,2 %

2003	4 463	3 533	26,3 %
2004	6 170	4 769	29,4 %
2005	7 493 *	5 731	30,7 %
2006	8 934 *	6 569	36,0 %
2007	11 956 #	8 255	44,8 %

* Estimations revues, # Estimation préalable

5.   Comme la nouvelle méthode utilisera en permanence les derniers chiffres trimestriels partiellement révisés des RDE transmis par la RBI, l'écart entre les estimations du MT et de la RBI sera aussi probablement minime dans l'avenir.

6.   Le site du ministère du Tourisme du gouvernement de l'Inde sur la Toile (www.tourism.gov.in) donne des précisions sur la méthode.

INDONESIE

(5.2,5.4,7.2,7.4,9.3,9.4) Hôtels homologués seulement; (9.1,9.2) Toutes formes d'hébergement commercial; (9.3) Chambres. Sources: (1.2-5.4,7.2,7.4,8.1,9.1-9.4) "Ministry of Culture and Tourism" et "BPS Statistics Indonesia"; (6.1-6.3,8.2-8.4) Fonds monétaire international.

IRAN, REPUBLIQUE ISLAMIQUE D'

(3.3) Y compris chemin de fer; (5.2,7.2) Hôtels seulement; (9.1,9.2) Hôtels seulement, 21 mars - 20 mars; (9.3) Estimations (Places-lit). Sources: (1.2-5.4,7.1-7.4,8.1,9.1-9.4) "Iran Cultural Heritage and Tourism Organization (ICHTO)"; (6.1-6.3,8.2-8.4) "Central Bank of Islamic Republic of Iran".

IRLANDE

(1.2,2.3,3.3,4.1-4.3,5.4) Y compris les touristes en provenance de l'Irlande du Nord; (3.3) Y compris chemin de fer; (8.1) Y compris les visiteurs de la journée (excursionnistes); (9.1) À l'exclusion des hôtelleries; (9.3) Chambres, hôtels seulement. Sources: (1.2-5.4,7.1-7.4,8.1,9.1-9.3) "Fáilte Ireland"; (6.1-6.3,8.2-8.4) Fonds monétaire international.

ISLANDE

(1.2,2.1-2.4) Touristes non résidents dans tous types d'établissements d'hébergement; (3.1,3.4) Arrivées de touristes non résidents aux postes-frontières islandais. Note: Suite à l'application des accords de Schengen à partir de mars 2001, la collecte des données sur les arrivées et les départs aux postes-frontières islandais a subi des changements. Depuis 2002, le "Icelandic Tourist Board" est chargé de la collecte de ces données. Sources: (1.2-2.4,5.1-5.4,7.1-7.4,9.1-9.4) "Hagstofa Íslands Statistics Iceland"; (3.1,3.4) "Icelandic Tourist Board"; (6.1-6.3,8.2-8.4) Fonds monétaire international.

ISRAEL

(1.1) Arrivées de visiteurs non résidents aux frontières nationales; à l'exclusion des nationaux résidant à l'étranger; (1.2,2.1-4.3) Arrivées de touristes non résidents aux frontières nationales; à l'exclusion des nationaux résidant à l'étranger; (3.3) Y compris nouvelles entrées de touristes après une visite au Sinaï d'un maximum de 7 jours; (3.4) Y compris les membres de la marine des Etats-Unis en visite de courtoisie; (4.3) Y compris visites à des parents et amis et pèlerinages; (5.1) Hôtels de touristes et aparthôtels; (6.2) Y compris les dépenses des travailleurs étrangers en Israël (Mn $E.U.):
2002: 1.125
2003:   997
2004:   904
2005:   847
2006:   909
(9.3) Taux d'occupation/lits dans hôtels et établissements assimilés ouverts; (9.4) Tourisme récepteur dans hôtels touristiques. Sources: (1.1-5.4,7.1-7.3,8.1,9.1-9.4) "Ministry of Tourism"; (6.1-6.3,8.2-8.4) Fonds monétaire international.

ITALIE

(1.1,3.1-4.3) Arrivées de visiteurs non résidents aux frontières nationales; à l'exclusion des travailleurs saisonniers et frontaliers; (1.1-4.3,8.1) Enquête aux frontières de l'"Ufficio Italiano dei Cambi"; (1.2,2.1-2.6) Arrivées de touristes non résidents aux frontières nationales; à l'exclusion des travailleurs saisonniers et frontaliers; (1.3) Y compris les passagers en croisière; (5.1,5.2) Hôtels seulement; (8.1) Nombre de touristes résidents (visiteurs qui passent la nuit) voyageant à l'étranger; (9.3) Places-lit. Sources: (1.1-4.3,8.1) "Ufficio Italiano dei Cambi"; (5.1-5.4,7.1-7.4,9.1-9.4) "Statistiche sul Turismo - Istituto Nazionale di Statistica (ISTAT)"; (6.1-6.3,8.2-8.4) Fonds monétaire international.

JAMAHIRIYA ARABE LIBYENNE

(1.1,2.1-2.6) Y compris tous voyageurs (visiteurs et autres voyageurs non définis comme visiteurs par l'OMT); (3.1-3.4) Arrivées de visiteurs non résidents aux frontières nationales; (4.1-4.3) Arrivées de touristes non résidents aux frontières nationales.
Note 2002-2004: Données préliminaires.
Sources: "General People's Committee for Tourism"; (6.1-6.3,8.2-8.4) Fonds monétaire international.

JAMAIQUE

(1.2,2.1-4.3) Arrivées de touristes non résidents par voie aérienne; y compris les nationaux résidant à l'étranger; cartes E/D; (5.3) Données obtenues en multipliant la durée moyenne du séjour par le nombre d'escales dans chacun des pays d'origine; (5.4) Durée de séjour prévue; (9.3) Chambres; (9.4) Nuitées dans les hôtels seulement.
Sources: (1.1-5.4,9.1-9.4) "Jamaica Tourist Board"; (6.1-6.3,8.2-8.4) Fonds monétaire international.

JAPON

(1.1,2.1-2.6,4.1-4.3) Arrivées de visiterus non résidents aux frontières nationales; à l'exclusion des nationaux résidant à l'étranger; (3.1,3.4) Arrivées de visiteurs non résidents aux frontières nationales; y compris les résidents étrangers au Japon; (5.4) Jours; (6.2,8.3/2003) La méthode de calcul a changé depuis janvier 2003; (6.2,8.3/2006) La méthode de calcul a changé depuis janvier 2006; (7.1,9.1/2005) À partir de 2005 les données ne sont pas disponibles; (9.1) Hôtels homologués et non homologués, ainsi que "ryokans" (auberges); (9.3) Taux d'occupation des principaux hôtels gouvernementaux homologués (chambres); (9.3/2006) À partir de 2006 les données ne sont pas disponibles.
Sources: (1.1-5.4,7.1,8.1,9.1,9.3) "Japan National Tourist Organization"; (6.1-6.3,8.2-8.4) Fonds monétaire international.

JORDANIE

(1.1-1.3) Y compris les nationaux résidant à l'étranger; (2.1-2.6) Arrivées de touristes non résidents aux frontières nationales; à l'exclusion des nationaux résidant à l'étranger; (3.1-3.4) Arrivées de visiteurs résidents et non résidents; (5.4) Circuits organisés seulement; (9.3) Chambres.
Sources: (1.1-5.4,7.1-7.4,8.1,9.1-9.4) "Ministry of Tourism and Antiquities"; (6.1-6.3,8.2-8.4) Fonds monétaire international.

KAZAKHSTAN

(2.1-2.6,3.1-4.3) Arrivées de visiteurs non résidents aux frontières nationales.
Sources: (1.1-5.4,7.1,8.1,9.1-9.3) "Agency of Statistics of the Republic of Kazakhstan"; (6.1-6.3,8.2-8.4) Fonds monétaire international.

KENYA

(1.1,2.1-4.3) Arrivées de visiteurs non résidents à travers tous les postes frontière; à l'exclusion des nationaux résidant à l'étranger; (9.3) Places-lit; (9.4) Jours.
Sources: (1.1-5.4,7.1,7.4,9.1-9.4) "Kenya Tourist Board"; (6.1-6.3,8.3) Fonds monétaire international.

KIRGHIZISTAN

(1.2,2.2-2.5,8.1/2003-2006) Nouvelle source d'information: Département du Contrôle douanier.
Sources: (1.1-5.2,7.1,7.2,8.1,9.1,9.2) "National Statistical Committee"; (6.1-6.3,8.2-8.4) Fonds monétaire international.

KIRIBATI

(1.2,2.2-2.4,3.1) Arrivées par voie aérienne. 2002/2003/2006: Tarawa et Ile Christmas. 2004/2005: Tarawa uniquement; (4.1-4.3) Arrivées par voie aérienne. Tarawa uniquement.
Source: "Kiribati National Tourism Office, Ministry of Communication, Transport and Tourism Development".

KOWEIT

(1.1,2.1-2.6,3.1-3.4) Arrivées de visiteurs non résidents aux frontières nationales; (1.2,4.1-4.3) Touristes non résidents dans les hôtels et établissements assimilés.
Sources: (1.1-5.4,8.1,9.1,9.2) "Ministry of Planning"; (6.1-6.3,8.2-8.4) Fonds monétaire international.

LESOTHO

(1.1,2.1-4.3) Arrivées de visiteurs non résidents aux frontières nationales; (10.1-10.3) Cette section comprend uniquement le poste « voyages » parce que le poste « transport de passagers » ne figure pas dans les données du Fonds monétaire international qui ont servi à la préparation de la présente édition du Compendium.
Sources: (1.1-4.3,9.1-9.4) "Lesotho Tourism Development Corporation"; (6.2,8.2-8.4) Fonds monétaire international.

NOTES DES PAYS

LETTONIE

(1.1,3.1-3.4) Arrivées de visiteurs non résidents aux frontières nationales. Données provenant de la Police d'Etat aux frontières; (1.2-1.4,2.1-2.6,4.1-4.3) Départs des non-résidents. Enquête auprès des personnes qui traversent les frontières du pays; (1.3) Y compris les passagers en croisière; (4.3) Y compris les visites à des parents et amis et traitement médical; (5.3,7.3) Nuitées dans tous les établissements d'hébergement collectif; (5.4) Durée moyenne du séjour des visiteurs non résidents passant une ou plusieurs nuits; enquête auprès des personnes qui traversent les frontières du pays; (8.1) Données provenant de la Police d'Etat aux frontières; (9.3) Places-lit.
Sources: (1.1-5.4,7.1-7.4,8.1,9.1-9.4) "Transport and Tourism Statistics Section - Central Statistical Bureau"; (6.1-6.3,8.2-8.4) Fonds monétaire international.

LIBAN

(1.2) À l'exclusion des ressortissants syriens.
Sources: (1.2-5.4,9.1-9.3) Ministère du Tourisme; (6.1-6.3,8.2-8.4) Fonds monétaire international.

LIECHTENSTEIN

(1.2,2.1-2.4) Touristes non résidents dans les hôtels et établissements assimilés; (9.3) Places-lit.
Source: "Liechtenstein Tourismus".

LITUANIE

(2.1-2.4) Touristes non résidents dans tous types d'établissements d'hébergement; (3.1-3.4,4.1-4.3) Arrivées de touristes non résidents aux frontières nationales; (5.1,5.2,7.1,7.2,9.1,9.2) Hôtels et motels; (9.3) Chambres.
Sources: (1.1-5.4,7.1-7.4,8.1,9.1-9.4) "Lithuanian State Department of Tourism"; (6.1-6.3,8.2-8.4) Fonds monétaire international.

LUXEMBOURG

(1.2,2.2,2.3) Touristes non résidents dans tous types d'établissements d'hébergement; y compris auberges de jeunesse, hébergement touristique privé et autres; (5.1,7.1) Nuitées dans hôtels, auberges et pensions de famille; (5.3,7.3) Y compris l'hébergement touristique privé et autres; (9.3) Chambres.
Sources: (1.2-5.4,7.1-7.4,9.1-9.4) Office National du Tourisme et STATEC; (6.1-6.3,8.2-8.4) Fonds monétaire international.

MACAO, CHINE

(1.1,2.1-4.3) Arrivées de visiteurs non résidents aux frontières nationales; (1.1-1.3,2.4,3.1-3.4) Y compris chinois de souche provenant de "Hong-Kong, Chine"; (1.2,1.3) Estimations; (3.1) Y compris les arrivées en hélicoptère; (6.1) Les données de dépense sont celles que le pays a fournies à l'OMT car il s'agit d'une série plus complète que celle obtenue du Fonds monétaire international (FMI) pour la préparation de la présente édition du Compendium. Y compris les recettes en provenance du jeu; (8.1) Circuits organisés; (9.1,9.2) Hôtels, pensions de famille et "pousadas" (auberges); (9.3) Chambres; (10.1-10.3) Cette section n'a pas pu être remplie parce que les postes « voyages » et « transport de passagers » ne figurent pas dans les données du Fonds monétaire international qui ont servi à la préparation de la présente édition du Compendium.
Source: "Macau Government Tourist Office" et "Statistics and Census Service".

MADAGASCAR

(1.2,2.1-2.4,3.1,4.1-4.3) Arrivées de touristes non résidents par voie aérienne; (9.3) Chambres.
Sources: (1.2-5.4,9.1-9.4) Ministère des Transports et du Tourisme; (6.1-6.3,8.2-8.4) Fonds monétaire international.

MALAISIE

(1.2,2.1-2.6) Arrivées de touristes non résidents aux frontières nationales; y compris les résidents de Singapour qui traversent la frontière par le Johore Causeway; (3.1-3.4,4.1-4.3) Péninsule de Malaisie seulement; (8.1) Déplacement des Malaisiens péninsulaires; y compris les départs par voie terrestre utilisant le Johore Causeway; (9.1) Hôtels avec 10 chambres et plus; (9.3) Chambres.
Sources: (1.1-5.2,7.2,8.1,9.1,9.3) "Tourism Malaysia"; (6.1-6.3,8.2-8.4) Fonds monétaire international.

MALAWI

(1.2-4.3) Départs; (5.3/2004) Donnée provisoire; (9.3) Places-lit.
Sources: (1.2-5.4,9.1-9.4) "Ministry of Information and Tourism"; (6.1-6.3,8.2-8.4) "Reserve Bank of Malawi".

MALDIVES

(1.2,2.1-2.6) Arrivées par voie aérienne; (5.1,9.1-9.4) Centres touristiques et hôtels; (9.4) Jours; (10.1-10.3) Cette section comprend uniquement le poste « voyages » parce que le poste « transport de passagers » ne figure pas dans les données du Fonds monétaire international qui ont servi à la préparation de la présente édition du Compendium.
Sources: (1.2-5.1,8.1,9.1-9.4) "Ministry of Tourism"; (6.2,8.2-8.4) Fonds monétaire international.

MALI

(1.2) Arrivées par voie aérienne; (2.1-2.6) Touristes non résidents dans les hôtels et établissements assimilés; (9.3) Chambres.
Sources: (1.2-5.4,7.1-7.4,9.1-9.4) Office malien du tourisme et de l'hôtellerie (O.MA.T.HO); (6.1-6.3,8.2-8.4) Fonds monétaire international.

MALTE

(1.2,2.1-2.6,3.1,3.4/2002/2003) Arrivées de touristes non résidents aux frontières nationales; (1.2,2.2-2.6,3.1,3.4/2004-2006) Départs par voies aérienne et maritime; (4.1-4.3,5.1-5.3/2003-2006) Départs de touristes par voie aérienne; (8.1/2002-2004) Par voie aérienne uniquement; (9.3) Places-lit.
Sources: (1.1-5.4,8.1,9.2-9.4) "Malta Tourism Authority" et "National Statistics Office"; (6.1-6.3,8.2-8.4) Fonds monétaire international.

MAROC

(1.2,3.1-4.3) Arrivées de touristes non résidents aux frontières nationales; y compris les nationaux résidant à l'étranger; (2.1-2.6) Arrivées de touristes non résidents aux frontières nationales; à l'exclusion des nationaux résidant à l'étranger; (5.1,5.2,7.1,7.2,9.1-9.3) Hôtels homologués, villages de vacances et résidences touristiques; (9.3) Chambres; (9.4) Touristes étrangers.
Sources: (1.1-5.2,7.1,7.2,8.1,9.1-9.4) Ministère du tourisme; (6.1-6.3,8.2-8.4) Fonds monétaire international.

MARTINIQUE

(1.2,2.2,2.3,4.1-4.3) Arrivées de touristes non résidents aux frontières nationales; (6.1) Les chiffres de dépense sont ceux que le pays a fournis à l'OMT mais ils ne figurent pas dans les données du Fonds monétaire international qui ont servi à la préparation de la présente édition du Compendium; (9.1) Hôtels et villages de vacances (Club Méditerranée); (9.3) Chambres dans les hôtels et établissements assimilés.
Source: Comité Martiniquais du Tourisme.

MAURICE

(1.2,2.1-3.4) Arrivées de touristes non résidents aux frontières nationales; (4.1-4.3) Arrivées de visiteurs non résidents aux frontières nationales; (5.4) Grands hôtels; (9.3) Chambres.
Sources: (1.1-5.4,8.1,9.1-9.3) "Ministry of Tourism and Leisure"; (6.1-6.3,8.2-8.4) Fonds monétaire international.

MEXIQUE

(1.2,2.2-4.3) Arrivées de touristes non résidents aux frontières nationales; y compris les nationaux résidant à l'étranger; (1.3) Y compris les visiteurs de la frange frontalière avec les Etats Unis avec séjour inférieur à 24h; (2.2/2004) États-Unis et Canada uniquement; (2.2,2.3/2002-2004) Données compilées par pays de résidence; (2.2-2.4/2005/2006) Données compilées par nationalité; (2.4/2005/2006) Japon et République de Corée uniquement ; (3.3) Y compris chemin de fer; (5.1) Sélection de centres touristiques; (5.2,7.2) Hôtels seulement; (9.3) Chambres; (9.4) Tourisme étranger seulement.
2006: Données préliminaires.
Sources: (1.1-5.4,7.1,7.2,8.1,9.1-9.4) "Secretaría de Turismo de México (SECTUR)"; (6.1-6.3,8.2-8.4) Fonds monétaire international.

MICRONESIE (ETATS FEDERES DE)

(1.2,2.2-2.4,4.1-4.3) Arrivées dans les États de Kosrae, Chuuk, Pohnpei et Yap; à l'exclusion des citoyens de EFM; (6.1,8.2) Les chiffres de dépense sont ceux que le pays a fournis à l'OMT mais ils ne figurent pas dans les données du Fonds monétaire international qui ont servi à la préparation de la présente édition du Compendium. Années fiscales (1 octobre - 30 septembre).
Source: "Department of Economic Affairs".

MONACO

(1.2,2.1-4.2) Touristes non résidents dans les hôtels et établissements assimilés.
Source: Direction du Tourisme et des Congrès.

MONGOLIE

(1.2,2.1-2.5,4.1-4.3) Arrivées de touristes non résidents aux frontières nationales. Sont exclus les diplomates et les étrangers qui résident en Mongolie.
Sources: (1.1-4.3) "Tourism Department - Ministry of Road, Transport and Tourism"; (6.1-6.3,8.2-8.4) Fonds monétaire international.

NOTES DES PAYS

MONTENEGRO

(1.2,2.2-2.4) Touristes non résidents dans tous types d'établissements d'hébergement.
Source: "MONSTAT - Statistical Office of the Republic of Montenegro".

MONTSERRAT

(10.2,10.3) Cette section comprend uniquement le poste « voyages » parce que le poste « transport de passagers » ne figure pas dans les données du Fonds monétaire international qui ont servi à la préparation de la présente édition du Compendium.
Sources: (1.1-5.2) "Statistics Department Montserrat"; (6.2,8.3) Fonds monétaire international.

MOZAMBIQUE

Sources: (1.1-4.3,9.1-9.4) "Ministry of Tourism"; (5.1,5.2,7.1,7.2) "Instituto Nacional de Estatística"; (6.1-6.3,8.2-8.4) Fonds monétaire international.

MYANMAR

(1.2,2.2-2.6) Comprenant les arrivées de touristes aux postes-frontières de Yangon; (4.1-4.3) Arrivées de visiteurs non résidents aux frontières nationales; (5.1,9.4) Hôtels et établissements assimilés gérés uniquement par l'Etat; (9.1,9.2) Hôtels gérés par l'Etat et pensions de famille privées homologuées; (9.3) Chambres.
Sources: (1.1-5.4,9.1-9.4) "Ministry of Hotels and Tourism"; (6.1-6.3,8.2-8.4) Fonds monétaire international.

NAMIBIE

(2.1-4.3) Arrivées de touristes non résidents aux frontières nationales; (2.2) Etats-Unis uniquement; (2.4) Australie uniquement; (9.3) Places-lit.
Sources: (1.1-5.4,7.1-7.4,9.1-9.4) "Ministry of Environment and Tourism"; (6.1-6.3,8.3) Fonds monétaire international.

NEPAL

(1.2) Y compris les arrivées en provenance de l'Inde; (3.3) Voie terrestre; (9.1,9.2) Hôtels à Katmandou et à l'intérieur du pays; (9.1,9.2/2006) À l'exclusion des hôtels en cours de construction.
Sources: (1.2-5.4,8.1,9.1,9.2) "Nepal Tourism Board"; (6.1-6.3,8.2-8.4) Fonds monétaire international.

NICARAGUA

(1.2,2.1-4.3) Arrivées de touristes non résidents aux frontières nationales; (1.2/2002-2004) (2.1-2.5) Nationaux résidant à l'étranger exclus; (1.2/2005/2006) Nationaux résidant à l'étranger compris; (5.1,7.1) Principaux établissements d'hébergement dans l'ensemble du pays (7); (5.3,7.3) Total de établissements dans l'ensemble du pays; (9.1,9.2) Hôtels et établissements assimilés classés en catégories supérieures; (9.4) Tous types d'établissements d'hébergement, tourisme récepteur.
Note 2006: (1.1-4.3,8.1) Estimations préliminaires.
Sources: (1.1-5.4,7.1-7.4,8.1,9.1-9.4) "Instituto Nicaragüense de Turismo (INTUR)"; (6.1-6.3,8.2-8.4) Fonds monétaire international.

NIGER

(5.4,7.4,9.4) Jours.
Sources: (1.2-5.4,7.1,7.2,9.1-9.4) (6.2,8.2-8.4/2006) Ministère du Tourisme et de l'Artisanat; (6.1-6.3,8.2-8.4/2002-2005) Fonds monétaire international.

NIGERIA

(1.1,2.1-2.6,3.1-3.4) (4.1-4.3/2006) Arrivées de visiteurs non résidents aux frontières nationales; (1.2,4.1-4.3) Arrivées de touristes non résidents aux frontières nationales.
Sources: (1.1-4.3,9.2,9.3) "Nigerian Tourism Development Corporation"; (6.1-6.3,8.2-8.4) Fonds monétaire international.

NIOUE

(1.2) Arrivées par voie aérienne; y compris les nationaux résidant normalement en Nouvelle-Zélande; (8.1) Retours des résidents.
Source: "Statistics Niue".

NORVEGE

(1.1-4.2) Les chiffres se fondent sur "l'enquête auprès de la clientèle" de l'Institut d'économie des transports; (2.2-4.2) Arrivées de touristes non résidents aux frontières nationales; (2.2) Etats-Unis seulement; (2.4) Japon seulement; (5.1) Nuitées dans les

établissements classés; (5.1,9.1,9.2) Les chiffres des hôtels et établissements assimilés se réfèrent aux établissements de 20 places-lit et plus tout au long de l'année; (8.1) Voyages pour vacances; (9.3) Places-lit.
Sources: (1.1-5.3,7.1-7.3,8.1,9.1-9.4) "Statistics Norway" et "Institute of Transport Economics"; (6.1-6.3,8.2-8.4) Fonds monétaire international.

NOUVELLE-CALEDONIE

(1.2,2.1-4.3) Y compris les nationaux résidant à l'étranger; (4.1) Vacances et visites à des parents; (4.2) Affaires uniquement; (5.1,5.2,7.1,7.2) Hôtels de Nouméa uniquement; (8.1) Retours des résidents; (9.3) Chambres à Nouméa; (9.4) Jours, hôtels de Nouméa; (10.2,10.3) Cette section comprend uniquement le poste « voyages » parce que le poste « transport de passagers » ne figure pas dans les données du Fonds monétaire international qui ont servi à la préparation de la présente édition du Compendium.
Sources: (1.1-5.4,7.1,7.2,8.1,9.1-9.4) Institut de la Statistique et des Études Économiques (ISEE); (6.2,8.3) Fonds monétaire international.

NOUVELLE-ZELANDE

(1.1,3.1-4.3) Arrivées de visiteurs non résidents aux frontières nationales; nationaux résidant à l'étranger compris; (2.1-2.6) Arrivées de visiteurs non résidents aux frontières nationales, nationaux résidant à l'étranger exclus; (5.3,7.3) Estimation à partir du total des nuitées de clients des établissements d'hébergement commerciaux ayant un chiffre d'affaires annuel d'au moins NZ$30.000, sur la base du pourcentage moyen de clients du tourisme international et du tourisme interne en jan, avr, juil et oct; (8.1) Départs pour peu de temps de résidents de NZ (année civile); (9.1) Il s'agit de la capacité des « unités de séjour » des hôtels, motels et pensions de famille; (10.1-10.3) Cette section comprend uniquement le poste « voyages » parce que le poste « transport de passagers » ne figure pas dans les données du Fonds monétaire international qui ont servi à la préparation de la présente édition du Compendium.
Sources: (1.1-5.3,7.3,8.1,9.1-9.4) "Ministry of Tourism"; (6.2,8.3) Fonds monétaire international.

OMAN

(1.1-1.3,4.1-4.3,5.3,5.4) Enquête du tourisme récepteur; (2.1-2.6) Touristes non résidents dans les hôtels et établissements assimilés; (4.1-4.3) Arrivées de visiteurs non résidents aux frontières nationales; (8.1) Enquête du tourisme émetteur; y compris les visiteurs de la journée (excursionnistes); (9.3) Chambres.
Sources: (1.1-1.3,4.1-4.3,5.3,5.4,8.1) "Ministry of National Economy and Ministry of Commerce and Industry"; (2.1-2.6,5.1,5.2,7.1,7.2,9.1-9.3) "Directorate General of Tourism - Ministry of Tourism"; (6.1-6.3,8.2-8.4) Fonds monétaire international.

OUGANDA

Sources: (1.2-5.3,8.1,9.1,9.2) "Ministry of Tourism, Trade an Industry" et "Uganda Bureau of Statistics"; (6.1-6.3,8.2-8.4) Fonds monétaire international.

OUZBEKISTAN

(6.1-6.3) Les chiffres de dépense sont ceux que le pays a fournis à l'OMT mais ils ne figurent pas dans les données du Fonds monétaire international qui ont servi à la préparation de la présente édition du Compendium.
Source: "National Company "Uzbektourism".

PAKISTAN

(5.4) Jours.
Sources: (1.2-5.4,7.1,7.2,9.1-9.4) "Pakistan Tourism Development Corporation - Ministry of Tourism"; (6.1-6.3,8.2-8.4) Fonds monétaire international.

PALAOS

(1.2-4.3) Arrivées par voie aérienne (aéroport international de Palau); (6.1,8.2) Les chiffres de dépense sont ceux que le pays a fournis à l'OMT mais ils ne figurent pas dans les données du Fonds monétaire international qui ont servi à la préparation de la présente édition du Compendium. Années fiscales.
Source: "Office of Planning and Statistics, Bureau of Budget and Planning - Ministry of Finance".

PALESTINE

(1.2,2.1-2.6) Touristes non résidents dans les hôtels; (5.1,5.2,7.1,7.2) Hôtels seulement; (10.1-10.3) Cette section comprend uniquement le poste « voyages » parce que le poste « transport de passagers » ne figure pas dans les données du Fonds monétaire international qui ont servi à la préparation de la présente édition du Compendium.
Sources: (1.2-5.2,7.1-7.4,9.1-9.4) "Palestinian Central Bureau of Statistics"; (6.2,8.3) Fonds monétaire international; (6.2,8.3,10.1-10.3) Cisjordanie et Gaza.

NOTES DES PAYS

PANAMA

(1.1) Arrivées de visiteurs non résidents, aéroport international de Tocúmen (AIT), frontière de Paso Canoa (FPC) et ports de Cristóbal et Balboa (PCB); (2.2-2.4) Arrivées de visiteurs non résidents, AIT; (3.1-3.4) Arrivées de touristes non résidents, AIT, FPC et PCB; à l'exclusion des arrivées à d'autres ports d'entrées (non spécifiés):
2002: 34.996
2003: 39.870
2004: 51.295
2005: 53.818
2006: 53.638
(4.1-4.3) Arrivées de touristes non résidents, AIT; (5.1) Hôtels de Panama-City; (9.1,9.2) Chambres/places-lit recensées pour le tourisme international; (9.3) Chambres.
Sources: (1.1-5.4,8.1,9.1-9.4) "Instituto Panameño de Turismo"; (6.1-6.3,8.2-8.4) Fonds monétaire international.

POPOUASIE-NOUVELLE-GUINEE

Sources: (1.2-4.3,8.1,9.1,9.2) "Papua New Guinea Tourism Promotion Authority"; (6.1-6.3,8.2-8.4) Fonds monétaire international.

PARAGUAY

(1.1-3.4,8.1) Cartes d'embarquement et de débarquement à l'aéroport Silvio Petirossi et comptages des passagers lors du franchissement des frontières nationales – Police nationale et SENATUR; (1.2,2.2-4.3) À l'exclusion des nationaux résidant à l'étranger et membres des équipages; (3.4) Voie fluviale; (9.3) Places-lit.
Sources: (1.1-5.4,8.1,9.1-9.4) "Secretaría Nacional de Turismo - SENATUR"; (6.1-6.3,8.2-8.4) Fonds monétaire international.

PAYS-BAS

(1.2-2.4) Touristes non résidents dans tous types d'établissements d'hébergement; (5.1,7.1) Hôtels et pensions; (8.1) Départs en vacances des ressortissants nationaux; (8.1/2002) Nouvelle enquête; (9.2) Hôtels; (9.3) Places-lit; (9.4) Tous types d'établissements d'hébergement.
Sources: (1.2-5.4,7.1-7.3,8.1,9.1-9.4) "Statistics Netherlands"; (6.1-6.3,8.2-8.4) Fonds monétaire international.

PEROU

(1.2) Y compris les passagers en croisière qui passent la nuit; (1.2,2.1-2.5) À partir de 2002, nouvelle série estimée comprenant les touristes avec une pièce d'identité autre qu'un passeport ; (1.4) Passagers en croisière qui passent la nuit; (3.4) Comprend les arrivées par voie fluviale et lacustre.
Note 2003-2006: Estimations préliminaires.
Sources: (1.2-4.3,8.1) "Dirección General de Migraciones y Naturalización (DIGEMIN)"; (5.1-5.4,7.1,7.2,9.1-9.4) "Ministerio de Comercio Exterior y Turismo (MINCETUR)"; (6.1-6.3,8.2-8.4) Fonds monétaire international.

PHILIPPINES

(1.2,3.1-4.3) Arrivées de touristes non résidents aux frontières nationales; y compris les nationaux résidant à l'étranger; (2.1-2.6) Arrivées de touristes non résidents aux frontières nationales; à l'exclusion des nationaux résidant à l'étranger; (4.1-4.3) Arrivées par voie aérienne; (8.1) Y compris les travailleurs sous contrat en provenance d'outre-mer; (9.1,9.2) Hôtels homologués seulement; (9.3,9.4) Hôtels homologués dans la région de Manille seulement.
Sources: (1.2-5.4,8.1,9.1-9.4) "Department of Tourism"; (6.1-6.3,8.2-8.4) Fonds monétaire international.

POLOGNE

(1.1,2.1-3.4) Arrivées de visiteurs non résidents aux frontières nationales; (4.1-4.3) Arrivées de touristes non résidents aux frontières nationales, d'après les enquêtes de l'Institut du tourisme; (5.4) Établissements d'hébergement collectif et privé, d'après les enquêtes de l'Institut du tourisme; (8.1) Voyages du tourisme émetteur enregistrés aux frontières; (9.3) Chambres.
Sources: (1.1-5.4,7.1-7.4,8.1,9.1-9.4) "Institute of Tourism"; (6.1-6.3,8.2-8.4) Fonds monétaire international.

POLYNESIE FRANÇAISE

(1.2,2.2-4.3) Arrivées de touristes non résidents aux frontières nationales; à l'exclusion des nationaux résidant à l'étranger; (5.2) Hôtels seulement; (5.4,9.4) Jours; (9.1) Hôtels seulement; au 31 décembre de chaque année; (9.3) Chambres dans hôtels.
Sources: (1.2-5.4,9.1-9.4) Service du Tourisme; (6.1-6.3,8.2-8.4) Fonds monétaire international.

PORTO RICO

(1.2) Arrivées de touristes non résidents par voie aérienne; (2.2) Iles Vierges Américaines et Etats-Unis seulement; (5.1,5.4) Y compris résidents et non résidents; (6.1,8.2-8.4) Les chiffres de dépense sont ceux que le pays a fournis à l'OMT mais ils ne figurent pas dans les données du Fonds monétaire international qui ont servi à la préparation de la présente édition du

Compendium; (9.1) Chambres classées par la "Compañía de Turismo" de Porto Rico; (9.1/2006) Y compris 2.927 chambres non-homologués; (9.3) Chambres; y compris les chambres occupées par des résidents de Porto Rico.
Données: Années fiscales (juillet-juin).
Sources: (1.1-3.4,6.1,8.1,8.2-8.4,10.1-10.3) "Junta de Planificación de Puerto Rico"; (5.1,5.2,5.4,7.2,9.1,9.3,9.4) "Compañía de Turismo de Puerto Rico".

PORTUGAL

(1.1-4.3) La méthodologie a été modifiée et pour cela, à partir de 2004 les données ne sont pas comparables avec celles des années précédentes; (1.1,3.1-3.4,4.1-4.3) Arrivées de visiteurs non résidents aux frontières nationales; (1.1-3.4/2002/2003) À l'exclusion des nationaux résidant à l'étranger; (1.1-4.3/2004-2006) Y compris les nationaux résidant à l'étranger; (1.2,2.2-2.5) Arrivées de touristes non résidents aux frontières nationales; (1.4) Y compris les passagers par voie maritime en transit; (5.1-5.4,7.1-7.4,9.1-9.4) Depuis 2002, nouvelle méthodologie; (5.1-5.4,7.1-7.4/2006) Données provisoires; (9.3) Places-lit; (9.4) Tous types d'établissements d'hébergement.
Sources: (1.1-5.4,7.1-7.4,8.1,9.1-9.4) "Direcçao-Geral do Turismo (DGT)"; (6.1-6.3,8.2-8.4) Fonds monétaire international.

QATAR

(1.2-5.4,9.1-9.3) Hôtels seulement; (6.2,8.3) Les chiffres de dépense sont ceux que le pays a fournis à l'OMT mais ils ne figurent pas dans les données du Fonds monétaire international qui ont servi à la préparation de la présente édition du Compendium; (6.2,8.3/2006) Estimations préliminaires; (9.3) Places-lit.
Sources: (1.2-5.4,9.1-9.3) "The Planning Council - Statistics Department" et "Qatar Tourism Authority"; (6.2,8.3) "Qatar Central Bank".

REPUBLIQUE ARABE SYRIENNE

(1.1,2.1-4.3) Arrivées de visiteurs non résidents aux frontières nationales; à l'exclusion des arrivées des nationaux résidant à l'étranger; (9.3) Chambres.
Sources: (1.1-5.4,7.1,7.2,8.1,9.1-9.4) "Ministry of Tourism" - Source des données: enquête du tourisme récepteur en 2002 et 2004; (6.1-6.3,8.2-8.4) Fonds monétaire international.

REPUBLIQUE CENTRAFRICAINE

(1.2,2.1-2.6,4.1-4.3) Arrivées par voie aérienne à Bangui uniquement.
Note 2006: Estimations.
Sources: (1.2-5.4,7.1-7.4,8.1,9.1-9.4) (6.1,8.2/2003/2004) Ministère du Développement du Tourisme et de l'Artisanat; (6.1,8.2/2002) Banque des Etats de l'Afrique Centrale (B.E.A.C.).

REPUBLIQUE DE MOLDOVA

(1.1-4.3,8.1) (5.1,7.3/2002/2003) Visiteurs qui ont bénéficié des services des agents économiques officiellement enregistrés avec le type d'activité tourisme et des unités d'hébergement qui leur appartiennent.
Note: À l'exception de la rive gauche de la rivière Nistru et de la municipalité de Bender.
Sources: (1.1-5.4,7.1-7.4,8.1,9.1-9.4) "National Bureau of Statistics"; (6.1-6.3,8.2-8.4) Fonds monétaire international.

REPUBLIQUE DEMOCRATIQUE DU CONGO

(1.2,2.1-2.4,4.1-4.3/2002-2004) Arrivées par voie aérienne uniquement; (9.1) Hôtels homologués.
Note 2005-2006: Données provisoires.
Source: Office National du Tourisme.

REPUBLIQUE DEMOCRATIQUE POPULAIRE LAO

(1.2) Arrivées de touristes non résidents aux frontières nationales; (2.2-2.5,3.1,3.3,4.1-4.3) Arrivées de visiteurs non résidents aux frontières nationales; (5.4) Jours; (10.1-10.3) Cette section comprend uniquement le poste « voyages » parce que le poste « transport de passagers » ne figure pas dans les données du Fonds monétaire international qui ont servi à la préparation de la présente édition du Compendium.
Source: "National Tourism Authority".

REPUBLIQUE DOMINICAINE

(1.2) Arrivées par voie aérienne uniquement; y compris les nationaux résidant à l'étranger; (1.4) Toutes les arrivées par voie maritime; (2.2-2.4) Arrivées par voie aérienne; à l'exclusion des nationaux résidant à l'étranger; (2.2-2.4,4.1-4.3/2002) À l'exclusion des passagers de l'aéroport de Herrera; (4.1-4.3) Arrivées par voie aérienne uniquement; y compris les nationaux résidant à l'étranger; (9.1,9.2) Hôtels; (9.3) Chambres; (10.1-10.3) Cette section comprend uniquement le poste « voyages » parce que le poste « transport de passagers » ne figure pas dans les données du Fonds monétaire international qui ont servi à la préparation de la présente édition du Compendium.
Note 2006: Données provisoires.
Sources: (1.1-5.4,8.1,9.1-9.4) "Secretaría de Estado de Turismo"; (6.2,8.2-8.4) Fonds monétaire international.

REPUBLIQUE TCHEQUE

(1.2,2.1-2.4) Touristes non résidents dans tous types d'établissements d'hébergement.
Sources: (1.2-5.4,7.1-7.4,9.1-9.4) "Department of Conception and International Cooperation in Tourism - Ministry for Regional Development"; (6.1-6.3,8.2-8.4) Fonds monétaire international.

REPUBLIQUE-UNIE DE TANZANIE

Sources: (1.1-5.3,7.3,9.1-9.4) "Tourism Division - Ministry of Natural Resources and Tourism" et "National Bureau of Statistics"; (6.1-6.3,8.2-8.4) Fonds monétaire international.

REUNION

(5.4) Jours; (6.1) Les chiffres de dépense sont ceux que le pays a fournis à l'OMT mais ils ne figurent pas dans les données du Fonds monétaire international qui ont servi à la préparation de la présente édition du Compendium.
Sources: Institut National de la Statistique et des Études Économique - INSEE et Comité du Tourisme de la Réunion.

ROUMANIE

Sources: (1.1-5.4,7.1-7.4,8.1,9.1-9.4) "National Authority for Tourism - Ministry of Transports, Constructions and Tourism"; (6.1-6.3,8.2-8.4) Fonds monétaire international.

ROYAUME-UNI

(3.2) Tunnel; (5.4) Jours; (9.3) Places-lit (Angleterre seulement).
Sources: (1.1-4.3,5.3,5.4,7.3,8.1,9.3) "VisitBritain"; (5.1,5.2,7.1,7.2,9.1,9.2) "EUROSTAT (New Cronos)"; (6.1-6.3,8.2-8.4) Fonds monétaire international.

SABA

(1.3) Principalement de St. Martin.
Sources: "Saba Tourist Bureau", "Caribbean Tourism Organization" et "Central Bank of the Netherlands Antilles".

SAINT-EUSTACHE

(1.2,2.2,2.3) À l'exclusion des résidents des Antilles Néerlandaises.
Source: "Central Bank of the Netherlands Antilles".

SAINT-KITTS-ET-NEVIS

(1.2,2.2) Arrivées de touristes non résidents par voie aérienne; (1.4,3.4) Arrivées en yacht et en bateau de croisière; (10.1-10.3) Cette section comprend uniquement le poste « voyages » parce que le poste « transport de passagers » ne figure pas dans les données du Fonds monétaire international qui ont servi à la préparation de la présente édition du Compendium.
Sources: (1.1-3.4,9.1,9.2) "Statistics Department - Ministry of Sustainable Development"; (6.2,8.3) Fonds monétaire international.

SAINT-MARIN

(1.1) Y compris les visiteurs Italiens; (1.2) Touristes non résidents dans les hôtels et établissements assimilés; y compris les touristes Italiens; (9.1,9.2) Hôtels seulement.
Note: Nouvelle méthodologie à partir de 2005.
Source: "Segreteria di Stato per il Turismo, lo Sport, le Telecomunicazioni, i Trasporti e la Cooperazione Economica".

SAINT-MARTIN

(1.2,2.2,2.3) Par voie aérienne; y compris les arrivées à Saint-Martin (côté français de l'île); (3.1) Arrivées à l'aéroport "Juliana" (y compris les visiteurs à destination de Saint-Martin (côté français); (6.2,8.3) Y compris estimations pour Saba et Saint-Eustache; (9.1,9.2) Hôtels, pensions de famille et appartements.
Sources: (1.1-3.4,9.1-9.3) "St. Maarten Tourist Bureau"; (6.2,8.3) "Central Bank of the Netherlands Antilles".

SAINT-VINCENT-ET-LES-GRENADINES

(1.2,2.2-2.3,4.1-4.3) Arrivées de touristes non résidents par voie aérienne; (3.4) Y compris les passagers en croisière et en yacht; (9.1) Hôtels, appartements, bungalows, villas et pensions de famille; (10.1-10.3) Cette section comprend uniquement le poste « voyages » parce que le poste « transport de passagers » ne figure pas dans les données du Fonds monétaire international qui ont servi à la préparation de la présente édition du Compendium.
Sources: (1.1-5.4,9.1,9.2) "Ministry of Tourism and Culture"; (6.2,8.3) Fonds monétaire international.

SAINTE-LUCIE

(1.1) À l'exclusion des arrivées de passagers en yacht; (1.2,2.2-4.3) Arrivées de touristes non résidents aux frontières nationales; à l'exclusion des nationaux résidant à l'étranger; (9.3) Chambres; (10.1-10.3) Cette section comprend uniquement le poste « voyages » parce que le poste « transport de passagers » ne figure pas dans les données du Fonds monétaire international qui ont servi à la préparation de la présente édition du Compendium.
Sources: (1.1-5.2,9.1-9.4) "Saint Lucia Tourist Board"; (6.2,8.3) Fonds monétaire international.

SAMOA

Sources: (1.2-4.3,9.1,9.2) (6.2/2002/2003) "Samoa Tourism Authority" et "Statistical Services Division (Ministry of Finance)"; (6.1-6.3,8.2-8.4/2004-2006) Fonds monétaire international.

SAMOA AMERICAINES

(1.2,2.4,4.1-4.3) Y compris le Samoa occidental; (4.3) Visites à des parents, amis.
Source: "American Samoa Government - Department of Commerce - Statistics Division".

SAO TOME-ET-PRINCIPE

(10.1-10.3) Cette section comprend uniquement le poste « voyages » parce que le poste « transport de passagers » ne figure pas dans les données du Fonds monétaire international qui ont servi à la préparation de la présente édition du Compendium.
Sources: (1.2-4.3) "Direcçao do Turismo e Hotelaria"; (6.2,8.2-8.4/2002) Fonds monétaire international; (6.2/2003-2005) "Banco Central".

SENEGAL

(1.2/2002) (2.1-2.6/2002/2003) Touristes non résidents dans les hôtels et établissements assimilés; (1.2/2003-2006) (2.1-2.3/2004-2006) Arrivées de touristes non résidents aux frontières nationales; (5.1,5.2,7.1,7.2,9.1,9.2) Hôtels et villages de vacances; (9.3) Places-lit.
Sources: (1.1-5.4,7.1,7.2,9.1-9.4) Ministère du Tourisme et des Transports Aériens; (6.1-6.3,8.2-8.4) Fonds monétaire international.

SERBIE

(1.2,2.2-2.4) Touristes non résidents dans tous types d'établissements d'hébergement; (6.1,8.2) Les chiffres de dépense sont ceux que le pays a fournis à l'OMT mais ils ne figurent pas dans les données du Fonds monétaire international qui ont servi à la préparation de la présente édition du Compendium.
Source: "Statistical Office of the Republic of Serbia".

SEYCHELLES

(1.2,2.1-4.3) Arrivées de touristes non résidents aux frontières nationales; (5.4) Chiffres des nuitées élaborés à partir des départs; (9.1,9.2) Hôtels et pensions de famille; (9.3) Places-lit.
Sources: (1.1-5.4,7.1,8.1,9.1-9.3) "National Statistics Bureau"; (6.1-6.3,8.2-8.4) Fonds monétaire international.

SIERRA LEONE

(1.2,2.1-2.6,4.1-4.3) Arrivées par voie aérienne; (9.1,9.2) Hôtels seulement; (10.1-10.3) Cette section comprend uniquement le poste « voyages » parce que le poste « transport de passagers » ne figure pas dans les données du Fonds monétaire international qui ont servi à la préparation de la présente édition du Compendium.
Sources: (1.2-5.4,8.1,9.1-9.4) "National Tourist Board"; (6.2,8.2-8.4) Fonds monétaire international.

SINGAPOUR

(1.1) À l'exclusion des arrivées de Malaisiens par voie terrestre; y compris les visiteurs de la journée (excursionnistes); (5.4,9.4) Jours; (9.1) Hôtels (homologués et non-homologués); (9.3) Chambres; hôtels homologués seulement; (10.1-10.3) Cette section comprend uniquement le poste « voyages » parce que le poste « transport de passagers » ne figure pas dans les données du Fonds monétaire international qui ont servi à la préparation de la présente édition du Compendium.
Sources: (1.1-5.4,8.1,9.1-9.4) "Singapore Tourism Board"; (6.2,8.3) Fonds monétaire international.

SLOVAQUIE

(1.2,2.1-2.5) Touristes non résidents dans tous types d'établissements d'hébergement.
Sources: (1.1-5.4,7.1-7.4,8.1,9.1-9.4) "Department of Tourism - Ministry of Economy" et "Statistical Office"; (6.1-6.3,8.2-8.4/2002/2003) Fonds monétaire international.

SLOVENIE

(1.1) Y compris toutes les catégories de voyageurs, quel que soit le motif de la visite; (1.2,2.1-2.4) Touristes non résidents dans tous types d'établissements d'hébergement; (3.1-3.4,4.1-4.3) Touristes non résidents dans tous types d'établissements d'hébergement; données provenant de l'enquête (été) auprès des touristes étrangers en Slovénie portant sur 3 années; (8.1) Enquête trimestrielle des voyages de la population résidente.
Sources: (1.1-5.4,7.1-7.4,8.1,9.1-9.4) "Statistical Office - Information Society and Tourism Statistics"; (6.1-6.3,8.2-8.4) Fonds monétaire international.

SOUDAN

(1.2-4.3/2005/2006) Arrivées de touristes non résidents aux frontières nationales; y compris les nationaux résidant à l'étranger; (6.1) Pour la dépense, le pays fournit à l'OMT des niveaux d'agrégation qui diffèrent de façon significative des données du Fonds monétaire international utilisées pour la préparation de la présente édition du Compendium. Les données du pays sont les suivantes :
2002:   62
2003:   63
2004:   68
2005: 316
2006: 409
(10.1-10.3) Cette section comprend uniquement le poste « voyages » parce que le poste « transport de passagers » ne figure pas dans les données du Fonds monétaire international qui ont servi à la préparation de la présente édition du Compendium.
Sources: (1.2-4.3,9.1-9.4) "Ministry of Tourism and Wildlife"; (6.2,8.3) Fonds monétaire international.

SRI LANKA

(1.2,2.1-4.3) Arrivées de touristes non résidents aux frontières nationales; à l'exclusion des nationaux résidant à l'étranger; (9.1,9.2) Hôtels, motels, auberges, pensions de famille et apart-hôtels; (9.3) Chambres.
Sources: (1.1-5.4,7.1,8.1,9.1-9.3) "Sri Lanka Tourist Board"; (6.1-6.3,8.2-8.4) Fonds monétaire international.

SUEDE

(1.1-4.3) Données reposant sur l'enquête IBIS (auprès des visiteurs du tourisme récepteur) portant sur les années 2001 à 2003 (aucune donnée n'a été collectée avant 2001 ni après 2003). Source: "Swedish Tourist Authority" et "Statistics Sweden"; (1.2,2.1-4.3) Arrivées de touristes non résidents aux frontières nationales; (3.2) Transport ferroviaire et autres modes de transport compris; (5.1,7.1,9.1,9.2) Hôtels seulement; (9.3) Places-lit.
Sources: (1.1-5.4,7.1-7.4,8.1,9.1-9.3) "NUTEK - The Swedish Agency for Economic and Regional Growth"; (6.1-6.3,8.2-8.4) Fonds monétaire international.

SUISSE

(1.2,2.1-2.6,5.1,5.2,7.1,7.2,9.1,9.2/2002-2004) Hôtels, motels et auberges; (1.2,2.1-2.6,5.1,5.2,7.1,7.2,9.1-9.4/2005/2006) Hôtels et établissements de cure; (9.3) Taux d'occupation nets (places-lit disponibles).
Sources: (1.2-5.3,7.1-7.3,8.1,9.1-9.4) "Swiss Federal Statistical Office"; (6.1-6.3,8.2-8.4) Fonds monétaire international.

SURINAME

(1.2,2.2-2.4,4.1-4.3,5.2/2002/2003) (3.1) (5.2/2004) Arrivées à l'aéroport de Zanderij; (1.2,2.2-2.4,4.1-4.3/2004/2005) Arrivées à l'aéroport de Zanderij, aéroport Zorg en Hoop, Albina et Nickerie; (1.4/2003) (3.4) Arrivées au port Nw. Nickerie.
Sources: (1.1-1.4,2.2-2.4,4.1-4.3,5.2/2002/2003) (3.1,3.4/2002-2004) "General Bureau of Statistics (ABS)"; (1.2,2.2-2.4,4.1-4.3,5.2/2004/2005) (3.1,3.4/2005) (9.1) "Suriname Tourism Foundation"; (6.1-6.3,8.2-8.4) Fonds monétaire international.

SWAZILAND

(1.1) (2.1-2.5,4.1-4.3/2005/2006) (3.1,3.3) Arrivées de visiteurs non résidents aux frontières nationales; (1.2,4.1-4.3/2002) (2.1-2.4/2002-2004) (5.2) Arrivées dans les hôtels seulement; (9.3) Places-lit.
Sources: (1.1-5.4,7.1,7.4,8.1,9.1-9.4) "Swaziland Tourism Authority" et "Ministry of Tourism, Environment and Communications"; (6.1-6.3,8.2-8.4) Fonds monétaire international.

TAIWAN (PROVINCE DE CHINE)

(1.1) Y compris les nationaux résidant à l'étranger; (2.1-2.6) À l'exclusion des nationaux résidant à l'étranger.
Sources: (1.1-5.4,8.1,9.1,9.3) "Planning Division Tourism Bureau - Ministry of Transportation and Communication"; (6.1-6.3,8.2-8.4) Fonds monétaire international.

TCHAD

(1.2,2.1-2.6,5.2) Touristes non résidents dans les hôtels et établissements assimilés; (9.3) Chambres.

NOTES DES PAYS

Sources: (1.1-5.4,7.1,8.1,9.1-9.4) Direction des Études et de la Programmation - Ministère du Développement Touristique; (6.1,8.2) Banque des Etats de l'Afrique Centrale (B.E.A.C.).

THAILANDE

(1.2,3.1-3.4/2002-2005) Y compris les arrivées des nationaux résidant à l'étranger; (1.2,3.1-3.4/2006) (2.1-2.6,4.1-4.3) À l'exclusion des arrivées des nationaux résidant à l'étranger; (3.3) Y compris chemin de fer; (5.4) Jours; (9.3) Dans les principales destinations touristiques seulement.
Sources: (1.2-5.4,8.1,9.1,9.3) "Tourism Authority of Thailand (TAT)"; (6.1-6.3,8.2-8.4) Fonds monétaire international.

TOGO

(1.2) Touristes non résidents dans les hôtels et établissements assimilés; (9.3) Chambres.
Sources: (1.2-5.4,7.1-7.4,9.1-9.4) Ministère de l'Environnement, du Tourisme et des Ressources Forestières; (6.1-6.3,8.2-8.4) Fonds monétaire international.

TONGA

(1.2,2.2-2.4,4.1-4.3) Arrivées par voie aérienne; (10.1-10.3) Cette section comprend uniquement le poste « voyages » parce que le poste « transport de passagers » ne figure pas dans les données du Fonds monétaire international qui ont servi à la préparation de la présente édition du Compendium.
Sources: (1.1-4.3) "Tonga Visitors Bureau"; (6.2,8.3) Fonds monétaire international.

TRINITE-ET-TOBAGO

(1.2,2.1-2.5,4.1-4.3) Arrivées par voie aérienne; (4.1) Y compris les visites à des parents et amis.
Sources: (1.1-5.4,9.1,9.3) "Central Statistical Office - Ministry of Planning and Development"; (6.1-6.3,8.2-8.4) Fonds monétaire international.

TUNISIE

(1.2,2.1-3.4) Arrivées de touristes non résidents aux frontières nationales; à l'exclusion des nationaux résidant à l'étranger; (9.1,9.2) Hôtels homologués et non-homologués, pensions et villages de vacances; (9.3) Places-lit.
Sources: (1.1-5.4,7.1-7.4,8.1,9.1-9.4) Ministère du Tourisme - Office National du Tourisme et Institut National de la Statistique; (6.1-6.3,8.2-8.4) Fonds monétaire international.

TURQUIE

(1.1,3.1-3.4) Arrivées de visiteurs non résidents aux frontières nationales; (1.3) Arrivées par mer (à l'exclusion d'une frontière terrestre depuis 1989); (2.1-2.6) Arrivées de touristes non résidents aux frontières nationales; (3.4) Y compris les passagers en croisière; (4.1-4.3) Départs de visiteurs non résidents; (5.3) Enquête auprès des établissements d'hébergement homologués par le Ministère du Tourisme; (5.3,7.3) Y compris les terrains de camping; (6.2) Y compris les dépenses des nationaux résidant à l'étranger; (9.3,9.4) Hôtels homologués; à l'exclusion des terrains de camping; (9.3) Places-lit; (10.1-10.3/2002-2004) Cette section comprend uniquement le poste « voyages » parce que le poste « transport de passagers » ne figure pas dans les données du Fonds monétaire international qui ont servi à la préparation de la présente édition du Compendium.
Sources: (1.1-3.4,5.1-5.4,7.1-7.4,8.1,9.1-9.4) (6.2/2002) "Ministry of Culture and Tourism"; (4.1-4.3) "Departing Visitors Survey - Turkish Statistical Institute (TURKSTAT)"; (6.1-6.3/2003-2006) (8.2-8.4) Fonds monétaire international.

TURKMENISTAN

Source: "State Committee for Tourism and Sport".

TUVALU

Source: "Central Statistics Division - Ministry of Finance, Economic Planning and Industry".

UKRAINE

(2.1-2.6) Arrivées de touristes non résidents aux frontières nationales; (3.1-3.4/2002) Arrivées de visiteurs non résidents aux frontières nationales; (3.1-3.4/2003-2006) Arrivées de touristes non résidents aux frontières nationales; (4.1-4.3) Arrivées de visiteurs non résidents aux frontières nationales.
Sources: (1.1-5.4,7.1,7.3,8.1,9.1-9.4) "State Tourism Administration"; (6.1-6.3,8.2-8.4) Fonds monétaire international.

URUGUAY

(1.1,4.1-4.3) Y compris les nationaux résidant à l'étranger; (2.2-3.4) À l'exclusion des nationaux résidant à l'étranger; (3.3) Y compris chemin de fer; (5.4) Jours; (9.1,9.2/2005/2006) À l'exclusion des hôtels non-homologués.
Sources: (1.1-5.4,8.1,9.1-9.4) "Ministerio de Turismo y Deporte"; (6.1-6.3,8.2-8.4) Fonds monétaire international.

VANUATU

(5.4) Jours; (9.3) Chambres.
Sources: (1.1-5.4,8.1,9.1-9.4) "Vanuatu National Statistics Office"; (6.1-6.3,8.2-8.4) Fonds monétaire international.

VENEZUELA

(1.2,2.1-4.3) Arrivées de touristes non résidents aux frontières nationales; (9.1,9.2/2002-2004) Hôtels et Parador/"Pousadas"; (9.1,9.2/2005/2006) Hôtels uniquement.
Sources: (1.1-5.4,7.4,8.1,9.1-9.3) "Ministerio del Poder Popular para el Turismo"; (6.1-6.3,8.2-8.4) Fonds monétaire international.

VIET-NAM

(1.1) Y compris les nationaux résidant à l'étranger; (1.4,3.4) Y compris les arrivées de passagers en croisière et par voie maritime; (2.2-4.3) Arrivées de visiteurs non résidents aux frontières nationales; (6.1) Les chiffres de dépense sont ceux que le pays a fournis à l'OMT mais ils ne figurent pas dans les données du Fonds monétaire international qui ont servi à la préparation de la présente édition du Compendium.
Source: "Viet Nam National Administration of Tourism".

YEMEN

(1.2,2.1-2.6,5.2) Touristes non résidents dans les hôtels et établissements assimilés; (10.1-10.3) Cette section comprend uniquement le poste « voyages » parce que le poste « transport de passagers » ne figure pas dans les données du Fonds monétaire international qui ont servi à la préparation de la présente édition du Compendium.
Sources: (1.2-5.4,7.1,7.2,9.1,9.2) "Ministry of Tourism"; (6.2,8.2-8.4) Fonds monétaire international.

ZAMBIE

(5.4) Jours; (9.3) Chambres; (10.1-10.3) Cette section comprend uniquement le poste « voyages » parce que le poste « transport de passagers » ne figure pas dans les données du Fonds monétaire international qui ont servi à la préparation de la présente édition du Compendium.
Note 2002: Données provisoires.
Sources: (1.2-5.4,7.1,9.1-9.3) "Ministry of Tourism, Environment and Natural Resources"; (6.2,8.2-8.4) Fonds monétaire international.

ZIMBABWE

(2.1-2.6,3.1,3.3,4.1-4.3) Arrivées de visiteurs non résidents aux frontières nationales; (3.1,3.3/2002/2003) Y compris les personnes en transit; (6.1) Les chiffres de dépense sont ceux que le pays a fournis à l'OMT mais ils ne figurent pas dans les données du Fonds monétaire international qui ont servi à la préparation de la présente édition du Compendium; (9.1,9.2) Hôtels classés uniquement; (9.3) Places-lit.
Source: "Zimbabwe Tourism Authority - ZTA".

ALBANIA

(1.1,2.2-4.3) Visitantes y otros viajeros; (1.2,5.2,7.2) Llegadas en hoteles únicamente; 5.4,7.1-74,9.1-9.4/2004-2006) Encuesta trimestral: hoteles con 5 habitaciones o más; (4.3) Tránsito.
Fuentes: (1.1-5.4,7.1-7.4,9.1-9.4) "Institute of Statistics - INSTAT"; (6.1-6.3,8.2-8.4) Fondo Monetario Internacional.

ALEMANIA

(1.2,2.1-2.6) Turistas no residentes alojados en todo tipo de establecimientos de alojamiento; (9.3) Plazas-cama; (9.4) Turismo receptor, hoteles y establecimientos asimilados.
Fuentes: (1.2-5.4,7.1-7.4,8.1,9.1-9.4) "Statistiches Bundesamt"; (6.1-6.3,8.2-8.4) Fondo Monetario Internacional.

ANDORRA

Fuente: Ministerio de Turismo y Medio Ambiente.

ANGOLA

(5.1,5.2,7.1,7.2) Hoteles únicamente.
Fuentes: (1.2-5.3,7.1-7.3,9.1-9.4) "Ministério de Hotelaria e Turismo - Gabinete de Estudos, Planeamento e Estatística"; (6.1-6.3,8.2-8.4) Fondo Monetario Internacional.

ANGUILA

(1.1,3.1-4.3) Llegadas de visitantes no residentes en las fronteras nacionales; (1.2,2.2,2.3) Llegadas de turistas no residentes en las fronteras nacionales; excluidos los nacionales residentes en el extranjero; (4.3) Visitantes del día (excursionistas); (9.1) Hoteles, casas de huéspedes y apartamentos/ villas; (9.3) Habitaciones; enero-mayo; (10.2,10.3) Este apartado incluye únicamente la partida "viajes" debido a que la partida "transporte de pasajeros" no figura en los datos del Fondo Monetario Internacional utilizados para la preparación de esta edición del Compendio.
Fuentes: (1.1-5.4,9.1-9.4) "Statistical Department - Ministry of Finance"; (6.2,8.3) Fondo Monetario Internacional.

ANTIGUA Y BARBUDA

(1.1) Excluidas las llegadas de pasajeros en yate; (2.2,2.3,3.1,4.1-4.3) Llegadas por vía aérea; excluidos los nacionales residentes en el extranjero; (3.4) Pasajeros en crucero únicamente; (10.1-10.3) Este apartado incluye únicamente la partida "viajes" debido a que la partida "transporte de pasajeros" no figura en los datos del Fondo Monetario Internacional utilizados para la preparación de esta edición del Compendio.
Fuentes: (1.1-5.4,9.1) "Ministry of Tourism"; (6.2,8.3) Fondo Monetario Internacional.

ARABIA SAUDITA

(9.1/2002/2003) Hotels únicamente; (6.1-6.3,8.2-8.4) Las cifras de gasto corresponden a las facilitadas por el país a la OMT y que, sin embargo, no figuran en los datos del Fondo Monetario Internacional utilizados para la preparación de esta edición del Compendio.
Fuente: "The Supreme Commission for Tourism".

ARGELIA

(1.1,3.1-3.4) Incluidos los nacionales residentes en el extranjero:
2002   736.915
2003   861.373
2004   865.157
2005   1.001.884
2006   1.159.224
(2.1-2.6,4.1,4.2) Excluidos los nacionales residentes en el extranjero; (6.1,8.2) Las cifras de gasto corresponden a las facilitadas por el país a la OMT y que, sin embargo, no figuran en los datos del Fondo Monetario Internacional utilizados para la preparación de esta edición del Compendio.
Fuentes: "Ministère de l'Aménagement du Territoire, de l'Environnement et du Tourisme" y "Office National des Statistiques".

ARGENTINA

A partir del año 2004, como resultado de la importancia de la "Encuesta de Turismo Internacional" se modificaron las estimaciones de la serie de la cuenta "Viajes" de la Balanza de Pagos. Por este motivo, los datos no son rigurosamente comparables con los años anteriores.
Nota 2005-2006: Datos provisionales.
Fuentes: (1.2-5.4,7.1,7.2,8.1,9.1-9.3) Dirección de Estudios de Mercado y Estadística - Secretaría de Turismo de la Nación; (6.1-6.3,8.2-8.4) Fondo Monetario Internacional.

NOTAS DE LOS PAISES

ARMENIA

Fuentes: (1.2-5.4,7.1-7.4,8.1,9.1-9.4) "Tourism Department - Ministry of Trade and Economic Development"; (6.1-6.3,8.2-8.4) Fondo Monetario Internacional.

ARUBA

(1.2,2.2-4.3) Llegadas de turistas no residentes en las fronteras nacionales; (5.4) Turistas no residentes alojados en hoteles y establecimientos asimilados; (9.3) Habitaciones.
Fuentes: (1.1-5.4,9.1-9.3) "Aruba Tourism Authority"; (6.1-6.3,8.2-8.4) Fondo Monetario Internacional.

AUSTRALIA

(1.1) Excluidos los nacionales residentes en el extranjero y miembros de tripulaciones; (1.2,1.3) Llegadas por vía aérea; (2.1-4.3) Llegadas de visitantes no residentes en las fronteras nacionales; (9.1,9.2/2002-2004) Hoteles, moteles, casas de huéspedes y apartamentos de servicio hotelero con 15 habitaciones o más; (9.1,9.2/2005/2006) Hoteles, moteles, casas de huéspedes y apartamentos de servicio hotelero con 5 habitaciones o más; (9.3) Habitaciones.
Fuentes: (1.1-4.3,8.1,9.1-9.4) "Australian Bureau of Statistics"; (6.1-6.3,8.2-8.4) Fondo Monetario Internacional.

AUSTRIA

(1.2-2.6) Turistas no residentes alojados en hoteles y establecimientos asimilados; (5.1,5.2,7.1,7.2) Incluidos los complejos vacacionales; (5.3,7.3) Excluido el alojamiento privado; (8.1) A partir de 2003, nueva metodología. Incluye viajes al extranjero por vacaciones y negocios con al menos una pernoctación; (9.1) Sólo hoteles; (9.2) Hoteles y complejos vacacionales; (9.3) Basado en la temporada de verano; (9.4) Duración media de la estancia en hoteles y establecimientos asimilados; incluidos los complejos vacacionales.
Fuentes: (1.2-5.4,7.1-7.4,8.1,9.1-9.4) "Department for Tourism and Historic Objects - Federal Ministry of Economics and Labour"; (6.1-6.3,8.2-8.4) Fondo Monetario Internacional.

AZERBAIYAN

Fuentes: (1.2-5.2,7.1,7.2,8.1,9.1,9.2) "Ministry of Culture and Tourism"; (6.1-6.3,8.2-8.4) Fondo Monetario Internacional.

BAHAMAS

(1.2,2.1-2.6,4.1-4.3) Llegadas de turistas no residentes en las fronteras nacionales; (5.2) Llegadas en hoteles únicamente; (9.1,9.2) Hoteles, apartamentos, bungalows y villas - Establecimientos homologados únicamente; (9.3) Habitaciones.
Fuentes: (1.1-5.4,9.1-9.4) "Bahamas Ministry of Tourism"; (6.1-6.3,8.2-8.4) Fondo Monetario Internacional.

BAHREIN

(1.1,2.1-4.3) Llegadas de visitantes no residentes en las fronteras nacionales; excluidos los nacionales residentes en el extranjero; (3.1) Llegadas al aeropuerto internacional de Bahrein; (3.3) Llegadas a través del "King Fahad Causeway"; (3.4) Llegadas al puerto Mina Salman; (5.1,9.1,9.2) Únicamente hoteles clasificados.
Fuentes: (1.1-5.4,9.1-9.3) "Tourism Affairs - Ministry of Information"; (6.1-6.3,8.2-8.4) Fondo Monetario Internacional.

BANGLADESH

Fuentes: (1.2-5.4,8.1,9.1-9.3) "Bangladesh Parjatan Corporation"; (6.1-6.3,8.2-8.4) Fondo Monetario Internacional.

BARBADOS

(1.2,2.1-4.3) Llegadas de turistas no residentes en las fronteras nacionales; (9.1,9.2) Hoteles, hoteles-apartamento, apartamentos y bungalows, casas de huéspedes; (9.3) Habitaciones.
Nota 2006: Datos provisionales.
Fuentes: (1.1-5.4,9.1-9.4) "Barbados Tourism Authority"; (6.1-6.3,8.2-8.4) Fondo Monetario Internacional.

BELARUS

(1.2,2.2-2.6) Turismo organizado.
Fuentes: (1.1,3.1-3.3,4.1-4.3) "State Committee of Frontier Troops"; (1.2,2.2-2.6,5.1,5.2,7.1,7.2,8.1,9.1-9.4) "Ministry of Statistics and Analysis"; (6.1-6.3,8.2-8.4) Fondo Monetario Internacional.

BELGICA

(1.2,2.1-2.6,4.1-4.3) Turistas no residentes alojados en todo tipo de establecimientos de alojamiento; (5.1,5.2,7.1,7.2) Hoteles únicamente; (9.1,9.2) Hoteles y poblados de vacaciones.
Fuentes: (1.2-5.3,7.1-7.3,8.1,9.1,9.2) "Institut National de Statistique"; (6.1-6.3,8.2-8.4) Fondo Monetario Internacional.

NOTAS DE LOS PAISES

BELICE

(1.3) Pasajeros en tránsito y cruces de frontera; (2.2-4.2) Llegadas de turistas no residentes en las fronteras nacionales; (10.1-10.3) Este apartado incluye únicamente la partida "viajes" debido a que la partida "transporte de pasajeros" no figura en los datos del Fondo Monetario Internacional utilizados para la preparación de esta edición del Compendio.
Fuentes: (1.1-5.4,7.3,9.1-9.4) "Belize Tourist Board"; (6.2,8.2-8.4) Fondo Monetario Internacional.

BENIN

(1.2,2.1-2.6) Llegadas de turistas no residentes en las fronteras nacionales.
Nota 2003-2006: Estimaciones.
Fuentes: (1.1-5.3,7.3,9.1-9.4) "Direction du développement touristiques - Ministère de la culture, de l'artisanat et du tourisme"; (6.1-6.3,8.2-8.4) Fondo Monetario Internacional.

BERMUDA

(1.1) Excluidos los nacionales residentes en el extranjero; (1.2,2.2-2.4,4.1-4.3) Llegadas por vía aérea; (5.3) Incluidas las pernoctaciones en casas particulares; (6.1,8.2) Las cifras de gasto corresponden a las facilitadas por el país a la OMT y que, sin embargo, no figuran en los datos del Fondo Monetario Internacional utilizados para la preparación de esta edición del Compendio; (9.3) Habitaciones.
Fuente: "Bermuda Department of Tourism".

BHUTAN

(6.1) Las cifras de gasto corresponden a las facilitadas por el país a la OMT y que, sin embargo, no figuran en los datos del Fondo Monetario Internacional utilizados para la preparación de esta edición del Compendio.
Fuente: "Department of Tourism - Royal Government of Bhutan".

BOLIVIA

(1.2) Llegadas de turistas no residentes en las fronteras nacionales; (2.1-2.4) Turistas no residentes alojados en hoteles y establecimientos asimilados; (3.4) Llegadas por vía lacustre; (4.1-4.3) Datos procedentes de encuestas; (5.1-5.,7.1-7.4,9.1,9.2) Capitales de departamento únicamente; (9.3) Plazas-cama (hoteles); (9.4) Días, hoteles y establecimientos asimilados, turismo receptor.
Nota 2003-2006: Datos preliminares.
Fuentes: (1.2-5.4,7.1-7.4,8.1,9.1-9.4) Viceministerio de Turismo - Ministerio de Producción y Microempresa; (6.1-6.3,8.2-8.4) Fondo Monetario Internacional.

BONAIRE

Fuentes: (1.1-5.4,9.1-9.4) "Tourism Corporation of Bonaire (TCB)"; (6.2,8.3) "Central Bank of the Netherlands Antilles".

BOSNIA Y HERZEGOVINA

(1.2,2.2-2.4) Turistas no residentes alojados en todo tipo de establecimientos de alojamiento; (2.5,2.6) Menos de 500 llegadas; (9.1,9.2) Excluida la República Srpska.
Fuentes: (1.2-5.3,7.3,9.1,9.2) "Agency for Statistics of Bosnia and Herzegovina"; (6.1-6.3,8.2-8.4) Fondo Monetario Internacional.

BOTSWANA

Fuentes: (1.1-5.2,7.2,9.1-9.4) "Department of Tourism - Ministry of Environment, Wildlife and Tourism"; (6.1-6.3,8.2-8.4) Fondo Monetario Internacional.

BRASIL

(1.2-4.3) Incluidos los nacionales residentes en el extranjero; (3.4) Incluidas las llegadas por vía fluvial.
Nota 2006: Estimaciones.
Fuentes: (1.2-4.3,8.1) "Instituto Brasileiro de Turismo (EMBRATUR)"; (6.1-6.3,8.2-8.4) Fondo Monetario Internacional.

BRUNEI DARUSSALAM

(1.2,2.2-2.4,3.1) Llegadas por vía aérea; (10.1-10.3) Este apartado incluye únicamente la partida "viajes" debido a que la partida "transporte de pasajeros" no figura en los datos del Fondo Monetario Internacional utilizados para la preparación de esta edición del Compendio.
Fuentes: (1.1-5.2,9.1-9.3) "Brunei Tourism - Ministry of Industry and Primary Resources"; (6.2,8.3) Fondo Monetario Internacional.

BULGARIA

(1.3) Visitantes en tránsito; (3.4) Mar y ríos del interior del país; (5.1,5.3,5.4,7.1,7.3,9.2-9.4) Cubre prácticamente el antiguo alojamiento del sector público y de propiedad del Estado. Una parte considerable del sector privado (más del 70 por ciento en 1998) no está incluido en los datos; (9.2) Hoteles únicamente; (9.3) Plazas-cama en los hoteles.
Fuentes: (1.1-5.4,7.1-7.3,8.1,9.2-9.4) "National Statistical Institute - State Agency for Tourism"; (6.1-6.3,8.2-8.4) Fondo Monetario Internacional.

BURKINA FASO

(1.2,2.1-2.6,5.2) Turistas no residentes alojados en hoteles y establecimientos asimilados; (4.1-4.3) Incluido el turismo interno; (9.3) Habitaciones.
Fuentes: (1.2-5.4,7.1,7.2,9.3) "Service de l'analyse statistique et de la Coopération touristique - Ministère de la Culture, des Arts et du Tourisme"; (6.1-6.3,8.2-8.4) "Banque Centrale des Etats de l'Afrique de l'Ouest".

BURUNDI

(1.2-4.3) Llegadas de turistas no residentes en las fronteras nacionales; incluidos los nacionales residentes en el extranjero; (3.4) Llegadas por vía lacustre.
Fuentes: (1.2-4.3,9.1,9.2) "Office National du Tourisme"; (6.1-6.3,8.2-8.4) Fondo Monetario Internacional.

CABO VERDE

(1.2,2.1-2.6,5.2) Non-resident tourists staying in hotels and similar establishments.
Sources: (1.2-5.2,7.1,7.2,9.1,9.2) "Ministère du Tourisme"; (6.1-6.3,8.2-8.4) International Monetary Fund.

CAMBOYA

(1.2) Llegadas de turistas internacionales por todo el conjunto de medios de transporte; (2.2-2.5,3.1-3.4/2004-2006) Excluidas las llegadas a la provincia "Phreah Vihear": 2004: 67.843; 2005: 88.615; 2006: 108,691; (3.3/2002) Llegadas por tierra y barco; (3.4) Llegadas por barco; (4.1-4.3/2002) Llegadas por vía aérea; (4.1/2002) Incluidas las llegadas al aeropuerto de Siem Reap en vuelos directos: 202.791; (4.3/2005/2006) Incluidas las llegadas a la provincia "Phreah Vihear"; (5.4) Días.
Fuentes: (1.2-5.4,8.1,9.1-9.3) "Ministry of Tourism"; (6.1-6.3,8.2-8.4) Fondo Monetario Internacional.

CAMERUN

(1.2,2.1-2.6,5.2) Turistas no residentes alojados en hoteles y establecimientos asimilados.
Fuentes: (1.2-5.2,7.1,7.2,9.1,9.2) "Ministère du Tourisme"; (6.1-6.3,8.2-8.4) Fondo Monetario Internacional.

CANADA

(1.1,1.3) Datos basados en la contabilidad aduanera, ajustándola en función de los resultados de las encuestas; (1.2,2.1-4.3) Llegadas de turistas no residentes en las fronteras nacionales; (4.2) Incluye congresos; (8.1) Viajes-persona (una/varias noches).
Nota 2006: Datos provisionales.
Fuentes: (1.1-4.3,5.3,7.1,7.3,8.1) "Canadian Tourism Commission" y "Statistics Canada"; (6.1-6.3,8.2-8.4) Fondo Monetario Internacional.

CHAD

(1.2,2.1-2.6,5.2) Turistas no residentes alojados en hoteles y establecimientos asimilados; (9.3) Habitaciones.
Fuentes: (1.1-5.4,7.1,8.1,9.1-9.4) "Direction des Études et de la Programmation - Ministère du Développement Touristique"; (6.1,8.2) "Banque des Etats de l'Afrique Centrale (B.E.A.C.)".

CHILE

(5.1,5.2,7.1,7.2) Las cifras de 2005 no son comparables con años anteriores debido a una actualización del Censo con cobertura nacional de Establecimientos de Alojamiento Turístico.
Fuentes: (1.2-5.4,7.1,7.2,8.1,9.1-9.4) Servicio Nacional de Turismo - SERNATUR; (6.1-6.3,8.2-8.4) Fondo Monetario Internacional.

CHINA

(1.1,2.1-2.6,3.1-3.4) Incluidas las llegadas de personas de origen étnico chino procedentes de "Hong Kong, China", "Macao, China", "Taiwán (Provincia de China)" y de ultramar, la mayor parte de excursionistas proceden de "Hong Kong, China" y "Macao, China"; (4.1-4.3) Excluidas las llegadas de turistas de origen étnico chino procedentes de "Hong Kong, China", "Macao, China", "Taiwán (Provincia de China)" y de ultramar; (7.1,9.1,9.2) Referido sólo a los hoteles clasificados con estrellas; (8.1) Incluidos los miembros de las tripulaciones y otros miembros de las fuerzas armadas; (9.3) Habitaciones; (9.4) Turismo receptor.

Fuentes: (1.1-5.4,7.1,8.1,9.1-9.4) "National Tourism Administration"; (6.1-6.3,8.2-8.4) Fondo Monetario Internacional.

CHIPRE

(1.2,2.1-2.6) Llegadas de turistas no residentes en las fronteras nacionales; (1.3) Incluidos los pasajeros en crucero y en tránsito; (3.4) Incluidos los pasajeros en crucero; (5.4) Datos extraídos de la encuesta de gastos turísticos (salidas) referidos a la estancia y al tipo de alojamiento; (9.3) Plazas-cama; (9.4) A partir de 2000, los cálculos de la duración media de las estancias se basan en las pernoctaciones y en las llegadas a hoteles y establecimientos asimilados.
Fuentes: (1.1-5.4,7.1-7.4,8.1,9.1-9.4) "Cyprus Tourism Organization"; (6.1-6.3,8.2-8.4) Fondo Monetario Internacional.

COLOMBIA

(1.1,2.1-2.6,3.1-3.4,4.1-4.3) Llegadas de visitantes no residentes en las fronteras nacionales. Excluidos los pasajeros en crucero; (9.3) Habitaciones.
Nota 2006: Datos provisionales.
Fuentes: (1.1-4.3,8.1) Dirección de Extranjería - Departamento Administrativo de Seguridad (DAS); (6.1-6.3,8.2-8.4) Fondo Monetario Internacional; (9.1-9.3) Dirección de Turismo - Ministerio de Comercio, Industria y Turismo, Asociación Hotelera de Colombia (COTELCO).

COMORAS

(6.1,8.2) Las cifras de gasto corresponden a las facilitadas por el país a la OMT y que, sin embargo, no figuran en los datos del Fondo Monetario Internacional utilizados para la preparación de esta edición del Compendio.
Fuentes: "Direction Nationale de la Promotion du Tourisme et de l'Hôtellerie - Ministère du Transport, Tourisme, Postes et Télécommunications" y "Banque centrale des Comores".

COREA, REPUBLICA DE

(1.1) Incluidos los nacionales residentes en el extranjero y miembros de las tripulaciones; (2.1-2.6) Excluidos los nacionales residentes en el extranjero; (3.1,3.4/2002-2005) Excluidos los nacionales residentes en el extranjero y miembros de las tripulaciones; (8.2) El país facilita a la OMT niveles agregados de gasto que son significativamente diferentes a los datos del Fondo Monetario Internacional utilizados para la preparación de esta edición del Compendio (excluidos los gastos de los estudiantes que realizan sus estudios fuera del país). Los datos del país son:
2002:   9.038
2003:   8.248
2004:   9.856
2005: 12.025
2006: 14.336
(9.1) Hoteles únicamente; (9.3) Habitaciones.
Fuentes: (1.1-5.4,8.1,9.1,9.3) "Ministry of Culture and Tourism"; (6.1-6.3,8.2-8.4) Fondo Monetario Internacional.

COSTA RICA

(4.1) Viajes de placer y visita a familiares; (5.4) En la zona central del país; (9.3) En establecimientos de "cinco categorías" en el Gran Área Metropolitana de San José (estudio por muestreo).
Fuentes: (1.1-5.4,8.1,9.1,9.3) Instituto Costarricense de Turismo; (6.1-6.3,8.2-8.4) Fondo Monetario Internacional.

CROACIA

(1.2,2.2-2.4) Turistas no residentes alojados en todo tipo de establecimientos de alojamiento; incluidas las llegadas a los puertos de turismo náutico; (3.1-3.4) Llegadas de visitantes no residentes en las fronteras nacionales; (3.4/2004) Desde 2004 se aplicó una nueva metodología y cobertura y por lo tanto la información no es comparable con años anteriores; (5.3,7.3) Incluidas las pernoctaciones en puertos de turismo náutico; (9.4) Turismo interior (interno y receptor) en todos los medios de alojamiento (incluidos los puertos de turismo náutico).
Fuentes: (1.1-5.4,7.1-7.4,9.1-9.4) "Central Bureau of Statistics"; (6.1-6.3,8.2-8.4) Fondo Monetario Internacional.

CUBA

(1.1,2.1-2.6) Llegadas de visitantes no residentes en las fronteras nacionales; (1.2,4.1-4.3) Llegadas por vía aérea; (1.3) Incluidos los pasajeros en crucero; (5.1,7.1,9.1,9.2) Hoteles, moteles y aparthoteles; (5.3,7.3) Hoteles, moteles, aparthoteles, terrenos de camping/caravaning y otros; (6.1-6.3) Las cifras de gasto corresponden a las facilitadas por el país a la OMT y que, sin embargo, no figuran en los datos del Fondo Monetario Internacional utilizados para la preparación de esta edición del Compendio; (8.1) Comprende sólo giras controladas por el Instituto del Turismo; (9.3) Habitaciones.
Fuente: Oficina Nacional de Estadísticas.

CURAÇAO

(1.2,1.3,2.2,2.3,3.1,4.1-4.3) Llegadas por vía aérea; (3.4) Llegadas de pasajeros en crucero; (4.1-4.3) Diferencias en los totales globales debido a la falta de datos completos en las tarjetas de embarque y desembarque de los visitantes; (6.1) Las cifras de

gasto corresponden a las facilitadas por el país a la OMT y que, sin embargo, no figuran en los datos del Fondo Monetario Internacional utilizados para la preparación de esta edición del Compendio; (9.1) Hoteles, casas de huéspedes y apartamentos; (9.3) Habitaciones.
Fuente: "Curaçao Tourist Board".

DINAMARCA

(1.2,2.2-2.4) Turistas no residentes alojados en todo tipo de establecimientos de alojamiento; (1.2-5.3,7.1-7.3,8.1) Nueva metodología a partir de 2004; (5.2,7.2) Hoteles únicamente; (9.1-9.3) Únicamente hoteles y alojamientos de vacaciones con 40 camas o más; (9.3) Plazas-cama; (10.1-10.3) Este apartado incluye únicamente la partida "viajes" debido a que la partida "transporte de pasajeros" no figura en los datos del Fondo Monetario Internacional utilizados para la preparación de esta edición del Compendio.
Fuentes: (1.1-5.4,7.1-7.4,8.1,9.1-9.3) "Statistics Denmark"; (6.2,8.3) Fondo Monetario Internacional.

DJIBOUTI

(1.2) Turistas no residentes alojados en hoteles; (9.3) Habitaciones; (10.1-10.3) Este apartado incluye únicamente la partida "viajes" debido a que la partida "transporte de pasajeros" no figura en los datos del Fondo Monetario Internacional utilizados para la preparación de esta edición del Compendio.
Fuentes: (1.2,5.1,5.2,9.1-9.3) "Office national du tourisme"; (6.2,8.2-8.4) Fondo Monetario Internacional.

DOMINICA

(1.2,2.2-2.4,4.1-4.3) Llegadas de turistas no residentes en las fronteras nacionales; (3.1,3.4) Llegadas de visitantes no residentes en las fronteras nacionales; excluidos los pasajeros en crucero; (5.4) Días; (10.1-10.3) Este apartado incluye únicamente la partida "viajes" debido a que la partida "transporte de pasajeros" no figura en los datos del Fondo Monetario Internacional utilizados para la preparación de esta edición del Compendio.
Fuentes: (1.1-5.4,9.1) "Central Statistical Office - Ministry of Finance"; (6.2,8.3) Fondo Monetario Internacional.

ECUADOR

(1.1) Excluidos los nacionales residentes en el extranjero.
Fuentes: (1.1-3.4,8.1,9.1,9.2) Ministerio de Turismo; (6.1-6.3,8.2-8.4) Fondo Monetario Internacional.

EGIPTO

(1.1,2.1-3.4) Llegadas de visitantes no residentes en las fronteras nacionales; (4.1-4.3) Llegadas de turistas no residentes en las fronteras nacionales; (7.1) Hoteles únicamente en las principales regiones: Cairo, Giza, Sur del Sinaí, Mar Rojo, Luxor, Aswan, Alejandría; (8.1) Viajes por turismo y no-turismo (más del 50% por motivo de trabajo); (9.3) Habitaciones.
Fuentes: (1.1-5.4,7.1-7.4,8.1,9.1-9.4) "Ministry of Tourism"; (6.1-6.3,8.2-8.4) Fondo Monetario Internacional.

EL SALVADOR

(1.2,2.1-4.3) Llegadas de turistas no residentes en las fronteras nacionales; (6.1) El país facilita a la OMT niveles agregados de gasto que son significativamente diferentes a los datos del Fondo Monetario Internacional utilizados para la preparación de esta edición del Compendio. Los datos del país son (millones $EE.UU.):
2002: 342
2003: 373
2004: 425
2005: 644
2006: 862
Dicho gasto turístico es obtenido en base a investigaciones conjuntas con el Banco Central de Reserva de El Salvador y la Corporación Salvadoreña de Turismo para la identificación de un Perfil Básico de Turista internacional que visita El Salvador. (9.3) Plazas-cama.
Fuentes: (1.1-5.4,8.1,9.1-9.4) Corporación Salvadoreña de Turismo (CORSATUR) - Ministerio de Turismo; (6.1-6.3,8.2-8.4) Fondo Monetario Internacional.

EMIRATOS ARABES UNIDOS

(1.2) Llegadas en los hoteles únicamente. Incluido el turismo interno y los nacionales residentes en el extranjero; (2.1-2.6) Llegadas en los hoteles únicamente. Excluido el turismo interno y los nacionales residentes en el extranjero; (5.1) Pernoctaciones en los hoteles únicamente. Incluido el turismo interno y los nacionales residentes en el extranjero; (6.1,8.2) Las cifras de gasto corresponden a las facilitadas por el país a la OMT y que, sin embargo, no figuran en los datos del Fondo Monetario Internacional utilizados para la preparación de esta edición del Compendio; (9.1,9.2) Hoteles únicamente; (9.3) Habitaciones alquiladas.
Fuente: "Ministry of Economy and Planning - Planning Sector".

NOTAS DE LOS PAISES

ERITREA

(1.1) Incluidos los nacionales residentes en el extranjero; (2.1-2.6) Excluidos los nacionales residentes en el extranjero; (5.1,7.1) Únicamente hoteles y establecimientos asimilados en las tres principales ciudades: Asmara, Karen y Massawa; (6.1) Los datos de gastos corresponden a los facilitados por el país a la OMT, por tratarse de una serie más completa que la facilitada por el Fondo Monetario Internacional (FMI) para la preparación de esta edición del Compendio; (9.1,9.2/2002-2004) Únicamente en las principales ciudades de Eritrea: (9.1,9.2/2005) Todos los hoteles y establecimientos asimilados en Eritrea; (10.1-10.3) Este apartado no se ha podido completar debido a que las partidas "viajes" y "transporte de pasajeros" no figuran en los datos del Fondo Monetario Internacional utilizados para la preparación de esta edición del Compendio.
Fuente: "Ministry of Tourism".

ESLOVAQUIA

(1.2,2.1-2.5) Turistas no residentes alojados en todo tipo de establecimientos de alojamiento.
Fuentes: (1.1-5.4,7.1-7.4,8.1,9.1-9.4) "Department of Tourism - Ministry of Economy" y "Statistical Office"; (6.1-6.3,8.2-8.4/2002/2003) Fondo Monetario Internacional.

ESLOVENIA

(1.1) Incluidas todas las categorías de viajeros por cualquier motivo de visita; (1.2,2.1-2.4) Turistas no residentes alojados en todo tipo de establecimientos de alojamiento; (3.1-3.4,4.1-4.3) Turistas no residentes alojados en todo tipo de establecimientos de alojamiento; datos procedentes de la encuesta sobre 3 años realizada en verano entre los turistas extranjeros llegados a Eslovenia; (8.1) Encuesta trimestral de los viajes de la población residente.
Fuentes: (1.1-5.4,7.1-7.4,8.1,9.1-9.4) "Statistical Office - Information Society and Tourism Statistics"; (6.1-6.3,8.2-8.4) Fondo Monetario Internacional.

ESPAÑA

(1.1) Llegadas de visitantes no residentes en las fronteras nacionales; incluidos los nacionales residentes en el extranjero; (2.2-4.3) Llegadas de turistas no residentes en las fronteras nacionales; incluidos los nacionales residentes en el extranjero; (2.4) Japón únicamente; (5.1,7.1) Pernoctaciones en hoteles y hostales; (5.3,7.3) Pernoctaciones en hoteles, hostales, terrenos de camping, apartamentos turísticos y alojamientos/casas rurales; (5.4,7.4,9.1-9.4) Hoteles y hostales únicamente; (8.1) Desde 2005 se aplicó una nueva metodología y por lo tanto la información no es comparable con años anteriores; (9.3) Plazas-cama.
Fuentes: (1.1-4.3,8.1) Instituto de Estudios Turísticos; (5.1-5.4,7.1-7.4,9.1-9.4) Instituto Nacional de Estadística; (6.1-6.3,8.2-8.4) Fondo Monetario Internacional.

ESTADOS UNIDOS

(1.2,2.2) Incluidos los mexicanos que pasan una noche o más en EE.UU.; (3.1-3.4) Estimaciones preliminares; (3.3) Incluye un muy pequeño porcentaje (0.2%) de viajeros cuyo modo de transporte no se conoce; (4.1-4.3) Principal motivo del viaje; (4.1-4.3,5.2) Ultramar únicamente; excluido México (los datos no están disponibles); (6.2,8.3) El país facilita a la OMT datos de gasto que son significativamente diferentes a los datos del Fondo Monetario Internacional utilizados para la preparación de esta edición del Compendio. Los datos del país son:

	6.2	8.3
2002:	66.605	58.715
2003:	64.359	57.447
2004:	74.546	65.750
2005:	81.799	68.970
2006:	85.694	72.029

(8.1) Incluidos los americanos que pasan una o varias noches en México.
Fuentes: (1.2-5.2,8.1) "Office of Travel and Tourism Industries"; (6.1-6.3,8.2-8.4) Fondo Monetario Internacional; (9.1,9.3) "American Hotel & Lodging Association (AHLA)".

ESTONIA

(1.1,3.1-3.4) Llegadas de visitantes no residentes en las fronteras nacionales; (1.1-1.3,3.1-3.4,8.1/2004) A partir de 2004 no se recopilan las estadísticas de fronteras; (1.2/2004-2006) Calculado en base a las estadísticas de alojamiento y a la "Foreign Visitor Survey" realizada por la "Statistical Office of Estonia"; (2.1-2.4) Turistas no residentes alojados en todo tipo de establecimientos de alojamiento; (9.1-9.4) Se incluyen los datos de complejos de salud que ofrecen un servicio de alojamiento.
Fuentes: (1.1-5.4,7.1-7.4,8.1,9.1-9.4) "Estonian Tourist Board / Enterprise Estonia"; (6.1-6.3,8.2-8.4) Fondo Monetario Internacional.

ETIOPIA

(1.2) Llegadas a todos los puestos fronterizos; incluidos los nacionales residentes en el extranjero; (2.1-2.6,3.1-3.3,4.1-4.3) Llegadas a todos los puestos fronterizos; (9.1,9.2/2002/2003/2005) Excluidos los hoteles sin homologar; (9.3) Plazas-cama; (9.4) Años fiscales etíopes.
Fuentes: (1.2-5.1,9.1-9.4) "Ethiopian Tourism Commission"; (6.1-6.3,8.2-8.4) Fondo Monetario Internacional.

NOTAS DE LOS PAISES

EX REPUBLICA YUGOSLAVA DE MACEDONIA

(1.2,2.2-2.4) Turistas no residentes alojados en todo tipo de establecimientos de alojamiento; (3.1-3.3) Llegadas de visitantes no residentes en las fronteras nacionales; (9.4) Duración media de la estancia en todos los establecimientos de alojamiento.
Fuentes: (1.1-5.4,7.1-7.4,9.1-9.4) "State Statistical Office"; (6.1-6.3,8.2-8.4) Fondo Monetario Internacional.

FEDERACION DE RUSIA

(1.1,2.1-4.3) Llegadas de visitantes no residentes en las fronteras nacionales; (9.1,9.2) Alojamiento en hoteles y en otros establecimientos de carácter turístico.
Fuentes: (1.1-5.4,7.1-7.4,8.1,9.1-9.4) "Russian Federal Agency for Tourism"; (6.1-6.3,8.2-8.4) Fondo Monetario Internacional.

FIJI

(1.2,2.2-4.3) Llegadas de turistas no residentes en las fronteras nacionales; excluidos los nacionales residentes en el extranjero; (1.2-4.3,5.4/2004-2006) Datos provisionales; (5.4) Días; (9.3) Habitaciones.
Fuentes: (1.1-5.4,7.1,8.1,9.1-9.3) "Fiji Islands Bureau of Statistics"; (6.1-6.3,8.2-8.4) Fondo Monetario Internacional.

FILIPINAS

(1.2,3.1-4.3) Llegadas de turistas no residentes en las fronteras nacionales; incluidos los nacionales residentes en el extranjero; (2.1-2.6) Llegadas de turistas no residentes en las fronteras nacionales; excluidos los nacionales residentes en el extranjero; (4.1-4.3) Llegadas por vía aérea; (8.1) Incluidos los trabajadores con contrato procedentes de ultramar; (9.1,9.2) Hoteles homologados únicamente; (9.3,9.4) Hoteles homologados en Metro Manila.
Fuentes: (1.2-5.4,8.1,9.1-9.4) "Department of Tourism"; (6.1-6.3,8.2-8.4) Fondo Monetario Internacional.

FINLANDIA

(1.1,2.1-4.3) Llegadas de visitantes no residentes en las fronteras nacionales. Encuesta en las fronteras; (1.2) Llegadas de turistas no residentes en las fronteras nacionales; (5.1-5.3,7.1-7.3) Debido a un cambio en la metodología, la información de 2004 no es comparable con años anteriores; (8.1) Viajes al extranjero, incluidos los cruceros con pernoctaciones a bordo.
Fuentes: (1.1-5.4,7.1-7.4,8.1,9.1-9.4) "Tourism Statistics - Statistics Finland"; (6.1-6.3,8.2-8.4) Fondo Monetario Internacional.

FRANCIA

(1.1-4.3,5.3) Estimaciones basadas en encuestas en fronteras (1996-2004); (1.1-4.3,5.3,5.4/2005) Ruptura de serie, datos no comparables con años anteriores; (4.1) Vacaciones y visitas a parientes, amigos; (4.2) Negocios, recreo; (4.3) Tránsito y otros motivos; (5.1,5.2,7.1,7.2,9.1-9.4) 2002/2003: únicamente hoteles 0 a 4 estrellas. 2004-2006: incluidos hoteles sin clasificar. 2006: renovación de la encuesta, datos no comparables con años anteriores; (5.3,7.3) Todo tipo de alojamiento; (5.4) Duración media de la estancia del turismo receptor; (7.1-7.4/2005/2006) Población residente de 15 años o más; (9.3) Tasa neta de ocupación de las habitaciones.
2005: Datos revisados; 2006: Datos provisionales.
Fuentes: (1.2-5.4,7.1-7.4,8.1,9.1-9.4) "Bureau des études, des statistiques et des comptes économiques - Direction du Tourisme"; (6.2,8.3)
Fondo Monetario Internacional; (6.3,8.4) "Banque de France".

GABON

(1.2,2.1,3.1) Llegadas de turistas no residentes al aeropuerto de Libreville.
Fuentes: (1.1-5.1,8.1,9.1,9.3) "Centre Gabonais de Promotion Touristique (GABONTOUR)"; (6.1-6.3,8.2-8.4) Fondo Monetario Internacional.

GAMBIA

(1.2,2.1-2.3,3.1,4.1-4.3) Llegadas en vuelos fletados únicamente.
Fuentes: (1.1-4.3,8.1,9.1-9.4) "Gambia Tourism Authority"; (6.1-6.3,8.2-8.4) Fondo Monetario Internacional.

GEORGIA

(4.1-4.3) Llegadas en hoteles únicamente.
Fuentes: (1.1-4.3,8.1) "Department of Tourism and Resorts - Ministry of Economic Development"; (5.2,7.2,9.1,9.2) "State Department for Statistics - Ministry of Economic Development"; (6.1-6.3,8.2-8.4) Fondo Monetario Internacional.

GHANA

(1.2) Incluidos los nacionales residentes en el extranjero; (2.1-2.6) Excluidos los nacionales residentes en el extranjero.
Fuentes: (1.2-4.3,9.1-9.3) "Ghana Tourist Board" y "Ministry of Tourism and Modernisation of the Capital City"; (6.1-6.3,8.2-8.4) Fondo Monetario Internacional.

NOTAS DE LOS PAISES

GRANADA

(1.2,2.1-4.3) Llegadas de turistas no residentes en las fronteras nacionales; (9.1,9.2) Hoteles, bungalows/ apartamentos y casas de huéspedes; (9.3) Habitaciones; (10.1-10.3) Este apartado incluye únicamente la partida "viajes" debido a que la partida "transporte de pasajeros" no figura en los datos del Fondo Monetario Internacional utilizados para la preparación de esta edición del Compendio.
Fuentes: (1.1-5.4,9.1-9.4) "Grenada Board of Tourism"; (6.2,8.3) Fondo Monetario Internacional.

GRECIA

(1.1,3.1-3.4) Llegadas de visitantes no residentes en las fronteras nacionales; (1.2,2.1-2.6) Llegadas de turistas no residentes en las fronteras nacionales; información procedente de datos administrativos; (3.4) Incluidos los pasajeros en crucero.
Fuentes: (1.1-5.4,7.1-7.4,9.3) "National Statistical Service"; (6.1-6.3,8.2-8.4) Fondo Monetario Internacional; (9.1,9.2) "Hellenic Chamber of Hotels".

GUADALUPE

(1.2) Llegadas por vía aérea; excluidas las islas del norte (San Martín y San Barthelemy); (1.2/2003/2004) Turistas no residentes alojados en hoteles únicamente; (1.2,2.3,3.1/2005) Datos obtenidos en una encuesta realizada en el aeropuerto de Guadalupe; (5.2) Hoteles únicamente; (9.1) Hoteles; (9.3) Habitaciones.
Fuente: "Comité du Tourisme des Îles de la Guadeloupe".

GUAM

(1.2) Llegadas por vías aérea y marítima; (2.2-2.4) Llegadas por vía aérea únicamente; (4.1-4.3) Llegadas de civiles por vía aérea únicamente; (9.1) Habitaciones disponibles.
Fuente: "Guam Visitors Bureau".

GUATEMALA

(8.2) El país facilita a la OMT niveles agregados de gasto que son significativamente diferentes a los datos del Fondo Monetario Internacional. Los datos del país son:
2002: 517
2003: 601
2004: 735
2005: 754
2006: 789
Fuentes: (1.2-4.3,8.1,9.1-9.4) Instituto Guatemalteco de Turismo - INGUAT; (6.1-6.3,8.2-8.4) Fondo Monetario Internacional.

GUINEA

(1.2,2.1-2.6,4.1-4.3/2003/2005/2006) Llegadas por vía aérea al aeropuerto de Conakry; (5.2) Hoteles únicamente; (6.2) Los datos de gastos corresponden a los facilitados por el país a la OMT, por tratarse de una serie más completa que la facilitada por el Fondo Monetario Internacional (FMI) para la preparación de esta edición del Compendio.
Fuentes: (1.2-5.4,6.2,9.1-9.4) "Division Observatoire du Tourisme - Ministère du Tourisme, de l'Hôtellerie et de l'Artisanat"; (6.3,8.2-8.4) Fondo Monetario Internacional.

GUINEA-BISSAU

(1.2,2.1-2.6,4.1-4.3) Llegadas al aeropuerto "Osvaldo Vieira".
Fuentes: (1.2-4.3) "Ministério do Turismo e do Ordenamento do Território"; (6.1-6.3,8.2-8.4) Fondo Monetario Internacional.

GUYANA

(1.2,2.2,2.3,3.1) Llegadas al aeropuerto de Timehri únicamente.
Fuentes: (1.2-3.1) "Guyana Tourism Authority"; (6.1-6.3,8.2-8.4) Fondo Monetario Internacional.

GUYANA FRANCESA

(1.2,6.1/2005) Encuesta 2005 en el aeropuerto de Cayenne-Rochambeau a la salida.
Fuentes: "Comité du Tourisme de la Guyane" e "INSEE Guyane".

HAITI

(10.1-10.3) Este apartado incluye únicamente la partida "viajes" debido a que la partida "transporte de pasajeros" no figura en los datos del Fondo Monetario Internacional utilizados para la preparación de esta edición del Compendio.
Fuentes: (1.1-3.4) "Ministère du Tourisme"; (6.2,8.2-8.4) Fondo Monetario Internacional.

NOTAS DE LOS PAISES

HONDURAS

(1.2,2.1-4.3) Llegadas de turistas no residentes en las fronteras nacionales.
Fuentes: (1.1-5.4,8.1,9.1-9.4) Instituto Hondureño de Turismo; (6.1-6.3,8.2-8.4) Fondo Monetario Internacional.

HONG KONG, CHINA

(6.1-6.3) Las datos de gastos corresponden a los facilitados por el país a la OMT, por tratarse de una serie más completa que la facilitada por el Fondo Monetario Internacional (FMI) para la preparación de esta edición del Compendio. (Fuente: "HKTB Visitors Survey"); (8.1) Incluidos los residentes de Hong Kong viajando a Macao y China; (9.1) Hoteles (tarifas altas/medias) y albergues/ casas huéspedes; (9.3) Habitaciones.
Fuentes: (1.1-8.1,9.1,9.3) "Hong Kong Tourism Board"; (8.3) "Census and Statistics Department".

HUNGRIA

(1.1/2002/2003) (3.1-3.4) Salidas de visitantes no residentes; (1.1-1.4,4.1-4.3/2004) Nueva serie; (2.1-2.4) Turistas no residentes alojados en todo tipo de establecimientos de alojamiento; (3.4) Por vía fluvial; (9.3) Habitaciones, Julio-Junio.
Fuentes: (1.1-5.4,7.1-7.4,8.1,9.1-9.4) "Hungarian Central statistical Office"; (6.1-6.3,8.2-8.4) Fondo Monetario Internacional.

INDIA

(1.2,2.1-4.2) Llegadas de turistas no residentes en las fronteras nacionales: excluidos los nacionales residentes en el extranjero; (4.1) Incluye otros motivos; (8.1) Salidas de nacionales del país únicamente, por cualquier motivo de visita; (9.1,9.2) En hoteles homologados; (9.3) Habitaciones.
Fuentes: (1.1-4.2,8.1,9.1-9.3) "Market Research Division - Government of India"; (6.1-6.3,8.2-8.4) Fondo Monetario Internacional.

Nota sobre la revisión de la metodología para la estimación de los ingresos de divisas por turismo en la India mes a mes

1.   El Reserve Bank of India (RBI), banco central de ese país, compila las estimaciones oficiales de ingresos de divisas por turismo con regularidad trimestral como parte de las estadísticas de la balanza de pagos. La estimación trimestral preliminar, difundida en un plazo de 3 meses, suele revisarse dos veces (denominándose "estimación parcialmente revisada") antes de la revisión final. Para preparar las estimaciones mensuales de los ingresos de divisas por turismo en un plazo inferior a una semana, el Ministerio de Turismo ha desarrollado una metodología. Los principales insumos en esta metodología fueron: los promedios de los ingresos de divisas por visitante de Bangladesh y Pakistán, el ratio del total de ingresos de divisas por turismo y llegadas de turistas extranjeros de países distintos a Bangladesh y Pakistán; el número total de llegadas de turistas extranjeros en el mes para el que se han de compilar las estimaciones de ingresos de divisas; y el índice de precios al por mayor. Este método adolecía de dos deficiencias importantes. En primer lugar, los promedios de los ingresos de divisas por visitante de Bangladesh y Pakistán se basaban en cifras muy antiguas. En segundo lugar, el ratio de ingresos totales de divisas por turismo por visitante de países distintos a Bangladesh y Pakistán, derivado de los datos de ingresos de divisas del RBI, no se actualizaba de forma continua utilizando las últimas cifras finales disponibles. Estas deficiencias hacían que las estimaciones del Ministerio de Turismo fueran sustancialmente inferiores a las estimaciones del RBI y esta subestimación se incrementó del 9% en 2000 al 26% en 2003 y a más del 36% en 2006.

2.   Para garantizar la mínima variación posible en las estimaciones finales de ingresos de divisas por turismo facilitadas por el RBI, en diciembre de 2007 se empezó a revisar la metodología empleada por el Ministerio de Turismo. Las principales medidas adoptadas en la revisión de la metodología fueron las siguientes:

(vi) La última estimación trimestral parcialmente revisada de ingresos de divisas por turismo que tiene el RBI se divide proporcionalmente utilizando las cifras mensuales de llegadas de turistas extranjeros en ese trimestre, a fin de obtener las estimaciones mensuales de ingresos de divisas.

(vii) El ratio de ingresos de divisas y llegadas de turistas extranjeros del último mes del trimestre mencionado en el punto a) se infla utilizando la cifra del índice de precios de consumo para empleados urbanos no manuales, a fin de obtener el ratio del último mes para el que se están preparando las estimaciones de ingresos de divisas.

(viii) El ratio mencionado en el punto b) se multiplica por el número de llegadas de turistas extranjeros para ese mes a fin de obtener la estimación de ingresos de divisas en rupias indias para dicho mes. Esas estimaciones reciben el nombre de "estimaciones avanzadas".

(ix) Utilizando los tipos de cambio de que dispone el RBI, la estimación de ingresos de divisas en rupias indias se convierte a dólares de los Estados Unidos.

(x) Tan pronto como se dispone de una estimación parcialmente revisada del RIB de los ingresos de divisas para un trimestre más reciente, se emplea para calcular las estimaciones mensuales de los meses siguientes.

3.   Las estimaciones avanzadas de ingresos de divisas para un año se revisarán dos veces al año cuando se disponga de las estimaciones parcialmente revisadas del RBI para los distintos trimestres de ese año. Estas cifras revisadas volverán a revisarse para obtener las cifras finales una vez se disponga de las estimaciones definitivamente revisadas del RBI para todos los trimestres del año.

4.   A partir de la nueva metodología, se han revisado las estimaciones del Ministerio de Turismo de los ingresos de divisas por turismo para los años posteriores al año 2000. La adopción de la nueva metodología ha reducido la variación entre las

estimaciones avanzadas del Ministerio de Turismo y las cifras del RBI hasta un nivel de alrededor del 5%, frente a la anterior divergencia de hasta un 40%. A continuación, se muestra una comparación de las estimaciones de ingresos de divisas según la nueva metodología y según la antigua.

Año	Nueva metodología	Metodología antigua	Porcentaje de variación
(1)	(2)	(3)	(4)
2000	3460	3168	9.2%
2001	3198	3042	5.1%
2002	3103	2923	6.2%
2003	4463	3533	26.3%
2004	6170	4769	29.4%
2005	7493 *	5731	30.7%
2006	8934 *	6569	36.0%
2007	11956 #	8255	44.8%

(Millones de dólares de los Estados Unidos)

* Estimaciones revisadas, # Estimaciones avanzadas

5.   Puesto que la nueva metodología utilizará siempre las últimas cifras trimestrales parcialmente revisadas del RBI de ingresos de divisas, cabe esperar que la divergencia entre las estimaciones del Ministerio de Turismo y del RBI será mínima también en el futuro.

6.   Los pormenores de la metodología empleada pueden consultarse en la web del Ministerio de Turismo del Gobierno de la India (www.tourism.gov.in).

INDONESIA

(5.2,5.4,7.2,7.4,9.3,9.4) Únicamente hoteles clasificados; (9.1,9.2) Conjunto de los medios comerciales de alojamiento; (9.3) Habitaciones.
Fuentes: (1.2-5.4,7.2,7.4,8.1,9.1-9.4) "Ministry of Culture and Tourism" y "BPS Statistics Indonesia"; (6.1-6.3,8.2-8.4) Fondo Monetario Internacional.

IRAN, REPUBLICA ISLAMICA DEL

(3.3) Incluye ferrocarril; (5.2,7.2) Hoteles únicamente; (9.1,9.2) Hoteles únicamente, 21 de Marzo-20 de Marzo; (9.3) Estimaciones (plazas-cama).
Fuentes: (1.2-5.4,7.1-7.4,8.1,9.1-9.4) "Iran Cultural Heritage and Tourism Organization (ICHTO)"; (6.1-6.3,8.2-8.4) "Central Bank of Islamic Republic of Iran".

IRLANDA

(1.2,2.3,3.3,4.1-4.3,5.4) Incluidos los turistas procedentes de Irlanda del Norte; (3.3) Incluye ferrocarril; (8.1) Incluidos los visitantes del día (excursionistas); (9.1) Excluidos los hostales; (9.3) Habitaciones, hoteles únicamente.
Fuentes: (1.2-5.4,7.1-7.4,8.1,9.1-9.3) "Fáilte Ireland"; (6.1-6.3,8.2-8.4) Fondo Monetario Internacional.

ISLANDIA

(1.2,2.1-2.4) Turistas no residentes alojados en todo tipo de establecimientos de alojamiento; (3.1,3.4) Llegadas de turistas no residentes a las fronteras islandesas.
Nota: Debido a la introducción del Schengen en marzo de 2001, la recopilación de datos sobre entradas y salidas en las fronteras islandesas sufrió cambios. A partir de 2002 la recopilación de estos datos es realizada por "Icelandic Tourist Board".
Fuentes: (1.2-2.4,5.1-5.4,7.1-7.4,9.1-9.4) "Hagstofa Íslands Statistics Iceland"; (3.1,3.4) "Icelandic Tourist Board"; (6.1-6.3,8.2-8.4) Fondo Monetario Internacional.

ISLAS CAIMAN

(1.2,2.2-2.4,4.1-4.3) Llegadas por vía aérea; (5.4,9.4) Días; (6.1) Las cifras de gasto corresponden a las facilitadas por el país a la OMT y que, sin embargo, no figuran en los datos del Fondo Monetario Internacional utilizados para la preparación de esta edición del Compendio. Incluidos los gastos de los pasajeros en crucero; (5.2,9.1,9.2) Hoteles y apartamentos; (9.3) Hoteles (habitaciones).
Fuente: "Cayman Islands Department of Tourism".

ISLAS COOK

(1.2,2.2-2.4,4.1-4.3) Llegadas por vías aérea y marítima; (6.1) Las cifras de gasto corresponden a las facilitadas por el país a la OMT y que, sin embargo, no figuran en los datos del Fondo Monetario Internacional utilizados para la preparación de esta edición del Compendio; (9.3) Habitaciones.
Nota 2006: Datos provisionales.
Fuente: "Cook Islands Tourism Corporation" y "Cook Islands Statistics Office".

ISLAS MARIANAS SEPTENTRIONALES

(1.1,2.2-2.4) Llegadas de visitantes no residentes en las fronteras nacionales; (1.2) Llegadas por vía aérea; (2.2) Incluye Guam; (9.1) Cubre el 68 por ciento del total de habitaciones censadas.
Fuente: "Marianas Visitors Authority".

ISLAS MARSHALL

(1.2,2.2-2.4,4.1-4.3/2002/2003/2006) Llegadas por vía aérea; (1.2,2.2-2.4,4.1-4.3/2004/2005) Llegadas por vías aérea y marítima; (6.1,8.2) Las cifras de gasto corresponden a las facilitadas por el país a la OMT y que, sin embargo, no figuran en los datos del Fondo Monetario Internacional utilizados para la preparación de esta edición del Compendio. Años fiscales (1 octubre - 30 septiembre).
Fuente: "Marshall Islands Visitors Authority".

ISLAS SALOMON

(1.2,2.2-2.4/2005) Excluido el 1er trimestre.
Fuentes: (1.2,2.2-2.4) "Solomon Islands National Statistics Office"; (6.1-6.3,8.2-8.4) Fondo Monetario Internacional.

ISLAS TURCAS Y CAICOS

(6.1) Las cifras de gasto corresponden a las facilitadas por el país a la OMT y que, sin embargo, no figuran en los datos del Fondo Monetario Internacional utilizados para la preparación de esta edición del Compendio.
Fuente: "Turks and Caicos Tourist Board".

ISLAS VIRGENES AMERICANAS

(2.1-2.4) Turistas no residentes alojados en hoteles y establecimientos asimilados; (3.1) Llegadas de visitantes por vía aérea; excluidas las llegadas de residentes y el tráfico entre las islas pero incluidos los excursionistas; (3.4) Pasajeros en crucero; (5.3) Incluido el turismo interno (cerca del 40% del total); (6.1) Las cifras de gasto corresponden a las facilitadas por el país a la OMT y que, sin embargo, no figuran en los datos del Fondo Monetario Internacional utilizados para la preparación de esta edición del Compendio; (9.1,9.3) Hoteles y condominios o villas; (9.3) Habitaciones.
2006: Datos provisionales.
Fuente: "Bureau of Economic Research".

ISLAS VIRGENES BRITANICAS

(1.1-9.4/2004/2005) Estimaciones; (6.1) Las cifras de gasto corresponden a las facilitadas por el país a la OMT y que, sin embargo, no figuran en los datos del Fondo Monetario Internacional utilizados para la preparación de esta edición del Compendio; (9.3) Habitaciones.
Fuente: "The Development Planning Unit - Ministry of Finance".

ISRAEL

(1.1) Llegadas de visitantes no residentes en las fronteras nacionales; excluidos los nacionales residentes en el extranjero; (1.2,2.1-4.3) Llegadas de turistas no residentes en las fronteras nacionales; excluidos los nacionales residentes en el extranjero; (3.3) Incluidas las nuevas entradas tras una visita de hasta 7 días en el Sinaí; (3.4) Incluido el personal de la flota de EE.UU. en visita de cortesía; (4.3) Incluidas las visitas a familiares y amigos y peregrinaciones; (5.1) Hoteles turísticos y apart-hoteles; (6.2) Incluidos los gastos de los trabajadores extranjeros en Israel (Millones de $EE.UU.):
2002: 1.125
2003: 997
2004: 904
2005: 847
2006: 909
(9.3) Tasa de ocupación/camas en hoteles y establecimientos asimilados abiertos; (9.4) Turismo receptor en hoteles turísticos.
Fuentes: (1.1-5.4,7.1-7.3,8.1,9.1-9.4) "Ministry of Tourism"; (6.1-6.3,8.2-8.4) Fondo Monetario Internacional.

ITALIA

(1.1,3.1-4.3) Llegadas de visitantes no residentes en las fronteras nacionales; excluidos los trabajadores estacionales o fronterizos; (1.1-4.3,8.1) Encuesta en fronteras del "Ufficio Italiano dei Cambi"; (1.2,2.1-2.6) Llegadas de turistas no residentes

en las fronteras nacionales; excluidos los trabajadores estacionales o fronterizos; (1.3) Incluidos los pasajeros en crucero; (5.1,5.2) Hoteles únicamente; (8.1) Número de turistas residentes (visitantes que pernoctan) que viajan al extranjero; (9.3) Plazas-cama.
Fuentes: (1.1-4.3,8.1) "Ufficio Italiano dei Cambi"; (5.1-5.4,7.1-7.4,9.1-9.4) "Statistiche sul Turismo - Istituto Nazionale di Statistica (ISTAT)"; (6.1-6.3,8.2-8.4) Fondo Monetario Internacional.

JAMAHIRIYA ARABE LIBIA

(1.1,2.1-2.6) Incluidos todos los viajeros (visitantes y otros viajeros no definidos como viajeros por la OMT); (3.1-3.4) Llegadas de visitantes no residentes en las fronteras nacionales; (4.1-4.3) Llegadas de turistas no residentes en las fronteras nacionales. Nota 2002-2004: Datos preliminares.
Fuente: "General People's Committee for Tourism"; (6.1-6.3,8.2-8.4) Fondo Monetario Internacional.

JAMAICA

(1.2,2.1-4.3) Llegadas por vía aérea de turistas no residentes; incluidos los nacionales residentes en el extranjero; tarjetas E/D; (5.3) Datos obtenidos multiplicando la duración media de la estancia por el número de escalas en cada uno de los países de origen; (5.4) Duración de estancia prevista; (9.3) Habitaciones; (9.4) Pernoctaciones en los hoteles únicamente.
Fuentes: (1.1-5.4,9.1-9.4) "Jamaica Tourist Board"; (6.1-6.3,8.2-8.4) Fondo Monetario Internacional.

JAPON

(1.1,2.1-2.6,4.1-4.3) Llegadas de visitantes no residentes en las fronteras nacionales; excluidos los nacionales residentes en el extranjero; (3.1,3.4) Llegadas de visitantes no residentes en las fronteras nacionales; incluidos los residentes extranjeros en Japón; (5.4) Días; (6.2,8.3/2003) El método de cálculo ha sido cambiado desde enero de 2003; (6.2,8.3/2006) El método de cálculo ha sido cambiado desde enero de 2006; (7.1,9.1/2005) A partir de 2005 los datos no están disponibles; (9.1) Hoteles homologados y no homologados así como "ryokans" (posadas); (9.3) Tasa de ocupación de los principales hoteles gubernamentales homologados (habitaciones); (9.3/2006) A partir de 2006 los datos no están disponibles.
Fuentes: (1.1-5.4,7.1,8.1,9.1,9.3) "Japan National Tourist Organization"; (6.1-6.3,8.2-8.4) Fondo Monetario Internacional.

JORDANIA

(1.1-1.3) Incluidos los nacionales residentes en el extranjero; (2.1-2.6) Llegadas de turistas no residentes en las fronteras nacionales; excluidos los nacionales residentes en el extranjero; (3.1-3.4) Llegadas de visitantes residentes y no residentes; (5.4) Para visitas organizadas únicamente; (9.3) Habitaciones.
Fuentes: (1.1-5.4,7.1-7.4,8.1,9.1-9.4) "Ministry of Tourism and Antiquities"; (6.1-6.3,8.2-8.4) Fondo Monetario Internacional.

KAZAJSTAN

(2.1-2.6,3.1-4.3) Llegadas de visitantes no residentes en las fronteras nacionales.
Fuentes: (1.1-5.,7.1,8.1,9.1-9.3) "Agency of Statistics of the Republic of Kazakhstan"; (6.1-6.3,8.2-8.4) Fondo Monetario Internacional.

KENYA

(1.1,2.1-4.3) Llegadas de visitantes no residentes a través de todos los puestos fronterizos; excluidos los nacionales residentes en el extranjero; (9.3) Plazas-cama; (9.4) Días.
Fuentes: (1.1-5.4,7.1,7.4,9.1-9.4) "Kenya Tourist Board"; (6.1-6.3,8.3) Fondo Monetario Internacional.

KIRGUISTAN

(1.2,2.2-2.5,8.1/2003-2006) Nueva fuente de información: Departamento de Control Aduanero.
Fuentes: (1.1-5.2,7.1,7.2,8.1,9.1,9.2) "National Statistical Committee"; (6.1-6.3,8.2-8.4) Fondo Monetario Internacional.

KIRIBATI

(1.2,2.2-2.4,3.1) Llegadas por vía aérea. 2002/2003/2006: Tarawa e Isla Christmas. 2004/2005: Tarawa únicamente; (4.1-4.3) Llegadas por vía aérea. Tarawa únicamente.
Fuente: "Kiribati National Tourism Office, Ministry of Communication, Transport and Tourism Development".

KUWAIT

(1.1,2.1-2.6,3.1-3.4) Llegadas de visitantes no residentes en las fronteras nacionales; (1.2,4.1-4.3) Turistas no residentes alojados en hoteles y establecimientos asimilados.
Fuentes: (1.1-5.4,8.1,9.1,9.2) "Ministry of Planning"; (6.1-6.3,8.2-8.4) Fondo Monetario Internacional.

NOTAS DE LOS PAISES

LESOTHO

(1.1,2.1-4.3) Llegadas de visitantes no residentes en las fronteras nacionales; (10.1-10.3) Este apartado incluye únicamente la partida "viajes" debido a que la partida "transporte de pasajeros" no figura en los datos del Fondo Monetario Internacional utilizados para la preparación de esta edición del Compendio.
Fuentes: (1.1-4.3,9.1-9.4) "Lesotho Tourism Development Corporation"; (6.2,8.2-8.4) Fondo Monetario Internacional.

LETONIA

(1.1,3.1-3.4) Llegadas de visitantes no residentes en las fronteras nacionales. Datos procedentes de la Policía Estatal de Fronteras; (1.2-1.4,2.1-2.6,4.1-4.3) Salidas de no residentes. Encuesta realizada en los puestos fronterizos del país; (1.3) Incluidos los pasajeros en crucero; (4.3) Incluidas las visitas a parientes y amigos y tratamientos de salud; (5.3,5.4) Pernoctaciones en todos los establecimientos de alojamiento colectivo; (5.4) Duración media de la estancia de visitantes no residentes que pernoctan; encuesta realizada en los puestos fronterizos del país; (8.1) Datos procedentes de la Policía Estatal de Fronteras; (9.3) Plazas-cama.
Fuentes: (1.1-5.4,7.1-7.4,8.1,9.1-9.4) "Transport and Tourism Statistics Section - Central Statistical Bureau"; (6.1-6.3,8.2-8.4) Fondo Monetario Internacional.

LIBANO

(1.2) Excluidos los nacionales de Siria.
Fuentes: (1.2-5.4,9.1-9.3) "Ministère du Tourisme"; (6.1-6.3,8.2-8.4) Fondo Monetario Internacional.

LIECHTENSTEIN

(1.2,2.1-2.4) Turistas no residentes alojados en hoteles y establecimientos asimilados; (9.3) Plazas-cama.
Fuente: "Liechtenstein Tourismus".

LITUANIA

(2.1-2.4) Turistas no residentes alojados en todo tipo de establecimientos de alojamiento; (3.1-3.4,4.1-4.3) Llegadas de turistas no residentes en las fronteras nacionales; (5.1,5.2,7.1,7.2,9.1,9.2) Hoteles y moteles; (9.3) Habitaciones.
Fuentes: (1.1-5.4,7.1-7.4,8.1,9.1-9.4) "Lithuanian State Department of Tourism"; (6.1-6.3,8.2-8.4) Fondo Monetario Internacional.

LUXEMBURGO

(1.2,2.2,2.3) Turistas no residentes alojados en todo tipo de establecimientos de alojamiento; incluye albergues de juventud, alojamientos turísticos privados y otros; (5.1,7.1) Pernoctaciones en hoteles, albergues y casas de huéspedes; (5.3,7.3) Incluidos los alojamientos turísticos privados y otros; (9.3) Habitaciones.
Fuentes: (1.2-5.4,7.1-7.4,9.1-9.4) "Office National du Tourisme" y "STATEC"; (6.1-6.3,8.2-8.4) Fondo Monetario Internacional.

MACAO, CHINA

(1.1,2.1-4.3) Llegadas de visitantes no residentes en las fronteras nacionales; (1.1-1.3,2.4,3.1-3.4) Incluidas las personas de origen étnico chino procedentes de "Hong Kong, China"; (1.2,1.3) Estimaciones; (3.1) Incluidas las llegadas en helicóptero; (6.1) Los datos de gastos corresponden a los facilitados por el país a la OMT, por tratarse de una serie más completa que la facilitada por el Fondo Monetario Internacional (FMI) para la preparación de esta edición del Compendio. Incluidos los ingresos procedentes del juego; (8.1) Viajes organizados; (9.1,9.2) Hoteles, casas de huéspedes y "pousadas"; (9.3) Habitaciones; (10.1-10.3) Este apartado no se ha podido completar debido a que las partidas "viajes" y "transporte de pasajeros" no figuran en los datos del Fondo Monetario Internacional utilizados para la preparación de esta edición del Compendio.
Fuente: "Macau Government Tourist Office" y "Statistics and Census Service".

MADAGASCAR

(1.2,2.1-2.4,3.1,4.1-4.3) Llegadas de turistas no residentes por vía aérea; (9.3) Habitaciones.
Fuentes: (1.2-5.4,9.1-9.4) "Ministère des Transports et du Tourisme"; (6.1-6.3,8.2-8.4) Fondo Monetario Internacional.

MALASIA

(1.2,2.1-2.6) Llegadas de turistas no residentes en las fronteras nacionales; incluidos los residentes de Singapur que cruzan la frontera por la Johore Causeway; (3.1-3.4,4.1-4.3) Península de Malasia únicamente; (8.1) Salidas de malasios peninsulares, incluidas las salidas por carretera a través de la frontera Johore Causeway; (9.1) Hoteles con 10 habitaciones y más; (9.3) Habitaciones.
Fuentes: (1.1-5.2,7.2,8.1,9.1,9.3) "Tourism Malaysia"; (6.1-6.3,8.2-8.4) Fondo Monetario Internacional.

MALAWI

(1.2-4.3) Salidas; (5.3/2004) Dato provisional; (9.3) Plazas-cama.

NOTAS DE LOS PAISES

Fuentes: (1.2-5.4,9.1-9.4) "Ministry of Information and Tourism"; (6.1-6.3,8.2-8.4) "Reserve Bank of Malawi".

MALDIVAS

(1.2,2.1-2.6) Llegadas por vía aérea; (5.1,9.1-9.4) Centros turísticos y hoteles; (9.4) Días; (10.1-10.3) Este apartado incluye únicamente la partida "viajes" debido a que la partida "transporte de pasajeros" no figura en los datos del Fondo Monetario Internacional utilizados para la preparación de esta edición del Compendio.
Fuentes: (1.2-5.1,8.1,9.1-9.4) "Ministry of Tourism"; (6.2,8.2-8.4) Fondo Monetario Internacional.

MALI

(1.2) Llegadas por vía aérea; (2.1-2.6) Turistas no residentes alojados en hoteles y establecimientos asimilados; (9.3) Habitaciones.
Fuentes: (1.2-5.4,7.1-7.4,9.1-9.4) "Office malien du tourisme et de l'hôtellerie (O.MA.T.HO)"; (6.1-6.3,8.2-8.4) Fondo Monetario Internacional.

MALTA

(1.2,2.1-2.6,3.1,3.4/2002/2003) Llegadas de turistas no residentes en las fronteras nacionales; (1.2,2.2-2.6,3.1,3.4/2004-2006) Salidas de turistas por vías aérea y marítima; (4.1-4.3,5.1-5.3/2003-2006) Salidas de turistas por vía aérea; (8.1/2002-2004) Por vía aérea únicamente; (9.3) Plazas-cama.
Fuentes: (1.1-5.4,8.1,9.2-9.4) "Malta Tourism Authority" y "National Statistics Office"; (6.1-6.3,8.2-8.4) Fondo Monetario Internacional.

MARRUECOS

(1.2,3.1-4.3) Llegadas de turistas no residentes en las fronteras nacionales; incluidos los nacionales residentes en el extranjero; (2.1-2.6) Llegadas de turistas no residentes en las fronteras nacionales; excluidos los nacionales residentes en el extranjero; (5.1,5.2,7.1,7.2,9.1-9.3) Hoteles homologados, ciudades de vacaciones y residencias turísticas; (9.3) Habitaciones; (9.4) Turistas extranjeros.
Fuentes: (1.1-5.2,7.1,7.2,8.1,9.1-9.4) "Ministère du tourisme"; (6.1-6.3,8.2-8.4) Fondo Monetario Internacional.

MARTINICA

(1.2,2.2,2.3,4.1-4.3) Llegadas de turistas no residentes en las fronteras nacionales; (6.1) Las cifras de gasto corresponden a las facilitadas por el país a la OMT y que, sin embargo, no figuran en los datos del Fondo Monetario Internacional utilizados para la preparación de esta edición del Compendio; (9.1) Hoteles y ciudades de vacaciones ("Club Méditerranée"); (9.3) Habitaciones en hoteles y establecimientos asimilados.
Fuente: "Comité Martiniquais du Tourisme".

MAURICIO

(1.2,2.1-3.4) Llegadas de turistas no residentes en las fronteras nacionales; (4.1-4.3) Llegadas de visitantes no residentes en las fronteras nacionales; (5.4) Grandes hoteles; (9.3) Habitaciones.
Fuentes: (1.1-5.4,8.1,9.1-9.3) "Ministry of Tourism and Leisure"; (6.1-6.3,8.2-8.4) Fondo Monetario Internacional.

MEXICO

(1.2,2.2-4.3) Llegadas de turistas no residentes en las fronteras nacionales; incluidos los nacionales residentes en el extranjero; (1.3) Incluidos los visitantes de la franja fronteriza con los Estados Unidos y estancia inferior a 24h; (2.2/2004) Estados Unidos y Canadá únicamente; (2.2,2.3/2002-2004) Datos compilados por país de residencia; (2.2-2.4/2005/2006) Datos compilados por nacionalidad; (2.4/2005/2006) Japón y República de Corea únicamente; (3.3) Incluye ferrocarril; (5.1) Centros turísticos seleccionados; (5.2,7.2) Hoteles únicamente; (9.3) Habitaciones; (9.4) Turismo extranjero únicamente.
2006: Datos preliminares.
Fuentes: (1.1-5.4,7.1,7.2,8.1,9.1-9.4) Secretaría de Turismo de México (SECTUR); (6.1-6.3,8.2-8.4) Fondo Monetario Internacional.

MICRONESIA (ESTADOS FEDERADOS DE)

(1.2,2.2-2.4,4.1-4.3) Llegadas en los Estados de Kosrae, Chuuk, Pohnpei y Yap; excluidos los ciudadanos de EFM; (6.1,8.2) Las cifras de gasto corresponden a las facilitadas por el país a la OMT y que, sin embargo, no figuran en los datos del Fondo Monetario Internacional utilizados para la preparación de esta edición del Compendio. Años fiscales (1 octubre - 30 septiembre).
Fuente: "Department of Economic Affairs".

MONACO

(1.2,2.1-4.2) Turistas no residentes alojados en hoteles y establecimientos asimilados.
Fuente: "Direction du Tourisme et des Congrès".

NOTAS DE LOS PAISES

MONGOLIA

(1.2,2.1-2.5,4.1-4.3) Llegadas de turistas no residentes en las fronteras nacionales. Excluidos los diplomáticos y extranjeros residentes en Mongolia.
Fuentes: (1.1-4.3) "Tourism Department - Ministry of Road, Transport and Tourism"; (6.1-6.3,8.2-8.4) Fondo Monetario Internacional.

MONTENEGRO

(1.2,2.2-2.4) Turistas no residentes alojados en todo tipo de establecimientos de alojamiento.
Fuente: "MONSTAT - Statistical Office of the Republic of Montenegro".

MONTSERRAT

(10.2,10.3) Este apartado incluye únicamente la partida "viajes" debido a que la partida "transporte de pasajeros" no figura en los datos del Fondo Monetario Internacional utilizados para la preparación de esta edición del Compendio.
Fuentes: (1.1-5.2) "Statistics Department Montserrat"; (6.2,8.3) Fondo Monetario Internacional.

MOZAMBIQUE

Fuentes: (1.1-4.3,9.1-9.4) "Ministry of Tourism"; (5.1,5.2,7.1,7.2) "Instituto Nacional de Estatística"; (6.1-6.3,8.2-8.4) Fondo Monetario Internacional.

MYANMAR

(1.2,2.2-2.6) Incluidas las llegadas de turistas a través de los puntos de entrada fronterizos a Yangon; (4.1-4.3) Llegadas de visitantes no residentes en las fronteras nacionales; (5.1,9.4) Hoteles y establecimientos asimilados administrados por el Estado únicamente; (9.1,9.2) Hoteles administrados por el Estado y casas de huéspedes privadas homologadas; (9.3) Habitaciones.
Fuentes: (1.1-5.4,9.1-9.4) "Ministry of Hotels and Tourism"; (6.1-6.3,8.2-8.4) Fondo Monetario Internacional.

NAMIBIA

(2.1-4.3) Llegadas de turistas no residentes en las fronteras nacionales; (2.2) Estados Unidos únicamente; (2.4) Australia únicamente; (9.3) Plazas-camas.
Fuentes: (1.1-5.4,7.1-7.4,9.1-9.4) "Ministry of Environment and Tourism"; (6.1-6.3,8.3) Fondo Monetario Internacional.

NEPAL

(1.2) Incluidas las llegadas procedentes de la India; (3.3) Vía terrestre; (9.1,9.2) Hoteles en Katmandú y en el interior del país; (9.1,9.2/2006) Excluidos los hoteles en proceso de construcción.
Fuentes: (1.2-5.4,8.1,9.1,9.2) "Nepal Tourism Board"; (6.1-6.3,8.2-8.4) Fondo Monetario Internacional.

NICARAGUA

(1.2,2.1-4.3) Llegadas de turistas no residentes en las fronteras nacionales; (1.2/2002-2004) (2.1-2.5) Excluidos los nacionales residentes en el extranjero; (1.2/2005/2006) Incluidos los nacionales residentes en el extranjero; (5.1-5.4,7.1-7.4,9.4/2005) Datos preliminares; (5.1,7.1) Principales establecimientos de alojamiento del país (7); (5.3,7.3) Total de establecimientos del país; (9.1,9.2) Hoteles y establecimientos asimilados ubicados en categorías superiores; (9.4) Todo tipo de establecimientos de alojamiento, turismo receptor.
Nota 2006: (1.1-4.3,8.1) Estimaciones preliminares.
Fuentes: (1.1-5.4,7.1-7.4,8.1,9.1-9.4) Instituto Nicaragüense de Turismo (INTUR); (6.1-6.3,8.2-8.4) Fondo Monetario Internacional.

NIGER

(5.4,7.4,9.4) Días.
Fuentes: (1.2-5.4,7.1,7.2,9.1-9.4) (6.2,8.2-8.4/2006) "Ministère du Tourisme et de l'Artisanat"; (6.1-6.3,8.2-8.4/2002-2005) Fondo Monetario Internacional.

NIGERIA

(1.1,2.1-2.6,3.1-3.4) (4.1-4.3/2006) Llegadas de visitantes no residentes en las fronteras nacionales; (1.2,4.1-4.3) Llegadas de turistas no residentes en las fronteras nacionales.
Fuentes: (1.1-4.3,9.2,9.3) "Nigerian Tourism Development Corporation"; (6.1-6.3,8.2-8.4) Fondo Monetario Internacional.

NOTAS DE LOS PAISES

NIUE

(1.2) Llegadas por vía aérea, incluidos los nacionales de Niue que residen normalmente en Nueva Zelandia; (8.1) Residentes que regresan.
Fuente: "Statistics Niue".

NORUEGA

(1.1-4.2) Las cifras se basan en "The Guest Survey", un estudio realizado por el "Institute of Transport Economics"; (2.2-4.2) Llegadas de turistas no residentes en las fronteras nacionales; (2.2) Estados Unidos únicamente; (2.4) Japón únicamente; (5.1) Pernoctaciones en establecimientos homologados; (5.1,9.1,9.2) Las cifras para hoteles y establecimientos asimilados se refieren a establecimientos con 20 camas o más durante todo el año; (8.1) Viajes por vacaciones; (9.3) Plazas-cama.
Fuentes: (1.1-5.3,7.1-7.3,8.1,9.1-9.4) "Statistics Norway" e "Institute of Transport Economics"; (6.1-6.3,8.2-8.4) Fondo Monetario Internacional.

NUEVA CALEDONIA

(1.2,2.1-4.3) Incluidos los nacionales residentes en el extranjero; (4.1) Vacaciones y visitas a parientes; (4.2) Negocios únicamente; (5.1,5.2,7.1,7.2) Hoteles en Noumea únicamente; (8.1) Residentes que regresan; (9.3) Habitaciones en Noumea; (9.4) Días, hoteles en Noumea; (10.2,10.3) Este apartado incluye únicamente la partida "viajes" debido a que la partida "transporte de pasajeros" no figura en los datos del Fondo Monetario Internacional utilizados para la preparación de esta edición del Compendio.
Fuentes: (1.1-5.4,7.1,7.2,8.1,9.1-9.4) "Institut de la Statistique et des Études Économiques (ISEE)"; (6.2,8.3) Fondo Monetario Internacional.

NUEVA ZELANDIA

(1.1,3.1-4.3) Llegadas de visitantes no residentes en las fronteras nacionales; incluidos los nacionales residentes en el extranjero; (2.1-2.6) Llegadas de visitantes no residentes en las fronteras nacionales; excluidos los nacionales residentes en el extranjero; (5.3,7.3) Estimación a partir del número total de pernoctaciones en establecimientos comerciales hoteleros con un volumen de negocio anual de al menos 30.000 dólares neozelandeses, y basada en el porcentaje medio de huéspedes internacionales e internos en enero, abril, julio y octubre; (8.1) Salidas de residentes de NZ de corta duración (año civil); (9.1) Referencia a la capacidad de "unidades de estancia" en hoteles, moteles y casas de huéspedes; (10.1-10.3) Este apartado incluye únicamente la partida "viajes" debido a que la partida "transporte de pasajeros" no figura en los datos del Fondo Monetario Internacional utilizados para la preparación de esta edición del Compendio.
Fuentes: (1.1-5.3,7.3,8.1,9.1-9.4) "Ministry of Tourism"; (6.2,8.3) Fondo Monetario Internacional.

OMAN

(1.1-1.3,4.1-4.3,5.3,5.4) Encuesta de turismo receptor; (2.1-2.6) Turistas no residentes alojados en hoteles y establecimientos asimilados; (4.1-4.3) Llegadas de visitantes no residentes en las fronteras nacionales; (8.1) Encuesta de turismo emisor; incluidos los visitantes del día (excursionistas); (9.3) Habitaciones.
Fuentes: (1.1-1.3,4.1-4.3,5.3,5.4,8.1) "Ministry of National Economy and Ministry of Commerce and Industry"; (2.1-2.6,5.1,5.2,7.1,7.2,9.1-9.3) "Directorate General of Tourism - Ministry of Tourism"; (6.1-6.3,8.2-8.4) Fondo Monetario Internacional.

PAISES BAJOS

(1.2-2.4) Turistas no residentes alojados en todo tipo de establecimientos de alojamiento; (5.1,7.1) Hoteles y pensiones; (8.1) Salidas de nacionales por vacaciones; (8.1/2002) Nueva encuesta; (9.2) Hoteles; (9.3) Plazas-cama; (9.4) Todo tipo de establecimientos de alojamiento.
Fuentes: (1.2-5.4,7.1-7.3,8.1,9.1-9.4) "Statistics Netherlands"; (6.1-6.3,8.2-8.4) Fondo Monetario Internacional.

PAKISTAN

(5.4) Días.
Fuentes: (1.2-5.4,7.1,7.2,9.1-9.4) "Pakistan Tourism Development Corporation - Ministry of Tourism"; (6.1-6.3,8.2-8.4) Fondo Monetario Internacional.

PALAU

(1.2-4.3) Llegadas por vía aérea (aeropuerto internacional de Palau); (6.1,8.2) Las cifras de gasto corresponden a las facilitadas por el país a la OMT y que, sin embargo, no figuran en los datos del Fondo Monetario Internacional utilizados para la preparación de esta edición del Compendio. Años fiscales.
Fuente: "Office of Planning and Statistics, Bureau of Budget and Planning - Ministry of Finance".

PALESTINA

(1.2,2.1-2.6) Turistas no residentes alojados en hotels; (5.1,5.2,7.1,7.2) Hoteles únicamente; (10.1-10.3) Este apartado incluye únicamente la partida "viajes" debido a que la partida "transporte de pasajeros" no figura en los datos del Fondo Monetario Internacional utilizados para la preparación de esta edición del Compendio.
Fuentes: (1.2-5.2,7.1-7.4,9.1-9.4) "Palestinian Central Bureau of Statistics"; (6.2,8.3) Fondo Monetario Internacional; (6.2,8.3,10.1-10.3) Cisjordania y Gaza.

PANAMA

(1.1) Llegadas de visitantes no residentes: Aeropuerto Internacional Tocúmen (AIT), frontera de Paso Canoa (FPC) y puertos de Cristóbal y Balboa (PCB); (2.2-2.4) Llegadas de visitantes no residentes, AIT; (3.1-3.4) Llegadas de turistas no residentes, AIT, FPC y PCB; excluidas las llegadas a otros puertos de entrada (sin especificar):
2002: 34.996
2003: 39.870
2004: 51.295
2005: 53.818
2006: 53.638
(4.1-4.3) Llegadas de turistas no residentes, AIT; (5.1) Hoteles de la Ciudad de Panamá; (9.1,9.2) Habitaciones/ plazas cama inventariadas para turismo internacional; (9.3) Habitaciones.
Fuentes: (1.1-5.4,8.1,9.1-9.4) Instituto Panameño de Turismo; (6.1-6.3,8.2-8.4) Fondo Monetario Internacional.

PAPUA NUEVA GUINEA

Fuentes: (1.2-4.3,8.1,9.1,9.2) "Papua New Guinea Tourism Promotion Authority"; (6.1-6.3,8.2-8.4) Fondo Monetario Internacional.

PARAGUAY

(1.1-3.4,8.1) Tarjetas E/D en el aeropuerto Silvio Petirossi y planillas de pasajeros en los puestos terrestres - Policía Nacional y SENATUR; (1.2,2.2-4.3) Excluidos los nacionales residentes en el extranjero y miembros de tripulación; (3.4) Vía fluvial; (9.3) Plazas-cama.
Fuentes: (1.1-5.4,8.1,9.1-9.4) Secretaría Nacional de Turismo - SENATUR; (6.1-6.3,8.2-8.4) Fondo Monetario Internacional.

PERU

(1.2) Incluye a los pasajeros en crucero que pernoctan; (1.2,2.1-2.5) A partir de 2002, nueva serie estimada incluyendo a los turistas con un documento de identidad diferente al pasaporte; (1.4) Pasajeros en crucero que pernoctan; (3.4) Incluye las llegadas por vía fluvial y lacustre.
Nota 2003-2006: Estimaciones preliminares.
Fuentes: (1.2-4.3,8.1) Dirección General de Migraciones y Naturalización (DIGEMIN); (5.1-5.4,7.1,7.2,9.1-9.4) Ministerio de Comercio Exterior y Turismo (MINCETUR); (6.1-6.3,8.2-8.4) Fondo Monetario Internacional.

POLINESIA FRANCESA

(1.2,2.2-4.3) Llegadas de turistas no residentes en las fronteras nacionales; excluidos los nacionales residentes en el extranjero; (5.2) Hoteles únicamente; (5.4,9.4) Días; (9.1) Hoteles únicamente; al 31 de diciembre de cada año; (9.3) Habitaciones en hoteles.
Fuentes: (1.2-5.4,9.1-9.4) "Service du Tourisme"; (6.1-6.3,8.2-8.4) Fondo Monetario Internacional.

POLONIA

(1.1,2.1-3.4) Llegadas de visitantes no residentes en las fronteras nacionales; (4.1-4.3) Llegadas de turistas no residentes en las fronteras nacionales, según encuestas del Instituto de Turismo; (5.4) Establecimientos de alojamiento colectivo y privado, según encuestas del Instituto de Turismo; (8.1) Viajes de turismo emisor registrados en las fronteras; (9.3) Habitaciones.
Fuentes: (1.1-5.4,7.1-7.4,8.1,9.1-9.4) "Institute of Tourism"; (6.1-6.3,8.2-8.4) Fondo Monetario Internacional.

PORTUGAL

(1.1-4.3) Debido a un cambio de metodología, a partir de 2004 los datos no son comparables con los años anteriores; (1.1,3.1-3.4,4.1-4.3) Llegadas de visitantes no residentes en las fronteras nacionales; (1.1-3.4/2002/2003) Excluidos los nacionales residentes en el extranjero; (1.1-4.3/2004-2006) Incluidos los nacionales residentes en el extranjero; (1.2,2.2-2.5) Llegadas de turistas no residentes en las fronteras nacionales; (1.4) Incluidos los pasajeros por mar en tránsito; (5.1-5.4,7.1-7.4,9.1-9.4) Desde 2002, nueva metodología; (5.1-5.4,7.1-7.4/2006) Datos provisionales; (9.3) Plazas-cama; (9.4) Todo tipo de establecimientos de alojamiento.
Fuentes: (1.1-5.4,7.1-7.4,8.1,9.1-9.4) "Direcçao-Geral do Turismo (DGT)"; (6.1-6.3,8.2-8.4) Fondo Monetario Internacional.

PUERTO RICO

(1.2) Llegadas de turistas no residentes por vía aérea; (2.2) Únicamente Islas Vírgenes Americanas y Estados Unidos; (5.1,5.4) Incluye residentes y no residentes; (6.1,8.2-8.4) Las cifras de gasto corresponden a las facilitadas por el país a la OMT y que, sin embargo, no figuran en los datos del Fondo Monetario Internacional utilizados para la preparación de esta edición del Compendio; (9.1) Habitaciones endosadas por la Compañía de Turismo de Puerto Rico; (9.1/2006) Incluye 2.927 habitaciones sin clasificar; (9.3) Habitaciones; incluidas las habitaciones ocupadas por residentes de Puerto Rico.
Datos: Años fiscales (julio-junio).
Fuentes: (1.1-3.4,6.1,8.1,8.2-8.4,10.1-10.3) Junta de Planificación de Puerto Rico; (5.1,5.2,5.4,7.2,9.1,9.3,9.4) Compañía de Turismo de Puerto Rico.

QATAR

(1.2-5.4,9.1-9.3) Hoteles únicamente; (6.2,8.3) Las cifras de gasto corresponden a las facilitadas por el país a la OMT y que, sin embargo, no figuran en los datos del Fondo Monetario Internacional utilizados para la preparación de esta edición del Compendio; (6.2,8.3/2006) Estimaciones preliminares; (9.3) Plazas-cama.
Fuentes: (1.2-5.4,9.1-9.3) "The Planning Council - Statistics Department" y "Qatar Tourism Authority"; (6.2,8.3) "Qatar Central Bank".

REINO UNIDO

(3.2) Túnel; (5.4) Días; (9.3) Plazas-cama (Inglaterra únicamente).
Fuentes: (1.1-4.3,5.3,5.4,7.3,8.1,9.3) "VisitBritain"; (5.1,5.2,7.1,7.2,9.1,9.2) "EUROSTAT (New Cronos)"; (6.1-6.3,8.2-8.4) Fondo Monetario Internacional.

REPUBLICA ARABE SIRIA

(1.1,2.1-4.3) Llegadas de visitantes no residentes en las fronteras nacionales; excluidas las llegadas de nacionales residentes en el extranjero; (9.3) Habitaciones.
Fuentes: (1.1-5.4,7.1,7.2,8.1,9.1-9.4) "Ministry of Tourism" - Fuente de los datos: encuesta del turismo receptor en 2002 y 2004; (6.1-6.3,8.2-8.4) Fondo Monetario Internacional.

REPUBLICA CENTROAFRICANA

(1.2,2.1-2.6,4.1-4.3) Llegadas por vía aérea a Bangui únicamente.
Nota 2006: Estimaciones.
Fuentes: (1.2-5.4,7.1-7.4,8.1,9.1-9.4) (6.1,8.2/2003/2004) "Ministère du Développement du Tourisme et de l'Artisanat"; (6.1,8.2/2002) "Banque des Etats de l'Afrique Centrale (B.E.A.C.)".

REPUBLICA CHECA

(1.2,2.1-2.4) Turistas no residentes alojados en todo tipo de establecimientos de alojamiento.
Fuentes: (1.2-5.4,7.1-7.4,9.1-9.4) "Department of Conception and International Cooperation in Tourism - Ministry for Regional Development"; (6.1-6.3,8.2-8.4) Fondo Monetario Internacional.

REPUBLICA DE MOLDOVA

(1.1-4.3,8.1) (5.1,7.3/2002/2003) Visitantes que se beneficiaron de los servicios de los agentes económicos registrados oficialmente en la actividad turística y en el alojamiento.
Nota: Excluido el margen izquierdo del río Nistru y la municipalidad de Bender.
Fuentes: (1.1-5.4,7.1-7.4,8.1,9.1-9.4) "National Bureau of Statistics"; (6.1-6.3,8.2-8.4) Fondo Monetario Internacional.

REPUBLICA DEMOCRATICA DEL CONGO

(1.2,2.1-2.4,4.1-4.3/2002-2004) Llegadas por vía aérea únicamente; (9.1) Hoteles homologados.
Nota 2005-2006: Datos provisionales.
Source: "Office National du Tourisme".

REPUBLICA DEMOCRATICA POPULAR LAO

(1.2) Llegadas de turistas no residentes en las fronteras nacionales; (2.2-2.5,3.1,3.3,4.1-4.3) Llegadas de visitantes no residentes en las fronteras nacionales; (5.4) Días; (10.1-10.3) Este apartado incluye únicamente la partida "viajes" debido a que la partida "transporte de pasajeros" no figura en los datos del Fondo Monetario Internacional utilizados para la preparación de esta edición del Compendio.
Fuente: "National Tourism Authority".

REPUBLICA DOMINICANA

(1.2) Llegadas por vía aérea únicamente; incluidos los nacionales residentes en el extranjero; (1.4) Todas las llegadas por mar; (2.2-2.4) Llegadas por vía aérea; excluidos los nacionales residentes en el extranjero; (2.2-2.4,4.1-4.3/2002) Excluidos los pasajeros del aeropuerto de Herrera; (4.1-4.3) Llegadas por vía aérea únicamente; incluidos los nacionales residentes en el extranjero; (9.1,9.2) Hoteles; (9.3) Habitaciones; (10.1-10.3) Este apartado incluye únicamente la partida "viajes" debido a que la partida "transporte de pasajeros" no figura en los datos del Fondo Monetario Internacional utilizados para la preparación de esta edición del Compendio.
Nota 2006: Datos provisionales.
Fuentes: (1.1-5.4,8.1,9.1-9.4) Secretaría de Estado de Turismo; (6.2,8.2-8.4) Fondo Monetario Internacional.

REPUBLICA UNIDA DE TANZANIA

Fuentes: (1.1-5.3,7.3,9.1-9.4) "Tourism Division - Ministry of Natural Resources and Tourism" y "National Bureau of Statistics"; (6.1-6.3,8.2-8.4) Fondo Monetario Internacional.

REUNION

(5.4) Días; (6.1) Las cifras de gasto corresponden a las facilitadas por el país a la OMT y que, sin embargo, no figuran en los datos del Fondo Monetario Internacional utilizados para la preparación de esta edición del Compendio.
Fuentes: "Institut National de la Statistique et des Études Économique - INSEE" y "Comité du Tourisme de la Réunion".

RUMANIA

Fuentes: (1.1-5.4,7.1-7.4,8.1,9.1-9.4) "National Authority for Tourism - Ministry of Transports, Constructions and Tourism"; (6.1-6.3,8.2-8.4) Fondo Monetario Internacional.

SABA

(1.3) Principalmente desde San Martín.
Fuentes: "Saba Tourist Bureau", "Caribbean Tourism Organization" y "Central Bank of the Netherlands Antilles".

SAINT KITTS Y NEVIS

(1.2,2.2) Llegadas de turistas no residentes por vía aérea; (1.4,3.4) Llegadas en yates y cruceros; (10.1-10.3) Este apartado incluye únicamente la partida "viajes" debido a que la partida "transporte de pasajeros" no figura en los datos del Fondo Monetario Internacional utilizados para la preparación de esta edición del Compendio.
Fuentes: (1.1-3.4,9.1,9.2) "Statistics Department - Ministry of Sustainable Development"; (6.2,8.3) Fondo Monetario Internacional.

SAMOA

Fuentes: (1.2-4.3,9.1,9.2) (6.2/2002/2003) "Samoa Tourism Authority" y "Statistical Services Division (Ministry of Finance)"; (6.1-6.3,8.2-8.4/2004-2006) Fondo Monetario Internacional.

SAMOA AMERICANA

(1.2,2.4,4.1-4.3) Incluye Samoa Occidental; (4.3) Visitas a parientes, amigos.
Fuente: "American Samoa Government - Department of Commerce - Statistics Division".

SAN EUSTAQUIO

(1.2,2.2,2.3)Excluidos los residentes de las Antillas Neerlandesas.
Fuente: "Central Bank of the Netherlands Antilles".

SAN MARINO

(1.1) Incluidos los visitantes italianos; (1.2) Turistas no residentes alojados en hoteles y establecimientos asimilados; incluidos los turistas italianos; (9.1,9.2) Hoteles únicamente.
Nota: Nueva metodología a partir de 2005.
Fuente: "Segreteria di Stato per il Turismo, lo Sport, le Telecomunicazioni, i Trasporti e la Cooperazione Economica".

SAN MARTIN

(1.2,2.2,2.3) Por vía aérea; incluidas las llegadas a San Martín (parte francesa de la isla); (3.1) Llegadas al aeropuerto "Juliana" (incluidos los visitantes con destino a San Martín (parte francesa); (6.2,8.3) Incluidas las estimaciones para Saba y San Eustaquio; (9.1,9.2) Hoteles, casas de huéspedes y apartamentos.
Fuentes: (1.1-3.4,9.1-9.3) "St. Maarten Tourist Bureau"; (6.2,8.3) "Central Bank of the Netherlands Antilles".

SAN VICENTE Y LAS GRANADINAS

(1.2,2.2-2.3,4.1-4.3) Llegadas de turistas no residentes por vía aérea; (3.4) Incluidos los pasajeros en crucero y en yate; (9.1) Hoteles, apartamentos, bungalows, villas y casas de huéspedes; (10.1-10.3) Este apartado incluye únicamente la partida "viajes" debido a que la partida "transporte de pasajeros" no figura en los datos del Fondo Monetario Internacional utilizados para la preparación de esta edición del Compendio.
Fuentes: (1.1-5.4,9.1,9.2) "Ministry of Tourism and Culture"; (6.2,8.3) Fondo Monetario Internacional.

SANTA LUCIA

(1.1) Excluidas las llegadas de pasajeros en yate; (1.1,2.2-4.3) Llegadas de turistas no residentes en las fronteras nacionales; excluidos los nacionales residentes en el extranjero; (9.3) Habitaciones; (10.1-10.3) Este apartado incluye únicamente la partida "viajes" debido a que la partida "transporte de pasajeros" no figura en los datos del Fondo Monetario Internacional utilizados para la preparación de esta edición del Compendio.
Fuentes: (1.1-5.2,9.1-9.4) "Saint Lucia Tourist Board"; (6.2,8.3) Fondo Monetario Internacional.

SANTO TOME Y PRINCIPE

(10.1-10.3) Este apartado incluye únicamente la partida "viajes" debido a que la partida "transporte de pasajeros" no figura en los datos del Fondo Monetario Internacional utilizados para la preparación de esta edición del Compendio.
Fuentes: (1.2-4.3) "Direcçao do Turismo e Hotelaria"; (6.2,8.2-8.4/2002) Fondo Monetario Internacional; (6.2/2003-2005) Banco Central.

SENEGAL

(1.2/2002) (2.1-2.6/2002/2003) Turistas no residentes alojados en hoteles y establecimientos asimilados; (1.2/2003-2006) (2.1-2.3/2004-2006) Llegadas de turistas no residentes en las fronteras nacionales; (5.1,5.2,7.1,7.2,9.1,9.2) Hoteles y ciudades de vacaciones; (9.3) Plazas-cama.
Fuentes: (1.1-5.4,7.1,7.2,9.1-9.4) "Ministère du Tourisme et des Transports Aériens"; (6.1-6.3,8.2-8.4) Fondo Monetario Internacional.

SERBIA

(1.2,2.2-2.4) Turistas no residentes alojados en todo tipo de establecimientos de alojamiento; (6.1,8.2) Las cifras de gasto corresponden a las facilitadas por el país a la OMT y que, sin embargo, no figuran en los datos del Fondo Monetario Internacional utilizados para la preparación de esta edición del Compendio.
Fuente: "Statistical Office of the Republic of Serbia".

SEYCHELLES

(1.2,2.1-4.3) Llegadas de turistas no residentes en las fronteras nacionales; (5.4) Pernoctaciones basadas en las salidas; (9.1,9.2) Hoteles y casas de huéspedes; (9.3) Plazas-cama.
Fuentes: (1.1-5.4,7.1,8.1,9.1-9.3) "National Statistics Bureau"; (6.1-6.3,8.2-8.4) Fondo Monetario Internacional.

SIERRA LEONA

(1.2,2.1-2.6,4.1-4.3) Llegadas por vía aérea; (9.1,9.2) Hoteles únicamente; (10.1-10.3) Este apartado incluye únicamente la partida "viajes" debido a que la partida "transporte de pasajeros" no figura en los datos del Fondo Monetario Internacional utilizados para la preparación de esta edición del Compendio.
Fuentes: (1.2-5.4,8.1,9.1-9.4) "National Tourist Board"; (6.2,8.2-8.4) Fondo Monetario Internacional.

SINGAPUR

(1.1) Excluidas las llegadas de ciudadanos malasios por vía terrestre; incluidos visitantes del día (excursionistas); (5.4,9.4) Días; (9.1) Hoteles (homologados y no homologados); (9.3) Habitaciones; hoteles homologados únicamente; (10.1-10.3) Este apartado incluye únicamente la partida "viajes" debido a que la partida "transporte de pasajeros" no figura en los datos del Fondo Monetario Internacional utilizados para la preparación de esta edición del Compendio.
Fuentes: (1.1-5.4,8.1,9.1-9.4) "Singapore Tourism Board"; (6.2,8.3) Fondo Monetario Internacional.

SRI LANKA

(1.2,2.1-4.3) Llegadas de turistas no residentes en las fronteras nacionales; excluidos los nacionales residentes en el extranjero; (9.1,9.2) Hoteles, moteles, albergues, casas de huéspedes y aparthoteles; (9.3) Habitaciones.
Fuentes: (1.1-5.4,7.1,8.1,9.1-9.3) "Sri Lanka Tourist Board"; (6.1-6.3,8.2-8.4) Fondo Monetario Internacional.

NOTAS DE LOS PAISES

SUDAFRICA

(1.1,3.1-3.4) Excluidos los nacionales residentes en el extranjero. Incluidas las llegadas por motivo de vacaciones, negocios, estudios, trabajo, tránsito, tráfico fronterizo y trabajadores con contrato; (1.2,2.1-2.6,4.1-4.3) Llegadas de turistas no residentes en las fronteras nacionales; excluidas las llegadas por trabajo y los trabajadores con contrato; (9.1) Las cifras de 2002 y 2003 se basan en la encuesta "Hoteles: estadísticas comerciales" que se interrumpió en marzo de 2004. Esa encuesta fue sustituida en septiembre de 2004 por la de "Alojamiento turístico". Las cifras de 2004, 2005 y 2006 se basan en la encuesta de "Alojamiento turístico" y no son comparables con las cifras de la encuesta sobre "Hoteles: estadísticas comerciales". Las cifras de 2004 y 2005 se han revisado debido al cálculo retrospectivo basado en la muestra de 2006 para la encuesta de "Alojamiento turístico"; (9.1,9.3) Las cifras de 2006 son estimaciones preliminares; (9.3) Habitaciones (hoteles).
Fuentes: (1.1-4.3,8.1,9.1-9.3) "Statistics South Africa" y "South African Tourism"; (6.1-6.3,8.2-8.4) Fondo Monetario Internacional.

SUDAN

(1.2-4.3/2005/2006) Llegadas de turistas no residentes en las fronteras nacionales; incluidos los nacionales residentes en el extranjero; (6.1) El país facilita a la OMT niveles agregados de gasto que son significativamente diferentes a los datos del Fondo Monetario Internacional utilizados para la preparación de esta edición del Compendio. Los datos del país son:
2002:   62
2003:   63
2004:   68
2005: 316
2006: 409
(10.1-10.3) Este apartado incluye únicamente la partida "viajes" debido a que la partida "transporte de pasajeros" no figura en los datos del Fondo Monetario Internacional utilizados para la preparación de esta edición del Compendio.
Fuentes: (1.2-4.3,9.1-9.4) "Ministry of Tourism and Wildlife"; (6.2,8.3) Fondo Monetario Internacional.

SUECIA

(1.1-4.3) Datos según la encuesta IBIS (visitantes llegados a Suecia) durante los años 2001 a 2003, (no se han recopilado datos anteriores a 2001 ni posteriores a 2003). Fuente: Autoridad de Turismo de Suecia y Estadísticas de Suecia; (1.2,2.1-4.3) Llegadas de turistas no residentes en las fronteras nacionales; (3.2) Los datos incluyen ferrocarril y otros medios de transporte; (5.1,7.1,9.1,9.2) Hoteles únicamente; (9.3) Plazas-cama.
Fuentes: (1.1-5.4,7.1-7.4,8.1,9.1-9.3) "NUTEK - The Swedish Agency for Economic and Regional Growth"; (6.1-6.3,8.2-8.4) Fondo Monetario Internacional.

SUIZA

(1.2,2.1-2.6,5.1,5.2,7.1,7.2,9.1,9.2/2002-2004) Hoteles, moteles y posadas; (1.2,2.1-2.6,5.1,5.2,7.1,7.2,9.1-9.4/2005/2006) Hoteles y establecimientos de cura; (9.3) Tasa neta de ocupación (plazas-cama disponibles).
Fuentes: (1.2-5.3,7.1-7.3,8.1,9.1-9.4) "Swiss Federal Statistical Office"; (6.1-6.3,8.2-8.4) Fondo Monetario Internacional.

SURINAME

(1.2,2.2-2.4,4.1-4.3,5.2/2002/2003) (3.1) (5.2/2004) Llegadas al aeropuerto de Zanderij; (1.2,2.2-2.4,4.1-4.3/2004/2005) Llegadas al aeropuerto de Zanderij, aeropuerto Zorg en Hoop, Albina y Nickerie; (1.4/2003) (3.4) Llegadas al puerto Nw. Nickerie.
Fuentes: (1.1-1.4,2.2-2.4,4.1-4.3,5.2/2002/2003) (3.1,3.4/2002-2004) "General Bureau of Statistics (ABS)"; (1.2,2.2-2.4,4.1-4.3,5.2/2004/2005) (3.1,3.4/2005) (9.1) "Suriname Tourism Foundation"; (6.1-6.3,8.2-8.4) Fondo Monetario Internacional.

SWAZILANDIA

(1.1) (2.1-2.5,4.1-4.3/2005/2006) (3.1,3.3) Llegadas de visitantes no residentes en las fronteras nacionales; (1.2,4.1-4.3/2002) (2.1-2.4/2002-2004) (5.2) Llegadas en los hoteles únicamente; (9.3) Plazas-cama.
Fuentes: (1.1-5.4,7.1,7.4,8.1,9.1-9.4) "Swaziland Tourism Authority" y "Ministry of Tourism, Environment and Communications"; (6.1-6.3,8.2-8.4) Fondo Monetario Internacional.

TAILANDIA

(1.2,3.1-3.4/2002-2005) Incluidas las llegadas de nacionales residentes en el extranjero; (1.2,3.1-3.4/2006) (2.1-2.6,4.1-4.3) Excluidas las llegadas de nacionales residentes en el extranjero; (3.3) Incluye ferrocarril; (5.4) Días; (9.3) En los principales destinos turísticos únicamente.
Fuentes: (1.2-5.4,8.1,9.1,9.3) "Tourism Authority of Thailand (TAT)"; (6.1-6.3,8.2-8.4) Fondo Monetario Internacional.

TAIWAN (PROVINCIA DE CHINA)

(1.1) Incluidos los nacionales residentes en el extranjero; (2.1-2.6) Excluidos los nacionales residentes en el extranjero.
Fuentes: "(1.1-5.4,8.1,9.1,9.3) "Planning Division Tourism Bureau - Ministry of Transportation and Communication"; (6.1-6.3,8.2-8.4) Fondo Monetario Internacional.

TOGO

(1.2) Turistas no residentes alojados en hoteles y establecimientos asimilados; (9.3) Habitaciones.
Fuentes: (1.2-5.4,7.1-7.4,9.1-9.4) "Ministère de l'Environnement, du Tourisme et des Ressources Forestières"; (6.1-6.3,8.2-8.4) Fondo Monetario Internacional.

TONGA

(1.2,2.2-2.4,4.1-4.3) Llegadas por vía aérea; (10.1-10.3) Este apartado incluye únicamente la partida "viajes" debido a que la partida "transporte de pasajeros" no figura en los datos del Fondo Monetario Internacional utilizados para la preparación de esta edición del Compendio.
Fuentes: (1.1-4.3) "Tonga Visitors Bureau"; (6.2,8.3) Fondo Monetario Internacional.

TRINIDAD Y TABAGO

(1.2,2.1-2.5,4.1-4.3) Llegadas por vía aérea; (4.1) Incluidas las visitas a familiares y amigos.
Fuentes: (1.1-5.4,9.1,9.3) "Central Statistical Office - Ministry of Planning and Development"; (6.1-6.3,8.2-8.4) Fondo Monetario Internacional.

TUNEZ

(1.2,2.1-3.4) Llegadas de turistas no residentes en las fronteras nacionales; excluidos los nacionales residentes en el extranjero; (9.1,9.2) Hoteles homologados y no homologados, pensiones y ciudades de vacaciones; (9.3) Plazas-cama.
Fuentes: (1.1-5.4,7.1-7.4,8.1,9.1-9.4) "Ministère du Tourisme - Office National du Tourisme" e "Institut National de la Statistique"; (6.1-6.3,8.2-8.4) Fondo Monetario Internacional.

TURKMENISTAN

Fuente: "State Committee for Tourism and Sport".

TURQUIA

(1.1,3.1-3.4) Llegadas de visitantes no residentes en las fronteras nacionales; (1.3) Llegadas por mar (excluida una frontera terrestre desde 1989); (2.1-2.6) Llegadas de turistas no residentes en las fronteras nacionales; (3.4) Incluidos los pasajeros en crucero; (4.1-4.3) Salidas de visitantes no residentes; (5.3) Encuesta en establecimientos de alojamiento homologados por el Ministerio de Turismo; (5.3,7.3) Incluidos los terrenos de camping; (6.2) Incluidos los gastos de los nacionales residentes en el extranjero; (9.3,9.4) Hoteles homologados, excluidos los terrenos de camping; (9.3) Plazas-cama; (10.1-10.3/2002-2004) Este apartado incluye únicamente la partida "viajes" debido a que la partida "transporte de pasajeros" no figura en los datos del Fondo Monetario Internacional utilizados para la preparación de esta edición del Compendio.
Fuentes: (1.1-3.4,5.1-5.4,7.1-7.4,8.1,9.1-9.4) (6.2/2002) "Ministry of Culture and Tourism"; (4.1-4.3) "Departing Visitors Survey - Turkish Statistical Institute (TURKSTAT)"; (6.1-6.3/2003-2005) (8.2-8.4) Fondo Monetario Internacional.

TUVALU

Fuente: "Central Statistics Division - Ministry of Finance, Economic Planning and Industry".

UCRANIA

(2.1-2.6) Llegadas de turistas no residentes en las fronteras nacionales; (3.1-3.4/2002) Llegadas de visitantes no residentes en las fronteras nacionales; (3.1-3.4/2003-2006) Llegadas de turistas no residentes en las fronteras nacionales; (4.1-4.3) Llegadas de visitantes no residentes en las fronteras nacionales.
Fuentes: (1.1-5.4,7.1,7.3,8.1,9.1-9.4) "State Tourism Administration"; (6.1-6.3,8.2-8.4) Fondo Monetario Internacional.

UGANDA

Fuentes: (1.2-5.3,8.1,9.1,9.2) "Ministry of Tourism, Trade an Industry" y "Uganda Bureau of Statistics"; (6.1-6.3,8.2-8.4) Fondo Monetario Internacional.

URUGUAY

(1.1,4.1-4.3) Incluidos los nacionales residentes en el extranjero; (2.2-3.4) Excluidos los nacionales residentes en el extranjero; (3.3) Incluye ferrocarril; (5.4) Días; (9.1,9.2/2005/2006) Excluidos los hoteles sin homologar.
Fuentes: (1.1-5.4,8.1,9.1-9.4) Ministerio de Turismo y Deporte; (6.1-6.3,8.2-8.4) Fondo Monetario Internacional.

UZBEKISTAN

(6.1-6.3) Las cifras de gasto corresponden a las facilitadas por el país a la OMT y que, sin embargo, no figuran en los datos del Fondo Monetario Internacional utilizados para la preparación de esta edición del Compendio.

Fuente: "National Company "Uzbektourism".

VANUATU

(5.4) Días; (7.1) Habitaciones.
Fuentes: (1.1-5.4,8.1,9.1-9.4) "Vanuatu National Statistics Office"; (6.1-6.3,8.2-8.4) Fondo Monetario Internacional.

VENEZUELA

(1.2,2.1-4.3) Llegadas de turistas no residentes en las fronteras nacionales; (9.1,9.2/2002-2004) Hotels y Paradores/"Pousadas"; (9.1,9.2/2005/2006) Hoteles únicamente.
Fuentes: (1.1-5.4,7.4,8.1,9.1-9.3) Ministerio del Poder Popular para el Turismo; (6.1-6.3,8.2-8.4) Fondo Monetario Internacional.

VIET NAM

(1.1) Incluidos los nacionales residentes en el extranjero; (1.4,3.4) Incluidas las llegadas de pasajeros en crucero y por vía marítima; (2.2-4.3) Llegadas de visitantes no residentes en las fronteras nacionales; (6.1) Las cifras de gasto corresponden a las facilitadas por el país a la OMT y que, sin embargo, no figuran en los datos del Fondo Monetario Internacional utilizados para la preparación de esta edición del Compendio.
Fuente: "Viet Nam National Administration of Tourism".

YEMEN

(1.2,2.1-2.6,5.2) Turistas no residentes alojados en hoteles y establecimientos asimilados; (10.1-10.3) Este apartado incluye únicamente la partida "viajes" debido a que la partida "transporte de pasajeros" no figura en los datos del Fondo Monetario Internacional utilizados para la preparación de esta edición del Compendio.
Fuentes: (1.2-5.4,7.1,7.2,9.1,9.2) "Ministry of Tourism"; (6.2,8.2-8.4) Fondo Monetario Internacional.

ZAMBIA

(5.4) Días; (9.3) Habitaciones; (10.1-10.3) Este apartado incluye únicamente la partida "viajes" debido a que la partida "transporte de pasajeros" no figura en los datos del Fondo Monetario Internacional utilizados para la preparación de esta edición del Compendio.
Nota 2002: Datos provisionales.
Fuentes: (1.2-5.4,7.1,9.1-9.3) "Ministry of Tourism, Environment and Natural Resources"; (6.2,8.2-8.4) Fondo Monetario Internacional.

ZIMBABWE

(2.1-2.4,3.1,3.3,4.1-4.3) Llegadas de visitantes no residentes en las fronteras nacionales; (3.1,3.3/2002/2003) Incluidas las personas en tránsito; (6.1) Las cifras de gasto corresponden a las facilitadas por el país a la OMT y que, sin embargo, no figuran en los datos del Fondo Monetario Internacional utilizados para la preparación de esta edición del Compendio; (9.1,9.2) Sólo hoteles clasificados; (9.3) Plazas-cama.
Fuente: "Zimbabwe Tourism Authority - ZTA".

ALBANIA

Transportation

Passenger. To obtain data for sea, air, and other kinds of transport, BOA uses bank reports.

Travel

BOA compiles credits and debits for the travel category (business and personal) by combining results from the travel survey (conducted by BOA and INSTAT three times a year) with data on arrivals and departures of Albanians and foreign travelers from the Ministry of Internal Affairs. BOA uses the travel survey for estimating average duration of stay and average daily expenditures per traveler.

ANGOLA

Services

This category covers the following components: transportation, travel, building, insurance, royalties and license fees, other business services, and government services not included elsewhere. The information is obtained through (1) the surveys of oil and diamond companies and also from various companies rendering services, such as construction, insurance, carriers, Angola Multichoice, and Use of the Medium Kwanza office (GAMEK), and (2) BNA data on execution of the cash plan and treasury draft orders.

ANGUILLA

See East Caribbean.

ANTIGUA AND BARBUDA

See East Caribbean.

ARGENTINA

Transportation

INDEC compiles statistics on transportation. For passenger fares, on-board services, and excess baggage charges, it obtains data from surveys of the sea, air, and road passenger transport companies operating in Argentina. Data include both the international operations of resident carriers (credit) and the domestic operations of nonresident carriers (debit).

For passenger road transport, the estimates are based on the number of international trips provided by the companies and on the cost of the tickets. They are also based on surveys conducted monthly of departing and incoming buses to ascertain information on the average occupancy rate of the vehicles and the percentage of resident and nonresident passengers.

Travel

This item is calculated on the basis of the estimated number of passengers entering and departing Argentina, the number of days they stay, and the estimated average expenditure per person. To improve the estimates for this account, INDEC conducted surveys at main border crossings in 1996. (For more details, see *Estimación de la Cuenta Viajes del Balance de Pagos*–May 1999.)

ARMENIA

Transportation

In addition to the estimates made for the transportation of imported goods referred to above, the BPD gathers additional data from other sources, such as surveys of transportation companies. These surveys collect information on both freight and passenger fares. BPD derives the estimates from the statistical survey on services conducted in 1999.

Travel

For travel, the BPD collects data from surveys carried out by the NSS.
To estimate the total amount of receipts and payments related to travel, the BPD collects data on the number of foreign arrivals and resident departures, the countries of origin and destination, length of stays, and cost of transportation, hotel, meals, and incidental costs. These estimates include expenditures in Armenia by nonresidents and by Armenians in foreign countries on short-term work assignments (that is, for periods of less than one year). The BPD derives the estimates from the statistical survey on services conducted in 2001.
Government ministries and agencies also provide data on expenditures on business trips abroad.

ARUBA

Transportation

The item comprises harbor dues and fees, freight, and passenger fares.

Travel

This item includes receipts from transactions in foreign currency, travelers' checks, and credit cards, as well as goods carried out of Aruba by tourists and paid for in foreign currency, travelers' checks, or credit cards. However, because of the difficulty of obtaining a breakdown for the expenses of resident credit card holders, the item also includes their local expenses. Steps will be taken to adjust the data on travel for these expenses.

The item also includes payments related to medical treatments abroad and expenditures of students abroad.

AUSTRALIA

Transportation

Passenger. Data cover passenger services provided by sea and air. The main source of data is the quarterly ABS Survey of International Trade in Services (SITS). From the September quarter 1994 onward, for confidentiality reasons, the credit series also includes all non-freight earnings of resident transport operators and the expenses in Australia of nonresident transport operators. For confidentiality reasons, before the September quarter 1997, the debit series includes cruise fares. From the September quarter 1997 onward, these cruise fares are included in travel debits.

Travel

The ABS derives travel credits largely from data collected in the International Visitor Survey conducted by the Bureau of Tourism Research. ABS uses these data in conjunction with results from its monthly overseas arrivals and departures statistics, which it compiles from information collected by the Department of Immigration and Citizenship from arriving and departing international travelers.

Travel credits also include the receipts by domestic airlines from international airlines for the on-carriage, in Australia, of foreign visitors who have purchased tickets abroad. The source is the ABS SITS. Also included is the estimated expenditure of foreign military personnel on rest and recreation in Australia.

ABS compiles information on students' expenditure in Australia from student numbers and their associated fees, provided by the Department of Education, Science and Training, and estimated average expenditures on other goods and services sourced from a survey of foreign students.

Benchmark estimates for travel debits are compiled from a periodic household survey of returning Australian travelers. The survey provides a dissection of the average expenditure per travelers by purpose of travel (business and personal), by income earned abroad and cash taken abroad.

Between these surveys, the bureau compiles estimates using data from the SITS, which covers businesses providing travel finance and outbound travel and collects data on prepaid tours, credit card usage, and traveler's checks issued. As with travel credits, the ABS uses these data in conjunction with results from its monthly overseas arrivals and departures statistics.

AUSTRIA

Transportation

This item covers freight revenues and expenditures, as well as international passenger transport and auxiliary services.

Travel

Travel now excludes international passenger transport. One of the most important sources for the credit side of travel is the official statistics on overnight stays and arrivals of nonresident visitors to Austria.

Furthermore, studies and sources provided by other institutions are used, for instance the new Austrian Guest Inquiry "T-Mona"—an instrument that measures the average daily expenditure of foreign tourists in Austria.

The main source for measuring the expenditure of Austrians abroad is a quarterly household survey operated by Statistics Austria.

Credit card data are mainly used for plausibility checks on the data from the above-mentioned sources and for compiling the geographical breakdowns on a detailed country level.

Various supplementary data sources are used in the compilation process to provide the necessary data that cannot be obtained from the main sources. These sources are used to measure directly specific variables; for example direct imports of cars by households are taken from the car registration statistics. The expenditure of "fuel tourists" contributing to the credit side of the travel item is relatively high; a model is therefore used to measure it.

Concerning the debit side of the travel item, expenditure on health services abroad—in particular related to "dental tourism"—is significant. Because this kind of travel is not or only partly covered by the household survey, an estimation model is employed, which takes into account the supply structure of dentists near the Austrian border (in particular the border with Hungary).

Supplementary data sources are also used to corroborate the reliability of outcomes of highly important variables that depend on weaker data sources. Examples of supplementary sources are data provided by other countries or institutions, such as Eurostat or the World Tourism Organization (UNWTO), data from private institutions, or other macroeconomic indicators such as GDP, the consumer price index, and statistics on wages studies on the mobility of students.

AZERBAIJAN

Transportation

This category covers freight and passenger transportation, and port services for all modes of transport. Data on passenger fares and port service charges are based mainly on information the SSC collects from marine shipping, airline, railway, and road transport companies.

Travel

Data for the travel component are estimated by combining the SCC data on the number of foreign visitors entering Azerbaijan and Azerbaijan residents traveling abroad with data collected from the commercial banks on the average per capita expenditures of travelers.

BAHAMAS

Transportation

The data on freight and passenger services cover all modes of transport and port services. CBOB obtains entries for transportation services from surveys of both foreign and resident shipping and airline companies.

Travel

Regarding travel credit, CBOB compiles entries using the Ministry of Tourism's tourist expenditure estimates, which are in turn based on exit surveys of foreign visitors (cruise and stopovers) conducted by the Ministry of Tourism. Estimates are compiled by taking the product of the number of foreign visitors and an estimate of an average expenditure per visit.
Regarding travel debit, CBOB compiles entries using exchange control records.

BAHRAIN

Transportation

For transportation service credits, FSD derives entries from information provided by Gulf Air for tickets sold by its offices outside Bahrain and payments received by port and airport authorities against services provided to foreign ships and airlines.

Travel

Credits. Tourists and business travelers coming via air and sea and 10 percent of Saudi tourists coming to Bahrain via the causeway are assumed to stay in hotels and other apartments. FSD obtains data from MOF on gross output (revenue) of hotels (covering room rent and other revenue) and restaurants (sales). All rental revenue of hotels is assumed to be earned from nonresidents, while assumptions are made on the proportion of other revenue of hotels and sales of restaurants ascribable to nonresidents.

Using these estimates and data on the number of persons staying in hotels, obtained from the Tourism Directorate, FSD derives estimates of per capita expenditure. A lower estimate of per capita expenditure is applied to the number of tourists not staying in hotels. In addition, FSD makes an allowance for miscellaneous expenditures (e.g., taxi fares, purchases of souvenirs, etc.). Ninety percent of Saudis arriving via the causeway are considered day travelers and assumed to spend about BD 40 per person.

Debits. Bahrainis crossing the causeway are assumed to spend, on average, BD 30 per person. In addition, FSD makes an allowance for the overseas training costs of Bahraini officials. The directorate also uses survey reports on bank transactions, covering records on foreign currency notes and traveler's checks sold to residents (e.g., tourists, businessmen, students studying abroad).

INTERNATIONAL MONETARY FUND (IMF) NOTES

BANGLADESH

Transportation

Transportation covers those services performed by residents in one economy for those of another, by all modes of transportation that are involved with carriage of passengers, movement of goods (freight), charter of carriers with crew, and other related supporting and auxiliary services.

Travel

The Statistics Department collects data on travel transactions through the banks. It records as credits the receipts from foreign visitors, and as debits the residents' expenditures abroad.

BARBADOS

Transportation

For passenger service debits, which represent sea and air fares paid by Barbadians to nonresident carriers, CBB estimates the entries from survey forms returned by nonresident carriers. The credit entries cover receipts of domestic carriers for similar services.
The port and airport authorities provide data on other transport services.

Travel

CBB obtains these estimates from BSS estimates. The BSS obtains values representing travelers' expenditures from information derived from surveys of travelers on the length of stay and type of accommodation. For the credit entries, the compilers apply estimated average daily expenditures to the number of visitors recorded. For the debit entries, CBB supplements the data with exchange record information.

In the case of business travel, the credit entries include expenditures by foreign seasonal workers in Barbados, and the debit entries include expenditures abroad by resident seasonal workers. The Ministry of Labor provides these data.

In the case of personal travel, compilers classify the data by purpose of travel into health, education, and other. Compilers base credit estimates for students and health-related travelers on a survey of colleges and hospitals; they base debit entries on exchange record data.

BELARUS

Transportation

The main sources of information for freight and transport services are the MSA surveys of transport companies and the estimates made to convert imports from the c.i.f. to the f.o.b. basis.

Travel

The main sources of data are (1) the MSA surveys of hotels and tourist companies, (2) the Frontier Troops State Committee for information on the number of foreign visitors and residents of the Republic of Belarus who enter and leave the country, and (3) other official sources of information, such as the MOF and the SCC.

The NBB estimates travel services on the basis of estimated average per diem expenditures, the number of residents traveling abroad and nonresidents traveling in the Republic of Belarus, and the estimated duration of their stay. The Frontier Troops State Committee provides data on the number of travelers, country of origin (for inward travelers), country of destination (for outward travelers), and types of travel (private, business, tourism, transit, etc.).

Travel debits include the estimated value of vehicles imported by resident individuals of the Republic of Belarus for noncommercial use. The SCC registers the number of vehicles and provides data on the aggregate value of vehicles brought into the country by natural persons.

BELGIUM

Transportation

Source data distinguish the means of transportation (sea, air, and other transport) and provide, within each category, a breakdown into passenger, freight, and other transport services. A further breakdown of transportation by five supplementary types is available.

Travel

Sources include data related to the use of credit cards. Some adjustments are made to consider the impact of border workers.

BELIZE

Transportation

Since Belize has no international shipping lines or international airline, credit entries contain only revenues collected from foreign carriers. The CBB collects these data from annual surveys of the International Airport and Port Authorities.

Regarding freight debit, CBB calculates it as 8 percent (derived from the survey of customs declaration forms) of the c.i.f. value of merchandise imports as reported by the CSO. It subtracts the value of banana and papaya boxes from the import numbers before the calculation of freight charges. No attempt is made to disaggregate freight services by air and land since the use of these types of transportation for imports is minimal.

The credit information represents revenues from foreign shipping companies to the port for services and to domestic agents for commission payments and other services rendered. The CBB deducts from these inflows and outflows the money sent to the shipping agencies to pay the nonresident crew of foreign vessels.

For air transport–passenger debit, the entry consists only of payments for air tickets sold by airline agents. The ticket sales from branch offices of foreign airlines in Belize are not recorded here, since the branch offices are treated as resident companies; therefore, remittances abroad are recorded under profits in income.

Travel

For travel credits, the CBB derives information by estimating expenditures of five main categories of nonresidents—seasonal and border workers, business, students, cruise ship passengers, and stay-over tourists.

For seasonal and border workers in the country, CBB estimates their expenditures at 69 percent of the income earned by them. This percentage was derived from a 2004 survey of nonresident workers. No information is collected on residents working temporarily abroad.

Regarding stay-over tourists and cruise ship passengers, in 2005, CBB replaced estimates of tourist expenditure, previously based on the 2000 Visitor Expenditure and Motivational Survey (VEMS), with actual inflows reported in the commercial banks' foreign exchange purchases report under line item "Tourist Related Purchases." The change was necessary because purchases of foreign exchange from tourist establishments by commercial banks significantly exceeded tourist expenditure estimates obtained using the 2000 VEMS results. The inflows data are cleaned out to add/remove misclassified transactions. An upward adjustment of 5 percent is made to reflect tourism inflows not captured in the banking system.

Before 2005, CBB obtained its estimate of national tourism expenditures using stay-over tourist arrival numbers from the Immigration Department, cruise ship arrival numbers from the BTB, and estimates of average daily expenditure and average length of stay derived from the visitor expenditure survey.

Owing to the large numbers of people who move daily between Belize and Guatemala and between Belize and Mexico, it is necessary to adjust downward the number of arrivals through these two land borders. Certain ratios, developed during the expenditure surveys, are used to estimate the actual numbers of stay-over visitors. These ratios removed people traveling in-transit, adjusted for tourists who traveled for a short day trip to a neighboring country and were recorded as entering the country twice (called multiple-entry tourist), and removed seasonal/border workers and students that are accounted for elsewhere. At the international airport, citizens who reside abroad but travel to Belize using their Belizean passports are added, while in-transit visitors are excluded.

Regarding business travel, based on previous estimates, approximately 97 percent of total tourism inflows accounted for personal, nonbusiness expenditures, while the balance of 3 percent is considered to be expenditure by business travelers. CBB obtains expenditure by business and official visitors by taking the cleaned out "Tourist Related Purchases" data from the commercial banks' foreign exchange purchase report and multiplying it by 3 percent. The debit reflects expenditure on business travel by the public service (as recorded in the Overseas Expenditure of the Public Service database) and the public (as recorded in the database of all outflows of foreign currency from the banking system).

Regarding students, CBB obtains expenditure data on foreign students from the annual BOP survey of educational establishments and the commercial banks' reported inflows to educational institutions not covered by the annual BOP survey. The total obtained is assumed to represent 90 percent of foreign student coverage, so the number is adjusted accordingly.

Travel debits consist of the total number of residents traveling through the international airport and multiplying this number by an average expenditure of BZ$1,795 per person. This number is checked by comparing the outflows on vacation travel and outbound credit card payments recorded by the commercial banks. Only part of the credit card outflows is attributed to travel, since businesses use credit cards to pay for imports.

BENIN

Transportation

This item covers freight and insurance relating to international shipping, other passenger transportation services (regardless of the mode of transport used), and port services. BCEAO estimates transportation services based on data gathered from the Joint

Benin-Niger Railways and Transportation Organization, port authorities, shipowners and shipping agents, foreign airlines, and the Air Navigation Safety Agency.

Travel

BCEAO derives credit entries from surveys of hotels and travel agencies conducted by the Tourism and Hotel Business Directorate. Estimates are calculated based on the number of visitors, the number of overnight stays, and the estimated average expenditure by tourists.

Debit entries are drawn from data on pilgrimages provided by the Islamic Union of Benin, data on mission expenditures of government officials provided by the General Directorate of the Budget and Equipment, and an estimate of the holiday expenditures of technical assistants and other nonresidents.

These credit and debit entries are supplemented with the amounts obtained from the breakdown, by economic type, of exchanges of BCEAO banknotes between West African Economic and Monetary Union (WAEMU) member countries.

BOLIVIA

Transportation

This account covers freight and passenger services for all modes of transport. The BCB obtains transportation services data from surveys it conducts for this purpose.

Travel

Since 2000, this information is obtained through an annual survey conducted by the INE. This is in accordance with an agreement signed by the BCB, the Vice Ministry of Tourism, the National Service of Migration, and the INE. Travel transactions are broken down between business and personal travel.

BOSNIA AND HERZEGOVINA

Transportation

CBBH calculates the value of freight transportation services on the basis of the estimated difference between the value of imported goods at c.i.f. and f.o.b. values. Out of this amount, a part related to the services provided by nonresident carriers is estimated. The compilers derive passenger transportation services from Sarajevo airport statistics on air traffic of local and foreign carriers and from CBBH research on transport of nonresidents by bus.

Travel

CBBH estimates business trips according to its research on transactions of nonresident experts and staff of foreign embassies, as well as international civil and military organizations in BH.

For private travel, CBBH derives the estimates from data on foreign tourists from statistical institutes in BH, and data of other countries on BH tourists abroad, with estimates for unregistered inflows and outflows from tourism.

BOTSWANA

Transportation

Transportation services cover air, road, and rail transport for freight, passenger, and courier services. Annual surveys of transport companies (both private and parastatals) provide much of these data, but the surveys are supplemented by data captured from foreign exchange forms. Some of the freight data are estimated using data from customs.

Travel

In the past, travel estimates were based on amounts reported on Forms A and S in a bank's exchange reporting system. These estimates were considered likely to be understated particularly on the credit side, because of the incidence of pre-paid travel settled offshore and the likelihood that expenditure by nonresident visitors while in Botswana will not be classified to the travel item.

To improve the estimates on the credit side, a methodology was established using arrival statistics and the results of a Department of Tourism Visitor Survey. The TSU compiles arrival statistics from migration cards, which classify noncitizen visitors according to their reasons for entering Botswana, based on the Visitor Survey. The survey was first conducted for 1998 and is now being repeated approximately every two years. It also provides useful measures of lengths of stay and average expenditure in various categories of visitor. Estimates are made using information on the average length of stay and expenditure data for each category of visitor applied to the appropriate arrivals data.

The BOB derives data on travel by Botswana government officials from the MFDP's Cash Flow Unit.

On the debt side, the coverage of the item has been improved by the addition of a number of categories of expenditure that were not previously measured. These include

- student expenditure abroad (derived from Ministry of Education disbursements);
- expenditure abroad by resident air travelers (estimated from air departures and assumptions about length of stay and average expenditure); and
- similar expenditure abroad by resident land travelers (estimated from purchases of foreign exchange for travel reported on Form A, less the amount estimated for air travelers).

BRAZIL

Transportation

For transportation of goods, the BCB uses data provided directly by Brazilian seagoing shipping companies, International Air Transportation Agency, and the National Waterways Transportation Agency, supplemented by ITRS data. Staff monitor separately the operations involving air, sea, and other (river/land) modes of transportation.

The source of data on passenger transport is the ITRS. For charters, the BCB uses data from the ITRS and data provided by the National Waterways Transportation Agency, which along with companies also supplies data on freight and cross-trade. Data on other transportation services are either reported by companies or based on the ITRS.

Travel

To compile the travel account, the BCB uses ITRS data. The data cover revenues and expenditures regarding sales and purchases by means of international credit cards, currency transactions between travelers and authorized exchange operators, and receipts and payments between domestic and foreign travel operators.

BULGARIA

Transportation

Passenger. Credit and debit entries are based on BNB estimates.

Travel

The BNB compiles estimates using a data model that combines data on numbers of travelers to and from Bulgaria with estimates of per capita expenditure to calculate the total credit and debit entries.

BURUNDI

Transportation

For passenger services, BRB compiles data on the basis of a survey of air carriers conducted by BRB's Financial Operations Department. The data are drawn exclusively from receipts from these companies and are recorded in the settlement statement.

Travel

BRB derives the entries for travel from a survey of hotels, foreign tourist spending in Burundi, and spending abroad by residents (BRB statement of exchange transactions).

CAMBODIA

Transportation

Separate estimates are made for air and sea transportation services.

For *air* transportation services, freight on imports carried by nonresident airlines are estimated by applying an average freight rate per ton to the quantity of imports. The same methodology is used to estimate details of freight on exports carried by the resident airline.

Passenger fares paid by residents to nonresident airlines are estimated by combining information on the number of passengers collected from the Ministry of the Interior on the numbers of resident and nonresident arrivals and departures, an average weighted airfare, and passenger loadings by the different airlines serving Phnom Penh. Passenger fares paid by nonresidents to the resident airline are estimated in the same manner.

Other air transportation services are estimated from information provided by the resident airline for expenditure in foreign ports and from information provided by the Civil Aviation Authority for expenditure in Cambodia by nonresident airlines.

For *sea* transport, freight on imports carried by nonresident carriers is estimated by deducting freight on air imports from the estimate of freight on total imports and applying to the result the share of nonresident shipping. Freight on exports carried by resident carriers is estimated by multiplying an average freight rate for exported goods by the proportion of the tonnage of exports estimated to be carried by residents. ITRS data are used to estimate passenger fares for sea transport.

Other sea transportation services are estimated from information provided by resident shipping agents and port authorities.

For 2003 onwards, ITRS data are used to estimate other transport: freight, passenger fares, and other transportation services.

Travel

For travel credits, separate estimates are made for expenditures by gamblers, tourists, business travelers, and diplomats and official travelers. For example, for tourists and business travelers, data on the number of arrivals are combined with data on the length of stay and the average pattern of expenditure, collected from the NBC International Visitors Survey conducted in 2005 and 2006, Ministry of Tourism, and travel agents. For short-term employees of international organizations in Cambodia and employees of aid agencies, estimates are based on the number of such staff and the pattern of expenditure.

Travel debits include estimates based on numbers of departures of residents obtained from Ministry of Interior and Ministry of Tourism data, and their estimated length of stay abroad and their pattern of expenditure from the NBC Returned Cambodian Travelers' Survey conducted in 2005 and 2006. The distinction between business and personal travel is not disseminated.

CAMEROON

Services

The balance of payments staff prepare the data on the various types of services using the settlement balance obtained from bank forms—reports prepared by commercial banks concerning the transactions of their customers.

To supplement the information in the settlement balance, staff use the data obtained, on the one hand, from questionnaires sent to consignees and to airline and insurance companies and, on the other hand, from the annual reports of reporting entities.

CANADA

Transportation

For *passenger* transport, BOPD relies on monthly administrative data, combined with estimates of average passenger fares from a quarterly sample survey of expenditure characteristics by the Culture, Tourism, and Center for Education Statistics Division (CTCES) of Statistics Canada. Included with passenger transport is coverage of cruise fares, which international standards define as travel.

Travel

The CTCES Division compiles the basic Canadian travel statistics. CTCES derives these statistics from a combination of census data and sample counts of travelers crossing the border, coupled with sample surveys used to collect specific information from travelers, including their expenditures and main purpose of visit. Beginning with the reference year 2000, a new air exit survey introduced on-site interviews for foreign travelers at eight key Canadian airports.

Travel is subdivided into travel for business reasons and travel for personal reasons: *Business* travel covers expenditures by cross-border workers, but insufficient data bar their identification as such in the Canadian statistics. Also, as a result of data limitations, cruise fares as noted above are recorded under transportation services rather than travel. As part of the business travel item, the CTCES calculates estimates of spending by crews (of airplanes, ships, boats, trains, and trucks).

For *personal* travel, data for health-related travel consist of foreign spending for hospital services in Canada. CTCES records these data from the annual hospital survey of the Canadian Institute for Health Information, projecting data for recent years where survey results are not yet available. With the 1995 reference year, CTCES introduced estimates for physician services linked to U.S. data on the payments side. Also starting in 1995, access to U.S. sources has enabled a fuller estimate covering payments, beyond provincial health plans, at major medical centers and university hospitals located in the United States.

On the receipt side of the education series, CTCES produces the estimates by combining the time series on the number of students with average tuition rates and adding estimates of other expenditure. For expenditures of Canadian students in the United States, the data have been supplied by the U.S. BEA from 1981 onward and were linked with balance of payments data for prior years. CTCES updates the data on student expenditures overseas to incorporate volume and expenditure estimates.

CAPE VERDE

Transportation

Staff derive the data on passenger and other transportation services from the exchange record and surveys of the national airline, fuel suppliers, and port and airport authorities.

Travel

Entries in the travel category include tourism, business travel, students, civil servants, and other travelers. Staff collect data from the exchange record.

CHILE

Transportation

Passenger. Credit and debit entries for passenger services are estimated on the basis of information obtained from quarterly forms provided by resident carriers (i.e., shipping companies and airlines) and by representatives of nonresident transport companies. The CBC supplements the data with information from annual surveys of resident carriers, a benchmark survey of other carriers, and data on vehicles crossing the border. Before complete information is obtained from the forms and surveys, preliminary estimates are made.

Travel

Both credit and debit entries are estimated by combining monthly data provided by immigration authorities on the number of foreign visitors and Chilean travelers who enter and exit the country, with data on average expenditures and length of stay obtained from surveys, which cover tourism by both incoming and outgoing travelers. The surveys are undertaken in accordance with an agreement between the CBC and the National Tourism Service, a government agency.

CHINA

Transportation

Until 1995, the SAFE obtained credit entries for transportation (shipment) and port services from the Ministry of Communications and the Ministry of Railways, among other sources. Beginning in 1996, the SAFE derives credit entries from the ITRS. Debit entries are drawn from import statistics compiled by Customs and from information derived from the ITRS.

Travel

The compilers obtain data on travel credits from the National Tourism Administration (NTA). The NTA collects the data through sample surveys conducted by the National Bureau of Statistics. Travel debits are calculated using data from the Immigration Administration Department of the Ministry of Public Security and relevant receipts of main international travel destinations (countries or areas) outside China.

COLOMBIA

Transportation

Regarding passenger services and other transportation, BR compiles credit and debit entries on the basis of data supplied by national and foreign airlines. It bases freight credit entries on data supplied by national airlines and shipping companies. It bases freight debit entries on data supplied by DIAN for imports of goods.

Travel

The travel component measures nonborder travel (via airports) and cross-border travel (through land-border crossing points). The data for nonborder travel are estimated on the basis of information on international passenger movements provided by the Civil Aviation authorities and the Administrative Department of Security. Regarding cross-border travel, BR derives data from quarterly surveys conducted at five land-border crossing points.

CONGO

Transportation

BEAC values shipping costs either directly, based on the reports of enterprises, the postal administration, and banks, or, if this is not available, by assuming that shipping costs are 18 percent of the c.i.f. value of imports.
Other transportation entries include services rendered by carriers, mainly for the international transportation of passengers, and goods and services purchased by carriers and consumed in the course of their business.

Travel

Credit and debit: Credit entries include expenditure in the Republic of Congo by foreign travelers, and debit entries include current expenditure by residents traveling abroad, regardless of the nature of the travel. The postal administration (SOPECO) and banks report the amounts for both types of entries; the banks report transactions in foreign banknotes, travelers' checks, transfers of travel agencies, tourists transiting the Republic of Congo, etc.

BEAC also collects the information by means of questionnaires sent to the United Nations and its affiliated agencies, the Congolese Public Treasury, and embassies (for scholarships paid directly abroad). It supplements these figures by an estimate of flows of BEAC and franc zone currency notes and an estimate of expenditure by technical assistants during their leave abroad.

COSTA RICA

Transportation

The CBCR obtains data on freight, passenger, and other transportation services, as well as on other international transactions by air, land, and sea transportation companies, from information reported in the questionnaires it sends to such companies.

Travel

The CBCR bases estimates on data the ICT reports on the number of foreigners visiting Costa Rica and residents traveling abroad. It also uses data from ICT sample surveys on per capita spending and average length-of-stay. The Directorate General of Migration and Foreign Travel provides the ICT with monthly data on the number of nonresident travelers entering Costa Rica and the number of residents leaving the country. The ICT undertakes surveys quarterly to derive the average amount spent and the average stay.

CÔTE D'IVOIRE

Transportation

For passenger services, the data are collected from the national airline, Air Ivoire, and the offices of nonresident airlines.

Travel

Credit entries are obtained primarily from statistics on arrivals of foreign tourists and hotel occupancy, provided by the Ministry of Tourism and Crafts (formerly High Commission for Tourism). A direct survey of hotels is also conducted.

Debit entries are based on estimates and mainly cover expenditure of non-Ivoirien residents while out of the country. These figures are derived from the income of nonnationals working in the private sector, the wages of technical assistants and non-Ivoirien staff of international organizations with offices in Côte d'Ivoire, and the length of the leave of such persons.

Figures on government missions are obtained from the Payroll Directorate.

The expenditure of Ivoirien students abroad is primarily taken from surveys of donors for foreign scholarships and of the Ministry of Higher Education for scholarships granted by the Ivoirien government.

CROATIA

Transportation

This category covers the international transportation of passengers, goods, and other transportation services.

From 1993–98, the data sources were the ITRS and questionnaires that CNB received from enterprises engaged in the international transportation of goods and passengers. Expenditures on transportation services also included 1) part of the differences between c.i.f. and f.o.b. imports, pertaining to services provided by nonresidents, and 2) estimates of the operating costs of Croatian transportation companies in international transportation.

As of the first quarter 1999, the CNB compiles revenues and expenditures from transportation services on the basis of data from the new CNB survey on international transportation services, with two exceptions: First, revenues and expenditures from road transport are still compiled from ITRS data, and second, data on c.i.f./f.o.b. adjustments for nonresident carriers are obtained from the questionnaires on transportation costs related to imports of goods, classified by modes of transportation and residency. From the first quarter of 1999, a breakdown by mode of transportation is available.

Travel

The travel component shows income from services rendered to foreign travelers and tourists, as well as expenditures incurred by domestic travelers and tourists abroad. Beginning with the second half of 1998, the CNB has conducted a survey of consumption by foreign travelers in Croatia and domestic travelers abroad. Since early 1999, the CNB data compilers have combined the results of this survey (stratified sample) with the Ministry of the Interior data on the total number of foreign and domestic travelers, along with the data on distribution of foreign travelers by countries contained in the CBS report on tourism for compiling the travel component.

CYPRUS

Transportation

This category covers freight and passenger services provided by sea and air transport operators. CBC derives debit entries for freight services from the estimates made to convert imports from a c.i.f. to an f.o.b. basis (i.e., freight and insurance are assumed to equal 8 percent of imports c.i.f.).

Concerning passenger transport, banks report the data through the settlements system. With respect to credits, CBC cross-checks the figures with data obtained from an annual survey of major resident passenger transport operators. The staff supplement settlement data for supporting, auxiliary, and other transport services with data from the financial statements or reports of international business companies engaged in such activities.

Travel

For travel credits for tourism, the central bank obtains data from CYSTAT, which conducts a monthly frontier survey on tourist expenditure in Cyprus. To obtain geographical allocation for travel credits, the CBC combines per person expenditure derived from the survey with the number of tourist arrivals, as given by the frontier survey of incoming travelers, which CYSTAT also conducts.

With regard to education-related revenue, CBC conducts an annual survey among those colleges that provide educational services to nonresidents and compares the survey results with data reported by banks under the settlements system.

In 2004, CYSTAT launched a new survey to measure the expenditures of nonresidents in their residential properties in Cyprus. The results of the survey are included in the "travel" item.

For travel debits, CBC obtains the value from the settlements system. Reported data include foreign exchange allowances issued to resident travelers for tourism purposes, foreign exchange issued for education, private medical spending abroad, payments by resident travel agents, and foreign exchange outflows through credit or debit cards.

CZECH REPUBLIC

Transportation

For 1993–2003, the CNB collected data on air transport of goods and passengers directly from transportation companies. For other kinds of transport, the data were based on the commercial banks' records. Additional data were required from companies involved with transporting natural gas through the territory of the Czech Republic to Western Europe (credit) and transporting gas and oil through the Slovak Republic to the Czech Republic (debit).

For data on freight services connected with exports and included in the contractual export price, the CNB made estimates from customs declarations and reported them under *transportation–credits*. The cost of transportation for imports, when included in the import price, remained part of the trade balance with a debit entry.

A new system for collecting data on transport services via the CZSO is used from the first quarter of 2007. Data from a CZSO pilot survey-based project have been used for a 2004–06 revision.

Travel

For 1993–98, the CNB compiled the travel item using data the CZSO provided on the number of travelers; the CZSO obtained the information from police on the arrivals of foreign visitors and on the trips of Czech residents abroad.

For average expenditures by foreigners during their stay in the Czech Republic and of Czech tourists during their trips abroad, the CNB based estimates on regular inquiries at selected border crossings. The estimates were also based on information from the banking sector on purchases of Czech currency by nonresidents and foreign currency by residents, on the use of credit and payment cards, and on the receipts and expenditures of hotels and travel agencies.

Since 1999, the banking statistics, complemented by the CZSO survey of travelers at accommodation establishments, have been the main source of information used to compile the travel item. From 1998 onwards, CNB has supplemented the travel data with data on personal expenditures on goods and services by foreigners in the Czech Republic and Czechs employed abroad for less than one year. Starting from 2001, the CNB produces data showing the split between business and personal travel.

DENMARK

Services

Statistics Denmark conducts a combined monthly (covering approximately 400 enterprises) and quarterly (covering approximately 1,200 enterprises) sample survey on trade in services and transfers. The sample has been drawn on the basis of the settlement system, using partly a cut-off method (monthly reporters) and partly a stratified sample method (quarterly reporters).

In the future, the sample will be considered fixed, but an update of the sample will be made each year to secure representativeness, that is, to replace enterprises that can no longer be a part of the sample. This update will be made on the basis of sources including the VAT (value added tax) Register, merchandise trade statistics, and the General Business Register. The survey incorporates a full breakdown by countries.

The import of travel is primarily based on a separate survey on personal and business travel.

The export of travel is based partly on accommodation statistics combined with a survey on overnight travelers' spending in Denmark and partly on different border surveys covering travelers on same-day visits.

The rest of the travel item is based on the general survey of trade in services.

Monthly data on services are estimated from information from the monthly reporters to the survey of trade in services and from extrapolations for the quarterly reporters, and by adding estimates for the travel item.

DOMINICA

See East Caribbean.

DOMINICAN REPUBLIC

Transportation

The BCRD's International Department compiles and classifies credit and debit entries by mode of transportation (sea, air, and land) and category of transportation (freight, passenger, and other transportation services). For freight services obtained by importers, compiling staff base entries on data recorded in customs declarations. For freight obtained from nonresidents, they derive the value from estimates for freight services provided by residents. For passenger transportation, they base data on the quarterly surveys of resident shipping and airline companies. They also collect data on port services from the port authorities.

Travel

The International Department staff derive estimates by combining data on numbers of travelers with estimates of the average stay and expenditure of nonresident and resident travelers. The department obtains the number of travelers from the BCRD's daily records of arrivals and departures of travelers at national airports. Staff crosscheck the data with data from the National Statistics Office and the Secretariat of State for Tourism. Data from the National Migration Office are not used because of the delay in their availability. Staff obtain average stay and expenditure estimates from quarterly surveys undertaken by the BCRD's National Accounts Department.

EAST CARIBBEAN

Transportation

The estimates for passenger services cover receipts and payments for the transportation of passengers. The ECCB obtains the data from an annual balance of payments survey of airline companies and agencies, carried out by the CSOs and the ECCB.

Travel

On the credit side, this item covers total expenditures by visitors to countries in the East Caribbean region. The ECCB derives the figures by combining data on the number of visitors and their average length of stay (obtained from the immigration departments of member countries), with an estimate of the average daily expenditure per category of visitor. The latter component is obtained through benchmark surveys of visitor expenditures, conducted periodically and adjusted annually for inflation.

Estimates of travel debits are obtained from commercial banking statistics on sales of foreign exchange for travel purposes, as well as official sources providing data on student maintenance overseas and on travel to attend international conferences.

ECUADOR

Transportation

For credits and debits on sea transport, the CBE uses its quarterly and annual surveys of shipping companies operating in Ecuador. To supplement that data, it uses information on passengers and cargo from the Merchant Marine and Coastal Administration (Dirección de la Marina Mercante y del Litoral, DIMERC)—the government regulatory authority for maritime traffic in Ecuador.

For air transport, the CBE uses information supplied by the Civil Aviation Administration (Dirección General de Aviación Civil, DAC). The CBE also obtains data from its merchandise trade database, containing information about f.o.b. and c.i.f. goods imports.

Travel

The National Migration and Aliens Office (Dirección Nacional de Migración y Extranjería) supplies data on inbound and outbound tourism, obtained through nationwide surveys based on type of visa and place of entry/exit (ports and airports). Only nonimmigrant visas are considered for balance of payments purposes. These sources will be supplemented by surveys of hotels, travel agencies, etc. to be carried out by the Ministry of Tourism.

For travel expenditures, the CBE estimates data from information derived from surveys on travelers and hotels on the length of stay and type of accommodation. The CBE applies the estimated average daily expenditure to the number of visitors recorded.

EGYPT

Transportation

The credit entries for transportation cover amounts received by Egyptian shipping and airline companies for freight and passenger services. Other transportation covers receipts of Suez Canal dues and receipts of the Suez Mediterranean oil pipeline for transporting foreign companies' oil through pipeline services.

The debit entries for transportation cover amounts transferred to foreign shipping and airline companies for freight and passenger services, as well as payments for freight on imports estimated from the c.i.f. value of imports (10 percent). The entries also include payments made for maintenance and repair of Egyptian ships and aircraft at foreign ports and airports.

Travel

For travel credit, compilers base the entries on the number of nights spent by tourists in Egypt (data from the Ministry of Tourism) and the average expenditure per night (CBE estimates based on a survey conducted by the Ministry of Tourism). Separate details are not available for business and personal travel.

The debit entries for travel cover expenditures of government officials and private employees traveling abroad, pilgrimage, expenditures of students studying abroad, training, technical and educational missions, and expenditures abroad for medical care.

EL SALVADOR

Transportation

The item includes freight and all modes of passenger transportation, including rental of transportation equipment with crew.

For freight transportation, CRB derives the credit data from surveys of enterprises operating in this field. It obtains debit data from customs forms, after deducting freight transportation carried out by resident enterprises.

For other forms of transportation, the credit data correspond to expenditure in the country by nonresident carriers. CRB obtains these data by means of surveys of these enterprises, supplemented with information from the Autonomous Executive Port Commission (CEPA). The debit data record expenditure abroad by resident enterprises.

For land and air transportation, CRB obtains the data from various resident and nonresident enterprises surveyed.

Travel

Credit and debt entries are based on travel surveys, conducted by a private enterprise. In turn, the data are based on the number of foreign visitors to the country and average stay and expenditure obtained from the travel survey.

ESTONIA

Transportation

The transportation services item is compiled mainly on the basis of the transportation companies survey and data from the ITRS. Information on resident passenger services rendered by nonresident companies is obtained mainly from the SSO. The BOPD conducts the transportation survey each quarter with nearly 400 local transport companies that provide international freight and passenger services. Most of these companies are involved in road transport, followed in importance by sea transport, air transport, and rail transport.

Travel

The main sources of information for travel services are the travel border survey conducted by SSO, in cooperation with the Eesti Pank, and border statistics, provided by the Board of Border Guard. These sources provide data on sales and purchases of travel packages, as well as on the number of foreign tourists visiting Estonia and the length of their stay. The same sources provide information on the number of Estonian residents visiting foreign countries and the length of their stay.

Relying on results of sample surveys, BOPD compiles cost-per-day estimates of such visits. Using statistical models, BOPD also models the number of citizens of EU countries and other Schengen Treaty participants who visit Estonia. As a result, the total amount of travel receipts and payments can be calculated.

The credit and debit entry for travel also includes approximately 50 percent of the net wages and salaries earned by nonresidents who have worked in Estonia and residents who have worked abroad for less than one year. Health-related and educational expenditures made by medical patients and students are treated as travel services.

Regular bilateral comparison is carried out every year and corrected if needed.

ETHIOPIA

Transportation

The NBE obtains data from transportation companies. A survey form prepared by the NBE's Balance of Payments Division is sent to these companies and compiled quarterly by the staff of the division. Data on freight debits are estimated as 9.24 percent of imports c.i.f., which is 8.95 percent for freight and 0.29 percent for transit fees on imports.

Travel

The FESMD provides data on travel receipts, while travel payment data reflecting payments made by residents to nonresident transport companies are obtained both from FESMD and Ethiopian Airlines (EAL).

FIJI

Transportation

FBS derives the data largely from its balance of payments survey covering resident and nonresident airlines, ports, and airports. Fiji's only resident airline, Air Pacific, operating on international routes, reports its passenger fare earnings from nonresidents. Ports and airport agencies provide aviation fees and charges, port dues, pilotage, and stevedoring. Foreign airlines provide figures on passenger fares earned from residents.

Travel

FBS derives travel credit entries from estimates of tourist expenditures and the per diem information, obtained from the International Visitor Survey (IVS), conducted by the Ministry of Tourism and Civil Aviation. Until the IVS results become available, FBS derives estimates of tourist expenditure per diem for the current reference period by inflating the per diem derived from the last IVS results by an index (referred to as the tourism expenditure index [TEI]). This index is calculated from the results of an FBS quarterly survey of hotels (TEI survey).

Travel debits are sourced entirely from the OET system.

FINLAND

Transportation

This category covers freight and passenger services by all modes of transport and port services. For sea transport, the BOF derives data from a quarterly survey of shipping companies; the survey seeks information on freight earnings from foreign traffic, passenger transport, and port expenditures abroad. For the estimates of freight that are deducted from imports in the trade statistics on the debit side (the cif-fob adjustment), the BOF derives the data from a survey conducted by the National Board of Customs.

For air transport and railway traffic, the BOF obtains data from Finnair, the National Board of Aviation, and the State Railways, respectively.

Travel

From 1999 onward, the data are based on border interviews and other tourism statistics conducted and compiled by Statistics Finland. Until 1998, data were derived from settlements reported by domestic banks; they included purchases of foreign currency by residents at home and abroad and sales of Finnish markkas to nonresidents in Finland and abroad. In addition, an estimate of foreign exchange transactions by Finnish residents abroad was added to travel income and expenditure. Other sources of information on travel included the use of travelers' checks and credit cards.

FRANCE

Transportation

The data are broken down by sea, air, and other transport and when significant, passenger and merchandise transportation services. The latter comprise an estimate of the portion of costs of transportation included in merchandise payments.

Travel

Data on travel are derived from payments by credit card and from two surveys on inward and outward travel. Since 2003, a distinction is made between business and other travel.

GABON

Transportation

For passenger services, the entries cover earnings of air, sea, and land carriers.

Travel

Entries cover expenditures in Gabon by foreign travelers (credit) and expenditures of Gabonese residents traveling abroad (debit) for all purposes (tourism, business, study, holiday, medical care, official missions, etc.) and by any means of payment (banknotes, checks, credit transfers, money orders, etc.).

GAMBIA

Transportation

Data for transportation services are derived from returns provided by the Gambia ports authority and Civil Aviation Authority. Credit entries comprise services provided to nonresidents through the Trans-Gambia and the Banjul-Barra ferries, airport fees, landing and parking fees, and port services. Debit entries cover freight services acquired by importers estimated to be 12.4 percent of the value of imports c.i.f., remittances for air tickets and port services, and foreign expenditure of the above-mentioned enterprises.

Travel

In calculating travel credit, a model based approach is used. The CBG's Economic Research Department uses data provided by the Gambia Tourism Authority (GTA). The estimated average out-of-pocket expenditure is equivalent to 500 dalasis per tourist multiplied by tourist arrivals to obtain total tourists expenditure. This is added to income from hotel beds and arrival and departure fees. Travel debits are derived from data supplied by parastatals and government departments on staff travel and education-related expenditures.

GEORGIA

Transportation

In addition to the estimates of freight mentioned above, the main data sources are information from the Georgian Railways Limited and from the Georgian ports and airports. The BPD also uses as data sources the indirect estimates based on information from the Department of Border Defense, regarding the means of transport and number of individuals entering and leaving the country.

Travel

The BPD compiles travel data on the basis of information from the regular household survey. It collects information on business travel from governmental institutions (ministries, departments, the NBG, etc.), as well as from the banking sector.

The BPD also uses, as data sources, the indirect estimates based on (1) information from the Department of Border Defense regarding the number of individuals entering and leaving the country, (2) expenses abroad of those individuals engaged in export-import operations in goods, and (3) expenses of those working abroad for less than one year.

GERMANY

Transportation

The ITRS provides data on passenger services and some basic information on freight services, broken down by modes of transport. For freight, reported data are not in all cases sufficiently detailed and need to be supplemented by estimates. These estimates are based on ratios, dating back to 1992, of freight services to the value of imports and exports of goods, broken down by mode of transport and by country. The ratios were derived from very detailed information that used to be available from foreign trade statistics before the introduction of the Intrastat system in 1993 and have remained constant since then.

Travel

For travel expenditures, the Bundesbank introduced a household sample survey in 2001 to cover for the loss of information on banknote transactions resulting from the introduction of the euro.

Formerly, most travel transactions were estimated on the basis of the following: bank reports on the purchase and sale of foreign currency (banknotes, travelers' checks) by residents and of domestic currency by nonresidents, reports on bank transfers by travelers and travel agencies, as well as credit and debit card transactions of residents abroad and of nonresidents in Germany.

The sample survey is conducted by a private institute on behalf of the Bundesbank on a continuous basis. Since the results are only available with a time lag of five to six months after the reference quarter, preliminary figures are based on Auto-Regressive Integrated Moving Average (ARIMA)-based estimates and are cross-checked with developments in monthly credit/debit card transactions.

For the travel credit side, Bundesbank compiles the account from ITRS reports and supplements it by partner country data and other secondary data sources, including the accommodation statistics of the FSO. The item includes the purchase of goods and services by border workers but excludes their income.

For the debit side, a breakdown between business travel and personal travel is available.

GHANA

Transportation

This category covers freight and passenger services by air, land, and sea transport, as well as services rendered and acquired at the ports. BOG's BOP Office therefore estimates entries for transportation services from information provided by the port authorities, airlines, and shipping companies, both local and foreign.

Entries for freight debits are estimated based on merchandise imported into the country within a given period. Freight for non-oil imports are estimated using 9 percent (covering both freight and insurance) of f.o.b value of the imports. In the future, the BOG will source estimates for freight directly from the trade reporting system. For oil imports, the office collects information on freight on imported oil from TOR, VRA, and AMOC, using 2.4 percent of the f.o.b value of imports. It estimates freight credits based on information provided by transportation companies.

Travel

The Ghana Tourist Board (the regulatory and monitoring governmental agency for tourism) has since 2005 been reporting data on estimates of expenditures abroad of returning Ghanaian residents and anticipated expenditures of nonresidents in Ghana.

GREECE

Transportation

BoG compiles the transportation items on the basis of settlements, supplemented with estimates derived from the conversion of imports from c.i.f. to f.o.b. Data are broken down by means of transport (sea, air, rail, and other means) as well as by transportation category (freight and passengers). The main category is sea transport-cross trading activity.

Travel

Prior to 2002, BoG compiled travel data on the basis of settlements. The introduction of the euro called for methodological changes in the compilation of travel data for balance of payments purposes. On a pilot basis in May 2002, BoG started a monthly frontier travel survey aimed at estimating travel expenditure and, since January 2003, has conducted the survey on a permanent basis.

GRENADA

See East Caribbean.

GUATEMALA

Transportation

For passenger services and other transportation services, the data source is the foreign exchange statistics.

Travel

For credits and debits, the BOG compiles the entries by combining the data on tourists arrivals and departures (provided by the Migration Directorate) with the following: estimates of their average daily expenditures and their average length of stay (provided by the Guatemalan Institute of Tourism, for credits) and the estimation on the amounts carried by Guatemalan travelers outside the country (from the foreign exchange statistics, and the Guatemalan Institute of Tourism, for debits).

The foreign exchange statistics also provide information on business travel, travel for medical treatment, study abroad, and official travel.

INTERNATIONAL MONETARY FUND (IMF) NOTES

GUINEA

Transportation

The central bank asks banks and mining companies to perform their own surveys to estimate freight and insurance for imports they have reported on a c.i.f. or cost & freight basis. Otherwise, the central bank makes the estimates.

With respect to other imports (chiefly grants and loans related to projects), compilers proceed in the manner described in *Goods* above.

Travel

The central bank uses this category to record over-the-counter exchange transactions conducted through the banking system, as well as mission expenses of civil servants and staff of the semipublic mining companies. When the travel purpose is not clear, compilers list the amounts under *personal travel*.

GUINEA-BISSAU

Transportation

This category covers freight and passenger services on all modes of transport, as well as port services. Debit entries are estimated on the basis of freight and insurance data obtained from the pre-import registration slip. Transportation costs are not usually declared on this slip. When necessary, expenditure on freight and insurance is estimated at 17.5 percent of c.i.f. imports.

Travel

For credit, compilers derive entries from surveys of commercial banks and hotels concerning the expenditure of foreign visitors. For debit, they derive entries from the records of banks and ministries.

GUYANA

Transportation

This category covers freight and passenger services for sea and air transport. Surveys are conducted to obtain these data.

Travel

Credit entries include all receipts from transactions in foreign currency at bank and nonbank cambios and travelers' checks encashed. Debit entries comprise purchases of travelers' checks and foreign currency sold at cambios.

HAITI

Transportation

Data on transportation services are estimated on the basis of information provided by the port and airport authorities and on the basis of annual surveys carried out at Haitian and foreign airlines and at shipping agencies. The debit entry for freight on imports includes insurance and is estimated at 7 percent of imports, c.i.f.

Travel

The Secretariat of State for Tourism gathers monthly statistics on the number of tourists in Haiti. Estimated income from travel is distributed under separate headings for tourists arriving by air, ship, and road, respectively. For those arriving by air, the number of tourists recorded during the period in question is multiplied by the average duration of their stay and by their estimated daily expenditures. Data coming from the airport authority related to the number of travelers are also used by the IED.

For those arriving by ship and spending a maximum of 24 hours in Haiti (excursionists), the number is multiplied by an estimate of the sum spent on the day in question. The number of tourists crossing the border is obtained from data of the central bank's Tax Operations Division on tolls paid at counters.

Travel debits are estimated based on the number of Haitians leaving the country.

HONDURAS

Transportation

This category covers freight and passenger services by all modes of transport, plus port services. The Economic Research Department derives the credit entries for transportation services from information provided by airport and seaport authorities and annual surveys of Honduran airline and shipping companies. It obtains debit entries for freight from information on freight and insurance reported in customs declaration forms, received monthly. The Economic Research Department obtains debit entries for passenger transportation by a survey of foreign airlines.

Travel

The department bases credit and debit entries for travel on surveys conducted by the Tourism Institute and the General Department of Migratory Policy. Estimates are compiled by combining the number of foreign visitors with estimates of average expenditures.

HONG KONG, CHINA

Services

The C&SD collects data on trade in services primarily from the *Annual Survey of Imports and Exports of Services* (ASIES), supplemented by results from other annual or quarterly surveys and administrative data sources. Data from administrative sources include those from the Hong Kong Tourism Board, the Immigration Department, and the Treasury. The value of financial intermediation services is indirectly measured using the "reference rate" method. Services data for 2006 presented in this *Yearbook* contain only the net balance and total credits and debits. A full breakdown of 11 service items will be compiled when the ASIES results for 2006 become available.

HUNGARY

Transportation

Up to 2004, MNB compiles the data. The primary data source (reports of monetary institutions) provided a breakdown by transportation category (passenger, freight, and other) but did not distinguish the means of transportation (sea, air, or other).

Since 2005, data have been compiled by the HCSO. The main source is the direct reporting of companies. Additionally, administrative data are used.

In addition to the primary information sources, which record transportation services on separate accounts, an adjustment (related to the change in the terms of delivery of goods) relies on the data derived from the external trade statistics. Transportation services are adjusted with a value equal to the adjustment in the terms of delivery of goods, but with the opposite sign. The estimation of the terms of delivery correction and its allocation between debits and credits for transportation services are based on bills of clearance. The estimation and allocation are carried out by the HCSO, and the data obtained are used by the MNB.

Travel

Since 2004, the travel item (both inbound and outbound) of balance of payments is compiled from results of border surveys. In the course of these surveys, Hungarians returning from abroad and foreigners leaving Hungary are asked about their travel-related expenses. Data include part of international transport fares and some other package tour elements (commission). Based on the survey results, the ITRS-based time series on travel have been revised going back to 2000.

Up to 2003, settlement data (reports by the MNB, commercial banks, exchange offices, and companies holding accounts abroad) were used for compiling travel services. Up to 2003, travel-related flows reported by banks and exchange offices were corrected with the following:

• The balance of cash transactions affecting households' foreign exchange accounts held at resident banks, as well as the balance of forint/foreign currency exchange transactions carried out at banks, were recorded under travel. As of 2003, relying on a direct survey of account holders (2000) and natural indicators, the MNB estimated separately the breakdown by various components (travel, income, current transfers, real estate investment) of the credit and debit entries for these cash transactions. It recorded the transaction values obtained under the appropriate items in the balance of payments. Simultaneously with the methodological switch, it had revised the time series going back to 1995.

• MNB primarily classified as travel the foreign exchange bought by exchange offices from residents. Therefore, as of 1998, travel receipts included the excess of foreign currency purchased by exchange offices from residents over a "benchmark" value (of a similar item in 1997 for the period between 1998 and 2000, and from 2001, an amount equaling 5 percent of travel expenditures in the previous month). Before 1998, MNB treated these transactions as re-exchange of foreign exchange previously bought for travel purposes by residents. It recorded them as correction entries to travel debit.

ICELAND

Transportation

The entries for transportation, freight, passenger, and port services are based on surveys of the main Icelandic airlines and shipping companies and estimates of other companies' data, based on bank reports on foreign exchange transactions.

Travel

Hospital, educational, and other travel services are estimated from the foreign exchange transactions reported by banks and payment card companies. Iceland is not able to distinguish between business and personal travel services from prevailing data sources.

INDIA

Transportation

This category covers all modes of transport and port services; RBI bases the data mainly on the receipts and payments reported by the banks in respect of transportation items. In addition to the foreign exchange transactions records, a source is the survey of unclassified receipts.

These sources are supplemented by information collected from major airline and shipping companies in respect of payments from foreign accounts. The RBI also uses a benchmark *Survey of Freight and Insurance on Exports* to estimate freight receipts on account of exports.

Travel

For travel, the RBI obtains data from foreign exchange transactions records, supplemented by information from the surveys of unclassified receipts. The estimates of travel receipts also use the information on foreign tourist arrivals and expenditure, received from the Ministry of Tourism, as a cross-check of the foreign exchange transactions and survey data.

INDONESIA

Transportation

This category covers freight, passenger, and other by all modes of transport. Entries for the value of freight debits are mainly estimated on the basis of information on freight furnished in customs declaration forms.

For passenger and freight credits, the BI collects data from the ITRS. Data on passenger transportation debits are estimated based on a survey of travelers and average air fares derived from a survey of travel agencies.

Other transportation includes foreign exchange receipts for use of seaport and airport facilities. The seaport and airport authorities report these data.

Travel

For travel credits and debits, BI derives entries from censuses and surveys conducted by the Ministry of Tourism and the Central Bureau of Statistics. Estimates are made by combining the number of foreign visitors and the number of Indonesian travelers abroad with estimation of their average expenditures. It should be noted that part of the travel debit item is accounted for by *hajj* pilgrimages.

IRAN, ISLAMIC REPUBLIC OF

Services

The entries for transactions in services cover passenger services, freight and insurance, travel, and other public and private services—most of which are derived from the foreign exchange records of the banking system and from reports on receipts and payments provided by banks. The largest debit items are freight, other business services, and insurance, whereas the largest credit items are government and other business services.

Freight and insurance services are estimated based on the information on transportation undertaken by residents, which the central bank obtains from the foreign exchange records of the banking system. To compare and adjust this figure, the CBI uses reports from the major land transportation companies. It also includes an adjustment on the basis of statistics supplied by maritime transportation companies.

For other services items, the central bank obtains data from the foreign exchange records of the banking system, which are recorded on a cash basis. Other services items include travel (university students and patients), other transport services (transportation companies), public services (including membership fees paid to international organizations), commissions, financial services, and cultural services (purchase of books and articles from abroad).

To derive the travel entreis, the CBI uses statistics released by the Iran Touring and Tourism Organization (prepared for the World Tourism Organization) and a household budget questionnaire.

IRELAND

Transportation

Because merchandise imports have been valued on an f.o.b. basis since 1998, the freight element of the c.i.f. to f.o.b. adjustment on merchandise imports is now split and included under the transportation and insurance service headings. Apart from this, the CSO collects data primarily by means of quarterly inquiries to resident airline and shipping companies.

Passenger fares paid by residents of Ireland to foreign transport companies generally cannot be distinguished and are instead included in the travel (debit) item. Disbursements in Irish ports and airports by foreign carriers, time charters, and other receipts from abroad by Irish carriers are included in the air and sea transport items. These data are collected from administrative sources.

Travel

Data are based on estimates of the number of travelers and their per capita expenditures, provided internally by the CSO's Tourism and Travel Section. These estimates of the number of travelers cover those traveling by public carriers (based on information supplied by sea, air, and land transport companies operating in international traffic) and those traveling privately by road across the Northern Ireland border.

Expenditures by Irish residents abroad and by foreign visitors to Ireland are estimated from information from the large sample survey of travelers (i.e., the *Passenger Card Inquiry*) conducted by the CSO, as well as information from CSO's *Household Travel Survey*. See also information under *Transportation* above.

ISRAEL

Transportation

The major sources for freight and transportation are Israeli companies that operate ships and aircraft on international routes, foreign shipping and aviation companies that operate in Israel, the Ports Authority in Israel, ship and aircraft repair companies, companies that supply food and bunker oil to ships and aircraft, and the Civil Aviation Service of the Ministry of Transport.

Transactions include receipts resulting from the transport of cargo by foreign carriers temporarily leased by Israeli companies. The data also include receipts and payments by ships owned by Israeli subsidiaries under a foreign flag (convenience flag), operated by Israeli agents only.

Some reports of Israeli shipping and aviation companies include a detailed breakdown of expenditures according to type of currency and not according to the location of the expenditures—in Israel or abroad. Compilers correct or adjust the item *other expenditures* in these reports (which includes information from other sources), such as the purchase of tickets for travel abroad by Israelis in foreign currency or the purchase in Israel of bunker oil in foreign currency.

Beginning in 1971, repairs of Israeli ships and aircraft performed abroad by foreign insurance agents have been included in expenditures of Israeli shipping and aviation companies. At the same time, these expenditures have been recorded as income from insurance claims in the insurance item. Until 1971, this listing, as well as that included in the insurance item, was a net figure.

Travel

For estimation of credit entries, compilers use a semiannual survey of foreign tourists, conducted by the Ministry of Tourism and under the supervision of the Central Bureau of Statistics (CBS). The survey provides the average expenditure per tourist during each half year, while the total expenditure of foreign tourists is estimated according to the average expenditure and the total number of tourists leaving Israel each quarter. (This latter figure is obtained from the statistics of the CBS Demography Department.)

Debits are estimated on the basis of a quarterly updated survey conducted by the CBS for 1997, regarding the average expenditure per tourist, and on current data on departures abroad of Israel residents, published by the CBS.

ITALY

Transportation

Passenger transport items were estimated on the basis of the sample survey of transport enterprises and the UIC sample survey of international tourism (for data on the number of passengers). Starting from 2002, both passengers' transport costs and number of passengers are derived from the survey on international tourism.

Travel

Up to 1989, the data were compiled from transfers related to international trips for tourism, business, health, and education purposes and from credit card transactions. A monthly sample survey of travelers, introduced in 1996 and covering about 60 border points, has now become the main source of data for travel services. The survey provides a detailed breakdown by purpose of the travel, according to the supplementary items indicated in *BPM5*. Historical data for 1990–95 have been revised and adjusted in a linear manner with the results of the survey.

JAMAICA

Transportation

This category covers freight and passenger services by all types of transportation. The Port and Airport Authorities of Jamaica provide data for port services. The BOJ also derives data from annual surveys of the national airlines, foreign airlines, and shipping companies. It obtains information on passenger services from surveys of national airlines and foreign airlines. Data for freight are estimated at 15 percent of non-oil imports (c.i.f.) and 4 percent of oil imports (c.i.f.).

Travel

Compilers derive travel credits from expenditure surveys carried out by the Jamaica Tourist Board. Credit data also come from immigration statistics on the number of visitors and their average length of stay. Travel debits are compiled from banking records and from data supplied by the Ministry of Labor.

JAPAN

Transportation

Regarding payments for transportation services, the data compilers obtain the data mainly from the reports submitted by international shipping and airline companies, as well as the Payments Reports. This item includes the value of freight, deducted from the value of imports in the trade statistics. Distinctions between subitems, such as *sea transportation* and *air transportation*, depend on types of transportation methods.

Travel

The main sources of data, used to estimate the amount of the goods and services acquired from an economy by travelers, are survey results on expenditures of foreign travelers in Japan and Japanese overseas travelers. The data on per capita expenditure of these travelers are estimated by utilizing the number of such travelers, released by the Japan National Tourist Organization.

Other expenditures, not covered by this survey, are estimated by utilizing data from other sources. For example, data on the expenditures of long-term international students are estimated by using data published by government agencies. In addition, data on large amounts of medical expenses are obtained from the Payments Reports. The distinction between business and personal travel is made by detailed information of the survey results and other sources.

JORDAN

Transportation

For credit and debit entries for transportation services (freight and passenger), CBJ derives data from information provided by Aqaba Port Authority and by airline shipping and land companies, respectively. CBJ records entries for freight credits on the basis of data on freight and other transportation extracted from ITRS forms.

The breakdown between "passengers" and "other transportation" is estimated based on available information and indicators from the main transportation companies. Entries for freight debits are estimated at 9 percent of c.i.f. imports.

Travel

For travel, CBJ bases entries on the number of departures and arrivals, provided by the Ministry of Tourism and Antiquities in cooperation with the Ministry of Interior, and on the results of tourism surveys, conducted by DOS. These surveys provide information on the average expenditure of foreign tourists coming into Jordan and resident tourists traveling abroad, and on the average duration of stay.

Compilers use data on the number of Jordanians studying abroad—sourced from the Ministry of Higher Education—to estimate education expenditures abroad; these estimates are included in the travel debits.

KAZAKHSTAN

Transportation

This category covers all modes of transport and port services. NBK bases the data for passenger fares and port charges mainly on reports it collects from marine shipping, airline, railway, and road companies.

Freight includes the data reported by cargo enterprises and estimated transportation of goods carried from/to the frontier countries and the rest of the countries. Freight estimates for frontier countries and for the rest of the countries are based on the yearly survey and used for the data beginning in 2000.

Travel

NBK estimates data on travel on the basis of estimated average expenditures, number of residents traveling abroad and nonresidents traveling in Kazakhstan, and the estimated duration of their stay. Also available is information on travelers by country of origin or destination and type of travel.

KENYA

Transportation

This category covers passenger fares, freight services by all modes of transport, and port services. The credit entries are derived from information obtained from Kenya Railways, sea transport, air road, inland waterway (Lake Victoria), and pipeline transport firms. Data on passenger fares, port services, and leases are obtained from Kenya Airways (KA), the Kenya Airport Authority (KAA), Nairobi Airport Services, bus companies, and Kenya Ports Authority. Port services include services to shipping lines.

Travel

Data are obtained from CBK returns on invisible transactions. Plans are underway to conduct a sample survey of departing visitors, to which regular monthly data on travel receipts from the CBK's foreign exchange record can be benchmarked.

KOREA, REPUBLIC OF

Transportation

For transportation services, the BOK derives entries from the KFX and surveys of resident airlines and shipping companies. The KFX data provide a breakdown by transportation category (i.e., passenger transportation, freight, or other transportation).

Travel

The KFX data include both nonresidents' sales of foreign currency in Korea and residents' purchases of foreign currency in Korea. The KFX also covers the use of traveler's checks and credit cards. Business and personal travel will be distinguished from 2006 onward.

KUWAIT

Transportation

The KAC provides information on passenger tickets. For the freight component, CBK calculates estimates as a percentage of imports. The CBK's estimates for shipping services on imports allocate 95 percent of estimated freight services and 80 percent of estimated insurance services as balance of payments flows to foreign carriers and providers. For credit entries, CBK compiles estimates for transportation services provided to nonresidents from reports provided by the KOTC and other shipping companies.

For the *other transportation* item, CBK compiles estimates of expenses abroad on the basis of data provided by the KAC and Kuwaiti shipping companies. On the credit side, CBK compiles estimates from questionnaires and reports provided by the KAC, Kuwaiti shipping companies, the Kuwait Ports Authority (for port dues), and the General Directorate of Civil Aviation (for airport dues). These estimates include transport and storage services provided to the international coalition forces stationed in Kuwait and Iraq from 2003 onwards.

Travel

The central bank compiles estimates of travel debits on the basis of questionnaires answered by travel agencies, surveys implemented by CBK (the last of which took place March-September 2000), and reports submitted by government agencies on expenses paid for education, conferences, training, medical treatment, and official missions abroad. For credit entries, the CBK calculates estimates based on the number of nonresident visitors to Kuwait and their average expenditures. The Immigration Department provides a figure on the number of nonresident visitors.

KYRGYZSTAN

Transportation

The NSC collects data from domestic airlines, railway, and road transportation companies. NBKR supplements these data with information it collects from enterprises and ITRS. It derives freight on imports provided by nonresidents from the estimated freight included in the c.i.f. value of imports and adjusted to exclude transportation provided by resident carriers.

INTERNATIONAL MONETARY FUND (IMF) NOTES

Travel

The NSC assesses travel services on the basis of the estimated average per diem expenditures, number of residents traveling abroad and nonresidents traveling in the Kyrgyz Republic, and the estimated duration of their stay. The SCI provides data on the number of travelers, country of origin (for foreign travelers), country of destination (for domestic travelers), and types of travel (private, business, etc.).

LAO PEOPLE'S DEMOCRATIC REPUBLIC

Transportation

This item covers freight, passenger transportation by overflights, and other types of transportation. The BOL's Operation Department provides data on overflights, and the remaining elements are based on BOL staff estimates.

Travel

Credit entries are derived from information in surveys conducted by the National Tourism Authority of Lao P.D.R., including the number of visitors arriving in the country, the number of overnight stays, and the estimated average expenditure.

Debit entries are derived from data from the Receipts and Payments reporting system provided by the commercial banks, and some data are estimated by BOP staff.

LATVIA

Transportation

Compilers obtain data from the quarterly survey of transportation and intermediary services and the statistics on nonbanks' external payments (ITRS). Data cover transportation services rendered/received by mode of transport. In addition, staff use foreign trade statistics to obtain, in accordance with the calculation methodology described in the section "Goods," the difference between c.i.f. and f.o.b. values of imported goods. The share of transportation services carried out by nonresidents is set apart from the obtained figure and included under transportation in the balance of payments.

For credit entries for passenger transportation by air, reporting agents declare total amounts received for the international carriage of passengers in the quarterly survey on transportation and intermediary services. The compilers use the data on the monthly number of residents and nonresidents crossing the state border, broken down by mode of transportation, for calculating the proportion of nonresidents in total border crossings. They use this ratio to determine the nonresident part of the international carriage of passengers broken down by mode of transportation.

Debit entries are obtained by calculation, using 1) data on the number of departing passengers by airlines, submitted by the Riga international airport, 2) CSB data on the monthly number of residents and nonresidents crossing the state border by air, and 3) information on the average prices of airline tickets.

Travel

Compilers derive the data on travel from the CSB aggregated data on persons entering and leaving the country. Travelers are polled at border control points four times a year to obtain information about nonresident spending in Latvia and resident spending abroad. Using mathematical methods, the compilers calculate the average spending of a traveler and, thereafter, obtain travelers' total spending. The number of travelers is available from the State Border Guard of the Republic of Latvia, which registers persons entering and leaving the country.

For personal travel credit entries, compilers estimate expenditures of students, using the number of foreign students in Latvia, submitted by the Ministry of Education and universities. For debit entries, compilers use the information submitted by foreign embassies in Latvia on the number of Latvia's students and average expenditures by country.

LEBANON

Transportation

Only public sector operations are recorded before 2003. Using the information obtained from the ITRS, as of 2003, ESS also includes data on private sector transactions (banks, the nonbank financial sector, and the private sector, comprising households and private companies). This section also comprises freight transactions, estimated by applying a 7.5 percent average rate on the value of imports c.i.f. The obtained figure is subdivided among the sea, air, and other transport sections according to the weights obtained from the records of goods by the different ports of entry.

Travel

ESS bases estimates on the General Directorate of General Security data on arriving and departing travelers through all borders and on an evaluation of the average spending per individual.

It also derives statistics from basic circular #1564, dated October 3, 1997, decision # 6754. (This circular was replaced by circular #63, dated June 10, 1999, decision #7299, amended for the last time with intermediary circular #24, dated August 26, 2002, decision #8216, related to ATMs and credit cards.) ESS adds these statistics to the data with the aim of improving the estimate of tourist expenditures and revenues. This circular covers all transactions done via automated teller machines (ATMs), as well as debit and credit cards, to keep track of nonresident expenditures in Lebanon and resident expenditures abroad.

As of 2003, data from the ITRS have been added, giving this item a wider statistical coverage.

LESOTHO

Transportation

Data on passenger services/air travel are obtained through a continuous survey covering travel agencies in Lesotho. Data on port services are obtained from the Department of Civil Aviation.

Travel

Data on expenditure by foreign visitors to Lesotho are obtained from the Lesotho Tourism Development Corporation (LTDC), which phased out the old Lesotho Tourist Board (LTB). Data on expenditure by Lesotho residents on trips abroad are obtained from foreign exchange declaration forms. Data on expenditure by government funded Basotho students studying abroad are obtained from the National Manpower Development Secretariat. Data on expenditure by private funded Basotho students studying abroad are obtained from the exchange control records.

The National University of Lesotho and the Center for Accounting Studies provide data on foreign students studying in Lesotho. Lesotho Agricultural College and Lesotho College of Education (formerly known as the National Teachers Training College) also provide information on fees and living expenditures by foreign students, although the figures are small.

LIBYAN ARAB REPUBLIC

Transportation

The item includes passenger and freight services. CBL derives the data mainly from commercial bank records.

Travel

CBL obtains data on travel (for tourism, education, and medical expense) credits and debits from its records and commercial banks.

LITHUANIA

Transportation

This category includes cargo and passenger transportation services using all means of transportation, including seaport and airport services. The primary data source is the quarterly survey of the cross-border transactions of nonbank entities with nonresidents, conducted by SL. The quarterly survey is supplemented by a comprehensive annual survey of small road transport operators, covering their quarterly and annual transactions. Approximately 1,000 enterprises provide the data.

Travel

Travel services include all goods and services acquired by travelers in foreign countries. (A person living in a country in which he/she is not a resident for less than one year is considered a traveler.) Services for international passenger transportation (i.e., the transportation of passengers between countries) are not included in the travel item. Such services belong to the category of passenger transportation services.

Data on travel services are calculated on the basis of (1) the monthly data on the number of incoming foreigners from non-EU countries and departing residents from Lithuania, provided by the State Border Guard Service at the Ministry of the Interior; (2) the Department of Tourism's annual selective research on incoming foreigners and their average expenditure and length of stay; (3) the SL selective research on Lithuanian travelers and their average expenditure and length of stay; and (4) the data of quarterly surveys of enterprises providing accommodation services (hotels, health spa, etc.) and of enterprises involved in sales of touring packages.

LUXEMBOURG

Travel

The main sources are surveys, other statistics, and administrative data. Compilers record under business travel the personal expenditures on goods and services by nonresident cross-border workers.

MACAO, CHINA

Transportation

The data on passenger, freight, and other transportation are obtained from statistics of various activity surveys and national accounts. Because the current survey system does not differentiate the value of this service among different modes of transportation, no breakdown on the type of transportation is available.

Travel

Credit entries for travel are mainly derived from national account statistics that include travelers' expenditures on gaming, accommodation, and other expenses, utilizing data of the Visitor Expenditure Survey, Hotel Survey, and administrative records on hotel and gaming receipts. Gaming expenditures of nonresidents are estimated based on an appropriate method and proportion applied to the gross gaming receipts on administrative records.

Travelers' expenditures on accommodation are estimated from the number of room nights sold and the average room rates, whereas expenditures on other areas are estimated by using the number of visitor arrivals, per capita spending of visitors, and other tourism data. The split between business and personal travel is based on purpose of visit reported by interviewed visitors.

Entries for business travel (debit) are mainly derived from the enterprise surveys and activity surveys, whereas those for personal travel (debit) are principally extracted from national account statistics that are mainly estimated from the Household Budget Survey and other statistics.

MALAWI

Transportation

The main subcomponents of transport are passenger, freight, and landing fees. Credits on passenger and freight transportation relate mostly to air transport, collected from the sole domestic airline operator, Air Malawi.

Debits are derived from the adjustment of imports c.i.f. to f.o.b. by applying a 15 percent fixed factor for freight and insurance, which is fully attributed to air freight. In the medium term, the 15 percent will be split between freight and insurance so that the latter can be classified under insurance services in accordance with *BPM5*.

Statistics on landing fees are obtained from the Civil Aviation Department for the credit side, and from Air Malawi for the debit side.

Travel

Data on travel debits are obtained from the exchange control records through forms that are completed for purchases and sales of foreign currency from authorized dealers. Credits are compiled on the basis of exit cards completed by tourists returning abroad to their original economies. The data tend to underestimate credits on travel.

MALAYSIA

Transportation

This category covers freight and passenger services by all modes of transport and port services. For transportation services, DSM derives entries from quarterly information provided by airport and seaport authorities, Malaysian airline and shipping companies, and an annual survey of foreign airline companies in Malaysia.

Travel

For travel credits, the DSM derives entries from expenditure surveys of foreign visitors carried out by the Tourism Malaysia. Estimates are compiled by combining the number of foreign visitors with estimates of average expenditures.

For travel debits, the DSM derives entries from the BNM records, supplemented with information provided by the Pilgrimage Fund Board and other ministries and agencies.

MALDIVES

Transportation

This category covers transportation of passengers, freight, and other items. ERSD obtains data on passenger services and port services from MACL, Maldives Ports Authority, and Maldives National Shipping Limited (MNSL).

Travel

Travel credits (receipts) are MMA estimates based on data obtained from MOTCA regarding tourist arrivals, tourist bednights, and room rates in resorts and hotels. Estimates are adjusted for seasonality.

MMA calculates travel receipts in three parts: receipts by tour operators, purchases at resorts, and expenditure outside of resorts. The first item, receipts by tour operators, is calculated by multiplying bed nights by an estimated average daily expenditure. The other two items are aimed at covering the cost of incidentals, souvenirs, and similar—that is, any expenditure other than what is spent on the tour package. MMA calculates purchases at resorts on the basis of a per diem estimate, while it bases estimates of expenditure outside of resorts on numbers of arrivals.

For travel debits, MMA obtains estimates from various sources: Business travel covers expenditures relating to government travel and travel for tourism fairs, data for which are obtained from the foreign exchange records maintained by MMA and the MOTCA, respectively. For personal travel, the health-related expenditure component is also obtained from the foreign exchange records of MMA and includes social security releases made for medical treatment.

For expenditure on education-related travel, MMA obtains estimates from the Ministry of Higher Education, Employment, and Social Security (MHES), which provides information on expenses associated with scholarships under the Education and Training project.

For other travel, estimates are derived as the sum of total expenditure on hajj travel (obtained from hajj tour organizers and relevant government authorities) and the residual between the estimate of total expenditures by Maldivian travelers and travel under the other categories.

MALI

Transportation

Data on passenger services are collected from national and foreign airlines.

Travel

The amounts posted as credits to this account are determined from the results of surveys of the Tourism Commissioner's Office and of hotels concerning arrivals of foreign tourists and hotel occupancy.

The debits posted are mainly expenditure by non-Malian residents on leave. This expenditure is estimated on the basis of the income of expatriates working in the private sector, compensation of technical assistance personnel and non-Malian permanent staff in international organizations, as well as the length of leave of these groups of persons.

However, the figures pertaining to government missions are sourced from the National Directorate of the Treasury and Public Accounting.

Expenditure by Malian students abroad is estimated from scholarships. Data on these scholarships, whether foreign or granted by the Malian government, are basically collected from the Ministry of Higher Secondary Education and Scientific Research.

MALTA

Transportation

The source for passenger transportation, separated by mode of transport, is the monthly survey of airline and shipping companies.

Travel

Regarding travel, NSO derives gross earnings from tourism from its frontier surveys—TOURSTAT and CRUISTAT. Data have been revised back to 1995 for comparability.

Gross expenditure by residents traveling abroad is derived from information provided by the Tourism unit within the NSO. This is replacing the previous source, emanating from foreign currency transactions that banking institutions and other authorized dealers reported to the CBM on a monthly basis.

MAURITIUS

Transportation

The main data sources are the survey of airline and shipping companies (quarterly since 1999; half-yearly prior to then) and the CSO. Transportation credits measure receipts by domestic carriers from passenger fares, freight on exports and shipments between other countries, and other port disbursements. Transportation debits measure payments made to nonresident carriers for passenger fares, freight on imports, and other port disbursements.

Travel

Travel credits are estimated from purchases by banks of foreign exchange from tourists, business travelers, hotels, cash dealers, and traders. Travel debit estimates are derived from the banking records of banks.

MEXICO

Transportation

For passenger fares, BM estimates the entries from information provided by the resident airlines on their total earnings on international transportation. It supplements these estimates with information from migration statistics on the number of residents and nonresidents traveling by air and from travel surveys on expenditures on ticket purchases by travelers.

Travel

BM bases credit entries on the immigration authorities' reports on the number of nonresidents visiting Mexico and on its own sample surveys on travelers' average expenditure. It obtains the debit entries using a similar procedure.

Travel is broken down into tourists and excursionists (one-day visitors). Tourists are defined as those who have spent at least one night in the host country and as those who, having not spent at least one night in the host country, have visited it beyond the border area; excursionists are defined as those who have not spent the night in the host country. No distinction is made between business and personal travel.

MONGOLIA

Transportation

Mongolian Railways and Mongolian Airlines (MIAT) report information for the credit and debit entries for passenger fares and other distributive and auxiliary services. From imports c.i.f. to an f.o.b. conversion, 10.0 percent of the total import data are estimated to add to the debit side of transportation.

Regarding port services credits, the ID derives entries from ITRS data, as well as from the report of Mongolia's Civil Aviation Authority. It derives the debit entries from MIAT. The credit entries for port services represent payments by foreign airlines for the use of facilities at the airport in Ulaanbaatar.

Travel

Up to 1996, the ID derived credit and debit entries for travel from the foreign exchange record. From 1997 onward, travel is estimated on the basis of information on the number of travelers combined with an estimate of the average duration of stay and an estimate of the per capita expenditures. The General Authority for Border Protection of Mongolia compiles the data on the number of travelers, while the National Tourism Agency of the Ministry of Roads, Transportation, and Tourism estimates and provides the average number of nights per visit and the average daily expenditure.

MONTSERRAT

See East Caribbean.

MOROCCO

Transportation

This item records, on both the credit and debit sides, payments relating to the transportation of goods and passengers, broken down by means of transportation: sea, air, and other.

Travel

Travel credits correspond to receipts from abroad received by tourism sector operators (travel agencies, hotels, clubs, tourist transportation, etc.). Receipts include encashment of travelers' checks and international credit card payments, as well as foreign currency banknotes exchanged via the banking system by tourists during their stay in Morocco. These credits also include part of the foreign currency banknotes exchanged by Moroccans residing abroad that are used to cover their board and lodging in Morocco.

Debit entries cover the various allocations of foreign banknotes to residents when they travel for purposes of tourism, business, education, medical care, training and missions, or pilgrimages. Debits also cover bank or postal transfers made to cover expenses incurred during this travel.

MOZAMBIQUE

Transportation

The BM compiles data on transportation services from reports presented by the authorized foreign exchange banks and from balance of payments surveys. Since 1995, it has introduced specific surveys of selected transportation companies (railways, national airlines, and shipping). Very recently, owing to the process of improving the collection of transportation data by the Balance of Payment Service of the BM, the response rate of the surveys has improved substantively.

Travel

Data on travel credits and debits are based on reports presented by the authorized foreign exchange banks, exchange bureaus, central bank, and the country's main tourism authorities. A specific survey has been introduced in various hotels in the country. However, the response rate is low.

MYANMAR

Transportation

This item includes freight and passenger services for all modes of transport and port services. The source is the ITRS.

Travel

In compiling the travel item, the CBM uses the ITRS source, supplemented with estimates derived from data from the Immigration and Population Department for the number of tourists and from the Ministry of Hotels and Tourism for total travel expenditure.

NAMIBIA

Transportation

This component is estimated from the external trade data and data from a survey of airlines. In 1995, a specific survey was instituted, but the response rate was very low, owing to a lack of cooperation from the reporting units (i.e., the national airlines, railways, and road transport operators) and the lack of awareness of the importance of balance of payments statistics among the respondents. However, RD is now able to obtain a reasonable response rate from the main airlines.

Travel

Data on travel credits and debits are estimated on the basis of the Exit Survey 2002 contracted by the Ministry of Environment and Tourism because of the absence of comprehensive data. Estimates of data on travelers arriving in and departing from Namibia are made on the basis of information from a variety of sources, including the Ministry of Home Affairs, national airlines, and various hotels in the country.

NEPAL

Transportation

This category includes freight and passenger services by all modes of transport. The data are collected from commercial banks, the NRB, Indian airlines having offices in Nepal, and domestic airlines for three main categories—freight, passenger services, and other transportation. The main credit items are the foreign exchange earnings of local airlines on passenger services and enterprises engaged in land transport. Debits reflect mainly freight charges, passenger services, and payments made to the foreign transport companies.

Travel

Data on travel are collected from the ITRS and the NRB's Foreign Exchange Management Department. This item includes, as credits, the receipts from foreign visitors in the form of cash, travelers' checks, drafts, etc. and the foreign exchange earnings from nonresidents of local hotels, travel agencies, and certain service agencies.

The item includes, as debits, the residents' expenditures abroad for business and personal travel, education expenses, medical treatment, and passport facilities (foreign exchange facilities provided to Nepalese passport holders going abroad).

NETHERLANDS

Services

As of the second quarter of 2003, Statistics Netherlands has been producing quarterly data on international trade in services. To that end, it adopted a new quarterly survey. In 2005 the reporting population for this survey comprised a sample of about 2,200 reporting agents (approximately 7 percent of the total population). A small number of large entities directly reports. In addition,

Statistics Netherlands surveys a larger number of small and medium enterprises with less detail. The results are grossed up to a national level.

NEW ZEALAND

Transportation

The main types of transportation services data collected are for the carriage of goods (freight) and passengers. Also included under transportation services are charters of carriers, tugboat services, airport and harbor fees, and goods consumed by carriers in the course of their operations, including bunkering and provisioning. These data are provided from quarterly and annual surveys of resident airlines and shipping companies, nonresident airlines (through their New Zealand offices), and New Zealand agents acting for nonresident ship operators.

Travel

Data on the expenditure of overseas tourists in New Zealand are derived from the International Visitors' Survey (IVS), conducted by a marketing company for the New Zealand Ministry of Tourism. In January 2003, the sampling in the IVS was changed to a "flight-based" basis. Flight-based sampling is a nonrandom method of sampling, allowing the specific targeting of passengers with certain characteristics that are to be represented in the sample of international visitors. Data on the characteristics of passengers are generated from the departure cards of passengers. The sample is selected from departing visitors at New Zealand's three largest international airports—Auckland, Wellington, and Christchurch.

Estimates are also made for expenditure on education- and health-related travel by nonresidents. The estimates for education-related travel are derived from a Survey of English Language Providers and New Zealand Ministry of Education data. Health expenditure is derived from Crown Health Entity data.

Information on the expenditure of New Zealand residents traveling overseas is derived from a model that uses information obtained from a benchmark survey of returned New Zealand travelers.

NICARAGUA

Transportation

Credit entries for freight are estimated on the basis of information provided by Customs. For freight services obtained by importers, BCN uses data recorded in the customs declarations. For air passenger services, it bases the data on an annual enterprise survey. Data on other transport include services reported by the National Ports Enterprise.

Travel

To estimate credit and debit entries, BCN combines information provided by the Directorate General of Migration and Aliens (on the number of nonresident and resident travelers and the average stay) with information derived from the annual survey undertaken by the Institute of Tourism (on the travelers' expenditures) plus the BCN's External Programming Department's estimates.

NIGERIA

Transportation

This category of services covers all modes of transportation plus port services. In the non-oil sector, credit entries reflect receipts from freight, passenger services, and port services that Nigeria provides to nonresidents. RSD obtains the data from bank returns made to the TED. Debit entries cover freight charges accruable to foreign carriers; these are estimated by adjusting the derived freight value for local components. Currently, freight cost is estimated at 10 percent of the c.i.f. value of imports.

Travel

For non-oil sector travel data (private), RSD obtains data from authorized dealers' returns to the TED, not broken down into the relevant components. Thus, the item does not provide separately the data on personal and business travel. The FOD cash flow statement captures foreign exchange disbursements on official travel. The oil sector travel item is estimated to move in tandem with the level of crude oil production activities.

NORWAY

Transportation

The estimation of receipts from the provision of maritime freight and passenger services of nonresidents is based on the ocean transport survey compiled by SN. Compiled both on an annual and quarterly basis, the ocean transport survey is based on reports from shipping companies on both operating income and expenditures broken down by type of transportation.

Travel

Through 2004, entries for travel were based almost entirely upon data supplied by NCB on the sale of local currency in exchange for foreign currency, supplemented with data from credit card companies. From 2005 onward, the sources have been changed toward tourist statistics (i.e., accommodation statistics, passenger transport statistics) and travel surveys.

OMAN

Transportation

Data on transportation credits reflect the value of services provided to nonresidents at Omani ports. The CBO takes these data, representing payments of port dues, stevedoring, and demurrage charges, from the annual statements of the Port Services Corporation Ltd. Debit entries include estimated freight values on imports.

Travel

Travel credit estimates are based on the number of foreign tourist arrivals as provided by the immigration authorities, multiplied by the average expenditure per tourist as estimated through a comprehensive survey.

Travel debits represent the estimated expenditure of students studying abroad, Omani pilgrims abroad, and health treatment received by Omani nationals abroad. Debits include estimates of expenditure by Omani residents abroad.

In 2003, a change in the methodology to compile statistics on travel data took into account the findings of a new tourism survey.

PAKISTAN

Transportation

This component covers all modes of transport and port services. Surveys of foreign shipping companies and airlines and the reporting of Pakistani shipping companies and airlines provide data for the freight, passenger, and other services components.

Travel

Data for both business and personal travel are collected through receipts and payments of the banking sector, plus the inward and outward remittances on travel through the exchange companies operating in Pakistan.

Further, the travel expenses of the crews of foreign shipping companies and airlines while on stay in Pakistan and the travel expenses of the crews of local shipping companies and airlines while on stay abroad are collected through surveys of the respective companies/airlines.

PALESTINE (WEST BANK/GAZA)

Transportation

This item consists of the transportation costs of passengers and goods, as well as auxiliary services, such as storage, cargo handling, etc. The data are obtained from economic surveys conducted by the PCBS. The data also include an estimate for the freight element of the c.i.f./f.o.b. adjustment to the foreign trade statistics, namely, 8 percent of the c.i.f. value of imports.

Travel

The main sources used to compile the data on travel credits and debits are economic surveys, a hotel survey, the Balance of Payments Annex with a labor force survey (LFS), and data from the Ministry of Islamic Affairs, the Ministry of Health, and the Ministry of High Education.

These surveys and administrative records cover (for the debit data) all travel transactions of residents abroad, such as students abroad, medication costs abroad, part of the wages of Palestinian border workers in Israel, and the expenditure of pilgrims.

The credit data cover nonresidents coming to the Palestinian Territories, such as tourists, foreign employees of consulates, representatives, international organizations, and those visiting relatives, etc.

PANAMA

Transportation

DSC derives information on freight on imports from customs declarations. It obtains data on passenger services from surveys of national airlines and agents of foreign airlines. For port services, it obtains data from agents of foreign air and shipping lines, national airlines, container terminals ports, and the Panama Canal Authority (for tolls and other services to Canal users).

Travel

DSC bases data on sample surveys it conducts in conjunction with the Panamanian Tourism Institute, on the expenditures of foreign visitors in Panama and of Panamanian residents on their trips abroad, and on information derived from migration statistics on the number of travelers.

PAPUA NEW GUINEA

Transportation

Transportation services include receipts and payments from freight, port handling, or other transportation-related services on traded goods.

Travel

Travel data cover passenger services by all modes of transport and port services related to the transportation of passengers. The data include tickets, hotel rooms, airport taxes, and other travel expenses and receipts. A separate component of travel shows education-related expenditures, including all tutorial fees and remittances or receipts associated with education at all levels.

PARAGUAY

Transportation

The main sources for freight data are shipment documents and surveys of land, air, and inland waterway transportation companies. Other sources to compile this item include the report on soya exports of the Paraguayan Chamber of Cereals and Oleaginous Products Exporters, regional reports prepared by the Ministry of Public Works, and the report on goods exported via inland waterways from the State Merchant Marine. The CBP obtains data to compile passenger services from the Capital Police, which reports the number of passengers entering and leaving the country using different carriers (air or land), multiplied by the ticket prices collected in surveys of local tourism operators.

Travel

Concerning inward tourism, the CBP obtains data monthly from the Directorate General of Tourism on the number of excursionists (mainly related to cross-border shopping) and tourists (who stay in the country for more than 24 hours). The central bank multiplies these data by an estimated daily expenditure based on UN estimates.

For outward tourism, the Capital Police provide data on the number of Paraguayan nationals leaving the country and, for air travel, their points of departure and destination. To calculate expenditure, the CBP uses a UN schedule of expenditure together with estimates based on interviews with tourism agents on cross-border shopping.

PERU

Transportation

CRBP bases the credit and debit entries on its quarterly survey of international transport companies and agents. It surveys all national companies and foreign airlines. Transactions of foreign shipping companies are reported by their agents or representatives in Peru.

The survey provides data on freight charges, sale of passenger fares, and supporting and auxiliary services by mode of transport (air, sea, and other transport). Compilers also use the import freight charges recorded in customs declaration forms after they adjust the data to subtract freight services provided by resident enterprises.

Travel

Data are estimated on the basis of tourism surveys (inward and outward) that the CRBP and PROMPERU conduct at the Jorge Chavez International Airport, the Santa Rosa post on the Chilean border, and the Yunguyo post on the Bolivian border. These surveys provide estimates on the average expenditure of nonresident travelers in Peru and resident travelers abroad.

The number of international travelers is provided by the Directorate General of Migration and Naturalization, an agency of the Ministry of the Interior. Data include travelers that cross the border and spend more than a night abroad and same-day visitors abroad (outward tourism) or in Peru (inward tourism). Debit entries also include the contra-entry of scholarships recorded as current transfers.

PHILIPPINES

Transportation

Transportation refers largely to data on merchandise freight, sourced from the foreign trade statistics. For other components of transportation services, the ITRS and the CAB company reports, obtained from the CBTS, provide the data.

Travel

For travel receipts, DES bases estimates on the Visitors Sample Survey (VSS), conducted by DOT. The VSS provides information on the average expenditure of foreign tourists and the average length of stay in the Philippines. For tourist-related travel expenditure abroad by residents, DES bases data on the ITRS.

Beginning with the 1999 report, travel credits include expenditure in the Philippines of nonresident OFWs during home visits. Travel debits include expenditures of resident OFWs in the host countries.

POLAND

Transportation

Data provided by the banking system on payments and by the surveys on enterprises for transportation services include services broken down by type (sea, air, railway, and other). These data are broken down by passenger transportation, freight, and other forms. Data received from the c.i.f./f.o.b. adjustment of the goods item are also included in freight transportation services. The value of these services is compiled as a fixed rate of the value of goods imports in the foreign trade statistics.

Travel

The travel item is compiled using data of the Institute of Tourism, which come from border surveys. The NBP receives data on travelers' expenditures: foreigners in Poland and Poles abroad.

When compiling monthly data, NBP makes estimates using information of the Border Guard (on numbers of arrivals and departures) and payments data (including settlements on travel items recorded in the banking system and also purchases and sales of foreign banknotes).

PORTUGAL

Transportation

BdP bases transportation data on the settlement statistics, supplemented with the estimates (see above) used to convert c.i.f. to f.o.b. valued goods. Data distinguish the means of transportation (sea, air, rail, or other transport) and provide a breakdown by transportation category (passenger, freight, or other transportation).

Travel

Travel data are based on settlements (e.g., bank transfers, cash, travelers' checks, debit and credit cards, and other means of settlement), on information provided by travel agencies, and on estimates produced by the BdP based on real indicators and prices of tourist activity (tourism statistics provided by the INE).

REPUBLIC OF MOLDOVA

Transportation

Besides the estimates made for transportation payments related to imported goods, referred to above, additional data are obtained from other sources. The main sources are the ITRS and the NBS' data on transportation services, which are collected from companies that provide transportation services, as well as the data on fees resulting from the pipeline transportation through Moldova. Disaggregating is done by type of transportation (air, sea, rail, road, and pipeline) and by category of services (freight, passenger, and other).

Travel

Data on travel are compiled using information provided by the NBS, the banking system, institutions that provide travel, and accommodation services. Estimates are also calculated of expenditures abroad by persons engaged in the export/import of goods, by business travelers, and by workers residing abroad for less than one year. Estimates of students' travel expenditures are made from data provided by the Ministry of Education and Youth.

ROMANIA

Transportation

Banking records are the main source for compilation of export freight services. The credit side of the transportation balance is recorded on the basis of banks' customers' declarations.

In the case of import freight services, an estimation method is used to determine the value of the freight services provided by nonresident carriers to residents. Assuming that the difference in c.i.f./f.o.b. of imported goods refers to transportation and insurance expenses, it is important to assess the weight of transportation services provided by nonresidents in total transportation payments.

Insurance costs are calculated by applying an average insurance rate to imports calculated on a c.i.f. basis, and finally deducted from the c.i.f./f.o.b. difference. A breakdown of imports by carrier and by mode of transportation is available from the National Authority for Customs (NAC). Therefore, it is possible to assess, from the remaining part of the c.i.f./f.o.b. difference, the freight services performed by nonresident operators only.

Travel

Data are based on information obtained from the banks, on an individual basis (transaction-by-transaction data collected from bank customers), supplemented by additional data based on the transactions of the exchange offices, compiled by the SD.

Estimates are made of the amounts of foreign exchange used by residents traveling abroad. The foreign exchange transactions of nonresidents made through bureaus of exchange (credits) are derived as the difference between the amounts of foreign exchange sold and purchased by nonresidents in the reporting period.

RUSSIAN FEDERATION

Services

The BR derives the data on transportation, royalties and license fees, and operational leases from enterprise surveys conducted by Rosstat.

Compilers estimate travel services via a model, using data on the number of border crossings classified by purpose of travel, average time of stay, and average expenditure per trip. The model uses data obtained from Rosstat surveys, the Federal Frontier Service of Russia, the Minfin of Russia, the Federal Migration Service of the Ministry of Internal Affairs, and sampling observations of offers by hotels and travel agencies conducted by the BR. Also used are partner country and mass media data. Besides, the BR estimates the number of cars imported for personal use—the costs of such cars being recorded under the travel debit item.

The BR obtains the data on all other services mainly from the ITRS. BR also uses, supplementary to ITRS, the information from the Minfin of Russia, local governments, and international organizations, for calculating financial services. It also uses data from the Minfin of Russia and other ministries for compiling government services.

RWANDA

Transportation

Passenger. Transportation services include the (1) transportation of nonresident passengers by the national airlines and road-transport companies and (2) transportation of resident passengers by foreign airlines.

Travel

The NBR derives credit entries from surveys conducted at hotels, guesthouses, and the Rwanda Office of Tourism and National Parks and from the exchange records. The amounts entered as debits are also drawn from the exchange records, supplemented with information from the ministries of National Education, Foreign Affairs and Cooperation, and the Interior's Immigration and Emigration Service.

These data were not gathered for 1994–2000, and the balance of payments for those years were compiled on the basis of estimates. Beginning in 2001, survey data have been used to compile this item.

SAINT KITTS AND NEVIS

See East Caribbean.

SAINT LUCIA

See East Caribbean.

SAINT VINCENT AND THE GRENADINES

See East Caribbean.

SAMOA

Transportation

For transportation services, CBS derives entries from the ticket system (mainly for data on services transactions of foreign shipping companies, the local shipping company, and the local airline) and from a monthly survey of all foreign airlines.

Travel

Monthly entries for travel credits are estimated on the basis of tourist arrivals and the average tourist expenditure derived from the Western Samoa Visitor Survey conducted in 1990. The estimates are subsequently adjusted for price changes using the consumer price index. (Travel credits captured in the ticket system are replaced by the above entries.)

SAO TOME AND PRINCIPE

Services

Exports

Travel and tourism: Based on the information provided by the immigration and customs services, and taking the years 2001–03 as a baseline, it was inferred, by evaluating rates of change, that the proportions of business travel and personal travel were 40 percent and 60 percent, respectively.

SAUDI ARABIA

Transportation

This item covers all air, marine, and land transport services and includes passenger, freight, and other services. Data on air, marine, and land transport are obtained from the Saudi Arabian Airlines, the Presidency of Civil Aviation, the General Ports Authority, and the Saudi Land Transportation Company. Data on freight are estimated.

Travel

Foreign visitors are mainly pilgrims and Umrah performers year-round—especially those who visit Saudi Arabia around the months of Dhul-Hijjah and Ramadan each year. Expenditures are estimated on the basis of data received from the Ministry of Interior on actual numbers of pilgrims and other visitors. Data on travel by residents of Saudi Arabia abroad are obtained from the commercial banks, which record the purpose for sales of foreign exchange.

SENEGAL

Transportation

This item covers freight, passenger services, and port services. Freight costs are estimated at 10 percent of c.i.f. imports, after adjustments. Passenger transportation information is obtained from airline companies. Port services data are obtained from surveys of port and airport authorities and from the consignees of shipping companies.

Transportation receipts consist essentially of National Railroad Company receipts (Société Nationale des Chemins de Fer du Sénégal) from merchandise in transit to neighboring countries.

Travel

Credit entries are taken from surveys of hotels, tourist sites, etc. by the Ministry of Tourism. Estimates are based on the number of foreign visitors, their estimated average expenditure, and their average length of stay.

Debit entries are obtained from statements of tourist allocations (including pilgrimage operations) granted by banks, plus data collected from airport authorities.

SEYCHELLES

Transportation

This item consists mainly of revenue from passenger services, port services, and freight. Passenger services represent air transportation only; data are obtained from Air Seychelles and agents of foreign airlines based in Seychelles. Port revenue includes data on general marine and port charges and agency service income, obtained from shipping agents. Air Seychelles provides data on airport handling fees. Aircraft landing fees are obtained from the MOF. Payments in respect of freight are estimated at 12.5 percent of c.i.f. imports. Receipts for carriage of foreign cargo by Air Seychelles are obtained directly from the airline.

Travel

Until 1991, revenue from travel was based on commercial bank records and a tourism expenditure survey carried out by NSB. Since 1992, however, the emergence of a parallel market for foreign exchange has reduced the coverage of commercial bank records, and total revenues from 1992 to 1995 are based on the NSB survey, although commercial bank receipts are also shown as part of overall revenue. From 1996 onwards, revenue includes commercial bank receipts and an estimate of inflows outside the official banking system.

For foreign travel, bank records remain the source of data. In June 2001, with the introduction of exchange control regulations, these records have increased in importance.

SIERRA LEONE

Transportation

This category covers freight and passenger services for all modes of transport and port services. BSL derives data for transport services from an annual survey of airline and shipping companies that operate in Sierra Leone. It draws data on seaport charges and airport fees from information provided by the seaports and airport authorities.

Travel

BSL compiles estimates of travel credits by combining data on tourist arrivals with estimates of their average expenditures—both of which are provided by the Sierra Leone Tourist Board.

Regarding government travel, banking records provide information.

SINGAPORE

Transportation

Transportation covers freight, passenger, and port services. The credit entries for freight cover freight earnings of local shipping lines and airlines. Data are obtained from the TIS. The debit entries cover payments to nonresidents for freight services provided. The total cost of freight on imports is estimated by applying freight factors to the value of imports (c.i.f.). These factors come from a survey of importers. Data on passenger and port services are obtained from the TIS and accounts of harbor and airport authorities.

Travel

The main source of information on expenditure by visitors who come in by air and sea is the Survey of Overseas Visitors to Singapore conducted by the Singapore Tourism Board. Estimates are also made for the expenditure of visitors coming to Singapore by road and rail. Entries for travel debits are derived from the number of returning Singapore residents and the estimated average expenditure per person.

SLOVAKIA

Transportation

This category covers all modes of transportation, including transit and passenger services. NBS generally obtains the transportation data from the "monthly report on foreign exchange income and payments" and the "monthly report on receipts and payments for the account of nonresidents." Individual respondents (such as pipeline operators) also directly report several items, including pipeline transit.

SLOVENIA

Transportation

Transportation services are broken down by categories of transport (sea, air, road, rail, other transport) and services (passenger, freight, other). The main source for recording transportation services is the ITRS.

Travel

The ITRS sources used in compiling the "incoming travel" category include (1) health- and education-related services; (2) payments made by nonresidents to Slovenian tourist agencies; (3) net withdrawals in tolars from nonresident accounts; (4) money spent in casinos by nonresidents; (5) data on sales of goods to nonresidents in duty-free shops and consignment warehouses; (6) payments with credit cards; and (7) sales of tolars to nonresidents abroad.

Regarding sales of tolars to nonresidents in Slovenia, the Bank of Slovenia estimates the data based on the number of border crossings of foreign travelers and on the number of nights spent in the country by foreign tourists.

Data for the category "expenditure on travel" come from the ITRS and estimations.

SOLOMON ISLANDS

Transportation

Included here are passenger and freight services. Data are derived mainly from FET records.

Travel

Data on travel credits and debits are compiled from FET records. The disaggregation into business and personal travel is available from 1998.

SOUTH AFRICA

Transportation

This category covers freight and passenger services; information is obtained from the SARS, transport operators, and other organizations involved in these transactions.

Travel

Estimates are based on statistics compiled by Statistics South Africa, regarding the number of foreign tourists visiting South Africa and the number of South African tourists traveling abroad. Data are taken from periodic surveys conducted by the South African Tourism Board and from questionnaires completed during buying and selling of foreign exchange.

SPAIN

Travel

In 2006, the border spending survey, EGATUR, was implemented as the only information source for the estimation of the credits.

Since 2007, and for data from January 2005 onwards, a statistical factor model has been implemented for the estimation of the credits side. The model combines the historical information on travel credits and a set of relevant credit tourist indicators, including the border spending survey and nonresident visitors among others. The weights of the indicators in the estimation method take into account the dynamic correlation between the indicators and the travel credits. For the time being, only evolution rates have been incorporated.

SRI LANKA

Transportation

This category covers all modes of transport and port services, divided into subcategories of passenger fares, freight, other (port and other) earnings and expenditure, and other related transactions.

The main source of data is the International Transactions Reporting System (ITRS) of commercial banks, which records values of transactions by purpose and currency of each transaction. In addition, for port-related services and passenger fares, CBSL obtains data from relevant institutions, using a sample survey to check the consistency of data recorded by the ITRS.

Travel

This category includes receipts and payments on official, business, medical, and educational travel. The ITRS is the main source of data. CBSL makes necessary adjustments to receipts on travel, based on SLTB data on the number of tourist arrivals, their average duration of stay, and their average daily expenditure.

SUDAN

Transportation

Freight and passenger services. This category covers all modes of transport and port services. The CBOS, the Ministry of Energy and Mining, commercial banks, and Sudan Customs are the main sources of data for freight and passenger services.

INTERNATIONAL MONETARY FUND (IMF) NOTES

Travel

Sources are the reports of the commercial banks, hotels, and the foreign exchange bureaus; the reports include purchases of foreign currencies by residents at home and abroad and sales of Sudanese dinars to nonresidents in Sudan and abroad. The use of travelers' checks and credit cards is another source of information on travel.

SURINAME

Transportation

For the transportation component, CBS derives information from the ITRS, which provides a breakdown (i.e., sea transport, air transport, and other transportation). Adjustments are made with data received from the national airline company.

Travel

For the travel component, CBS derives data from the ITRS. Adjustments are made to include data provided by the national carrier.

SWAZILAND

Transportation

Transportation services include freight and passenger transportation by all modes of transportation and other distributive and auxiliary services, including rentals of transportation equipment with crew. This includes international passenger services. Data for this sector are derived from various sources (domestic airline, railway corporation, freight companies, etc.). The main source is a survey of transportation companies and their agencies. The ITRS provides supplementary data.

Travel

Most of the data are obtained from surveys of travel agents. The ITRS provides additional data. The item covers goods and services, including those related to health and education, acquired across frontiers for business and personal purposes. Students and medical patients are treated as travelers, regardless of the length of stay.

Tourism data are compiled from a variety of sources. The BOP-IEO conducts surveys of car rental agencies and educational institutions. Banking statistics are another source (mainly for official travel) including a hotel survey carried out by the Domestic Economy Unit within the Research Department.

SWEDEN

Transportation

Transportation data are based on a survey compiled by Statistics Sweden.

Travel

For the travel component, Sveriges Riksbank uses three sources: (1) reports from banks and currency dealers on sales and purchases to/from the public of banknotes and travelers' checks; the report also covers banks' sales and purchases of Swedish banknotes vis-à-vis foreign banks; (2) reports on transactions made with credit cards; the estimation is made on gross flows of Swedish banknotes exchanged abroad by travelers from Sweden and resold to the public by foreign banks; and (3) quarterly surveys covering, for example, travel agencies.

A recurrent supplementary household survey serves as a basis for estimation of a split between tourism and business travel; it also supplies information for geographical breakdown estimates.

SWITZERLAND

Transportation

The data cover passenger transportation and transport services for goods exported and imported, for goods traffic through Switzerland on behalf of nonresidents, and for supporting services provided in connection with air and rail travel. The modes of transport include rail, air, sea, and transport by the Rhine fleet. The data sources are the annual and quarterly surveys carried out by the SNB.

Travel

The data cover business and personal travel, stays at health resorts and hospitals, travel related to studies, same-day travel, and transit travel, as well as adjustments for small volumes in cross-border traffic, duty-free shops, and consumption expenditure by cross-border commuters and holders of short-term residence permits. The data sources are surveys carried out by the Federal Statistical Office (FSO) and the SNB.

SYRIAN ARAB REPUBLIC

Transportation

For passenger services, CBS derives the data from information provided by the Syrian airline company (for credits) and foreign airlines (for debits). It cross-checks these data with information obtained from the foreign exchange records.

Travel

For travel, CBS estimates credits using the information on the number of arriving foreign travelers, their nationality, the class of hotel, and standard expenditure samples obtained from an annual survey conducted by the Ministry of Tourism.

For travel debits, CBS uses a similar survey, determining typical expenditures of Syrian residents traveling abroad. The travel debits also include goods purchased abroad by Syrian travelers and recorded by Customs.

THAILAND

Transportation

For passenger services, BOT derives estimates from the ITRS and reports from Thai Airways International. For other transportation, entries are derived from the ITRS.

Travel

For travel credits, BOT compiles entries by combining the number of foreign visitors and their average length of stay, obtained from the Tourism Authority of Thailand (TAT), with adjusted estimates of average expenditures per person per day. The estimates are adjusted annually before 1999, and quarterly since, and the average expenditures per capita are based on expenditure surveys of foreign visitors carried out by the TAT.

Since 1992, BOT travel receipts have been adjusted upward by approximately 5 percent from the TAT baseline figures. This is to reflect the difference in the coverage and concepts used by the two institutions (i.e., the TAT defines the length of stay as between one and ninety days, whereas the BOT's definition is up to one year to conform with *BPM5*).

For travel debits, the central bank derives entries from foreign exchange records and quarterly surveys of Thai travelers carried out by the TAT.

THE FORMER YUGOSLAV REPUBLIC OF MACEDONIA

Transportation

The NBRM obtains data on transportation from the ITRS, allowing disaggregation by type of transportation (air, sea, rail, and road) and by category of services (freight, passenger, and other). An adjustment is made to freight debits based on the c.i.f./f.o.b. factor, and an adjustment is made to freight credits based on the difference between the statistical and the invoice value of exports.

Travel

The source of the data is the ITRS.

TOGO

Transportation

Other transportation services. Data relate to port services and passenger services, excluding freight. Staff make entries on the basis of questionnaires sent to the port, airlines and shipping companies, domestic carriers, transit and consignment companies, etc. The data also include ticket issues, leased transportation, fueling, etc.

Travel

This component covers tourism transactions and expenditure on business travel and pilgrimages. It also covers the expenditure of Togolese students abroad. The sources of these data are the hotels, Ministry of Tourism, Directorates of Finance and of Scholarships and Training Courses, organizations dealing with pilgrimages to the holy places, university and regional schools, etc.

TRINIDAD AND TOBAGO

Transportation

Subsumed under this category are passenger services, port services, and the provision of freight services by the national airline. Passenger fares (credit) relate to the passenger fares and excess baggage receipts accruing from nonresidents. Passenger fares (debit) pertain to similar payments by residents to foreign-owned carriers, as reported in the airline surveys. The national airline also supplies information on the value of freight services it provides to nonresidents (credit).

Travel

Compilers derive the estimates of travel credits from expenditure surveys conducted by the Central Statistical Office and from tourist arrival and departure information from the same source. Also included are estimates of expenditures by foreign students enrolled at the University of the West Indies. For travel debits, the compilers source the data from banking records.

TUNISIA

Transportation

In collecting the data, SDBP uses periodic surveys of airlines and shipping lines operating in Tunisia, in addition to the bank settlement statements.

Travel

For operations not subject to a settlement in connection with studies and internships, SDBP obtains data from surveys of the pertinent government agencies and organizations.

TURKEY

Transportation

TURKSTAT provides freight and insurance expenses, decomposed by the residency of operations and modes of transportation. Since freight and insurance income data become available with a one-year lag, these data are estimated based on the previous years' ratios.

Regarding air transportation, CBRT obtains data from the domestic airline operators and agencies of foreign airline operators.

Travel

For travel, CBRT bases data on sample surveys conducted by TURKSTAT in cooperation with the Ministry of Culture and Tourism and the CBRT. These surveys cover the expenditure per capita of foreign visitors and citizens living abroad and of residents on their trips abroad.

Estimates are then computed by multiplying the number of foreign visitors, citizens living abroad, and residents traveling abroad by the related average expenditure, obtained from surveys. In the surveys, business and personal travel are identified separately.

TURKMENISTAN

Transportation

For transportation services, CBT sources data from bank payment documents, as well as from information supplied by transport companies and other sources. Data on freight on imports are not separately available; they are estimated at 9 percent of the c.i.f. value to bring them to an f.o.b. price.

Travel

Data come from the banking system on settlements between national and foreign travel agencies for group and individual travel, payments made by credit cards, and expenses for business, training, and health trip costs.

The CBT survey also includes data obtained from hotels and tourist agencies and from the National Institute of Statistics and Information of Turkmenistan.

UGANDA

Transportation

This category is intended to cover all modes of transport. Passenger transportation is reported for air and road. Air passenger debits are reported with effect from January 2006 and are derived as the product of (1) the monthly number of resident travelers departing from Entebbe Airport by destination, provided by UBOS, and (2) the average return air fare for respective destination. The average airfare is computed as the average for all airlines that fly out of Entebbe to the respective destination. No credits are reported since there is no operational resident-owned airline.

Road passenger credits and debits have been revised back based on a similar methodology. In the past they have been estimated by growing a survey estimate obtained in 1995 using GDP growth. However, these data have been revised backwards for credits by multiplying the number of nonresident travelers (both arrivals and departures) through Malaba, Busia, and other border posts by the average transport fare quoted by different bus companies and the share of resident buses to the total number of buses that ply the respective route.

In the case of debits for transportation by road, passenger debits have been obtained by multiplying the number of resident travelers (both arrivals and departures) through Malaba, Busia, and other border posts by the average transport fare quoted by different bus companies and the share of nonresident-owned buses to the total number of buses that ply the respective route. The average route fare is computed as the average for all buses plying the respective destination. Debit entries are the freight and auxiliary service amounts obtained after adjusting imports from c.i.f. to f.o.b. values.

Travel

Travel (credit) estimates are projected forward from results of a survey conducted in 1993–94 for the years up to 1999. These estimates were derived from data on the number of travelers (recorded in immigration forms) with estimates for the average length of stay and the daily expenditures of foreign travelers.

Figures for 1999–2002 are based on results from a survey conducted by the Ministry of Trade Tourism and Industry (MTTI) in 2001, while figures for 2003 onwards are based on results from a survey conducted by the MTTI in 2003 and data on travel (arrivals of nonresidents) provided by UBOS compiled from data provided by the Immigration Department.

Total travel credits are then computed as a product of the weighted average expenditure by the inward travelers computed by the MTTI and the number of travelers per quarter. The total expenditure figures have been increased to take account of expenditures by travelers who arrive through other border posts not considered by UBOS.

There are currently no travel debits up to 2003, but estimates for 2004 onwards are obtained from the product of average expenditure of Ugandan residents returning from abroad obtained through surveys conducted by BOU and data from UBOS on the number of travelers.

In addition, a distinction is made between official and personal travel, based on the immigration statistics provided by UBOS. In the case of travel credits a further breakdown of personal travel into education and other personal is estimated from 2003 onwards based on surveys of nonresident students in Ugandan education institutions. The survey, however, covers a sample of secondary and tertiary institutions and omits primary education institutions, most of which provide free education under the government Universal Primary Education for residents.

UKRAINE

Transportation

For freight and passenger services, the main sources of data are banking reports and the SSC survey of transportation companies. However, coverage is incomplete, and it is necessary to estimate missing information, especially for the debit entries. These estimates for freight are used in the conversion of data on c.i.f. imports from Customs to an f.o.b. basis.

Travel

Up to 2004, entries for this item were obtained by combining information derived from an SCSU quarterly survey on the basis of reports supplied by hotels and tour companies, and banks' reports on the purchase/sale of foreign currency and travelers' checks. Starting from 2004, the estimation of exports/imports of travel services is based on quarterly data on the number of nonresidents and Ukrainians crossing the border (classified by country and purpose of travel), average length of stay, and average expenditure per trip.

Data on the number of travelers are obtained from Ukraine's State Border Administration. Sources of data for estimating average length of stay and average expenditure per trip are the Cabinet of Ministers' regulations on the reimbursement of expenditures on business trips, SCSU survey data, data from the State Service on Tourism and Resorts of Ukraine's Ministry of Culture and Tourism, the Internet, and the mass media.

UNITED KINGDOM

Transportation

For passenger fares paid to nonresident operators, ONS derives estimates from its IPS.

Travel

This item covers goods and services provided to U.K. residents during trips of less than one year in foreign countries (and provided to nonresidents during similar trips to the U.K.), net of any purchases made with money earned or provided locally.

ONS bases the estimates primarily on the IPS, which seeks information on expenditure from samples of foreign visitors leaving the U.K. and of U.K. residents returning from abroad. The survey distinguishes several purposes of visits, which are then aggregated as either business or personal.

For package tourists, ONS deducts estimates of the transport elements from the reported total package costs. For expenditure by U.K. residents on personal imports of cars, ONS derives estimates from the data received by HMRC.

UNITED REPUBLIC OF TANZANIA

Transportation

The main entry under transportation relates to freight transactions. For freight and insurance imports, the national compilers compute data as ratios of total imports. The ratios are derived from detailed data on imports, obtained from an inspection company. Currently, 9 percent of total imports is assumed to cover payments of both freight and insurance services (with freight accounting for about 97 percent of that amount, and insurance accounting for the remaining 3 percent).

Travel

For travel debits, compilers obtain data from commercial banks' exchange records and from bureaus of exchange.

For travel credits, the Ministry of Tourism and Natural Resources, in collaboration with the BoT, the National Bureau of Statistics, the Immigration Department, and the Zanzibar Commission for Tourism, conducts a tourism sector exit survey to obtain data.

UNITED STATES

Transportation

For passenger services, BEA bases estimates on data on numbers of travelers (provided by the Department of Homeland Security) and estimates of average passenger fares (developed from a travel survey administered by the U.S. Department of Commerce).

Travel

BEA prepares travel estimates (except for transactions with Canada and Mexico) by combining data on numbers of travelers, provided by the Department of Homeland Security, with estimates of average expenditures, obtained from a travel survey administered by the U.S. Department of Commerce. BEA derives estimates of travel transactions between the U.S. and Canada and between the U.S. and Mexico from data prepared by Statistics Canada and the Bank of Mexico.

URUGUAY

Transportation

DPF derives data for passenger fares from the annual survey of resident land, sea, and air transport companies and agents of foreign companies. It also conducts a survey of the main carriers on a quarterly basis.

Travel

For both travel credits and debits, the Ministry of Tourism compiles estimates on the basis of sample surveys of both inward and outward tourism, supplemented with data the National Migration Directorate provides on the number of travelers.

VANUATU

Transportation

The category covers freight and passenger services by all modes of transport (i.e., sea and air) and port services. For transportation services, RBV derives entries from information provided by airport and seaport authorities, Air Vanuatu, and stevedoring companies.

Travel

For travel credits, RBV derives the entries from information on the number of foreign visitors, their average daily expenditures, and their average length of stay. The expenditure estimates are based on the 2005 Visitor's Survey conducted by National Statistics Office through the collaboration of the RBV, the National Tourism Office, and the Tourism Council of the South Pacific and are rated forward, using CPI movements. On the number of visitors, RBV obtains data quarterly from migration statistics published by the Statistics Office.

For travel debits, RBV derives entries from an average expenditure figure provided by the Department of Finance and the residents' departure numbers from the Statistics Office. Also included is 70 percent of the value of training scholarships (the contra-entry is included in *current transfers, general government*).

VENEZUELA

Transportation

This item includes the national oil industry's income and the private air companies' freight services and sale of tickets for international flights. The CBV uses surveys to gather both sets of data. The item also includes income from ports, airports, and navigation routes received by the national oil industry, the National Institute of Canals, and the principal ports and airports of the country. The CBV obtains these data through questionnaires and administrative registries.

Debit entries are registered for freight, estimated through a coefficient applied to total imports of goods f.o.b., according to the nandina (Andean Community customs tariff), modality of transportation, region, etc. The item also includes payments for passenger transport on nonresident airlines and payments for port and airport services that the public oil industry and private airline companies make, estimated through surveys and indicators of volume of aircraft that the principal airport of the country reports.

Travel

For travel, the CBV measures credits and debits through a sample survey the INE and CBV carry out every quarter in the principal airport of the country. Compilers obtain data on average daily spending in U.S. dollars by category of traveler and reason for visit, average number of nights spent, and other indicators that allow an evaluation of the general profile of the traveler. These sample data are extrapolated by the total number of foreign visitors reported by the airports.

In addition, the category includes expenses for scholarships and missions that the public petroleum sector and nonpetroleum public sector incur abroad. The CBV validates the estimate through indicators of the activity, interviews for opinions in the principal hotels and travel agencies of the country, and reports and specialized journals.

YEMEN

Transportation

Data on debit entries for freight and insurance are estimated at 10 percent of the c.i.f. value of imports. BOPD records the data it collects from airport authorities as credit entries under other air transportation, while it records data it collects from seaport authorities as credit entries under other sea transportation.

Travel

The Ministry of Tourism collects data from the immigration authorities on the number of foreign tourist arrivals. Number of tourist nights is estimated through a comprehensive survey to estimate the travel receipts. The BOPD reflects the data obtained from the Ministry of Tourism in the balance of payments statistics.

Travel debits are estimated from the CBY records and the monthly international transactions reporting survey (ITRS) of commercial banks for students studying abroad, Yemeni pilgrims, and health treatments of Yemeni nationals abroad.

ZAMBIA

Transportation

Credit data comprise freight services only, estimated as 5.5 percent of the c.i.f value of nontraditional exports, plus data on inland freight reported by the mining companies on their metal exports.

Debits comprise estimates for freight, passenger, and other transport services. Freight debits are estimated as 10 percent of the c.i.f value of imports. Data on passenger transport and other transport services are estimated based on historical data. The BoZ plans to launch two enterprise surveys that would form the basis of compiling estimates of passenger and other transport services. These would consist of a quarterly survey of resident transportation companies and a survey of agents of nonresident airlines, primarily designed to capture data on passenger transportation.

Travel

Prior to June 1999, the BoZ compiled data on travel credits from reports the Zambia National Tourist Board (ZNTB) submitted. In June 1999 the MOT took over from ZNTB the task of conducting surveys of enterprises involved in providing travel services. The BoZ, collaborating with the MOT, has designed quarterly survey forms to capture, primarily, tourism revenues from hotels and companies involved in tours, car hire, and air charters. The first survey was launched in October of 2000 but has not been undertaken consistently, owing to a lack of funding and staff shortages.

Travel debits are estimated based on data on government employees' travel allowances and on government and quasi-government employees studying abroad. However, the BoZ is establishing reporting arrangements with the Ministry of Finance, the Ministry of Education, and the Cabinet Office for data on official expenditure on travel for purposes of education, medical, and training.

In the past, this information was captured from the banks and the exchange bureau reporting system on purchases and sale of foreign exchange. However, the liberalization of the foreign exchange market in Zambia resulted in incomplete coverage. That is, banks are no longer obliged to report all their foreign exchange transactions, and ordinary customers are not legally required to declare the purpose of the foreign currency that they purchase from banks and bureaus of exchange.